INSIDERS' GUIDE® TO
NORTH CAROLINA'S OUTER BANKS

Help Us Keep This Guide Up to Date

Every effort has been made by the author and editors to make this guide as accurate and useful as possible. However, many things can change after a guide is published—establishments close, phone numbers change, hiking trails are rerouted, facilities come under new management, etc.

We would love to hear from you concerning your experiences with this guide and how you feel it could be improved and be kept up to date. While we may not be able to respond to all comments and suggestions, we'll take them to heart and we'll also make certain to share them with the author. Please send your comments and suggestions to the following address:

The Globe Pequot Press
Reader Response/Editorial Department
P.O. Box 480
Guilford, CT 06437

Or you may e-mail us at:

editorial@globe-pequot.com

Thanks for your input, and happy travels!

INSIDERS' GUIDE® SERIES

Insiders' Guide®
to North Carolina's
Outer Banks

TWENTY-THIRD EDITION

By Molly Perkins Harrison

Guilford, Connecticut
An imprint of The Globe Pequot Press

The prices and rates in this guidebook were confirmed at press time. We recommend, however, that you call establishments before traveling to obtain current information.

Cover photograph courtesy Charlie Borland, Index Stock

Back cover photographs (left to right) courtesy of Artville, Brian Horsley, Molly Perkins Harrison, Brian Horsley, Brian Horsley, Brian Horsley

Maps by Geografx © The Globe Pequot Press

ISBN: 0-7627-2256-8
ISSN: 1082-9458

Manufactured in the United States of America
Twenty-third Edition/First Printing

Contents

Directory of Maps

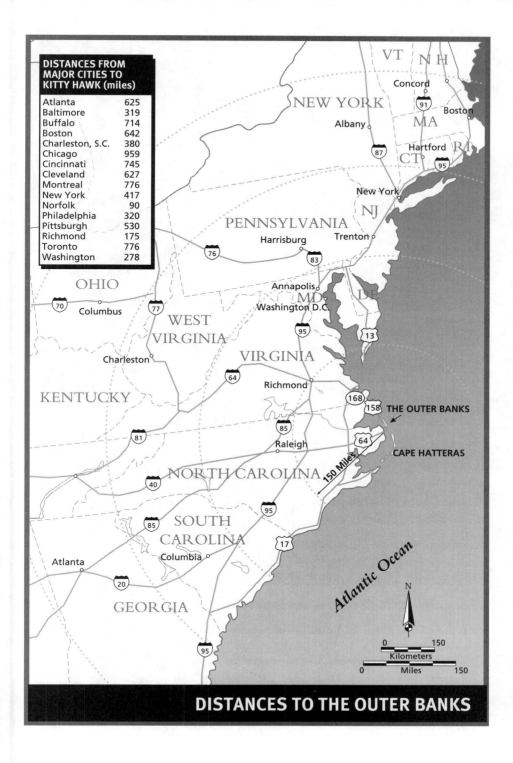

DISTANCES FROM MAJOR CITIES TO KITTY HAWK (miles)

Atlanta	625
Baltimore	319
Buffalo	714
Boston	642
Charleston, S.C.	380
Chicago	959
Cincinnati	745
Cleveland	627
Montreal	776
New York	417
Norfolk	90
Philadelphia	320
Pittsburgh	530
Richmond	175
Toronto	776
Washington	278

THE OUTER BANKS

CAPE HATTERAS

150 Miles

Atlantic Ocean

N

Kilometers
Miles

DISTANCES TO THE OUTER BANKS

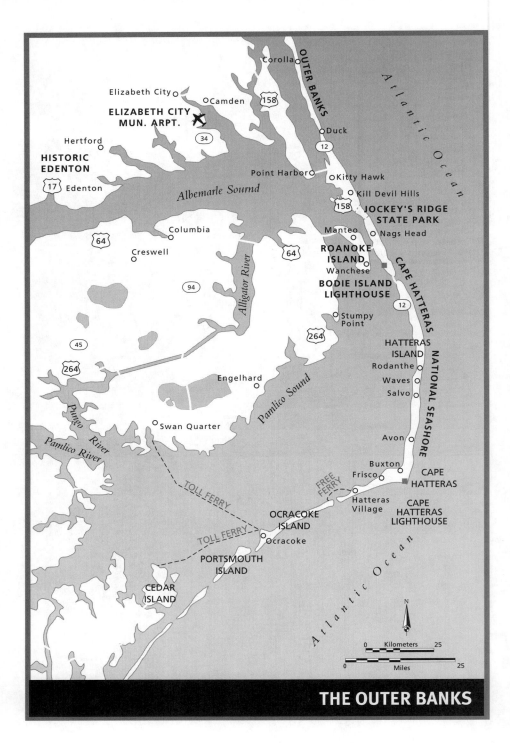

THE OUTER BANKS

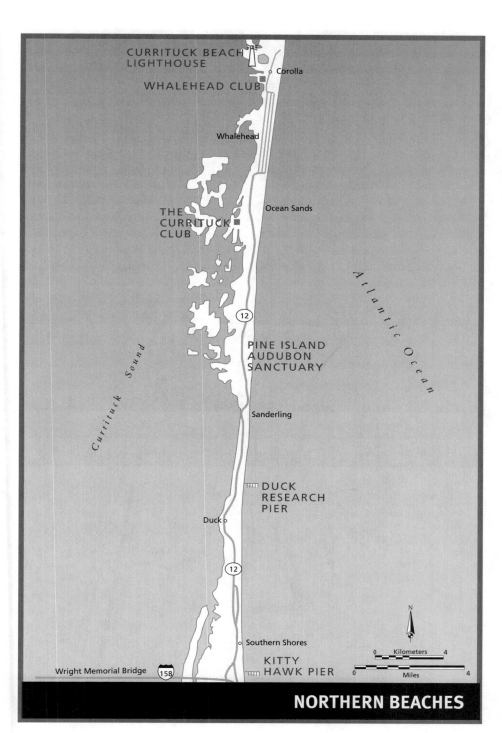

CURRITUCK BEACH
LIGHTHOUSE

Corolla

WHALEHEAD CLUB

Whalehead

Ocean Sands

THE
CURRITUCK
CLUB

12

Currituck Sound

PINE ISLAND
AUDUBON
SANCTUARY

Atlantic Ocean

Sanderling

DUCK
RESEARCH
PIER

Duck

12

N

Southern Shores

KITTY
HAWK PIER

Wright Memorial Bridge   158

0   Kilometers   4

0   Miles   4

NORTHERN BEACHES

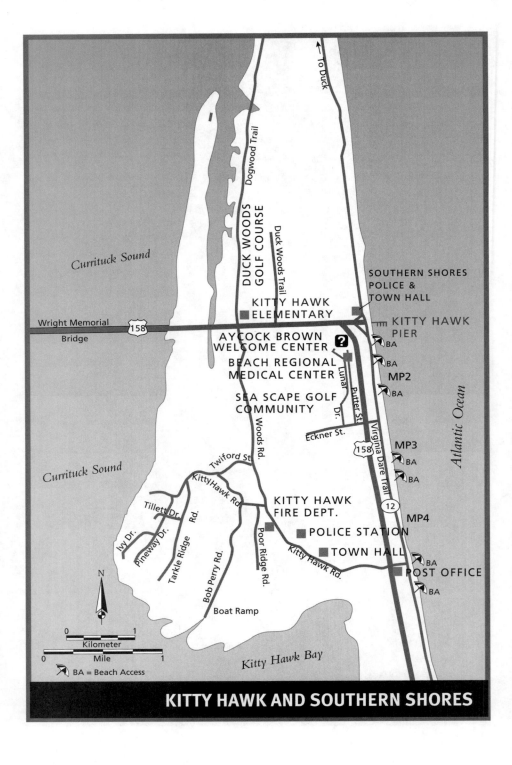

Currituck Sound

To Duck

Dogwood Trail

DUCK WOODS GOLF COURSE

Duck Woods Trail

KITTY HAWK ELEMENTARY

SOUTHERN SHORES POLICE & TOWN HALL

Wright Memorial
Bridge

158

KITTY HAWK PIER

AYCOCK BROWN WELCOME CENTER

BA

BEACH REGIONAL MEDICAL CENTER

BA

Lunar Dr.

Putter St.

MP2

BA

SEA SCAPE GOLF COMMUNITY

Eckner St.

Atlantic Ocean

Currituck Sound

Woods Rd.

158

MP3

Twiford St.

Virginia Dare Trail

BA

BA

KittyHawk Rd.

KITTY HAWK FIRE DEPT.

12

MP4

Tillett Dr.

Ivy Dr.

Pineway Dr.

Tarkle Ridge Rd.

Bob Perry Rd.

Poor Ridge Rd.

POLICE STATION

Kitty Hawk Rd.

TOWN HALL

BA

POST OFFICE

BA

Boat Ramp

Kitty Hawk Bay

N

0   Kilometer   1

0   Mile   1

BA = Beach Access

KITTY HAWK AND SOUTHERN SHORES

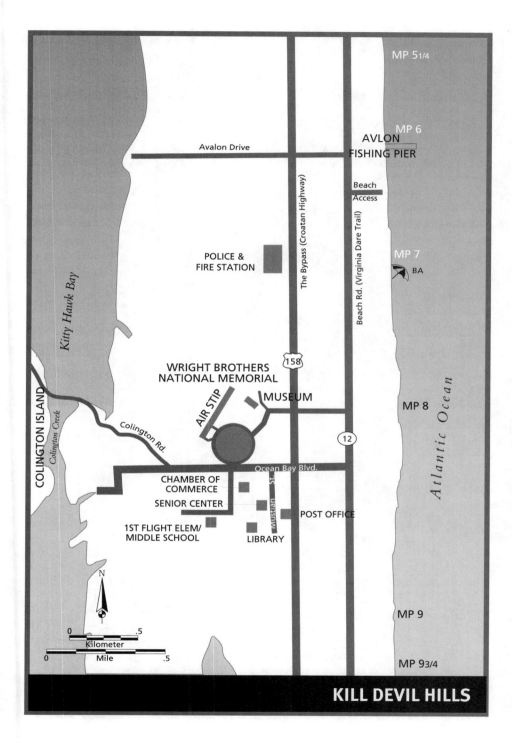

KILL DEVIL HILLS

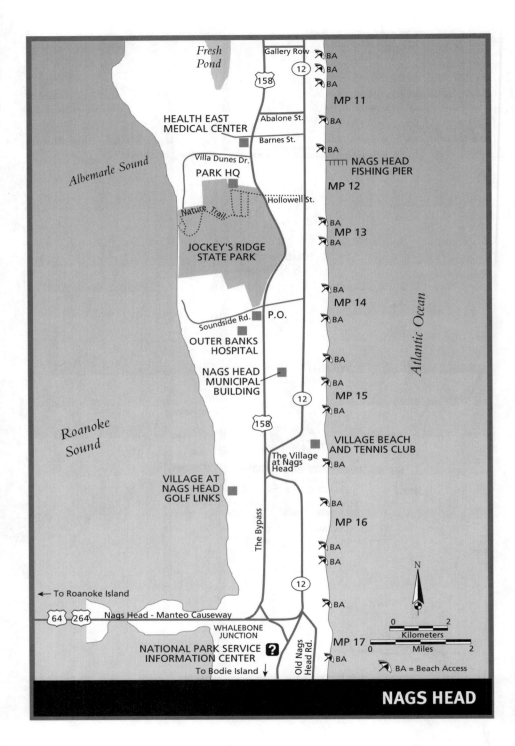

Fresh Pond

Gallery Row

🪁 BA
🪁 BA
🪁 BA

158

12

MP 11

Albemarle Sound

HEALTH EAST MEDICAL CENTER

Abalone St.   🪁 BA

Barnes St.   🪁 BA

Villa Dunes Dr.

PARK HQ   🪁 BA ┅┅┅ NAGS HEAD FISHING PIER

MP 12

Nature Trail

Hollowell St.

🪁 BA MP 13
🪁 BA

JOCKEY'S RIDGE STATE PARK

🪁 BA MP 14

Soundside Rd.   P.O.   🪁 BA

OUTER BANKS HOSPITAL

🪁 BA

NAGS HEAD MUNICIPAL BUILDING

🪁 BA

158   🪁 BA MP 15

12   🪁 BA

VILLAGE BEACH AND TENNIS CLUB

Roanoke Sound

The Village at Nags Head

🪁 BA

VILLAGE AT NAGS HEAD GOLF LINKS

🪁 BA MP 16

The Bypass

🪁 BA
🪁 BA

12

🪁 BA

N

To Roanoke Island →

64 264 Nags Head - Manteo Causeway

WHALEBONE JUNCTION

NATIONAL PARK SERVICE INFORMATION CENTER ❓

To Bodie Island ↓

Old Nags Head Rd.

MP 17   🪁 BA

0   2
Kilometers
0   Miles   2

🪁 BA = Beach Access

Atlantic Ocean

NAGS HEAD

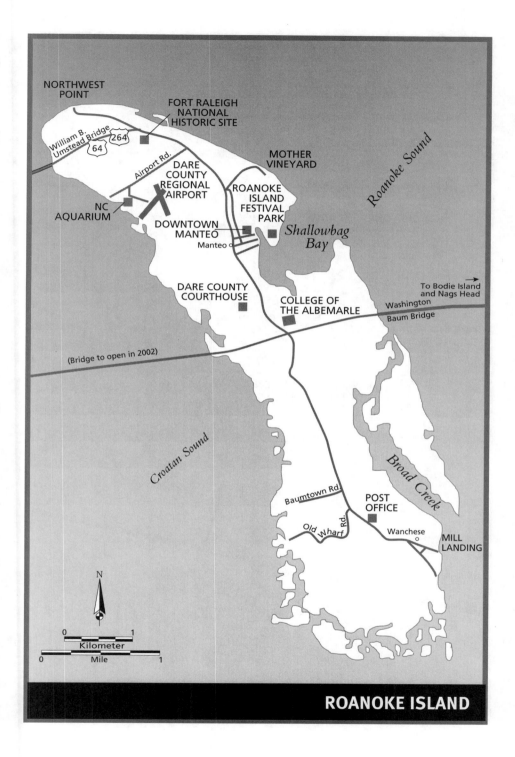

NORTHWEST
POINT

FORT RALEIGH
NATIONAL
HISTORIC SITE

William B.
Umstead Bridge 264
64

Airport Rd.

MOTHER
VINEYARD

DARE
COUNTY
REGIONAL
AIRPORT

ROANOKE
ISLAND
FESTIVAL
PARK

Roanoke Sound

NC
AQUARIUM

DOWNTOWN
MANTEO

Manteo

Shallowbag
Bay

DARE COUNTY
COURTHOUSE

COLLEGE OF
THE ALBEMARLE

To Bodie Island
and Nags Head

Washington
Baum Bridge

(Bridge to open in 2002)

Croatan Sound

Broad Creek

Baumtown Rd.

POST
OFFICE

Old Wharf Rd.

Wanchese

MILL
LANDING

N

0   1
Kilometer
0   1
Mile

ROANOKE ISLAND

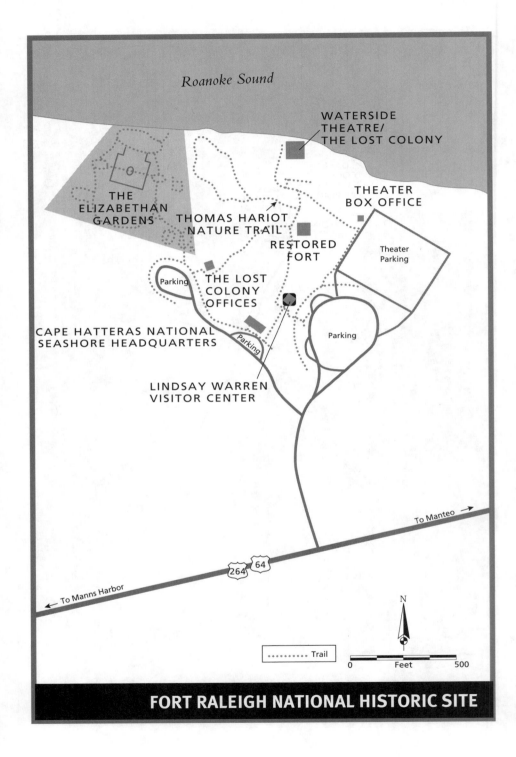

Roanoke Sound

WATERSIDE THEATRE/ THE LOST COLONY

THEATER BOX OFFICE

THE ELIZABETHAN GARDENS

THOMAS HARIOT NATURE TRAIL

RESTORED FORT

Theater Parking

Parking

THE LOST COLONY OFFICES

CAPE HATTERAS NATIONAL SEASHORE HEADQUARTERS

Parking

Parking

LINDSAY WARREN VISITOR CENTER

To Manteo

264 64

To Manns Harbor

.... Trail

N

0 Feet 500

FORT RALEIGH NATIONAL HISTORIC SITE

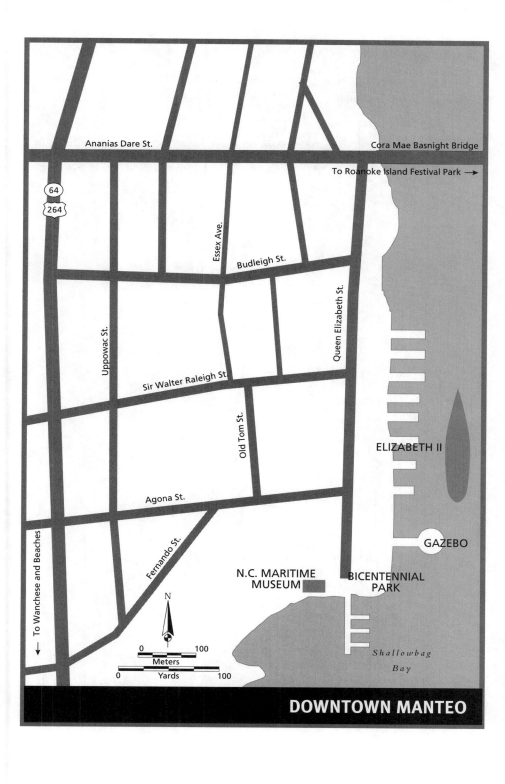

Ananias Dare St.

Cora Mae Basnight Bridge

To Roanoke Island Festival Park →

64
264

Essex Ave.

Budleigh St.

Queen Elizabeth St.

Uppowac St.

Sir Walter Raleigh St.

Old Tom St.

ELIZABETH II

Agona St.

To Wanchese and Beaches

Fernando St.

GAZEBO

N.C. MARITIME
MUSEUM

BICENTENNIAL
PARK

N

0   100
Meters
0   100
Yards

Shallowbag
Bay

DOWNTOWN MANTEO

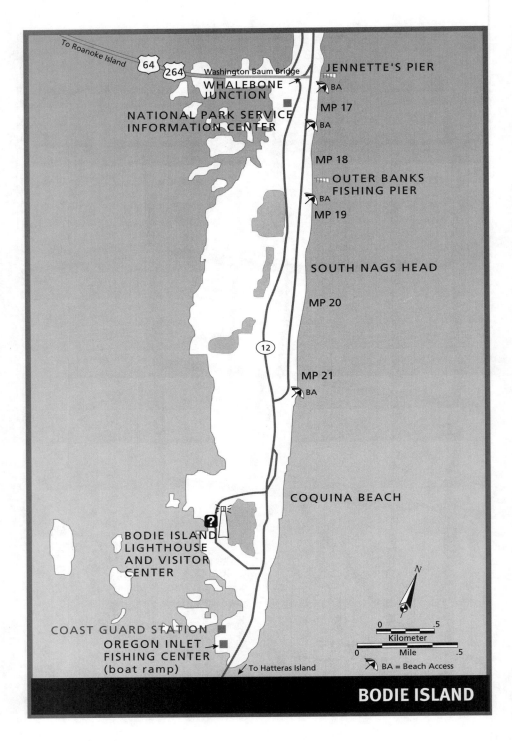

To Roanoke Island

64 264

Washington Baum Bridge

JENNETTE'S PIER

WHALEBONE
JUNCTION

BA

NATIONAL PARK SERVICE
INFORMATION CENTER

MP 17

BA

MP 18

OUTER BANKS
FISHING PIER

BA

MP 19

SOUTH NAGS HEAD

MP 20

12

MP 21

BA

COQUINA BEACH

?

BODIE ISLAND
LIGHTHOUSE
AND VISITOR
CENTER

N

COAST GUARD STATION

OREGON INLET
FISHING CENTER
(boat ramp)

To Hatteras Island

0   .5
Kilometer
0   Mile   .5

BA = Beach Access

BODIE ISLAND

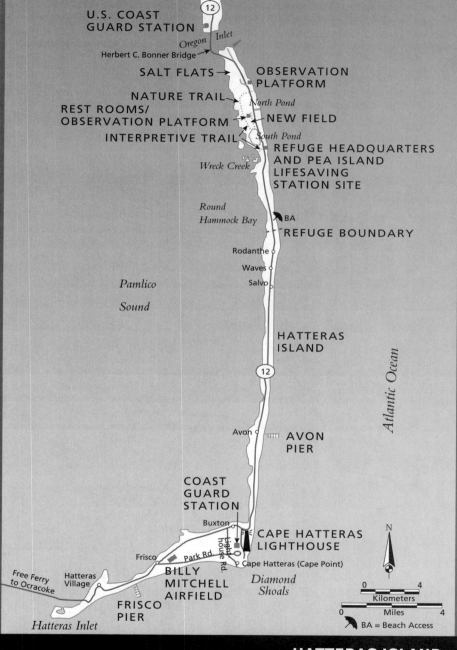

U.S. COAST
GUARD STATION

Oregon Inlet

Herbert C. Bonner Bridge

SALT FLATS →

OBSERVATION
PLATFORM

NATURE TRAIL

North Pond

REST ROOMS/
OBSERVATION PLATFORM

← NEW FIELD

INTERPRETIVE TRAIL

South Pond

REFUGE HEADQUARTERS
AND PEA ISLAND
LIFESAVING
STATION SITE

Wreck Creek

*Round
Hammock Bay*

BA

REFUGE BOUNDARY

Rodanthe

Waves

Salvo

*Pamlico

Sound*

HATTERAS
ISLAND

Atlantic Ocean

Avon

AVON
PIER

COAST
GUARD
STATION

Buxton

CAPE HATTERAS
LIGHTHOUSE

Frisco

Park Rd.

Lighthouse Rd.

Cape Hatteras (Cape Point)

Free Ferry
to Ocracoke

Hatteras
Village

BILLY
MITCHELL
AIRFIELD

*Diamond
Shoals*

N

FRISCO
PIER

Hatteras Inlet

0   4
Kilometers
0   4
Miles

BA = Beach Access

HATTERAS ISLAND

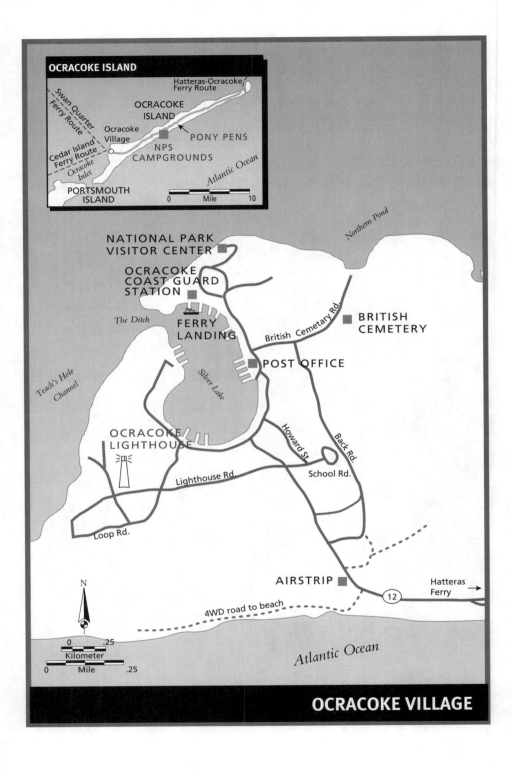

OCRACOKE ISLAND

Hatteras-Ocracoke
Ferry Route

Swan Quarter
Ferry Route

OCRACOKE
ISLAND

Ocracoke
Village

Cedar Island
Ferry Route

Ocracoke
Inlet

PORTSMOUTH
ISLAND

PONY PENS

NPS
CAMPGROUNDS

Atlantic Ocean

0   Mile   10

Northern Pond

NATIONAL PARK
VISITOR CENTER

OCRACOKE
COAST GUARD
STATION

The Ditch

FERRY
LANDING

British   Cemetary Rd.

BRITISH
CEMETERY

Teach's Hole
Channel

Silver Lake

POST OFFICE

OCRACOKE
LIGHTHOUSE

Howard St.

Back Rd.

Lighthouse Rd.

School Rd.

Loop Rd.

N

AIRSTRIP

Hatteras
Ferry

12

4WD road to beach

0   25
Kilometer
0   Mile   .25

Atlantic Ocean

OCRACOKE VILLAGE

Preface

Part of the Outer Banks's charm is the remoteness of the area. Since it's only accessible by ferry or by driving over one of the bridges that connects it to the mainland, once you're here, you have the feeling of being far removed from the rest of the world. It's really not that far. And in recent years, with an ever-growing tourism industry, goods and services have come to us. It's fascinating to hear locals tell of long drives to stores on the mainland to buy groceries or to receive medical care back in the old days. The "old days," however, were less than two decades ago! Those of us who live here year-round still make excursions to nearby cities for specific services, shopping, and cultural events, but we wouldn't trade island life for anything. Living here is a trade-off that is heavily weighted toward the good life; we're blessed, and we know it.

On NASA aerial maps, our strand of sand may look like the continent's after-thought, but our land was the welcome mat to the first English-speaking settlers in the country. The Outer Banks is stranded farther away from its main coast than any other barrier islands in the world. Although our shore has very slowly over the centuries crept west, it still stubbornly and mysteriously maintains its crooked post miles out into the Atlantic. Pounded century after century by storms—many escorted in by the nearby mighty Gulf Stream—the geology of these narrow, low-slung islands is unique in its steadfast adaptability. Its inhabitants have been no less resilient. When you step foot on these sandy shores, you join a legion of steely adventurers, renegade thinkers, and rugged survivors who have been captivated by the unbidden forces of nature.

Welcome to the land of beginnings! Feast your senses on wide beaches, whispering sea oats, and undulating dunes—a land where the pace of life is geared to the unceasing sand-sharpened breezes and wild winds. From the gifts and punishment of the glorious and untamed waters of these indomitable islands have sprung heroes, pioneers, pirates, and inventors. Tales of courage and creativity, bloody battles and savage shipwrecks, resourcefulness and compassion: all are part of the mystique of the Outer Banks.

Here, the first English colonists set up camp. Blackbeard and his band of buccaneers anchored sloops along the shallow sounds. Wilbur and Orville Wright also flew the world's first airplane, buoyed by stiff winds and brazen determination.

From remote national wildlife refuges, sheltered seashores, and protected maritime forests to upscale resort communities, these strips of shifting sand offer both peaceful retreat and awesome adventure. Kitesurf or JetSki. Surf fish or stroll the endless beaches. Charter a deep-sea fishing boat to fight an ocean giant. Grab the binoculars, and watch birds. Soar from the East Coast's highest sand dune in a hang glider. Catch some waves, and surf some of the best swells on the Atlantic Seaboard as the breakers barrel toward the beach. It's all here for the choosing, and boredom is not an option.

Only in the last 15 years or so have these ribbons of sand confronted the rapid-fire development that other coastal areas saw years earlier. One of only four states in the nation that forbids hard structures like seawalls, which can cause severe narrowing of beaches, North Carolina learned the tough lessons of coastal management by watching the mistakes of other ocean states. To a large extent, the Outer Banks owes its still healthy, wide beaches to the luck of its relatively late bloom. Isolated geographically by fences of water, the barrier islands were accessible only by boat until the 1930s, when the first major bridges from the mainland were constructed. Once travel improved, word of

A quiet creek is the perfect place to find solace in nature. PHOTO: HORSLEY/GARDNER

the Outer Banks's lovely weather and beautiful beaches spread, and vacationers and transplants poured in a steady stream over the shallow sounds, fishing rods and bathing suits at the ready.

Life on the Outer Banks has changed dramatically since then, but much of the beauty and color remains unsullied. Native families, many descendants of shipwreck survivors, still make their livings through commercial fishing. Much of the seafood for which we are so famous is caught locally by fifth-generation watermen. A visitor to Colington, Wanchese, Hatteras Island, or Ocracoke will mingle among people who speak with the distinctive Outer Banks brogue, an accent carried over by English settlers and sustained by centuries of isolation.

Four lighthouses (Currituck's red brick beacon, the mid-island light at Bodie Island, Cape Hatteras's famous candy-striped tower, and the squat, whitewashed watchdog on Ocracoke Island), once sentinels for sailors traversing the shipwreck-strewn Graveyard of the Atlantic, dot these storm-swept shores.

Wild horses roam the northernmost protected refuges, descendants, some believe, of Spanish mustangs that swam ashore from shipwrecks more than three centuries ago. Waterfowl abound throughout these islands, attracting bird-watchers, hunters, and long-lens photographers. The East Coast's best fishing also awaits anglers on the decks of offshore charter boats, atop numerous piers and bridges, and off miles of ocean and sound shores.

There are plenty of biking and in-line skating paths along flat roadways, and horses can be rented for leisurely strolls along the ocean and dirt roads through the island marshlands.

Painters, sculptors, potters, and other artisans open their galleries to browsers in almost every local village. Musicians, comedians, and poets provide evening entertainment in a variety of cafes and nightclubs. The entire family can cuddle up under the stars at Roanoke Island's Waterside Theatre and watch the acclaimed historical production *The Lost Colony,* the longest-running outdoor summer theater drama in the nation.

Despite its rise as a favorite resort destination, the Outer Banks continues to be a kickback kind of place. You don't have to dress up here. Shorts and sandals are the accepted garb in even the finest locales. Shrimp, crab, and dozens of species of fresh-caught fish (often hauled in that very day by Outer Banks fishermen) are available at nearly every one of the slew of restaurants that serves tourists and locals alike.

While you're trekking the dunes, frolicking in the pristine waters, or enjoying the Carolina blue skies and eye-popping sunsets, don't forget that the magic of these overgrown sand bars has inspired some of the most dramatic moments in American history. Remember that you are walking the sands of some of the most dynamic barrier islands on Earth.

Some things have stayed the same since Sir Walter Raleigh's party first laid eyes on Roanoke Island more than 400 years ago. These barrier beaches still startle visitors as well as natives with their rugged beauty and capricious topography. The fragile landscape remains at the mercy of the sea, furious with storm one season, calm the next.

Summer isn't the only time to enjoy the Outer Banks, although the season from Memorial Day through Labor Day is by far the most packed with people and things to do. Fall offers fabulous fishing and windsurfing; spring brings bird-watching and bicycling. And winter is deliciously devoid of almost everyone.

Spend a little time here, and you'll understand why many of us came back to stay—or never left. We hope this book helps you find exactly what you want in your visit to our vibrant barrier beaches.

The stark beauty of nature will stop you in your tracks on the Outer Banks. PHOTO: HORSLEY/GARDNER

Acknowledgments

I am not the sole author of this book. After 23 years in publication, this book is a compendium of the work of many authors, all of whom have left their impressions on it in one way or another. While the changeable facts are updated every year, much of the text is still peppered with each author's voice, forming a melting pot of insights and perceptions. I've added my own voice, to be sure, but I also recognized that some authors have already said it better than I ever will. As I read the text, I recognized the distinct alliteration of Lane DeGregory, the poetry of Mary Ellen Riddle, the spice of Cate Kozak, the wit of Linda Lauby, the passion of Liz Corsa, the practicality of Karen Bachman. Now that I know what they've been through, I commend and thank these and all the other former authors of this book for their hard work.

Beth Storie and Michael McOwen command my admiration for creating this book 23 years ago. Starting with one book and launching it into a national series from Manteo, North Carolina, has given many Outer Bankers the confidence to pursue bigger dreams. Though they are no longer publishing the series, they left behind a legacy.

Working for Beth when she was publisher of the series was one of the most educational experiences of my life, and I thank her for believing in me.

Updating this book has been a challenge and a joy. At times it felt like I had a telephone growing out of my ear as I tried to track down all the facts. What made this bearable was all of the friendly and helpful people I spoke with. After we'd talked business, many Outer Bankers wanted to talk about the weather or the crowds of tourists, and they often put me onto another lead. I sincerely thank all the people who took time out of their busy lives to help me.

Researchers Karen Brown and Brant Harrison helped me more than they know by reducing the number of phone calls I had to make, and for that I am very grateful. Thanks to Quinn Capps of the Outer Banks Visitors Bureau for always being willing to promptly look up a fact for me.

I must thank Jackie Thomas, who kept me abreast of everything she heard as she sold the advertising for this book. Huge thanks go to the folks at Silver Lake Inn on Ocracoke for putting me up for the weekend while I researched their wonderful island. Gratitude goes to my sister, Laura Catoe, for giving me whatever information was stored in her head and for letting me vent when I needed to, and to Karen Bachman for all of her advice and friendship. Thanks to friends Brian Horsley and Sarah Gardner for donating many of the photographs that appear in this book. Thanks to editors Lynne Arany and Gillian Belnap for their guidance.

I'm especially grateful to my old dog, Rowdy, for stalwartly lying by my side on my office floor, a symbol of patience and just about the only thing that kept me from leaping from my chair and running out into the sunny, 70-degree days that dominated the whole fall of 2001. I'm also grateful to my puppy, Jeke, whose silliness and spontaneity provided much-needed comic relief during this project. I bless my lucky stars for my husband, Patrick, who fostered in me a love of nature that I never knew I had and who was the source of much information for this book. Finally, I want to express how absolutely grateful I am to be living here on the edge of the continent, where the surroundings inspire me every day.

— Molly

The Outer Banks is all about water—and being in it or on it however you can. PHOTO: GINGER CARSLAKE

How to Use This Book

Continuing the 23-year tradition of the *Insiders' Guide® to North Carolina's Outer Banks*, we've updated, revised, and added to our extensive collection of favorite restaurants, shops, attractions, events, getaways, and much more.

Most information in our guide is arranged geographically from north to south. Besides introducing you to the area's fascinating history and hidden treasures, we provide practical information on medical services, camping, real estate, vacation rentals, ferry schedules, fishing sites, and other areas of interest. You'll also discover information on local media, children's activities, worship sites, and retirement, plus valuable tips that you could only get from an Insider. We've designed *The Insiders' Guide® to North Carolina's Outer Banks* as a handy reference for all aspects of life here. Keep it in hand, and let us accompany and guide you along every step of your Outer Banks journey. We make sure there's always a copy ready to lend to visiting relatives and friends. While researching new businesses, we were surprised to find out how many people had copies of the *Insiders' Guide* that they were using as a relocation resource.

We begin with colorful overviews about each area along these barrier islands, from the sand-trail villages of Carova (at the Virginia–North Carolina border) to the windswept shores of Ocracoke Island; after that come a chapter on the various ways to get to and around on the Outer Banks and a chapter on our history. Comprehensive chapters tailored to meet your personal needs follow. You'll find Accommodations, Real Estate, Arts and Culture, Annual Events, Kidstuff, Recreation, and more—there are more

Catch a sunrise before catching some waves on the Outer Banks. PHOTO: COURTESY OF BOB REARDON

than 25 information-packed chapters. If you're looking for a cozy dinner spot, browse through our Restaurants chapter. If you want to spend the afternoon in search of a special souvenir, turn to Shopping. If you've always wanted to try scuba diving, parasailing, or surfing, all the information you'll need is waiting in Watersports.

We've arranged this book so you can read it bit by bit, turning to those particular pages that pique your interest while breezing by those that don't. But please go back and thumb through any parts you may have skipped at first. We bet you'll learn something and maybe even discover some new favorite spots or pastimes along the way. Be sure to note the passel of excellent maps tucked in here at the book's beginning as well.

Finally, feel free to mark up this guide. Jot down your own discoveries, observations, and experiences, and let us know about them. We'd love to hear any suggestions or comments you have that will help us improve our effort to make the most of your time on the Outer Banks. Reach us online at our Web site (www.insiders.com) or write us at this address:

The Globe Pequot Press
P.O. Box 480
Guilford, CT 06437-0480

Area Overview

The Outer Banks is a world of islands, linked to the rest of civilization only by a few bridges and ferries. This fact lends a separatist character to the Outer Banks, with residents who are proud to not be caught up in the trappings of the mainland and vacationers who come here to forget the city life. Time seems to lose meaning as one slips into the indescribable realm of "island time," which gets more surreal the farther south you go.

Cultural traditions and norms seem to fall by the wayside once one has crossed over onto one of the islands. Suddenly, it's perfectly acceptable to go barefoot all day, to wear your bathing suit to the grocery store, to get buried up to your neck in sand, to spend hours on the porch staring at the water, to stop activity and come to rest to watch the sun set. When I moved to the Outer Banks, one of the first things that let me know I was someplace wonderfully different was when I attended a Nags Head Board of Commissioners meeting and one of the town commissioners was wearing a coat and tie, wrinkled khakis, and Teva sandals, his toes peeking out from under the boardroom table.

The area is a chain of several islands—Roanoke, Colington, Bodie, Hatteras, and Ocracoke—stretching over 100 miles along eastern North Carolina. Bodie Island, the largest landmass of the Outer Banks, encompassing the land from the north side of Oregon Inlet through Carova, is technically not an island. Physically, it's connected to Virginia and is therefore a peninsula. However, since the state border is closed to land crossings, Bodie is, in many minds, an island.

Some people also consider the islands south of Ocracoke Island, from Cape Lookout and through Bogue Banks, to be part of the Outer Banks. But for the purposes of this book, the Outer Banks are just from the Virginia line through Ocracoke.

Bodie, Hatteras, and Ocracoke Islands are barrier islands, separated from the mainland by a system of wide, shallow sounds. The barrier islands are like reefs of sand protecting the mainland from the ravages of the Atlantic Ocean. What keeps the barrier islands from just wasting away in the face of all that power is their ability to shift and move, to go with the flow of nature. On the other hand, vegetation plays a huge part in the stabilization of the islands, making them fit for human occupation. Roanoke Island and Colington Island are floating in the sound west of the barrier islands.

The Albemarle-Pamlico Sounds system that separates the Outer Banks from the mainland is the second largest estuary in the United States, second only to the Chesapeake Bay. These sounds have 3,000 square miles of surface water and 30,000 square miles of watershed. The system is made up of seven sounds—Albemarle, Pamlico, Currituck, Croatan, Roanoke, Bogue, and Core. These sounds are fed by inlets, cuts of water that slice through the skinny islands from the ocean, and by five major rivers. The Albemarle-Pamlico system is one of the most biologically productive estuaries in the United States, and it supports a huge variety of wildlife, fish, shellfish, and plants.

Three counties lay claim to these barrier islands—Currituck, Dare, and Hyde. Dare is the largest county, with 391 square miles of land, 509 square miles of water, and over

31,000 residents. Dare County stretches from north of Duck to the tip of Hatteras Island, including Roanoke Island and a huge chunk of mainland. Currituck County encompasses 255 square miles of land, most of it on the mainland and a small portion of barrier island from north of Duck up to the Virginia border. Currituck County has a population of 19,500. Hyde County's Outer Banks portion is Ocracoke Island, a 13- by 2-mile island with 700 residents. The 50,000 or so year-round residents of these islands host over seven million visitors a year.

Due to bridges and air travel, the Outer Banks is now more easily accessible than ever. This has led to rapid development, along with a dramatic increase in the availability of goods and services. Residents definitely have all the accoutrements needed for a comfortable way of life, including a thriving economy with low unemployment; affordable housing; retail stores offering almost everything they could possibly want; an abundance of restaurants, arts, and entertainment; a hospital; and recreational opportunities. With all this, however, no one will deny that the pulse of life on these barrier islands is still set by wind and water. The weather and the natural world play intimate roles in the lives of barrier island residents.

Part of what makes the Outer Banks so special is the Cape Hatteras National Seashore, which encompasses over 50 miles of rugged, undeveloped beaches, dunes, marshes, and flatlands. With commercial and residential development continually increasing on the barrier islands, the Cape Hatteras National Seashore—the first national seashore in the nation by the way—is treasured and appreciated more than ever. Three national wildlife refuges further protect a portion of the Outer Banks from development.

Whether it's the sunrise, the sunset, or what goes on between, the Outer Banks offers the most extraordinary of what island life has to offer. "The sunsets here are the prettiest I have ever seen," Orville Wright wrote to his sister in 1900. "The clouds light up with all colors, in the background, with deep clouds of various shapes fringed with gold before. The moon rises in much the same style, and lights up the pile of sand almost like day." We have more than just good looks and personality, though: We have history. We have drama. We have lots of good stories to tell.

In this chapter we offer overviews of the areas that make up the Outer Banks, taking you on a north-to-south tour of Corolla and Currituck's beaches, Sanderling and Duck, Southern Shores, Kitty Hawk, Kill Devil Hills, Nags Head, Roanoke Island, Hatteras Island, and Ocracoke Island.

Corolla and Currituck's Beaches

Fewer than 20 years ago, Currituck County's Outer Banks beaches were the barrier islands' outback. Seeming to stretch infinitely from north of Duck to the Virginia border, wide windswept expanses of sandy terrain lay virtually untouched except by winds, blue herons, and wild horses (see our Close-up in the Attractions chapter). While other island communities on the Outer Banks became boomtowns in the late 1970s, the northern beaches remained virtually untouched. For many years, the area was blocked to vehicles on both ends—by the state of Virginia on the north end and by a private developer on the south end. In 1984 the state opened up NC 12 into the tiny village of Corolla, and it wasn't long before developers and vacationers started setting their sights on the Currituck Outer Banks.

From these barren dunes harboring a few fishing shacks and a handful of private homes, thousands of upscale houses, including 5,000-square-foot mansions, have sprung up on miles of recently paved subdivision roads. A family-owned convenience store that once supplied the only local goods for fewer

Now a private cottage, the Old Whaleshead Lifesaving Station has been moved to a four-wheel-drive area.

PHOTO: LINDA LAUBY

than 100 permanent residents has been overshadowed by a modern chain grocery store. A lighthouse completed in 1875 has become more important as a landmark for tourists than as a guide for sailors. Dozens of eateries offer a variety of cuisine, and three quality resort shopping plazas are available to fulfill almost every desire of the hundreds of thousands of visitors that flock to the northernmost Outer Banks in the summertime.

In a span of 10 short years, the permanent population of the Corolla-area beaches grew from 171 residents in 1985 to 620 residents in 1995; meanwhile, the seasonal population skyrocketed from 4,271 to 19,370 in the same period. Within that decade, 70 permanent houses and 563 seasonal rental houses expanded to 255 permanent homes and 2,039 seasonal houses. By the year 2000, the number of seasonal homes had jumped to 2,750.

The tiny community where everyone knew everyone else has undergone enormous change in its transformation into a favorite travel destination, but development has been tasteful and aesthetically pleasing. (And everyone still knows everyone else.)

It has only been in recent years that people referred to the whole of the Currituck Outer Banks as "Corolla." Technically, Corolla is only the tiny, old village that sits on the west side of the island near the lighthouse. The Currituck Outer Banks has no incorporated towns and consists of several planned developments. From north to south, these are Ocean Hill, Corolla Light, Monteray Shores, Whalehead Beach, Buck Island, Crown Point, Ocean Sands, Ocean Sands South, and Pine Island.

From Fishing Village to Vacation Destination

The remoteness of Currituck's Outer Banks kept these spectacular sea oat–strewn dunes isolated long after the barrier islands' southern beaches had grown in leaps and bounds. The lack of a permanent population and the accompanying services put a built-in damper on tourism and growth. In 1972 coastal officials called Currituck County's 23 miles of beaches "the longest undeveloped strip of coastal land on the Eastern Seaboard." One telephone, which only allowed outgoing calls, served the entire area. The spit island was not even connected to line-distributed electricity until the 1950s. Families placed weekly food orders with the postmaster, who ran a tiny general store in his house. The few visitors to Corolla traveled on a sandy lane or the beach at low tide.

Winston-Salem developer Earl Slick saw possibilities in the vast stretches of untouched beach and soundfront, and in 1973 he changed the face of the northern Outer Banks. For $2 million, he and his Coastland Corporation purchased 636 acres just north of the Dare County line from Texas oil tycoon Walter B. Davis.

Slick proceeded two years later to erect a wooden guardhouse at the southern tip of his property, barring all but residents or landowners from entering Currituck beaches. Impassioned protests, which at times came to blows, eventually put the matter in the hands of the North Carolina Supreme Court. Finally, on November 1, 1984, the state took over the road that stretched from the Dare County line north. As security guards watched, bulldozers toppled the guard post, opening free passage all the way to Corolla and clearing a path for widespread development.

Despite its relative isolation before Slick's arrival, the northern beaches have always had their own unique history and allure. After the Civil War, Currituck Beach was the largest community on the Outer Banks between Kitty Hawk and Virginia. Fishing families lived in small wooden houses near the sound. The area's reputation as "Sportsmen's Paradise" had its genesis at this time, when hunters discovered the plentiful waterfowl inhabiting the Currituck Sound.

In 1874, the U.S. government put Currituck's beaches on the map by building the Currituck Beach Lifesaving Station and the Currituck Beach lighthouse. The lifesaving station, one of the Outer Banks's original seven outposts, was first named Jones Hill, then Whalehead, and finally, Currituck Beach. The 150-foot-tall, red-brick beacon lifesaving station, the last major lighthouse built on North Carolina's barrier islands, is known as the Currituck Beach Lighthouse.

The tiny fishing community was officially named Corolla the following year, when the federal government installed a modest post office down the road a bit from the lighthouse. Three names were rejected before a local teacher suggested that postal officials name the village after the inner petals of a flower, the corolla (pronounced "ka-RAH-la" by locals).

Throughout the early 1900s, Currituck County's barrier islands grew in popularity as a retreat for recreational hunters who flocked to the dense marshlands each fall for the annual waterfowl migration. You can still spot crudely built duck blinds along the swampy shores. Historic structures have been turned into resort community clubhouses, real-estate offices, retail shops, restaurants, and county-owned tourist attractions. The Whalehead Club, the largest and most magnificent of all the Outer Banks hunting lodges, is being restored with tourism tax profits, a project that is nearing completion. This Currituck County facility is open for tours daily throughout the summer season. (See our Attractions chapter.)

Putting aside its appeal as premier hunting and fishing grounds, Corolla was unsentimentally regarded as little more than a wasteland of sand. Until about 25 years ago, Currituck County was even known to give tracts of barrier island land away with purchases of mainland tracts.

Getting to Currituck County's Outer Banks

In the 1950s Virginia and North Carolina officials began talking about building a road from Sandbridge, in Virginia, to Corolla, traversing a long spit of solid sand

and the state line. That route, however, was never started. Today, only longtime property owners with special permits can drive through the protected lands that lie between Carova Beach and Sandbridge. Fences and metal gates prevent access to anyone other than pass-holders. The rest of the populace must drive up NC 12 from the south to get to Currituck's beaches. Turn onto NC 12 at its junction with US 158 in Kitty Hawk, 1.5 miles east of the Wright Memorial Bridge's eastern terminus; then, travel through Southern Shores, Duck, and Sanderling, and you'll hit the county line. Although it's only about 10 miles from Kitty Hawk to the Currituck County border, and another 12 miles to the end of the paved road at Corolla, the trip can take up to an hour or more on weekends during the peak season.

Once you pass through Duck, you'll notice the roadside starts opening up and the terrain looks sparser and wilder. Watch your speed limit, because police are on the lookout for speeders who forget themselves on the straight two-lane road when traffic is light.

Much debate has taken place over whether to construct a two-lane, 4.8-mile bridge spanning the Currituck Sound from the mainland to Corolla. The proposed project would cut about 40 miles off the trip from US 158 in Currituck County to NC 12 in Corolla.

Corolla Today

No Outer Banks community has changed as much in the past decade as has Corolla. Less than 10 years ago, NC 12 took an abrupt right turn toward Whalehead Beach and continued on a circuitous route to Corolla Village. Now, Monteray Plaza—a huge shopping center housing a Food Lion grocery store, a movie theater, and a variety of restaurants and stores—stands where a sign on a vacant lot once welcomed visitors to Whalehead. Across the road, TimBuck II shopping center lures visitors to its specialty stores, eateries, and entertainment

options. NC 12 doesn't veer off to the right anymore but continues northward past Monteray Shores, on through Corolla Light, Corolla Village, Ocean Hill, and the Villages at Ocean Hill.

The northern beaches are home to some of the most luxurious rental properties on the Outer Banks. Although the area still has no home mail delivery, you won't have any trouble finding upscale shopping and dining, medical services, amenities galore, and entertainment other than that provided by nature. And despite the fact that Corolla's popularity is continually rising, you'll discover that you still feel far away from the rest of the world while visiting this northern destination.

In the past decade, developers and individuals have built thousands of homes between the Dare County line and the Virginia border, and at least 100 businesses have opened their doors. The Currituck Club, a Corolla subdivision, opened in July 1996. The community boasts an 18-hole, 6,800-yard championship golf course, designed by world-renowned golf course architect Rees Jones (see our Golf chapter). The 3.7 miles of soundside property will eventually include 600 patio homes, single-family homes and condominiums situated on half-acre lots. The gated community also has beach oceanfront access. (See our Real Estate chapter for more information.)

Most visitors to Currituck's beaches tend to rent the huge homes that straddle the undulating sand dunes. The average Corolla house sleeps 10 to 15 people, includes more than 3,000 square feet of living space, has a pool and hot tub, and is available for weekly rentals. Many of the contained communities also offer exercise facilities, racket or golf clubs, indoor and outdoor swimming pools, boardwalk beach accesses, and trolley services. The area's first chain hotel, a Hampton Inn, is opening on the oceanfront in Pine Island, south of Corolla, in the spring of 2002.

Retail stores scattered throughout this upscale area sell items ranging from handmade hammocks to custom-designed jewelry. Restaurants appeal to all tastes from

The interior of the Currituck Beach Lighthouse in Corolla is a photographer's dream. PHOTO: COURTESY OF MARY ELLEN RIDDLE

raw or steamed seafood to elegant European dining. And watersports—kayaking, windsurfing, sailing, and more—are popular from early spring through fall (see our Shopping, Restaurants, and Watersports chapters for details).

Although tourists flock to the northern beaches during the summer tourism season, the permanent population of Currituck County's Outer Banks is still small, estimated at about 500 people. A county satellite office keeps them connected with Currituck's services, but children who live in Corolla year-round travel more than one hour by bus to attend Dare County schools—the closest ones to their resort community.

Currituck National Wildlife Refuge

A few miles north of the Currituck Beach Lighthouse, the multistory mansions become more sparse and the paved two-lane highway dead-ends at a sand hill. Here, a wildlife sanctuary provides a safe haven for endangered piping plover, wild boar, and other wildlife. A 4-foot-tall fence stretching a mile from sound to sea marks the southern barrier of this 1,800-acre sanctuary, where most of Corolla's wild horses still range (see the Close-up in our Attractions chapter). People can walk through the fence, however, and four-wheel-drive vehicles can cross over a cattle grate.

Once Corolla's most popular tourist attraction, the wild horses no longer roam freely in the populated village. The Corolla Wild Horse Fund is headquartered at county satellite offices, where membership information is available.

Isolated Outposts North of the Road's End

There is no paved route from Corolla to the Virginia border. Still, a few hundred homes line this expanse of sand. On summer afternoons, more than a thousand four-wheel-drive vehicles create their own paths on the beach as they drive into and around a community called Carova—where North Carolina meets Virginia. Note that Carova's name is a melding of both states.

In May 1998 a new ordinance requiring permits to drive all-terrain vehicles (ATVs) to Carova went into effect. Call the county satellite office at (252) 453-8555 for more information.

About 300 permanent residents reside along these remote beaches, and new homes go up every year. Residents negotiate tides and beach not only in off-road and four-wheel-drive vehicles, but also in regular cars with big deflated tires. Bicyclists sometimes manage at dead low-tide to scoot around the fence into Sandbridge, Virginia, which natives in pre-fence days did routinely.

Despite being relatively protected from civilization, the area is patrolled by county, state, and federal officers. A system of dirt roads behind the dune line allows residents access to their homes. Most residents and visitors to Swan Beach, Carova, North Swan Beach, and the Seagull subdivisions drive on the beach above the waterline or on well-tread tracks at the base of the dune line.

If you don't have a four-wheel-drive vehicle, you probably shouldn't risk the tricky business of driving on the beach. Local guides will be glad to show you around in off-road vehicles. Two companies offer guided tours of the area (see our Recreation chapter). Watch out for tree stumps, though. An ancient forest that historians say grew along the sound more than 800 years ago still thrusts its sea-withered trunks through the waves at an area known as Wash Woods.

Whether you're staying in one of Currituck Beach's exclusive rental homes or camping somewhere on the southern Outer Banks, Corolla and the four-wheel-drive area are well worth exploring.

Duck

What makes Duck unique is its village-like atmosphere and the incredible water views that run along the main street of town. In this upscale resort community, you'll find wonderful waterfront boutiques, art galleries, and a variety of fine restaurants and casual eateries within easy strolling distance of one another and within walking or biking distance of many of Duck's neighborhoods. In the busy season, Duck teems with visitors and traffic crawls along the two-lane highway that runs north to Corolla, but if you're staying elsewhere, it's well worth a special trip. The Travel Channel voted Duck as one of the Top 10 Beaches in Americain 2002.

Duck is the latest Dare County community to incorporate. In the November 2001 elections, the citizens of Duck voted in favor of incorporating into the town of Duck rather than adhere to the county rules as it has always done. Incorporation will allow the town to create its own zoning laws as well as receive a higher percentage of tax revenues. The town of Duck

Insiders' Tip

The Army Corps of Engineers Research Pier north of Duck is the only oceanographic research pier of its kind in the world. See our Attractions chapter for information on touring this facility.

will not be official until May 2002, with elections planned for November 2002.

Tourism was slow to find Duck. It began to catch hold in the early 1980s, but once it did, the town grew rapidly (too rapidly, according to many locals). Two decades ago, T-shirts that read "Stuck in Duck" seemed to speak for a lot of the young people who craved more excitement than could be found in this sleepy town. Today, it is affluent, busy, and thriving. In addition to the usual beach fare, you can find some real treasures, authentic and one-of-a-kind items to bring home as souvenirs. Plan to enjoy at least one meal here: Duck boasts many outstanding restaurants, and some offer outdoor tables. Two bed-and-breakfast inns accommodate nightly guests, but don't expect to find strings of motels. Most every visitor rents a vacation home in Duck.

Duck makes an excellent jumping-off point for the full range of watersports. You'll find places to rent kayaks, canoes, windsurfing equipment, sailboats, JetSkis, and Wave Runners, and you can launch very close to restaurants and shops. For extra exhilaration, try a few hours of kayaking followed by lunch or dinner at a soundside table.

The town grew up on one of the most slender strips of sand on the Outer Banks. The ocean and the sound are close enough here so that many cottages offer extraordinary views of both, and, when the weather turns nasty, NC 12 floods quickly in many sections around town. The neighborhoods in and around Duck are a pleasing mixture of graceful older cottages and luxurious new homes. The gently rolling terrain is in contrast to many of the flatter areas of the Outer Banks, and this is the place to look if you crave a shady, tree-lined escape or a hilltop retreat where you can watch the sun rise and set from two sides of the same home.

A Growing Economy

Like most barrier island beach communities, Duck started out as a small fishing village. Families lived in rough-hewn wooden houses set atop 2-foot blocks that kept the floors above the level to which the sea or sound had been known to rise during storms. With more trees and thicker underbrush here than in other areas of the Outer Banks, many Duck residents farmed small garden plots to supplement their seafood and waterfowl diets. Hogs, cows, and chickens were raised in the woods while watermen worked from dawn until dark, netting fish from the beach with long-haul seines, taking dories out in the sound to set pound nets, and trapping crabs with wooden crates. Whole crews of women, men, and children toiled together for days mending heavy cotton fishing nets, sometimes garnering up to 25 cents an hour for their trouble. During the Great Depression, children, and sometimes grown-ups, made a decent living catching "peelers"—blue crabs that had shed their shells. The business of harvesting these soft-shell crabs, still a major fishing enterprise on the Outer Banks, first cropped up in Duck. Eel pots also were prevalent along the shallow shores and shoals. Made of thin wood and more rounded than the crab pots, these contraptions' contents gave local fishermen an item to export. They packed the long, snakelike creatures in salt, stored them in barrels, and trucked them along the sand trails to Hampton Roads markets, where eel were once eaten in abundance.

The first post office opened in Duck in 1909, when postmaster Lloyd Toler gave the community its charming moniker in honor of the area's abundant waterfowl. The facility was abandoned by 1950. Year-round residents today have to travel to Kitty Hawk for their mail, though residents and visitors can mail letters and postcards from the little postal station now located in the Barrier Island Shops.

Little changed in Duck until the late 1970s. Single-family homes were sparsely scattered throughout the thick shrubbery, and small wooden boats bobbed from tree trunks turned into pilings.

Tourism took over about 1980, when small shops began lining up along the two-lane road through town and larger houses sprang from the beach areas. Barrier Island Station, among the biggest and most popular timeshare resorts on the Outer Banks, now houses a new restaurant and includes an indoor and outdoor pool, tennis courts, a communal hot tub, and live evening entertainment on a covered waterfront deck.

In 1990 you had your choice of five restaurants between Kitty Hawk and Corolla. Today more than 25 locally owned establishments offer breakfast, lunch, and dinner: a coffeehouse, a pizza parlor, an upscale deli with unusual home-made salads, scads of sandwich shops, bistros, and a marvelous wine bar and cafe. Shopping runs the gamut of galleries, boutiques, and colorful shops offering offbeat wares, crafts created by local artisans, and quality sea-themed souvenirs (see our Restaurants and Shopping chapters for more details).

Recreational offerings abound here, too, and are being added to every season. You can learn to windsurf or rent a sailboat or a trimaran. Speed across the sound on a JetSki, paddle around a marsh island in a canoe or kayak, or bounce about the waves on an inflatable banana boat.

No matter what your tastes in food, fashion, or fun, you will find something to enjoy in the now-bustling village of Duck.

Getting to Duck

If you're heading to Duck from the northern Outer Banks, turn left onto NC 12 at its junction with US 158 in Kitty Hawk, 1.5 miles from the Wright Memorial Bridge's terminus. Travel past the flattop homes of Southern Shores, and wind around the dunes on the two-lane highway. On good days, Duck is a 10-minute drive from Kitty Hawk. In heavy summer traffic, bottlenecks form in the village, causing backups that last for miles and, sometimes, more than 30 minutes.

NC 12 curves through the center of Duck. All the commercial development is along this road, confined to the highway by zoning ordinances, landscaped with lovely local foliage. Drive slowly—even we locals are astounded by the fetching sights around every bend.

The sea is quite close to Duck, as is the sound; so, many rental homes provide the rare opportunity for viewing both bodies of water from upstairs open-air decks. Wild beans, peas, and cattails cover the marshy yards, most of which are at least partially wooded, with the houses tucked between the trees.

True to its name, Duck is home and passageway for a variety of nesting and migrating shore birds and waterfowl. Streets are named after these feathered creatures, which often come to call. Loons, cormorants, gannet, and flocks of terns and gulls soak up the sun's warmth near the water's edge. You can sometimes see swans and mallards swimming in the sound at sunrise as well as otters playing in the sound.

On the northern edge of Duck, a U.S. Army Corps of Engineers research facility occupies the site of a former Navy bombing range. Military weapons recovery crews have dug up thousands of unexploded ordnances around here, and an 1,800-foot-long pier now provides scientists with an important opportunity to track subsurface currents, study the effects of jetties and beach nourishment projects, and chart the movements of the slender strips of sand. (Turn to our Attractions chapter for more information.)

Beyond the pier, heading north toward Corolla, you'll find the Duck Volunteer Fire Department, the Dare County Sheriff's Office northern beach station, and the Duck Recycling Center.

About 5 miles north of Duck, through an open wilderness area, Sanderling is the northernmost community on Dare County's beaches—an isolated, exclusive, upscale enclave with 300 acres stretching from sound to sea.

The community itself was initiated in 1978, setting a precedent for excellence among vacation destinations. These neighborhoods, barely visible from the road, approach land planning sensitively, preserving as much natural vegetation as possible and always aiming for architectural excellence. They are well worth searching out.

In 1985, the Sanderling Inn and Restaurant opened in the restored Caffey's Inlet Lifesaving Station, built in 1874. With cedar-shake siding, natural wood interiors, and English country antiques, it has the appearance of turn-of-the-20th-century Nags Head resorts and the ambiance of a European escape. It's large and airy, with wide porches that provide plenty of room for conversation, drinks, and soaking in the sunrise in wooden rocking chairs. (See our Accommodations and Restaurants chapters for details.)

North of Sanderling, Palmer's Island Club is a 35-acre development with 15 oceanfront one-acre lots and at least eight estates ranging from 6,000 to 10,000 square feet each. The homes are engineered to withstand 120 mph winds. Signature architectural embellishments are scaled to match the grandeur of the natural environment.

Southern Shores

Stretching from sound to sea, Southern Shores is heralded as one of the most beautiful, well-thought-out developments on the Outer Banks. Interwoven with canals, maritime hardwood forests, dunes, and private beaches, its scenic beauty is hard to match. Real estate agents call Southern Shores property one of the best Outer Banks values for long-term investment.

Southern Shores is south of Duck and north of Kitty Hawk. You can enter this community via NC 12, South Dogwood Trail, which runs alongside Kitty Hawk School, or by Juniper Trail, which runs perpendicular to the Marketplace shopping center.

Yesteryear and Today

Southern Shores was the first planned community on the northern Outer Banks and a pioneer for underground utilities. The visionary Frank Stick—developer, artist, outdoorsman, and self-trained ichthyologist—bought the land in 1947 for $30,000. Today it is worth more than $430 million.

Stick worked eight years developing the northern Outer Banks community,

and his care is evident throughout the town today. He had his hands full designing and building cottages and homes, supervising the platting of lots and the installation of roads. A master illustrator, who studied under the distinguished Howard Pyle, Stick later shared the task of developing the virgin land with his son, David. Much like a watercolor from the era in which the senior Stick thrived, Southern Shores was developed to resemble a *Wind in the Willows* paradise.

Home to cardinals, finches, mockingbirds, Canadian grosbeaks, woodpeckers, quail, raccoons, deer, and squirrels, this idyllic place with seas of white dogwoods blooming in spring speaks to the Sticks' love and dedication for preserving the natural habitat. Perhaps nowhere else on the Outer Banks better illustrates the harmonious coexistence of human development and nature.

The small oceanside community consists of approximately four square miles and lies alongside NC 12 as it stretches through the northern Outer Banks. As you

Sea oats and grasses help stabilize the dunes by preventing erosion—never pick them. PHOTO: HORSLEY/GARDNER

drive through the town along this winding, two-lane road, you'll see open skies, dunes with low scrub vegetation, vacation homes including old-style cottages with the vintage flattops, intermittent with large, expensive beach homes. If you turn off the highway away from the ocean onto one of the side roads, the landscape changes dramatically. Here you'll find neighborhoods of year-round homes, green lawns, hardwood trees draped with Spanish moss, dogwoods, and a sprawling golf course.

A Haven of Solitude

Comprising mostly single-family homes, Southern Shores is predominantly a residential town uncluttered by the commercial aspects of other Outer Banks areas, making it the perfect place to seek solitude. Residents enjoy canoeing or kayaking in the canal system designed by the younger Stick, a local historian and published author. Though not the painter his father was, David's artistic talent was in full swing when he created these panoramic lagoons that connect interior properties to Jean Guite Bay and Currituck Sound.

The community includes two private marinas, soundside picnic and bathing areas, and ocean beach accesses situated every 600 feet. The accesses are available only to residents and vacationers staying in the area (make sure you display the proper permit), affording every beachgoer enough elbow room to comfortably spread a blanket or throw a Frisbee. A soundside wading beach on North Dogwood Trail is a favorite spot for families because the shallow sound water is a safer place for children to swim than the ocean. In the summer, the picnic area has toilet facilities on site. Paved and unpaved bike trails meander through the town. Anyone can use the facilities, but to park you must belong to the civic association or get a town sticker. In either case, you have to be a property owner or guest to park in Southern Shores.

The golf course at Duck Woods Country Club winds its way through a residential neighborhood of Southern Shores, offering outstanding play in a pristine setting among tall pines, dogwoods, and other foliage. The 18-hole course is the oldest on the Outer Banks and accepts public play year-round (see our Golf chapter).

The 40 original families who inhabited Southern Shores formed the town's first civic association. The Southern Shores Civic Association acts like a parks and recreation department. It owns, operates, and maintains the marinas, playgrounds, beach accesses, and crossovers for residents, property owners, and guests. Membership dues cover costs, but most of the physical upkeep is done by volunteers in the community.

Today the population has expanded to more than 2,500 year-round residents, with retirees accounting for a large percentage of the population. The occupations of working residents vary greatly. The town hall is on a small hill off US 158 on Skyline Road.

It's been 52 years since Stick first purchased Southern Shores, but the slow pace of development means there still is real estate available. Raw land on the oceanfront or soundfront is hard to come by these days, but those wanting to purchase property can obtain homes or land in the beach zone, dunes, or woods. Due to careful planning, Southern Shores has land reserved for a future civic center and several plots to be developed for other town needs.

The town's only retail establishment, The Marketplace, includes a movie theater, a Food Lion, and a multitude of smaller shops (see our Shopping chapter). This complex sits at the edge of Southern Shores, just east of the base of the Wright Memorial Bridge. However, the shops, restaurants, and services of Kitty Hawk and Duck are only minutes away.

Southern Shores was incorporated in 1979 and growth has occurred in the development over the last 52 years, but the developers' spirit of conservation is felt with every bike ride, every sunset, and every tour of the waterways that weave together flora, fauna, and humankind. The town continues to be environmentally conscious and is the first Outer Banks community to offer curbside recycling.

Kitty Hawk

If you access the Outer Banks from North Carolina's Currituck County mainland, the first town you'll reach is Kitty Hawk. This beach municipality begins at the eastern end of the Wright Memorial Bridge over the Currituck Sound and stretches sound-to-sea for about 4 miles. Within its town limits are a maritime forest, fishing pier, golf course, condominiums, and a historic, secluded village where Wilbur and Orville Wright stayed while conducting experiments on their famed flying machines.

Southern Shores forms the northern boundary of Kitty Hawk and Kill Devil Hills is to the south. Milepost (MP) markers offer the best means of finding your destination. Most rental cottages, shops, restaurants, attractions, and resorts in this area can be located by green milepost markers along US 158 (Insiders call this the Bypass) and NC 12 (Insiders call this the Beach Road). The first milepost marker is in Kitty Hawk where the highway splits near the Aycock Brown Welcome Center.

With its name bonded to aviation history and its positioning as one of the gateways to the reputed wide, undeveloped beaches of the Outer Banks, Kitty Hawk might not be what you expect—at least at first glance. Much of the 4 miles of beachfront here is narrower and appears more developed than any other place on the barrier islands. Even though Wilbur and Orville Wright certainly disembarked and stayed with the locals in the village of Kitty Hawk, they didn't actually fly here. Their experiments and successful flights were accomplished a few miles down the road in Kill Devil Hills.

Now that we've got that straight, enjoy Kitty Hawk for what it is: a vacation getaway offering lots of family-oriented activities, a fishing pier, some great eateries, convenient shopping, and all the fun you could want on a clean beach. Plus, tucked

away within the borders of Kitty Hawk's 12 square miles are some of the loveliest and most exclusive communities in the central beach area.

Keep in mind that when you just feel like taking a ride, the Beach Road through Kitty Hawk is one of the few stretches on the entire Outer Banks where you can see the ocean right out your car window. As you cruise south along the beach, you'll start noticing some weather-beaten houses perched tenuously on the shoreline. At high tide and in stormy weather, waves crash under the house pilings and wash out truckloads of sand. The ocean plays chicken every year with these tired beach cottages, and just about every year a cottage cries uncle and collapses into the pounding surf. After every "big blow," local gossip (we love to talk weather here) inevitably comes around to an update on the Kitty Hawk cottages. You've likely gotten a good view of one of them on The Weather Channel, which, to the Visitor Bureau's chagrin, seems to delight in showing the wreckage of a Kitty Hawk beach house clinging pitifully to the sands during a storm. Once they're gone, they're gone, as federal coastal management law now forbids building closer than 60 feet from a coastline's first line of vegetation.

By one popular version, Kitty Hawk owes its colorful name to a derivation of local Indians' references to goose hunting season as "killy honker" or "killy honk." Eighteenth-century documents record this northern beach community as "Chickahauk," a name adopted by the community between Kitty Hawk and Southern Shores. Other theories say the name evolved from "skeeter hawk," mosquito hawks that were prolific in the area, or from ospreys or similar raptors preying on the area's kitty wren.

The History of "A Hospitable People"

Primarily a fishing and farming community from the late 18th century through the early 1900s, Kitty Hawk Village grew up along the wide bay that juts into the barrier

Set aside a day (or night) for fishing from one of the many piers in the area. PHOTO: COURTESY OF BOB REARDON

islands along Albemarle Sound. By 1790 a builder, a merchant, a shoemaker, a minister, a planter, and a mariner all owned deeds to the sandy, sloping marshlands that now constitute Kitty Hawk. The community received additional goods from ships and ferries arriving from Elizabeth City, North Carolina, and Norfolk, Virginia.

In 1874 one of the Outer Banks's seven original lifesaving stations was built on the beach at Kitty Hawk. A U.S. Weather Bureau opened there the following year and remained in service until 1904. This weather station provided the Wright brothers with information about local wind patterns, which was the impetus for the Ohio bicycle shop owners to test their wings at Kill Devil Hill.

The first families of Kitty Hawk were named Twiford, Baum, Etheridge, Perry, and Hill. These hearty folk were self-sufficient, building their own boats, fishing, farming, and raising livestock on the open range. Many descendants of these early inhabitants still live on the west side of Kitty Hawk. A drive along winding Kitty Hawk Road, which begins just north of the 7-Eleven, will lead you to other streets with such names as Elijah Baum Road, Herbert Perry Road, and Moore Shore Road. Along the latter is a monument that designates the spot where Orville and Wilbur Wright assembled their plane before successfully completing their historic flight a few miles away in 1903.

"I assure you, you will find a hospitable people when you come among us," Kitty Hawk Lifesaving Station Capt. Billy Tate wrote to Wilbur Wright in 1900. Tate described the local terrain as "nearly any type of ground you could wish . . . a stretch of sandy land 1 mile by 5 with a bare hill in the center 80 feet high, not a tree or a bush anywhere to break the wind current." The winds, he wrote, were "always steady, generally from 10 to 20 miles velocity per hour. If you decide to try your machine here and come, I will take pleasure in doing all I can for your convenience and success and pleasure."

Wilbur arrived at Kitty Hawk in September of that year. He traveled by rail from Dayton, Ohio, to Elizabeth City, where he boarded *The Curlicue* bound for the Outer Banks. (Before the Wright Memorial Bridge was built, visitors to the Outer Banks arrived by boat from Elizabeth City.) The boat trip took two days in hurricane winds. Wilbur stayed with the Tates until Orville arrived, and then the two set up camp in Kitty Hawk Village.

Members of the Kitty Hawk Beach Lifesaving Station crew assisted the brothers with their early experiments. Even though many of the first flights were conducted near the town of Kill Devil Hills, the Wrights' first Outer Banks visit—and their letters carrying a Kitty Hawk postmark—etched this town's name in the annals of history around the world. It's not surprising that many visitors think the Wright Brothers National Monument is in Kitty Hawk, instead of 3 miles south atop Kill Devil Hill.

The first post office in Kitty Hawk opened November 11, 1878. A second one was established in 1905 to serve the western section of the community. In 1993 the biggest post office facility on the Outer Banks was built on the eastern side of US 158 in Kitty Hawk.

Residents of this town floated their own $7,000 bond in 1924 to build a school. Housed in a single building, the grammar and high school served fewer than 100 students until a Dare County high school consolidated Outer Banks children at a single facility in Manteo. Today, Kitty Hawk still has its own elementary school. Middle-school students travel by bus to Kill Devil Hills to attend First Flight Middle School, and high-school students still ride to Manteo, almost an hour's commute for some. Today there are close to 3,000 residents in this town.

The Transition to Vacation Destination

Unlike Nags Head, which has been a thriving summer resort since before the Civil War, Kitty Hawk didn't become a vacation destination until about 65 years ago. A group of Elizabeth City businessmen bought 7 miles of beach north of Kitty Hawk Village in the late 1920s and formed the Wright Memorial Bridge Company. By 1930 they had built a 3-mile wooden span across the Currituck Sound from Point Harbor to the Outer Banks. Now travelers could finally arrive at the barrier island beaches by car from the mainland. Kitty Hawk land became popular—and a lot more pricey. Summer visitors streamed across the new bridge, paying $1.00 per car for the privilege.

With the sudden boom in tourism, development shifted from the protected soundside hammocks to the open, windswept beaches. Small wooden cottages sprung from behind dunes on the oceanfront. As the beach eroded over the years, wind and water had its way with many of the beachfront homes. Since 1993 more than a half-dozen houses have been swept away during hurricanes and nor'easters, providing newfound ocean frontage for the neighbor cottage across the street.

Even the original Kitty Hawk Lifesaving Station had to be jacked up and moved to a more protected site on the west side of the Beach Road to prevent tides from carrying it to a watery grave as well. The station is now a private residence, but travelers can still recognize the original Outer Banks gabled architecture of this historic structure.

In the western reaches of this community, the maritime forest of Kitty Hawk Woods winds for miles over tall ridges and blackwater swamps. Here, primarily year-round residents make their homes on private plots and in new subdivisions. Some lots are much larger here than in other central beach communities. The twisting vines, dripping Spanish moss, and abundant tall trees also offer a seclusion and shelter from the storms not found in the expansive, open oceanfront areas. On summer days, locals often ride horses around the shady lanes of old Kitty Hawk Village, reminiscent of the days before bridges.

Although you'll find some businesses tucked back in the trees of Kitty Hawk Village, at the western end of Kitty Hawk Road near the sound, most of this town's commercial outposts are along the Bypass and the Beach Road. The Outer Banks's only Wal-Mart is in Shoreside Center near the end of the Wright Memorial Bridge. And Regional Medical Center at MP 1½ offers a full range of emergency and outpatient services.

If you're headed for the beach, you'll find a public bathhouse at MP 4½. The public is also welcome to use the Dare County boat launch at the end of Bob Perry Road, where locals and visitors can set sail during a hot summer day and watch the dolphins frolic in Kitty Hawk Bay.

From waterskiing to fishing, Kitty Hawk presents exceptional recreational possibilities. With all the water fun rounded out with a fine selection of dining establishments, convenient shopping, and medical services, along with history and natural beauty, it's obvious why Kitty Hawk is a favorite beach retreat for young families, retirees, and college students.

Kill Devil Hills and Colington Island

Even among all the other romantic and striking names of Outer Banks communities, Kill Devil Hills swirls a little longer in the imagination. The sand dune where the Wright Brothers revolutionized transportation, Kill Devil Hill, legend has it, was named after the wretched-tasting kill-devil rum that may have been washed up in barrels from shipwrecks in early Colonial days. Another tale has the three hills named after a rogue called Devil Ike, who blamed the theft of shipwrecked cargo on the devil, whom he claimed to have chased to the hills and killed. Other local lore tells of a Banker who, atop one of the dunes, tried to kill the devil he had traded his soul to for a bag of gold.

The Outer Banks's first incorporated town, Kill Devil Hills is bookended by Kitty Hawk and Nags Head. Spanning the barrier island from sound to sea, this beach community is the geographic center of Dare County, with about 6,000 permanent residents. Hundreds of thousands of tourists also visit this bustling beach town each summer. Indeed, the intersection of Ocean Bay Boulevard and Colington Road—where the Wright Memorial, a beach bathhouse, the post office, the town municipal center, the county chamber of commerce, the library, and the entrance to the only road to Colington Island are grouped—is the busiest junction in the county.

Despite the trend toward bigger and more exclusive resort homes and amenities elsewhere on the Outer Banks, Kill Devil Hills remains attached to its place in history as a family-oriented beach for visitors and a centrally located town of moderately priced housing for the permanent population. Kite flying, sea kayaking, windsurfing, sunbathing, air flight tours, shopping, restaurants, motels, churches, and schools combine to make this town a top choice for many, as it has been for more than a half-century.

Condominiums and franchise hotels dot the 5 miles of once-barren dunes. More than 41 miles of paved roads have replaced sandy pathways. Fast-food restaurants have sprung up along the five-lane US 158, forming the Outer Banks's commercial hub, known locally as French Fry Alley.

The Wright Brothers monument in Kill Devil Hills is a popular stop for tourists. PHOTO: COURTESY OF J. AARON TROTMAN

Building Bridges to the Tourist Trade

Kill Devil Hills' population did not really begin to grow until new bridges were constructed from the mainland across the sounds in the early 1930s. Kitty Hawk and Nags Head both had docks for steamer ships bringing passengers from Elizabeth City and Norfolk. Kill Devil Hills was seldom visited until cars could more easily reach the Outer Banks.

The federal government built a lifesaving station in Kill Devil Hills in 1879. At the time Wilbur and Orville Wright arrived from Ohio to test their famed flying machine at the turn of the 20th century, the few permanent residents living along the barren central beaches were mainly lifesavers, fishermen, and salvagers. Even on December 17, 1903, when the Wrights made their first historic flight on windswept flatland below Kill Devil Hill, only a handful of local people watched in awe as the airplane finally soared under its own power.

Schoolchildren and their parents going back and forth to First Flight Elementary and First Flight Middle Schools are treated to the sight of the Wright Brothers Memorial every day, looming under its varied sun- or moon-drenched shadows. Motorists can spy it from the Bypass or Colington Road. A 2-mile bike path was constructed on the outskirts of the landmark, and now in-line skaters, bikers, and joggers exercise in range of the spell of history.

In the summer of 1952, U.S. Representative Lindsay C. Warren, D-N.C., was vacationing at the Croatan Inn on the Outer Banks. One night, historians say, Warren met Kill Devil Hills Coast Guard Capt. William Lewark on the hotel's sprawling deck. The men looked around them at the four dozen wooden "beach box" houses that had sprung from the sand over the past 20 years. Warren warned of overexpansion. He told Lewark that his seaside village ought to be zoned. He told the captain to create a town. So Lewark drafted a petition, called on his neighbors, and convinced 90 of the area's 93 voters to support incorporation. On March 6, 1953, the General Assembly officially recognized Kill Devil Hills as the first town on Outer Banks beaches.

The new town almost died in infancy though. On May 4, 1955, the day that Emily Long Mustian, the town's first elected mayor, was scheduled to take office, the new town ceased to be a town. Fed up with taxes that had jumped to 30 cents from 10 cents per $100 of property value since incorporation, citizens passed a referendum repealing the town charter.

Kill Devil Hills was reborn, however. On February 29, 1956, the North Carolina Supreme Court ruled that the petition by which the referendum had been conducted was invalid and reversed the repeal vote. In the mid-1950s Kill Devil Hills' founders began planning their town hall on a site on the Beach Road. Newly elected officials struggled to provide fire and police protection while residents balked at climbing taxes.

Residents of neighboring communities began looking for similar services but worried that the municipality might expand to encompass them. A 1955 newspaper report said that Kill Devil Hills commissioners refused to let their "new" 1925 fire truck respond to a call in neighboring Nags Head because the blaze was outside town limits. Nags Head was incorporated six years later.

Developers, meanwhile, aimed at selling prime properties in the newly incorporated town of Kill Devil Hills. Lots in Avalon, one of the Outer Banks's first subdivisions, used to be sold by developers who sat at card tables under beach umbrellas at the piers, hawking the plots for $250 each. Most of the property purchasers had their permanent homes in Hampton Roads.

By the 1970s, business was booming in Kill Devil Hills—with summer cottage rentals, motel traffic, and year-round residents. The Outer Banks's first fast-food restaurant, McDonald's, opened in 1978. The next year, Pizza Hut set up shop on a nearby Bypass lot. The rest of what locals call French Fry Alley developed in the late '70s and early '80s. As developers began stacking condominiums on the beaches as fast as they could, county commissioners hastily enacted a 35-foot building height moratorium to prevent spoiling the eye-appeal of the barrier beaches.

In 1986 commissioners financed streetlights for the town's 5 miles of highway, giving their municipality a glow at night. The neighboring towns have yet to put up continuous streetlights. By the end of the '80s, Kill Devil Hills employees had moved into a new complex on Veterans Drive, and the town had gotten its first large-scale shopping center. Complete with a full-size Food Lion, The Dare Center completed the town's self-sufficiency in late 1989.

By the time the town turned 40, four years later, about 98 percent of Kill Devil Hills' private property already had been platted. Some residents began looking for ways to retain their small-town feeling while becoming increasingly citified. Others expressed amazement at the ways in which their community was developing: adding a new soccer field for children, creating adult recreation programs, and welcoming new retail shops each summer.

Colington Island

In 1633 Colington Island became the first land in Carolina to be deeded to an individual. Today this 2-mile-long, 2.5-mile-wide island, although developing rapidly, is one of the last of the Outer Banks communities to experience growth.

The east end of Colington Island lies a mile west of the Wright Brothers memorial, linked by a bridge over Colington Creek, which separates the island from Kill Devil Hills and the Dare County beaches. Colington's other borders are surrounded by open water. Kitty Hawk Bay is to the north and Buzzard Bay is to the south. The mouths of four sounds (Currituck, Albemarle, Croatan, and Roanoke) converge on the west side of this family community.

Colington, named after its first proprietor Sir John Colleton, was originally tilled to grow grapes for a winery shortly after settlers in 1664 founded the first Outer Banks community. The grapes, along with crops of tobacco, fruits, and vegetables, all eventually failed after three successive hurricanes. But by the early 1800s, a thriving fishing community had sprung up on what was now two halves of the island: Great Colenton and Little Colenton, cleaved in 1769 by the Dividing Creek. Fishing, crabbing, and hunting sustained islanders generation after generation. Eventually, years behind the rest of the barrier islands, Colington natives got paved roads, telephones, and electric service.

Now, they have tourism. Just like the four- or five-generation families that live

Commercial crabbing is a traditional occupation on Colington Island. PHOTO: HORSLEY/GARDNER

here, Colington Island has its own unique Outer Banks identity. High, uneven dunes meet dank, brackish swamplands. Thick groves of pine, dogwood, live oak, beech, and holly drip Spanish moss over expanses of sandy shoreline. Thin creeks widen to unexpected harbors and bays. In the summer months, soft-shell crab holding pens illuminate strips of scrubby yard along the sounds at night, the naked light bulbs glaring out of the darkness like a Reno casino. Advertisements for waterfront property in pricey new subdivisions are posted not far from where trailers and campgrounds line the twisting road. Mansions are barely evident perched on their sandy shelves overlooking Colington Road, the most heavily traveled secondary road in Dare County.

Since Colington Harbour, the island's first subdivision, was built in 1965, numerous other subdivisions have been constructed along canals, marshlands, and soundfronts and in woodlands throughout Colington Island. After a year of weighing benefits and risks, newcomers and natives hammered out a reasonable zoning plan. Several restaurants, a storage garage, and a go-cart track mingling with crab shedders and fish houses along the road illustrate the conflict and challenges this sheltered community faced over dramatic change. With new development being approved every year, residents have accepted that growth is inevitable. The future face of Colington will be determined by the strength of the zoning plan and the people who molded it.

Nags Head

Home of the Outer Banks's first resort, the community of Nags Head is south of Kill Devil Hills and north of Oregon Inlet. It stretches from the Atlantic Ocean to the Roanoke Sound and has remained a popular vacation destination for more than 150 years. Many first-time vacationers mistakenly refer to the whole middle-Banks area as "Nags Head," lumping the town together with the neighboring Kill Devil Hills and Kitty Hawk. This is likely historically based, due to the fact that at one time Nags Head was the only true destination on the middle Banks.

The booming summer scene was once anchored by cottages towering over the shallow sound, elaborate hotels facing the mainland, and calm-water canoeing, crabbing, and conversation. This relaxed style of soundside vacationing has long since been overrun with shifting sands and varying values.

Nags Head History and the Story Behind the Name

The primary resort destination on these barrier islands for more than a century, Nags Head has been the official name of the area since at least 1738 when it first appeared on maps. Historians say the beach town got its name from the free-range horses that once roamed throughout the islands. The much more colorful legend we Insiders prefer is that Nags Head was derived from a custom locals used to lure ships to the shores with clever trickery. Securing a lantern from a Banker pony's neck, residents would drive the horse up and down the beach, the light swinging with the same motion as a sailboat. The unsuspecting offshore vessel would then steer toward the light and proceed to get grounded, often wrecked, on the shoals. The locals would then promptly ransack what was left of the hapless ship. This is only one of many stories about how the town got its name.

In the early 1830s, a Perquimans County planter explored the then-deserted Outer Banks "with the view of finding a suitable place to build a summer residence where he and his family could escape the poisonous miasma vapors and the attendant fevers," wrote author and historian David Stick in *The Outer Banks of North Carolina.* "He explored the beach and the sound shore and picked his house site overlooking the latter, near the tallest of the sand hills." The planter paid $100 to an unknown Banker for the 200 acres and built the first summer house on the Outer Banks in Nags Head.

In 1838 the Outer Banks's first hotel was built in Nags Head midway between the sound and the sea. A two-story structure, the grand guesthouse had accommodations for 200 travelers, an elaborate ballroom, a bowling alley, covered porches, and a 5-foot-wide pier that extended from the hotel's front a half-mile into the sound.

The 1850 census showed that 576 people, including 30 slaves, lived year-round in Nags Head, but hundreds more came each summer. By that time the soundside community had become a well-known watering hole for the families of mainland farmers, bankers, and lawyers.

Elizabeth City doctor William Gaskins Pool was the first person to build a home on the seaside in 1866, according to a 19th-century journal kept by Outer Banks resident Edward R. Outlaw Jr. On September 14, 1866, Pool purchased 50 acres "at or near Nags Head, bordering on the ocean, for $30" and constructed his one-story cottage 300 feet from the breakers. "But over there by themselves, his family was very lonely," Outlaw writes in his book, *Old Nag's Head.*

Seeing that the Pools could survive beside the sea, more people began building their houses on the eastern edges of Nags Head. By the early 1900s, homeowners were erecting their cottages on logs so they could roll them back from encroaching tides. Some of the houses moved three or four times during residents' lifetimes. Oceanfront house moving is still a common practice in Nags Head today. The houses are jacked up, mounted onto a flatbed truck, and slowly inched away from the encroaching sea.

The Nags Head Post Office has a confusing history. It was established in 1884, but the name was changed to Naghead in 1893. A second post office in the area opened in 1909 and was called Griffin. Within a few years, the Naghead Post Office was closed, and all mail was handled through Griffin, a move that caused

Cottages such as this one—on pilings with darkened cedar-shake siding, covered porches, and multiple rooflines—are referred to as "Old Nags Head style." PHOTO: MOLLY HARRISON

much confusion and therefore the changing of the name back to Naghead and finally to Nags Head.

Nags Head became an incorporated town in 1961. As it did more than a century ago, this beach area continues to attract anglers and surfers, nature lovers and shoppers, families and fun-seeking adventurers. A half-century ago, Newman's Shell Shop opened as the first store on the beach. Charter boat captains Sam and Omie opened a restaurant at Whalebone Junction more than 50 years ago to serve breakfast to their fishing parties. The small wooden eatery across from Jennette's Pier still bears their names—and still serves some of the best she-crab soup around.

Nags Head Today

Today, Nags Head is home to more than 2,700 residents. Hotels, restaurants, piers, rambling residences, and luxurious vacation cottages line Nags Head's oceanfront, which is still predominantly vacation oriented. Local residents live in the middle

and on the west side of the island, away from the harsh elements of the sea. The sound shores are lined with private cottages, except in one portion of lower Nags Head that's a recreational wonderland with watersports outfitters, go-cart tracks, and mini-golf galore. South Nags Head, stretching from MP 17 to MP 21, is an exclusively residential area with no commercial development, home to hundreds of houses, most of them vacation rentals, on the oceanfront or backing up to National Park Service property.

Jockey's Ridge State Park is Nags Head's most popular attraction, next to the beach. The best kite flying, hang gliding, and sunset views are found atop this natural phenomenon, which is the largest sand dune on the East Coast. Every summer day, the sprawling dune is dotted with hundreds of people who climb to the top for recreation and for the expansive views of sea and sound.

Another of Nags Head's natural attractions is the Nags Head Woods Preserve, really in both Nags Head and Kill Devil

Hills. Hikers, bird-watchers, and nature lovers delight in this wooded anomaly, where diverse flora and fauna can be enjoyed in stunning silence (see our Natural Wonders chapter).

Nags Head is well known for its recreational opportunities. A paved bike path stretches almost the entire length of the town. A Scottish links–style golf course, The Village at Nags Head Golf Links, is one of the area's most beautiful and challenging courses. It stretches along the Roanoke Sound, offering sound views and the opportunity to see a variety of water birds and wildlife. Companies offering dolphin tours, airboat rides, boat rentals, JetSki rentals, kite-boarding lessons, windsurfing, and sailing are all offered on the sound in lower Nags Head, around MP 16 and on the Nags Head–Manteo Causeway. Minature golf and go-cart tracks are also clustered in this area. One of the barrier islands' few amusement parks, Dowdy's, has a Ferris wheel, bumper cars, and a merry-go-round at MP 11. Nags Head has the largest movie theater in the area and the area's only bowling alley.

Shoppers flock to Nags Head's namebrand outlet stores and to its several strip malls and grocery stores. Nags Head is home to many art galleries, including an artists' enclave known as Gallery Row (see our Arts and Culture chapter). Restaurants and nightspots lure diners and revelers to Nags Head. Owens' Restaurant has been a Nags Head institution for more than 50 years; Kelly's Tavern is the longest-running nightspot on the Outer Banks.

Since it's centrally located on the Outer Banks, Nags Head is a favorite destination of people who want to take daytrips to Hatteras Island and Corolla. If you don't want to get in the car again once you've arrived at your vacation destination, you can get everything you want within walking distance of most Nags Head hotels and cottages.

Whether you're looking to escape the bustle of the beach by taking a quiet hike through the Nature Conservancy's Nags Head Woods Ecological Preserve or dance the night away at a tropical tavern, this Outer Banks beach town remains one of the area's most popular resorts.

Roanoke Island

Nestled between the Outer Banks and the North Carolina mainland, Roanoke Island is one of the most historic places in America. People sometimes confuse our island's history with that of Jamestown, Virginia, where the first permanent English colony thrived in the early 17th century. The confusion between the two revolves around the word "permanent." Roanoke Island is the site of England's earliest attempts to plant a permanent colony in the New World. Beginning in 1584, Sir Walter Raleigh dispatched a series of voyages carrying adventurous souls to settle in the New World. These journeys culminated in a colony of 117 men, women, and children, sent here in 1587, only to disappear mysteriously (see our History chapter); hence the lack of "permanence." Despite having a slippery foothold on history, the Lost Colony has left a permanent puzzle. Theories concerning the colonists' fate abound, as our History chapter outlines, but until archaeologists dig up some real proof, we'll continue to wonder what really happened to these early settlers.

For those who appreciate concrete links to the past, relics exist that have been retrieved from the waters surrounding Roanoke Island—artifacts that may provide clues to centuries-old puzzles. Many locals and archaeologists alike have combed the island for treasures from the Native American culture, earliest English settlements, and Civil War times (read our History chapter for more information on these Roanoke Island highlights). Old English coins, a powder horn, a vial of quicksilver, weapons, bottles, iron fragments, pottery, and arrowheads have been discovered here. In the winter of 1998–99, a strong nor'easter blew so much water out of the sound that some creek beds and sound bottoms were exposed for the first time in many decades. Locals harvested

adorn the bushes alongside the road. They really stand out in the winter when the leaves have left trees barren. Scan the creeks in the warm months, just before entering Roanoke Island from the west, and you can see turtles lined like soldiers on half-sunken logs and along the banks. Crossing the Washington Baum Bridge from the east, we regularly spot osprey flying overhead, clutching dangling snakes or fish in their claws. (Try not to remove your eyes from the road too long, and definitely do not stop on the bridge!) Of course, a wide variety of fish, such as spot, croaker, pigfish, sea mullet, sheepshead, and stripers, inhabit the surrounding waters. Boats and recreational water vehicles of all sorts share the sounds and bays in fair weather. Crabbers, windsurfers, sailors, JetSkiers, and operators of small fishing crafts and big charter vessels cross paths on a daily basis.

By land, you can experience a walk back into time at Roanoke Island Festival Park, formerly the *Elizabeth II* State Historic Site in Manteo. You can also examine history at Fort Raleigh. Make sure to explore the park's nature path, the Thomas Hariot Trail. Hariot, a 16th-century author, wrote the first book about the New World in Elizabethan English. His book is a study of the Native Americans and a survey of the area's natural resources. Only six copies are said to exist of his literary treatise.

Getting Here

Roanoke Island is west of Nags Head and due east of Williamston, North Carolina. It certainly is easier and quicker to get here now than it was centuries or even decades ago due to the construction of several bridges and new highways. While you won't have to forge a path through reeds, as our ancestors did, you still can reach the island by water. If a car is your mode of transportation, you can choose from at least four routes; all are scenic. Some wend through more remote regions than others. One two-lane road, US 64/264, has always carried all the local traffic plus vacationer

numerous arrowheads from the exposed muddy tracts. Some remnants can be seen at Fort Raleigh National Historic Site on the north end of the island (see our Attractions chapter), while others found their way into personal collections. Roanoke Island native Hubby Bliven opened The Roanoke Heritage Gallery and Museum on the island mostly with artifacts he's been collecting since his youth. Archaeologists continue to search today for clues to the bygone era. Speculation exists that an ongoing dig occurring on Hatteras Island could uncover some indication that the Roanoke colony left the island with friendly Croatan Indians and relocated on Hatteras.

Although this tiny island measures a mere 3 miles wide by 12 miles long, there's a lot of history packed into this little land mass. With a little imagination, its history comes alive. Bordered by the Roanoke and Croatan Sounds and threaded throughout by canals, creeks, bay, and marsh, the natural geography inspires romantic visions in visitors and locals alike.

Roanoke Island tends to bring out the nature lover in all of us. In the spring, summer, and fall, early mornings and late afternoons find marsh rabbits nibbling roadside grasses. Red-winged black birds, looking much like holiday ornaments, traffic right down the spine of Roanoke Island, creating backups and bottlenecks that make being in a hurry an unfortunate condition to find yourself in. That will all change in the summer of 2002, however, when a new 5-mile bridge that bypasses Roanoke Island is completed. This bridge, the longest in the state, will steer vacationer traffic and much of the local traffic away from the island. One end of the bridge is in Manns Harbor and the other is at the Manteo-Wanchese junction, which leads right to the beaches. If you wish to travel by air, the Dare County Regional Airport is on the north end of Roanoke Island. Private pilots fly into this airport on a daily basis, and charter services are available. It's not unusual to see visitors riding in on bicycles. The Outer Banks's flat terrain makes for excellent bicycle touring. For specific routes and directions see our Getting Here, Getting Around chapter.

Island Economy and Tourism

At the heart of Roanoke Island life is the inhabitants' desire/conflict to preserve a small-town feeling while finding ways to make a living. Islanders mostly work in tourist- and service-oriented businesses, at fishing-related jobs, as writers and artists, in local government, and in the public school system.

With the fluctuating financial climate in mind, it's fortunate Roanoke Island has history we can market. Our Attractions chapter describes the island's top sites: The Elizabethan Gardens, The North Carolina Aquarium, Fort Raleigh National Historic Site, The Outer Banks History Center, Roanoke Island Festival Park, the N.C. Maritime Museum, and *The Lost Colony* outdoor drama.

An interesting place to read up on Roanoke Island lore and view old photographs and maps is at the Outer Banks History Center, housed at Roanoke Island Festival Park (see our Arts and Culture chapter).

Don't overlook the main branch of the Dare County Library on US 64, just across from Manteo Elementary School, as a source for more island information. You'll discover that a great number of books in the North Carolina reference section are written by Insiders. For overall Outer Banks information, such as maps, brochures, and other local data, stop in at the Outer Banks Visitors Bureau on US 64/264. The staff is friendly and helpful, and there's even a convenient drive-through window if you find it's too hard to get the kids and paraphernalia out of the car.

Talk with some of our old-timers for some really entertaining inside information. Conversation with lifelong locals is bound to reveal a colorful tale or two. There are plenty of boat captains who can fill your ear with tales. Stories by natives bring to life the days when islanders drove horses and buggies through the mud to catch a movie downtown and how it felt to venture offshore to fish for the first time. You'll hear tales of pregnant women who delivered their babies with the help of a midwife at the local doctor's house and spent time recuperating there. Pick up a copy of *Memories of Manteo and Roanoke Island, N.C.,* by Suzanne Tate as told by the late Cora Mae Basnight, if you're unable to make a personal connection. This oral history, from the mouth of a much-loved native and the late mother of the current Senator Pro Tem of the North Carolina Senate, Marc Basnight, is a delightful book accented by interesting photographs. Ms. Basnight, according to Tate's book, held the record for playing the same role longer than any actress in American Theater, that of Agona, a Native American woman, in *The Lost Colony.* Many consider her the quintessential Agona. Another fantastic, more thorough history of the town and island is *Manteo, A Roanoke Island Town* by Angel Ellis Khoury. It's filled with fascinating stories, anecdotes, and facts about this area.

Lots of exciting tales revolve around *The Lost Colony,* the historic outdoor drama that outlines the story of the first English settlement and its disappearance. Pulitzer

Prize-winning playwright Paul Green wrote the drama, which debuted in 1937, and it has played a major role in the lives of local folk ever since (see our Arts and Culture chapter). In 1997 the production observed its 60th anniversary, drawing former Lost Colony thespians and production members the world over to reminisce and celebrate the occasion. In 1998 a stunning $2 million renovation to the historic Waterside Theatre was completed.

Generations of families grew up acting in the annual play. From representing the infant Virginia Dare to playing the role of Gov. John White or Chief Manteo, many a Roanoke Island resident nurtured a love of history through the play and a love of theater as a result. And Andy Griffith, who played Sir Walter Raleigh in his first acting stint, is a Roanoke Island resident.

William S. Powell's *Paradise Preserved* is the definitive source where you can study the history of the Roanoke Island Historical Association, perpetuators of the historic play. Powell offers an exciting account of the creative endeavors of Mrs. Mabel Evans Jones, the author and producer of local pageants on Roanoke Island that predate Green's play. Evans Jones, the former Superintendent of Schools in Dare County, ran a summer arts camp on the island back in the early 1920s. As it is with an archaeologist, the more you dig, the more you're likely to uncover something concerning Roanoke Island's roots and tales of the people who called the island home.

Yesteryear and Today

Prior to the settling of Manteo in the 1860s, islanders had established two sparsely populated residential settlements on Roanoke Island called the Upper End and the Lower End. The Upper End referred to the north end of Roanoke Island, and the lower end described the area that is now called Wanchese. About 100 years later, a third settlement was formed by former slaves and has been referred to as California. Manteo and the village of Wanchese were named after two Native Americans who befriended the early English explorers.

When the black residents of the island's north end were forced to relocate in the 1930s, they settled in a section of Manteo west of US 64. Between Shallowbag Bay and Croatan Sound, south of the Dare County Regional Airport, California referred to land that stretched from Bowserstown Road to Burnside Road. At the turn of the century, the tract was bought by 11 black men and divided among them. Nobody is sure why the area was named California, but its history includes an account of children tacking a hand-painted sign to a tree in a fig orchard on the west side of the community, christening it as such.

California history shines with memories of blacks and whites ignoring Jim Crow laws to pass back and forth between communities via White Cross Way, also called Bay Street, to help one another. The isolation of Roanoke Island may have helped islanders weather the postwar civil rights conflict without mayhem. Skin color did not prevent neighbors from delivering baskets of fruits and vegetables to anyone in need.

More on Manteo

In 1999 the town of Manteo celebrated its centennial. Manteo became Dare County's seat in 1870 and was incorporated as a town in 1899. Islanders soon erected the first courthouse and established a post office. The white-columned brick courthouse that stands in downtown Manteo today was built in 1904 to replace the original wooden structure. One of the earliest private homes built on the Upper End in the 1780s was the Etheridge home, also referred to as Drinkwater's Folley. It was moved in the 1930s from a wooded area between Heritage Point and the Elizabethan Gardens to its present location on US 64 at the Morrison Grove turnoff. Another private home that bears note is the Colonial-style dwelling built in Manteo in 1872 that later became the Tranquil House, whose rooms entertained Thomas Edison and radio pioneer Reginald Fessenden. The Tranquil House also did a tour of duty as a barracks during World War II. The original Tranquil House is gone now, but the name lives on at a different location. Today there's a Tranquil House Inn operating in downtown Manteo on The Waterfront. The Tranquil House is built in the style of 19th-century Outer Banks inns, but it has 21st-century conveniences, including an in-house, world-class restaurant, 1587.

In the late 1800s Roanoke Island acted as a prominent port. Large boats from Old Dominion Steamline of Norfolk, Virginia, made daily stops on the west end of the island at Skyco (between Manteo and Wanchese), while Manteo's Shallowbag Bay was a busy port for smaller boats. In 1906 Shallowbag Bay was dredged, allowing access to larger boats such as the river steamer *Trenton*. For nearly 20 years, mail, freight, and passengers arrived daily on this vessel.

As new infrastructure tied the island to other areas, Roanoke Island became less remote and things began to change. In 1928 the Washington Baum Bridge was completed, linking Roanoke Island to the Outer Banks beaches. Two years later the Wright Memorial Bridge was constructed to tie those beaches to Currituck from the north. New roads were built from Elizabeth City and Manteo, and as the automobile became more popular, boat usage declined somewhat.

Fire has ravaged the Manteo waterfront five times since 1920. Oil that was brought to the island by barge was stored in tanks on the waterfront. The presence of all that oil caused great problems when the town caught fire. All that was available to put out the early fires was an old-fashioned bucket brigade, with volunteers forming a line and handing buckets of water from one person to another. During the course of these five fires, various sections of town were destroyed, including the old Hotel Roanoke. The only mercantile building to survive all the fires is the little white building on Budleigh Street that now operates as E.R. Midgett Insurance. Adequate fire-fighting equipment, a modern water system, and brick construction were introduced to the town when rebuilding began in the 1930s.

Manteo continues to be the hub for Dare County's business. From 1983 through 1987, major renovations took place in the town as part of America's Quadricentennial. Fifteen hundred live oaks and flowering crape myrtle trees were planted on the island's main corridor along US 64. Buildings and streets were restored, bringing new glory to the town.

On July 13, 1984, Manteo entertained Princess Anne of England, North Carolina Gov. James B. Hunt Jr., and newsman Walter Cronkite as part of America's 400th Anniversary Celebration. A memorial stone on the waterfront commemorates the event.

Manteo today does a good job reflecting its history. The downtown Manteo Waterfront complex featuring shops, restaurants, and private residences is built in old-style architecture. You can sit at outdoor picnic tables or benches along the docks or in one of the window-lined restaurants and view the *Elizabeth II* (see our Attractions chapter), which is berthed across the bay from the Manteo waterfront at Roanoke Island Festival Park. Reminders of our Native American and English heritages are evident in many of the town's street names including: Ananias Dare, Wingina, Sir Walter Raleigh, Queen Elizabeth, Essex, and Uppowac. Traveling these byways threading through historic Manteo are a number of structures worth noting.

In Manteo proper on Budleigh Street, you'll find the English Tudor-style Pioneer Theatre, the oldest family-operated movie theater in the United States, which celebrates its 67th year in 2001 (see our Attractions chapter). You can actually get a bag of popcorn here for 50 cents, and that's after paying only $4.00 to get in. The Theodore S. Meekins house on Sir Walter

Raleigh Street that now operates as the White Doe Inn (see our Accommodations chapter) is one of Manteo's most elegant buildings. The basic structure of the house was built before 1900. Featuring long porches and bowed windows in its turrets, the white, three-storied inn is listed in the National Register of Historic Places. A reference for historic Manteo sites is *The Manteo Walking Tour,* available at the Manteo branch of the Dare County Library on US 64 or in local bookshops.

There are just over 1,000 residents in Manteo. The town continues to grow as it annexes outlying properties, and as far as new building, Manteo proper—the historic downtown area—is fairly well developed with only a few select lots left. People are drawn to the charm and the quaintness and the small-town atmosphere here. The absence of serious crime in the town also reflects its desirability. If there is any significant future growth to Manteo, which is currently home to five churches and four schools, expansion would be to the south, but that's very indefinite.

Wanchese

Wanchese, on the southern end of Roanoke Island, has a more isolated feel than Manteo. For years it's operated as a fishing port. Drive the streets and you'll see wooden houses, built in some cases 80 to 100 years ago, that have been lovingly maintained. In many backyards you still find boats in various sizes and states of repair, linking their owners with the ever-important sea and sounds.

Many old seagoing vessels fill Wanchese Harbor, living out their last days in a place generations of men have used as a regular point of departure. While time will always bring change in the fishing industry—change in species, seafood quantities, boat styles, and government regulations—in Wanchese today, you can track family occupations established long ago when men in the industry navigated solely by the stars. Still living today are at least three or four generations of anglers—men and women alike—from families who have at one time or another called Wanchese home.

The fishing fleet in Wanchese supplies fish to the world. PHOTO: JOSH CORSA

The Tilletts, Baums, and Etheridges, names you'll notice a lot on the Outer Banks, are just a few. Some have crossed over from commercial fishing to become sport fishermen, and many work as boat builders.

Today, as many as 50 fishing trawlers from up and down the East Coast use Wanchese Harbor, as do hundreds of smaller commercial and sport-fishing boats. The village features several seafood companies that ship fish all over the country. Most seafood caught in Dare County goes through Wanchese, and an estimated $27.5 million worth, or 39 million pounds, was landed in the county in 1995 (this is the latest figure available on record). Boats fish North Carolina's offshore and inshore waters and also depart Wanchese Harbor to fish off New England in the winter. On the east side of the harbor is the state-owned Wanchese Seafood Industrial Park where seafood and marine-related industries are based (see our Attractions chapter). The park features boat-maintenance facilities, seafood plants, boat builders, and state fisheries operations.

Wanchese has 852 registered voters out of an estimated 1,875 people living in the small fishing community. An average of only three to four homes and/or buildable lots comes available annually. There is plenty of undeveloped land in Wanchese that is buildable, but it is privately owned.

Boatbuilding

A section on Roanoke Island would be incomplete without a nod to a very special livelihood shared by native islanders. Boatbuilding was and continues to be a major part of Roanoke Island living. From the small bateau put together in a backyard shed to the 72-foot yachts constructed at major boatbuilding operations, Manteo and Wanchese share in this rich heritage.

In 1998 the North Carolina Maritime Museum opened in the old George Washington Creef Boathouse on the Manteo waterfront as a tribute to the area's boatbuilding heritage. Here, you can watch old crafts being restored and view a variety of boat exhibits.

George and Benjamin Creef operated the facility as the Manteo Machine Shop and Railways in the 19th century. The shop was built in 1884, and boats were hauled out of the water and serviced there. It was at this location that "Uncle Wash" Creef built the first shad boat, now documented as one of the most important fishing vessels of its time because its design allowed it to effectively work nets and carry weight and still ride well in the water. Winters of the past would find many fishermen holed up in shops crafting juniper vessels that would take them farther from home than many had ever imagined. The Sharpie and the Shallowbag Shad Boat were designed and built in Manteo.

Boats are still built on Roanoke Island today—huge, sleek vessels with their hulls buffed to a sun-splintering shine. Each spring these brand-new 50-foot-plus boats emerge from private building barns and are tugged slowly down the highway to Wanchese to be put in the water for the first time. On board the boat, members of the construction crew carefully lift power lines as their vessel moves down the road, invariably delaying traffic. Smiles wreathe the faces of the crew: After six to eight months of hammering, sanding, and painting, they are ready to christen the fruit of their labor. It is a tense time, too, for no one really relaxes until everyone sees that the boat sits and moves "just right" in the water. You can hear the admirers exclaim "pretty work" as the vessel begins her maiden voyage. The crowd always includes family members and friends who wouldn't miss the celebration.

Hatteras Island

The sea is a strong tonic that humans sometimes crave at the expense of security. Nowhere is this desire more obvious than in the people who live on this little stretch of sand that juts precariously out into the Atlantic Ocean just off North Carolina's coast. Hatteras Island residents accept the stresses of living with a seasonal economy, storm damage, and cultural isolation

On Roanoke Island it's not uncommon to see enormous boats being hauled down the road. PHOTO: PATRICK HARRISON

while carving out solid lives in the shifting sand. The decision to live on the threshold of land and sea forges an intimate relationship with nature. Like passionate lovers, each contributes joys and sorrows that cannot easily be put asunder. Why live in an ever-changing environment? Because blood is thicker than water. And locals know it's really Mother Nature's wind, sea, and salt that courses through every Hatteras Islander's veins.

Hatteras Island is south of Nags Head and north of Ocracoke Island. It measures 60 miles from Oregon Inlet to Hatteras Inlet and consists of seven small towns. Running north to south they are Rodanthe, Waves, Salvo, Avon, Buxton, Frisco, and Hatteras Village. You can enter the island from the north by car via NC 12 by crossing the Herbert C. Bonner Bridge or from the south by ferry via Ocracoke Island. As with our other townships and islands, you can also reach the area by air—setting down on a small airstrip in Frisco—or by boat. (See our Getting Here, Getting Around and Fishing chapters for airfield, marina, and ferry information.)

Island Living, Economy, and Tourism

Overall, Hatteras's residents live and work supported mostly by tourism, fishing, real estate, teaching, and government employment. Because of the seasonal economy, weather-related economic setbacks, and lack of corporations and industries that hire mass amounts of people, it's not unusual for residents to have more than one job. Cleaning cottages on the side provides extra money, and you may find that your waiter during the summer months is a professional from another trade altogether.

Necessity also provokes creativity, and many locals sell their carvings or paintings in local shops and galleries. One thing remains clear about most barrier island residents: They choose to be here.

Families thrive despite typical small-town inconveniences. They pattern their living styles accordingly. You won't find a Kmart on the island, but mail-order companies get their share of business. A sense of community is evident in the packed stands at the Cape Hatteras High School basketball games (even folks with no kids attend). The Cape Hatteras team, appropriately called the Hurricanes, made it to the state playoffs in 1997 and 1998. Part of their success has been attributed to the fact that the players grew up playing basketball together and have a strong rapport with their hometown coach. With a school that has only 95 to 100 male high school students to choose from (it's the smallest school in its state athletic classification), the fervor generated at home and away games is award-winning in and of itself. Word has it that the away games have their share of Hatteras fans in the stands, which says a lot coming from islanders whose ancestors had to be pried from their homes during hurricane evacuations.

It only has been during recent years that Hatteras residents have left the island in large numbers during county-mandated hurricane evacuations. We have national footage of damage to other areas from Hurricane Hugo and Andrew to thank for it. Weather plays a regular role in Hatteras life. When the island is evacuated during a hurricane warning, it's not unusual for the locals to lose a week's worth of income. This creates great financial hardship for businesses when you consider that their annual income is made primarily during the 12 weeks of summer.

Even smaller storms cause delays when the roads flood. A recent nor'easter found parts of NC 12 under water during high tide for four days, and Hurricane Dennis devastated the island, ripping up part of NC 12 and literally relocating houses that had moved back from the water so as not to be damaged in a storm. It's not uncommon to find a pair of boots left by the front and back doors of an islander's home. When the Herbert C. Bonner Bridge, which spans Oregon Inlet, was hit and damaged by an unwieldy dredge during a storm in October 1990, islanders who worked on the mainland or who needed to leave had to travel off Hatteras by boat or ferry. Long days ensued, as travel time greatly multiplied. The Bonner

Insiders' Tip
Cape Hatteras National Seashore was the first national seashore in the nation. Proposed in 1933 and authorized in 1937, it was not established until 1953 and was dedicated in 1958.

Bridge is greatly in need of repairs that necessitate closing the bridge for several weeks at a time. When that happens, Hatteras Islanders will have to be ferried off the island. No one knows at this time when that will happen, but you can bet it won't be during the summer months!

Nature and islanders are so entwined, it's hard to tell where the sea mist ends and the foggy breath of life begins. Despite the imposing tone Mother Nature can cast over the barrier island (the county's evacuation policy ensures that visitors leave the island in plenty of time), visitors flock here annually to enjoy its beauty and seclusion. Today there are enough conveniences, restaurants, and diversions within reach to entertain even sophisticated vacationers. The Cape Hatteras School, with help from the local arts council, brings in cultural events for the residents. There are also several noteworthy art galleries on the island (see our Arts and Culture chapter).

History tells us, though, that even without these modern additions, folks would still come to relax Hatteras-style, away from the busier pace of the towns farther up the barrier islands to do a little crabbing, clamming, fishing, beach walking, bird-watching, or chatting with the old anglers who relax at the docks. Many a modern-day adult vacationer has been coming to the Outer Banks since childhood. In fact, generations of families can call Hatteras Island their summer home.

A weatherworn, abandoned Coast Guard station stands at the northernmost tip of Hatteras Island.
PHOTO: MOLLY HARRISON

The island has obvious drawing cards: the sea and unique landscape. Both natural and artificial recreational activities abound. Some of the best wind-surfing and surfing in North America can be done in the waters along Hatteras Island (see our Recreation, Attractions, and Watersports chapters). Surfers from all over the East Coast come to Hatteras Island to surf the breakers, especially during strong nor'easters. Surfers look forward to hurricane season from June through November, when big northern swells push the waves to 8 feet and sometimes higher. National surfing championships are held in Buxton (see our Annual Events chapter).

Hatteras Island is famous as an East Coast fishing hot spot. Moving through the ocean about 40 miles offshore are the Gulf Stream, a shelf current, and the Deep Western Boundary Current, all of which cross near the Continental Shelf's edge. The influence of this convergence is both positive and negative. These crossing currents spawned Diamond Shoals, creating the groundwork for danger but also supplying a rich habitat for game fish (see our Natural Wonders chapter).

While the watery Graveyard of the Atlantic gives Hatteras a bad rap, with shipwrecks lining almost the entire length of the underwater coastline, the wide variety of fish traveling up the Gulf Stream have given this area the reputation of "Billfish Capital of the World." World-record fish have been caught both offshore and in the surf at Cape Hatteras Point, where red drum come to feed. Much of the tip of Hatteras is lined with marinas where recreational charter boats take visitors to the inshore and offshore waters (see our Fishing chapter). Full-service tackle shops, staffed with knowledgeable Insiders, speckle the barrier island.

North of Rodanthe and just south of Oregon Inlet is the Pea Island National Wildlife Refuge, and a unique maritime forest lies farther south in Buxton (see our Attractions and Natural Wonders chapter for descriptions of both).

There are three National Park Service campgrounds on Hatteras Island (at Oregon Inlet, Frisco, and Cape Point) offering more laid-back and less expensive camping than the rest of the Outer Banks's camping facilities. Several private campgrounds also are established in the island communities (see our Camping chapter).

If Mother Nature hasn't sold you on Hatteras Island's perks, check out our Recreation chapter for those artificial amusements that can be enjoyed by the whole family.

Yesteryear and Today

Thousands of years ago, Native Americans settled on Hatteras Island and called it Croatan. Originally marked Cape S. John on 16th-century maps, the island's history is filled with diverse tales of Civil War battles, fabulous fishing stories, shipwrecks, and lifesaving efforts (see our History and Fishing chapters).

The residents of this 33-mile-long barrier island, who could only reach the outside world by boat until the Bonner Bridge was built to span Oregon Inlet in 1963, were a people so isolated that their speech today still maintains the direct flavor of their ancestors. Need was the driving force behind livelihood choices. Everyone fished for food, and seafood was traded on the mainland for provisions and corn. Windmills, a profusion of which dotted the landscape, provided the power to turn corn into flour. Commercial fishermen harvested whale oil, turtles, oysters, and even seaweed. And the island was once covered with roving livestock gobbling up protective vegetation.

The village of Kinnakeet, now Avon, was the heart of a thriving shipbuilding industry. Materials were gathered from the oak and cedar forests on the sound side of the island. The islanders built their homes there, in the woody hammocks, seeking safety from high waters and winds. Timbers also were used to fashion clipper ships. Kinnakeet was a base for a large fleet of small schooners, many of which were used to harvest oysters.

The Cape Hatteras Lighthouse in Buxton has towered over the island's low-lying terrain since 1870. Rising 208 feet, it is the tallest brick lighthouse in the nation (see our History, Natural Wonders, and Attractions chapters). Within reach of the light shed by the tower are the treacherous and ever-changing Diamond Shoals, where hundreds of vessels met their demise. Lifesaving teams, at one time riding horse-drawn carts through the sand, saved thousands of seafarers' lives off these shores. Today, modern equipment aids in navigation, and the Cape Hatteras Light still operates, but the power of the sea, shuffling weather patterns, and changing inlets still cause captains to traverse the waters with care.

Much of Hatteras Island is undeveloped National Park Service property. But scattered north to south along the coast are the seven villages, hugging what is loosely termed as "Highway 12," a thin strip of blacktop often covered with sand and water. More often than not, it seems the children of Hatteras's old-timers stay or return to carry on family traditions in these villages. This may be why the flavor of the area has not changed too drastically over the years despite the influx of vacationers and outsiders looking for summer homes. Most of the people who move here are seeking just what the island presents: the domination of nature coupled with the feel of a small community.

Insiders' Tip

Pea Island is not an island now, but it used to be. The inlet separating it from Bodie Island closed in 1837. The name is said to derive from the wild peas that grow there.

The Cape Hatteras Lighthouse is a cherished icon of the Outer Banks. PHOTO: ELAINE FOGARTY

dents are now able to maintain a steady water flow even when storms knock out the power. Utility lines have been upgraded over the last few years, so power outages are not as frequent. Hatteras Island has plenty of real estate available, and its infrastructure, including its school, is being expanded to accommodate new residents.

Birds and fish rendezvous in our wetlands and coastal waters, and residents board up windows or open their doors depending upon the season; what remains unchanged is the desire to be a part of the flow, Hatteras-style.

Hatteras Island Communities

Rodanthe is Hatteras Island's northernmost village, situated about 12 miles from the northern tip of the island. Rodanthe blends seamlessly with Waves and Salvo to form what is sometimes referred to as the Tri-Village area. The three towns were once one, called Chicamacomico, but by the early 1900s they had separated into three distinct villages. Of the three, Rodanthe has the most commercial offerings, including restaurants, an amusement park, gas stations, a shopping center, and tackle shops, but still it is primarily a residential and vacation village. Rodanthe is home to the restored 1874 Chicamacomico Lifesaving Station, a historic tourist attraction that offers many activities. It also has a fishing pier.

Waves is a sleepy little village with predominantly vacation homes. It's hard to know when you are actually in Waves because there are no signs welcoming you. Surfers stole those so often that the villagers finally gave up installing them. This village was known as South Rodanthe until 1939, when it got its own post office and a new name.

Salvo, too, has nebulous village boundaries. The locals know them though, and that's all that matters. Salvo is vacation oriented, although just accommodations-wise. There aren't many commercial offer-

There are more than 5,000 year-round residents living on Hatteras Island. With the blink of an eye, you can drive past these tiny villages, ending up in Hatteras Village at the island's tip. This is where you pick up the ferry to Ocracoke Island. The majority of churchgoers attend Methodist or Assembly of God services, but there is also a Catholic church in Buxton.

While 75 percent of Hatteras Island is National Park land, lots and homes are available for purchase, and each village has a mix of low- to high-price choices. The addition of a reverse-osmosis water plant on the north end of the island breathed new life into the Rodanthe, Waves, and Salvo communities in the spring of 1996, allowing many additional parcels to be built upon. Formerly using electric-generated water pumps, the resi-

ings in Salvo. Originally called Clark, this village was reportedly named for a salvo (simultaneous firing of cannon) it was given by Union soldiers during the Civil War. At the south end of the village is a National Park Service day-use area that's great for soundside picnicking, swimming, and windsurfing.

Avon is about 10 miles south of Salvo, separated from the northern villages by a long, beautiful stretch of undeveloped National Park Service property. Avon was originally called Kinnakeet, a name that is still used by many old-timers. The name changed when the village got a post office in 1883. Avon offers a wealth of vacation rental homes, hotels, and commercial offerings. It's home to the island's only large chain grocery store and movie theater. It has many shops, restaurants, watersports rentals, and a pier. One of the most well-known wind- and kite-surfing spots in the world, Canadian Hole, is on the south end of Avon. Old Avon Village, on the west side of the island, offers a chance to see the local life. Turn toward the sound at the stoplight and take a drive down there to see the wonderful old-school cottages, fishing paraphernalia, boats, and friendly people.

Buxton is at the widest part of the island, on a point of land that juts into the sea and is known as Cape Point. Buxton is the hub of Hatteras Island, with the only school, medical facilities, and Dare County satellite offices. Hotels, restaurants, shops, and small-town grocery stores line the highway. Tackle shops are abundant here because fishing at Cape Point is rightly famous, as is surfing. The 200-foot-tall, black-and-white candy-striped Cape Hatteras Lighthouse towers over the village and is, of course, the most popular attraction here. Buxton Woods, a rare maritime forest, provides a shady element to the village. When Buxton got its post office in 1873, it was called simply The Cape. The name changed in 1882.

Frisco is the next town you reach when heading south. Quiet Frisco is the perfect place to get away from it all. There are many vacation rental homes, a couple of great art galleries, a pier, some shops and restaurants, and a Native American museum, but mostly it is the fishing, uncrowded beaches, and solitude that attract people to Frisco. Frisco was originally known as Trent or Trent Woods, but the name was changed when the village got its first post office in 1898.

Hatteras Village, at the southernmost end of the island, is a picture-book fishing village and the ferry embarkation point for Ocracoke Island. When people say they're going to Hatteras, they mean the village, not the lighthouse, the cape, or the inlet. With its proximity to the Gulf Stream, Hatteras is a world-famous fishing locale, especially renowned for its bluefin tuna fishery in winter. Several marinas and charter fishing vessels call Hatteras Village home. The village has always had a quaint, homespun appeal, with independently run restaurants and shops, small motels geared to anglers, and simple homes. Lately, however, Hatteras Village has seen the addition of upscale oceanfront homes, a fancy shopping complex, and the first chain hotel on the island, a Holiday Inn. The much-anticipated Graveyard of the Atlantic Museum, at the southernmost point of the village, plans to open in 2003. Hatteras Village rose up along the shores of Hatteras Inlet after the inlet was opened in a storm in 1846. A post office was established here in 1858, and in 1861 the Hatteras area was the first portion of the Confederacy to fall to Union troops.

Ocracoke Island

Insiders generally see Ocracoke as a tourist hot spot during the warm months and romantic hideaway during the off-season, but they grab any chance they have to visit, regardless of the calendar. There's just no place like this quaint island with its pristine beaches and homey atmosphere. The small-town flavor results from most of the island being protected land. Because nearly all development surrounds Silver Lake, it makes for a nucleus of commerce and housing. The land is but a slender strip of sand, geographically much like the other Outer Banks islands. At its widest the 16-mile-long island is only about 2 miles across, narrowing in some spots to a half-mile, where sound and sea are both visible from the two-lane road.

After disembarking from the Hatteras ferry, you are released onto NC 12 toward the village. Sea oats and dunes line the left side of the road. The right side of the road is lined with marshland grasses, and exquisite creeks meander toward the sound. Occasionally you'll see some old fishing skiffs tied up on the creeks, giving you the first hint at human life on Ocracoke Island. The drive along this road alone makes the journey to Ocracoke worthwhile. The northern beaches are sparsely populated, while the surf along the southern beaches is usually lined with four-wheel-drive vehicles and anglers, especially in the fall when fishing is best.

Despite our enthusiasm for the drive, it's not easy to discuss all that makes Ocracoke Island so special. The obvious is that it's beautiful, off the beaten track, and much of it is protected as a National Seashore and therefore undeveloped. But there's so much history embedded in this land and embraced by the people that it's hard to find words to express that which is almost vaporous. You can absorb the unspoken by quietly walking the beaches and back roads of the village. Breathe deeply of the salty air that has filled the lungs of its inhabitants for centuries, and be prepared for a lifelong love affair with this southern isle.

Getting Here

Access to Hyde County's Ocracoke Island is limited to sea and air. A free 45-minute ferry ride across the waters of Pamlico Sound transports islanders and visitors to the north end of Ocracoke from Hatteras Island. Once you hit land, it's a 12-mile drive past undeveloped marshlands and dunes to the village. Two toll ferries connect the island with the mainland. The Cedar Island and Swan Quarter ferries, each a two-and-a-half-hour ride and costing $10, arrive and depart from the heart of downtown Ocracoke on the southern end of the island. A small airfield allows private planes to land just outside of Ocracoke Village (see our Getting Here, Getting Around chapter).

Island Economy and Tourism

Vacationers flock to Ocracoke during the warm months. Once a simple fishing village where islanders primarily lived off the sea and her bounty, Ocracoke today operates as a vacation resort about nine months out of the year. Tourism and traffic have changed the pace of this traditional fishing village, but the influx of visitors is necessary to maintain a healthy economy.

While many Ocracokers work at tourist-related businesses, year-round residents also are employed by the National Park Service, in the local school, in the building industry, or as commercial and recreational fishermen. The island's natural beauty and easy pace act as a magnet for artists, craftspeople, and writers.

Ocracoke Island offers a variety of sightseeing options that radiate from a core village atmosphere. You can ride bikes all over the quaint island, and it's best to explore the village by foot. You can park your vehicle after you arrive on the island and not use it again until you leave. Make sure you stroll through the town that surrounds Silver Lake. Wander around on the back roads: Specialty shops, galleries, and old island cottages are just waiting to be discovered. Casually elegant restaurants and come-as-you-are eateries offer several opportunities for a meal, and friendly natives will make recommendations and point you in the right direction (we outline more than a dozen spots in our Restaurants chapter).

Sailboats moor in the protected cove of Silver Lake, and charter and fishing boats fill the downtown docks. You can

NC 12 stretches down the spine of Ocracoke Island, past 14 miles of undeveloped National Park Service property, before reaching the tiny village. PHOTO: HORSLEY/GARDNER

book half- and full-day fishing excursions year-round. All accommodations—bed-and-breakfast inns, hotels, rental cottages, and private campgrounds—are close to the activity of the island. (See our Shopping, Fishing, and Accommodations chapters for details.)

On the oceanside about halfway to the village, you'll see tents and camping trailers dotting the secondary dunes. This popular National Park Service campground is open from late spring to early fall and requires advance reservations (see our Camping chapter). Our Attractions chapter outlines the island's historic hot spots in detail. Make sure you take in the British Cemetery (see our Annual Events chapter) and the stately Ocracoke Inlet Lighthouse. Come January, the flow of visitors subsides, and islanders take a break from long, seven-day workweeks. Off-season tourists still can find available accommodations. Howard's Pub is the only restaurant that stays open year-round.

Yesteryear and Today

It is said that when the first English explorers arrived at Ocracoke, the island was attached to Hatteras Island and jointly they bore the name of Croatan. Obsolete maps indicate that Ocracoke may once have been connected to its southern neighbor, Portsmouth Island, and together the islands were called Wokokon.

Names are great history trackers, and while there are many stories as to how Ocracoke was named, two theories hold most popular. One is that the name descended from Wokokon, not a far stretch from the island's current moniker. The Wokokons, a tribe of Native Americans, journeyed to Ocracoke to feast on seafood, historians say. In 1657 a survey map showed the island as Wococock. A more fanciful story surrounds the legend of Blackbeard, the pirate. It is said that on the morning of his demise, Blackbeard's assassin impatiently awaited the dawn and the coming of his enemy, looking ashore to the island and yelling, "O Crow Cock Crow! O Crow Cock!" The legendary Blackbeard, or Edward Teach, is only a small part of Ocracoke history. And while there are several shops and a museum dedicated to his legend, some Ocracokers today don't care to place importance on the 18th-century villain. His fleet included four boats and 400 crewmen, and by the mid-1700s he'd plundered at least 25 ships.

During Blackbeard's era it became clear to the colonists of North Carolina that there was a need to improve trade and navigation along the coast. The Colonial assembly passed an act in 1715 to establish Ocracoke Island as a port and to maintain pilots and their assistants who helped guide ships safely from sea to shore at "Ocacock Inlett."

It was not until 1730 that the pilots actually came. Their numbers increased over the years, and 33 years later these "squatters" were given 20 acres of land for themselves and their families. By November 1779 the Ocracoke Militia Company was established to protect the inlet (see our History chapter).

Ocracoke was initially owned by several inhabitants. Three successions of absentee owners followed. The fourth owner, William Howard, bought the island in 1759 and at his death deeded all his land to his son, Wallace Howard. Land was sold by both Howards to various families on the island. Descendants of the Howards reside on the island today. A family graveyard is near Village Craftsmen on Howard Street, a craft and gift shop run by Philip Howard. Walking down Howard Street is like stepping back in time. With its stately live oaks, the Howard Cemetery, the oldest homes on Ocracoke Island, right down to the oyster shells embedded in the narrow and rutted dirt road, it evokes an immediate sense of quietude.

In 1770 Ocracoke was annexed to Carteret County and remained there until it was transferred to Hyde County in 1845. By the year 1850 there were 536 residents on Ocracoke Island. Thirty-six of them were employed as pilots.

Ocracoke history is filled with stories of shipwrecks and lost lives. The islanders worked to rescue stranded sea travelers and ships, and housed and fed those who survived. Crabs and a wide variety of seafood kept their bellies full. While the island inhabitants were forced to witness the ocean's wrath as she smashed ships and stole human life, as if in repayment she provided for them, though sometimes in the most unlikely way. Wrecked ships tossed up a variety of goods, including lumber, shoes, clothing, and bananas. But these luxuries were small in contrast to the toll the sea took as the churning waters swallowed not only sailors but also women and children. The year 1823 saw the construction of the Ocracoke Inlet Lighthouse. The white brick structure has stood steady in Ocracoke Village for 174 years, guiding sailors to safety and housing residents during hurricanes (see our Attractions chapter). Several lifesaving stations were also built on the island in the late 1800s and early 1900s. In 1940 a Coast Guard station was erected. Coast Guardsmen continue to watch over Ocracoke waters today, but the island lost eight Coast Guard families within the last few years when federal budget cuts forced a closing of the island's Coast Guard building. Service is still provided around the clock by a rotating group of 10 men, but the families were relocated to Hatteras Island. Modern technology has helped diminish the number of wrecks these days. When accidents do occur, they usually involve offshore fishing vessels caught in foul weather.

The dredging of Cockle Creek and creation of Silver Lake Harbor in 1931 played a role in Ocracoke's development as host to a sizable fishing industry. Access to the village was improved, and fairly large boats now could safely enter and dock at the village. In 1953 most of the island became part of the Cape Hatteras National Seashore, with the exception of the village. The first hard-surfaced

Make sure to catch a harbor sunset when visiting the Outer Banks. PHOTO: COURTESY OF JACKIE THOMAS

road was constructed four years later connecting the village to a spot near Hatteras Inlet. These changes came during a decline in the fishing industry.

Though tourism now replaces fishing as Ocracoke's main source of income, islanders continue to ply the sea for food and fun. Two fish houses operate throughout the year, and a variety of species including Spanish and king mackerel, bluefish, red drum, cobia, amberjack, tuna, and billfish are caught in sound, inlet, and ocean waters.

Gas and water shortages in the '70s and '80s caused a decline in Ocracoke's boating traffic. Gas shortages were, of course, widespread, but water shortages were specific to Ocracoke Island. At that time, the only freshwater sources were from individual wells and cisterns that collected rainwater. With increased tourism and more demand placed upon wells, so much water was drawn from wells that it caused saltwater intrusion. The ensuing severe water restrictions limited personal use to specific times of the day and forbade any outside use. Therefore, no water was available at the boat docks. The water district has since constructed a water desalination plant, and now the island has enough of this resource for

locals, tourists, and boaters. As on any island, electrical outages are not uncommon. Many local businesses now operate their own electrical generators, and a municipal generator ensures that there is a power supply in the event of extended outages due to storms. The generator is used in the event that an outage lasts more than four hours. The year-round population of Ocracoke has not changed dramatically since 1850. Today between 600 and 700 people call Ocracoke Island home. Public school children, grades K–12, attend classes at the Ocracoke School. And community concerns are aired at the Ocracoke Community Center where the Ocracoke Civic and Business Association meets. Welcome progress to the barrier island includes the addition of several vegetable stands, and today the once-isolated community supports two grocery stores and a True Value Hardware Store.

The real estate market is busy on Ocracoke Island. A recent revaluation brought about tax increases of 200 to 300 percent for some property owners. There's only a limited amount of property available, and what's there is in high demand. The few lots are mostly inland, and it's rare to find a waterfront lot for sale. Only one to two canalfront lots sell per year. The island's beauty and isolation will always be a major drawing card. On the eastern flyway of migrating land and water birds, Ocracoke is a birder's paradise, with brown pelicans flying in formation over the waves, sandpipers leaving thin footprints in the sand, herons gracing the salt marsh, and warblers, grosbeaks, and cardinals adorning the trees. Live oaks lend majesty and a sense of strength to the fragile isle.

Famous for its legendary wild ponies, Ocracoke has 180 fenced-in acres set aside for the small herd to roam, and visitors to the island can see a group of them at a special lookout midway down NC 12. The National Park Service rotates four ponies at a time from the range to a pen to let admirers get a close-up view (see our Attractions chapter).

To learn more about Ocracoke Island, we suggest you pick up a copy of *Ocracokers* by Alton Ballance. He speaks beautifully of the history of his home, giving words to the salty spirit of the islanders as no one else has. All proceeds from this literary gem go to the Ocracoke School. Other worthwhile reading includes environmental anthropologist Pat Garber's books *Ocracoke Odyssey* and *Ocracoke Wild*. Both offer wonderful insight into the island's fascinatingly diverse wildlife population. A Richmond, Virginia, native, Garber is (among other occupations) a wildlife rehabilitator on the island she now calls home. Ann Sebrell Ehringhaus's book *Ocracoke Portrait* is another gem that should make its way to your bookshelves. Filled with duotone photographs of Ocracokers, animals, fishing scenes, venerable trees, and water shots, it's supplemented by a delightful collection of interviews that illustrate people's love of the island. A great source for local books (plus other literature and unique gifts) is Books to be Red on NC 12 in Ocracoke Village (see our Shopping chapter for more information).

Getting Here, Getting Around

In the not-so-distant past, it was an ordeal to travel to the Outer Banks. Before the bridges were built, many visitors gained access to these barrier islands by ferry from Elizabeth City, and some people with four-wheel-drive vehicles drove down the beach from Virginia. Both of those routes are now obsolete. Thankfully, we now have two bridge access points, one in Kitty Hawk, used most by travelers from the north, and one from Roanoke Island to Nags Head, used most by visitors from the south and west. North Carolina's Department of Transportation has spent considerable time and money improving state routes, making it increasingly easier to drive to the bridges. Another access point is via long ferry rides from the North Carolina mainland to Ocracoke Island. In fact, ferry travel is still the only way to reach Ocracoke Island—outside of private motorboat or private plane—and we don't foresee any changes there.

Besides the state-run ferries to Ocracoke, there is no public transportation to the Outer Banks. The nearest Amtrak station is in Newport News, Virginia, and the nearest bus stations are in Elizabeth City, North Carolina, and Norfolk, Virginia. The nearest commercial airport is in Norfolk. Once you arrive by bus, train, or plane, however, you must either rent a car and drive to the Outer Banks or hire a private plane or shuttle service to pick you up.

This chapter outlines the best routes for getting here by land, sea, and sky. Once you arrive, however, know that you will need some form of transportation—a motorcycle, a car, a bicycle, a scooter, or at least enough money for a cab—if you plan to venture around a bit. Don't even think of complaining about the lack of public bus transportation. Instead, while you're still unwinding from your trip, venture on down to the beach. Remove your shoes, take off your socks, and walk in the tideline. Now, are you really concerned about bus transportation? If so, you haven't walked far enough. When you decided to come to the Outer Banks, you decided to exchange some of the accoutrements of city life for the simple pleasures that come with leisure.

Within this chapter you'll find information not only for getting here, but also for getting around once you've arrived. As most of our visitors choose to drive, we initially guide you here by car, and then share with you some alternatives to driving.

Getting Here

By Land

You can't get to these islands without spanning water, and thankfully we have many bridges that do just that. Crossing bridges provides you with that magical taste of salty air and sea winds. As your car wheels rhythmically click along the bridge dividers, by all means roll down your car windows and inhale the smell of the beach. Of course, as thrilling as it is to be driving over a bridge eastbound, there's always a sinking feeling when you're traveling westbound. No one ever wants to leave the Outer Banks.

During a state of emergency, such as a hurricane evacuation, our bridges are the only ways off the island. In these times of mass egress, local officials sometimes close the bridges to incoming traffic and use all the lanes to expedite evacuation. In peak travel times (read: summer weekends), the bridges, especially the Wright Memorial Bridge, can be bottlenecks, so drive cautiously.

In the following entries, **Arriving from the South** will take you through Manteo on Roanoke Island to the Washington Baum Bridge, and **Arriving from the North** will direct you to the Wright Memorial Bridge. **Arriving from the West** gives you routes to both the Washington Baum and the Wright Memorial. Directions to points on the Outer Banks from each bridge follow the three "Arriving From" sections.

Arriving from the North:
To the Wright Memorial Bridge

Since so many of our visitors are from Pennsylvania, New York, New Jersey, Connecticut, and Washington, D.C., we'll begin this section with directions from Richmond, Virginia, which visitors from the North can reach on Interstate 95 South. If you're coming from north of the Outer Banks but south of Richmond, read through the directions and select the route nearest your location.

From Richmond, follow Interstate 64 East to Interstate 664 East and take the Monitor-Merrimac Bridge/Tunnel across the James River to I-64. The new VA 168 Bypass, completed in 1999, allows you to skirt all the traffic lights and congestion on Battlefield Boulevard in Chesapeake, thus easing your drive to and from the Outer Banks. From I-64, take exit 291 to VA 168 South. VA 168 will turn into US 158 in North Carolina; don't worry, both refer to the same road. You now have two options for traveling on VA 168, but both will get you to the same place. The new VA 168, linking US 64 in Chesapeake with US 158 to the Outer Banks, is known as the Chesapeake Expressway and is a faster, four-lane

The Wright Memorial Bridge provides the final link to the Outer Banks from the north. PHOTO: COURTESY OF JEANNE REILLY

option, though there is a toll of $1.00 per axle to use it. From VA 168, it's a straight shot to the Wright Memorial Bridge, which crosses the Currituck Sound to Kitty Hawk on the Outer Banks. The road from the North Carolina/Virginia border is now, thankfully, a four-lane highway the entire distance. The drive will take you about an hour, though you may wish to stop at the many antiques shops, thrift stores, and wonderful produce stands. You'll pass Mel's Diner, a 1950s-style diner in Grandy that does a booming tourist trade and has a loyal local following as well. If you just can't wait for some Carolina barbecue, Dixie Bar-B-Q Pit in Powells Point and Saul's Cafe in Harbinger are good options. For good ol' Southern cookin' and great value, Pot's On 'N' Kitchen, about 1.5 miles north of the Wright Memorial Bridge, is an excellent choice.

Another option to traveling through Chesapeake if you're coming from the north is to take US 17 South from I-64 in

Virginia. This stretch of highway flanks the Intracoastal Waterway through the aptly named Great Dismal Swamp. Follow US 17 South to South Mills, where you'll take NC 343 to Camden, following signs to US 158 and the Outer Banks.

Arriving from the West:
To the Washington Baum Bridge

From I-95 in North Carolina, take US 64 East toward Rocky Mount. US 64 will take you through Williamston, Jamesville, Plymouth, Creswell, Columbia, over the Alligator River, through East Lake and Manns Harbor to Roanoke Island.

The bridge over the Alligator River, part of the Intracoastal Waterway, is an old-fashioned drawbridge, opened as needed by an on-site bridge tender. If you're lucky enough to get caught by a bridge opening, do what everyone else does: Get out of the car and enjoy the unique vantage of peering over the railings into the water. As you enter the Alligator River National Wildlife Refuge, US 64 is lined with canals and creeks. The reflection of trees and the sun sparkling on the water create dazzling views. It is a sparse area with few stops between Plymouth and the Outer Banks, so fuel up before you leave either Williamston (approximately 1 hour and 45 minutes from Manteo) or Plymouth, especially if you're traveling at night. If you have to pull off the road, do so carefully and choose a wide shoulder if possible. In areas where canals alternate sides of the road, pull off on the side without the canal. The N.C. Department of Transportation installed guardrails alongside the canals to make travel on this road safer.

Along this route watch for deer, black bears, red wolves, and a wide variety of birds. You'll spot an occasional blue heron wading in the roadside creeks. The state adorns the byways with an abundance of colorful poppies and other wildflowers. It's tempting to pick the lush beauties, but it's illegal to do that, so please leave them in place for the next traveler to enjoy.

Continuing east on US 64, you'll cross the William B. Umstead Bridge or as locals call it, the Manns Harbor Bridge, to Roanoke Island. The Roanoke Island Visitor Center at Fort Raleigh is the first information center from this direction. (See the section on visitor centers later in this chapter.) In a few minutes, you'll pass through the quaint town of Manteo, which celebrated its 100-year anniversary in 1999. By the summer of 2002, there will be a new bridge option for getting from the mainland to the beaches. The Croatan Sound Bridge (its colloquial name; it was not yet officially named at this writing) stretches from the mainland at Manns Harbor to the Manteo–Nags Head Causeway, completely bypassing Roanoke Island. This 5.2-mile bridge, the longest in the state, will shave 20 minutes or so from the trip to the beaches because it will avoid the two-lane bottleneck through Manteo. A new welcome center and rest area of the Outer Banks Visitors Bureau will be open at the bridge's eastern terminus by the summer of 2002. However, the old Manns Harbor Bridge will remain open and should be used if you want to visit the attractions, restaurants, and shops of Roanoke Island and Manteo.

Once through Manteo, if you wish to go to the fishing village of Wanchese, turn right at the junction of US 64 and NC 345 (referred to by locals as Midway). For Outer Banks beaches, Cape Hatteras, Nags Head, and points north, veer left after passing through Manteo, remaining on US 64. Overhead signs make getting lost a difficult endeavor, but if you find yourself off your intended route, just blame it on the scenery. US 64 will take you across the Manteo–Nags Head Causeway and the Washington Baum Bridge.

To the Wright Memorial Bridge from the West

Let's backtrack to Williamston for a minute to explore an alternate route to the Outer Banks: Instead of traveling on US 64 along the southern route, you can choose to take US 17 to Elizabeth City. Either route takes about the same amount of traveling time. From Elizabeth City, follow signs on US

158 to Nags Head and Manteo, and you'll arrive on the island from the north, crossing the Wright Memorial Bridge. US 17 seems to be the route preferred by most visiting Virginians.

Arriving from the South

From points south, take I-95 North to Rocky Mount, North Carolina, then take US 64 East to Williamston, following directions as stated in Arriving from the West. An alternate southern route would be to follow the coastline north to Morehead City and on up to Cedar Island, where you can board a toll ferry to Ocracoke Island. You could also follow US 17 from Wilmington, North Carolina, north through Jacksonville and New Bern to Washington. From Washington, take US 264 East to Swan Quarter and follow signs to the Swan Quarter toll ferry, which will take you to Ocracoke Island. The route will take you through the Swan Quarter National Wildlife Refuge, with gracious old cedars lining the way. From Ocracoke, follow NC 12 to the Ocracoke-Hatteras ferry and gain passage to Hatteras Island

and points north. For ferry schedules and further information, see the Ferries section of this chapter.

Crossing the Wright Memorial Bridge

No matter which route you choose, the destination is well worth the journey. Because the Wright Memorial Bridge is the main thoroughfare to and from the Outer Banks, bear in mind that summer season peak travel time (going to the island) is from noon to 6:00 P.M. on Saturdays and Sundays. This is rush hour traffic, Outer Banks–style. Peak travel time leaving the island is from about 8:00 A.M. to noon on the same days. Delays are possible from Memorial Day to Labor Day; for your convenience, travel advisories are posted on a flashing sign at the bridge.

Once you cross the bridge into Kitty Hawk, you can't miss the brand-new, bigger-than-life signs that will lead you to your destinations. If you're going to Southern Shores, Duck, Sanderling, Corolla, or Carova, turn left on NC 12 and head north. For destinations south of Kitty Hawk, continue on US 158 to Kill Devil Hills and Nags Head. Just over 16 miles south of the bridge, the road veers right toward Roanoke Island and Manteo and branches left toward Oregon Inlet and the Cape Hatteras National Seashore. Follow NC 12 on Hatteras Island to the communities of Rodanthe, Waves, Salvo, Avon, Buxton, Frisco, and Hatteras. In Hatteras Village, you can board a ferry to Ocracoke Island.

At the junction of US 158 and NC 12 in Kitty Hawk is the Aycock Brown Welcome Center. Stop here for a wealth of information and for a break from driving. Another great information stop is the Outer Banks Chamber of Commerce, located on Ocean Bay Boulevard about one block west of US 158 in Kill Devil Hills.

Crossing the Washington Baum Bridge

The Washington Baum Bridge from Roanoke Island will lead you to South Nags Head, where you can choose to travel north toward Nags Head, Kill Devil Hills,

Kitty Hawk, Duck, and Corolla, or south to Hatteras Island and Ocracoke Island. The Cape Hatteras turnoff will be on your right just about a mile from the bridge's eastern terminus. At this intersection—referred to as Whalebone Junction—you can bear left onto US 158 in Nags Head or go straight to connect with the Beach Road (NC 12), either of which will take you north from Nags Head through Kitty Hawk. (Note that South Nags Head is accessed in this area via Old Nags Head Road.) A right turn at Whalebone Junction puts you on NC 12 toward Bodie Island, the Oregon Inlet Fishing Center, and points south. If you continue on NC 12 across the Herbert C. Bonner Bridge onto Hatteras Island, the road will take you through Rodanthe, Waves, Salvo, Avon, Buxton, Frisco, and Hatteras Village. A ferry in Hatteras Village will take you (and your vehicle) to Ocracoke Island.

By Air

Airports and Airstrips

Note to pilots: Several Outer Banks airstrips are unattended, as explained in this section. Please call the State Division of Aviation at (919) 571-4904 for information not covered in the following entries.

Dare County Regional Airport
Airport Rd., Roanoke Island
(252) 473-2600

If you'd like to fly your own plane to the Outer Banks, this is the airport to call. Dare County Regional Airport's two runways measure 3,300 feet and 4,300 feet, and both are lighted. Jet-A and 100 LL fuels are available, as is unleaded auto fuel. Operating hours are 8:00 A.M. to 7:00 P.M. daily. This airport has a terminal VOR, DME, and NDB, plus automated weather updates through AWOS, which you can access at radio frequency 128.275 or by calling (252) 473-2826.

Flightline Aviation, (800) 916-3226, and Outer Banks Airways, (252) 441-7677, are local carriers offering charter service to and from Dare County Regional Airport.

Car rentals are available at Dare County Regional Airport; call in advance.

First Flight Airstrip
Wright Brothers National Memorial
US 158, MP 8, Kill Devil Hills
(252) 441-4460

Every pilot visiting the Outer Banks should make a point of signing in at least once at this historic location. At First Flight your stay is limited to 24 hours. This unattended 3,000-foot strip is maintained by the National Park Service. Since there are no lights, take-offs and landings are permitted only during daylight hours. Reservations are not necessary, and a sign-up book is on premises. No fuel is available.

Billy Mitchell Airstrip
NC 12, Frisco
(252) 995-3735

Also known as Hatteras Mitchell Field, this Hatteras Island airport is on National Park Service land. As the airport is unattended, call the telephone number listed above for an automated weather observation report. Billy Mitchell Airstrip's unlighted runway is approximately 3,000 feet long, and fuel is not available. There is a parking lot. A shelter on the premises has a phone and toilets. Taxi and rental-car services are available through Buxton Under the Sun, (252) 995-6047.

Ocracoke Island Airstrip
NC 12, Ocracoke Island
(252) 928-9901

Yet another airstrip maintained by the National Park Service, this location on Ocracoke is an unattended strip with no lights; there is a parking lot and a pay telephone. The runway is 3,000 feet long and has brush and 25-foot sand dunes at either end. Call for Hatteras area weather updates.

Norfolk International Airport
2000 Norview Ave., Norfolk, VA
(757) 857-3351
www.norfolkairport.com

Norfolk International Airport is open 24 hours a day and offers air service on

American, Continental, Delta, Northwest, United, and USAirways. Major rental car companies have offices at the airport. For main passenger information, call the above number. For private charter information, see the following entries.

Air Service

Burris Flying Service
Hatteras Village
(252) 986-2679
paradise@outer-banks.com

Burris Flying Service, operating from the Billy Mitchell Airport, offers air tours, charter service, and aerial photography for the Outer Banks.

Flightline Aviation
(252) 338-5347, (800) 916-3226
www.flightlineair.com

You can get charter service to the Outer Banks or eastern North Carolina from most anywhere with Flightline Aviation. Flightline will deliver you in comfort to Manteo, First Flight, Pine Island, Hatteras, Ocracoke, or any local airport. Just call for current prices and they'll gladly fill you in on all the details.

Outer Banks Airways
1714 Bay Dr., Kill Devil Hills
(252) 441-7677

Outer Banks Airways offers charter service from just about anywhere you want to fly. Most of its passengers choose to land at Dare County Regional Airport, First Flight Airstrip in Kill Devil Hills, or the private Pine Island airstrip between Duck and Corolla.

Outer Banks Airways is affiliated with Kitty Hawk Aero Tours, which offers sightseeing flights. (See our Attractions chapter for information on advance reservations.)

Pelican Airways
Ocracoke Island
(252) 928-1661

Pelican Airways offers flights to and from Ocracoke as well as services all along the East Coast. It also offers sight-seeing air tours and instrument flight lessons. Call the number listed for specifics.

Southeast Air
Ocracoke Island
(252) 928-5555

Southeast Air offers professional, top-quality air service to and from Ocracoke Island. Air service is also available to and from Norfolk, New Bern, Raleigh, and other East Coast destinations.

By Water

The best way to beat the traffic—and to see some incredible scenery while you're at it—is to arrive at the Outer Banks by boat. You may wish to discuss your trip with a local sailor or captain while making your plans, and be sure to pick up a copy of the *Mid-Atlantic Waterway Guide*; it provides the most detailed information available about the area's waterways. Current chart numbers from the Intracoastal Waterway to Manteo on Roanoke Island are 12204 and 12205. Chart 12204 is a large map of the North River, and chart 12205 is a strip map that includes both the Alligator and North Rivers. Both charts cover the inlet, although 12205 provides a bit more detail.

From the North

If you're boating from points north, you can enter the Intracoastal Waterway (ICW) in Norfolk, Virginia. In fair weather and with a fast boat, you can make it to the Outer Banks in five to six hours; if you're sailing, you may wish to spend your first night at the Coinjock Marina. Be prepared for choppy and shallow waters in the Albemarle Sound. As long as you remain within the ICW markers, you won't have to worry about depth.

Any of the following three routes will lead you to the Outer Banks. One will take you from Norfolk, Virginia, across the Currituck Sound to Coinjock, North Carolina, the North River, and the Albemarle Sound. From the ICW mid-sound marker,

Many folks choose to arrive on the Outer Banks the traditional way—by water. PHOTO: KAREN BACHMAN

head in an easterly direction and look for day markers leading to the waterfront town of Manteo on Roanoke Island.

An alternate route from Norfolk takes you to Deep Creek, Virginia, through the Great Dismal Swamp to Lake Drummond, North Carolina. From there, you'll travel through South Mills to the Pasquotank River, where the ICW—locally known as "The Ditch"—joins the Albemarle Sound. Refer to your charts for navigating across the Albemarle Sound to the Alligator River, and then follow either the Croatan Sound or the Roanoke Sound to Manteo. The trip from Norfolk to Manteo is about 80 nautical miles.

The third—and probably the easiest—route takes you from the end of the North River into the Albemarle Sound. Look for marker number 173, then bear left and follow the day markers leading you behind Powell's Point. The first marker you'll come to is number 4; from there look for number 2 and then MG (the middle ground marker). From MG you'll be heading nearly due south. Look for another number 2 day marker, which will take you from the north end of East Lake toward Manns Harbor Channel. From there, follow the day markers to the Roanoke Island Channel. (All these markers will be present on your charts.)

From the South

If you are traveling to the Outer Banks from the south, pick up the Intracoastal Waterway (ICW) between Beaufort and Morehead City, North Carolina, and follow the ICW to the Neuse River. Take the ICW north from the Neuse River across the Pamlico River to Belhaven on the Pungo River. Take the time to stop in Belhaven at the River Forest Manor, a country inn, restaurant, marina, and shipyard. At this worth-it stop you can fuel up while you tour the turn-of-the-century Southern plantation mansion and even get a bite to eat in its historic restaurant. Sunday brunch alone is worth the trip. An alternative stop is the new Dowry Creek Marina, with slips and fuel. After you leave Belhaven, continue north on the ICW to the Alligator River, then travel easterly until you spot the Roanoke Sound day markers, which will lead you on to Manteo on Roanoke Island.

If seas aren't rough, the fastest route from the south is to go through the Pamlico Sound from either the Pamlico or Neuse River. After you pass under the Manns Harbor Bridge, look for the Roanoke Sound day markers leading you to Manteo.

Roanoke Island Marinas

Manteo has several docks within walking distance to restaurants and attractions. Locations and amenities are as follows. Also see the Boating section of our Watersports chapter.

Waterfront Marina
Manteo Historic District
(252) 473–3320

The Waterfront Marina provides public docking facilities with water and power at each slip. Charges are on a per-foot basis for semi-annual, annual, and transient boaters. Call ahead or radio the dockmaster on your approach to the marina. Laundry and shower facilities are available. The marina's boardwalk extends along the waterfront, and you're within walking distance of shops, restaurants, and other diversions. In Manteo you'll

find friendly merchants and interesting sights, and if you'd like a break from your berth, there are several lovely inns. A brief stroll across the bridge takes you to Roanoke Island Festival Park, where there are a host of exhibits, activities, and entertainment (see our Attractions chapter for more information).

Pirate's Cove Marina
Roanoke Sound, between Manteo and Nags Head
(252) 473-3906

Open year-round, Pirate's Cove can accommodate boats from 25 to 110 feet in 180 slips. Transients are welcome, and many slips are rented year-round. Daily rates are $1.50 per foot. Monthly rates are $16.00 per foot on-season and $10.00 per foot in the off-season. Annual rates are $100 to $150 per foot. Electricity is rated per cord or metered. Slip rental includes showers, water, cable TV hookup, and laundry facilities. Pirate's Cove offers one courtesy car that boaters can use on a limited basis to make a run for supplies or other necessities. Boaters can use the tennis courts and pool and other on-site facilities.

The on-site ship's store and restaurant are open to the public, as is the fuel dock. You really can't beat the scenery from the top deck of Hurricane Mo's Restaurant & Raw Bar, where you can have a beer and some steamed shrimp while getting a bird's-eye view of one of the area's most beautiful sportfishing fleets. Make sure you're on hand in the afternoon to watch the fleet come in and to ogle each boat's catch.

Salty Dawg Marina
US 64/264, Manteo
(252) 473-3405
www.saltydawgmarina.com

This top-notch facility sports 55 slips, all with power and water, plus a modern, air-conditioned bathhouse. On site is a ship's store, dry dock, and repair facilities, and you can fuel up with either diesel or plus. Salty Dawg added a new lift in 1999 to accommodate larger boats. If you get into a spot of bother out on the water, radio in for Salty Dawg's commercial towing service. Salty Dawg monitors Channel 16, the hailing and distress frequency on marine radios. The marina is just minutes from downtown Manteo and is within walking distance of a laundromat, drug store, grocery store, and several excellent restaurants. A courtesy car is available. The marina is open every day year-round; you're advised to call ahead for reservations on holidays.

Ferries

Landlubbers can also enjoy an Outer Banks arrival by boat thanks to the North Carolina Ferry System. One picturesque route is to follow US 70 East from New Bern to Havelock. Pick up NC 101, follow to NC 306, and then take the ferry to Bayview near historic Bath. Follow NC 99 to Belhaven, where you pick up US 264 to Swan Quarter. Choose an overland course along NC 94 across Lake Mattamuskeet, then US 64 to Manteo—or select another ferry from Swan Quarter to Ocracoke Island. It sounds complicated, but signs will guide you.

An alternate route follows US 70 through Havelock to Beaufort. US 70 continues from Beaufort to Harkers Island, following the Core Sound to NC 12, where you can board the Cedar Island Ferry to Ocracoke Island. The voyage across the Pamlico Sound is well worth the time it takes to arrive in Ocracoke. Cross Ocracoke Island from south to north, and pick up the Hatteras Island Ferry to the upper Outer Banks.

Ferry passage is a good way to reduce your driving time if you're heading to the southern portion of the Outer Banks. It also gives you a chance to stretch and move around while still making progress. Unless you have your own boat or plane, it's the only way to reach picturesque Ocracoke Island. The ferries transport cars to the island, although we suggest that you park your car after arriving on Ocracoke and get around on foot or by bike.

Following is information on the Outer Banks ferry services. Although it is rare to have a time change, you may wish to call ahead and verify departure times. You can get more information by writing to Director, Ferry Division, Morehead City, North Carolina 28557, or by calling

Relax and enjoy the 40-minute ride on the Hatteras-Ocracoke Ferry. PHOTO: COURTESY OF GEORGIA BEACH

(800) BY FERRY. Truckers: For information about weight and size limitations, call the specific ferry location. Toll-free numbers are operable east of the Mississippi River only.

Hatteras Inlet (Ocracoke) Ferry

This free, state-run service links the islands of Hatteras and Ocracoke. The 40-minute crossing carries you from Hatteras Village past Hatteras Inlet across the Pamlico Sound. Hatteras-Ocracoke ferries accommodate 30 vehicles—including cars and large camping/recreational vehicles—and are run frequently during the summer to avoid excessive delays. The Hatteras ferry does not require reservations, although reservations are recommended if you plan on taking either the Swan Quarter or Cedar Island ferries to Ocracoke Island. Public restrooms are at the Hatteras dock, and heads are on board. The information number for Hatteras is (800) 368-8949 or (252) 986-2353.

Summer Schedule
May 1–October 31

Leave Hatteras	Leave Ocracoke
5:00 A.M.	5:00 A.M.
6:00 A.M.	6:00 A.M.
7:00 A.M.	7:00 A.M.
7:30 A.M.	8:00 A.M.
Then every 30 minutes until . . .	
7:00 P.M.	7:00 P.M.
8:00 P.M.	8:00 P.M.
9:00 P.M.	9:00 P.M.
10:00 P.M.	10:00 P.M.
11:00 P.M.	11:00 P.M.
Midnight	Midnight

Winter Schedule
November 1–April 30

Ferries leave Hatteras and Ocracoke every hour on the hour from 5:00 A.M. to midnight. Additional departures may be scheduled as needed.

Swan Quarter and Cedar Island

Make a reservation to avoid possible delays in boarding the Ocracoke–Cedar Island toll ferry and the Ocracoke–Swan Quarter toll ferry. You can reserve space in person at the departure terminal or by calling the ferry location from which you're departing. The reservationist will ask you to supply the driver's name and vehicle license number. For reservations from Ocracoke, call (800) 345-1665 or (252) 928-3841; from Cedar Island, call (800) 856-0343 or (252) 225-3551; and from Swan Quarter, call (800) 773-1094 or (252) 926-1111. Office hours are usually 6:00 A.M. to 6:00 P.M., but the office stays open later during the summer.

Reservations may be made up to 30 days in advance of departure date and are not transferable. You must claim your reservation at least 30 minutes prior to departure time. Information on tolls and vehicle weight limits follows the ferry information.

Ocracoke–Swan Quarter Toll Ferry

This 28-car ferry connects Swan Quarter in Hyde County on the mainland with Ocracoke Island and takes two-and-a-half hours to cross the Pamlico Sound. It's a scenic trip offering a wonderfully relaxing break from driving. See Arriving from the South for directions to Swan Quarter.

Summer Schedule
May 22–September 3

Leave Ocracoke	Leave Swan Quarter
6:30 A.M.	*7:00 A.M.
12:30 P.M.	9:30 A.M.
*4:00 P.M.	4:00 P.M.

Winter Schedule
September 4–May 21

Leave Ocracoke	Leave Swan Quarter
6:30 A.M.	9:30 A.M.
12:30 P.M.	4:00 P.M.

*Additional departures: Memorial Day through Labor Day. One-way fares and rates are listed at the end of this section.

Ocracoke–Cedar Island Toll Ferry

This ferry provides a popular link between Cedar Island and Ocracoke Island. It accommodates 50 cars and has a crossing time of two hours and 15 minutes. Take along a good book and something to eat, and enjoy the view. See Arriving from the South for directions to Cedar Island.

Summer Schedule
May 22–September 30

Leave Cedar Island	Leave Ocracoke
7:00 A.M.	7:00 A.M.
8:15 A.M.	—
9:30 A.M.	9:30 A.M.
—	*10:00 A.M.
—	10:45 A.M.
Noon	Noon
*1:00 P.M.	—
1:45 P.M.	—
3:00 P.M.	3:00 P.M.
—	4:40 P.M.
6:00 P.M.	6:00 P.M.
8:30 P.M.	8:00 P.M.

*Additional departures: Memorial Day through Labor Day.

Spring and Fall Schedules
April 10–April 31 and October 1–October 31

Leave Cedar Island	Leave Ocracoke
7:00 A.M.	7:00 A.M.
9:30 A.M.	9:30 A.M.
Noon	Noon
3:00 P.M.	3:00 P.M.
6:00 P.M.	6:00 P.M.
8:30 P.M.	8:30 P.M.

Winter Schedule
January 1–April 9 and November 1–December 31

Leave Cedar Island	Leave Ocracoke
7:00 A.M.	7:00 A.M.
10:00 A.M.	10:00 A.M.
1:00 P.M.	1:00 P.M.
4:00 P.M.	4:00 P.M.

Toll Ferry One-Way Fares

• Pedestrians, $1.00

• Bicycles and Riders, $2.00

• Single vehicles or combinations 20 feet or less in length, and motorcycles (minimum fare for licensed vehicle), $10.00

• Vehicles or combinations from 20 to 40 feet in length, $20.00

• All vehicles or combinations 40 to 55 feet in length having a maximum width of 8 feet and height of 13 feet, 6 inches, $30.00

Vehicle Gross Load Limits

The following weight limits apply for all crossings:

• Any axle, 13,000 pounds

• Two axles (single vehicle), 24,000 pounds

• Three or more axles, 36,000 pounds (single or combination vehicle)

Getting Around by Auto

We've gotten you here; now let's get you around.

Let's get the traffic report out of the way first. Being a resort community, we experience a dramatic increase in the number of travelers on our roads during the summer. Traffic more than triples from Memorial Day through Labor Day, offering a great contrast to that of the other nine months. We realize that visitors enrich our economy, and we welcome you—cars, trucks, sport-utilities, and all. If you're used to big-city driving, you'll find the summer traffic tolerable. Naturally, roads get very congested during hurricane evacuations, but county authorities do a good job with advance warnings (refer to the Waves and Weather: How to Stay Safe chapter for more). Bear in mind the following tips, and you should experience smooth driving.

The northern route up NC 12 through Duck and Corolla can get bogged down on summer weekends and during lunch and dinner hours Monday through Friday. If the weather's bad, everyone will be out shopping, so prepare for heavier traffic when the skies are gray. As a rule of thumb, if it's not a good beach day, it's a crowded shopping day. Just remember to allow an extra half-hour or so when traveling to the northern Outer Banks on summer weekends.

The Herbert C. Bonner Bridge spans Oregon Inlet, connecting Hatteras and Bodie Islands. PHOTO: MOLLY HARRISON

You may want to call the various municipalities or radio stations to see when traffic is heaviest during holidays. And if you must travel during high traffic hours, don't panic and try not to lose your cool. There are plenty of places to stop for food, drinks, and shopping, though you may also want to pack some snacks, especially if you have young children.

While we do have congested spots to deal with from time to time, we have a simple road layout that makes getting lost almost impossible. These barrier islands, including Roanoke Island to the west, have only three major roadways. US 158 crosses the Wright Memorial Bridge into Kitty Hawk and winds through the center of the island to Whalebone Junction in Nags Head. This five-lane highway (the center lane is for turning vehicles only) is also called the Bypass, Croatan Highway, or the Big Road. In this book, we will refer to it as the Bypass or US 158.

NC 12 runs along the beach, parallel to US 158. A two-lane road, it stretches from the southern border of the Currituck

National Wildlife Refuge at the Villages at Ocean Hill development in Corolla to the ferry docks at Hatteras Island's southernmost tip. NC 12 picks up again on Ocracoke, spanning the length of the tiny island, ending in picturesque Ocracoke Village. NC 12 is also called Ocean Trail in Corolla, Duck Road in Duck and Southern Shores, Ocean Boulevard in part of Southern Shores, and either Virginia Dare Trail or the Beach Road from Kitty Hawk through Nags Head. In this book, we will refer to it as NC 12 (or occasionally as the Beach Road, when talking about that stretch from Kitty Hawk through Nags Head).

On Roanoke Island, US 64/264 is also called US 64 or Main Highway. This stoplight-filled road begins at the Nags Head–Manteo Causeway and runs across the Washington Baum Bridge through Manteo, across the William B. Umstead Bridge and through Manns Harbor on the mainland. School traffic clogs US 64/264 on weekday mornings and afternoons. Also, on rainy days in summer, this road is extremely congested with visitors headed to Roanoke Island's attractions and shops. The new Croatan Sound Bridge, scheduled to open in summer 2002, should alleviate some of the congestion on US 64/264 through Manteo.

US 158 and NC 12 run mainly north and south. Smaller connector streets link seaside rental cottages to year-round neighborhoods west of the Bypass. Most locals will be glad to point you in the right direction.

If you truly want to relax and spend your vacation days island-style, kick off your shoes and travel on foot. You can walk for miles down the beaches, collecting shells and wading, and stopping at various beach accesses that will take you back to the Beach Road (NC 12). There are plenty of restaurants and fishing piers running the length of the Outer Banks, so you're usually not far from food and drink. Most spots welcome casual diners. When walking the Beach Road, watch out for vehicles with projecting mirrors—the road is narrow. It is not the best choice for biking, except in Nags Head, where there is a bike path. You can easily explore Manteo on foot, and biking is a safe alternative in that town.

By Bike

The Outer Banks boasts several paved bike paths. Running the length of Roanoke Island is a 7-mile asphalt path with benches alongside. The path has awakened the athlete in many locals, young and old, who are now regularly seen walking, riding bikes, and in-line skating. It's a wide, safe path that we are grateful to have.

An 11-mile bike path runs along NC 12 almost the entire length of the town of Nags Head. In South Nags, the path is concrete, and in the rest of the town it is asphalt. The town of Kill Devil Hills sports a scenic asphalt route along Colington Road, running down the National Park Service property past the Wright Brothers National Memorial. Kitty Hawk has a bike path meandering through the maritime forest along Woods Road, off US 158 between the Wright Memorial Bridge and the Kitty Hawk Wal-Mart Shopping Center.

A great place to go for a ride is through Southern Shores and Duck. A bike path runs the entire length of NC 12 in Southern Shores and Duck. Duck's path extends through town to just north of Sanderling. Call each township for specific bike path restrictions.

If you're going to enjoy these paths or bike anywhere else on the Outer Banks, please wear a helmet. You can rent bikes at several rental services, and many accommodations offer bikes and helmets as a courtesy (see our Recreation and Accommodations chapters). Watch out for the sand that blows on the road. This can get in your eyes as you pass the dunes and can be slippery when you brake. Follow the normal rules of the road that apply to cars, stopping at lights and stop signs and yielding to pedestrians. There is a lot of foot traffic near the beach, so whether you're on a bike or in a car, watch out for that rolling beach ball, which is usually followed by a child.

Taxis, Limos, and Tours

Even though you won't find any public transportation here, you do have a number of alternatives. Since demand for taxicabs and limousines can be great at times, make sure to call in advance.

Insiders' Tip
When riding or walking on the bike paths, be sure to keep a lookout for traffic coming out of driveways that cross the bike path. They're supposed to look for you, too, but they don't always do it.

A Stretch of the Beach
(252) 457–1099

This Corolla-based limousine service offers limousines and town cars for special occasions and airport transportation to any city. Weddings, nights on the town, concerts, and shopping trips to Norfolk are just some of the special events this company has handled.

Bayside Cab
(252) 480–1300

Bayside is on US 158 at MP 6 and offers point-to-point service 24 hours a day. The company offers service between the Outer Banks and Norfolk International Airport with 24-hour notice, and has three nine-passenger station wagons.

Beach Cab
(252) 441–2500, (800) 441–2503

The familiar sky-blue taxis of Beach Cab offer 24-hour service and Norfolk International Airport pickups.

Buxton Under the Sun
(252) 995–6047

"We'll go just about anywhere," say the accommodating folks at Buxton Under the Sun. They offer 24-hour taxi service and shuttle service to anywhere within 250 miles, including Norfolk Airport and bus station, Newport News Airport, and Raleigh-Durham. Anglers take note: Buxton Under the Sun will take you to your favorite surf-fishing spot or to your charter boat, and then they'll arrange to pick up you and your catch.

Coastal Cab Company
(252) 449–8787

Coastal Cab offers radio-dispatched 24-hour service on the Outer Banks. Service to airports in Norfolk and Raleigh is offered with advance reservations. Credit cards are accepted.

The Connection
(252) 473–2777

The Connection is a shuttle service that operates between Norfolk and the Outer Banks. It offers door-to-door shared-ride and private service to Norfolk International Airport, the bus station, and Amtrak. The vehicles are full-size, air-conditioned passenger vans that can accommodate groups, families, bicycles, surfboards, sailboards, etc. They are fully licensed and insured and use professional drivers. Reservations are recommended.

Historically Speaking's Outer Banks Tours for Motor Coaches
(252) 473–5783
nikndug@aol.com

Historically Speaking offers year-round step-on tour guiding and receptive tour services (lodging, meals, attractions) for bus groups, conferences, and conventions, featuring entertaining commentary on the natural and cultural history of Roanoke Island and the Outer Banks. Call for your personalized tour consultation. Step-on guides are CPR-certified. Fun-filled itineraries are individually designed. Private evening programs offer traditional Outer Banks music and sea song sing-alongs as well as costumed living history performances of Elizabethan music and culture from the time of Sir Walter Raleigh's Roanoke colonies (see our Attractions chapter). You can e-mail for more information.

Island Hopper Shuttle
(252) 995–6771

Island Hopper Shuttle serves Hatteras Island with transportation to and from Norfolk International Airport, plus courier service on weekdays to Nags Head and Manteo. They'll even deliver your dry cleaning.

Island Limo
(252) 441–LIMO, (800) 828–LIMO

If it's a stretch limo you want, Island Limo has a selection to suit your every need. Island Limo provides transportation to and from Norfolk International Airport via private sedan and limousine year-round.

Car Rentals

Whether you simply need something to get around town in or you need something more substantial, like a four-wheel-drive vehicle, to really explore the island, you have a number of rental options.

Cars Only

Dare County Regional Airport, on Roanoke Island, off Airport Road, (252) 473-2600

B&R Rent-A-Car at R.D. Sawyer Motor Company, US 64 in Manteo, (252) 473-2141

Cars and Four-Wheel-Drive Vehicles

Buxton Under the Sun, NC 12 in Buxton on Hatteras Island, (252) 995-6047

Outer Banks Chrysler, Plymouth, Dodge, Jeep, Eagle, US 158 at MP 5 in Kill Devil Hills, (252) 441-1146

U-SAVE Auto Rental, US 158, one mile north of the Wright Memorial Bridge in Point Harbor, (252) 491-8500, (800) 685-9938

Beach Driving

Off-road access is possible on the Outer Banks but only in designated spots and at certain times of the year. It is mandatory that you use a four-wheel-drive (4WD) vehicle. Check with each township for specific rules; some places even require a permit.

Generally you can drive on the beach in Kill Devil Hills and Nags Head from October 1 through April 30. You must have a permit to do so in Nags Head. Southern Shores and Kitty Hawk prohibit driving on the beach at all times. As far north as Corolla and Carova in Currituck County, there are designated spots where you can drive on the beach. Hatteras Island operates under the guidance of the National Park Service, (252) 473-2111, so any questions you have concerning off-road driving can be referred to them.

Driving is not allowed on the beach at Pea Island National Wildlife Refuge (the area from Rodanthe Pier north to Oregon Inlet), but as you move south, you will see access areas marked by a picture of a jeep where you can travel on the beach.

You can take it all with you when you drive out onto the beach at Oregon Inlet for a day of fishing and lazing around in the sun. PHOTO: MOLLY HARRISON

Obviously those jeeps with an X marked through them are spots where beach driving is prohibited. It's a good idea to stop at one of the National Park Service visitor centers or campgrounds and chat with a ranger before you take to the beach by wheels. Rangers can supply up-to-date information on unusual conditions, such as eroded beach areas, that could prove hazardous to you and your vehicle.

Year-round Beach Driving Areas–NPS

Here is a list of areas that are open year-round in the National Park for beach driving:

• From ramp 23 to ramp 34, the area that stretches from the south end of Salvo to the north side of Avon.

• The beach around Cape Point, which continues all the way to Frisco Campground. You can also enter the beach at Cape Point Campground and head north to the Point or south to Frisco.

• Hatteras Ferry dock to Hatteras Inlet.

• The north end of Hatteras Inlet, depending on how much beach front is available.

• The south end of Ocracoke Island toward the village to the beach behind the airport.

Seasonal Beach Driving Areas–NPS

These National Park areas are open to vehicular traffic on a seasonal basis:

• Ramp 20 to ramp 23, from Rodanthe to Salvo, closed from the end of May until the second week in September.

• Ramp 34 to ramp 38, the area in front of the village of Avon, closed from the end of May until the second week in September.

Driving Rules and Safety Tips

The maximum speed for beach driving is 25 mph, but even that can be too fast on a crowded day. The speed limit is strictly enforced by park rangers and local law officials. In some spots where the sand is soft, you may have to drive even slower than 25 mph.

Beach drivers follow the same rules that apply when driving on asphalt: keep to the right, pass on the left, etc. All vehicles must be street legal with valid plates, insurance, and inspection stickers, and driven by a licensed individual. Seat belts must be worn by anyone in the front seat. Standing is not allowed in any vehicle. If you are riding in the back of a pickup truck, you must sit on the bed, not on the side rail or wheel well. Jeep passengers must be seated and may not stand and hold on to the roll bar. No open containers of alcohol are allowed in the vehicle.

Pedestrians have the right-of-way at all times on the beach, regardless of where they are in relation to your vehicle. Look out for children, pets, sunbathers, and anglers. Many folks fall asleep on the beach and are groggy as a result. Expect the unexpected. The wind can hamper hearing, so use caution when approaching pedestrians. If the wind is blowing away from them and toward you, they may not hear your approach.

When leaving the sand, please keep your eye on pedestrian traffic on the road also. The edge of the Beach Road sometimes grabs the wheels a bit and can pull you to one side or another abruptly. Just make sure you give a wide berth to anyone walking near you.

And a note to pedestrians: wear light clothing at night if you intend to walk near car traffic. While most drivers respect driving safety rules, some come to the beach to really let their hair down. Pedestrians need to be as conscientious as drivers on both sand and roadways.

Vehicle Preparation

Many, many drivers get stuck because they don't let air out of their tires before driving on the beaches. The National Park Service says its rangers generally drive with 20 pounds of pressure in their tires. This applies to vehicles of any size, from large trucks to smaller sedans. Lowering the pressure also helps prevent the engine from overheating when traveling through soft sand. Make sure to use a tire gauge when inflating and deflating; in fact, the process can seem a bit time-consuming when you're raring to get out on the beach, so you may want to buy two gauges and put one of your passengers to work. Rangers advise reinflating tires when returning to the paved roads.

Please don't block the beach ramps to lock hubs or deflate tires. We suggest pulling well off to the side of the ramp or using the parking areas found at most vehicle accesses.

Driving on Sand

Once on the beach, try to drive on the firm, wet section of the beach below the high-tide line and follow in someone else's tracks if you can. Areas that don't have any tracks might have been avoided for good reason. Watch out for areas of the beach with shell-laden, reddish sand and depressions where there is just a bit of standing water. These areas can be very soft.

Restricted Areas

You are not allowed to drive on, over, or in between the dunes for any reason at any time. The dunes and their fragile vegetation create our protective barrier and are extremely vital to the delicate ecology of animal and plant life.

Please obey all the area designations that you'll find on the beaches. Often, portions of the beach are roped off to allow shorebirds and turtles to nest. These areas change throughout the seasons, so areas that were open in April could be closed in August. Through traffic can be curtailed by these closings, especially at high tide. Stay alert for the changes, and respect the limitations. There are substantial fines for violators.

When driving down by the waterline, always drive behind surf anglers. You don't want to snap their nearly invisible monofilament fishing line or upset their fishing activity.

Welcome and Visitor Centers

Aycock Brown Welcome Center at Kitty Hawk
US 158, MP 1½, Kitty Hawk
(252) 261-4644

Constructed in the style of an old lifesaving station, this center is called "Outer Banks at a Glance" and includes 17 state-of-the-art displays, a theater, and a brochure gazebo. By combining computers, photography, video graphics, period music, and sound effects, the displays give you an entertaining overview of the Outer Banks, and the well-informed local staff members are ready to answer any questions you might have. Named for a 1950s photographer who has since become a local legend, this building sits a mile east of the Wright Memorial Bridge at the juncture of US 158 and NC 12. It is one of three such welcome centers operated by the Outer Banks Visitors Bureau.

Resources include area maps, tide charts, ferry schedules, and brochures. Free community newspapers such as *The Coast,* published by *The Virginian-Pilot,* and the locally published *North Beach Sun* offer features that highlight the local area.

The center is open daily 8:30 A.M. to 5:30 P.M. from Memorial Day through September and 9:00 A.M. to 5:00 P.M. daily from October through April. It is closed Thanksgiving Day, Christmas Day, and New Year's Day. The building and the public restrooms are wheelchair-accessible, and the picnic area is a welcome sight for those who have been riding a long time. Contact the Outer Banks Visitors Bureau at (800) 446-6262 for more information.

Outer Banks Chamber of Commerce
101 Town Hall Dr., Kill Devil Hills
(252) 441-8144
www.outerbankschamber.com

On the south side of Colington Road, near the corner of US 158 at MP 8, a wooden building with a covered porch houses the Chamber of Commerce in Kill Devil Hills. This center overflows with free information that's helpful to both visitors and permanent residents. It's a clearinghouse for written and telephone inquiries, and the friendly staff can give information on activities, accommodations, and annual events.

The mailing address is P.O. Box 1757, Kill Devil Hills, North Carolina 27948. The center is open year-round Monday through Friday from 9:00 A.M. to 5:00 P.M.

Outer Banks Visitors Bureau
704 US 64/264, Manteo
(252) 473-2138, (800) 446-6262
outerbanks.org

The Outer Banks Visitors Bureau will be relocating in the summer of 2002, so its location will vary depending on your time of visit. At this writing, the Visitors Bureau is located in a former bank building, complete with a drive-up information window, on US 64/264 in Manteo. In the summer of 2002, the Visitors Bureau will move down the road to a new 10,000-square-foot facility near the eastern terminus of the new Croatan Sound Bridge. The new location, housing both the Outer Banks Welcome Center and the Bureau's administrative offices, will make it much more convenient for visitors coming to the Outer Banks from the south and west. The Outer Banks Visitors Bureau is equipped to help visitors and residents find almost any Outer Banks information. The Bureau has a huge collection of brochures, maps, and promotional materials about area offerings, and

Insiders' Tip

When on Ocracoke Island, do yourself a favor and abandon your vehicle. Explore on foot and on bicycle to experience the true flavor of the island.

Sometimes it's best to get around in a simple way. PHOTO: MOLLY HARRISON

the staff can answer most questions quickly. They can also offer data on demographics and business opportunities on the Outer Banks. The new Welcome Center will be technologically advanced to allow visitors to make reservations on-site, and it will have a rest area, toilets, and an RV dump station.

The Outer Banks Visitors Bureau offices are open year-round. Current hours are 8:00 A.M. to 6:00 P.M. Monday through Friday and noon to 4:00 P.M. Saturday and Sunday. Welcome Center hours may be extended when the Visitors Bureau moves to its new location. For specific information and a free, detailed vacation guide, write to the Outer Banks Visitors Bureau at 704 US 64/264, Manteo, North Carolina 27954, call the toll-free number shown above, or visit the Web site.

Nags Head Visitor Center at Whalebone
Whalebone Jct., Nags Head
(252) 441–6644
Operated by the Outer Banks Visitors Bureau, this welcome center sits just south

of the Whalebone Junction intersection on NC 12. It's open daily 9:00 A.M. until 5:00 P.M. from Memorial Day through September. From October through Thanksgiving, it is open Friday, Saturday, and Sunday from 9:00 A.M. until 5:00 P.M. It closes during December, January, and February and reopens in the spring around Easter time. The staff can answer all kinds of questions about southern destinations along the Outer Banks. These restrooms are also some of the few you'll find on this remote stretch of NC 12. The wooden structure also serves as a hunter contact station.

Pea Island Visitor Center
NC 12, Pea Island
(252) 987–2394
The Pea Island Visitor Center offers information, free public restrooms, and paved parking. Wildlife and waterfowl exhibits enhance the public building. There are plenty of nature-related gifts to choose from and an excellent assortment of wildlife books for all ages. In summer the

center is open daily from 9:00 A.M. to 4:00 P.M. Off-season you can visit Thursday through Sunday from 9:00 A.M. to 4:00 P.M. It's closed Christmas Day. This also is an exciting stop for birders. A nature trail winds through the refuge, which is a haven for a wide variety of seasonal and year-round species. Pick up a free nature trail map at the center. Pea Island trails and beaches are open year-round during daylight hours.

Hatteras Island Visitor Center
Off NC 12, Buxton
(252) 995-4474
About 300 yards south of Old Lighthouse Road, past the Texaco station and Sharky's Grill & Pizzeria, a large wooden sign welcomes visitors to the Cape Hatteras National Seashore and Cape Hatteras Lighthouse Historic District. Turn left toward the wooden fence if you are coming from the north and follow the winding road past turtle ponds and marshes.

At the four-way intersection, turn left and you'll be led to the original lighthouse location, marked by a circle of granite stones that are etched with the names of 83 former lighthouse keepers. Back at the four-way intersection, turn right and park the car in the parking area while you explore the lighthouse in its new location. The visitor center, called the Museum of

the Sea, and the bookstore, both housed in the historic former keepers' quarters, were moved to this location before the lighthouse was moved. Restrooms are located here as well. If you continue past the parking area, you'll pass the picnic area and the Buxton Woods Nature Trail. If you continue on, you'll come to the Cape Point Campground and off-road vehicle ramps. The beach here is great for swimming, sunbathing, surfing, and fishing, and you can take four-wheel-drive vehicles along many sections of the beach year-round. Park rangers and volunteers are willing to answer questions and can be found in the visitor center and on the historic district grounds. Visitor center and bookstore hours are 9:00 A.M. to 5:00 P.M. daily, except for Christmas Day.

Ocracoke Island Visitor Center
Near the Cedar Island and Swan Quarter
Ferry Docks, Ocracoke Island
(252) 928-4531
This visitor center at the southern end of NC 12 is a clearinghouse of information about Ocracoke Island. It's located across from Silver Lake and operated by the National Park Service. If you're arriving on the island from the Hatteras ferry, stay on the main road until you reach the T intersection at Silver Lake. Veer right and continue around the lake, counterclockwise,

until you see the low brown building on your right. Parking is available at the visitor center.

Inside you'll find an information desk, helpful staff, a small book shop, and exhibits about Ocracoke. You can pick up maps of the winding back roads that make great bicycle paths and arrange to use the Park Service's docks.

The visitor center is open daily 8:30 A.M. to 6:00 P.M. June through Labor Day, 8:30 A.M. to 5:30 P.M. after Labor Day through October, and 9:00 A.M. to 5:00 P.M. November to June. Rangers offer a variety of free summer programs through the center, including beach and sound hikes, pirate plays, bird-watching, night hikes, and history lectures. Check at the front desk for changing weekly schedules. Restrooms are open to the public during peak season.

History

The narrow strand of barrier islands known as North Carolina's Outer Banks stretches for more than 90 miles along the coast from Virginia's border down through Ocracoke and Portsmouth Islands. Bordered by bodies of brackish water on the west (known as "sounds") and by the Atlantic Ocean on the east, these fragile islands are accessible by plane, boat, or by driving over one of several bridges that provide links to the mainland. At the narrowest points, the islands are less than a half-mile wide, and in some areas, they extend out more than 20 miles east of the North Carolina mainland. Despite the apparent inaccessibility, the Outer Banks has historically been an alluring destination. Although today's year-round population barely tops 46,000 people, the area draws nearly 250,000 people each week during the height of the summer season. Many consider the area a vacation paradise, owing to its wide sandy beaches, unspoiled natural terrain, abundant clean water, and warm temperatures. Aside from the beach allure, recreational activities include swimming and watersports, the best surfing on the East Coast, world-class sport fishing, and world-class golf. And, since the towns of Kitty Hawk and Kill Devil Hills are home to the world's first powered flight, the area is a magnet for aviators. It's a place where adventure is still possible, where romance thrives, and where tide charts, seagulls, and wild ponies take precedence over convention and pretense.

In the Beginning

About 18,000 years ago, when continental glaciers held much of the world's ocean water, sea levels were almost 400 feet lower than they are today. North Carolina's coastline was 50 to 75 miles east of its present-day location. At that time, the region's principal rivers—the Neuse, Tar, Currituck, and Chowan—flowed across the continental shelf and emptied into the Atlantic Ocean.

When the sinking sea reached its lowest level and winds began carrying sediment from the west, a high ridge of sand dunes formed on the easternmost edge of the mainland. As glaciers began to melt, causing the sea level to rise, the land's vast forests and marshes began a slow retreat from the rising waters. In their wake, they left huge river deltas that ultimately formed the Outer Banks.

Sea levels continued rising over the next few thousand years, but the newly formed barrier islands that paralleled Carolina's coast weren't covered by the higher tides. Instead, an unusual combination of winds, waves, and weather enabled the Outer Banks to maintain its elevation above the ocean and to migrate as a unit.

Today, the islands' eastern edges still move backward in response to rising waters. The land builds up on the western side and creeps further west, slowly narrowing the sound waters that separate the barrier islands from the mainland.

Ocean levels rise about a foot every 100 years. The shoreline moves westerly at a rate of 50 feet to 200 feet per century along most of North Carolina's coast.

Although these figures aren't startling, there are parts of Hatteras Island where the Atlantic eats 14 feet of beach each year.

Geologists refer to the Outer Banks and similar land forms as "barrier islands" because they block high-energy ocean waves and storm surges, thus protecting the coastal mainland. Barrier islands are common to many parts of the world, and many have similar features, yet no two are alike. Winds, weather, and waves give each its own personality. Inlets from the sounds to sea are ever shifting, opening new channels to the ocean one century, closing off primary passageways the next. If you travel from one area of the Outer Banks to another, you'll soon realize that even along this small stretch of sand there is a vast variety of topography, flora, and temperatures (see our Natural Wonders chapter). An examination of the 16th-century paintings, drawings, and maps created by explorer Gov. John White reveal this same diversity. Even more important, they provide valuable documentation suggesting what the land was like, and when compared to today's geological maps, they illustrate the transformations that have occurred since the first English explorers arrived here.

Early Explorers

Jutting far into the ocean near the warm waters of the Gulf Stream, the Outer

The Elizabeth II *is the state ship of North Carolina.* PHOTO: COURTESY OF DARE COUNTY TOURIST BUREAU

Banks was the first North American land reached by English explorers. A group of colonists dispatched by Sir Walter Raleigh set up the first English settlement on North American soil in 1587. But Native Americans inhabited these barrier islands long before white men and women arrived.

Historians say humans have been living in North Carolina for more than 10,000 years. Three thousand years ago, people traveled throughout the Outer Banks hunting, fishing, and living off the land. The Carolina Algonkian culture, a confederation of 75,000 people divided into distinct tribes, spread across 6,000 square miles of northeastern North Carolina.

Archaeologists believe that as many as 5,000 Native Americans could have inhabited the southern end of Hatteras Island from 1000 to 1700. These Native Americans formed the only island kingdom of the Algonkians. Isolation afforded these people protection and the sole use of the island's seemingly limitless resources. The Croatan, as they were known, lived comfortably for more than 800 years in the protection of the Buxton Woods Maritime Forest at Cape Hatteras. Contact with Europeans proved fateful, however. Disease, famine, and cultural demise had eliminated all traces of the Carolina Algonkians by the 1770s.

Early ventures to America's Atlantic seaboard proved difficult for European explorers because of the high winds, seething surf, and shifting sandbars. In 1524 Giovanni de Verrazzano, an Italian in the service of France, plied the waters off the Outer Banks in an unsuccessful search for the Northwest Passage. Verrazzano thought the barrier islands looked like an isthmus and the sounds behind them, an endless sea. According to historian David Stick, the explorer reported to the French king that these silvery salt waters must certainly be the "Oriental sea . . . which is the one without doubt which goes about the extremity of India, China and Cathay." This explorer's misconception—that the Atlantic and Pacific Oceans were separated by only the skinny strip of sand we now call the Outer Banks—was held by some Europeans for more than 150 years.

About 60 years after Verrazzano's visit, two English boats arrived along the Outer Banks, searching for a navigable inlet and a place to anchor away from the ocean. The captains, Philip Amadas and Arthur Barlowe, had been dispatched by Sir Walter Raleigh to explore the New World's coast. They were hoping to find a suitable site for an English settlement.

The explorers finally found an entrance through the islands, well north of Cape Hatteras, probably at the present-day Ginguite Creek in northern Kitty Hawk. Passing through the inlet, they sailed south through the sounds to Roanoke Island. There, they disembarked, met the natives and marveled at the abundant wildlife and cedar trees. Their expedition had been successful, and they reported to Raleigh on the riches they had found and the kindness with which the Native Americans had received them.

During the next three years, at least 40 English ships visited the Outer Banks, more than 100 English soldiers spent almost a year on Roanoke Island, and Great Britain began to gain a foothold on the continent, much to the dismay of Spanish sailors and fortune-seekers.

Lost Colonists

In May of 1587 three English ships commanded by naturalist John White set sail for the Outer Banks with Sir Walter Raleigh's (thus Queen Elizabeth's) blessing and backing. Earlier explorers had dubbed the land "Virginia," in honor of the virgin queen Elizabeth. The expedition, which included women and children for the first time, arrived at Roanoke Island on July 22. Colonists worked quickly to repair the cottages and military quarters left by the earlier British inhabitants. They rebuilt a fort the soldiers had abandoned on the north end of the island and made plans for a permanent settlement. Less than a month later, the first English child was born on

Eleanor Dare and her baby, Virginia, two of the 1587 colonists who disappeared on Roanoke Island, are portrayed in The Lost Colony *outdoor drama.* PHOTO: COURTESY OF ROANOKE ISLAND HISTORICAL ASSOCIATION

American soil. Virginia Dare, granddaughter of Gov. John White, was born on August 18, a date still celebrated with feasts and festivities at Fort Raleigh.

One week after his granddaughter was baptized, John White left her and 110 other colonists on the Outer Banks while he returned to England for food, supplies, and additional recruits for the Roanoke Island colony. A war with Spain, meanwhile, had broken out. So when White was again ready to set sail for the Outer Banks the following spring, his queen refused to let any large ships leave England, except to engage in battles. White did not return to the American settlement until three years later, in 1590. By then, it had disappeared.

The houses were gone, destroyed and deserted. White's own sea chests had been dug from their shallow hiding places in the sand, broken open, and their contents raided. His daughter, granddaughter, and all the other English colonists had vanished—leaving no trace except for two cryptic carvings in the bark of Roanoke Island trees. "CRO" was scratched into the trunk of one tree near the bank of the Roanoke Sound. "CROATOAN" was etched into another, near the deteriorating fort. White thought these mysterious messages meant the settlers had fled south to live with the friendly Croatan Indians on Hatteras Island.

The abandoned settlement site showed no signs of a struggle, no blood, bodies, or even bones. Some say the colonists were killed by natives or carried away in a skirmish. Others think they were lost at sea, trying to sail home to England. Still others believe they skirted west across the sounds and began to explore the Carolina mainland. Or perhaps they headed to other areas of the Outer Banks, their footprints scattered in the blowing sands.

Historians have debated the "Lost Colony's" fate for more than 400 years. Archaeologists continue to dig on Roanoke Island's eastern edges, scouting for clues to "history's greatest mystery." Scholars from across the country gather to discuss the strange disappearance and even have established a special research office on the subject at East Carolina University in Greenville. Archaeologist David S. Phelps, former director of East Carolina University's Coastal Archaeology Office, dug on the Outer Banks for more than a decade.

Erosion from Hurricane Emily in 1993 unearthed remnants of a Croatan Indian civilization in Buxton. Phelps's team uncovered artifacts that could prove that some members of Sir Walter Raleigh's "Lost Colony" migrated south to Hatteras Island from the Fort Raleigh area. The discovery of lead bullets, fragments of European pottery and brass, and copper coins indicate a mingling of the Croatan and English cultures.

Each summer, for more than 60 years, actors have re-created the unsolved mystery in America's longest running outdoor drama, *The Lost Colony*, held at the settlement site in Waterside Theatre (see our Attractions chapter for more information about the play).

Shipping and Settlement into the 1700s

A century passed before English explorers again attempted to establish settlements along the Outer Banks. Throughout this time, however, European ships continued to explore the Atlantic seaboard, searching for gold and conquerable land. Scores of these sailing vessels wrecked in storms and on dangerous shoals east of the barrier islands. Spanish mustangs, some say, swam ashore from the sinking ships on which they were being transported overseas. Descendants of these wild horses roam in the Currituck National Wildlife Refuge. Others are corralled in a National Park Service pen on Ocracoke Island.

Although the Outer Banks beaches had few permanent people until the early 1700s, small colonies sprouted up across the Virginia coast and what is now the Carolina coast during the late 1600s. The barrier islands' inlets, with their ever-shifting sands, blocked deep-draft ships from sailing into safe harbors, where they needed to anchor and unload supplies for mainland settlers. Smaller vessels, fit for navigating the shallow sounds, transported goods from the Outer Banks to the mainland. People passed through these strips of sand long before they settled here.

Ocracoke Inlet, between Ocracoke and Portsmouth Islands, was the busiest North Carolina waterway during much of the Colonial period. The inlet was a vital yet delicate link in the trade network, and it was deeper than most other area egresses. Navigational improvements to the inlet began as early as 1715 when the British government made it an official port of entry. Pilot houses were established at Ocracoke to dock the small transport boats and to temporarily house goods that were headed inland. Commercial traffic increased along this Outer Banks waterway for many years.

Countless inlets from sea to sound have formed and closed since the barrier islands first formed, many due to hurricanes and nor'easters. More than two dozen inlets appear in the historical record and on maps dating from 1585, yet only six inlets are currently open between Morehead City and the Virginia border. Studies of geographic formations and soil deposits indicate that at some point, inlets have covered nearly 50 percent of the Outer Banks. Attempts to harness the inlets have proven costly and, for the most part, have been doomed to failure. Even today, recreational and commercial watermen continue to fight environmentalists for the rights and federal funding to build $97 million jetties in an effort to stabilize Oregon Inlet, which separates Nags Head and Bodie Island from Hatteras Island.

The first land the British government granted in North Carolina was what is now Colington Island, a small spit of earth surrounded by the Currituck, Albemarle, and Roanoke Sounds, between Kill Devil Hills and the mainland. Sir John Colleton, for whom the island is named, set up a plantation on the island's sloping sand hills in 1664. His agents planted corn, built barns and houses, and carried cattle across by boat to graze on the scrubby marsh grasses. According to historians, this was the beginning of the barrier islands' first permanent English settlement.

Over the next several decades, stockmen and farmers set up small grazing stocks and gardens on the sheltered sound side of the Outer Banks. Runaways, outlaws, and entrepreneurs also arrived in small numbers, stealing away in the isolated forests, living off the fresh fish and abundant waterfowl, and running high-priced hunting parties through the intricate bogs and creeks. Inhabitants also engaged in salvaging: When a shipwrecked vessel floated onto the shore, local residents made quick work of appropriating the wood off the boat, loosening sails from the masts, and scavenging anything of value that was left on board. If victims were still struggling ashore, the locals helped them, even setting up makeshift hospitals in their humble homes.

The inaccessibility of the barrier islands and the wealth of goods that passed through the ports made the Outer Banks a prime target for plundering pirates. The most infamous of all high seas henchmen was Edward Teach, better known as Blackbeard, a rum-drinking Englishman whose

up, as the people finally had found some steady occupation and were assured of regular wages.

In 1757 the barrier islands' first tavern opened amidst a sparse string of wooden warehouses and cottages on Portsmouth Island. About 11 years later, a minister made the first recorded religious visit to the Outer Banks when he baptized 27 children in the sea just south of the tavern. Today, a Methodist church and a few National Park Service–supervised cottages are all that remain on Portsmouth Island (see our Daytripping chapter).

War and Statehood

As much of a hindrance as the string of barrier islands and their surrounding shoals and sounds had been to shipping, the Outer Banks proved equally invaluable as a strategic outpost during the Revolutionary War.

Only local pilots in small sailing sloops could successfully navigate the shifting sands of the often unruly inlets that provided the sole passageways between the Atlantic Ocean and the North Carolina mainland. Consequently, big British warships could not anchor close enough to sabotage most North Carolina ports. Colonial crafts, instead, ferried much-needed supplies through Ocracoke Inlet, and up inland rivers and small waterways, to the new American strongholds in New England.

By the spring of 1776, British troops began threatening the pilots at Ocracoke, even boarding some of their small sloops and demanding to be taken inland, where they could better wage war. Colonial leaders then hired independent armed companies to defend the inlets. They abandoned these small forces by autumn of the following year. British boats, however, continued to beleaguer the Outer Banks. Ships crept close to the islands, enabling sailors to steal cattle and sheep. The redcoats anchored off Nags Head, going inland for freshwater and whatever supplies

raucous crew set up shop on the south end of Ocracoke Island. After waylaying countless ships and stealing valuable cargo for more than two years, Blackbeard finally was beheaded by a British naval captain in 1718, in a slough off his beloved Ocracoke.

Settlement and sparse development continued through the early 1700s, and by 1722 almost all of the Outer Banks was secured in private ownership. Large tracts of land, often in parcels with 2,000 acres or more, were deeded to noblemen, investors, and cattle ranchers. Some New England whalers also relocated to the barrier islands after British noblemen encouraged such industry. The whaling industry supplied blubber, oil, and bones to overseas markets. The huge marine mammals were harpooned offshore from boats or merely harvested on the sand after dying and drifting into the shallow surf.

Although small settlements and scores of fish camps were scattered from Hatteras Village almost to the Virginia line, Ocracoke and the next island south, Portsmouth, continued to be the most bustling areas of the Outer Banks through the middle of the 18th century. British officials enlisted government-paid pilots to operate transfer stations at Ocracoke Inlet, between the two islands, and carry goods across the sounds to the mainland. A small town of sorts sprang

Kitty Hawk + Kill Devil Hills p. 14 p. 77, 118

Lighthouses p. 69

Attractions p. 291, 298, 307, 312, 319, 322

they could pilfer. They raided fishing villages, plundered small sailboats, and came ashore beneath the cloak of darkness. Ocracoke Inlet, especially, suffered under their persistent attacks.

In November 1779, North Carolina legislators formed an Ocracoke Militia Company and hired 25 local men as soldiers to defend their island's independence. This newly armed force was issued regular pay and rations. Its members successfully protected the inlet and American supplies until fighting finally stopped in 1783, six years after the United States declared its independence.

About 1,000 permanent residents made their homes on the Outer Banks by the time North Carolina became a sovereign state under the 1789 Constitution. Most of these people sailed down from the Tidewater area of Virginia or across from the Carolina mainland. These settlers lived primarily in two-story wooden structures with an outdoor kitchen and privy. They dug gardens in the maritime forests, built crude fish camps on the ocean, and erected rough-hewn hunting blinds along the waterfowl-rich marshlands. After frequent storms crashed along their coasts, the residents continued to find profit in the shipwrecks strewn along nearby shoals and shores.

Lighthouses along the Graveyard of the Atlantic

More than a dozen ships a day were carrying cargo and crew along Outer Banks waterways by the dawn of the 19th century. Schooners and sloops, sailboats and new steamers all journeyed around the sounds and across the oceans, often dangerously close to the coast in search of the ever-shifting and shoaling inlets.

At that time, waterways were the country's primary highways, and North Carolina's barrier islands were along most eastern routes.

Hurricanes and nor'easters, which still threaten the Outer Banks, took many boats by surprise, ending their voyages and hundreds of lives. Statesman Alexander Hamilton dubbed the ocean off the barrier islands "The Graveyard of the Atlantic" because its shoals became the burying grounds for so many ships. In an attempt to help seamen navigate the treacherous shoals, the federal government authorized the Banks's first lighthouses in 1794: one at Cape Hatteras in the fishing village of Buxton and the other in the Ocracoke harbor, on a half-mile-long, 60-mile-wide pile of oyster shells dubbed "Shell Castle Island." Shell Castle Lighthouse first illuminated the Atlantic in 1798. The Cape Hatteras beacon took a little longer to erect. It was finally finished in 1802. Two subsequent structures have sat on the same Buxton spot, but the Shell Castle beacon has long since succumbed to the sea.

Ship captains complained that the early lighthouses were unreliable and too dim. Vessels continued to smash into the shoals. So in 1823 the federal government financed a 65-foot-high lighthouse on Ocracoke Island. The squat structure was whitewashed, with a glass tower set slightly askew on its top. It is the oldest lighthouse still standing in North Carolina.

Officials raised the Cape Hatteras tower to 150 feet in 1854. Five years later, they built two new Outer Banks beacons, at Cape Lookout and on Bodie Island. Both of those lighthouses were improved and rebuilt in later years.

On December 16, 1870, the third lighthouse at Cape Hatteras was illuminated. Standing 208 feet tall and using a multifaceted lens to refract its whale-oil beam across miles of sea, this spiral-striped structure is the tallest brick lighthouse in the world. See our National Wonders and Attractions chapters for more information on the Hatteras Lighthouse and its relocation in 1999.

Currituck Beach's red-brick beacon was the last major lighthouse to be built on the barrier island beaches. The 150-foot tower was completed in 1875. It watches over the Whalehead Club, near the western shores of Corolla. It is the only unpainted lighthouse on the Outer Banks

The Currituck Beach Lighthouse, completed in 1875, was the last lighthouse constructed on the Outer Banks.
PHOTO: HORSLEY/GARDNER

and the only one held in private ownership (at least it still was at this writing). All other Banks beacons are owned by the National Park Service and operated by the U.S. Coast Guard.

Summer Settlements

In the early 1800s mainland farmers and wealthy families along Carolina's coast suffered each summer from malaria. This feverous condition was thought to be caused by poisonous vapors escaping from the swamps on hot, humid afternoons. Physicians recommended escaping to the seaside for brisk breezes and salt air.

Nags Head was established as a resort destination primarily by a Perquimans County planter who bought 200 acres of ocean-to-sound land for 50 cents an acre in the early 1830s. Eight years later the Outer Banks's first hotel sprang from the sand near the sound, near what is now Jockey's Ridge State Park. Guests arrived at Nags Head Hotel from across the sounds on steamships, disembarked at a long, low boardwalk behind the 200-room hotel, and spent weeks enjoying the beaches and the hotel's formal dining room, ballroom, tavern, bowling alleys, and casino.

In 1851 workers enlarged the hotel and added a mile-long track of rails so mule-pulled carts could ease vacationers' journeys to the ocean. The hotel burned down and was rebuilt; later, it was buried by sand. Jockey's Ridge dune, the East Coast's tallest, swallowed the two-story structure bit by bit. Hotel clerks offered discounts during the final years for those who didn't mind digging their way into their rooms.

Wealthier visitors who wanted to stay the whole summer built their own vacation cottages on the barrier islands' central plains and eventually on oceanfront property. Some fathers carried their entire households—cows, pigs, sheep, and all—across the sounds on small sailing sloops to spend the season at Nags Head. By 1849 a local visitor remarked that between 500 and 600 visitors were bathing daily at the barrier island beach.

Meanwhile, locals lived in small wooden houses in the woods, selling fresh fish and vegetables to the new tourists, thereby earning unexpected extra income each summer.

Civil War Skirmishes

Outer Banks inlets again proved important military targets after the War Between the States erupted in 1861. Union and Confederate troops stationed armed ships at Hatteras and Ocracoke Inlets and set up early encampments. North Carolina crews, who joined their Southern neighbors and seceded from the United States, captured boats filled with fruit, mahogany, salt, molasses, and coffee along the enigmatic inlets. Forts, too, were built along the barrier islands, although erosion and storms have long since erased all traces of such structures. Fort Oregon was constructed on the south side of Oregon Inlet; Fort Ocracoke on Beacon Island, inside Ocracoke Inlet. Fort Hatteras and Fort Clark were across from each other at Hatteras Inlet, by then the primary passageway between the ocean and sounds. Approximately 580 men defended Fort Hatteras and Fort Clark. Seven cannon were mounted inside, aimed across the inlet from one fort to the other in a cross-fire position so that the entire waterway could be covered from within the high walls.

By the fall of 1861, however, federal forces had overtaken Hatteras Inlet and controlled most of the Outer Banks and lower sounds. Confederate troops still ruled Roanoke Island and the upper sounds. They built three small fortresses on the north end of their stronghold to reinforce their position and to block all access through Croatan Sound.

Union troops also were massing. In January 1862 Gen. Ambrose Burnside led an 80-boat flotilla from Newport News to North Carolina's Outer Banks. Water was so scarce on this trip that some soldiers resorted to drinking vinegar out of sheer thirst. Others died of typhoid before the battle even began. But on February 7 more than 11,500 members of the federal army amassed for a Roanoke Island attack (an overlook at Northwest Point on the northern end of the island commemorates this site today). At least 7,500 men raided the shores at Ashby's Harbor that night, near Roanoke Island's present-day Skyco. About 1,050 Confederate soldiers fought to maintain their foothold.

After hours of battle around what is now the Nags Head–Manteo Causeway, rebel troops finally were forced to surrender. Union troops captured an estimated 2,675 of these Southerners. Federal forces held Roanoke Island, and most of the Outer Banks, for the rest of the Civil War.

A Settlement for Freed Slaves

After Roanoke Island fell to Union troops, Union leaders had to decide what to do with the slaves from the former Confederate camp. Gen. Benjamin F. Butler at Fortress Monroe set a precedent by declaring slaves as contraband, successfully using the notion against the rebels. Word spread of this action, and black women and children began flocking to Union camps where they were allowed to settle peacefully. Once word reached the under-

ground network of servants, abolitionists, and free blacks, the number of freedom-seeking individuals migrating to Dare and Currituck Counties increased. At the outbreak of the Civil War, only a few hundred slaves lived along the Outer Banks. But two months after falling to Union troops, Roanoke Island was filled with more than 1,000 runaway and recently freed slaves. Inhabitants of the colony worked as porters for Union officers and soldiers, and as cooks, teamsters, and woodcutters. The federal government offered these African-American men $8.00 per month plus rations and clothing to build a fort, Fort Burnside, on the north end of Roanoke Island. Women and children, who made up three-fourths of the population of blacks on the island at that time, collected only $4.00 a month, including clothing and ration benefits.

By June 1863, officials had established an official Freedmen's Colony on Roanoke Island, west of where the Elizabethan Inn now stands. The government granted all unclaimed lands to the former slaves and outfitted them with a steam mill, sawmill, grist mill, circular saws, and other necessary tools. About 3,000 African Americans lived here in a village with more than 600 houses, a school, store, small church, and hospital.

Union forces began accepting African-American troops soon after they established the settlement. By the end of July, more than 100 members of the Freedmen's Colony formed the nation's first African-American army regiment. The new colony would have survived were it not for the government's decision to return all lands to the original landowners after the war was over. The Freedmen's Colony was abandoned in 1866. Federal officials quickly transported many of the former slaves off the Outer Banks. Others remained on Roanoke Island to work the waters and the land.

Lifesaving Stations

After the war, normal life resumed on the barrier islands. Commerce began again along the ocean, increasing quickly with steamers now outnumbering sailboats and onetime warships joining private shipping companies. Storms, too, continued to wrack the shores and seamen, sometimes even sinking iron battleships into oblivion.

Seven U.S. Life-Saving Stations were established on the Outer Banks in 1874 in an attempt to help save sailors' lives, if not salvage some of the ships. The stations were located at Jones Hill near the Currituck Beach Lighthouse; Caffey's Inlet north of Duck; Kitty Hawk Beach south of the present pier; Nag's (sic) Head within current town boundaries; Bodie's (sic) Island south of Oregon Inlet; Chicamacomico, which is still open to visitors in Rodanthe and conducts simulated rescue drills each summer; and Little Kinnakeet, on the west side of NC 12 in Avon.

During their first season of employment, lifesaving station keepers were paid $200 per year to supervise six surfmen from December through March. Lifesavers lived in the sparse wooden stations, often sleeping six to a room, and kept constant watch over the Atlantic from inside elevated towers that poked out of the stations' roofs. The men walked the beach 24 hours a day. Two from each station would leave at the same time, one heading north, the other south. After 3 to 6 miles, they'd meet a surfman from the neighboring station, also walking either north or south, and exchange tokens to prove they had completed their patrol.

Stations were operated mostly by longtime Outer Bankers. Good swimmers and sea captains who knew the wild waters, these men risked their lives (and many perished) trying to pull others from the ocean. In March of 1876 the entire Jones Hill station crew was lost during an attempt to rescue seven sailors aboard the Italian ship *Nuova Ottavia*. It was dark when the rescue began, and the entire crew drowned when their surfboat capsized in the breakers.

Many complained that the lifesaving service had two major flaws, one being that they were only open for four months of the year. The second was that the seven stations were too far apart, up to 15 miles in some cases, for the surfmen to ade-

quately patrol the beaches on foot. In 1877–78, two major shipwrecks that resulted in the loss of 188 lives provoked the government to build more stations. The wreck of the USS *Huron* in Nags Head occurred in November 1877 when the Nags Head station was closed for the season. The wreck of the *Metropolis* in January 1878, 4.5 miles south of the Jones Hill Station, was a fiasco of a rescue operation, with 85 lives lost because it took more than five hours for the lifesaving station to respond. By 1879, 11 new stations were in operation on the Outer Banks at Deal's Island (later Wash Woods), Old Currituck Inlet (later Penny's Hill), Poyners Hill, Paul Gamiels Hill, Kill Devil Hills, Tommy's Hummock (north of Oregon Inlet and later named Bodie Island), Pea Island, Cedar Hummock, Big Kinnakeet, Creeds Hill, and Hatteras (later named Durants). The schedule was switched to eight months of the year at that time and then was later established year-round. The Pea Island Station was the only all-black lifesaving station in the nation.

Rescue techniques advanced with new equipment and the surfmen's experience in ocean survival. Before motorized rescue craft were available, lifesaving teams had to row deep-hulled wooden boats, often through overhead waves. If they made it through raging seas to shipwrecks, they sometimes couldn't carry all of the sailors back to shore in one trip. As a result, they devised a pulley system to haul men off the sinking vessels. Dubbed a "Britches Buoy," the device consisted of a pair of short pants sewn around a life preserver ring and hung on a thick rope by wide suspenders; the rope was wound around a handle crank mounted to a wooden cart on shore. Shipwreck victims struggled into the britches, usually with the assistance of surfmen in the rescue boat, and gave an "all-clear" tug on the rope. With the buoy sewn into the seams around their waists, these sailors didn't sink. Even in the highest seas, they could keep their heads above water while lifesaving crews back on shore reeled them safely onto the sand.

Surfmen at Outer Banks lifesaving stations saved thousands of lives during hurricanes and hellacious northeast blows. In 1915 the Lifesaving Service became part of the U.S. Coast Guard. Coast Guardsmen continue to aid barrier island boaters with a variety of state-of-the-art rescue craft stationed at modern Oregon Inlet and Hatteras Island stations. The old lifesaving stations are scattered around the Outer Banks today. Some have been moved and are now private homes. The Wash Woods station is a rental house north of Corolla. A store in Corolla, Outer Banks Style, occupies the old Kill Devil Hills Lifesaving Station, which was moved north. To see a restored lifesaving station and learn about the history of the service and the surfmen, visit Chicamacomico Lifesaving Station in Rodanthe (see our Attractions chapter).

Historic Happenings

Government jobs of lifesavers, lighthouse keepers, and postmasters employed increasing numbers of Outer Banks residents at the dawn of the 20th century. Other locals continued to profit from summer tourists. But most remained poor fishermen, farmers, stockmen, store clerks, hunters, and hunting guides. Currituck Sound was known as the premier hunting spot on the East Coast, and many hunt clubs were established along the northern Outer Banks. Market hunting was a huge business for the locals on the northern Outer Banks in the late 1800s and early 1900s. During this time it was legal for anyone to kill as many ducks and waterfowl as they could and sell them on the market, to be shipped through the mainland to Norfolk and on to bigger cities. Locals also made a living as hunting guides. According to the record book of the Pine Island Club, from 1888 to 1910 its members killed a total of 72,124 waterfowl, including geese, swans, snipes, black ducks, mallards, widgeon, gadwall geese, and Canada geese. The record kill for a day's hunt, according to David Stick in

Statuary at the Wright Brothers National Memorial in Kill Devil Hills reminds visitors of the momentous first flight that Outer Banks history proudly claims. PHOTO: COURTESY OF J. AARON TROTMAN

The Outer Banks of North Carolina, was 892 ruddy ducks by Russell and Van Griggs. This reckless killing decimated the numbers of waterfowl on the Currituck Sound, and market hunting was outlawed in 1918 by an act that made the selling of migratory waterfowl illegal. Much later, in the 1930s, game laws were passed that shortened the season and lowered the bag limit. Sport hunting continues along the Outer Banks today, but on a much smaller scale.

In 1902 the barrier islands recorded another first when Thomas Edison's former chief chemist began experimenting with wireless telegraphy. Radio pioneer Reginald Fessenden transmitted the first musical notes to be received by signal from near Buxton on Hatteras Island to Roanoke Island. He wrote to his patent attorney that the resulting sounds were "very loud and plain, i.e., as loud as in an ordinary telephone."

In 1900 Ohio bicycle shop owners Wilbur and Orville Wright arrived by boat at Kitty Hawk, drawn by accounts of prevailing winds, isolation, and soft landing spots. They spent some time in Kitty Hawk and received their mail there, but they camped and flew their glider on Kill Devil Hill. They brought with them a 17-foot glider, but when they flew it the wings generated less lift than they expected. Wilbur kept it aloft for only 10 seconds. In 1901 they returned with another glider but it failed to fly as they had hoped. In 1902 the Wright brothers, ever persistent, had another machine that flew over 1,000 glides. In 1903 the Wrights returned to Kill Devil Hills with a new 40-foot, 605-pound Flyer. They tested it on December 14, 1903, but the Flyer was damaged and had to be repaired. On December 17, 1903, the Wrights made a second attempt. The wind was blowing 27 miles an hour, but they went ahead with the test. Orville positioned himself in the flyer and at 10:35 A.M. left the ground. He kept the Flyer aloft for 120 feet, with Wilbur running alongside. The brothers took turns flying three more times that day, increasing their flight distance each time. The fourth and last flight of the day, Wilbur's second, was the best:

852 feet in 59 seconds. The site is now marked with a stone monument in a National Park set along the original runway. Replicas of the historic airplane, hangar, and brothers' shack are on display at the Wright Brothers National Memorial (see our Attractions chapter).

Modern Influences

In the 1930s, bridges linking the Outer Banks to the mainland brought thousands more tourists and profound changes to the islands. Visitors now could drive to popular summer resorts at Nags Head rather than rely on steamships. Hotels, rental cottages, and restaurants sprang up to accommodate the influx.

Post-Depression era politics promulgated the Civilian Conservation Corps (CCC), which set up six camps along the barrier islands. Throughout the '30s, these government workers performed millions of dollars' worth of dune construction and shoreline stabilization. The dunes you see along the east side of NC 12 did not

Hunt clubs, like this one on Duck Island, dot the soundside islands of the Outer Banks, providing access to the multitudes of waterfowl. PHOTO: MOLLY HARRISON

The First Flight Centennial Celebration

Dayton, Ohio, may have nurtured hometown boys Wilbur and Orville Wright into aviation pioneers, but it was the Outer Banks's perfect assemblage of elements—constant wind, favorable climate, a lone hill, and soft sand for landings—that facilitated the historic first flight of the 1903 Wright Flyer on December 17, 1903.

On that day, after years of trial and error, experiment and revision, the Wright brothers finally succeeded in flying, at Kill Devil Hill, near their base camp in Kitty Hawk. Orville made the first flight at 10:35 A.M., staying airborne for 12 seconds and covering 120 feet. Wilbur conducted the last flight, increasing the length of the flight to 852 feet and the time in the air to 59 seconds.

The 100th anniversary of this life-changing event is fast approaching. Flight celebrations and events are planned all over the nation throughout 2003, but the grand finale will be on December 17, 2003, at the exact spot of the first flights—the National Park Service's Wright Brothers National Memorial in Kill Devil Hills.

Anticipation is already rising for the First Flight Centennial Celebration, the grandest and largest event ever to occur on the Outer Banks. The events at Kill Devil Hills will be of worldwide interest, not only to those in the aviation world but also to those who are inspired by the Wright brothers' story. Plans are now in the works for a grand five-day festival and celebration, complete with celebrities and dignitaries, daily flyovers, educational displays, hands-on experiments, and more.

The National Park Service, which oversees the Wright Brothers National Memorial, is taking the lead in organizing the events, but several other groups are playing large roles in the planning, including local organizations, national- and state-appointed commissions, and foundations.

The First Flight Centennial Celebration will officially kick off on the 99th anniversary of flight—December 17, 2002. There will be flyovers, this time with 99 planes, and speeches and celebration. Throughout the year 2003, several events will be held on the Outer Banks, throughout North Carolina, in Dayton, Ohio, and around the nation. The culmination of the year's worth of events will be the five-day official First Flight Centennial Celebration from December 13 through 17, 2003.

Each day from December 13 through 16 will have a different theme, featuring flyovers, visits by celebrities and dignitaries, exhibits, and displays related to the theme. The kick-off day, December 13, will be General Aviation Day, followed by Commercial Aviation Day, Future Aviation Day, and Military Aviation Day. Sponsors, speakers, and events for each day will be announced at later dates.

The Big Event is on December 17, 2003, when the eyes of the world will turn to the Wright Brothers National Memorial. The highlight and focal point of the day will be a re-enactment of Orville Wright's first flight at 10:35 A.M. Activities will be geared around the re-enactment, with aviation celebrities and dignitaries speaking, flyovers, and much fanfare and celebration.

In order to re-enact Orville Wright's first flight, the Experimental Aircraft Association (EAA) has commissioned a team called The Wright Experience of Warrenton, Virginia, to build an accurate reproduction of the original 1903 Flyer. The reproduction flyer is part of EAA's Countdown to Kitty Hawk celebration, sponsored by Ford Motor Company. The Wright Experience is meticulously reconstructing the 1903 Flyer in hopes

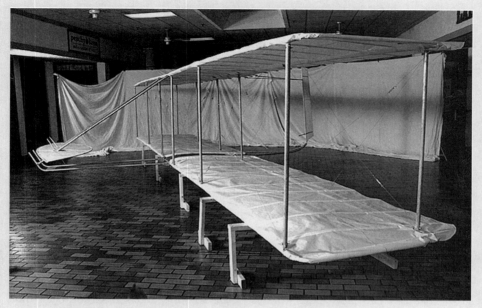

A replica of the Wright Brothers' 1902 glider was built by seven Outer Banks youths.
PHOTO: COURTESY OF J. AARON TROTMAN

of repeating Orville Wright's historic first flight exactly 100 years later, to the minute. The attempt at flying the reproduction flyer will be the only flight allowed by the National Park Service at the Kill Devils Hill at 10:35 A.M. The last time a Wright airplane flew was in 1934, and that plane is now at the Wright Institute in Philadelphia.

EAA will send the 1903 Flyer on a nationwide tour in 2003, with the plane ending up at the First Flight Centennial Celebration in Kill Devil Hills in December. In 2004 the 1903 Flyer reproduction will be installed at the Henry Ford Museum in Dearborn, Michigan.

The Wright Brothers National Memorial will serve as the educational center of the celebration. In addition to the site's regular exhibits and displays in its Visitor Center, a 20,000-square-foot supplementary building called the First Flight Centennial Pavilion will be constructed on the park service grounds.

A semipermanent structure, First Flight Centennial Pavilion will house special programs and exhibits. Pavilion exhibits will include: *The Outer Banks,* showing the Wright brothers' early campsite, the Outer Banks in the early 1900s, and a weather exhibit; *Precursors to Flight,* detailing the early flight experiments by humans and also the mythical and folk traditions of human flight; *The Wrights of Dayton,* showing Wilbur and Orville in their hometown life; *The Wrights as Engineers,* highlighting the brothers' engineering feats; *Glider Experiments,* showing the brothers' early experiments with flight; *Powered Flight,* retelling the hallmarks of powered flight; and *A Century of Flight,* detailing the aviation achievements of the century since the historic first flight.

EAA will also bring a 24,000-square-foot educational touring pavilion to the National Park Service site. The EAA pavilion will house the reproduction 1903 Flyer, multimedia displays, and hands-on educational exhibits. Microsoft has recently announced its plans to join EAA's Countdown to Kitty Hawk by developing a computer model of the Wright brothers' 1903 Flyer. The historically accurate model will enable a "pilot" to experience the 1903 Flyer just as Wilbur and Orville did. The pilot will lie on his or her stomach in front of a giant projection screen depicting the sand dunes at Kill Devil Hill. The pilot will use hand levers and a shifting hip mechanism to control the virtual flyer and practice take-offs and landings.

Other education exhibits will be set up in side venues on the Wright Brothers National Memorial site. One of the most interesting that is already lined up is NASA's mobile education learning unit.

A separate celebration venue known as Centennial Park will be established off-site, within walking distance of the memorial. Centennial Park will be the site of live performances, music, festivities, food, entertainment, and commercial offerings.

People have began planning their trips to the First Flight Centennial Celebration in December 2003. Many hotels and rental agencies are already taking reservations for this historic event. For more information, see the following Web sites: www.centennialofflight.gov, www.firstflightcentennial.org, www.firstflight.org, www.firstflightnc.com, www.nps.gov/wrbr, www.EAA.org, or www.outerbanks.org.

grow that tall naturally. CCC workers planted much of the grass and scrubby shrubbery to help stave off erosion along the ocean.

Although it was mostly waged continents away, World War II spread all the way across the ocean to the Outer Banks's doorstep. German U-boats lurked in near-shore shipping lanes, exacting heavy losses to Allied vessels. At least 60 boats fell victim to the submarines, though the Germans experienced losses of their own: The first U-boat sunk by Americans lies in an Atlantic grave off the coast of Bodie Island. Longtime barrier island residents recount having to pull their shades and extinguish all lights each night during the war so ships and submarines could not easily discern the shoreline.

Talk of the country's first national seashore began in the 1930s. By 1953, when the Cape Hatteras National Seashore finally was established under the auspices of the National Park Service, it stretched from Nags Head through Ocracoke Island.

Today, the Outer Banks is home to some of the most popular yet pristine beach resorts on the Atlantic coast. About 50,000 people make the barrier islands their permanent home. But seven million people visit our sandy shores each year. Please see our Area Overviews chapter for a modern portrait of our Outer Banks communities.

Restaurants

Corolla
Duck
Southern Shores
Kitty Hawk
Kill Devil Hills
Colinton Island
Nags Head
Roanoke Island
Hatteras Island
Ocracoke Island

When you visit the Outer Banks, be sure to bring your appetite. In this seemingly remote area of the world, we have the basic ingredients from which world-class cuisine is created. We have bounty from the mainland, the sounds, and the ocean. We have innovative, educated, experienced chefs and restaurateurs. We have a population for which a good wine has no substitute. And we have the terrain that lends itself to an eclectic variety of hip, funky, chic, laid-back, comfortable, rustic places. In short, we have cutting-edge cuisine and we know how to serve it.

Just across the Wright Memorial Bridge on the Currituck mainland grow the vegetable elements that you find on many Outer Banks menus: Silver Queen sweet corn, red bliss potatoes, sugar snap peas, luscious tomatoes, brightly colored bell peppers, slender green beans. And we can't forget about the fields of strawberries and melons or the orchards of trees laden with succulent peaches and figs. A little further inland is the source of smoke-cured country hams and the largest peanuts you've ever eaten. For those restaurants that don't have their own herb gardens, Wanchese Produce on Roanoke Island plays a starring role on a daily basis. Organic lettuce, mesclun mix, and armloads of fresh basil, thyme, rosemary, lemongrass, dill, and edible flowers are just a few of the fragrant wonders delivered to the back doors of kitchens all along this sandy bar.

And then there's the water. So much tuna is caught in the nutrient-rich warm waters of the Gulf Stream, that the tiny fishing village of Wanchese exports literally thousands of tons each year. In addition to tuna, local menus sport mahi mahi, wahoo, and mako shark from the Gulf Stream. From inshore ocean waters and our sound waters come fresh flounder, Spanish and king mackerel, bluefish, black grouper, drum, striped bass (locally known as rockfish), speckled trout, gray trout, oysters, clams, mussels, shrimp, and crabs. Along Colington Road and the streets of Kitty Hawk Village, you can easily spot the long wooden shedder beds, brightly lighted all night long, where soft-shell crabs are gathered as soon as they molt.

Big-city purveyors supplement our local seafood and produce; while the grocery stores may not carry as exotic a selection as you're used to, our restaurants make up for this lack with daring ingredients. The ratio of restaurants to say, traffic lights, is staggeringly weighted toward the former. In fact, Corolla and Ocracoke—which have no lights at all—have a bounty of excellent dining establishments. There's no shortage of eateries in between, either.

Wine has become one of our restaurants' biggest drawing cards. Wine dinners abound during the off-season, and many are attended by the vintners themselves. Wine-loving restaurateurs are happy to accommodate a variety of tastes, as evidenced by the increasing number of wines by the glass that we see cropping up on cellar lists. Lists of bottled wines lengthen each season, and restaurants along the northern beaches sometimes offer 100 or more varieties of the world's finest wines. A surprising number of Outer Banks restaurants annually receive coveted awards of excellence by *Wine Spectator* for their wine selections and for their pairing of wine with food.

Most area restaurants serve alcoholic beverages, at least for dinner; however, those in Southern Shores, and on Colington, Roanoke, Hatteras, and Ocracoke Islands are forbidden by law to offer mixed drinks and so serve only beer or wine. Some establishments allow brown bagging, however, whereby you can bring in your own liquor. Call ahead to make sure brown bagging is OK, and ask if they provide setups.

Increasingly, restaurants are opening earlier in the spring and staying open longer into the fall each year. The shoulder seasons have become popular times to dine out because the off-season offers the same friendly service and great food with fewer crowds. Most eateries open by March and don't close their kitchens until after Thanksgiving. Many even have decided to serve their full line of selections year-round.

Dinner isn't the only meal to eat out, of course. A variety of bakeries, diners, and even seafood restaurants now serve big breakfasts and weekend brunches. Most places are open for lunch throughout the summer, and some even serve bathing suit–clad customers just off the beach. The majority of restaurants, however, still require you to wear shirts and shoes. Many cooks will package any meal to go and some eateries deliver, with menus offering much more than just pizza.

If you're eating an evening meal out, feel free to dress as comfortably as you desire. Even most of the expensive, elite establishments welcome sundresses, sandals, and shorts. Nearly all restaurant managers say everything from evening gowns and suits to jeans and T-shirts is acceptable at their tables.

Reservations aren't taken at many restaurants. Others, however, suggest or even require them. The Blue Point, The Left Bank, and Elizabeth's Cafe in Duck, Carolina Blue in Southern Shores, Ocean Boulevard in Kitty Hawk, Colington Cafe on Colington Island, and 1587 in Manteo all get so booked up in the summer that it's best to call at least three days ahead to secure a table. The fare at these fabulous places, however, is well worth the wait.

If sticking to a budget is a concern, you can have homestyle meals from tuna steaks to North Carolina barbecue for less than $8.00 in many Outer Banks family-style restaurants. Sure, you'll find a few of the nationally recognized establishments, complete with drive-through windows, uniformed employees, and a known commodity in the so-called food category. There are enough of those places here to satisfy anyone's need for familiar foodstuff, and you may even want to pick up something there for the kids before you go out for an adult evening on the town. But if you're among the clientele who clamor for something ranging from a little bit different to downright extraordinary, read on. With our diversity of good restaurants, you're bound to find something to suit any appetite.

Seafood is, and probably always will be, one of the biggest draws for Outer Banks diners. Caught in the sounds, inshore ocean, and as far out as the Gulf Stream by local watermen, much of the fish served here lived or swam near the barrier islands. The fish often makes it to your plate less than two days after being landed. Some restaurants, however, are importing increasingly more fish from foreign countries. Ask your waiter where the seafood came from if you're fishing for Outer Banks–only food. If you want someone else to clean and cook your catch, Nags Head Pier Restaurant will gladly prepare your own "fish of the day" for you.

Raw bars always are great bets for relatively cheap, yet succulent, seafood. Oysters, clams, crab legs, and shrimp are served on the shell or slightly steamed, and some places even include vegetables. Soft-shell crabs also are an Outer Banks specialty worth raving about, served from Easter through early July. Don't be put off by the spidery legs hanging off these crustaceans. Just consume the entire creature, shell and all—it's a whole lot quicker and easier than having to pick the meat out of hard shells once the crabs stop molting later in the summer.

If you're into picking your own crabs, however, you'll probably want to spread out some newspaper on an outdoor picnic table to absorb the mess. You can buy the locally caught blue crabs already steamed, or you can cook them yourself in a big kettle. You can catch your own crabs in area sounds, inlets, and bays by dangling a chicken neck from a long string and letting the shellfish wrap its claws around the meat. Just be careful when you're taking it off the line to drop it in your bucket before it latches onto your finger. Always steam crabs while they're still alive, and don't eat the gray lungs or yellow mustard-like substance inside.

Restaurants in this chapter are arranged from north to south from Corolla through Ocracoke. Seasons and days of the week each place is open are included with each profile. Unless otherwise noted, these eateries accept at least MasterCard and Visa, and many accept other major credit cards as well.

We've also added some primarily carry-out and outdoor dining establishments that offer quick, cheap eats, cool ice-cream concoctions, and perfect items to pack for a picnic or offshore fishing excursion.

Whatever you're hungering for, you'll find it here.

Price Code

For your convenience, we've included a pricing guide with each restaurant listing to give you a general idea of what to expect when the tab comes. The costs are based on entrees for two people, excluding appetizers, dessert, and alcoholic beverages. Many area eateries also have senior-citizen discounts and children's menus to help families cut costs. Most entrees include at least one vegetable or salad and some type of bread. Prices vary, obviously, if you select the most or least expensive items on the menu; this guide is a generalization hitting the mid-range prices of restaurants' most popular meals. Here's our breakdown:

$ .... Less than $25
$$ .... $25 to $45
$$$ .... $45 to $75
$$$$ .... More than $75

Price ranges do not reflect North Carolina's 6 percent sales tax or the gratuity, which should be 15 percent to 20 percent for good service. Some restaurants offer early evening dining discounts to encourage patrons to avoid peak dining hours. Most have at least two or three daily specials that change depending on the availability of food and the whims of the chef.

Corolla

Corolla Pizza & Deli $
Austin Complex, NC 12, Corolla
(252) 453–8592

This take-out-only deli serves hot and cold subs and sandwiches, Philly cheese steaks, and pizza by the pie or slice for lunch and dinner. Each pizza is made to order on hand-tossed dough. Regular red sauce and gourmet white pizzas, including the ever-popular chicken pesto pizza, are available. During the summer season, Corolla Pizza offers free delivery. You can walk in or call ahead to have your order waiting. Corolla Pizza is open seven days a week in summer. Call for off-season hours.

Nicoletta's Italian Cafe $$$
Corolla Light Village Shops, NC 12, Corolla
(252) 453–4004

Since opening almost a decade ago, Nicoletta's Italian Cafe has been a cornerstone of fine dining on the northern Outer Banks. White linen tablecloths, long-stemmed roses, and a view of the Currituck Beach Lighthouse please the eye as sounds of classical jazz mix with Sinatra and friends to set the mood in the dining room. This upscale Italian eatery combines casual, elegant dining with Old World charm.

homemade, from Key lime pie to sopapillas drizzled with honey.

The decor here fits the theme. Bull horns, wool rugs, cacti, and, of course, horseshoes line the walls. A Mexican-tile bar offers a cool place to sit a spell and sip one of 25 kinds of beer served. The wine list is extensive too.

Horseshoe Cafe serves breakfast, lunch, and dinner seven days a week in summer. Sandwiches are available for a light supper along with the full entree offerings. A children's menu offers smaller portions and prices, and the wait staff even provides crayons to keep your tykes entertained. The restaurant is open Easter through October. Large parties can be accommodated.

Smokey's Restauran $
Monteray Plaza, NC 12, Corolla
(252) 453-4050

This down-home, family-style restaurant opened in 1991 and is a Corolla original. Its specialties include in-house barbecue true to the original North Carolina recipe, hickory-smoked barbecued pork ribs, half-pound burgers, Southern fried chicken, fresh yellowfin tuna steaks, homemade crab cakes, fried and steamed shrimp, and fried clams. They offer all the trimmings from coleslaw and baked beans to sweet potato sticks and onion rings. Many appetizers are available, including cheddar cheese–stuffed jalapeño peppers, buffalo wings, hush puppies, and their very own "Corolla Burst," a super colossal onion cut in the shape of a flower and deep fried. Salads are available throughout the day.

Smokey's offers a children's menu and will package most of its items for take-out. Desserts, wine, and beer are also available. This restaurant is open for lunch and dinner, March through December. In season, it serves seven days a week; call for off-season hours.

Nicoletta's menu features fresh seafood, certified Angus beef, milk-fed veal, free-range chicken, and gourmet pasta combinations, all prepared in the Italian tradition with a creative touch. An extensive wine list featuring more than 30 selections complements the fare, and sinful, ever-changing desserts end the meal with a smile. Nicoletta's was the winner of a 2001 *Wine Spectator* award. There is no children's menu at this restaurant.

Nicoletta's is open for dinner year-round. In season, they serve seven days a week; call for off-season hours. Dress is casual, and reservations are highly recommended. Catering and private parties are also available.

Horseshoe Cafe $$
Corolla Light Village Shops, NC 12, Corolla
(252) 453-8463

In 1992 Horseshoe Cafe brought Southwestern cuisine to the northern Outer Banks. Here you'll find homemade crab cakes seasoned lightly with chili powder for that Tex-Mex flair. Vegetarian chili also is a standout. There's also plenty of good seafood, steaks, chicken, and barbecue on the menu. All the desserts are

Bacchus Wine & Cheese $
Monteray Plaza, NC 12, Corolla
(252) 453-4333;
(252) 453-2429 to fax orders
www.bacchuswineandcheese.com

Bacchus Wine & Cheese carries more than 600 bottles of domestic and imported wines and beer plus some fantastic deli sandwiches, subs, and tortilla wraps. You can eat in the shop, at an outside table, or get anything to go. While your food is being prepared, you can browse through the wine racks or select a cold drink from the refrigerator cases. Cappuccino and espresso are available too. Owners Paul and Carolyn Sabo use Boar's Head meats and domestic and imported cheeses in their enormous innovative sandwiches. There's a nice selection of gourmet foods and gifts. Ask about the weekly wine tastings during the summer. You can also order special party platters and gift baskets. Bacchus is open for lunch and dinner daily in season; call for off-season hours.

Weeping Radish Brew Pub $
Monteray Plaza, NC 12, Corolla
(252) 453-6638
www.weepingradish.com

If you want a light meal and a mug of some of the best local microbrew beer, check out this little pub at the northern end of the Outer Banks. Like its big sister, the Weeping Radish Brewery and Bavarian Restaurant in Manteo (see this chapter's listing), this pub serves Weeping Radish beers on tap. The Fest, Corolla Gold, and Black Radish brews are always available, and the others vary depending on what's being brewed at the brewery in Manteo. For the teetotalers, there's a lip-smacking Weeping Radish root beer. The pub menu of sandwiches, hot dogs, German sausages, and burgers now includes a full dinner menu. Open until 9:00 P.M. in the summer; call for off-season hours.

Sundogs Sports Bar and Grill $-$$
Monterey Plaza, NC 12, Corolla
(252) 453-4263

Sundogs is one of the newest restaurants in Corolla. It's a sports bar, decorated in masculine hues with a long bar, a pool table, video games, and TVs. If there's a game on, customers like to sidle up to the bar, drink a few beers, and chow down on munchies, such as jumbo buffalo wings (hot or teriyaki) served with ranch or blue cheese dressing, beer-battered onion petals, jalapeño poppers, or mozzarella sticks. A steam bar offers shrimp and crab legs. For meals, try a seafood basket of fried fish, shrimp, or oysters served with fries or potato salad. Sandwiches, burgers (even a one-pounder!), barbecue, po'boys, and hotdogs are served, along with full meals of New York strip, ribs, and seafood. There is a children's menu. Sundogs is open year-round.

Jimmy's Seafood Buffet $$
Monteray Plaza, NC 12, Corolla
(252) 453-4345

A second location of the popular Kitty Hawk restaurant, Jimmy's is in front of the main Monteray Plaza on an upper level above a beach-rentals store. This buffet specializes in seafood—all you want of it. Buffet items include shrimp, fish, clams, and crab dishes, but there's also pork barbecue, hand-carved roast beef, ribs, chicken, a ton of vegetables, breads, and desserts. Jimmy's has 75 different frozen cocktail flavors to get your appetite rolling for all that chow. In season, Jimmy's is open every night for dinner starting at 4:00 P.M. Jimmy's also offers Seafood Buckets for take-out, which they will cook or give you instructions to cook yourself. See our Kitty Hawk section for more about Jimmy's Seafood Buffet.

North Banks Restaurant & Raw Bar $$
TimBuck II Shopping Village, NC 12, Corolla
(252) 453-3344
www.jksribs.com

This 50-seat restaurant and raw bar serves lunch and dinner year-round. Lobster, shrimp, oysters, clams, and mussels are available as well as JK's baby back ribs, lamb, veal, grilled beef, chicken, and even sandwiches. Diners will enjoy the waterside view from this upscale but casual restaurant that boasts 28-foot vaulted ceilings. If you have to wait for a table, you can wear a "patron pager" and stroll through TimBuck II Shopping Center until you're beeped. North Banks also offers desserts and appetizers as well as microbrewery beers, wine, and Black and Tans (that hearty, layered combination of Guinness and Bass Ale) to complement the fresh local seafood.

JK's $$$
TimBuck II Shopping Village, NC 12, Corolla
(252) 453–4336
www.jksribs.com

The name JK's has been synonymous with good food on the Outer Banks for longer than many of us can remember. Not only do they have a new location at MP 9 in Kill Devil Hills, but they're in Corolla as well, in the TimBuck II Shopping Center. JK's steaks, veal, lamb, ribs, chicken, and seafood are all cooked over a mesquite grill, bringing you aromatic wood cooking at its best. JK's eggless Caesar salads are to die for, and you can get them topped with shrimp or chicken. The fresh-made cornbread and French bread that accompany the meals are excellent too. Four or five different fish specials are offered each night, so the dinner menu really changes nightly. JK's is also known for its fine selection of wines. The restaurant serves dinner nightly during the summer; call for off-season hours.

Steamer's Shellfish To Go $
TimBuck II Shopping Village, NC 12, Corolla
(252) 453–3305
www.steamersshellfishtogo.com

The most innovative idea to hit the beach in a long time, Steamer's Shellfish To Go, is Corolla's version of the popular New England–style clam bake. This gourmet seafood market offers full take-out of the best the Outer Banks has to offer presented in a refreshingly different fashion. Steamer's offers the highest quality gourmet lunch and dinner entrees (grilled fish, chicken, baby back ribs, vegetarian lasagna to name a few), fantastic homemade soups, bountiful salads, and desserts as well as their ever famous Steamer Pots To Go. The pots are custom made-to-order and layered with seafood,

red bliss potatoes, yellow onion, and corn on the cob and include cocktail sauce, butter, lemon, and even the claw crackers. Choose from live Maine lobster, little neck clams, mussels, Alaskan snow crab legs, and jumbo king crab legs. Take home your Steamer Pot To Go, place it on the stove, add a cup of water and in 30 to 45 minutes, you'll have a seafood feast like no other! Steamer's also offers a full menu of steamed seafood for carry-out. The steamed spiced shrimp is a house specialty and not to be missed! Shellfish To Go is open in season for lunch and dinner, April 1 through Columbus Day weekend. There's a waterfront deck here for outdoor dining, if you'd like.

Neptune's Grill & Arcade $, no credit cards
TimBuck II Shopping Village, NC 12, Corolla
(252) 453–8645
www.corolla.net

A locals' favorite, this casual grill offers quarter-pound burgers, Philly cheese steaks, North Carolina barbecue, fried oysters, salads, veggie burgers, and a variety of sandwiches to eat in or carry out. French fries, cheese fries, frozen candy bars, and cookies also are available, as are beer and wine. One Insider says that Neptune's has the best fried fish sandwiches on the Outer Banks.

This is a low-key burger joint where you can sit at booths or tables. It features the only pool table north of Duck; pinball and foosball offer added family entertainment. Neptune's Grill is open for lunch and dinner year-round. In summer, Neptune's serves food seven days a week until 2:00 A.M.; during the off-season, lunch is served daily. See our Nightlife chapter for after-hours offerings.

Grouper's Grille & Wine Bar $$$
TimBuck II Shopping Village, NC 12, Corolla
(252) 453–4077

Tucked between handmade hammocks and quaint gift shops at this upscale shopping village, Grouper's opened in 1996 and visitors have been singing its praises ever since. This restaurant provides an array of

Leave the city behind and find a waterfront seat with some steamed local shrimp. PHOTO: J. AARON TROTMAN

enticing offerings in an atmosphere of understated elegance—and is well worth the 45-minute drive from Nags Head.

Angus beef, free-range chicken, fresh local seafood, and vegetarian entrees are made all the more mouthwatering with unusual spices and sauces. The menu changes seasonally so that only the freshest available ingredients can be used. Local seafood is served with an international twist. Pasta, chicken, lean-generation pork, and beef are all prepared with flair.

Each meal begins with fresh-baked bread. Huge appetizers include such temptations as Grouper's crab cakes, with mounds of jumbo lump crabmeat; seared tuna loin sashimi; Chardonnay-steamed little neck clams; homemade ravioli; goat cheese and smoked chicken-stuffed empanadas; or fresh mozzarella and vine-ripened tomatoes drizzled with a roasted red pepper puree. Organic salad greens are prepared with an assortment of delicious in-house dressings. Grouper's extensive wine list boasts more than 100 varieties by the bottle and a large by-the-glass selection. A generous number of domestic, imported, and microbrewed beers round out the drink choices. Don't forget dessert. It's made on the premises, and the selections are beyond sinful.

The atmosphere here is as delightful as the dinners, with open post-and-beam wooden ceilings, butter-colored tablecloths set with flickering candles, and large windows surrounding the dining room. Upscale but casual, the eatery makes diners comfortable in suit and tie or in blue jeans. Grouper's is open for dinner from March through October. Reservations are recommended.

Route 12 Steak & Seafood Co. $$
TimBuck II Shopping Village, NC 12, Corolla
(252) 453-4644

A sister restaurant to Grouper's, Route 12 Steak & Seafood Co. opened its doors during the summer of 1999 to a booming business. Located next to Brew Thru, the new restaurant is decorated with a restored 1938 Mobil gasoline pump, old Esso signs, and gas station memorabilia. In this casual roadhouse atmosphere, you can get fresh local seafood, certified Angus beef, barbecued chicken, and ribs that are fall-off-the-bone tender. This is a family-oriented restaurant, where kids are welcome and a children's menu is available. Dinner is served nightly; call for off-season hours.

Turf's Up $$
Timbuck II Shopping Village, NC 12, Corolla
(252) 453-8792
www.turfsupobx.com

With a stunning vista of the marsh and Currituck Sound, Turf's Up deserves a visit based on the view alone. But don't let that be the only reason you come. The food is good too. Appetizers are creative and indulgent. How about seared foie gras accompanied with truffled risotto and sliced pear? Or Arborio rice–crusted oysters served over baby spinach with a lemon-berry vinaigrette? Salads, including a warm spinach salad and a Caesar salad, are fresh, and the she-crab soup is divine. Turf's Up serves certified Angus beef, duck, local seafood, chicken, pasta, and a vegetarian option, all artfully prepared. For dessert you'll be tempted by tiramisu, crème brûlée, bananas foster with ice cream and homemade caramel, or lemon sorbet if you're being good. A good wine list, beer, and cappuccino and espresso are available.

Duck

The Sanderling Restaurant $$$
NC 12, Sanderling
(252) 449-6654
www.thesanderling.com

The Sanderling Restaurant, part of the Sanderling Resort north of Duck, is one of the Outer Banks's loveliest restaurants, housed in a restored 1899 lifesaving station that is a National Historic Landmark. The dining rooms reflect turn-of-the-20th-century coastal architecture and are enhanced with rich woods and brass, nautical antiques, and original artifacts of the lifesaving station. Contemporary American cuisine with an emphasis on local seafood is the specialty of the Sanderling Restaurant's executive chef Christine Zambito. The restaurant serves breakfast, lunch, and dinner every day to everyone, not just guests of the resort.

The Sanderling's breakfasts are more formal than your standard Outer Banks morning meals. A smoked salmon platter, waffles, eggs, and delicious scones are specialties. For lunch, expect fancy salads, crab cakes, seafood, and sandwiches. Dinner at the Sanderling is a special affair. Local fish, trout, salmon, lamb, venison, veal, beef, and vegetarian dishes are finely crafted with fresh ingredients. For example, a fresh-caught tuna steak is pan-seared and served over fresh fettuccine with a wild mushroom ragout. A favorite appetizer is the Sanderling Signature Seafood Chowder with corn, crab, and shrimp. Desserts are sinful.

The Sanderling has an award-winning wine list and a full bar. The upstairs Swan Bar and Lounge are good places to relax before or after your meal. A children's menu is available. Dinner reservations are highly recommended. All three meals are served seven days a week year-round. A dress code is required for this restaurant. T-shirts and jeans are not allowed at dinner, and tasteful attire is requested at breakfast and lunch.

The Left Bank $$$
(252) 261–8419, (252) 449–6654
www.thesanderling.com

New to the Sanderling resort complex, The Left Bank is a French-inspired restaurant with a focus on delicious simplicity. Housed in a contemporary version of the classic Old Nags Head style, its location on the Currituck Sound offers guests panoramic vistas of water and marsh grasses through a half-moon-shaped window wall. The interior is sublimely chic, like nothing else on the Outer Banks, with leather banquettes, mohair chairs, a bar top of blonde granite lit from underneath, a museum-quality collection of porcelain Doughty birds—and that spectacular view. A display kitchen affords diners a peek at the behind-the-scenes magic. The French-inspired American cuisine emphasizes the freshest regional foods available. Dishes are simple, focusing on the purity of each ingredient. For example, local rockfish topped with jumbo lump crabmeat, a preserved lemon béchamel, and snips of freshly cut herbs. Signature touches at the Left Bank include predinner canapés and *amuse bouche* and granita palate cleansers between courses. The wine list is a careful selection of boutique wines, and flight tastings are an option. A martini list is also available. Dinner is served every night

Insiders' Tip
It's not vacation if you spend the whole time in the kitchen. If you've got a houseful of people, consider hiring a personal chef while you're on vacation. You can choose from a chef who cooks all three meals in house or one who just drops off dinner every evening. Ask your rental company for suggestions.

year-round, and brunch is served on Sunday. Reservations are recommended. Blazers are appropriate dress for gentlemen.

Cravings Coffee Shoppe $
Duck Common Shopping Center, NC 12, Duck
(252) 261–0655

This delightful eatery is the perfect place to pop by for a quick breakfast before hitting the beach or to indulge yourself in a delectable dessert and coffee after dinner. You can eat inside or on an open-air deck, or take the tasty treats home with you. Table service is not available; you simply order and pick up your food from the counter.

Order a fresh New York–style bagel with one of six flavored cream cheeses. Homemade pastries and muffins also are baked each day. The ice cream is homemade as well. Out-of-town newspapers are available each and every morning.

For lunch, Cravings has a light-fare menu. Every type of coffee drink you can concoct is available, from several types of brewed coffee that change daily to espresso, cappuccino, mocha drinks, and other fancy combinations. Chai tea is served either iced or hot, and you can choose from a variety of iced blended coffee drinks and blended smoothies. Cravings is open year-round. In summer the eatery serves into the evening; it's open weekends only in winter. Call for off-season hours.

Sunset Grill and Raw Bar $$
NC 12, Duck
(252) 261–3901

New in 2001 from the owners of the popular Fishbones Raw Bar & Restaurant, Sunset Grill and Raw Bar is quickly becoming another favorite Duck dining spot. Aptly named, the restaurant sits on the Currituck Sound and is the prime sunset-watching spot in the village. Customers have been known to jump up from their meals to rush out to the docks and snap a photo of the setting sun. Sunset Grill is patterned after Fishbones, with Caribbean-influenced entrees and appetizers, moderately priced food, a fun atmosphere, and good service to locals and visitors alike.

Sunset, like Fishbones, is known for its extensive drink menu. Specialty drinks are served in novelty vessels, like a tiki god, a monkey, or a pineapple. The full bar list is available upstairs at a stunning horseshoe-shaped bar covered with coral tiles, downstairs at another bar and raw bar, and outside at a tiki bar. Meals are served upstairs or down or outside on the deck. Dinners focus mostly on seafood, and the blackened fish and conch fritters are standouts. The raw bar serves all the freshest Outer Banks favorites. For lunch, seafood, sandwiches, and burgers are served. Lunch and dinner are served every day year-round.

Sunset also offers breakfast, daily in season and on weekends in the off-season. Breakfast is not just the standard fare. There are also omelets, skillet dishes, smoked salmon bagels, and a wonderful banana French toast served with a vanilla-strawberry cream sauce. Sunset is a popular nighttime hangout, with live music four or five nights a week in the summer and one or two nights in the off-season. See our Nightlife chapter. Sunset offers catering and site rental for weddings and large parties.

Insiders' Tip
Elizabeth's Cafe in Duck has an annual wine auction the day after Thanksgiving. This could be your chance to pick up some unusual and coveted vintages.

Elizabeth's Cafe & Winery $$$
Scarborough Faire, NC 12, Duck
(252) 261–6145
www.elizabethscafe.com

Well known across the nation for its wine and wonderful cuisine—and perfectly matched combinations thereof—Elizabeth's has earned international acclaim from *Wine Spectator* magazine for consecutive years since 1991. Each year since 1993, this restaurant has been awarded the prestigious Best of the Award of Excellence.

Elizabeth's receives accolades from all the bigwigs in the business. In 1999 the International Restaurant and Hospitality Rating Bureau awarded it their International Award of Excellence. In 2000 executive chef Brad Price was recognized as one of America's Top 100 Chefs by the same organization. In 2001 Elizabeth's was awarded the coveted 2001 Sante Award as the Best Fine Dining Restaurant in the Southeast United States and the Best Wine and Spirits Dinner in the Southeast United States. Fine diners from all over the East Coast have been known to fly to the Outer Banks just for one of Elizabeth's fantastic meals.

Elizabeth's is a delight from ambiance to entrees. It's warm and casual inside, with a fireplace that's usually lit on chilly evenings. Service is always excellent. If you have trouble selecting a wine from the Russian novel–length wine list, owner Leonard Logan is always more than happy to help you select a vintage to complement any meal. Leonard loves a celebration and is always eager to pop open a cork of good champagne. On Wednesday evenings during July and August, featured dinners include special wine selections from the cellar.

Besides the regular menu offerings, which include country French and California eclectic foods that change continually, two prix fixe dinners (six-course meals and accompanying wines) are available every night. All the dishes are made with fresh ingredients, from seafood and steak to unusual pastas. Cold appetizers, cheeses, and croissants are served at the wine bar from late afternoon into the evening. A pastry chef creates different desserts daily: Elizabeth's Craving is sinfully delicious.

This cafe is very popular—and small, seating only about 40 diners. Reservations are highly recommended. In addition to some of the finest wines available, the restaurant also serves French beer and has a full bar. Patrons with disabilities can be accommodated. This is a nonsmoking establishment. Dinner is served seven nights a week in season; call for winter hours.

Fishbones Raw Bar & Restaurant $$
Scarborough Lane Shoppes, NC 12, Duck
(252) 261–6991

Specializing in locally caught seafood, this raw bar and grill opened in the summer of 1995 and won the Outer Banks chowder cook-off with an original recipe during its first year in business.

Midday items include sandwiches, crab cakes, fried seafood, and creamy soups such as tomato conch and, of course, chowder. Dinner entrees offer such Caribbean cuisine favorites as calypso eggplant and coconut shrimp, in addition to pastas with fresh clam sauce, lobster tails, crab legs, and more than a dozen raw bar selections. The hot crab dip, barbecue shrimp, and conch fritters all are outstanding appetizers. This is a casual place with a full bar, five types of beer on tap, 50 bottled beers from all over the world, a wine list, and several microbrews from which to choose. Desserts also are available.

Fishbones serves lunch and dinner seven days a week year-round, and specials change daily for both meals. Carry-out is available on all menu items. Reservations are not accepted.

The Blue Point Bar & Grill $$$
The Waterfront Shops, NC 12, Duck
(252) 261–8090

This waterfront bistro is one of our favorite places to dine on the Outer Banks. It's been open for dinner since 1989 and consistently receives rave reviews from magazines such as *Southern Living* and *Gourmet* as well as admiring local audiences. Here, regional Southern cooking brings a cosmopolitan flair to the area. A 1950s-style interior with black-and-white checkered floors, red upholstery, and lots of chrome provides an upbeat, bustling atmosphere. An enclosed porch not only overlooks the sound, it actually overhangs it. There's also a small bar facing the aromatic kitchen where you can watch your appetizers being prepared while sipping a cocktail as you wait for a table.

The Blue Point's menu is contemporary Southern cuisine and changes seasonally. Starters range from Hatteras tuna to fresh tomato-mozzarella stacks, each artistically arranged and flavored with the freshest combination of seasonings. Entrees include jumbo lump crab cakes served with rice and black beans and Currituck corn on the cob, homemade soups, unusual seafood dishes, steaks, salads, and perfect pastas. Desserts, like the bourbon pecan pie or the Key lime pie, are divine.

If you're into creative cooking that's sure to tantalize every taste bud—and awaken some you might not realize you have—this restaurant is a must-stop on the Outer Banks. It's open for dinner, and reservations are highly recommended. During the summer, dinner reservations are required. It's open seven days a week in season; call for off-season hours.

Roadside Bar & Grill $$
NC 12, Duck
(252) 261–5729

Occupying a renovated 1932 cottage, this restaurant is warm and homey, with hardwood floors inside and a patio dotted with umbrella-shaded tables out front. In season, live jazz and blues music is performed here three nights a week (see our Nightlife chapter).

A casual, fine-dining establishment, Roadside offers half-pound Angus burgers, fresh fish sandwiches, meat loaf, and a variety of salads and sandwiches for lunch. The Roadside clam chowder is chock-full of shellfish, and you can choose from steamed and seasoned shrimp by the pound or half-pound and steamed clams by the dozen. Weather permitting, you can opt for service on the patio and enjoy your meal while watching the summertime foot traffic in downtown Duck.

For dinner you can choose from a variety of starters, including Roadside's own shrimp and grits—sautéed Gulf shrimp and petite bananas served over jalapeño grits with an Amaretto syrup. In addition to mixed green and Caesar salads is our favorite: a warm salad of bay scallops, black beans, corn, and red bell peppers, with sesame-soy dressing. Dinners highlight fresh seafood, although you can choose from chicken, beef, and vegetarian pasta options as well.

In season, there's an oven-roasted half lobster, stuffed with crabmeat and served with wild rice and corn on the cob, or pan-seared cornmeal-encrusted black grouper with black sticky rice and mango-strawberry salsa. Beef lovers will appreciate the 10-ounce Angus whiskey-drenched filet mignon served with a hash of potatoes, andouille sausage, and portobello mushrooms over fresh arugula. Yes, the desserts are just as enticing. There's a full bar with a nice selection of microbrewed beers. The restaurant serves lunch and dinner year-round. Call for off-season hours. Reservations are not accepted.

Duck Deli $$
NC 12, Duck
(252) 261–3354

This casual deli on the east side of the highway opened in 1987 primarily to serve lunch to locals. Since then, Duck Deli has expanded to offer breakfast, lunch, and dinner seven days a week, year-round.

Barbecued pork, beef, chicken, and ribs are the specialties here. Sandwiches, Philly cheese steaks, and subs are served all day, as are side salads, garden burgers, and coleslaw. A full breakfast menu includes everything from eggs and pancakes to omelets. For dessert, you can get sweet on cherry and peach cobblers, homemade brownies, or a frozen yogurt bar with plenty of toppings. Everything is available to eat in or take out.

Herron's Deli and Restaurant $
NC 12, Duck
(252) 261–3224

With a full menu available for carry-out or to eat in, this casual deli serves breakfast and lunch seven days a week all year and adds dinner hours in the summer. Booths and tables are available indoors, and picnic tables allow you to enjoy outdoor dining. Hot and cold Italian subs, cheese steaks, cheeseburgers, and crab cakes are among the most popular items in the afternoon and evening. We recommend the soups, from chili specials to she-crab bisque and Hatteras-style chowder.

A big breakfast menu features French toast, sausage gravy, omelets, eggs, and homemade biscuits. Desserts range from cakes and brownies to homemade strawberry pie. Beer and wine are also available.

Swan Cove $$$
NC 12, Duck
(252) 255–0500

This elegant establishment opened in 1995 and has gained a reputation as one of the finer establishments in Duck. Unbelievable views are available from the soundfront dining room, where tablecloths and cut flowers grace each table and crystal glasses sparkle during sunset hours. There's a separate lounge with a full bar and an extensive wine list upstairs.

The menu changes daily and seasonally to incorporate new offerings. Swan Cove uses all local produce, seafood, and fresh herbs and specializes in low-fat, light cooking. Entrees might include duck, pastas, wild game, veal, baby back ribs, three kinds of Outer Banks fish, seafood bouillabaisse over saffron fettuccine, tenderloin steaks, and fresh salads.

A great bet for starters: shrimp stuffed with gouda, wrapped in bacon, and served with smoky barbecue sauce. And for dessert, try choosing between a chocolate layer cake, peanut butter pie, and seasonal fresh fruits drizzled with fabulous sauces.

Swan Cove is open seven days a week in season. Call for off-season hours. There is a children's menu. Reservations are highly recommended.

Southern Shores

Southern Bean $
The Marketplace, US 158, Southern Shores
(252) 261–JAVA

Opened in September 1995, this gourmet coffee shop caters to folk looking for healthful light meals in addition to a great cup of java. Southern Bean serves breakfast and lunch year-round. Three types of just-brewed coffee always are simmering here, filling the air with tantalizing aromas.

This comfortable place serves every type of specialty coffee drink imaginable, from espresso and cappuccino to iced lattes—even in decaf varieties. More than 30 flavors of freshly roasted coffee beans are sold by the pound here. You can eat inside at Southern Bean, sip a warm blend at an outdoor table, or order your drinks and your food to go. All menu items are either vegetarian or seafood, and sandwiches range from hummus to tuna salad to peanut butter and honey; try the Bean bagel topped with sun-dried tomatoes, pesto, red onion slices, cream cheese, and

sprouts. Muffins, croissants, cinnamon rolls, and other bakery items are available here, too. No sandwich costs more than $5.00. Southern Bean is also one of the few places on the Outer Banks where you can get your hands on fresh-squeezed juices and a wide variety of fruit smoothies.

Southern Bean is open seven days a week year-round from 7:00 A.M. to 6:00 P.M.

Carolina Blue Restaurant $$$
The Marketplace, US 158, Southern Shores
(252) 255–1543

Since opening night in June of 1998, Carolina Blue Restaurant has become the secret spot of locals and vacation homeowners alike. It's a surprise yet to be discovered in Southern Shores (yet its patrons hope that you'll still keep it a bit of a secret). Chef/owner Chip Smith brings to the Outer Banks an element of fine dining generally reserved for an adventure in a cosmopolitan area or a rendezvous in a quaint French village bistro. A graduate of the Culinary Institute of America in Hyde Park, New York, Chip had the great privilege of working with Larry Forgione of An American Place in New York City, Jean-Louis Palladin of the Watergate Hotel in D.C., and Patrick O'Connell of The Inn at Little Washington in Virginia's countryside before setting his sights on the Outer Banks. Chip's dedication to presenting food simply—albeit with elegance, finesse, and exquisite flavors—has delighted a loyal following of guests who keep on coming back for more.

The restaurant's menu changes frequently, but there are some staples not to be missed: Butternut squash risotto and crispy leeks; oven-roasted duck with apples, prunes, pearl onions, and exotic spiced couscous; salmon blanketed with horseradish and served with organic root vegetables and fresh herb gnocchi; or foie gras and other seasonal offerings. (Insiders' tip: All fish preparations are incredible.) All bread and desserts are made in-house and include such temptations as chocolate pots de crème, an old-fashioned six-layer coconut cake (to die for!), or, on occasion, Grand Marnier soufflé. The wine list is small, yet varied and eclectic, offering selections from various boutique vineyards, and there's a nice selection of beers. Service is friendly and professional.

Co-owner Tina Vaughn says her hand-painted walls are "the color of chanterelle mushrooms"—that is, golden and earthy. Her artistry is evident in the decor from the minute you peer in the wide windows. She's created an ambiance that's sophisticated and airy, yet intimate—though she's quick to add that the dining room merely serves to frame the open kitchen, the true focal point. Since there are only 11 tables, reservations are strongly recommended, especially during the high season.

Carolina Blue hosts special wine tastings and winemaker dinners, plus guest chef dinners year-round. There is no children's menu. Dinner is served Tuesday through Sunday in the summer, and Wednesday through Sunday in the off-season. Appropriate dress is required.

Kitty Hawk

Kitty Hawk Pier Restaurant $
NC 12, MP 1, Kitty Hawk
(252) 261–3151

One of the most popular breakfast places on the beach, this ultra-casual restaurant, which opened in 1954, is somewhere you'll feel comfortable just rolling out of bed and rolling into. Pancakes, eggs, sausage, French toast, omelets, biscuits, hash browns, grits, sausage, bacon, and anything else you could desire for a filling first meal of the day are cooked up beginning at 6:00 A.M.

Lunch specials, served Monday through Friday, change daily and include such local favorites as ham and cabbage, fried trout, shrimp, crab cakes, meat loaf, and turkey with dressing and yams. For dinner, try a seafood platter of flounder, scallops, oysters, mahi mahi, or Spanish mackerel, each served with a choice of two sides: hush puppies, rolls, coleslaw, beets, peas, beans, or other vegetables.

Kitty Hawk Pier Restaurant is a down-home place with lots of local patrons and flavor. You can find out what's biting here and even may see your dinner being reeled in off the nearby wooden planks. Most of the fish are caught right off the pier, within 200 feet of where you eat it. Better still, you can come as you are—even barefoot and in your bathing suit.

Desserts include homemade cobblers (peach, apple, blueberry, and cherry), strawberry shortcake, and a variety of pies. A children's menu is offered for the small fry. Everything is available to take out, but you'll enjoy eating in this oceanfront restaurant where salt spray coats the windows and a heavy surf combined with strong winds will rock the whole building.

The restaurant serves three meals a day every day in summer. In the off-season only breakfast and lunch are available. Kitty Hawk Pier Restaurant is open April through October.

Bessie's Kitchen & Spirits $$
NC 12, MP 1, Kitty Hawk
(252) 261–3700

Brought to you by the owners of Roadside Bar and Grill in Duck, Bessie's Kitchen and Spirits is in its third year of business. The big news at Bessie's is the new executive chef—Susan Holton Rogers, formerly of the acclaimed 1587 in Manteo. Rogers brings contemporary coastal cuisine to Bessie's, using only the freshest ingredients available. Her superb skills in the kitchen make this restaurant even more of a dining destination. Certified Angus beef and other meats, local seafood, pasta, and vegetarian options are prepared with the utmost care and attention, resulting in dishes that look almost too good to eat. Desserts are homemade, including pecan pie, chocolate bread pudding, and a Key lime–martini pie. New Orleans–style Sunday brunch is very popular here, with live jazz, bluegrass, or blues to accompany your morning meal. Bessie's is known for its wide array of specialty drinks. It's also kid-friendly and has a children's menu. Lunch and dinner are served. Live jazz and blues play here weekly; call for a schedule.

Rundown Cafe $$
NC 12, MP 1, Kitty Hawk
(252) 255–0026

Opened in 1993, this Caribbean-style cafe has been a big hit with locals, offering some spicy, unusual alternatives to traditional Outer Banks seafood. Named for a Jamaican stew, Rundown serves island entrees flavored with African and Indian accents. If you've been to the Rundown before, you may be surprised to see that it's not in the same building it used to be in. They've moved down the road a very short ways because a grocery store is supposed to be built on the old location.

Specials shift daily, and you'll find the enormous lunches the best deal on the beach. Try a huge platter of fish taco fixings, a big salad of mixed greens and vegetables with grilled beef, fresh fish, or the best fried conch sandwiches anywhere. Some say that Rundown's fries are the best on the beach too. There's a steam bar for shellfish of all sorts and vegetables. Dinner items include grilled chicken breasts with garlic-peppercorn cream sauce or Jamaican pork—dry jerk-marinated pork loin, grilled and served with a red pepper glaze and apple chutney. The food is always terrific.

There's a full bar, and the bartenders can come up with some pretty potent concoctions. Guinness Stout, Bass, Coors Light, Pyramid, and Harp beers are on tap. This is a casual, happening place, often featuring live blues and jazz in the summer (see our Nightlife chapter). The upstairs bar is a great place to soak in the sunset, catch a few rays, or just linger over a cool cocktail after a hot day in the sun. Lunch and dinner are available seven days a week. A kids' menu is available and take-out orders are welcome. Rundown is closed in December and January.

Ocean Boulevard $$$
NC 12, MP 2, Kitty Hawk
(252) 261–2546
www.ocean-boulevard.com

This warm, cozy, upscale eatery gives you a great feeling from the second you walk into the gold-walled dining room until you leave full and relaxed after consuming a fabulous meal. It opened in September 1995 and has quickly become one of the most popular places on the Outer Banks. Manteo residents drive 30 miles each way to treat themselves to a midweek dinner here. No wonder— it's owned by the same culinary masters who brought us the inimitable 1587 Restaurant in Manteo (see subsequent entry). Ocean Boulevard has an intimate atmosphere, and the food is sophisticated.

This restaurant occupies the former 1949 Virginia Dare Hardware store, and you won't believe what the builders and decorators have done with the place. It's accented with warm woods, burgundy fabrics, and forest-green chairs. Cobalt blue glasses grace every tabletop. There's even an open kitchen where you can watch the chefs work.

Selections are all prepared with locally grown herbs, spices, produce, and just-caught seafood. Influences and ideas from around the world give the food here a flavor all its own, and the menu changes according to the season. For an appetizer try the pan-seared house-made Stracota raviolis filled with braised short ribs, Manchego cheese with cranberry-fennel compote, and veal reduction, or the duck confit on ginger biscotti with a cinnamon root vegetable puree and mixed berries.

Entrees are exquisite, like the pan-seared sea scallops with a spring vegetable risotto, local greens, sweet peppers, parsley salad, and tamarind glaze, or the pan-roasted halibut over wheat noodles, applewood smoked bacon, and caramelized fennel in a shellfish broth with Mahogany clams. As well as the menu items, there are special nightly selections, which may include beef, duck, lamb, pasta, pork, and vegetarian options. Menus change seasonally, about six times a year.

Ocean Boulevard's wine list, which has won the *Wine Spectator* Award of Excellence, contains more than 100 selections. Microbrewed beers are available. The bar specializes in martinis.

Dessert offerings are to die for. We especially crave the white chocolate crème

With so many fine restaurants on the Outer Banks, a great meal is never hard to find. PHOTO: HORSLEY/GARDNER

brûlée and the macadamia nut torte with caramel ice cream. A full line of after-dinner coffee drinks and herbal teas is also served to top off your dining experience.

This elegant eatery will please even the most discriminating diners. It's open year-round for dinner only. During summers, doors are open seven days a week. Call for off-season hours. Reservations are highly recommended.

Art's Place $, no credit cards
NC 12, MP 2½, Kitty Hawk
(252) 261-3233

Serving good, basic meals for more than 20 years, this tiny eatery across from the ocean is a Kitty Hawk standby well known among locals. The food here isn't fancy, but it's inexpensive, filling, and all-American. Sausage gravy is the most popular breakfast entree, although Art's also serves the usual eggs, pancakes, and biscuits. The same entrees are available for lunch and dinner, along with daily spe-

cials such as fish, steaks, fried chicken, shrimp, clam strips, and cheeseburgers—each served with French fries, coleslaw, and a cucumber and onion salad. Jalapeño poppers are a hot bet for an appetizer, and calamari is also available most of the time. The eatery is open seven days a week year-round. Reservations are accepted but seldom are they necessary.

Max's Real Bagels $
US 158, MP 4, Kitty Hawk
(252) 255-3111
www.maxrealbagels.com

Southerners never knew a bagel could be this good. For a fresh yummy bagel like those our northern neighbors eat, head to Max's. Twelve varieties of bagels are baked fresh every day, in flavors like sundried tomato spinach, ET (everything), onion, cracked honey wheat, and salt. The Philadelphia cream cheese blends are made fresh every day, too, in flavors such as lox, veggie olive, scallion chive, jalapeño, and honey raisin. The Norweigan smoked salmon is the best on the beach. Homemade salads include a killer smoked whitefish salad. Sandwiches are served on bagels or fresh-baked breads. Pastries and gourmet coffee are also served. Max's is open year-round, seven days a week for breakfast and lunch. You can dine inside or take it all to go.

Jimmy's Seafood Buffet $$
US 158, MP 4, Kitty Hawk
(252) 261–4973

Celebrating its fourth season in 2002, Jimmy's Seafood Buffet specializes in food and fun. Some say that the only thing more exciting than the food is the atmosphere. Start your evening off on the open-air thatched-roof porch. There's a full bar, and eight frozen drinks are offered with a souvenir glass. "Kiddie cocktails" are available for the younger set. While you're relaxing on the porch, the kids can entertain themselves on the new playground.

Inside this tropical paradise you'll find all of your favorite seafood and all you'll want of it! Choose from crab, shrimp, oysters, and clams, or pick your own lobster from the tank. Landlubbers can opt for pork barbecue, ribs, chicken, and hand-carved roast beef, among other selections. A children's menu is provided, and there's a make-your-own-sundae bar with soft-serve ice cream. All shellfish is available to go in one of Jimmy's soon-to-be-famous buffet buckets. Pick and choose what you want, and they'll pack it up in a bucket to go. It's a great way to enjoy seafood at home, on the beach, or at a backyard party.

Jimmy's is open nightly for dinner starting at 4:00 P.M. in season; call for off-season hours.

Keeper's Galley $$
US 158, MP 4, Kitty Hawk
(252) 261–4000

Keeper's Galley is run by Rufus Pritchard Jr., the same fellow who owns the Dunes Restaurant in Nags Head (see subsequent entry). But the menu is slightly different here, and Keeper's Galley serves breakfast, lunch, and dinner seven days a week in season.

Breakfast, which is available until noon, features waffles, eggs, pancakes, country ham, grits, toast, biscuits, vegetarian breakfast sandwiches, and fish roe stirred into eggs. For lunch, try a cold plate, shrimp or tuna sandwich, homemade seafood gumbo, or a big bowl of clam chowder. Dinner entrees change daily but include such regular offerings as prime rib, crab cakes, seafood fettuccine, chicken, and a surf and turf platter. All desserts, including cheesecakes, are made from scratch. Keeper's Galley has a children's menu and a full bar. Reservations aren't accepted. Keeper's Galley is closed November through February or March. Call for off-season hours.

Capt'n Frank's $
US 158, MP 4, Kitty Hawk
(252) 261–9923

Capt'n Frank's is an institution on the Outer Banks. They've been puttin' on the dog for 26 years, serving three sizes of all-beef Oscar Mayer hot dogs with a variety of different accompaniments. First of all, decide among the regular dog, a quarter-pounder, or a foot-long. Then, choose from at least half a dozen specialty creations. The Chicago Dog tops the popularity list, with chili, mustard, onions, and slaw. Runner-up is the eight-item Junkyard Dog, topped with chili, cheese, sauerkraut, onions, mustard, ketchup, slaw, and relish. We're partial to the Mad Dog, served with chili and hot peppers.

If "going to the dogs" doesn't appeal to you, Capt'n Frank's also offers barbecue sandwiches and their addictive nacho fries—French fries with chili, cheese, hot peppers, and sour cream. Steamed shrimp is served nightly in season. Beer is available. Capt'n Franks serves lunch and dinner daily Memorial Day through Labor Day. Off-season, the restaurant is open daily for lunch.

Black Pelican Oceanfront Cafe $$
NC 12, MP 4½, Kitty Hawk
(252) 261–3171
www.blackpelican.com

This casual restaurant is in an old Coast Guard station and includes an enclosed deck overlooking the Atlantic. It's roomy and wide, with three separate levels, and features a huge bar with 12 TVs (see our Nightlife chapter). Hardwood floors, tongue-and-groove appointments, light gray accents, burgundy carpeting, and black bentwood chairs all add to the comfortable ambiance of this moderately priced eatery.

Here, gourmet pizzas are cooked before your eyes in a wood-hearth oven. Try the steamed shellfish fresh from the sea. An extensive selection of appetizers is made from scratch. Dinner offerings include pasta and seafood specials, grilled or blackened to suit your taste. A children's menu is also available. Black Pelican serves lunch and dinner seven days a week year-round.

Frisco's Restaurant $$
US 158, MP 4½, Kitty Hawk
(252) 261–7833

Chefs at this restaurant pride themselves on using only fresh local seafood, choice beef, poultry, and pasta. Entrees include traditional Outer Banks fish, great crab cakes, and shrimp jambalaya. Specials change daily. All the desserts, including chocolate chess pecan pie, are homemade. Frisco's dining room is light and open with greenery throughout. Well-tended terrariums and aquariums filled with fascinating fish line the walls and gargantuan bar (see our Nightlife chapter). Lunch and dinner are served seven days a week during the summer. Call for off-season hours because this restaurant is open year-round. A children's menu is available, and early bird prices are offered from 4:30 to 6:00 P.M.

Parents: Frisco's is very kid-friendly. Children love the decor, and your waitperson will hand each of the little ones crayons and a placemat to color.

John's Drive-In $, no credit cards
NC 12, MP 4¾, Kitty Hawk
(252) 261–2916

Home of the planet's best milk shakes, John's has been an Outer Banks institution for years. There are people who will drive two hours from Norfolk just to sip one of the fruit and ice cream concoctions, which are often so thick they won't even flow through the straw. Our favorite is the chocolate peanut butter and banana variety, but you'll have to sample a few first and create some of your own combinations before making that call for yourself.

You can't eat inside here, but plenty of picnic tables are scattered around the old concrete building across from the ocean. Everything is served in paper bags to go. While you're waiting for your food, check out the faded photographs of happy customers lining this diner's salt-sprayed windows. You may even recognize a few local friends.

Besides the milk shakes and ice cream sundae treats, John's serves delicious mahi mahi, trout, and tuna sandwiches or boats with the fish crispy-fried alongside crinkle fries. Dogs love this drive-in too. If your pooch waits patiently in the car, the worker behind the window probably will provide him or her with a free "puppy cup" of soft-serve vanilla ice cream. We can't think of a better doggie treat on a hot summer afternoon.

John's drive-in is open from May through September or October for lunch and early dinner. It's closed Wednesdays, unfortunately (we could eat there seven days a week).

La Fogata Mexican Restaurant $
US 158, MP 4½, Kitty Hawk
(252) 255–0934

A traditional Mexican restaurant, La Fogata got its name from the Spanish word for "campfire." All the owners, waiters, and cooks are Mexican natives, and almost all of them speak English. For the price, La Fogata serves the best ethnic food on the beach. After being open since 1994, people still wait in line to eat here on weekend nights. You'll see a lot of locals in here year-round.

Airy, bright, and decorated with Mexican art and photographs, the interior of this ultra-casual eatery usually hums with Latin tunes. The waiters bring baskets of crispy tortillas and carafes of homemade salsa as soon as they distribute the menus. All entree portions are generous, so save some room for the main course. Other appetizers we enjoy include the hot queso (cheese) dip and stuffed jalapeño peppers.

Specialties here are fajitas, beef and chicken tacos, enchiladas, and chiles rellenos. The cooks make the dishes hot or mild, depending on your desire. Selections come in every possible combination, vegetarian varieties, and à la carte if you want to try one of everything. (Actually, that's impossible here. The menu has more than 36 dinner selections, many starting at $6.00.) A full bar offers a wide selection of Mexican, American, and imported beers, and mixed-drink and margarita prices are among the lowest on the beach. La Fogata is open for lunch and dinner year-round, seven days a week.

Wrong Dog Bar and Grill $–$$
120 E. Kitty Hawk Rd.
(MP 4¼, between the highways), Kitty Hawk
(252) 255–DANE (3263)

The Wrong Dog Bar and Grill starts its fifth season on the Outer Banks offering the "Best of the Best" from various U.S. cities' cuisines. Owners Dawn "The Great Dane" Didriksen and Glenn "The Great Dane's Husband" Schumacher have made the blue building across from the Kitty Hawk Post Office a local's favorite for "The Best Lunches on the Beach," and have received raves from visitors as far away as Alaska! And why not? Dawn and Glenn's dog memorabilia and art collection, the comfortable atmosphere with flexible seating for 2 or 20, easy access a half block east of the Bypass (US 158), and great food all add up to an unforgettable experience for locals and visitors alike.

Breakfast is anything but ordinary. From the $1.99 "one egg, hash browns, &

biscuit" combo to eggs benedict done three different ways (ham, crab, or smoked salmon) to omelets or biscuit and muffin sandwiches, there is something for every taste. And breakfast take-out is available on selected items. Just call ahead.

It's a treat just to read the lunch menu at the deli. The 45 deli-style sandwiches are humorously named for famous dogs like "Old Yeller" and "The Snoopy." Featured as "Best of Show" are a selection of burgers, Greek gyros, NC pork BBQ, crab cakes, cheesesteaks, and reubens. You can also choose from side dishes, soups, salads, appetizers, desserts, and a great kid's menu. Eat in or take out.

The Wrong Dog Bar and Grill has something for every taste, and with the Dog House Bar's eight tap beers, selected wine list, and full ABC permits, something for every beverage taste, too. Open year-round for breakfast and lunch. Call for off-season hours.

Kill Devil Hills

Coastal Cactus $
Seagate North Shopping Center
US 158, MP 5, Kill Devil Hills
(252) 441–6600

Since 1993, Jim and Deby Curcio have been serving the best the Southwest has to offer to the Outer Banks. Visitors from Arizona, Texas, New Mexico, and California have raved about the authentic regional flavor of the menu offerings at this affordable, casual eatery. The menu has more than 60 choices of entrees, combination plates, and à la carte items. They prepare all their food from scratch daily using fresh vegetables and meats and hot-off-the-grill tortillas. Start your meal with nachos piled high on the plate and covered with cheese, jalapeños, onions, tomatoes, and your choice of beef, chicken, or beans. It's all smothered in the Coastal Cactus's own fresh homemade salsa, which is bottled for purchase if you want to take some home. All the herbs and spices used here are imported directly from the Southwest.

For an entree, select their signature dish: sizzlin' fajitas served still smoking in a cast-iron skillet. You can choose from shrimp, steak, tuna, chicken, pasta, ribs, lobster, or vegetarian combinations to fill them. Other offerings include tacos, enchiladas, burritos, chiles rellenos, tamales, and tequila-lime shrimp. Desserts all are tempting and retain the Tex-Mex theme. Fried ice cream, banana chimichangas, apple enchiladas à la mode, and coconut caramel flan are just some of the sweets from which you can choose.

Drinks are among our favorite features at Coastal Cactus. The golden margaritas are marvelous and made from scratch. There are also several other fresh-fruit varieties to sample. Wine, beer, and other mixed drinks also are available in this peach and teal colored restaurant accented with authentic Southwestern artifacts and art. A children's menu is available. Separate smoking and nonsmoking dining rooms are provided. A Southwestern general store on the premises features Navajo pottery, Hopi jewelry, hot sauces, and other unusual gift items. The Coastal Cactus is open seven days a week for dinner in season. Call for off-season hours.

Henry's Beef & Seafood Restaurant $
US 158, MP 5½, Kill Devil Hills
(252) 261–2025

Locals love this low-priced, homey restaurant that has been serving breakfast, lunch, and dinner for 12 years. Omelets, hotcakes, and egg combinations are filling ways to start the day, and they're served until 1:00 P.M. for late-risers. Lunch entrees include hamburgers, a variety of sandwiches, seafood platters, and several homemade soups. For dinner, there's prime rib, fried oysters, chicken dishes, pasta, shrimp, scallops, soft-shell crabs (in season), flounder, trout, clam strips, and daily specials. The hot fudge cake, apple pie, and cheesecake are rich and decadent dessert options.

There's nothing fancy about Henry's. The low booths that line the walls and the bare tabletops are clad with paper placemats, but the food is hearty and filling. Beer, wine, and mixed drinks are served here. Reservations are accepted for large parties. And all-you-can-eat dinners are offered daily. Henry's is open year-round, seven days a week.

Chilli Peppers $$
US 158, MP 5½, Kill Devil Hills
(252) 441–8081
www.chilli-peppers.com

World fusion with a Southwestern twist comes alive in the cooking at this fun, always bustling restaurant. Owner Jim Douglas has worked in Outer Banks eateries for years and has brought some of the most creative cooking around to Chilli Peppers. If being adventuresome is your style, you'll be wowed by the chefs' wild collaborations. If you prefer a milder meal, they can do that too and still tickle some untapped taste buds. The menu here changes frequently, with daily lunch and dinner specials sometimes stunning even the regulars. The chefs always come up with something to excite your taste buds. Weekly Tapas Nights, which feature little plates of dishes from a chosen worldly cuisine, are held on Thursday nights in fall, winter, and spring. One night you might taste samples of German food, the next week Italian, the next week Moroccan, and so on. This is always a big hit with the locals. Sushi nights are also popular.

A full bar separate from the cozy dining room was renovated and offers fresh-fruit margaritas, a nice wine selection, and more than a dozen varieties of bottled beer. Nonalcoholic fruit smoothies also are a great bet in the early afternoon. Happy Hour is held from 3:00 to 5:00 P.M. every day in the summer. Steamed seafood and veggies are served until closing. There's usually something going on here late at night too (see our Nightlife chapter). Chilli Peppers is an extremely progressive restaurant with a laid-back feel. Cacti, wooden chairs, and hand-painted accents all add to the casual atmosphere. Both lunch and dinner are served here seven days a week year-round. Sunday brunches, featuring a make-your-own Bloody Mary bar, are worth getting out of bed for. Also, you can take home a bottle of Chilli's award-winning original hot sauce, barbecue sauce, or hot salt. The T-shirts, too, make great memorabilia of a delicious meal.

Awful Arthur's $$
NC 12, MP 6, Kill Devil Hills
(252) 441–5955

An always-popular spot across from Avalon Pier, this raw bar and restaurant is usually crowded throughout the year. Wooden tables are laid out along the oblong room, and a bar stretches the entire length of the downstairs eatery. Upstairs, a separate lounge offers an ocean view. A live lobster tank and huge saltwater reef tank also offer interesting sea creatures to watch as you dine.

Awful Arthur's is a comfortably casual place where you won't mind peeling seasoned shrimp or picking the meat from succulent crab legs with sticky fingers. Seafood is the specialty here: everything from scallops and oysters to clams, mussels, homemade crab cakes, and daily entree specials. The bartenders are some of the fastest shuckers in town. Bass Ale and several other varieties of beer are on tap, or you can order from a full line of liquor and specialty drinks. For landlubbers, several nonseafood sandwiches are served.

At night, Awful Arthur's is usually packed. A late-night menu is available. Mondays are Locals' Nights, featuring drink and food specials all day. Awful Arthur's T-shirts have been seen all over the world and are also local favorites. This eatery is open seven days a week year-round for lunch and dinner.

Carolina Seafood $$$
NC 12, MP 6¼, Kill Devil Hills
(252) 441–6851

For an elaborate, all-you-can-eat seafood buffet where "fried has died," try Carolina Seafood. Here, you can enjoy 36 items for less than $19.95 a person: salad, soups, hush puppies, garlic crabs, crab legs, scallops, stuffed shrimp, and several types of fish served baked, broiled, blackened, steamed, or sautéed. You even see the whole loin of fish here. Roast beef is cut to order, and a variety of desserts are included in the price. If you're not feeling hungry enough to tackle the buffet, Carolina Seafood serves crabs, scallops, shrimp, and other seafood by the basket too. A children's menu also is available. This restaurant is open at 4:30 P.M. seven nights a week from May through September. Call for off-season hours.

Jolly Roger Restaurant $$
NC 12, MP 6¾, Kill Devil Hills
(252) 441–6530

Serving some of locals' favorite breakfasts, this lively restaurant is open for three meals a day 365 days a year. Besides the traditional eggs, pancakes, sausage, bacon, and toast, Jolly Roger has an in-house bakery that cooks up some of the biggest muffins and sticky buns you've ever seen. For lunch, choose from sandwiches, local seafood, or daily specials. Dinner entrees include homestyle Italian dishes, steaks, broiled and fried fish, and a popular $9.95 prime rib special each Friday. All the desserts are homemade, and special orders are accepted for items to go. The food isn't fancy, but the portions are enormous. You'll have no excuse if you leave here hungry. Jolly Roger also offers steamed spiced shrimp in the separate bar area each afternoon and is the karaoke headquarters of the Outer Banks seven nights a week.

Mako Mike's $$
US 158, MP 7, Kill Devil Hills
(252) 480–1919

Opened during the summer of 1995, this is the most outrageously decorated dining establishment on the Outer Banks. The fluorescent shark fins outside, decorated with swirls, stripes, and polka dots, don't give even a glimpse into what you'll see once you step inside. Some patrons have described the experience as similar to being underwater. We think it's almost like visiting an octopus's garden complete with three separate levels of dining, fish mobiles flying overhead, painted chairs, bright colors exploding everywhere, and murals all along the deep blue walls.

The menu is big and varied. Appetizers include hot crab dip and calamari. Dinner offerings are seasoned with Mediterranean, Cajun, Asian, and other exotic spices and include nine varieties of fresh pasta, seven wood-fired pizzas, several varieties of fresh blue-water fish, beef, pork, vegetarian stir-fries, mixed grills, scallops, shrimp, and dozens of other options.

This huge restaurant caters to couples, families, and large groups. A small meeting room is available for private parties. A separate bar serves daily frozen drink specials in addition to dozens of bottles of beer and wine. A children's menu is provided. A breakfast buffet is served Wednesday through Sunday in season, and dinner is served seven days a week year-round. Call for winter hours. Mako Mike's owner, Mike Kelly, also operates Kelly's Restaurant and Tavern and is part owner of Penguin Isle, both in Nags Head.

Goombays Grille & Raw Bar $$
NC 12, MP 7, Kill Devil Hills
(252) 441–6001
www.goombays.com

This island-style eatery is light and bright inside with plenty of cool artwork, an outrageous fish tank, and a wall-size tropical mural in the dining room. The ambiance is upbeat and casual, with wooden tables and chairs and a bare tile floor. The horseshoe-shaped bar, which is separate from the eating area, is a great place to try some of the delicious appetizers or drink specials that Goombays serves. We especially recommend the spicy crab balls and sweet coconut shrimp. Some of the drink offerings, both alcoholic and children's cocktails, come with zany toys to take home.

For lunch or dinner, try a fresh pasta entree, including everybody's favorite Rasta Pasta, locally caught seafood, a juicy burger topped as you wish, the Southwestern sampling, or one of the half-dozen daily specials that range from pork to barbecued shrimp and steak stir-fry. Everything here is reasonably priced and flavorful. A raw bar is open until 1:00 A.M., serving steamed shrimp, oysters, vegetables, and other favorites. Key lime pie is always a smart choice for dessert. Goombay's Jazzy Sunday Brunch was voted "best brunch on the beach" in a local newspaper poll. The New Orleans–inspired brunch menu, A.M. cocktails, and live jazz make for an excellent Sunday morning in the slower seasons. Brunch is served from 11:00 A.M. to 2:00 P.M. Goombays is open for lunch and dinner seven days a week in summer. Call for off-season hours.

The Good Life Gourmet $$
US 158, MP 7½, The Dare Center, Kill Devil Hills
(252) 480–2855

Aptly named, The Good Life offers home-made breads and pastries, sandwiches on house-made bread, soups and salads, and some incredibly decadent desserts. We're partial to the warm Cubana torta, a potato brioche roll filled with roast pork, country ham, jalapeño jack cheese, guacamole, and black beans. Vegetarian options include a black bean and three-cheese burrito with grilled vegetables, tomato salsa, and sour cream, or the Boulevard Brie sandwich, with sliced apples and grape vinaigrette on whole wheat. Another great sandwich is the hot roast beef with caramelized onions, Saga bleu cheese, and fig preserves on potato brioche. Good salads include spicy soy sesame noodles with mandarin oranges, toasted peanuts, red bell peppers, and scallions; mustard-grilled chicken salad with apples, raisins, and curry mayonnaise; cumin-lime coleslaw; and green salads and pasta salads.

Not only can you get a good cup of coffee, you can opt for espresso or cappuccino, as well as beer or wine. Wines are available by the glass, and there's a nice selection of retail bottled wines as well. While you're in the shop, tear yourself away from the pastry and dessert display and check out the selection of artisan cheeses, olives, olive oils, salsa, and sauces. Menu items are available for dining in or for take-out; special orders are accommodated and full-service catering is available. The Good Life is open for lunch and dinner. With new owners for 2002, there may be some changes in store for The Good Life Gourmet, though we hope it won't change much because it's perfect as it is.

Quagmires $$
NC 12, MP 7½, Kill Devil Hills
(252) 441-9188

With two oceanfront decks, an upstairs snack bar and large downstairs dining room overlooking the Atlantic, Quagmires is owned and operated by John Kirchmier and caters to almost every dining whim. If you're sunning yourself on the beach midday and start to hear your stomach grumble, you can get lunch to go from the upstairs grill without even putting on shoes or throwing a shirt over your wet bathing suit. If you'd rather wait to dress for dinner, you'll feel well cared for—and well fed—in the casual downstairs dining room. The giant U-shaped bar upstairs provides a great place to watch the waves and sip some of the best margaritas and frozen drinks on the beach. There's a kids' menu and special

treats just for the little ones. A volleyball court, horseshoe pit, and even ring toss are set up in the sand behind this eatery in case the younger set gets bored while their folks dawdle over dinner. Don't be misled, though: Those games are also open to adults. Better still, recently Quagmires added a new kids' playground.

The menu here features fresh local seafood, sandwiches, pasta, beef, chicken, and some Mexican favorites. The desserts are fresh and fabulous. Live acoustic music is offered throughout the summer (see our Nightlife chapter). Quagmires is open seven days a week for lunch and dinner in-season. Off-season hours vary.

Port O' Call $$$
Restaurant & Gaslight Saloon
NC 12, MP 8½, Kill Devil Hills
(252) 441-7484
www.outerbanksgifts.com

This antique-adorned restaurant offers fresh seafood cuisine with entrees including an array of seafood, veal, chicken, pasta, and beef. Blackboard specials change nightly. Each dinner comes with fresh-baked bread, fruit, and salads. The soups and chowders here are hot and succulent, and all the desserts are decadent. A children's menu is also offered.

Frank Gajar opened the restaurant in 1974, decorating it with a collection of Victorian furnishings. The dining room is warm and romantic, with flickering gaslights and brass accents. Special early bird dinners are served from 5:00 to 6:00 P.M. Live entertainment is offered in a large, separate saloon (see our Nightlife chapter). A full bar is available, and the gift shop/art gallery carries unusual, eclectic items. Port O' Call is open from mid-March through December.

The Thai Room $$
Oceanside Plaza
NC 12, MP 8½, Kill Devil Hills
(252) 441-1180

The Thai Room has been an Insiders' favorite for years. The fast-talking, fast-moving owner, Jimmy, lets his patrons choose their own level of spice—from mild to blow-your-brains-out. When he asks, "Very hot?"—think twice. He means it. Besides the daily specials, there's an in-season buffet dinner that allows you to sample several of the wonderful offerings. Don't miss an opportunity to try Thai Room's deep-fried soft-shell crabs when they're in season; they're perfectly crunchy and beyond description. More than a dozen American-style desserts are available. As for decor, it is unlike any other on North Carolina's barrier islands: authentically Thai with paper lanterns, Oriental portraits, and red-tasseled lamps. Family members prepare and serve each delectable meal—and they'll be happy to make suggestions if you're overwhelmed by all the options. The Thai Room is open for lunch and dinner March through December. All items are available for carry-out. The restaurant also has a full bar where you can indulge in exotic drinks and Thai beer while you wait for a table or take-out order.

Outer Banks Brewing Station $$
US 158, MP 8½, Kill Devil Hills
(252) 449–BREW

Everything about the Outer Banks Brewing Station is first class. Fine handcrafted brews, inspired cuisine, and noble yet subtle decor all work together to provide a sublime culinary experience. The Brewing Station opened in 2001 to rave reviews. Customers who expected standard brewhouse pub fare were pleasantly surprised to find contemporary, cutting-edge cuisine prepared by schooled chefs. The signature beers, made in house, have gone over well. Kolsch is the light summer brew; Hefewiezen II is a wheat beer with hints of banana and cloves; Mutiny Pale Ale is a crisp light-bodied dry ale; and The Old Alt is a lightly hopped, light-bodied golden brew. The owners say they believe that fine brewing deserves to be paired with revolutionary cuisine, and they certainly have the goods to prove it.

The food is outstanding. If I could eat it all in one sitting, my next visit's selections would start with cornmeal-dusted oysters, fried, on tossed Romaine with crumbled bacon and Tabasco-lemon aioli. I'd then move on to a pecan-honey-crusted goat cheese medallion on a bed of seasonal greens, succulent fall fruits, and Balsamic vinaigrette. The specials are always tempting, but the pan-seared colossal sea scallops with an Asiago cheese risotto, sautéed greens, brunoise vegetables, and a roasted garlic, herb shellfish broth are so good that I'd most likely order that again. Desserts are extremely tempting, but I'd likely not have room and save the space for a glass of tawny port. The excellent wine list here competes with the beers.

The Outer Banks Brewing Station occupies a most unique, church/barnlike building that was built especially for this use. Two silos anchor the building, prompting the owners to advertise their location as "between the silos in Kill Devil Hills." Inside, the cathedral ceilings, lined with tin, are over 20 feet high, with windows that reach to the ceiling along the front of the building. Rustic cement and brick floors, honey-toned walls adorned with Middle Eastern rugs, and warm woods create a comforting atmosphere. The serpentine bar stretches into the back of the restaurant, where a crowd of hip people gathers for drinks until the wee hours. Bands and acoustic music are staged here often; see our Nightlife chapter for more information. The Brewing Station is a year-round restaurant. Lunch and dinner are served daily in season.

JK's $$$
US 158, MP 9, Kill Devil Hills
(252) 441–9555
www.jksfoods.com

Fine-dinning Insiders love JK's selection of mesquite-grilled meats. JK's serves USDA Prime beef selected by Allen Brothers of Chicago, lamb and veal from Summerfield Farms in Virginia, and ribs from the Midwest. A seasoned and professional staff fits right in with the classy, comfortable dining room and bar. Three to four varieties of fresh fish are offered nightly. The menu varies, according to the best meats available, but generally has a prime rib chop, porterhouse steak, New York strip, Kansas City strip, top sirloin, veal rib chop, and lamb loin chops. Ribs and chicken are dry-marinated with JK's special seasoning, then mesquite-grilled. JK's has all ABC permits and an excellent wine list with some really good values. Dinner is served from 5:00 P.M. year-round. They also offer take-out.

Bob's Grill $
US 158, MP 9, Kill Devil Hills
(252) 441–0707

Bob serves big, cheap breakfasts all year seven days a week until 2:30 P.M. daily—and that's hard to find around here. The blueberry pancakes are so big, they fill a whole plate. Eggs are made any way you want 'em, and the hash browns flavored with onions and peppers are some of the best around.

For lunch, try a hamburger, tuna steak, or one of several traditional hot and cold sandwiches. Owner Bob McCoy cooks much of the food himself. A hot lunch special is available every day. You can't leave town without trying Bob's No. 1 seller—Philly steak and cheese. Dinners feature the biggest cuts of prime rib on the Outer Banks, Cajun beer batter–dipped shrimp, and fresh mahi mahi caught just offshore. The salads are also good here. Save room for the hot fudge brownie dessert.

Bob's has a casual, dinerlike atmosphere, with a regular-folk appeal that makes everyone comfortable. Even McCoy's well-known gruff motto, "Eat and get the hell out," has obviously not offended any locals, since the parking lot is packed with loyal customers more days than not. Service is fast and friendly, beer and wine are available, and everything can be ordered for carry-out. This grill closes from 2:30 to 5:00 P.M. daily, but it's open for three meals a day every day all year.

The Pit Surf Shop, Bar and Grill $
US 158, MP 9, Kill Devil Hills
(252) 480–3128
www.pitsurf.com

The Pit is the favorite counterculture hangout of the beach. It's the prime apres surf spot, where the food is good and cheap, the staff has personality, and board-sport videos are always running. The hallmarks of Pit dining are economy and portion size, and indeed, the West Coast–style wraps are big and filling. Beans, meats, cheese, veggies, and even mashed potatoes are blended into a variety of creative wraps, plus The Pit makes a mean quesadilla, hot sandwiches, salads in a fresh tortilla bowl, appetizers, fries, rings, wings, and more. Nothing costs more than $7.00. Drinks run the gamut from alcohol to up-to-the-minute So-Be flavors and everything in between. Food is served continuously from 11:30 A.M. until midnight, and delivery is offered on weekdays in the off-season. There are always people hanging around The Pit, killing time, meeting friends, or taking advantage of the free Internet access. See our Nightlife and Watersports chapters for more about The Pit.

Dirty Dicks Crab House $$
US 158, MP 9, Kill Devil Hills
(252) 480–3425
www.dirtydickscrabs.com

The litany of crab choices at Dirty Dicks Crab House reminds us of Bubba's roster of shrimp in *Forest Gump*. There are snow crab legs, soft-shell crab sandwiches, spiced crabs, crab cakes, and steamed crabs, plus steamed shrimp, clams, clam chowder, gumbo, jambalaya, and Cajun creole. The popular Dick Burger is a crab and shrimp patty with Cajun sauce. There are sandwich platter specials and offerings for the kids. You can even purchase Dicks special spice and famous Dirty Dicks T-shirts. Crustaceans are cooked to order for take-out. This location of Dirty Dicks is a sit-down restaurant. There's also a Dirty Dicks on the Beach Road that offers take-out only. You can get a big bushel of steamed blue crabs and take them home to your own picnic table and have at it. It takes a long time to clean and eat that many crabs so you might as well do it at home. Dirty Dicks has a third location—a sit-down crab house restaurant—on NC 12 in Avon, next to the Avon Pier. All locations are open seasonally; call for hours.

Dare Devil's Authentic Pizzeria $
NC 12, MP 9, Kill Devil Hills
(252) 441–6330, (252) 441–2353

This pizza parlor has been in business for more than a decade and is known for its superb stromboli and hand-tossed pizzas. Chicken wings, mozzarella sticks, nachos, Greek salads, and pizza bread are also available here, as are subs and salads. Dare Devil's also has four types of beer on tap served in frosty glass mugs. The interior is low-key, with laminated tables and a long bar where you can eat. A big-screen TV in the corner features whatever hot sporting event happens to be going on. You can also order any item to take out. Dare Devil's is open seven days a week for lunch and dinner from March through November.

Etheridge Seafood Restaurant $$
US 158, MP 9½, Kill Devil Hills
(252) 441–2645

The Etheridge family has long been synonymous with Outer Banks seafood, operating a commercial fishing fleet and wholesale fish company from the deep-draft docks in Wanchese. This 15-year-old restaurant serves almost all its fish right off the boats, so you know it's fresh. The casual, round dining room is nautically themed as well.

This is a real family-style restaurant where the waiters never stop pouring iced tea, and the food, though cooked to order, always seems to come fast. This is an ideal place to sample traditional Outer Banks–style seafood. For lunch, try a seafood pizza served with red or white garlic sauce. The Mill Landing egg rolls won the Wanchese Seafood cook-off several years ago and will win your approval too; they're deep-fried and stuffed with black olives, scallops, shrimp, and fresh vegetables. Crab cakes here are divine, filled with

fresh white meat and bursting with flavor. The sweet hush puppies are, in our opinion, some of the best on the beach.

For dinner, a five-course early bird special is served each day. Blackened Cajun crawfish with tomato basil sauce, broiled or fried platters with a sampling of several types of seafood, and any of the traditional fish specials are sure to please. Landlubbers, too, will find something to their liking here with several beef and chicken entrees from which to choose. The soups make great starters. Each evening meal comes with a basket of crackers, a crock of cheddar cheese, and the best seafood cheese spread you've ever tasted. There's even a children's menu, and a full bar is set off from the dining area. Etheridge's is open for lunch and dinner seven days a week from February through December.

Mama Kwan's $$
US 158, MP 9½, Kill Devil Hills
(252) 480–0967
www.mamakwans.com

Mama Kwan's is a favorite surf-style hangout in Kill Devil Hills, a haven of good food sandwiched between McDonald's and Pizza Hut on French Fry Alley. The atmosphere is laid-back and fun, with classic and current surf videos and occasional Elvis movies playing on TVs. Children are welcomed with a special menu and toys to keep them entertained.

Mama's features local seafood, land food, and veggies with touches from some of the world's best surf spots: Hawaii (blackened Hawaiian chicken seasoned with Jamaican and Hawaiian spices in a rum butter sauce with pineapple mango salsa), Indonesia (pad Thai and rice noodles), California (Cali-style fish tacos), and the Outer Banks (crab cakes). Mama recommends the Special Occasion Pasta: penne with red peppers, shiitake mushrooms, snow peas, and scallions in a soy cream sauce with or without tuna. The full bar serves beer, wine, and specialty frozen drinks in novelty glassware. Lunch and dinner are served daily. This is a popular nighttime hangout, and late-night food is served every night in the season and on weekends in the off-season. See our Nightlife chapter.

Peppercorns $$
Ramada Inn, NC 12, MP 9½, Kill Devil Hills
(252) 441–2151

With a wide, open dining room overlooking the Atlantic Ocean, Peppercorns has a traditional family menu with something for everyone.

Chef Greg Sniegowski prepares many Outer Banks favorites, including locally caught shrimp and crab cakes. The soup du jour is always filling and delicious. Entrees include prime rib crusted with spices, slow-roasted, and served au jus; Atlantic salmon stuffed with crabmeat; or Italian risotto with shrimp, scallops, and crabmeat. Each meal is served with several artfully prepared vegetables and a basket of interesting breads. Vegetarian entrees are always offered. There's a full bar and a children's menu. Peppercorns provides take-out food and room service for Ramada guests. This restaurant is open daily year-round for breakfast, lunch, and dinner. There's nightly entertainment in season on the outdoor tiki deck.

Pigman's Bar-B-Que $
US 158, MP 9½, Kill Devil Hills
(252) 441–6803
www.pigman.com

Pigman's rib-man, Bill Shaver, is locally famous for his corny cable television commercials. He's also known for serving succulent North Carolina–style barbecue and walking his pet potbellied pigs around town. At this counter-service eatery, you can get beef, pork, chicken, and barbecue. Try his new low-fat creations: catfish, turkey, and tuna barbecue. Each dinner comes with homemade coleslaw, homemade hush puppies, and baked beans and is served on disposable plates with plastic utensils. The sweet potato fries here are spectacular. Pigman's has a selection of gorgeous Southwestern jewelry and gifts for sale. You can also purchase hush puppy mix, all four Pigman barbecue sauces, and Pigman meat rub at the restaurant. Catering is available. Pigman's is open for lunch and dinner seven days a week. It's open year-round. Come on by and visit Pigman's critters behind the building. You might see one of his llamas, his miniature donkey or horse, or one of his smart, lovable potbellied pigs.

Flying Fish Cafe $$
US 158, MP 10, Kill Devil Hills
(252) 441–6894

This delightful restaurant serves an array of American and Mediterranean dishes. The interior is spruce green and adobe white with purple accents. Price's color photographs grace the walls. Brightly colored tablecloths adorn each table, illuminated by sconce wall lights crafted from wine boxes and by candles set in the center of each table or booth.

Chefs at Flying Fish roll their own pasta daily and offer an array of seafood, vegetarian entrees, and a variety of unusual grains and starches. Gourmet pot pies, eggplant parmesan, at least four types of fresh fish, and exceptional beef dishes are also always on the menu. Fresh fish is served four ways each night, and there's an Angus filet mignon, a veal chop, and pan-seared New York strip steak for meat lovers. All entrees come with a starch of the day, vegetables, and just-baked bread including focaccia. Appetizers include portobello mushrooms stuffed with shrimp, two types of soup, and hot seafood dip. For dessert, try to resist the Grecian Urn, a waffle filled with ice cream and topped with glazed fresh fruit and whipped cream. Chocoholics will love the Chocolate Hurricane, a flourless chocolate brownie with mousse and a liquid chocolate center, wrapped in a white and dark chocolate shell all topped with ganache and completed with a white chocolate flying fish jumping out of the top.

The Flying Fish Cafe has won the *Wine Spectator* Award of Excellence for the past three years. More than 40 types of wine are served either by the bottle or by the glass.

A children's menu also is available. Early bird dinner specials at $9.95 are served from 5:00 to 6:00 P.M. The Flying Fish offers dinner every day year-round. Reservations are recommended for dinner at this casual, innovative restaurant.

Colington Island

Colington Cafe $$
Colington Rd., 1 m. west of US 158, Kill Devil Hills
(252) 480-1123

Step back in time at this cozy Victorian cafe, nestled among live oaks on Colington Road. This popular restaurant is only a mile off the Bypass but once you've arrived, you'll feel worlds away from the bustling beach. It's tranquil and absolutely lovely in this restored old home set high on a hill. This is one of our favorite places to come for an intimate dinner, and the chefs prepare some of the most marvelous meals around for extremely reasonable prices. Three small dining rooms are adorned in tasteful decor. Even the black painted plates are unusual and artistic.

Hot crab dip slathered on buttery crackers and bowls of homemade she-crab bisque are outstanding appetizers. Nightly specials include wonderful pasta dishes, a mixed grill with hollandaise, gamefish, and tender filet mignon. Seafood entrees change depending on what's just been caught. Only fresh herbs and vegetables are used in cooking and as side dishes. Salads are served a la carte.

Owner Carlen Pearl's French heritage permeates her restaurant's delicious cream sauces, and she makes most of the irresistible desserts herself—from blackberry cobbler to chocolate tortes and crème brûlée. Restaurants in Colington may serve only beer or wine, by law, but you'll have plenty of choices at Colington Cafe. Check out the reserve wines and be sure to save room for a glass of port with your dessert. Colington Cafe is open for dinner only seven days a week, April through November. Call the number listed for off-season hours. Reservations are highly recommended.

Nags Head

Mrs. T's Deli $
US 158, MP 10, Nags Head
(252) 441-1220

This homey deli is a great bet for quick, satisfying lunches and some of the friendliest chatter in town.

Most of Mrs. T's three-dozen-plus sandwiches are named after friends and family members who eat here. We like the Stacy sub with four types of cheese. And the three varieties of veggie burger always get rave reviews. Club sandwiches are stacked so high they barely fit in your mouth. All the meats and cheeses are fresh out of the deli counter, which also offers items by the half-pound or more to take home. The Outer Banks curly fries, lightly seasoned and made to order, are wonderful. Each entree comes with a pickle. Cakes, pastries, and gourmet jelly beans are available for dessert, and lots of kosher food, including matzos, can be found all year. Mrs. T's serves lunch and dinner seven days a week from mid-March through early February. Everything here can be packaged to go.

Red Drum Grille and Taphouse $$
NC 12, MP 10, Nags Head
(252) 480-1095

Since it opened in 1998, the Red Drum Grille and Taphouse has been carving out its niche on the Outer Banks. The handsome red brick exterior presents an apt introduction to the tasteful decor: glossy, deep rust-colored tables and cozy oak booths give the room a warm, inviting feel. A gleaming redwood bar stretches along the length of the back wall and lures you in for one of 18 beers on tap. In the back room—away from the dining room—are a pool table and a Foosball table for those who want to stay and play after dinner.

The menu has something for everyone. For starters, try the Hatteras-style clam chowder, a quesadilla, or the shrimp con queso dip. The homemade stuffed jalapeños are just hot enough and full of flavor. Lunch fare from the steamer menu includes crab legs, shrimp, vegetables, clams, and oysters. Large burgers, a chicken sandwich with Smithfield ham and havarti cheese, fish and chips, and a gamefish burrito are some of the locals' favorites.

Dinner is a whole other ball game, with a simple country fare menu. It's reminiscent of the Outer Banks of old or of Mom's cooking taken a step further and served up with diligence and a smile. You'll find apple-glazed pork chops, ribs, steaks, a mixed grill of the day, and lots of fresh seafood, including seafood pasta with large shrimp and scallops and a fried seafood platter. Entrees are served with homemade mashed potatoes or wild rice. (Insiders' tip: The potatoes will knock your socks off.)

Grilled or fried fresh fish, pasta, and vegetarian dishes are also available on this unique menu.

The Red Drum Grille and Taphouse serves lunch and dinner from February through November. They also offer occasional entertainment into the wee hours of the night (see our Nightlife chapter). The Red Drum is closed in December and January.

Kelly's $$$
Outer Banks Restaurant & Tavern
US 158, MP 10½, Nags Head
(252) 441–4116
www.kellysrestaurant.com

Kelly's is an Outer Banks tradition and one of the most popular restaurants year-round. Owner Mike Kelly gives his personal attention to every detail, so the service and selections are always first-rate. This is a large, upscale eatery and a busy place. The decor reflects the area's rich maritime heritage and includes abundant examples of fish, birds, and other wildlife. The tavern is hopping seven nights a week, even during winter (see our Nightlife chapter).

Dinner is the only meal served here, and it's offered in several rooms upstairs and downstairs. Kelly's menu offers fresh seafood dishes, chicken, beef, and pastas. There's a raw bar for those who enjoy feasting on oysters and other steamed

shellfish. An assortment of delicious homemade breads accompanies each meal. Kelly's sweet potato biscuits are succulent—we usually ask for a second basket. Desserts are flavorful and filling. A separate children's menu is available, complete with crayons and special placemats to color. Kelly's also caters private parties, weddings, and any style event imaginable. The restaurant and lounge are open daily. Dinner is served daily.

Slammin' Sammy's Offshore Grille & Stillery $$
US 158, MP 10½, Nags Head
(252) 449–2255
www.slamminsammys.com

Slammin' Sammy's is the place to go for a frolicsome atmosphere of food, fun, and fuel. With 33 TVs plus four giant screens, you can get an eyeful of a lot of sporting events. There's also pool and tabletop shuffleboard if you're into a little more interaction. Sammy's is open for lunch and dinner, serving sandwiches, salads, "hot spot" jumbo baked potatoes loaded with plenty of extras, appetizers, prime rib, and pizza. Sandwiches include the Hogs Breath shrimp po'boy, the Incredible Edible crabcake sandwich, a Clubwater Club, and grilled gamefish. Slammin' Sammy's has daily chef's specials, a children's menu, and a full bar. Lunch and dinner are served daily year-round.

Mulligan's Oceanfront Grille $$
NC 12, MP 10½, Nags Head
(252) 480–2000

In restaurant polls by local newspapers, Mulligan's has taken the prize for "best burger on the beach" for four years running. Indeed, the burgers are big, juicy, and tasty and come with a variety of toppings. Mulligan's also serves steak, seafood, and an array of pasta entrees for lunch and dinner. Occupying the old 1949 Miller's Pharmacy building, the eatery is divided in half lengthwise by wooden and glass partitions. The south end is flanked by a long, low bar reminiscent of the TV show *Cheers*. Scores of old Outer Banks photographs, painted mirrors, and other memorabilia decorate this comfortable, inviting full-service bar, where appetizers and light dinners are available.

The north half of Mulligan's is the restaurant, where raw bar items, sandwiches, pasta, steak, and seafood are available. Bread, a salad, and potatoes or rice complete the main course, but be sure to save room for cheesecake and other delightful desserts. Live entertainment and karaoke are featured here year-round (see our Nightlife chapter). Mulligan's is open seven days a week all year long.

George's Junction $$
NC 12, MP 11, Nags Head
(252) 441-0606

Outside, George's Junction has a slightly exotic mystique, thanks to the unusual architecture of the former Restaurant by George. Inside, the expansive interior is a fitting setting for the largest all-you-can-eat seafood buffet on the Outer Banks. The dinner buffet offers 70 hot items and includes crab legs, hand-carved roast beef, ham, chicken, a variety of local seafood, a full salad bar, several varieties of bread and rolls baked daily, and a bar of delicious homemade desserts. One price includes everything, and a special price is set for children. The only restaurant big enough where customers can wait in line inside in the comfort of air-conditioning, George's includes a large lounge with a full bar. George's serves dinner seven days a week in season, with an early bird special from 4:00 to 5:00 P.M. The schedule varies in the off-season from March through November. Reservations are requested for parties of 10 or more.

Tortuga's Lie Shellfish Bar and Grille $
NC 12, MP 11, Nags Head
(252) 441-RAWW

A locals' favorite on the Outer Banks, this small, upbeat eatery is housed in a turquoise and white cottage across from the ocean near a great surf break. Tortuga's features an enclosed porch furnished with handmade wooden booths, table seating, and an expanded bar that seats more than two dozen people. There's a sand volleyball court out back where pickup games always are being played—and watched from the outdoor picnic tables. The bartenders and wait staff are some of the friendliest folk we know. The food is good and creatively concocted. The atmosphere inside is fun and casual, with turtle-themed batiks hanging from the white walls and more than 100 license plates, some with pretty unusual personal messages, from across the country tacked to the low ceiling beams.

The menu here offers everything from quick-fried fish bites to super-sized fish and black bean burritos plus sandwiches, seafood flavored with outrageous spices, and a full raw bar that always has something steaming. The French fries are among the best we've ever had. Dinner entrees include pork medallions, steak stir-fries, just-off-the-boat tuna steaks, succulent shrimp, and pasta plates. Most meals come with rice and beans, but the cooks will substitute fries if you ask. But we rarely choose anything from the menu because the daily specials are so tempting. Sushi is served on Wednesday nights, and the place usually is packed with locals. Desserts are delicious and change daily.

There's a full bar here with loads of specialty drinks. We also enjoy the Black and Tans, a combination of Bass Ale and Guinness Stout, combined in pint-sized glasses. If you're a beer lover and haven't discovered this duo yet, be sure to order one on your next trip to Tortuga's. This hip, laid-back eatery is open seven days a week for lunch and dinner from February through December. Call for winter hours. (See also our Nightlife chapter.)

Pier House Restaurant $
Nags Head Fishing Pier, NC 12, MP 11½, Nags Head
(252) 441-5141

Offering an amazing ocean view on the beach, this family-style restaurant allows patrons to sit right above the ocean. You can feel the salt spray if you dine on the screened porch, and even inside the air-conditioned building, waves sometimes crash beneath the wooden floor's slats. This is a great, laid-back place to enjoy a big breakfast before a day of fishing or to take a break from angling on a hot afternoon for lunch.

The staff at Pier House is friendly, and all three meals of the day are traditionally prepared. Lunch includes sandwiches, soups, and seafood specials. Dinner entrees include local fresh seafood, steaks, and chicken. All-you-can-eat dinners also are popular picks, which come with coleslaw, hush puppies, and French fries. You can have your fish grilled, broiled, or fried, and if you clean the fish you catch, the Pier House cooks will prepare it for you. Appetizers and desserts are also available. Free sightseeing passes come with supper so you can stroll along the long pier after your meal and watch the anglers and surfers. Pier House Restaurant is open seven days a week from March through November. Dinner is served until mid-October, and the restaurant has all liquor permits.

The Wharf $$
NC 12, MP 11½, Nags Head
(252) 441-7457

You can't miss this popular beach restaurant across from the Atlantic Ocean: It's the one with the long, long line of people out front. Diners arrive early for the ever-popular, all-you-care-to-eat buffet of Alaskan crab legs, fried shrimp, scallops, chowder, broiled catch of the day, clam strips, barbecue, prime rib, homemade yeast rolls, loads of vegetables, and desserts—all for $17.95 a person. The atmosphere is very informal. A reduced-price children's menu offers hamburgers, hot dogs, pizza, chicken tenders, clam strips, fried shrimp, a drink, and all-you-can-eat dessert served on a souvenir Frisbee. Kids three and younger eat for free. The Wharf is open from Easter through October. Doors open at 4:00 P.M. during the summer.

Don Gatos $-$$
NC 12, MP 11½, Nags Head
(252) 441-9330

This restaurant is fast becoming a local's favorite. Chef Amando brings his inspirations from Oaxaca, Mexico. He offers vegetarian dishes, chicken, beef, and fresh Outer Banks seafood dishes in an authentic Mexican atmosphere. The interior of the restaurant is quite beautifully decorated and evokes the feeling of an upscale cantina.

Daily specials like the delicious smoked tuna tostada are available. Lunch begins at 11:30 A.M., and dinner is served until 10:00 P.M. The food here is fresh, healthy, and filling. A favorite menu item is the Camarones al Mojo de Ajo (jumbo shrimp sauteed with onion and cilantro in a hearty garlic sauce). The ceviche and guacamole are stellar. You may want to sip a Mexican beer or a made-to-order margarita with your meal. A children's menu is available for the niños in your group.

Don Gatos is open year-round. Look for the bright orange building on the beach road with the surfer on the roof.

Jockey's Ribs $$
NC 12, MP 13, Nags Head
(252) 441-1141

For dining in or for take-out, Jockey's Ribs has been serving finger-licking barbecue for 16 years. Entrees include lean and meaty slabs of pork ribs, hot and spicy barbecued chicken wings, roasted chicken, steaks, chops, chicken and rib combos, and seafood. A variety of warm breads is served with each entree, along with hash browns or a baked potato. The seafood gumbo is always a favorite. If you're looking for a light dinner, sandwiches are served each evening, along with such appetizers as crab-stuffed mushroom caps and French onion soup. A children's menu is available. Dinner is served nightly from 5:00 to 10:00 P.M. in season. Call for off-season hours.

Country Deli $, no credit cards
Surfside Plaza, NC 12, MP 13, Nags Head
(252) 441-5684

A laid-back eatery with items only available for take-out, Country Deli offers breakfast breads plus some of the biggest sandwiches on the beach. The Killer is always a hit, with ham, turkey, havarti and muenster cheeses, and hot peppers spread on a sub roll. Our favorite is the Goesway, where five kinds of cheese are melted on thick slices of toast and topped with crispy strips of bacon. There's a full deli counter here, so you can create your own sandwiches. Side salads of macaroni, pasta, potato, and vegetables also are served. The owner offers several types of chips; sour pickles come free with every option. Brownies and cheesecake are tempting dessert selections.

Don't leave without checking out the philosophical ponderings employees leave on the blackboard behind the cash register—they could change the way you think about the world while you're trying to decide what to order. Country Deli is open for lunch and dinner seven days a week during the summer and offers free delivery to Nags Head and Kill Devil Hills. This eatery is open for lunch only during the off-season (call for hours and days).

Bad Barracuda's Raw Bar & Grille $$
US 158, MP 13, Nags Head
(252) 449–0223
www.badbarracudas.com

Brought to us in 1998 by the same folks who own Awful Arthur's, Bad Barracuda's Raw Bar & Grille serves up a broad assortment of just about any type of seafood you might be craving, plus clam chowder, seafood gumbo, lobster bisque, salads, pastas, and a variety of hearty dinner entrees. If you're looking for bar food and sandwiches, you won't be disappointed: The menu has a nice selection of appetizers and sandwiches, and there's a number of burger options. How about the Backfin Burger, topped with your choice of cheese and backfin crabmeat? Or, there's the Big "B" Burger ("the burger that Bad Barracuda eats"), made with one-half pound of freshly ground beef. The restaurant offers lunch and dinner specials daily and specializes in large parties. Bad Barracuda's has a full bar plus specialty

drinks (try the Awesome Barracuda), a nice wine selection, a children's menu, and soon-to-be-famous T-shirts. The restaurant is wheelchair-accessible. Insiders recommend that you save room for dessert, the double-cooked Key lime pie. The pie alone will lure you back.

Bad Barracuda's is open year-round, serving dinner nightly and lunch on the weekends.

The Clove Italian Pizza Kitchen & Pub $
Surfside Plaza, US 158, MP 13, Nags Head
(252) 480–1988

The Clove adds class and gourmet cooking to the traditional pizza parlor concept. Here, you don't just have beer with your pizza—you can choose from a whole list of microbrews. Pasta dishes, subs, sandwiches, salads, and a complete Italian-food menu are available, along with gourmet and traditional pizzas. The crust here is soft, chewy, and slightly sweet, which perfectly offsets the salty meats and tangy sauce. We like the vegetarian pie with artichoke hearts, spinach, red peppers, and feta. The Clove is open for lunch and dinner every day in season and closes in January and February. Call for off-season hours.

Grits 24 Hour Grill $
US 158, MP 14, Nags Head
(252) 449–2888

Just north of the Outer Banks Mall is the Outer Banks's only 24-hour eatery. Grits 24 Hour Grill has a strong local following. The restaurant has a standard fare breakfast and lunch menu served 'round the clock, plus fresh bakery items and fresh Krispy Kreme donuts. If you can't live without your Krispy Kremes, make sure you get to Grits early in the morning, for they sell out quickly. Grits 24 Hour Grill specializes in take-out orders and is open all year, but not 24 hours in the off-season.

La Fogata Mexican Restaurant $
US 158, MP 14, Nags Head
(252) 441–4179

At the front of the Outer Banks Mall, La Fogata joins its original Kitty Hawk sister restaurant with the same name in offering delicious Mexican food at affordable prices. These restaurants have a strong Outer Banks following, and the mall location has the same menu and similar decor as the first restaurant. See the listing earlier in our Kitty Hawk section for more information.

Bacu Grill $$
US 158, MP 14½, Nags Head
(252) 480-1892

Located across from Seamark at the Outer Banks Mall, the new Bacu Grill serves up authentic flavors from the East Coast to Cuba and beyond. The name Bacu comes from the Cuban-American term for a taste or sight that reminds one of home. At Bacu Grill, you'll find a homey atmosphere with a metropolitan feel.

You can get three different types of burgers for lunch: American, blackened, or with jerk seasonings. A variety of sandwiches is served, including soft-shell crab, blackened tuna, pit beef, and a Cuban mix. Side orders include Cuban beans and rice, chips and salsa, fries, and corn on the cob. The raw bar features stone crab, crab legs, clams, oysters, mussels, and spiced shrimp; fish, steak, seafood, and pasta dishes make up the dinner entrees. The popular porterhouse steak is 20 to 22 ounces, and is cooked Tuscan style—seared in olive oil and finished with garlic butter and cracked black pepper. For appetizers, try some West Indies coconut shrimp, cracked conch, hurricane wings, or baked Brie.

Bacu Grill has a world-class wine list, a full bar, nonsmoking dining, and a smoking lounge. Cigars and wines are sold in Bacu's retail shop. The restaurant is open year-round, serving lunch and dinner.

Taiko Japanese Restaurant and Sushi Bar $$
Outer Banks Mall, US 158, MP 14, Nags Head
(252) 449-8895

Finally! An Outer Banks restaurant that serves sushi all day, for lunch and dinner. Here in the land of the freshest seafood available, we thought it would come along a lot sooner than it did. Now we're just thankful it's here. Taiko's sushi is top-notch, rolled tightly and cut into perfect, bite-size pieces. Our favorite is the spicy tuna roll, with fresh raw tuna, a kick of spices, and a hint of crunch. We also like the spider roll special—fried soft-shell crab—and the Dragon roll with tuna, crab, and cucumber wrapped in masago, avocado, and eel. Yum. The miso and clear soups are to die for, as are the udon and soba noodle dishes and the refreshing seaweed salad. There are also Japanese-style entrees, such as steak teriyaki, shrimp tempura, and chicken sukiyaki. Lunch boxes combine sushi or sashimi with seaweed, rice, and a shrimp dumpling. The dining room is peaceful and serene, with soft music and tasteful, understated Asian decor. You can eat at the bar and watch the chefs prepare your meal or sit at a table. Saki, Kirin, Sapporo, plum wine, green tea, and many other beverages are served. Everything at Taiko is available for take-out, and they package everything with the utmost care so you don't have sauce all over your car seat by the time you get home. Taiko is open year-round and serves lunch and dinner daily in season. Call for off-season hours.

Outer Banx Steakhouse $$
US 158, MP 14½, Nags Head
(252) 449-4448

If you're craving a big juicy piece of meat, you might as well come to the place that devotes itself primarily to steak. Outer Banx Steakhouse serves certified Angus beef and cooks it to perfection. Center-cut sirloin, prime rib, rib eye, filet mignon, New York strip, porterhouse, and ribs are favorites here. To combine the best of both worlds, try the sirloin topped with fried oysters, the prime rib with broiled shrimp, or the half-rack of baby back ribs with stuffed shrimp. It's not all beef, though. Seafood entrees, like crab cakes, fish, and a seafood platter, and pasta are available. The side dishes range from fried oysters to sautéed onions to steak fries. The Steakhouse has full ABC permits, beer, and a wine list. A children's menu is available.

Penguin Isle Soundside Grille $$$
US 158, MP 16, Nags Head
(252) 441–2637
www.penguinisle.com

As night falls, waterfowl begin fluttering across the low-lying marshlands of Roanoke Sound, right outside the windows of this elegant soundside restaurant. Windsurfers in the distance cruise by beneath colorful sails, and brilliant sunsets abound. The sights outside the dining room are as lovely and tranquil as the ambiance inside. Penguin Isle is truly a peaceful place to enjoy a special, intimate meal.

Here, the decor is tasteful and creative, with displays of local art, hand-carved decoys, lighted authentic ship models, enormous mounted wine bottles, and light wood accents around the airy dining room. Linen tablecloths cover every table, and the lights and slow jazz music are soft and low.

Not only a premier place to dine, Penguin Isle is also a wine destination. The staff is very knowledgeable, and the much-heralded *Wine Spectator*'s Award of Excellence has identified this restaurant's wine list as "one of the best in the world" for the past 10 years. Seasonal wine dinners also are offered in the off-season with advance registration.

A separate window-walled lounge with full bar, an abbreviated menu, and small tables overlooks the sound. Patrons can also have a cocktail before dinner on the outdoor deck, and a lobby with comfortable couches affords an alternative place to await your table. Owner Mike Kelly, general manager Tom Sloate, and head chef Lee Miller combine their talents here to create a truly distinctive restaurant. Miller's reputation is well known on the Outer Banks, and the staff members are both friendly and professional.

Penguin Isle serves fresh local seafood, handmade pasta, certified Black Angus beef, chicken, duck, fresh-baked breads, and many other appetizing offerings. Creative food pairings, also called fusion cookery, is the chef's specialty, but the shrimp aristotle featuring shrimp with feta cheese, green onion, and fresh fettucini is hard to beat. We also recommend grilled Gulf Stream tuna over homemade fettuccine. The seafood gumbo and bean cakes are also delicious for starters here. Penguin Isle's portions are generous, especially for such an upscale restaurant. All of the desserts are delectable. The menu changes seasonally to make use of the freshest ingredients.

Only dinner is served here from March through December. Employees also will cater private parties, wedding receptions, and almost any occasion on-site. A children's menu is available, and early dining specials are offered from 5:00 until 6:00 P.M.; reservations are recommended.

Windmill Point $$$
US 158, MP 16½, Nags Head
(252) 441–1535

From Windmill Point's wide windows, you'll catch magnificent views of the sound at sunset, punctuated by the colorful sails of wind-surfers. Famous for its memorabilia from the elegant ocean liner SS *United States*, this restaurant provides excellent cuisine to match the outdoor sights. There are two dining areas, tastefully furnished down to the tablecloths, linen napkins, and comfortable chairs that hug rather than support you. Service is fast and unobtrusive. The upstairs lounge, which features the authentic kidney-shaped bar from the ship—complete with plaques from famous 1950s statesmen and actresses who sipped cocktails there—is a pleasant place to await your call to dinner.

Menu favorites include a seafood trio, poached or grilled with flavorful sauces, and a seafood pasta entree of lightly seasoned scallops. The chefs also prepare roasted prime rib, sauteed duck, fettuccine primavera, and capelli con scampi. Cooked with fresh herbs and creative sauces, the entrees get better each season. Windmill Point's menu features heart-healthy selections. A children's menu is available. Dinner is served seven nights a week. Windmill Point is open year-round; reservations are accepted.

The Dunes $
US 158, MP 16½, Nags Head
(252) 441-1600

When a large crowd or big family is gathering for a meal, this restaurant can accommodate all in its three huge dining rooms. Breakfast at The Dunes is a local's favorite—you can tell by the packed parking lot—where every early morning entree in every imaginable combination is offered. There's a popular breakfast bar here during weekends in the off-season and daily in the summer. Lunches include great burgers and homemade crab cakes served with fries and coleslaw. The rib-eye steak sandwich is also a good choice.

Dinners feature local, well-prepared seafood at moderate prices and a huge salad bar. All-you-can-eat specials are selected often. There are also plenty of desserts to choose from if you're not already too full. The Dunes serves beer and wine and has a children's menu for small fries. The service is fast and friendly. The Dunes is a nonsmoking establishment. The Dunes serves breakfast and lunch every day year-round. Dinner is served mid- February though November.

Owens' Restaurant $$$
NC 12, MP 16½, Nags Head
(252) 441-7309

The oldest Outer Banks restaurant owned and operated continuously by the same family, Owens' is a local legend. In 2002 this upscale eatery celebrated its 56th anniversary, marking over a half-century of good food and good service.

Clara and Bob Owens first owned a small hot dog stand in Manteo. In 1946 they opened a 50-seat cafe in Nags Head on the deserted strip of sand that's now filled with hotels, rental cottages, and thousands of vacationers who arrive each summer. The Owenses reared their two children, Bobby and Clara Mae, in the restaurant serving breakfast, lunch, and dinner during those early days. Today, Clara Mae and her husband, Lionel, run the family restaurant. R.V., Clara Mae's nephew, owns a restaurant by the same name on the Nags Head–Manteo Causeway. Clara Mae's daughter, Peaches, owns Clara's on the Manteo waterfront. Together, this food-loving family serves some of the best traditional Outer Banks–style seafood on the beach.

Owens' Restaurant now seats more than 200 people and offers only evening meals. More than 90,000 dinners are served from this Beach Road eatery each season. The atmosphere is still homey, yet upscale; the food is still fresh and homemade; and the large lobby overflows with memorabilia of the barrier islands and Owens family heritage. Even the building's architecture is reminiscent of the Outer Banks's past, patterned after an old Nags Head lifesaving station. The menu, however, combines modern tastes with traditional recipes. Owens' renowned Southern Thanksgiving buffet is worth experiencing just to sample the range of delights this restaurant is capable of creating.

Locally caught seafood, often fresh off the boat, is broiled, fried, sauteed, or grilled each evening. Coconut shrimp, "Miss O" crab cakes, and pasta are among the most popular entrees. There's a mixed grill for patrons who prefer prime rib with their fish. Live Maine lobsters, picked from the tank, are steamed just before they're placed on your plate. Homemade soups, including Hatteras-style clam chowder and lobster bisque, are delicious ways to start a meal. All of the homemade desserts are well worth saving room for.

There's a full bar upstairs in the Station Keepers' Lounge where beer, wine, mixed drinks, and special coffee concoctions are available. Light fare is also available upstairs. Owens' is open from mid-March through New Year's Eve. Dinner is served seven days a week. Reservations are not accepted.

Sam & Omie's $$
NC 12, MP 16½, Nags Head
(252) 441-7366

Begun as a place for early morning anglers to indulge in a big breakfast before the Oregon Inlet charter fishing fleet took off, Sam & Omie's is one of the oldest family restaurants on the barrier islands. In fact,

Crab, fresh from the waters of the Outer Banks, is hard to beat. PHOTO: J. AARON TROTMAN

the famed *Lost Colony* production and Sam & Omie's both celebrated their 60th anniversary in 1997. Omie Tillett recently retired his boat, *The Sportsman*, and he long ago sold this little wooden building at Whalebone Junction. The restaurant, however, retains its old beach charm and still serves hearty, homemade food cooked with traditional local recipes for breakfast, lunch, and dinner.

This is a very casual place with wooden booths and tables and a full-service bar. Local fishermen congregate to contemplate the day's catch, and families flock to enjoy the low-priced, filling meals. Photographs of famous Gulf Stream catches line the walls, and the TV usually is tuned in to some exciting sporting event. For breakfast, omelets are our favorite option. We like to make a meal of the rich she-crab soup and red chile poppers for lunch. Salads, sand-

wiches, hamburgers, fish fillets, turkey clubs, and daily specials also are served. A steamer was added recently for healthy steamed vegetables and fish. For dinner, try a soft-shell crab sandwich in season or a prime rib entree on Thursdays. Sam & Omie's is open from early March through November, at least. Call for winter hours.

RV's $$
Nags Head–Manteo Causeway, Nags Head (252) 441-4963

Opened in 1982, RV's is one of the most popular places on the beach for lunch and dinner. Just check the parking lot if you don't believe us. Owner R.V. Owens often stops by your table to greet you, offering his warm smile, a firm handshake, and maybe an opinion or two as an appetizer to an abundant meal. You can eat at the full-service bar in this casual restaurant or sit at a table in one of the sound-front dining rooms. The seafood stew is extremely tasty and filled to overflowing with shrimp and scallops. Marinated tuna is a must for fish lovers. There's also a gazebo raw bar on an attached deck overlooking the water that takes on a life of its own in the evening. Prices here are really reasonable, and the atmosphere is lively and fun. RV's is open from mid-February through Thanksgiving seven days a week.

Tale of the Whale $$
Nags Head–Manteo Causeway, Nags Head
(252) 441-7332
www.taleofthewhalenagshead.com

Family-operated and -owned for more than two decades, Tale of the Whale is situated on the Roanoke Sound. You can enjoy the delightful views either looking through the expansive windows inside while savoring dinner or out on the 75-foot deck and gazebo while sipping a refreshing cocktail. This roomy establishment is bright and airy, with big wooden booths lining the walls. Tables fill out the center of the two dining rooms, and a 40-foot bar is on the north side where diners can watch sunsets and bird life dance on the water.

Tale of the Whale serves a variety of the freshest available food in generous portions. Seafood, lots of pasta, steaks, chicken, and prime rib are staples of the menu. Specials, featuring everything from a mixed grill to broiled shellfish to lobster, are offered daily, and early-bird specials are available from 4:00 to 5:00 P.M. in season. Combination platters can be served fried or broiled. Desserts are homemade and baked on the premises. Tale of the Whale is open daily for dinner from April through November.

Basnight's Lone Cedar Cafe $$
Nags Head–Manteo Causeway, Nags Head
(252) 441-5405

Lone Cedar Cafe opened in the spring of 1996 to serve lunch and dinner with some pretty spectacular waterfront views. The Basnight family of Manteo operates this casual, upscale eatery where diners

wearing everything from shorts to suits are welcome. In fact, it's not unusual to see the president pro tem of the state senate himself, Marc Basnight, talking with guests and removing dinner plates. Checkered green-and-white tablecloths cover every table. You'll notice the hunting motif with duck decoys and fishing memorabilia in honor of the former barrier island hunt club for which the eatery is named.

Appetizers are plentiful, ranging from onion straws to clam chowder, seafood bisque, clam and oyster fritters, hot crab balls, and hot crab dip plus soups and other specials of the day. Lunch entrees start at $3.95 and include sandwiches and fresh local seafood. For dinner try Black Angus beef, homemade pasta, sliced duck breast, fried or broiled seafood, or order any of the evening specials. There's a full bar and an extensive wine list here. Desserts, homebaked daily, include pumpkin and pecan praline cheesecakes; pecan, peanut butter, lemon, or Key lime pie; banana fritters; and 16-layer chocolate cake.

This cafe offers a view of the water from every table and is open for lunch and dinner daily year-round. Vegetarian and children's offerings are available. Reservations are not accepted.

Roanoke Island

Manteo

Hurricane Mo's Restaurant & Raw Bar $$
Pirate's Cove Marina, Manteo–Nags Head
Causeway, Manteo
(252) 473-2266

This restaurant sits high atop Pirate's Cove Marina overlooking the Roanoke Sound. Owners Jeff and Maureen Ashworth, who have been in the restaurant business for more than 20 years, wanted a toned-down, classic feel with an authentic Outer Banks focus. The restaurant serves traditional fresh seafood, steaks, pasta, and some Cajun selections. There are also vegetarian choices and a children's menu as well as a steamed and raw shellfish bar. Beer and wine are served, and the establishment has a brown-bagging license for liquor, which will allow patrons to bring their own.

Inside the restaurant is a collection of mounted gamefish. From the covered outdoor porch, watch the fishing fleet return daily with their Gulf Stream catch, then enjoy dinner before continuing to *The Lost Colony* drama or sights in Manteo. Hurricane Mo's serves lunch and dinner in the summer. Call the number listed for off-season hours.

**The Weeping Radish Brewery &
Bavarian Restaurant $$
US 64, Manteo
(252) 473–1157
www.weepingradish.com**

Next to The Christmas Shop on the main highway in Manteo, this large Bavarian restaurant includes an outdoor beer garden, separate pub, children's playground, and two-story dining room. A European flavor prevails throughout. Traditional German meals include veal, sauerbraten, and a variety of sausages. Homemade noodles, also called spaetzle, and cooked red cabbage are flavorful side dishes offering tastes you won't find elsewhere on the Outer Banks. American and continental cuisine also is available.

The restaurant's name comes from the radish served in Bavaria as an accompaniment to beer. Cut in a spiral, it's sprinkled with salt and packed back together. The salt draws out the moisture and gives the radish the appearance of weeping. Beer isn't served with radishes here (except by special request), but the brews are certainly the best part about this place. A microbrewery opened at The Weeping Radish in 1986 offering pure, fresh, handcrafted German beer without chemical additives or preservatives. You can watch this "nectar of the gods" being brewed on-site. Ask about tours. Take home an extra pint to enjoy later. The Weeping Radish is open for lunch and dinner April through December, seven

days a week. The pub is open into the evening. Call for off-season hours.

**Garden Deli & Pizzeria $
US 64, Manteo
(252) 473–6888**

Shaded by pine trees, this tiny restaurant has a breezy outdoor deck perfect for summer dining. The cheerful, hometown crew has watched this Garden grow into one of the most popular lunch spots for the working crowd in Manteo. Here, New York–style stone-oven pizzas are cooked to order and packaged to go, if you wish. White pizza, one of our favorites, is topped with ricotta, mozzarella, parmesan, and romano cheeses, broccoli, and minced garlic. Traditional red sauce pizzas and specialty pizzas are also offered. The Philly cheese steaks, burgers, gyros, and a wide assortment of deli sandwiches, homemade salads, and antipasto salads are wonderful. Fresh tuna and chicken salad plates are just right for a light lunch or dinner.

Garden Pizzeria offers free delivery to Roanoke Island and Pirate's Cove. The restaurant is open for lunch and dinner Monday through Saturday year-round. Call about delivered boxed lunches for charter boat trips. Garden Deli specializes in party-boat catering.

**Big Al's Soda Fountain & Grill $
US 64, Manteo
(252) 473–5570**

You can't miss Big Al's, across from The Christmas Shop in downtown Manteo. The talk of the town since construction began the winter of 1996–97, locals eagerly awaited the early summer opening of this down-home eatery in the huge brand-new building. Owners Diana Croswait and Vanessa and Allan Foreman were originally planning to open a little ice cream parlor, but the concept expanded into a full-blown soda fountain and family restaurant. It's definitely a place to take the kids. With '50s decor and memorabilia, Big Al's is a great place to kick back and enjoy some good ol' American food and fountain treats. Plus, you can get fish so fresh, it's literally off-the-boat, says Vanessa Foreman. She should know because Allan catches most of it.

Children's meals are available for $3.25. Kids can also check out the game room, with a pinball machine, video games, and a jukebox. There's even a dance floor. Big Al's serves lunch and dinner daily.

Darrell's Restaurant $$
US 64, Manteo
(252) 473-5366

This down-home restaurant started as an ice cream stand more than 30 years ago and has been a favorite family-style eatery for the past two decades. It's common knowledge that the fried oysters at Darrell's are among the best in town. Menu items such as popcorn shrimp, crab cakes, grilled marinated tuna, and fried scallops are teamed with French fries, coleslaw, and hush puppies to provide more than enough to fuel you through the day. Soups such as Dare County–style clam chowder and oyster stew are hard to resist. Salads, sandwiches, and steamed and raw seafood are additional options for the hungry diner. Meat-eaters will be satiated by offerings such as Delmonico steak, barbecued minced pork, and grilled marinated chicken. Daily seafood specials are served for dinner; a children's and light-eater's menu is available. The hot fudge cake is a must for dessert. Beer and wine are served. Darrell's is open for lunch and dinner year-round but is closed Sundays.

Duncan's Bar-B-Q and Family Buffet $
US 64, Manteo
(252) 473-6464

The atmosphere is casual, and the food is spicy at this family-style restaurant known for its North Carolina–style hand-picked barbecue. The all-you-can-eat lunch and dinner buffets include fried chicken, coleslaw, and other vegetables—besides the barbecue, of course. Rose Bay oysters are available in season, and the fried and steamed shrimp on the dinner buffet are great. The ambiance is family

friendly. Eat in or call for take-out. Duncan's also caters off-site pig-pickin' parties and family barbecues. It's open Tuesday through Saturday for lunch and dinner in season. Call for winter hours.

Clara's Seafood Grill $$–$$$
The Waterfront Shops, Manteo
(252) 473-1727

Overlooking Shallowbag Bay and the state ship *Elizabeth II*, this is a favorite Manteo eatery for watching boats on the water or a romantic summer moon. It's a casual, relaxing restaurant with good service and equally admirable food. The dinner menu at Clara's has delicious hot soups, seasonal salads, and a selection of specials. All the dinners are excellent, especially tuna in parchment, prime rib, pan-seared salmon with pinenut pesto and citrus sauce, and an array of traditional fresh seafood. Other favorites include Clara's she-crab soup, Caesar salads, and Asian tuna salad. As a cool alternative on warm summer evenings, Clara's also offers a wide range of pasta dishes, like the hearty seafood puttenesca or pan-seared scallops with wild mushrooms in a rosemary cream sauce.

Historic photos lining the walls will remind you of what Manteo's waterfront looked like in the early days. Since this restaurant is less than a 10-minute drive from *The Lost Colony*, it's a good place to take in an early meal before the outdoor drama begins. Beer, wine, and champagne are available, and brown bagging is allowed. A children's menu is provided. Clara's Seafood Grill serves every night dinner from March through December.

Full Moon Cafe $$
Creef's Corner, Queen Elizabeth Ave., Manteo
(252) 473-MOON

This eclectic eatery opened in late 1995 and consistently overflows with local and visiting patrons. A Manteo favorite for lunch and dinner, this cozy cafe recently changed locations and is now occupying a more visible building on the corner of Queen Elizabeth Avenue and Sir Walter Raleigh Street. This location allows diners a view of the local streetscape, great for people-watchers and those who like being part of the waterfront scene. The innovative cuisine here has a nouveau-American flair. Most of the entrees and specials (which usually involve creative takes on pasta and seafood) are so unusual we haven't seen them anywhere else on the Outer Banks.

Hummus spread, baked Brie, and mushroom caps stuffed with shrimp are succulent appetizers. Lunch specials include gourmet sandwiches to satisfy everyone's tastes, vegetarian offerings, seafood, chicken, and homemade soups, such as Hungarian mushroom, curried spinach, and spicy tomato. Each entree is served with corn chips and Full Moon's own salsa. A separate dinner menu offers enticing seafood dishes, stuffed chicken breasts, roasted eggplant with other vegetables in marinara sauce and provolone cheese, and a beef dish with portobello mushrooms and a gorgonzola cheese sauce. Daily pasta specials are also available as a half-serving with a side salad. All the desserts are delightful. Beer (including some microbrews) and a good selection of wines are available. You can eat inside the dining room or dine outdoors in the courtyard if you take any meal to go. Reservations are accepted for parties of six or more.

Full Moon is open for lunch and dinner seven days a week in summer. Hours reduced off-season, so call for specific schedules.

Poor Richard's Sandwich Shop
$, no credit cards
The Waterfront, Manteo
(252) 473-3333

One of Manteo's favorite downtown eateries, Poor Richard's changed ownership in 1998. Owner Tod Clissold has not altered the easy charm and delicious food at this waterfront establishment. With half the workforce in Manteo making a beeline to Poor Richard's every day, this casual eatery is a local gathering spot for reasonably priced food with fast counter service and interesting offerings. Try the cucumber sandwich with cream cheese—a cool meal that surprises your palate. Cold and grilled sandwiches are made to order, and specials are offered daily. Homemade soups, meatless chili, hot dogs, salad plates, cookies, and ice cream are also available. Breakfast includes scrambled egg and bacon sandwiches, bagels and cream cheese, and fresh fruit. Steamed shrimp is available for lunch and dinner.

Whatever your mode of transportation—boat, bike, car, or legs—Poor Richard's is a worthy fueling station. You can eat inside at a roomy booth or take your meal out on the back porch and enjoy the waterfront view—there always seems to be enough room for everybody. Poor Richard's is open daily in the summer for breakfast, lunch, and dinner. Though it's open year-round, call for off-season hours.

1587 $$$
Tranquil House Inn, Queen Elizabeth St., Manteo
(252) 473-1587
www.1587.com

The owner of this critically acclaimed restaurant can make your mouth water just by reading his menu aloud. The offerings are unusual, upscale, cosmopolitan,

and some of the most ambitious of any
Outer Banks establishment. Ambiance is
elegant and romantic: the soft glow of intimate lighting, a gleaming copper-topped
bar in a separate lounge area, and polished
wood and mirrors that reflect the lights
sparkling off boats anchored in Shallowbag Bay. Executive Chef Donny King creates a constantly changing menu that's
always as fresh and fabulous as the food.

Homemade soups prepared each day
might include Mediterranean mussels
and crayfish with spring vegetables and
feta cheese in a light tomato broth. For
appetizers, select sesame-encrusted colossal scallops with spicy vegetable slaw, and
soy-wasabi cream or grilled portobello
mushroom on a zucchini podium with
balsamic-sautéed julienne vegetables.
Salads, served à la carte, offer Boston
bibb, romaine, and baby lettuce leaves
complete with spring vegetables and
herb-shallot vinaigrette.

Dinner entrees, each an artistic masterpiece, range from crispy cornmeal rockfish with Louisiana-style crayfish butter
sauce and chile-fried rice to an ocean
panache of tiger prawns, mussels, scallops,
and fish tossed with vegetables and orzo
pasta, finished with feta cheese. Another
excellent choice is grilled filet mignon
fanned with roasted garlic mashed pota-

toes and a wild mushroom, goat cheese,
and Cabernet ragout.

A children's menu offers simpler dishes
for younger tastes. Vegetarian requests are
welcome. The exquisite dessert creations
are well worth saving room for and are so
beautiful that you may want to take a snap-
shot before digging in!

Named for the first year English
colonists attempted to settle on Roanoke
Island, 1587 serves a wide selection of wine
and beer and permits brown bagging. This
outstanding restaurant is open for dinner
daily in the summer. Call for off-season
hours. Reservations are requested.

Magnolia Grille $
Magnolia Market, 408 Queen Elizabeth Ave., Manteo
(252) 475-9877

Magnolia Grille is a counter-service grill
serving up a variety of good eats. Hot
dogs, burgers, deli sandwiches, several vegetarian options, quesadillas, and daily specials are prepared as ordered. Appetizers
include chili cheese fries, onion rings, and
soups. The salads, with grilled chicken if
you like, are fresh. Kids can get grilled
cheese and other favorites. Order from the
counter, then eat at one of the few tables
or at a picnic table in the yard. If you're
headed to Roanoke Island Festival Park
for Summer Scenes concerts, this is a great
place to pick up a picnic on the way.

The Green Dolphin Restaurant and Pub $
Sir Walter Raleigh St., Manteo
(252) 473-5911

This downtown Manteo eatery has been
a popular pub for more than 20 years.
It's casual and comfortable inside, with
wooden booths and tables fashioned
from the hatch covers taken off old
ships. This storied pub suffered serious
smoke and water damage in a late summer fire in 1997, but the owners have the
Dolphin back in the swim of things,
complete with a new kitchen and remodeled bathrooms. Much of the same old
nautical memorabilia lines the walls, and
a long bar still stretches along the back
of the restaurant.

Food here is simple, satisfying, and a good value. Charbroiled hamburgers, she-crab soup (some say it's the best on the Outer Banks), crab cakes, lasagna, manicotti, Italian sausage, and French fries are just a few of the offerings served for lunch and dinner. Appetizers and desserts also are available, and the pub serves pizzas and small-fry portions for the kids. The Green Dolphin is open year-round daily except Sundays. Live entertainment is usually offered Fridays (see Nightlife).

The Coffeehouse on Roanoke Island $
106-A Sir Walter Raleigh St., Manteo
(252) 475-1295

Here is the perfect coffeehouse atmosphere: sofas, newspapers, local chatter, tables inside or on the deck, and a friendly owner who handles the busiest of morning rushes with aplomb. The coffee is just right, not overly strong, and the espresso and cappuccino drinks are expertly prepared. A selection of loose teas is available. Iced coffees are good for summer days, and there's a Chai milkshake that beats everything. Milkshakes and smoothies are large, and they'll give you the leftovers if they make one that's too big for your cup. For eats, The Coffeehouse serves heavenly cinnamon oat and blueberry scones, muffins, bagels, cinnamon bread, pastries, biscotti, granola, and fruit. You can have your granola with soy milk or yogurt, if you'd like. The Coffeehouse is open every day for breakfast, light lunches, and snacks.

Wanchese

Queen Anne's Revenge $$
Old Wharf Rd., Wanchese
(252) 473-5466

Named after one of Blackbeard's famous pirate ships that plied the waters off North Carolina's coast during the early 1700s, Queen Anne's Revenge is snuggled in a grove of trees in the scenic fishing village of Wanchese. The restaurant is well off the beaten path at the end of a winding lane. Wayne and Nancy Gray have operated this outstanding restaurant since 1978, serving seafood fresh from the Wanchese docks. They use only quality ingredients, and their attention to detail really shows.

The restaurant has three dining rooms, one with a fireplace that provides a cozy ambiance during cold winter months. A large selection of appetizers is offered, including bouillabaisse (full of fresh seafood) and black bean and she-crab soups. All the seafood here is excellent, from Blackbeard's Raving to the locally landed shellfish and fish served with the Wanchese platter. There's even Chateaubriand for two, carved at your table. Queen Anne's chefs make their own pasta; in fact, their fettuccine is a staple around Wanchese. All the desserts are homemade and served in generous portions. This lovely restaurant offers a children's menu and a nice selection of beer and wine. The dining room serves dinner seven days a week during the summer months. Enjoy the Sunday lunch buffet from January through May. Queen Anne's is open all year and is closed Tuesdays during the off-season.

Fisherman's Wharf $$
NC 345, Wanchese
(252) 473-5205

Overlooking the docks of this historical fishing village, the dining room of this family-owned restaurant offers the best views around of the Outer Banks's commercial fishing fleet. Windows form an entire wall of the dining room; chances are that the same seafood you watch being unloaded this afternoon may just be what you're served tonight. The fish here is as fresh and local as it gets.

The Daniels family of Wanchese fishing history fame opens this restaurant for lunch and dinner from late March through November. Seafood plates complete with homemade hush puppies and good coleslaw are the best selections from a variety of items on the menu. There's a grill, and landlubbers can order pasta and chicken entrees. You'll want to

save room for the homemade desserts. This is a casual eatery where families feel right at home. It is wheelchair accessible. A children's menu is available. Fisherman's Wharf is closed on Sunday. Call for off-season hours.

Hatteras Island

Rodanthe, Waves, and Salvo

Lisa's Pizza $
NC 12, Rodanthe
(252) 987–2525

Specialty pizzas, deli sandwiches, subs, calzone, chicken parmesan, and salads are among the most popular items at this 17-year-old restaurant. Lisa's also serves breadsticks, hot wings, and garlic and cheese bread. Beer and wine are available. There's also a separate children's menu. Lisa's offers lunch and dinner seven days a week beginning at 11:00 A.M. from early April through November. All items can be eaten inside the restaurant, carried out, or delivered. Call for off-season hours.

Down Under Restaurant & Lounge $$
NC 12, Rodanthe
(252) 987–2277

This Australian-style restaurant used to be at the Rodanthe Pier, but due to pier damage by hurricanes Irene, Floyd, and Dennis, the restaurant was moved to safer quarters, offering wonderful views of the sound. In its new site, the restaurant faces west and the bar faces east. Decorated with authentic Australian art and memorabilia, Down Under is one-of-a-kind on the Outer Banks. Lunch specialties include the Great Australian bite, similar to an Aussie burger, made with hamburger, a fried egg, grilled onions, cheese, and bacon. Spicy fish burgers, Vegemite sandwiches, and marinated chicken sandwiches are good authentic options too. Kangaroo, a delicious meat that is very popular at Down Under, is imported from Australia for 'roo stew, 'roo burgers, and kangaroo curry. And you've got to try stuffed jalapeños served with Down Under's famous sweet chile sauce.

Dinner selections include Down Under shrimp stuffed with jalapeño peppers and cream cheese wrapped in bacon.

We also enjoy a side order of the foot-high onion rings and a Foster's lager or Cooper's Stout. Parents will appreciate the children's menu, and kids will appreciate the extraordinary decor. Everyone will enjoy the view. Down Under is open seven days a week for lunch and dinner from April through October. The restaurant is wheelchair accessible.

Getaways Restaurant and Lounge $–$$
NC 12, Rodanthe
(252) 987–1243

Getaways offers soundfront dining for breakfast, lunch, and dinner. The food is simple and good, and the atmosphere is family friendly. Breakfast favorites include a wide range of omelets, eggs benedict, French toasts, rib-eye steak, and corned beef hash, served with home fries, grits, baked apples, or toast. For lunch there are sandwiches, including crab cake and club sandwiches, burgers, subs, seafood, and pasta. The Getaways Wraps, in a soft roll of bread, are popular. For dinner, select from prime rib, steaks, broiled or fried seafood platters, or pasta. Be sure to try the stuffed mushroom appetizer, overstuffed with crabmeat filling and baked. Yum. The blackened dishes are favorites. Wine and beer, including microbrews, are served. Getaways serves three meals a day year-round.

> ## Insiders' Tip
> If you're going to watch the entertainment under the stars at Illuminations Summer Arts Series at Roanoke Island Festival Park, Manteo restaurants and caterers will provide boxed picnics to take with you. Call Festival Park at (252) 475-1500 for information.

Top Dog Cafe $
NC 12, Waves
(252) 987–1272

Specializing in old-fashioned all-beef burgers that weigh up to one-and-a-half pounds, Top Dog Cafe also serves steamed seafood, Philly-style steak subs, shrimp and oyster baskets, all-beef hot dogs, salads, and appetizers. The restaurant has a casual atmosphere, and you can choose to eat on the shady screened porch or on the sound-view sundeck. Take-out is available, and there's a kids' menu too. Beer and wine are served. Open for lunch and dinner; call for hours and days.

Avon

Dirty Dicks Crab House $–$$
NC 12, Avon
(252) 995–3708
www.dirtydickscrabs.com

Right beside the Avon Pier, Dirty Dicks serves an incomparable selection of crabs. Snow crab legs, soft-shell crabs, spiced crabs, crab dip, crab cakes, and steamed crabs. The steamed, spiced crabs are superb, and Dicks offers its special spice for sale. The menu also includes steamed shrimp, clams, clam chowder, gumbo, jambalaya, and Cajun and Creole dishes. There are sandwich platter specials and offerings for the kids. The tasty Dick Burger is a crab and shrimp patty with Cajun sauce. Dirty Dicks T-shirts are popular for their suggestiveness, and you can buy them here. You can order any of the menu items and steamed crabs for take-out. Dirty Dicks has two other locations in Kill Devil Hills, one a sit-down affair like this one and the other for take-out only. Dirty Dicks is open for lunch and dinner in season and closes for a couple of months in the winter. Call for off-season hours.

Hodad's $–$$
NC 12, Avon
(252) 995–7866

This casual restaurant with surfboards, surfer pics, and a Dewey Webber board out front is the perfect place to have a good, filling meal without having to worry about changing out of your swim trunks and T-shirt. It is a great place to hang around the bar and shoot the breeze or to sit at a table with a group of friends. The list of appetizers is extensive. Fried pickles with horseradish sauce, anyone? If that's not your style, try the oven-baked Brie, shrimp roll-ups, conch fritters, hummus, rumaki, jalapeño poppers, or the Mondo Combo with a little taste of several things, including the pickles. Burgers, veggie burgers, crab cake sandwiches, fish sandwiches, and a Portobello sandwich are favorites here, but there's also a lighter side of offerings, including Hatteras clam chowder, a Caesar salad, a spinach salad, and a warm garlic shrimp salad. After 5:00 P.M. dinner-style entrees are offered. Try the flash-fried oysters, catch of the day, prime rib, or creative pasta dishes. Vegetarians will appreciate the Buddha Delight, stir-fried veggies and tofu over rice. If you've worked up a killer appetite on the waves, you might be able to tackle the Duke Seafood Combo, the size of the Pipeline with shrimp, scallops, crab cake, catch of the day, oysters, calamari...broiled or fried, if you dare. Beer and wine are served. Hodad's serves lunch and dinner every day from St. Patrick's Day through Thanksgiving.

The Mad Crabber Restaurant & Shellfish Bar $$
NC 12, Avon
(252) 995-5959

This lively place offers dinner nightly from April through November. It's not a fancy restaurant, but you'll find good, fresh seafood here and reasonable prices. It's a recipe for success that keeps people coming back—during summer the Mad Crabber usually is extremely busy. Steamed crabs and shrimp lead the way on the menu. Locally caught blue crabs, snow crabs, Dungeness crabs from the Pacific Northwest, and Alaskan king crabs also are on hand. Of course, delicious crab cakes are the specialty.

If you're not feeling "crabby," try a pasta dish, the vegetarian platter, or—for meat lovers—a thick burger or juicy steak. And you must try the famous "mad platters," a pizza pie plate overflowing with crab legs, shrimp, oysters, crawdads, clams, scallops, mussels, and, if requested, blue crab. All-you-can-eat specials are served on "Fat Tuesdays," along with $1.00 draft beers. Wine also is available. There's a special menu just for kids. A separate game room attached to the Mad Crabber has two pool tables and video games. Mad Crabber serves dinner and late-night snacks from 5:00 P.M. until midnight in season.

Buxton

Cape Sandwich Company $
NC 12, Buxton
(252) 995-6140

A popular spot with both tourists and locals, Cape Sandwich Company serves breakfast and lunch. The restaurant was recently moved to a new location on NC 12, next to the lighthouse entrance. Owners Bryan and Sylvia Mattingly have served a consistently good array of homemade soups, salads, subs and sandwiches, daily specials, and enticing desserts since 1993. Imported beer, gourmet coffees, and cappuccino are available, as are picnic items for the beach. Cape Sandwich Company serves breakfast and lunch all year, from 7:00 A.M. to 5:00 P.M. Breakfast is served all day.

Diamond Shoals Restaurant $$
NC 12, Buxton
(252) 995-5217

The parking lot at this eatery, which is within walking distance of several Buxton motels, always seems to be crowded around breakfast time. Here you'll find one of the best breakfasts on Hatteras Island, featuring all your early morning favorites. Diamond Shoals is closed for lunch; dinner offerings include plenty of local seafood choices, featuring fried and broiled seafood, a salad bar, and some good nightly specials. Steaks and other landlubber specials are also available.

Check out the remarkable 200-gallon saltwater aquarium stocked with tropical and Gulf Stream sea life. Diners can get an up-close-and-personal look at corals, anemones, and a variety of fascinating marine creatures. Diamond Shoals serves breakfast and dinner from March through December.

Tides Restaurant $$
NC 12, Buxton
(252) 995–5988

The driveway for this family-style restaurant is just south of the entrance to the Cape Hatteras Lighthouse, on the sound side. Traditional breakfasts are served here, with tasty homemade biscuits, omelets, and blueberry and pecan pancakes. Dinner selections include a fresh catch of the day, steaks, chicken, and ham. Try the chef's special shrimp gumbo. The stuffed potatoes are super. All the portions here are large, and the service is attentive. Beer and wine are available; brown bagging is allowed. This restaurant is open daily from Easter through Thanksgiving. Breakfast is served from 6:00 to 11:30 A.M. and dinner is served from 5:30 to 9:30 P.M.

Labrador Oceanic Bistro $$$
NC 12, Buxton
(252) 995–3348

The Labrador Oceanic Bistro is the place to come for a special dinner. The decor is warm and inviting, with purple carpeting and lavender ceilings playing up the natural light provided through lots of windows. With a focus on upscale New American cuisine on a seasonal menu, the restaurant offers fresh fish, beef, pork, chicken, pasta, and vegetarian entrees. A wide variety of microbrews and beers on tap is available, and there's an extensive wine list. Homemade desserts top it all off. A nonsmoking section is provided. Labrador Oceanic Bistro is open for dinner daily. The restaurant is closed for the month of December.

Orange Blossom Cafe and Bakery
$$, no credit cards
NC 12, Buxton
(252) 995–4109

The Orange Blossom starts the day offering an array of baked goods for breakfast and keeps serving until mid-afternoon. The famous Apple Uglies—huge apple fritter-style pastries piled high with fruit—are our favorite early morning treats. The sandwiches made with thick, homemade Italian bread always are a good bet. This little spot also caters to vegetarians, serving a wide selection of meatless salads, sandwiches, and entrees. This restaurant is open year-round, except for a spell during the winter, for take-out or eat-in. The bakery opens at 7:00 A.M. Monday through Saturday. Lunch at the Orange Blossom Cafe is served 11:30 A.M. to 1:30 P.M., Tuesday through Saturday.

Fish House Restaurant $$
NC 12, Buxton
(252) 995–5151

Can you tell this always-bustling eatery occupies a former fish house? If the simple wooden architecture and wharf-front location didn't give it away, you might notice something fishy when you glimpse down and see the slanted concrete floors sloped for easy washing so the fish scales could flow back into the sound. The Fish House is now a down-home restaurant where everything is casual and easygoing. Overlooking Buxton Harbor, it serves some of the best Outer Banks seafood prepared with traditional, local recipes. The tilefish is a popular choice, and we highly recommend the homemade crab cakes. All the seafood is fresh. Each entree comes with your choice of vegetables and hush puppies. Everything is served on disposable plates with plastic utensils. Beer and wine are served. It is open for lunch and for dinner daily from March through Thanksgiving.

The Pilot House $$$
NC 12, Buxton
(252) 995–5664

Set well off the road to capture spectacular, panoramic views of the sky, water, and sinking sun, The Pilot House offers soundside dining amid a decor that's unobtrusively nautical. The Captain's Lounge serves beer and wine, and if you bring your own liquor, they'll provide the setups. The Pilot House is a popular place, so you may have to wait for a table. But, believe me, you won't mind waiting when you see the view and the enormous outdoor porches where you can plop down in an Adirondack chair with a cool beverage. With this kind of view and the freshest seafood, this is the kind of dining experience you'd expect on Hatteras Island. Under new management, The Pilot House serves fresh local seafood, steaks and beef entrees, pastas, and vegetarian dishes. Nightly specials are offered. Don't pass up the opportunity to try the seafood bisque or one of the delectable desserts. The Pilot House serves only dinner seven days a week, from mid-April through late fall. Call for hours.

Frisco

Quarterdeck Restaurant $$
NC 12, Frisco
(252) 986–2425

Fresh, local seafood served broiled or fried, crab cakes packed with jumbo lump meat, and Hatteras or New England clam chowder are among the most popular offerings here. Crab puffs and stuffed flounder are house specialties. The Quarterdeck also has an 18-item salad bar and gives a discount to all diners who eat between 5:00 and 6:00 P.M. For dessert, the coconut cream, lemon meringue, and Key lime pies are delicious. Beer and wine are available, as is a children's menu. This low-key spot occupies a 70-year-old building that housed Hatteras Island's original bar. For more than 20 years, the same family has owned and operated the Quarterdeck, which is open for lunch and dinner daily (except on Saturdays, when they are not open for lunch) from mid-March through late November.

Gingerbread House Bakery
$, no credit cards
NC 12, Frisco
(252) 995–5204

From this tiny cottage flanked by gingerbread-style fencing, breakfast and dinner are served Tuesday through Sunday every week in season. To start the day, sample egg biscuits, French toast, omelets, or waffles. If you'd rather indulge yourself in delicious baked goods, try a frosted donut, cookie, or still-steaming bagel. By early evening, you can order a gourmet pizza made on the bakery's own homemade dough. Crusts range in thickness from hand-tossed to pan depth and are offered in white and whole wheat varieties. A whopping 30 toppings to choose from should satisfy virtually any craving. And a salad will round out your meal. Ice cream, brownies, and sweet breads all are great dessert options. You can eat inside this low-key little house or get your pizza and sweets to go. During the summer, the Gingerbread House also delivers from Buxton to Hatteras Village. And its bakers make super specialty cakes on a day's notice for any occasion. Call the number listed for off-season hours.

The South Shore Grill $
NC 12, Frisco
(252) 995–5535

Formerly the Frisco Sandwich Shop, the new owners of this casual eatery maintain the same quality and good food that hungry patrons depended on for more than 20 years at this favorite Hatteras Island establishment. The full range of popular appetizers and side dishes are offered. Fresh local seafood, steamed shellfish, certified Angus beef, chargrilled steaks, and daily specials are among the offerings. Vegetarian sandwiches are also on the menu, as is fresh local seafood. Comfortable and unassuming, South Shore Grill is a perfect place to stop on your way home from the beach. Beer is available. The restaurant is open Monday through Saturday for lunch and dinner through the summer; call the number listed for winter hours.

Bubba's Bar-B-Q $
NC 12, Frisco
(252) 995–5421

If you're in the mood for some genuine Carolina barbecue, you won't be able to miss Bubba's—just follow your nose to this famous roadside joint. The hickory fires start early here so the pork, chicken, beef, ribs, and turkey can cook slowly over an open pit. The late Larry "Bubba" Schauer and his wife Julie brought their secret recipe from West Virginia to Hatteras Island more than a decade ago—and the food has been drawing locals and tourists to their eatery ever since. Homemade coleslaw, baked beans, French fries, and cornbread round out the meal—and diners' bellies.

The homemade sweet potato and coconut custard pies, cobblers, and other desserts are delectable. Mrs. Bubba's Double Devil Chocolate Cake is approaching celebrity status. Bubba's has a children's menu and a nice selection of beer and soft drinks. All items are available for eating in or taking out. Bubba's Sauce is now a hot commodity with barbecue fans and is sold at retail and specialty shops across the Outer Banks. Bubba's is open daily for lunch and dinner from 11:00 A.M. to 9:00 P.M. during the summer. Call the number listed for winter hours. You'll find a second Bubba's, Bubba's Too, farther north on NC 12 in Avon, next to the Food Lion, (252) 995–4385.

Hatteras Village

Taste Buds Bakery & Deli $
NC 12, Hatteras Village
(252) 986-2500

Open for breakfast and lunch Monday through Saturday, Taste Buds serves a variety of fresh-baked items, including danish, muffins, donuts, bagels, fritters, and other pastries. It's a great place to stop in for salads, made-to-order breakfast and lunch sandwiches, or for fresh-baked bread, meats, and cheeses. Gourmet coffee is sold by the pound. There's also an Avon location; call (252) 995–3900.

The Channel Bass $$
NC 12, Hatteras Village
(252) 986-2250

Owned by the Harrison family, which is well known for its fishing heritage, this canal-side restaurant has been a Hatteras Village institution for more than 30 years. You'll notice all of Mrs. Shelby Harrison's fishing trophies in the foyer. The Channel Bass has one of the largest menus on the beach, loaded with seafood platters, crab imperial, crab cakes, veal, and charbroiled steaks that the chefs cut in house. The seafood is deep-sea and sound-caught. An old family recipe is used for the hush puppies, and all the salad dressings are homemade. Make sure you try the homemade Key lime pie. A private dining room is available, and large groups are welcome. The Channel Bass has early-bird discounts and different dinner specials every night. Beer and wine are served; brown bagging is allowed. A children's menu is available. The Channel Bass serves dinner seven days a week from Easter through Thanksgiving.

Harbor Seafood Deli $
NC 12, Hatteras Village
(252) 986-2331

Harbor Seafood Deli serves breakfast and lunch, including daily seafood specials, homemade pasta, scallop burgers, seafood salad, and a wonderful shrimp pasta salad. Homemade desserts are delicious and can be enjoyed on the enclosed porch (which gets very busy in the late afternoons when charter boats return to the adjacent marina). Steamed shrimp and other munchies are available during the late afternoon hours and hand-dipped Breyer's ice cream is a favorite dessert to sample while sitting in the hot sun. Beer and wine are also available at Harbor Seafood Deli.

One of the best aspects of this deli is that the owners will prepack breakfasts and lunches that you can pick up to take on a charter fishing trip. Just call in the afternoon or early evening before you're scheduled to depart and a hearty meal will be ready to go, probably even before you are. The deli opens at 5:30 A.M. daily and serves lunch until 6:00 P.M. Call the number listed for off-season hours.

Breakwater Island Restaurant $$
NC 12 at Oden's Dock, Hatteras Village
(252) 986–2733
www.breakwaterrest.com

If dining in a comfortable atmosphere with a stunning view of Pamlico Sound or relaxing with some live music on a deck at sunset sounds good, then this restaurant is the place for you. Here, a second-story dining room, deck, and bar overlook a small harbor and stone breakwater, providing a unique feel to this locally loved outpost.

The dinner menu features fresh, innovative seafood dishes, prime rib, veal, and pasta, all served in generous portions. Entrees are accompanied by a selection of vegetables, salad, and fresh-baked breads. Live entertainment is performed atop the deck on select evenings in summer. Dinner is served seven days a week during the season. A good selection of beer and wine is available, and brown bagging is allowed. Children's items are also offered. Check for winter hours.

Sonny's Restaurant $$
NC 12, Hatteras Village
(252) 986–2922

This casual, family-run eatery has served breakfast and dinner in Hatteras Village since 1976. Breakfast begins at 6:00 A.M. for the fishing crowd and includes hash browns, grits, sausage gravy, Western omelets, ham and cheese omelets, and hotcakes—just a few of Sonny's specialties. There's a seafood buffet each evening, with an 18-item salad bar, breads, crabmeat bisque, soft-shell crabs in season, sea scallops, popcorn and regular shrimp, prime rib, clams, oysters, macaroni and cheese, fettuccine alfredo, and desserts such as carrot and chocolate cake, rice pudding, and a soft-serve ice-cream bar. Salad bar, soup, and dessert are all included in the price. Regular menu items range from steaks to seafood to

pasta. Alcoholic beverages aren't served here, but you're welcome to bring your own. Sonny even will provide frosty beer mugs and wine glasses for you. Senior citizen and children's menus are offered. Reservations are accepted for large parties. Breakfast is served from 6:00 to 11:00 A.M., and dinner from 5:00 to 9:00 P.M. The restaurant is open year-round.

Sandbar & Grille $
NC 12, Hatteras Village
(252) 986–2044

The Sandbar & Grille is a popular Hatteras Village hangout. It's got a casual, college-bar–type atmosphere, with loud music, a long bar, a TV, neon beer signs, and low lighting. The Sandbar serves an array of appetizers, including nachos, jalapeño poppers, fried calamari, and steamed shrimp and clams. Soups, salads, fish sandwiches, burgers, Reubens, and other sandwiches make good lunch offerings, and there are also entrees, including linguine with little-neck clams, baby back ribs, veggie pasta, prime rib, and a rib eye. An early-bird menu is served from 5:00 to 6:00 P.M. The Sandbar often has live entertainment (see our Nightlife chapter).

Fish Tales $
NC 12, Hatteras Village
(252) 986–6516

Right next to the Sandbar in a jolly pink building, Fish Tales offers breakfast, lunch, and dinner daily in a friendly family-style atmosphere. The breakfasts are killer, with omelets, eggs, meats, Spanish home fries covered with cheese and salsa, and French toast. The pancake flavors will astound you: bacon, banana, blueberry, coconut, Carolina pecan, corn, chocolate chip, strawberry, and apple. There are even silver-dollar–size pancakes.

For lunch, Fish Tales serves appetizers, chili, salads, seafood salad, burgers, chicken and seafood sandwiches, subs, and more pancakes. For dinner, there are more appetizers, soups, salads, seafood platters, and landlubber dishes like steak, pork, chicken, and spaghetti. All entrees are served with hot rolls and butter and your choice of two vegetables. Seniors save $2.00 on all entrees, and there is a kids' menu. Fish Tales's food is well prepared, and the owners pay careful attention to customer satisfaction. They serve all three meals every day.

Austin Creek Grill $$
NC 12, Hatteras Landing
(252) 986–1511

Austin Creek Grill brings something unexpected to southern Hatteras Island: contemporary, artful Southern cuisine. This waterfront bistro opened at Hatteras Landing in February 2000, right on the docks with an awesome view of the fleet and the harbor. Executive chef Ed Daggers is a graduate of the Culinary Institute of America and has won numerous awards for his accomplished cooking skills. Before coming to Hatteras he was executive chef at some of the finest resorts, hotels, and clubs on the Eastern seaboard, including Sheraton Norfolk Waterside Hotel and Kingsmill in Williamsburg.

Daggers uses the bounty of the sea and region to create incomparable dishes you won't soon forget. For an appetizer, try a baby spinach, apple, and poached pear salad with caramelized pecans, red onion, Maytag blue, and warm bacon dressing. Or how about starting with pumpkin crab bisque? Entrees include such combinations as veal chop au poivre on Locatelli Romano risotto with fresh basil and garlic-sautéed spinach; Carolina chicken and dumplings with onion pan gravy and a puff pastry dome; or tortilla-crusted rockfish on sweet corn jalapeño sauce with fresh salsa and Spanish rice. They'll even cook your freshly caught fish for a fee if you bring it in. Dessert is worth saving room for. Some selections include white chocolate praline cheesecake with vanilla and caramel sauces, pecan apple cake with maple whipped cream and cinnamon Anglaise, and a double chocolate brownie torte with raspberry and chocolate sauces. All dishes are a work of art. The wine list has been carefully selected to accompany the meals, and beer is available as well.

Austin Creek Grill's atmosphere synchronizes well with the fare—it's lively and contemporary in a coastal way. Windows open up to spectacular water views, and nostalgic wall treatments, interior windows, blond woods, and sea blues give the feeling of dining in a well-heeled Martha's Vineyard cottage. Austin Creek Grill prepares lunches for charter boats if you call a day ahead. This restaurant is open for dinner Monday through Saturday. Call ahead in the off-season.

Ocracoke Island

The Fig Tree $
NC 12, Ocracoke Village
(252) 928–4554

The Fig Tree, a tiny delicatessen, offers both eat-in and carry-out cuisine. A variety of breakfast sandwiches, baked goods, specials, and a lunch menu are offered daily. The Fig Tree will pack picnics for ferry boat rides, fishing trips, and beach outings. Their spicy blue cheese coleslaw and sunflower seed bread are both out of this world. Veggie pockets here are stuffed to overflowing with lettuce, tomatoes, cucumbers, carrots, mushrooms, sprouts, and feta cheese and topped with a choice of homemade dressing. Shrimp and tuna salad are made with just-off-the-boat seafood. You can also design your own sandwich from numerous selections of meats and cheeses to be served on bakery-fresh bread, a hearty bagel, or inside a pita. Baked delights include jumbo cinnamon rolls, doughnuts, fruit and nut breads, breakfast biscuits, and gourmet cookies. Heavier dessert items, which are also outstanding, range from chocolate swirl cheesecake atop brownie crumb crust to Ocracoke's own fig cake. Both are available whole or by the slice. The Fig Tree also makes a traditional tomato sauce and cheese pizza, a white garden pizza, and a Greek tomato pie, all with homemade crusts. The Fig Tree is open from March through November.

Jason's Restaurant $
NC 12, Ocracoke Village
(252) 928–3434

On the north end of the village right as you come into town, Jason's has a casual, come-as-you-are atmosphere that welcomes islanders and vacationers alike. You can sit outside on the spacious screened porch or hang at the bar and watch the chefs at work. Standouts on the menu are pizzas and Italian specialties, including lasagna and vegetarian lasagna, spaghetti with meatballs, chicken parmesan, and fettuccine Alfredo. There's also a good selection of salads, sandwiches, and subs, plus dinner entrees such as New York strip, Jamaican jerk chicken, and seafood. If you just want a few munchies to get you by, try an appetizer. We liked the spinach and artichoke dip and shrimp quesadillas. To wash it down, choose from a wide variety of beers, including several on tap, and wines. Sushi is served here on Tuesday nights. Carry-out of all menu items is available. Lunch and dinner are served daily year-round.

Smacnally's Raw Bar and Grill $–$$
On Silver Lake, NC 12, Ocracoke Village
(252) 928–9999

Smacnally's is the coolest new gathering spot on the island. It's an outdoor establishment, right on the docks, with the smell of salt and fresh-caught fish coming off the water and the charter boats tied up practically to the bar. Fishermen walk off the boats and have a beer in their hand before they can say "Budwei . . . ." Patrons hang around the raw bar and at tables on the dock. Smacnally's claims to serve the coldest beer on the island. The raw bar serves fresh local seafood, including oysters, clams, and shrimp. This is also a grill serving burgers and the like. Lunch and dinner are served daily in the warm season, through November. The bar stays open until midnight. It's closed in the colder months. Steamed seafood buckets and boxed lunches are sold to go. Smacnally's is smack in the middle of the village action, at the Anchorage Inn Marina.

Pony Island Restaurant $$
NC 12, Ocracoke Village
(252) 928–5701

A casual, homey place that lots of people have come back to time and again since 1960, this restaurant features big breakfasts of biscuits, hotcakes, omelets, and the famous Pony Potatoes—hash browns covered with cheese, sour cream, and salsa. Dinner entrees include a variety of interesting fresh local seafood creations, pastas, steaks, and salads. They'll even cook your own catch of the day for you, as long as you've cleaned the fish first. Beer and wine are served, and homemade desserts add a great finishing touch to a tasty meal. The Pony Island Restaurant is adjacent to the Pony Island Motel. Breakfast is served from 7:00 to 11:00 A.M. The restaurant closes during lunchtime then reopens nightly for dinner from late March through November. Take-out orders are welcomed.

The Back Porch $$$
1324 Country Rd., Ocracoke Village
(252) 928–6401

Whether you dine on the wide screened-in porch or eat in the small nooks or open dining room of this well-respected restaurant, you'll find that dinners at The Back Porch are some of the most pleasant experiences on the Outer Banks. This older building was renovated and refurbished to blend with the many trees on the property. It's off the main road, surrounded by waist-high cacti, and is a quiet place to enjoy appealing entrees and comfortable conversation. Overall, it's one of our favorite restaurants on the 120-mile stretch of barrier islands. It's well worth the two-hour trip from Nags Head and the free ferry ride, just to eat here.

Advertising "original dishes with a personal touch," the menu is loaded with fresh vegetables and local seafood and changes seasonally to offer the freshest ingredients. All sauces, dressings, breads, and desserts are made right in the restaurant's huge kitchen. And each piece of meat is hand-cut. In addition to the quality ingredients, the chefs come up with some pretty outrageous taste combinations, and all of them seem to blend perfectly. The crab cakes with red pepper sauce are outstanding. And you won't want to miss the smoked bluefish or crab beignet appetizers. Non-seafood dishes are a tasty option as well. The Cuban black bean and Monterey jack cheese casserole is a perennial favorite.

Reduced prices and smaller portions are available. All the desserts are divine. Freshly ground coffee is served here, and the wine selections and imported beers are as ambitious as the menu. If you get hooked—like we are—you can try your hand at some of the restaurant's recipes at home after buying a *Back Porch Cookbook*. After reading the recipes you'll be even more impressed with the upscale culinary concoctions served in this laid-back island eatery. Dinner is offered nightly in season. Call for off-season hours.

The Back Porch Lunchbox, next to the Pony Island Motel, offers homemade bag lunches or picnics for the beach or ferry. Sandwiches, cold steamed shrimp, baked goods, drinks, and fruit are available. Call (252) 928–3651.

Thai Moon $
Spencer's Market, NC 12, Ocracoke Village
(252) 928–5100

Here's something new on Ocracoke Island: ethnic food, which can be a refreshing change of pace on the Outer Banks. Thai Moon offers authentic Thai specialties for carry-out only. You have to whet your appetite with Tom Yum Goong, hot and sour shrimp soup with lemongrass, straw mushrooms, Thai chili, lime juice, onions, and cilantro. Other appetizers include moon egg rolls, spring rolls with an addictive peanut sauce, and satay. If you love seafood, you'll love it even more prepared with Thai flair: an in-season fish fillet crispy fried with mushrooms, carrots, onions, and cashews; crabmeat fried rice with onion and basil; or Thai lo mein with shrimp, cabbage,

and scallions. Chicken, pork, beef, and vegetarian options are also available. Pad Thai and fried rice with choices of shrimp, chicken, or bean curd are specialties. Thai Moon is open for lunch and dinner Tuesday through Saturday and for dinner only on Sunday and Monday. Call for off-season hours.

Cap't. Ben's $$
NC 12, Ocracoke Village
(252) 928–4741

Serving Ocracoke locals and guests since 1970, Cap't. Ben's is a casual restaurant that offers lunch and dinner every day from April through mid-November. Owner and chef Ben Mugford combines Southern tradition with gourmet foods to achieve a well-balanced menu. Ben is especially revered for his crabmeat, prime rib, and seafood entrees. He also serves a mean Caesar salad and comes up with some good pasta and chicken creations. Sandwiches, crab cakes, and shrimp salad are good bets for lunch; each comes with chips or fries. Dinners come with soup, baked potato, and salad. And all the desserts are delicious and homemade. A large variety of domestic and imported beers is available, and the wine list complements the menu. The decor in this family eatery is nautical and friendly. The lounge and sundeck are comfortable places to relax if you have to wait for a table. Lunch and dinner are served daily. Call for off-season hours.

Howard's Pub & Raw Bar Restaurant $–$$
NC 12, Ocracoke Village
(252) 928–4441
www.howardspub.com

Always a fun, friendly place to go for a meal, Howard's Pub has continued to expand its floor space, seating capacity, and menu diversity. And don't let the selection of more than 200 imported, domestic, and microbrewed beers fool you: The crew at Howard's Pub has established its "little corner of paradise" as the choice hangout for families, couples, and individuals alike. The restaurant's various areas—including the long, wraparound

bar; main floor and game area; the large screened porch with Adirondack-style rockers; and the ocean-to-sound-view deck—provide plenty of room for your group to spread out.

Howard's Pub & Raw Bar Restaurant is the only Outer Banks place we know that can boast that it is open every day of the year—since 1991—including Thanksgiving, Christmas, Easter, and hurricane evacuations! Owners Buffy and Ann Warner hail from West Virginia, where he was a senator and she handled economic development for the governor. Their lifestyles have changed radically since moving here, and you can tell they truly love it. This place has become a must-stop for everyone visiting Ocracoke, with great local flavor and guaranteed good times. (See our Nightlife chapter for more on Howard's Pub.)

The restaurant boasts the only year-round raw bar on the island and is home to the spicy Ocracoke Oyster Shooter. We love these raw oyster, hot sauce, pepper, and draught combinations, especially when washed down with an unusual or hard-to-find imported beer. Food professional Larry Sidwell has completely taken over the kitchen and is intent on maintaining food quality, consistency, and variety. Appetizers range from soups, salads, and stone crab claws to hot wings, Southwestern black bean eggrolls, and Howard's famous peel-and-eat steamed shrimp. Larry has added steaks, barbecued ribs,

live Maine lobster, and various catch-of-the-day recipes, including blackened tuna, wahoo with tropical salsa, and marinated mahi mahi. With the menu taking a decided upturn, wine by the bottle has become a more popular option.

The new upstairs deck—a precursor to a planned second-floor bar and game room—affords breathtaking views of the ocean, sound, salt marshes, and sand dunes. On a clear day, you can even see Portsmouth Island! There are big-screen TVs and many smaller ones for viewing any number of events from just about anywhere in the restaurant. Board games, darts, a pool table, and coloring books for the wee ones, plus live music and a 17-speaker sound system guarantee that you and your party can party to your hearts' content. The full menu and drinks are served every day from 11:00 A.M. to 2:00 A.M.

Cafe Atlantic $$
NC 12, Ocracoke Village
(252) 928-4861

Bob and Ruth Toth opened Cafe Atlantic in this traditional beach-style building a few years ago. There's not much that's traditional about their innovative, fantastic food, however. Views from the dining room look out across marsh grass and dunes. The gallery-like effect of the restaurant is created with hand-colored photographs by local writer and artist Ann Ehringhaus and watercolors and oils by Debbie Wells.

Lunch and dinner are served at this upscale yet casual eatery seven days a week in season. And the Sunday brunches are among the best we've found. Brunch menus change weekly, but champagne and mimosas are always served. We're partial to the blueberry pecan pancakes, chicken and broccoli crepes, and the huevos rancheros served over black beans in a crisp tortilla shell. Hash browns come with almost every entree.

The Toths make all their soups, dressings, sauces, and desserts from scratch. Lunches feature a variety of sandwiches and salads. Dinner entrees include fresh Atlantic seafood, beef, pastas, and vegetarian entrees. Each meal is served with salad, rice or potato, and steaming rolls just out of the oven. You've got to leave room for dessert here—or take one of their outrageously ornate cakes, pies, or cobblers home. A children's menu is available, and the restaurant has a nice selection of wine and beer. Cafe Atlantic is open from early March through October. Lunches may vary off-season, so call for hours. This cafe, though isolated on tiny Ocracoke, is certainly among the best dining experiences the Outer Banks has to offer. It's a nonsmoking establishment.

Ocracoke Coffee $
Back Rd., Ocracoke Village
(252) 928-7473

The neatest place on the island to take care of those unavoidable caffeine and sugar needs, Ocracoke Coffee has

enjoyed tremendous success since opening for the 1995 season. The aromatic eatery is filled with bagels, pastries, desserts, brewed coffee drinks, espresso, shakes, whole bean and ground coffees, and loose tea. The shop is nestled under tall pines on Back Road, within an easy walk of most anything in the village. We know you'll find your way here in the morning (everyone does), but why not shuffle in after dinner for something sweet as well? The shop's feel is way hip, but it's also cozy and inviting, and the folks frothing your concoctions are friendly as can be. Look for more than 10 varieties of smoothie for a cool respite from the summer heat. Ocracoke Coffee is open daily from 7:00 A.M. to 9:30 P.M., and live music is offered during summer evenings on the deck. The shop closes December through March.

Island Inn Restaurant $$
Lighthouse Rd., Ocracoke Village
(252) 928-7821

This family-owned and operated restaurant at the Island Inn is one of the oldest establishments on Ocracoke. Its main dining room and airy porch are furnished in a traditional country style, with blue and white china to dine on and bright, nautical touches throughout. Breakfast and dinner are served here daily except in the dead of winter. Owners Bob and Cee Touhey make sure everyone is welcome to eat here; you don't have to be a guest at the inn. Standard breakfast fare, such as pancakes, eggs, and hash browns, is available. The cook also comes up with some unusual creations, such as oyster omelets with spinach and bacon and shrimp omelets loaded with melted jack cheese, green chiles, and salsa. For dinner, locally landed seafood and shellfish entrees can be grilled, fried, or broiled to your liking. Beef, pork, lamb, pasta, and stir-fry dishes also are available, as are vegetarian offerings. All the breads and soups are made daily at this restaurant, and homemade pies are perfectly delicious. Beer and a selection of wines are served here, and a children's menu is available. Reservations are needed for large groups; the owners are happy to accommodate private party requests. The Island Inn Restaurant is open for breakfast and dinner. Call the number listed for off-season hours.

Creekside Cafe $
NC 12, Ocracoke Village
(252) 928–3606

Overlooking Silver Lake Harbor from a second-story vantage point, this seven-year-old restaurant offers wonderful views. A covered porch that wraps around two sides of the wooden building has ceiling fans and breezes to cool afternoon diners. Inside, the eatery is casual and friendly, serving brunch items daily and lunch and dinner from a single menu between April and early November. Soups, salads, seafood, and pasta dishes are the afternoon and evening fare here. The blackened chicken sandwiches are so popular that the owners decided to package and sell the spices. French dips, fresh fish sandwiches, oyster baskets, crab cakes, and Greek-style linguine with feta cheese and black olives all are great choices. For brunch, we recommend the Tex-Mex: scrambled eggs, onions, peppers, tomatoes, and salsa served in a tortilla shell with a dollop of guacamole. Desserts include parfaits, cheesecakes, Key lime pie, Tollhouse pie, and pecan pie—all homemade. Beer and wine are available, and four champagne drinks offer unusual alcoholic creations. Creekside Cafe is open daily in season for lunch and dinner.

Jolly Roger Pub & Marina $$
NC 12, Ocracoke Village
(252) 928–3703

Jolly Roger is the perfect place to kick back and relax on Ocracoke Island. Although a roof, canopy, and umbrellas cover many of the dining tables, the entire restaurant is open, with tables on large decks overlooking the harbor. This is one of our favorite places for a casual meal in Ocracoke. There's nothing fancy here—wooden tables, paper plates, and plastic cutlery—but the service is good, the beer is cold, and the food is wonderful. The menu features homemade soups, sandwiches, salad plates, local seafood, and daily specials. Stop in for live entertainment at sunset; you'll hear the music wafting down the street as you stroll through the village. Beer and wine are served, and there's a good-sized bar on premises. Jolly Roger serves lunch and dinner daily in season.

Cat Ridge Deli $
Albert Styron's Store, Lighthouse Rd.,
Ocracoke Village
(252) 928–3354

This wonderful little deli is inside Albert Styron's Store, in an area known locally as "Cat Ridge." The deli offers gourmet take-out items, including wraps, sandwiches, salads, soups, and baked goods. Cat Ridge claims to have the best meatball sandwich on the planet. Thai-inspired foods are a specialty of the house, and you might find Choo Chee shrimp or spicy green beans

on the list of daily specials when you arrive. Everything you need to accompany a picnic is served here: drinks, chips, wine, beer, gourmet items, and chocolate—fine handmade chocolates, no less. The deli is open for lunch daily in season. Call for off-season hours.

The Pelican Restaurant   **$$**
NC 12, Ocracoke Village
(252) 928-7431

In an old home tucked under a grove of trees in the heart of the village, The Pelican serves breakfast, lunch, and dinner. There's a great patio where you can enjoy beers and 15-cent shrimp from 3:00 to 5:00 P.M. and enjoy live entertainment five nights a week in summer from 6:00 to 10:00 P.M. Outside is lively, inside is romantic and softly lit. Meals include seafood entrees, hand-cut prime steaks, and the most wonderful seafood pasta

swimming in a light lemon-butter broth. A good wine list is available. Sushi is served here on Thursday nights.

Nightlife

Corolla
Duck
Kitty Hawk
Kill Devil Hills
Colington Island
Nags Head
Roanoke Island
Hatteras Island
Ocracoke Island

For many of us who live here—and for many visitors as well—the best evening entertainment is watching the sun set over the sound waters. Soundfront decks, piers, gazebos, and public beaches are perfect spots to toast your friends and the setting sun. It's not uncommon for us to rush home in the evening, call our friends, and arrange for a rendezvous spot at which to watch the sunset. Many locals can be found sailing or motoring their boats out into the sound in anticipation of our favorite entertainment, provided free each day. Moonrise over the ocean is pretty spectacular too, and under a Carolina moon, just about anything is possible. Read on for some barrier island options.

The Outer Banks after hours isn't like other resort areas. So many families—and early-rising anglers—come here that many people are bedded down for the evening by 9:00 P.M. We don't have the huge strips of late-night entertainment joints that you find in many other vacation destinations, but there are a number of bars and dance floors across the barrier islands. If you are a night owl, or at least like to stretch your wings a bit on vacation, you will find fun and frolic in dozens of establishments from Corolla all the way to Ocracoke.

Families can enjoy a variety of early-evening entertainment options here. Miniature golf, go-cart tracks, movie theaters, bumper boats, even a small amusement park and a bowling alley are listed in our Recreation chapter. And don't forget *The Lost Colony* outdoor drama; that's detailed in our Attractions chapter.

There are plenty of places to shoot pool, catch sporting events on big-screen TVs, play interactive trivia, throw darts, listen to low-key acoustic music, or boogie the night away to a live band.

Outer Banks musicians play everything from blues to jazz to rock to hard-core alternative and country tunes. Both local and out-of-town bands take the stage often during the summer season. Several area nightclubs assess nominal cover charges at the door, usually ranging from $1.00 for dueling acoustic guitar duos to $10.00 or more for the national acts that grace these sands between mid-May and Labor Day. Many acoustic acts, however, can be heard for free.

If live music is what you're listening for, *The Virginian-Pilot*'s weekly *Coast* magazine—available free at area grocery and convenience stores and motels—has up-to-date listings in its "Club Hoppin'" section plus music scene info in the "After Dark" column by John Harper (see our Media chapter for more on the *Coast*). Local stations WVOD 99.1 FM and WOBR 95.3 FM give daily concert updates on evening radio broadcasts. (See our Annual Events and Arts and Culture chapters for more nighttime possibilities.)

Alcoholic beverages are available at most Outer Banks lounges until around 2:00 A.M. Beer and wine are offered throughout the barrier islands. In Southern Shores, and on Colington, Roanoke, Hatteras, and Ocracoke Islands, it is illegal to serve mixed drinks. However, with the exception of Colington Island, ABC stores sell liquor in each of these areas. Most nightclubs in areas that serve only wine and beer allow people to brown-bag and bring in their own alcohol for the evening. Call ahead to make sure that brown bagging is OK.

Several restaurants on the Outer Banks offer late-night menus or at least raw and steamed bar food until closing. Every nightclub operator will be glad to call a cab to take you home or to your hotel or rental cottage after an evening of imbibing. **Beware:** The legal drinking age in North Carolina is 21, and the blood-alcohol content necessary for a drunken-driving arrest is only .08. So even if you've only had a couple of cocktails, play it safe and take a taxi. Besides, we want your experience here to be memorable in a good way!

Although several area restaurants offer happy hour specials and most have bars within their establishments, we've only included those eateries that are open until at least midnight in this chapter. Check our Restaurants chapter for sunset entertainment options. Several spots also feature outdoor acoustic music until dark—but this section is for those who like to come out with the stars.

Corolla

Sundogs Sports Bar and Grill
Monteray Plaza, NC 12, Corolla
(252) 453–4263

Sundogs is the newest hangout in Corolla. It's a sports bar, so expect a lot of people hanging out watching Monday Night Football and the like. But it's also a gathering spot, where people linger at the bar until the late hours. A pool table and video games provide other entertainments.

Neptune's Grill & Arcade
TimBuck II Shopping Village, NC 12 , Corolla
(252) 453–8645

A laid-back burger joint offering dine in and take-out of good, cheap eats, this establishment has the only pool table north of Duck. Pinball, Foosball, and a variety of video games are available here, and 24 different beers and a good selection of wine are sold until 2:00 A.M. Dinners are served until 11:30 P.M. In the summer, live acoustic and electric music created by various local talent and bands is offered. Call ahead for schedules. Neptune's is open all year, seven days a week in season. Call for winter hours.

Duck

Sunset Grille & Raw Bar
Duck Rd. (NC 12), Duck
(252) 261–3901

Situated right on the Currituck Sound across from the entrance to Barrier Island Station, Sunset Grille & Raw Bar is the only place in Duck to see live bands. During the summer, Sunset has live music every night except Sunday and Monday. In the off-season, there's live music at least twice a week. The house band is a reggae act, JoMo Pimberton, who once played with Bob Marley. JoMo plays at least once a week. Other bands, including blues, rock, and a Jimmy Buffet–style act, play here as well. In season, the raw bar and sushi bar are open until at least 10:30 P.M., so you can get a bite before the bands really kick in.

Fishbones Raw Bar & Restaurant
Scarborough Lane Shops
Duck Rd. (NC 12), Duck
(252) 261–6991

This raw bar and restaurant is one of Duck's most popular evening hangouts. It's open daily and features a full bar with five beers on tap, 50 international bottled beers, various microbrews, and a wine list. During summer, deck parties are held outdoors when the weather is good. It's a casual place to catch up on conversation with old acquaintances—or to make new ones.

Roadside Bar & Grill
Duck Rd. (NC 12), Duck
(252) 261–5729

Low-key, casual, and serving great food, Roadside is a favorite early-evening hangout for locals and tourists alike. There's a full bar in this 1932 restored cottage, with

The Outer Banks's many piers make for laid-back nightlife—watch the fish surfacing, drop in a fishing line, or stargaze and listen to the waves. PHOTO: COURTESY OF ELAINE FOGARTY

hardwood floors and walls that give it a cozy, homey feeling. There's also an outdoor patio where you can hear live jazz and blues on Tuesday and Thursday evenings in the summer months. Appetizers and cocktails are served outside during the music. Roadside is open year-round, but call for off-season hours.

Kitty Hawk

Rundown Cafe
NC 12, MP 1, Kitty Hawk
(252) 255–0026

If you're looking for summertime blues and jazz—or just want to sip some frothy brews—this Caribbean-style cafe is always an exciting spot to hang out on the north end of the beach. It's a great place to relax with friends, listen to some of the best music on the Outer Banks several nights a week, or just sit a spell at the long bar. You'll be comfortable coming in here alone too. Outside, there's an enclosed bar that affords great views of the ocean and the opportunity to catch some cool breezes and conversation.

A variety of domestic and imported beers are on hand, and there is a full line of liquor (ask about the specialty rum and tequila drinks). Enjoy Guinness Stout, Bass Ale, and Harp Lager on tap. The steam and raw bar serves seafood and vegetables until closing. By the way, Rundown is a traditional Jamaican stew, and the decor reflects the cafe's unusual name. Call ahead for a rundown of the evening entertainment at Rundown, or just stop by and check out this happening haunt.

Bessie's Kitchen and Spirits
Ocean Center, NC 12, MP 1, Kitty Hawk
(252) 261–3700

Bessie's serves up gourmet low-country foods and live tunes on the northern end of the beach. Inside, deep-blue walls provide a comfortable place to listen to live jazz and blues. In the summer, there's a live band almost every night, and in the off-season you can catch the tunes on the weekends. If you didn't stay up too late on Saturday night, you might be able to make it in for the bluegrass Sunday brunch. Bessie's has a full bar.

Frisco's
US 158, MP 4, Kitty Hawk
(252) 261-7833

A popular nightspot for locals year-round, this restaurant features a large, three-sided bar and beautiful terrariums and aquariums throughout the dining area. It's open seven days a week. Frisco's is the local Parrothead gathering spot, so that should give you an idea of the kind of fun-loving crowd that hangs out here. Tuesday nights year-round is Pirates in Paradise, where the Parrotheads party with local musician Bruce Todd. If you're into public displays of amateur singing, you'll be glad to know that Frisco's has karaoke seven nights a week in the summer. Frisco's is popular all year-round with the 30-plus crowd of groups and singles. They're open until 2:00 A.M. in season, and a late-night munchies menu is served. There are tables of all sizes in the lounge, and drink specials are served late into the night. There's even a wide-screen TV for sports fans. Call for entertainment schedules.

Black Pelican Oceanfront Cafe
NC 12, MP 4, Kitty Hawk
(252) 261-3171

With 12 TVs and an enclosed porch overlooking the ocean, this Kitty Hawk hangout is a fun place to catch up on sporting events or just sit a spell at the bar. It's in a former Coast Guard station and still features hardwood floors, tongue-and-groove appointments, and light gray accents reminiscent of days gone by. In the evenings its upbeat atmosphere is anything but antique. Interactive TV trivia is available for the contemporary crowd. Gourmet pizzas are a great treat for late-night munchies. The Black Pelican is open year-round.

Kill Devil Hills

Chilli Peppers
US 158, MP 5, Kill Devil Hills
(252) 441-8081

World fusion food with a Southwestern twist is served at this small, innovative restaurant year-round. The separate bar area out front always is teeming with partying people. People often come here to eat and end up staying late, especially on sushi nights (Wednesday, Friday, and Saturday year-round) and tapas nights (Thursdays in the off-season). Chilli's has live bands or acoustic acts every Tuesday all year. Whether or not there's music, there's often a bar crowd hanging around and having fun. Seven nights a week, you can enjoy fresh fruit margaritas, a nice wine selection, and dozens of domestic and imported beers from the full bar. Bartenders also serve nonalcoholic beers and fruit smoothies. There's an outdoor patio if you want to sip your drinks under the stars, and steamed seafood and vegetables are served until closing.

Jolly Roger Restaurant
NC 12, MP 6, Kill Devil Hills
(252) 441-6530

Adorned with hanging plants and colorful lights, the lounge at this restaurant is separate from the dining area. This is a casual place with a long, distinctive bar inlaid with seashells. There's almost always something going on here late into the night. Most summer evenings, there's live acoustic entertainment or a band, which can range from blues to rock to country. The bar is open seven nights a week. There is also karaoke every night and interactive TV, featuring games from sports to movie trivia. Both draw a regular audience, and prizes are even awarded to some of the big winners. Locals love this place, and you'll find people from their early 20s to late 60s hanging out here.

Goombays Grille & Raw Bar
NC 12, MP 7, Kill Devil Hills
(252) 441–6001
www.goombays.com

This popular nightspot teems with tourists and locals year-round and is open seven nights a week. It's fun and colorful with a tropical island flair and flavor—and the bartenders all are local characters. Goombays is Caribbean and casual, the kind of hangout where you're sure to feel right at home even if you've never visited the Outer Banks.

On Wednesdays live bands play here for an increasingly crowded "Locals Night" year-round—visitors make it the-more-the-merrier in summer. Wednesday night bands begin at 10:30 P.M. A horseshoe-shaped bar is set to the side of the dining area, so you can lounge on a stool or high-backed chair in the bar area or have a seat at a nearby table after the dining room closes at 10:00 P.M. Goombays serves lots of imported and domestic beers, wine, and mixed drinks until 2:00 A.M. Be sure to try some of the special rum, vodka, and tequila combos that come with toys to take home. Steamed shrimp and veggies are served until 1:00 A.M.

Quagmires
NC 12, MP 8, Kill Devil Hills
(252) 441–9188

Once you step inside Quags, or out onto one of the biggest open-air oceanfront decks on the beach, you're bound to have a great time. Upstairs, a horseshoe-shaped bar faces the Atlantic—everyone sitting on a stool is guaranteed a gorgeous view. For an even better view, sit out on one of Quag's upstairs decks.

Frozen drinks are served outdoors or in, and the bartenders even pour pitchers of margaritas so you don't have to keep getting up to fill your thin-stemmed, salt-encrusted glass. Beer, wine, and mixed drinks are available, and there's a whole line of appetizers and munchies to sample through the night. Quagmires is open seven days a week in summer, featuring live acoustic music many nights and Sunday afternoons. On the sand below the bar, horseshoes, a ring toss, and a beach volleyball court beckon people to come play if they need a break from partying in the lounge. Quagmires is open daily April through October; call for the entertainment schedule.

Port O' Call Restaurant & Gaslight Saloon
NC 12, MP 8, Kill Devil Hills
(252) 441–7484

One of the area's most unusual places to hang out—and one of the few local nightclubs that attract national bands in summer—the Gaslight Saloon is decorated in an ornate Victorian style complete with overstuffed armchairs, antique wooden tables, and a long mahogany bar. There's a nice dance floor here and an upstairs lounge (with separate bar) that overlooks the stage.

Port O' Call features live entertainment seven nights a week in season and every weekend while the restaurant is open from mid-March through December. There's usually a cover charge here. Cover may be waived for diners. In recent years, Port O' Call has hosted such national acts as the ultra-hip, trailer-park boogie of Southern Culture on the Skids, hirsute blues legend Leon Russell, eclectic rockers Fishbone, Southern rock cliche-mongers Molly Hatchet, and an array of first-rate reggae artists. Beer, wine, and liquor are served until 2:00 A.M.

Shucker's Pub and Billiards
Oceanside Plaza, NC 12, MP 8, Kill Devil Hills
(252) 480–1010

This pub and billiard room serves more than 75 types of beer and features the only 9-foot pool tables on the Outer Banks. A dozen billiard tables offer people the chance to play by the game or by

A relaxing meal and a night out are a great way to follow a long day of fishing. PHOTO: COURTESY OF DARE COUNTY TOURIST BUREAU

the hour. Darts, Foosball, and pinball are popular pastimes, and there are plenty of TVs for sports fans. Would-be pool sharks who get beached by too much cigarette smoke will be happy to know that Shucker's operates heavy-duty electronic "smoke-eaters" in every room. It's open year-round, seven nights a week until 2:00 A.M. Wine is available, and Shucker's serves pizza and sandwiches until closing. You must be 21 or older to play in this pub after 9:00 P.M.

Outer Banks Brewing Station
US 158, MP 8½, Kill Devil Hills
(252) 449–BREW
www.obbrewing.com
Opened in 2001, this is the Outer Banks's hottest new restaurant and nightspot.

Outside, it looks like a big white barn with silos at either end (the silos are for making beer). Inside, it's absolutely inviting and city-chic, with a stretch-length bar, high ceilings, warm wood tones, an open kitchen, yummy house-made beers, well-chosen wines, and sublime food. The brew is a big draw, with selections like a Hefewiezen wheat beer, Mutiny Pale Ale, and Kolsch summer brew. After dinner hours, the Brewing Station stays open late to accommodate a crowd of lingerers. Live blues, jazz, and funk (and combinations thereof) bands and sometimes acoustic acts play here year-round on a stage at one end of the restaurant. Rhythm Quest Syndicate, a jazzy funk act, was the house band in 2001. You can watch the band from a table in front of the stage, from the bar area, or get a bird's-eye view from the upstairs loft. Expect large crowds on band nights. Live entertainment is held Friday, Saturday, and Monday year-round. You can also expect music on Sundays and Thursdays in the summer, possibly even seven days if the owners decide to do it. Sunday night jazz dinners are held once a month in the off-season. The Brewing Station is open until 2:00 A.M. seven nights a week in summer and on band nights in the off-season. Call or check the Web site for entertainment schedules.

The Pit Surf Shop, Bar and Grill
US 158, MP 9, Kill Devil Hills
(252) 480–3128
www.pitsurf.com

The Pit is a conglomerate surf shop, hangout, restaurant, cybercafe, bar, band venue, and teen scene. It's a popular, casual hangout spot all day and all night and has been called the Surf Chalet because its cozy, log-cabin–style interior is always filled with surfer types. Every summer night, and most off-season nights, something fun is happening at The Pit. Monday night is Mug Night with a DJ, where you pay $5.00, bring your own mug, and drink $1.00 beers all night. Bands play every Tuesday, Saturday, and Sunday, and The Pit consistently gets the biggest names in talent. Burning Spear, The Wailers, 2 Skinnee J's, The Connells, All Mighty Senators, and Everything are just a few of the bands that play here, plus all the funky, quirky bands you can think of. The sound and lighting production are state of the art. Band covers range from $5.00 to $20.00. The Pit serves food until midnight and has pool tables, Foosball, videos, Internet access, and board-sport videos to keep you otherwise entertained.

The Pit is one of the only places on the beach that welcomes the under-21 crowd. They give underage revelers three whole summer nights of their own—Tuesday, Wednesday, and Friday—(once in a while in the off-season) with no alcohol served at all, so parents can rest easy. These nights feature DJs or occasionally a band. Cover is $10.

Madeline's at the Holiday Inn
NC 12, MP 9, Kill Devil Hills
(252) 441–6333

A disc jockey spins Top 40 tunes here most summer nights, and there's a shag club on Mondays. Legendary local DJ Buzz Besette's local following blends in nicely with the hotel crowd in the summer months. The lounge serves beer, wine, and mixed drinks year-round and is a convenient place for guests of the hotel who don't want to worry about having to drive anywhere after enjoying an evening of fun.

Peppercorns at the Ramada Inn
NC 12, MP 9, Kill Devil Hills
(252) 441–2151

Enjoy a breathtaking ocean view from the plate-glass window wall while visiting with friends and listening to acoustic soloists or duos in the Ramada Inn's intimate lounge area. Live music is performed daily throughout summer and often starts earlier here than elsewhere on the Outer Banks—sometimes they get started at 8:00 P.M. This is an open, laid-back place with booths, tables, and a full bar. The music is never too loud to talk over. But if you'd rather listen, some of the best guitar talent on the beach shows up here in season. There's also a comedy club and karaoke in the summer.

Mama Kwan's Grill and Tiki Bar
US 158, MP 9½, Kill Devil Hills
(252) 441–7889

This retro-Hawaiian restaurant and bar is always packed late with young partiers. It's often the place local restaurant workers go when they get off work. In summer, a DJ spins tunes every Thursday night, and bands play on the weekends. Mama's keeps things going in the off-season too, usually with a band on Thursday nights. Tiki lights create an islandy atmosphere. The bar's specialty is frozen drinks served with surprises. It's open every night until 2:00 A.M.

Madison's Cafe and Lounge
Sea Holly Sq., NC 12, MP 9½
Kill Devil Hills
(252) 480–3667

Madison's hosts frequent live bands and karaoke in its small bar area. Bands play on Tuesday and Thursday nights year-round and on other days in summer. Seven TVs make this a lounging spot even when there's no live entertainment. Madison's is open until 2:00 A.M. seven nights a week and serves an ample late-night menu until closing.

Nags Head

Red Drum Grille and Taphouse
NC 12, MP 10, Nags Head
(252) 480–1095

Red Drum pours 18 beers on tap—these are no run-of-the-mill brews—try Sierra Nevada, J.W. Dundee's Honey Brown, Woodpecker Cider, Black Radish, or Pyramid-Hefeweizen. All the domestics are available as well, and you can get wine by the glass or the bottle. Red Drum also serves liquor from its beautiful long redwood-colored bar.

On some nights local and out-of-town bands play a variety of music ranging from rock, blues, and jazz to alternative. A min-imum cover is charged. Beer specials are offered all night. A pool table and Foosball table are in an adjacent bar area that's separate from the dining room. Why not try a little competition with the tunes?

Mulligan's Oceanfront Grille
NC 12, MP 10, Nags Head
(252) 480–2000

Mulligan's is heralded as a popular evening hot spot and maintains its image as the Outer Banks's own version of TV's *Cheers*. A wooden partition separates the long, three-sided wooden bar from the dining room, and loads of local memorabilia adorn the walls. Mulligan's serves microbrewed beers on tap or in iced-down bottles. Wine and liquor are available. Acoustic music is offered on weekends in the off-season, and Wednesday, Friday, and Saturday in summer.

Kelly's Tavern
US 158, MP 10, Nags Head
(252) 441–4116

Probably the most consistently crowded tavern on the Outer Banks, Kelly's offers live bands five nights a week in-season and an open-mike fest with a lip-synch contest and cash prizes on Tuesday. Even during fall and winter, rockin' bands take the stage, and fun people always fill this place.

A full bar serves everything from suds to shots, and folks often line up around its three long sides two or three people deep. The big dance floor is usually shaking after 10:00 P.M. If you're in the mood just to listen and watch, secluded booths surround the dance floor a few steps above the rest of the lounge, and tables are scattered throughout the tavern. A dartboard and fireplace adorn the back area, and beach memorabilia hangs in every corner. Featuring a tasty variety of foods served late into the night, a lounge menu offers appetizers and steamed shellfish. An old-fashioned popcorn popper even provides free munchies served in wicker baskets throughout the evening. Singles seem to really enjoy this tavern. *Playboy* magazine

Visitors and locals can enjoy a wide variety of evening entertainment on the Outer Banks. PHOTO: COURTESY OF THE ROANOKE ISLAND FESTIVAL PARK

rated Kelly's as the best place to pick up babes on the Outer Banks.

Slammin' Sammy's
US 158, MP 10, Nags Head
(252) 449–2255

Slammin' Sammy's is the area's only dedicated sports bar, with 41 TVs tuned to the sports du jour. If you'd rather play than watch, there are pool tables and darts. This bar attracts a bit of everyone—women, men, locals, tourists, whoever. It's right across the street from Kelly's Tavern, so people often hop back and forth between the two bars. Be careful crossing the highway at night! Slammin' Sammy's has a full bar and a late-night menu and is open until 2:00 A.M. every night.

Tortuga's Lie Shellfish Bar and Grille
NC 12, MP 11, Nags Head
(252) 441–7299

Our favorite place to meet friends for a laid-back evening—or to hang out alone to chat with long-lost local pals—Tortuga's offers probably the most comfortable atmosphere you'll find on the Outer Banks most of the year. There's no entertainment, but it's a popular hangout spot just the same. The bar winds around a corner to allow at least a half-dozen more stools to slide under the refurbished countertop. Old license plates are perched on the low, wooden ceiling beams, and the sand volleyball court remains ready for pickup games out back all summer. Bartenders serve Black and Tans in those same pint glasses—that's right, Tortuga's has Guinness and Bass Ale on tap. Longneck beers are served by the bottle or by the iced-down bucket. Shooters, mixed drinks, and tropical frozen concoctions are sure to please any palate.

The steamer is open until closing, so you can satisfy late-night munchies with shellfish or fresh vegetables. Whether you're new in town or here to stay, Tortuga's is one place you won't want to miss. Most nights, it remains open until 2:00 A.M. Tortuga's closes for a brief spell in December and January.

and comfortable, and it's made a great comeback after a summer 1997 fire caused considerable damage and closed its heavy wooden doors for several months.

There are wooden floors and booths, and the tables are made from old ship-hatch covers and Singer sewing machine stands. The staff is friendly, and locals like to hang out here. It's a fun place with a pool table and pockmarked dartboards set in a separate room. Check out the lovely old wooden cabinet with lockers—it's a holdover from the days when regulars used to brown-bag their liquor and keep it at the establishment. The restaurant serves appetizers and sandwiches late into the night. Call for seasonal schedules of entertainment. The Green Dolphin is open Monday through Saturday until 1:00 A.M.

Hatteras Island

Froggy Dog & Lounge
NC 12, Avon
(252) 995–4106

Late-night acoustic music plus bands and karaoke singers take the stage at this casual Hatteras Island eatery. Froggy Dog Lounge is open nightly in season, serving beer and wine. There's usualy entertainment on Wednesdays; call for schedule.

The Mad Crabber Restaurant & Shellfish Bar
NC 12, Avon
(252) 995–5959

This tiny crab shack shows surf videos on a big screen and provides live band entertainment on Saturdays during the season. A separate game room has two pool tables and video games. The lively dining room offers dinner nightly from April through November. Dinner and late-night snacks are served from 5:00 P.M. until midnight in season. There's a selection of wines, draft beers, imported beers, and microbrews.

Sandbar & Grille
NC 12, Hatteras Village
(252) 986–2044
www.sandbarandgrille.com

Bacu Grill
Outer Banks Mall, US 158, MP 14, Nags Head
(252) 480–1892

This Cuban-inspired restaurant and bar is about the only happening place in lower Nags Head. Blues and jazz bands play several nights a week in the summer and occasionally in the off-season. There might be a small cover for the bands. This is the favorite end-of-the-workweek gathering spot for Nags Head locals, so Friday nights are often packed. Bacu has a worldly wine list and a European beer engine that pours a perfect draft beer, such as Harp, Guinness, or Boddingtons. Appetizers and other munchies are served late.

Roanoke Island

The Green Dolphin Restaurant and Pub
Sir Walter Raleigh St., Manteo
(252) 473–5911

If you're looking for late-night fun in Manteo, this is the only place you're going to find it. Manteo is as still as a church mouse after dark, but The Green Dolphin is an oasis of fun in the midst of it. Acoustic guitarists perform here on Friday nights year-round, featuring jazz, rock, folk, and blues. There's a bar serving a variety of beer, and there's never a cover charge for live music. This pub is warm

The Sandbar has been a hit since it opened on New Year's Eve in 1997. Even when there's no band playing at this rustic, casual establishment, you can hear a fabulous range of music on one of the 83 satellite radio channels. The station is chosen to fit the crowd—the staff says there are even a select few stations that do a great job clearing the house when closing time comes around.

Bands that play everything from blues and rock to jazz are featured. The cover charge is $5.00. Sometimes there are solo acts and karaoke. Televised sports, pool, NTN trivia, and Foosball provide alternate distractions. Call for entertainment schedules and off-season hours. Lunch and dinner are served all day every day.

Ocracoke Island

Howard's Pub & Raw Bar Restaurant
NC 12, Ocracoke Village
(252) 928–4441
www.howardspub.com

This is our absolute favorite place to hear live bands. Featuring the friendliest crowd of locals and visitors around, Howard's Pub has an atmosphere and feeling all its own. Once you've visited, you'll plan to stop at this upbeat yet laid-back place at least once during every visit to Ocracoke. We try to return at least once a month to get a fix of fun and to get away from it all. Howard's is open 365 days until 2:00 A.M.—the only place on the Outer Banks that can make that claim, and has done so for over 10 years. It's also the only restaurant on Ocracoke open 365 days a year.

The pub serves more types of beer than any place we know—more than 200 varieties are available at this virtual oasis on the isolated island. There's a second-floor outdoor deck with breathtaking 360-degree, ocean-to-sound views, perfect for catching sunsets or falling stars. A huge, screened porch—complete with Adirondack rocking chairs for relaxing in the evening breezes—borders an entire side of the spacious wooden building. The dance floor has more than doubled in recent years. Two big-screen TVs and numerous smaller ones offer sports fans constant entertainment, along with the capacity to tune into multiple events simultaneously. Howard's has a dartboard, pool table, board games, and card games available free to playful patrons. The full menu, including pizza, sandwiches, and raw bar items, is available until 2:00 A.M.

Bands play most nights during the summer season and several times a week

Jolly Roger Pub
NC 12, Ocracoke Village
(252) 928-3703

A waterfront eatery with an open bar overlooking Silver Lake, this pub has a huge outdoor deck that's covered in case of thunderstorms. Local acoustic guitarists perform Caribbean and country music here with no cover charge Thursday and Friday nights. Jolly Roger serves beer, wine, and great food throughout the warm summer months.

Pelican Restaurant
NC 12, Ocracoke Village
(252) 928-7431

The Pelican features live acoustic entertainment on its outdoor patio on some summer nights. The Pelican's patio is right on the main road through the village, but it's tucked behind some trees to give the feeling that you're hiding away. You can kick back with a draft beer or share a pitcher with friends. The entertainment is usually early, until about 10:00 P.M.

during the winter. Music ranges from rhythm and blues to bluegrass, jazz, rock, and originals. The occasional open-mike and karaoke nights are favorites for locals and visitors alike. Howard's Pub never charges a cover, and even when electricity fails the rest of the island, this place is equipped with a generator so the crew can keep on cooking—and keep the beer cold.

Weekly & Long-term Cottage Rentals

Equipment Rentals
   and Related Services
Cottage Rental
   Companies
Corolla
Duck
Southern Shores
Kitty Hawk
Kill Devil Hills
Nags Head
Roanoke Island
Hatteras Island
Ocracoke Island
Year-round Rentals

If your idea of the perfect vacation is to settle down with all the comforts of a home away from home, the Outer Banks is a perfect choice for you. By far the most popular accommodations here are the thousands of private beach cottages available for rental. There are more than 8,000 rental cottages available in Dare County, and that's not including the thousands of cottages available in Corolla in Currituck County or on Ocracoke Island in Hyde County. From the unique off-road beaches of Carova just south of the Virginia line to the remote island of Ocracoke, accessible only by plane, boat, or ferry, you'll find a tremendous variety in price, location, and character. Although most vacationers stay for a week at a time, longer- and shorter-term rentals are available throughout most of the year.

Most beach cottages are owned by individuals and are represented by a property management firm. Normally the cottages reflect the individual tastes and preferences of their owners. Although property management firms or rental companies will set their own minimum standards for the homes they represent, you can still expect beach homes to vary widely in design, decor, and the amenities they offer. You can rent anything from a palatial nine-bedroom oceanfront mansion with a private pool, home office, and media room to a cozy little saltbox on the sound side of US 158.

There is a great deal of competition among rental companies to secure the greatest possible number of bookings for their owners, and the trend is to add more amenities to encourage guests to return year after year. In recent years, many companies have encouraged their cottage owners to add greater value to a week's vacation by including, as standard, amenities that used to be luxuries. Whirlpool baths, hot tubs, upscale interior decorating, book and video libraries, fireplaces, baby cribs, and playpens are becoming increasingly common, particularly in the newer properties. Veteran visitors to the Outer Banks are accustomed to bringing their own linens and towels, but the recent trend is toward more cottages coming equipped with linens. A few property management firms now require their owners to provide linens.

Of course, you'll pay more for these luxuries. Rental prices are based primarily on the season, the cottage's proximity to the ocean, the number of occupants it will "sleep," and the amenities it offers. The peak, most expensive, season runs from mid-June through the end of August. There are substantial discounts to be had in the fall and spring, considered "mid-season" by most companies, and, of course, the best bargains are from late November to late March. More vacationers are discovering the joys of the Outer Banks during seasons other than summer: With its temperate climate, the Outer Banks offers a great variety of outdoor activities to enjoy, even if the weather is too cold for ocean swimming or lounging on the beach.

Location, Location, Location!

An "oceanfront" cottage is one that sits right on the beach with no other cottages or lots to the east. Some, but not all, have private walkways to the ocean, an especially convenient feature if the cottage sits behind a dune. (Dunes are fragile and need protection. It's very poor form—and against the law—to trample them.) If your cottage doesn't have a private walkway, you'll have to use the community or public access; check on this when you make your reservation. Also, although most oceanfront cottages offer spectacular vistas, some have tall dunes obstructing the view from one or more levels. Oceanfront cottages without views are more the exception than the rule, but you won't encounter any nasty surprises if you double check this at the time of rental, assuming it's important to you!

There's no underestimating the convenience of an oceanfront cottage. You don't have to schlep the beach equipment very far, and when the little ones get cranky, you can sun yourself on your deck or patio and listen to the pounding surf while they take a nap inside.

The next best thing to oceanfront is "semi-oceanfront," which usually means one lot back from oceanfront. The distance to the Atlantic varies, but many semi-oceanfronts still offer good views of the water. In some areas, especially Kitty Hawk, Kill Devil Hills, and Nags Head, you'll have to cross the Beach Road (NC 12) to get to the shore.

When a cottage is described as being "between the highways," it is located between the Beach Road and US 158. The actual distance from the beach will vary, but you can expect a 5- to 15-minute hike. Cottages identified as "westside" are located west of US 158 in Kitty Hawk, Kill Devil Hills, and Nags Head. Those west of NC 12 in Corolla, Duck, and Southern Shores are referred to as "soundside." Of course, "soundfront" cottages are those with no houses or lots between them and the sound.

Westside or soundside cottages tend to be among the last to book and can offer an open-minded visitor a very affordable and pleasant alternative to costlier ocean-side cottages. Many communities offer pools, tennis courts, hiking trails, and other amenities on the soundside to enhance rentals. Some vacationers have come to prefer the soundside areas for their tranquillity and the convenience of certain watersports such as windsurfing and canoeing. Finally, many soundfront cottages offer views as spectacular as those on the ocean. It's the place to be if you prefer the sunset to the sunrise. (See our Real Estate chapter for more information on individual communities.)

Most rental companies identify, either in terms of number of lots from the beach or distance measured in feet, how close (or far) their cottages are to the ocean, so you should get an idea when you make your reservation how long a trek you can expect.

When and How to Reserve Your Cottage

As you might imagine, properties closest to the ocean are snatched up quickly. Many rental companies offer returning guests the opportunity to make advance reservations for the next year as they check out, so cottages in prime locations will often have several weeks reserved even before the New Year. Expect to make your reservation in January or February if you have your heart set on a particular cottage on the ocean. Otherwise, you'll still have a good variety from which to choose if you reserve by the end of March. Don't despair, however, if you can't make a decision until later. You might have to call around, but you can usually find something to rent, even at the last minute. (One caveat: the pickings will be slim for spur-of-the-moment trips in the month of August.)

Nearly all rental companies publish a color brochure or catalog describing their properties; the new editions typically are available from Thanksgiving on. You'll

Families can doubleup in many of the vacation homes on the Outer Banks. PHOTO: COURTESY OF JEANNE REILLY

find photos and property descriptions not only in a company's brochure, but on its Web site as well. Online availability and reservation booking capabilities are becoming increasingly popular.

The rental company's catalog or Web site will almost certainly cover the essential elements of the lease. Make sure you read these thoroughly before you make your reservation, and make a list of questions you want to ask the reservationist. You'd be surprised at how familiar many reservationists are with the properties they rent. This is also the right time to discuss any special needs anyone in your party may have. At the time of reservation, you'll typically be asked to secure your cottage with a deposit—usually 50 percent, with the balance due 30 days in advance of your visit.

Amenities

Rental companies will include a listing of the amenities offered at each cottage in their catalogs; some include this information on their Web sites. In addition, most

companies require their owners to supply certain amenities as standard. Typical standard items include air conditioning, a telephone, television, VCR, washer and dryer, barbecue, microwave—most appliances and items you'd expect to find in the typical residential home. Still, don't take anything for granted. Make sure you read the descriptions and your lease thoroughly so there's no misunderstanding.

Unless the lease stipulates that your rental is equipped with linens and towels, you'll need to bring your own. The cottage listing will tell you the sizes and number of beds in the home. You'll also need to supply your own toiletries, paper products, and cleaning supplies. It's a good idea to arrive with enough of the basics to get you through a half-day, until you can make that run to the grocery store.

If you don't feel like hauling a lot of extra stuff to the beach, you can rent just about anything you need, including linens, towels, beach equipment, bicycles, outdoor furniture, and recreational equipment. At the end of this chapter is a list of companies you can call in advance; many

A cottage by the sea means great fun for the little ones. PHOTO: COURTESY OF JACKIE THOMAS

will deliver the items you request right to your cottage.

Minimum Stays

During the mid- and off-seasons, you'll of course have more options than you will in the peak season, when occupancy runs at close to 100 percent. During the summer it's very difficult to find a cottage to rent for less than a week. Most rent from Saturday to Saturday or Sunday to Sunday. Some families enjoy renting for two or even more consecutive weeks, but don't expect a price break!

You'll have better luck finding a shorter term rental in the slower seasons. Most companies will offer what they call "partial" rentals from September through May or June. Some charge a flat fee for a three- or four-day period; others charge a nightly fee. Make sure you understand how the fee is determined. In the off-seasons, many rental companies get creative in order to increase bookings. That's the time to look for special getaway packages. As you might expect, the mid- and off-seasons offer some excellent bargains and are especially popular with vacationers who don't have school-aged children in tow. If you have the option of enjoying the Outer Banks during the slower seasons, you'll be delighted with the meandering pace. Most restaurants and shops now stay open at least through Thanksgiving, and more and more are extending their operating times well beyond. Visiting the Outer Banks during holidays throughout the year is becoming increasingly popular.

Advance Rents

Expect to pay an advance rent, typically 50 percent of the full lease amount, soon after you make your reservation. It's usually due within 10 days. Personal checks are usually accepted if the reservation is made in plenty of time for the check to clear. Some companies allow credit card transactions, but be aware that some will charge an additional fee to cover the extra costs charged by the bank that handles the card. In most cases, the balance of the lease amount is due 30 days prior to arrival. If payment is accepted at check-in, it's usually required in the form of a certified check or cash. Most rental companies will not accept a personal check upon arrival.

Security Deposits

Besides advance rents, most companies also require their guests to pay a security deposit. This, of course, is for the owner's protection. The amounts required will vary depending upon the company's policies. Cottages are typically inspected between check-ins to make sure everything is in order. If you notice any damage in a cottage after you've just arrived, make sure to inform your rental company immediately. They may already be aware of it, but a little extra caution on your part will help to prevent any misunderstanding about who caused the damage. Remember, please, that rental companies are anxious to please you, but they also answer to their owners.

If anything is damaged during your stay or is determined to be missing after you leave, expect to have an amount deducted from your security deposit. Cottages that allow pets usually require an extra deposit for possible pet damage and a standard fee for flea exterminating after you and your pet depart.

Hurricane Evacuation Refunds

Most rental companies now offer insurance with each reservation made. In accordance with North Carolina's Vacation Rental Act, if a guest buys vacation insurance, or if a guest is offered insurance but declines the offer, the real estate company is not required to reimburse that guest for any vacation days that he or she loses as a result of a hurricane evacuation. Each rental company sets its own policy governing refunds in the event of a hurricane. The few remaining companies that do not offer insurance generally will issue a partial or full refund in the event of a mandatory evacuation. Each area's local government officials are ultimately responsible for issuing evacuation orders. The County of Currituck has jurisdiction over Corolla and the four-wheel-drive beach areas; Hyde County has jurisdiction over Ocracoke; and Dare County governs everything in between.

The island of Ocracoke is usually evacuated before all other areas because access and egress is only by ferry or boat, and the choppy waters stirred up by a hurricane even miles away will make passage difficult or impossible as the storm approaches. The island of Hatteras also tends to be evacuated early because sections of NC 12 quickly flood when the waters rise. If a mandatory evacuation of your area is ordered, comply.

Most rental companies will not issue refunds for days you don't occupy the property once re-entry is permitted. Most Ocracoke property managers make exceptions for refunds in case the ferries aren't operating. These policies do vary from business to business, so make inquiries along with your reservation.

Consider buying travel insurance, which will protect your vacation investment in a variety of unexpected scenarios.

Handling and Inspection Fees

Some rental companies charge a handling fee for processing information and an inspection fee to check the cottage after you've checked out. This is a nonrefundable fee assessed in addition to other charges.

Taxes

A combined 10 percent tax, which includes the 6.5 percent state sales tax and a 4 percent local lodging tax, is charged on rents and fees.

Check-out is usually by 10:00 A.M.; check-in is usually at 4:00 P.M., give or take an hour. (These standard times account for the heavy traffic on Saturday and Sunday mornings and afternoons.) Most companies will allow you to take occupancy of your cottage earlier if it has been serviced properly, but don't arrive expecting this. If you want to travel during off-peak hours in the summer and plan to arrive several hours before check-in, head for one of the beach access areas that has showers and changing facilities, and just plan to spend the time relaxing. If you plan to check in after the rental company's office closes, most will make arrangements to leave your keys and cottage information in an outside box for pickup.

Be prompt when you check out. This is a courtesy to the rental company and the next guest, and you might be assessed an extra fee if you overstay your welcome!

Pet Rules and Costs

Some cottage owners allow guests to bring pets, within certain limits, but you'll be assessed extra fees for the privilege. You can usually count on an extra cleaning and extermination fee and a higher security deposit. Rental companies will often restrict the size of the pets accepted (for example, dogs up to 75 pounds), but if your pet does not conform to the restrictions, ask the rental manager if it's possible to make an exception. Many companies will contact the cottage owner to try to accommodate a reasonable request. Be aware, too, that some cottages will allow dogs but not cats and vice versa. Whatever you do, don't bring a pet "illegally"—this is almost always grounds for eviction without a refund.

Check-in and Check-out Times

Of course you're anxious to begin your vacation, but you'll save yourself (and others) some aggravation if you're courteous about observing check-in and check-out times. Rental companies need this time to clean and inspect the cottages and perform minor maintenance.

Occupancy

The number of people your cottage can accommodate will be listed in the description of the property in the rental brochure. This number is determined by the number and type of beds and the septic and water capacity. Do not exceed the maximum occupancy or you could risk eviction. Most rental companies rent to family groups only and will not rent to minors. Any violation of this policy could result in a ruined vacation—and no refund.

Mail, Telephone, and Fax Services

When you make a reservation, you can request the cottage's phone number to leave with those back home who may need to reach you. Most companies also print the cottage's physical address and telephone number on your lease, which you'll receive after making your initial payment. Almost all cottages have telephones these days, although a few of the older ones do not (and with the proliferation of cell phones, this may not be a problem for you). At any rate, the caveat once again is to know what you're renting. Of course you'll be required to pay for your own long-distance calls, and many homeowners have a block on their lines to prevent direct-dialed long-distance calls. Either bring along a calling card or buy a pre-paid phone card, but don't make calls from your cottage that will be charged to the homeowner.

If you expect to receive mail while you're on vacation, ask the reservationist for the proper mailing address and make sure you tell your correspondents to mark the envelope clearly with your name and cottage identification. The same common sense applies if you expect to receive faxes while you're on vacation. Most rental companies either have a fax machine set aside for guest use or will let you use theirs, but a fee is almost always charged. If you're expecting something important, it's a good idea to instruct the sender to call you when the fax has been sent so you can check to see if it has arrived. Rental companies are exceptionally busy during the summer and at peak holiday times, and your fax might be one of a few dozen that come in over the course of a day.

Trash Pickup and Recycling

Town or county garbage collectors gather the trash from in front of rental cottages at least twice a week during the summer and once a week during the slower seasons. Know which days the trash will be picked up. Your rental company will usually supply this information in your check-in packet. When you check out, bag your refuse securely and make sure the receptacle sits beside the road.

Recycling is usually the renter's responsibility. Some communities provide recycling service and the proper bins, but in most areas you'll need to carry your recyclables to one of the collection points. Ask your rental company for the location nearest your cottage and for instructions on sorting.

Many beach access areas now have recycling bins in addition to trash cans for you to deposit cans or bottles as you leave the shore.

Thank you for doing your part to help preserve these beaches for everyone.

Equipment Rentals and Related Services

If you'd rather not take everything with you to the beach, equipment rental companies from north to south can provide almost anything you need or want. Baby furniture, beach chairs, umbrellas, bicycles, linens, fishing gear, grills . . . you get the idea. You can also rent recreational "toys" such as personal watercraft, boogie boards, surfboards, and kayaks. Check the Watersports chapter for companies that specialize in these. The following listings cover companies that supply the widest variety of equipment and services.

At Your Service
(252) 261–5286, (800) 259–0229

With more than 10 years' experience on the Outer Banks, At Your Service will take on such tiresome chores as running errands and buying groceries by acting as your personal concierge. They can help in acquiring babysitters (it's the oldest babysitting and eldercare service on the Outer Banks), stocking your vacation cottage with groceries and other necessities before you arrive, providing linens and cleaning service, ordering flowers and theater tickets, and seeing to details to make a vacation run smoothly. Pamela Price, a former teacher and public relations professional, is the energetic owner of At Your Service, and she has a well-trained and competent staff of around 60 employees. For more information, see our Education and Child Care chapter.

Ocean Atlantic Rentals
(800) 635–9559 reservations
Corolla Light Village Shops, Corolla
(252) 453–2440
Duck Rd., Soundfront, Duck
(252) 261–4346
NC 12, MP 10, Nags Head
(252) 441–7823
NC 12, Avon
(252) 995–5868
www.oceanatlanticrentals.com

Ocean Atlantic will deliver from any of their locations. Beach umbrellas and chairs, bikes, cribs, TVs, VCRs, fax machines, kayaks, linens, skates, grills, videos, and watersports equipment are among the items this company leases.

Money's Worth Beach Home Equipment Rentals
(252) 453–4566, (252) 261–6999,
(800) 833–5233
www.mworth.com

With an advance minimum rental order of $20, all items are delivered to your vacation home on your check-in day and picked up after you check out. This company is the only one that services the real estate companies directly. It has a wide assortment of beach and sports equipment, TVs, VCRs, grills, baby items, and bicycles. You do not have to be present for delivery or pickup service.

Lifesaver Rent Alls
(800) 635–2764 information
US 158, MP 1, Kitty Hawk
(252) 261–1344
Lifesaver Shops, MP 9, Kill Devil Hills
(252) 441–6048
www.outer-banks.com/lifesaver

Delivery is available, or you can stop in the store to browse through numerous items. Beach equipment, bikes, baby supplies, linens, fishing supplies, and beach wheelchairs are among the items this company leases.

Metro Rentals
US 158 and Colington Rd., MP 8
Kill Devil Hills
(252) 480–3535
www.metrorentalsobx.com

This company specializes in wedding and catering needs, party supplies, party tents, construction equipment, and beach-combing devices such as metal detectors.

Beach Outfitters
NC 12, Ocracoke
(252) 928–6261, (252) 928–7411
www.ocracokeislandrealty.com

Beach Outfitters, at Ocracoke Island Realty, is open all year and accepts reservations. Free delivery and pickup are available on Ocracoke Island with full-week rental and prepayment. Items available to rent include beach chairs and umbrellas, towels and linens, bikes, rollaway beds, baby equipment, TVs, VCRs, and steamer pots and kitchen appliances.

Cottage Rental Companies

In this section, we've listed rental companies according to the physical location of their headquarters office. Many have more than one office, so check the text of the listing to see which areas they serve. Listings are from north to south.

A company's inventory of cottages will change somewhat from year to year, but almost all companies offer some accommodations that allow pets, a few wheelchair-accessible cottages, and partial week rentals in the mid- and off-seasons. In the following listings, we have concentrated on telling you which areas companies cover and approximately how many cottages they represent. We recommend that you call or e-mail companies directly for comprehensive information. Nearly all will supply you with a free brochure or catalog of all their rental properties.

Corolla

ResortQuest Outer Banks
(800) 962–0201

ResortQuest Outer Banks, part of ResortQuest International, is new to the Outer Banks. The company bought several of the best northern Outer Banks property management companies and rolled them into one. ResortQuest manages over 1,000 properties from Southern Shores to Corolla. Oceanfront, soundfront, and everything in between are available. Three check-in offices are available: one in Corolla at 1023 Ocean Trail; and two in Duck at 1316 Duck Road and 1184 Duck Road.

Karichele Realty
TimBuck II Shopping Village, NC 12, Corolla
(252) 453–4400, (800) 453–2377
www.karichele.com

Karichele Realty manages more than 145 properties in Corolla and the four-wheel-drive area. During the off-season, weekend packages are available. Pets are accepted in some units. Wheelchair-accessible cottages also are available.

Stan White Realty & Construction Inc.
812 Ocean Trail, Corolla
(252) 453–9619, (800) 753–6200
www.outerbanksrentals.com

This is the new northern beaches location for Stan White Realty, a longtime Nags Head company. The company manages over 725 properties on the Outer Banks. This location serves as the check-in office for rentals in and around Corolla.

Village Realty
50 Hunt Club Dr., Corolla
(252) 453–0409, (800) 548–9688
www.villagerealtyobx.com

The northern beaches' location of Village Realty rents homes from Pine Island north through the end of the paved road. They represent oceanfront, soundfront, and in-between homes in Pine Island, Ocean Sands Whalehead, Corolla Light, and the Currituck Club, the only golf community on the Currituck Outer Banks. Rentals at the Currituck Club include use of the pool, fitness center, and other amenities. Ask about golf packages.

Duck

Carolina Designs Realty
Village Sq., 1197 NC 12, Duck
(252) 261–3934, (800) 368–3825
www.carolinadesigns.com

Carolina Designs manages nearly 200 weekly rentals ranging in size from one-bedroom condos to eight-bedroom estates, with linens included. Properties are primarily from Corolla to Southern Shores and in the Village at Nags Head.

> ## Insiders' Tip
> Hurricane season lasts from late June through November. If you're renting a cottage on the Outer Banks in those months, you should seriously consider purchasing vacation insurance, which will protect your investment should a hurricane threaten during your vacation. Your rental agent will offer it to you upon booking.

Duck's Real Estate, A Stan White Company
1232 NC 12, Duck
(252) 261–4614, (800) 992–2976
www.outerbanksrentals.com

Duck's Real Estate manages 200 weekly rentals from Corolla to Southern Shores. Three-day golf packages also are available. Pets are accepted in some units. Some cottages are equipped for disabled guests.

Twiddy & Company Realtors
1181 NC 12, Duck
(252) 261–3521, (800) 489–4339 in Duck
1127A Schoolhouse La., Corolla
(252) 453–3341, (800) 789–4339 in Corolla
www.twiddy.com

Twiddy & Company manages more than 500 rental properties from Carova to Southern Shores from its offices in Duck and Corolla and offers several specialty properties that accommodate weddings, corporate retreats, and other special functions. A special events coordinator can be recommended. All of the company's cottages include linen and towel service as a standard amenity. A number of cottages allow pets. Many include private pools and spas.

Southern Shores

Southern Shores Realty
NC 12, Kitty Hawk
(252) 261–2111, (800) 334–1000
www.southernshores.com

Southern Shores Realty manages 480 year-round and weekly rentals from Southern Shores to Duck. Weekend packages also are available year-round. Dogs are accepted in some units. Ramps and elevators are offered in some cottages.

Kitty Hawk

Atlantic Realty
US 158, MP 2½, Kitty Hawk
(252) 261–2154, (800) 334–8401
(252) 453–4110, (800) 669–9245 in Corolla
www.atlanticrealty-nc.com

This company manages 250 properties from Corolla to South Nags Head for year-round and seasonal rental. Pets are accepted in some units.

Kitty Dunes Realty
US 158, Kitty Hawk
(252) 261–2171, (800) 860–3863
www.kittydunes.com

Kitty Dunes manages about 420 rental properties from Corolla to South Nags Head. Some can accommodate up to 22 people. Most properties rent by the week, but long-term rentals are offered in Colington Harbour. Three-night weekend packages are often available, even during the summer. Pets are accepted in many units, and a few cottages are wheelchair-friendly. Some properties include private pools and spas.

Joe Lamb Jr. & Associates
US 158, MP 2, Kitty Hawk
(252) 261–4444, (800) 552–6257
www.joelambjr.com

This company manages more than 200 properties, including year-round rentals from Duck to South Nags Head. Three-night packages are offered during the off-season. Pets accepted in some cottages.

Wheelchair-accessible rentals are also available. Units in some developments include pool access. Many have private pools.

Resort Central Inc.
US 158, MP 2½, Kitty Hawk
(252) 261–8861, (800) NAG–HEAD
www.resortcentralinc.com

Resort Central manages 75 weekly rental properties and 40 year-round rentals from Sanderling to South Nags Head. Advanced reservations are available in the off-season for weekend packages. Some cottages allow pets, and some units are equipped with elevators.

Prudential Resort Realty
791-A Sunset Blvd., Timbuk II, Corolla
(252) 453–3700
1248 Duck Rd., Duck
(252) 261–8888
3608 N. Croatan Hwy., Kitty Hawk
(252) 261–8232
2229 S. Croatan Hwy., Nags Head
(252) 441–5000, (800) 458–3830
www.resortrealty.com

Prudential Resort Realty manages over 350 weekly rental properties from Corolla to South Nags Head. Some three-night packages are available with a maximum of five days' notice. Some cottages allow pets.

Coldwell Banker / Seaside Realty
US 158, MP 2, Kitty Hawk
(252) 261–5500, (800) 395–2525
(252) 453–8030, (888) 267–6552 in Corolla
www.seasiderealty.com

Seaside Realty manages 225 year-round and weekly properties from Carova Beach to South Nags Head. At least 300 additional timeshares also are offered in that area. Three-night packages are available during the off-season. Some of these units allow pets. Some accommodations have elevators.

Wright Property Management
US 158, MP 4¾, 3719 N. Croatan Hwy, Kitty Hawk
(252) 261–2186, Fax (252) 261–5773
www.wpmobx.com

Wright Property Management offers 146

cottages and condominiums for weekly, partial week, or year-round rentals from Ocean Sands to South Nags Head. Some WPM units offer swimming pools, tennis facilities, hot tubs, and private pools; many units will accept pets.

Kill Devil Hills

Kitty Hawk Rentals/
Beach Realty & Construction
US 158, MP 6, Kill Devil Hills
(252) 441–7166, (800) 635–1559
(252) 261–6605 in Duck
(252) 453–4141 in Corolla
www.beachrealtync.com

This company manages more than 600 properties, a few of which are wheelchair-accessible, from Ocean Hill to South Nags Head. Some are available for year-round rental, but most rent by the week. Pets are accepted in some units. Outer Banks Golf Getaways, a Beach Realty division, offers weekend golf/accommodation packages in area homes and hotels. Call (800) 916–6244 for more information.

Ocean Breeze Realty
100 E. Third St., Kill Devil Hills
(252) 480–0093, (800) 633–4491
www.oceanbreezeobx.com

Ocean Breeze manages 200-plus weekly and year-round cottages, condos, duplexes, and townhouses from Kitty Hawk to South Nags Head. There are swimming pools and tennis courts available for use at the condos, and some units will accept pets.

Outer Banks Vacation Realty
3105 US 158, MP 5½, Kill Devil Hills
(252) 449–9034, (888) 685–9581
www.vacationouterbanks.com

Outer Banks Vacation Realty strives to be the most effective vacation rental company on the Outer Banks, preferring to remain comparatively small so that they can offer the best service possible to every guest. The company represents only a select group of vacation rental accommodations. Their properties range from Southern Shores to South Nags Head and include condomini-ums, cottages, and palatial oceanfront estates. Staff members have personally visited every property and can therefore make the best recommendations for a property based on a guest's needs.

Sun Realty
US 158, MP 9, Kill Devil Hills
(252) 441–7033, (800) 334–4745
www.sunrealty-nc.com

Satellite offices are at Corolla, Duck, Kitty Hawk, Salvo, and Avon. Sun Realty offers the largest inventory of rental properties on the Outer Banks, managing more than 1,250 properties from Corolla through Hatteras Island. Weekly, monthly, and year-round rentals are available. A special program for disabled guests is offered. Pets are accepted in some units.

Nags Head

Bodie Island Realty
NC 12, MP 17, Nags Head
(252) 441–2558, (800) 862–1785
www.bodieislandrealty.com

This R.C.I. affiliate manages timeshares and two wholly owned units in the Bodie Island Resort for weekly rental all year. Three-night rentals are offered during the off-season. An elevator is located in one building.

Outer Banks Resort Rentals
Pirate's Quay, US 158, MP 11, Nags Head
(252) 441–2134
www.outerbanksresorts.com

Marvin Beard represents the sales and rentals of timeshares from Duck to South Nags as well as a few in Hatteras.

Cove Realty
Between NC 12 and US 158, MP 13½,
Nags Head
(252) 441–6391, (800) 635–7007
www.coverealty.com

Cove Realty manages approximately 125 properties in Old Nags Head Cove and South Nags Head for year-round, weekly, and student rental. Pets are accepted in some units. Weekend packages are available

during the off-season. Guests have access, for a small fee, to a swimming pool as well as to tennis courts in Old Nags Head Cove.

Nags Head Realty
US 158, MP 10½, Nags Head
(252) 441-4315, (800) 222-1531
www.nagsheadrealty.com

Nags Head Realty manages about 200 weekly rentals from the Crown Point development in the northern beaches to South Nags Head. Three-day rentals are offered during the off-season. Some units accept pets.

Stan White Realty & Construction, Inc.
US 158, MP 10½, Nags Head
(252) 441-1515, (800) 338-3233
www.outerbanksrentals.com

Stan White Realty recently expanded its offerings with the purchase of two local realty companies. This brings the Stan White Realty number of rental properties to 725. Weekly and year-round rentals are available from Corolla through South Nags Head. Pets are allowed in some weekly rentals. Wheelchair-accessible units are available. Two other Stan White offices are on the northern beaches, one in Corolla and one in Duck, called Duck's Real Estate

(see the Corolla and Duck sections of this chapter).

Village Realty
US 158, MP 14½, Nags Head
(252) 480-2224, (800) 548-9688
www.villagerealtyobx.com

Village Realty manages about 450 vacation rental properties in the development of the Village at Nags Head. Special weekend and golf packages are available. Some units include access to a beach club with an outdoor swimming pool, tennis courts, a game room, and family activities. Golf and tennis lessons are available. A golf course, private oceanfront access, and two private soundside piers also are on the premises. Some cottages allow pets. Some have elevators and can accommodate disabled vacationers. Village Realty has a second office at The Currituck Club in Corolla.

Roanoke Island

Pirate's Cove Realty
Manteo–Nags Head Causeway, Manteo
(252) 473-6800, (800) 537-7245
www.piratescoverentals.com

Pirate's Cove Realty manages 140 properties in the Pirate's Cove development for weekly rentals. Two-night weekends also are offered during the off-season. Some cottages accept pets. All units include access to an outdoor swimming pool, tennis courts, playground, and free boat slips.

20/20 Realty Ltd.
516 S. Main Hwy., Manteo
(252) 473–2020
www.2020realtyltd.com

This company manages year-round rentals from Kitty Hawk to Manns Harbor.

Hatteras Island

Avon Cottages
NC 12, Avon
(252) 995–4123
www.avoncottages.com

Each of Avon Cottages' 26 rental homes has a magnificent view of the Atlantic Ocean. Eight are oceanfront, seven semi-oceanfront, and 11 are oceanside, ranging from one to five bedrooms. All cottages have a large combination living room/dining room/kitchen, plus central heat and air, a microwave oven, and remote color TV with HBO. Fully equipped kitchens include plates and utensils; you may bring your own sheets and towels or rent them on site. Also available are laundry facilities, outside showers, fish cleaning tables, and plenty of parking. Pets are allowed.

Colony Realty Corp.
NC 12, Avon
(252) 995–5891, (800) 962–5256
www.hatterasvacations.com

Colony handles about 100 weekly units and approximately 40 long-term rentals in Avon, Buxton, Frisco, and Hatteras. Most of the units, which are single-family cottages or condos, will accept pets. Three-day minimum stays can be arranged in the off-season. Several wheelchair-accessible units are available.

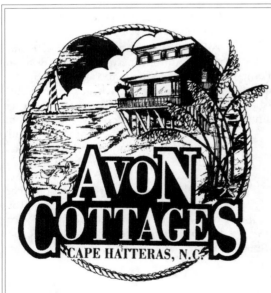

Dolphin Realty
NC 12, Hatteras Village
(252) 986–2562, (800) 338–4775
www.dolphin-realty.com

This company manages 70 properties, including homes and one-room efficiencies on Hatteras Island. Some are available for year-round rental. Pets are accepted in some units.

Hatteras Realty
NC 12, Avon
(252) 995–5466, (800) HATTERAS
www.hatterasrealty.com

Hatteras Realty manages over 375 properties on Hatteras Island for weekly rental only. Units may be rented by partial weeks during the off-season. Pets are accepted in some units. Wheelchair-accessible cottages are available. More than half of this company's units are furnished with hot tubs. Every guest has free access to the pool and tennis courts at Club Hatteras.

Midgett Realty
NC 12, Hatteras Village
(252) 986–2841, (800) 527–2903
www.midgettrealty.com

Midgett Realty manages more than 500 properties from Rodanthe to Hatteras Village for weekly rentals. Three-night rentals are available during the off-season, and some units accept pets. Several wheelchair-accessible units are offered.

Outer Beaches Realty
NC 12, Avon
(252) 995–4477 in Avon,
(252) 987–2771 in Waves, or (800) 627–3250
www.outerbeaches.com

Outer Beaches Realty manages nearly 500 rental cottages from Rodanthe to Hatteras Village. Weekly and three-day rentals are available. A few allow pets. Some wheelchair-accessible properties also are offered.

Surf or Sound Realty
NC 12, Avon
(252) 995–5801, (800) 237–1138
www.surforsound.com

The friendly staff at Surf or Sound Realty offers 300 cottages on Hatteras Island. Pets are accepted in some units. Wheelchair-accessible rentals also are available. You can make reservations on the Web site.

Old Nags Head: Authentic Outer Banks Architecture

For much of the 19th century, Nags Head was a getaway for the wealthy; a place to relax and recuperate; a safe haven from disease and so-called toxic vapors that doctors believed promoted illness. Summer after summer, growing families and networks of friends made this then-isolated beach one of the most popular of the East Coast's resort communities.

The Nags Head of yesteryear is still evident in a mile-long row of cottages that lines the oceanfront east of Jockey's Ridge. Weathered and stately, about a dozen homes built between 1860 and 1940 best characterize the unique Nags Head–style architecture that has become one of the signatures of the Outer Banks. The Nags Head Beach Cottage Row Historic District is one of the few turn-of-the-century resort areas remaining on the Eastern Seaboard that has maintained its original character, state historians say.

For the last few Septembers, Preservation North Carolina, a private nonprofit historic preservation group, has opened up many of the Nags Head cottages, with the owners' cooperation, for public tours. Scores of people eagerly took the group up on the offer, strolling from house-to-house and meeting the owners, some of whom spent almost every summer of their lives in the family's Nags Head oceanside retreat.

The beach cottages were designed to be functional and practical. Most notable for large porches lined with wind-proof built-in benches that wrap around three, even four, sides, the houses feature unpainted wooden siding, weathered by salt air to a deep brown, and angled porches and roofs. Shuttered windows offer ready shelter from sun and wind, but they are easily propped open with an attached stick. Pilings boost the floors away from encroaching waves. And if the ocean came a little too close for comfort, the houses were made to be moved easily. Some already have been moved away from the surf four times.

Most of the homes are one- or two-storied and have three or four bedrooms. Stairwells to the upstairs are narrow and the steps are creaky and often uneven. In some places on the ground floor, you can see through cracks to the scrubby plants and sand beneath the house. All houses now have flush toilets, rather than relying on the former outhouses, but many still depend only on the original outdoor shower installed away from the living quarters. Former servants' quarters have been changed into spare bedrooms, offices, or storage areas. Most cottages now have new kitchens in former breezeways, which separated the original kitchens from living space for safety reasons.

But what hasn't changed is the remarkable airiness and light that the rooms are effused in—and the way the steady slapping and sighing of ocean waves dominates the background sounds. The homes were all designed to foster air circulation; many cottage owners find no need for air conditioning. Sea breezes flip and billow tab curtains away from bedroom windows, affording occupants of one of these old beach cottages one of the best oceanfront vistas you can get on the Outer Banks.

Although there was already a thriving resort community near what is now Soundside Road in Nags Head, no one dared build near the Atlantic until 1866, when Dr. William Gaskins Pool decided to erect the first beachfront house on the Outer

Have a seat, relax, and enjoy the view. PHOTO: COURTESY OF DREW WILSON

Banks. Pool, according to historical documents, paid $30 for 50 acres of land along the ocean. In the interest of securing companionship, he gave 130-foot-wide lots away to friends, who built their own homes. Eventually, others followed, and one of the oldest beachfront settlements in the state took hold. The thirteen original Nags Head cottages were built between the end of the Civil War and World War II's onset.

Some cottages that have been part of the Preservation North Carolina tours include:

The Windemere
Built by well-known builder S.J. Twine, who constructed many of the cottages in the historic district. This one-story house was completed in the 1930s.

Fred Wood Cottage
This two-story house, also constructed by Twine, has two gable-end chimneys and a covered porch surrounding all four sides.

Whedbee Cottage
One of the few Civil War–era homes, this two-story frame home was finished in 1866.

Badham-Kittrell Cottage
Another house built by Twine, this 1928 home is one story with an L-shaped wing extending from the back of the house. The second level perches over the main living area.

Miss Mattie Midgett's Store

Moved from the soundside in 1933, this 1914 store supplied vacationers and locals with groceries, mail, and the area's only telephone. It still houses the booty from years of beachcombing done by Miss Mattie's daughter, Nellie Myrtle.

Martha Wood Cottage

Possibly the oldest of the historic district's cottages, this two-story house was likely built in 1870 or earlier. It has two projecting dormers on the beach side and a small, L-shaped addition in the rear.

The Silver Cottage

Built in 1883, this home's original owner paid $6.06 in annual taxes. The cottage was moved back farther from the ocean after the 1997–98 nor'easters.

For more information about future tours, please call Preservation North Carolina at (252) 832–1651 in Raleigh or (252) 482–7455 in Edenton.

Ocracoke Island

Ocracoke Island Realty Inc.
NC 12, Ocracoke Village
(252) 928–6261, (252) 928–7411
www.ocracokeislandrealty.com

A stroll on the beach is a mandatory part of your beach stay. PHOTO: COURTESY OF MARY ELLEN RIDDLE

Ocracoke Island Realty manages about 150 weekly rental properties on Ocracoke. Three-night packages are available during the off-season. A few of these cottages allow pets.

Sandy Shores Realty
NC 12, Ocracoke Village
(252) 928–5711
www.ocracoke-island.com

Sandy Shores manages 140 Ocracoke Island properties, one of which is wheel-chair-accessible. Only weekly rentals are available during the peak season. In the off-season, three-day minimums are available. Pets are accepted in some units.

Year-round Rentals

It can be quite a challenge to find a suitable property for long-term residential rental. It's not terribly difficult to find what most people on the Outer Banks refer to as a "winter rental," a time period that usually refers to the fall through early spring, when the cottage is not usually booked for weekly rentals. If you're looking for year-round residential or seasonal

accommodations during the summer, you'll need to begin your search as soon as possible.

Some rental companies deal lightly in long-term rentals, but few make it a specialty. It's worth some phone calls to the companies that specialize in the areas in which you're interested, but a better bet is probably to check the classifieds in the local newspapers. If you plan to spend the summer working on the Outer Banks, ask your employer for suggestions. If you don't have an employer yet, you should know that some smart business people are beginning to help their seasonal workers by offering housing.

Good places to look for long-term rentals are in Colington Harbour, on Roanoke Island, and between the highways in Nags Head, Kill Devil Hills, and Kitty Hawk. Southern Shores has a large year-round community. Currituck County, just north of the Wright Memorial Bridge, also offers some affordable options.

The following companies manage some year-round rentals. After the name of the company and phone number, we give the areas in which they have year-round options. Most of these companies are listed in greater detail either above or in our Real Estate chapter.

Atlantic Realty
(252) 261–2154, (800) 334–8401
Colington, Kill Devil Hills, and Kitty Hawk

Colony Realty
(252) 995–5891, (800) 962–5256
Avon, Frisco, and Hatteras

Cove Realty
(252) 441–6391, (800) 635–7007
Old Nags Head Cove and South Nags Head

Dolphin Realty
(252) 986–2241, (800) 338–4775
Hatteras Island

Kitty Dunes Realty
(252) 261–2171, (800) 334–3863
Colington Harbour, Kill Devil Hills, and Kitty Hawk

Kitty Hawk Rentals/Beach Realty & Construction
(252) 441–7166, (800) 635–1559
Duck, west of US 158, and between the highways in the central areas of the beach

Joe Lamb Jr. & Associates
(252) 261–4444, (800) 552–6257
Kitty Hawk to Nags Head

Jim Perry & Company
(252) 441–3051, (800) 222–6135
Duck to South Nags Head

Renting a cottage is a great way to accommodate the entire family. PHOTO: COURTESY OF JACKIE THOMAS

Resort Central Inc.
(252) 261–8861, (800) 334–4749
Kitty Hawk to Manteo

Seaside Realty
(252) 261–5500
Kitty Hawk to Nags Head

Southern Shores Realty
(252) 261–2111, (800) 334–1000
Duck to Kitty Hawk

Sun Realty
(252) 261–1152, (800) 334–4745
Corolla through Hatteras Island

20/20 Realty Ltd.
(252) 473–2020, (800) 520–2044
Kitty Hawk through Roanoke Island

Stan White Realty & Construction
(252) 441–1515, (800) 338–3233
Kitty Hawk to Nags Head

Wright Property Management
(252) 261–2186
Ocean Sands to South Nags Head

Accommodations

When it comes to accommodations, just like every other thing on the Outer Banks, you can have it as restful or as rowdy as you choose. Visitors looking to stay a night, several days, or a week can choose from a range of small, family-owned seaside motels to multiple-story franchises of national lodging chains. The farther south you go, the fewer chain-owned accommodations you'll see; in fact, they almost disappear. And north of Kitty Hawk, you'll find only two hotels and two bed-and-breakfasts. In recent years, upscale elegant inns and a variety of bed-and-breakfast establishments have opened their doors—offering a little more luxury and personal attention than the traditional barrier island hotels.

A few of these motels and hotels require two-night minimums on the weekends, and many accommodations require at least three-day stays for Memorial Day weekend, July Fourth weekend, and Labor Day weekend, since those are, by far, the busiest times on these barrier islands. A lot of Outer Banks hotels also have suites, efficiency apartments, and cottage units that rent by the day or week. Of course, you can stay in any room in any of these accommodations for a week or longer if you wish.

More and more, however, the Outer Banks is a vacation rental destination, where there are more private homes for rent by the week than there are hotel rooms for rent by the night. In Dare County alone (excluding the Currituck beaches and Ocracoke) there are approximately 8,066 rental cottages compared to 4,168 rooms or apartment-style rooms in hotels, bed-and-breakfast inns, and cottage courts. Modest, beachy cottages that offer comfort and convenience line the ocean from Kitty Hawk through Hatteras Village. Many families and groups of friends choose to rent these cottages for a week's vacation or longer. Companies that lease these properties are included in our Weekly and Long-term Cottage Rentals chapter.

If you're planning a summer stay on the Outer Banks, you should call early for reservations. Most accommodations are filled to capacity from early June through the first week of September. Usually, you can find walk-in rooms during the week; however, if you know the exact week or weekend that you're planning to visit, your best bet is to a room now.

Locations are indicated by milepost and town. Most of the hotels, motels, and inns are scattered along NC 12. A few line US 158, which is also called the Bypass. Roanoke and Ocracoke Islands also have several tucked beneath the trees off the beaten paths. Bed-and-breakfast inns are becoming more popular on the Outer Banks, with the largest numbers on Roanoke and Ocracoke Islands. There are 183 bed-and-breakfast rooms on the Outer Banks.

Rates vary dramatically from one area of the Outer Banks to another, from oceanfront rooms to those across the highway, between in- and off-season times, and especially depending on the amenities offered with each unit. In general, fall, winter, and early spring prices are at least one-third lower than midsummer rates—sometimes as little as $25 per night. The most expensive season, of course, is between mid-June and mid-August, when rates in general range from $50 a night for two people with two double beds to nearly $300 per night in some of the fancier establishments.

Many hotels and motels honor AARP and other discounts and oftentimes allow children to stay free with paying adults.

More and more accommodations providers are keeping their doors open all year to cater to fall fishing parties, spring visitors, and people who like the Outer Banks best in winter when few others are around. If you prefer isolation at the beach and don't mind wind and temperatures in the 40s and 50s, November through February would be a good time to come. September and October, however, are our favorite months. The ocean is still warm enough to swim in, the daytime temperature seldom drops below the mid-60s, most restaurants, attractions, and retail shops are still open, yet the prices are much cheaper and most of the bustle is gone once school starts up again.

Price Code

For your ease in checking our price ranges, we've created a dollar-sign key showing a range of the average cost for a double-occupancy one-night stay in a room with two double beds during peak summer season. Extra charges may apply for special weekends, additional people in the room, efficiency apartments, or pets. These prices do not include local and state taxes. Unless otherwise indicated in the listing, all accommodations accept major credit cards.

$ .... Less than $60
$$ .... $61 to $80
$$$ .... $81 to $125
$$$$ .... More than $126

Deposits and Check-in Times

Most motels and hotels require deposits to hold advance summer registration. Policies vary between properties, but the average amount is 25 percent to 35 percent of the total reservation cost or one night's rate. Ask about specific provisions when reserving your room, and call to confirm your reservations before leaving for the Outer Banks.

Many proprietors require the balance of your bill to be paid on arrival. Be prepared with cash, traveler's checks, or a credit card. Personal checks often are not accepted for this final payment. Again, ask

when booking your room. Automated teller machines (ATMs) are available at most local banks.

Before making reservations, be sure to check on the cancellation or refund policies. If you are concerned there might be a hurricane brewing during your visit, ask about refund policies in case of evacuation.

Check-in times also vary among accommodations. Most places won't allow you into their rooms before 2:00 P.M. but can hold them for you until 10:00 or 11:00 P.M. if necessary. If you know you'll get here earlier, ask about early check-in provisions or go ahead and just spend that first morning out on the beach. Public showers are provided at some beach accesses, so you can clean off before getting into your hotel room. Several motels, inns, and bed-and-breakfast establishments also offer outdoor showers for their guests. Check-out times in general are between 10:00 A.M. and noon. Sometimes, later stays can be accommodated. Ask for a late check-out if you know you'll want to linger that last day.

Locations and Amenities

In this chapter, oceanfront means that the property has at least some rooms facing the ocean right on the beach. Most of these units have balconies and picture windows. Rooms on the ground level or behind sand dunes, however, may not have views of the Atlantic, even if they're oceanfront. Ask about what's available, and clarify which type of location you'd prefer. Remember, you'll almost always pay more to watch the waves from your room.

Conveniences and luxuries included in rooms at motels, hotels, inns, efficiencies, and bed-and-breakfasts usually vary, even in the same structure. Some include kitchenettes, king-size beds, whirlpool baths, and fireplaces. Others may have double beds and an extra sleeper sofa for the kids. All, however, have air-conditioning, and places that remain open in the fall and winter include heat.

Many motels and hotels, especially the older beachfront structures and newer high-rise units, have meeting facilities, conference rooms, and large common areas to accommodate family reunions, business workshops, and tour groups. Although most newer accommo-

dations are wheelchair-accessible, many of the older motels and hotels are partially accessible or not at all. It is always a good idea when making your reservation to check that your particular needs can be met. If you are a pet owner and want the pooch to vacation with you, your pickings are going to be much slimmer. Most motels and inns do not allow pets, so assume that pets are not permitted unless otherwise noted. Many companies that rent cottages, however, welcome pets. See our Weekly and Long-term Cottage Rentals chapter.

Amenities run the gamut from the most basic (bed and shower only) to places that provide microwaves, refrigerators, televisions with free movie channels or videocassette recorders, telephones, fluffy bathrobes, fancy soaps, free coffee,

Curb the cost of the family vacation by choosing a hotel where kids can stay for free. PHOTO: COURTESY OF JACKIE THOMAS

also include volleyball courts, horseshoe pits, picnic tables, gas grills, and small putting greens on-site for their guests.

Area Profiles

Accommodations in the northern beaches are much more upscale than on the rest of the Outer Banks. Corolla has only two hotels that rent rooms by the night—the Inn at Corolla Light and the new Hampton Inn. The town of Duck boasts two by-the-night establishments, both of them bed-and-breakfast inns, and the Sanderling Inn Resort, between Duck and Corolla, offers hotel rooms in a classic resort atmosphere. All of these northern-beaches accommodations are elegant and guaranteed to make guests feel comfortable and well cared for; however, the majority of travelers on the northern beaches rent individual cottages by the week.

Nearly all accommodations in the northern beaches area are along the main artery, NC 12, which is known as Ocean Trail in Corolla and Duck Road in Duck.

Kitty Hawk was one of the first Outer Banks beach towns to develop a tourist trade, and some of the hotels and motels there are reminiscent of the early cottage courts. These primarily family-run businesses are small, clean, and often cheaper than nationally known hotels. There's also a Holiday Inn Express on US 158 and a couple of bed-and-breakfast inns west of the highway.

Kill Devil Hills is the most central—and most populated—place on the barrier islands. Many of its accommodations are in walking distance of restaurants, shopping, and recreational attractions. Quaint motels with fewer than two dozen rooms are common here, as are big chain establishments with oceanfront conference centers. Public beach and sound accesses abound in this town.

The Outer Banks's first resort destination was Nags Head, so here you'll find everything from a 1930s-era inn to the tallest hotel on the Outer Banks. Some accommodations retain the old-timey feel

Insiders' Tip

Memorial Day through Labor Day is the peak season for Outer Banks vacations, but fall and spring are becoming increasingly popular times of year to visit. Rates are lower in the spring and fall than during the summer, and there are far fewer crowds. Both of these seasons can offer remarkably warm weather and almost all of the amenities of the summer vacation—except warm ocean water.

cocktails and afternoon tea, gourmet breakfasts, bicycles, and golf clubs. A few hotels offer "big-city" advantages such as room service, assistance with luggage, and wake-up calls—but most don't, so read the descriptions carefully if you require such services, and call ahead with other specific questions.

All Outer Banks accommodations provide free parking for at least one vehicle per unit. Keep valuables with you rather than leaving them locked in the car. Some hotels offer safes in the main office for their guests to stow valued items.

Many motel, hotel, and inn managers will provide recreation packages with your room, especially during the off-season. For the most part, golf courses, tennis facilities, and health clubs are open year-round. Call about these special combinations, or ask the proprietor about special discounts that might be available to guests. Daily or weeklong memberships are offered at most private facilities. Some accommodations

of cedar-shake-shingled cottages, while others have gone for the ultramodern, multiple-floor look complete with elevators and room service from the in-house restaurant. Like Kill Devil Hills, but a lot more spread out and slightly less populated, Nags Head abounds with restaurants, retail shops, and recreation.

Roanoke Island's accommodations range from modest motels to fine, fabulous inns. All are just a bike ride away from the historic waterfront, and many are perfect for a romantic weekend getaway or cloistered honeymoon stay. Rental cottages aren't prevalent here because the large majority of the population, even in the summer, is made up of permanent residents; however, if you want to get away from the bustle of the beach and still be close to the sound, wetlands, and wonderful historic attractions this island has to offer, you won't have difficulty finding a room to suit your tastes here.

Motels and hotels on Hatteras Island are, in general, more laid-back than on other parts of the barrier islands. There are now two national chains on the island (one in Buxton and one in Hatteras), but family-owned and -operated places still dominate the accommodations here. Many of these units are no-frills without phones in the rooms or fancy furnishings,

but if you are looking for an affordable place to stay along the quieter stretches of beach, don't overlook Hatteras Island's short-term room, inn, and efficiency accommodation options.

Ocracoke Island's lodgings are, in general, the most personal on the Outer Banks. Here, you'll find old inns, newer motels, upscale bed-and-breakfast inns, efficiency apartments, and even a few folks who will rent you a room in their house, sometimes right next to their own. This laid-back little island is separated from the rest of the world by free ferry rides (see our Getting Here, Getting Around chapter). It's a great place to escape from it all. There are also plenty of accommodations, quaint boutiques, and great restaurants to please almost anyone here.

Corolla

The Inn at Corolla Light $$$$
1066 Ocean Trail, Corolla
(252) 453–3340, (800) 215–0772
www.corolla-inn.com
Located within walking distance of the Currituck Beach Lighthouse, The Inn at Corolla Light is a luxurious place where guests can plan their days around an incredible array of recreational activities

The inn furnishes bicycles to guests so they can take leisurely tours of the resort's landscaped grounds.

Sailing excursions, guided kayak trips, windsurfing, parasailing, and personal watercraft (JetSkis, Wave Runners, and others) are available at a watersports rental site on the resort. A championship golf course is also nearby. A must-do is to take the proprietor's wild horse tour by a four-wheel-drive Suburban into the off-road and largely undeveloped area north of Corolla. Bob White does many of these tours himself, and it's apparent that he loves the area. Although sparsely inhabited, the northern beaches are rich in history, local lore, and of course, wild horses (and plenty of other wild sights).

The inn's 43 guest rooms include kitchenettes, cable TVs, radios, VCRs, and private baths. Many also have fireplaces and whirlpool tubs. The rooms are designed for single or double occupancy, and many are equipped with sleeper sofas too. Guests can enjoy a free continental breakfast daily.

The Inn at Corolla Light has two- and three-night minimum stays on week-ends and charges $15 per night for each additional person. Special rate packages are offered throughout the year. Be sure to call their toll-free number for more information.

Hampton Inn and
Suites Outer Banks Corolla $$$$
NC 12, Pine Island (north of Duck)
(252) 453-6565, (800) HAMPTON
www.hamptoninn.com

Those looking for short-term lodgings on the northern Outer Banks have never had many options, but the fancy new ocean-front Hampton Inn now fills the void. Opened in May 2002, the inn has 123 sleeper rooms, a mix of guest rooms, and studio suites. Room decor has a coastal theme, plus ceiling fans and private bal-conies. Each room has a television, microwave, refrigerator, hair dryer, iron-ing equipment, coffeemaker, pay Nin-tendo, pay-per-view movies, and two two-line phones. Most rooms feature a

available nearly at their doorstep—or they may wish simply to relax in full view of the sparkling waters of Currituck Sound and bask in the serenity of this beautifully appointed facility.

The year-round inn opened during the 1995 season in the ocean-to-sound resort community of Corolla Light. This upscale development is laced with wooded walk-ing and biking trails and offers every leisure amenity a vacationer could dream of: an indoor sports center with an Olympic-size pool, hot tub, saunas, clay tennis courts, racquetball courts, and fit-ness equipment; an oceanfront complex that boasts two outdoor pools, a video game room, restaurant, and exclusive access to the beach; soundfront pools; play areas for basketball, shuffleboard, tennis, horseshoes, and more; and terrific shops and restaurants nearby (see our Shopping and Restaurants chapters). Guests of the inn have unlimited access to all of the resort's facilities. There is a nom-inal fee for use of the indoor tennis courts, but all other courts are free.

Guests may also use the inn's own waterfront swimming pool, hot tub, and private 400-foot pier on Currituck Sound.

pull-out sofa, and some have whirlpool tubs. Studio suites also feature a wet bar. The majority of rooms have an ocean view. Public areas include a heated indoor pool and whirlpool spa, an exercise room, a game room, four meeting rooms, coin-operated laundry facilities, and the Suite Shop with sundries, beach supplies, sodas, and snacks. Outdoors is a pool, kiddie pool, and a lazy river. Direct beach access is provided. Continental breakfast is served to guests each morning. This hotel is at Pine Island, just north of Duck and the Currituck County line.

Duck

Sanderling Inn Resort   **$$$$**
1461 NC 12, Duck
(252) 261–4111, (800) 701–4111
www.sanderlinginn.com

The Sanderling Inn Resort is situated on 12 acres of oceanside wilderness about 5 miles north of the town of Duck. Here, heavy strands of beach grass, sea oats, pines, fragrant olives, and live oaks provide a natural setting for an elegant, enjoyable vacation. The Sanderling was built in the style of the old Nags Head beach homes with wood siding, cedar-shake accents, dormer windows, and porches on each side. Rocking chairs line the wide porches, providing a relaxing way to pass sultry afternoons while overlooking the ocean or sound.

All 87 rooms at the Sanderling are comfortable, lush, and oh-so-accommodating. The inn provides all its guests with lounging robes, luxury soaps, toiletries, and a welcome gift featuring North Carolina products. A continental breakfast and afternoon tea also come with each room.

The main lobby and gallery of the Sanderling offer a warm welcome to weary travelers. Decorated in an English country theme, they're adorned with contemporary finishes and accented by polished wood floors and wainscotting. The inn's main building has 29 rooms, all with kitchenettes. Audubon prints and artwork line the walls. Another 32 rooms in Sanderling Inn North are filled with wicker furniture

and are now also equipped with kitchenettes. The 26 rooms in the newest South Wing each have a king-size bed, wet bar, and kitchenette. Six of the units in the South Wing are deluxe suites that feature two televisions with VCRs (one in the bedroom and one in the living area), a double sleeper sofa, a stereo with compact disc player and one-and-a-half baths. Some suites also have hot tubs. All Sanderling rooms have telephones and televisions and VCRs with remote control and cable.

Accommodations here are designed for the comfort and privacy of two guests per room, but sleeper sofas and cribs are available for an additional charge.

A separate building at the Sanderling houses excellent conference and meeting facilities as well as the Presidential Suite, complete with whirlpool bath, steam shower, and two decks—one overlooks the ocean and the other overlooks the sound. For an additional charge, the inn's housekeeping staff provides laundry service with a 48-hour turnaround. Room service is provided by the on-site, upscale Sanderling Restaurant (see our Restaurants chapter).

This is a complete resort with private beaches, a full-service spa, and state-of-the-art fitness center. There's an indoor pool, a separate whirlpool room, locker rooms, steam rooms, an outdoor pool, tennis courts, and a natural walking or jogging trail. The Audubon Wildlife Sanctuary and the Pine Island Tennis and Racquet Club are nearby. An eco-center offers kayaks for visitors to use. A seasonal outdoor pavilion and four three- and four-bedroom villas were also recently added to Sanderling's already extraordinary offerings. The villas are perfect for families.

The new spa houses six treatment rooms and offers an extensive menu of services, including manicures, pedicures, facials, massages, and more.

Full package deals are available for New Year's Eve, Valentine's Day, honeymoons, and winter escapes. Packages generally include one or more meals at the Sanderling Restaurant, full use of the fitness center and indoor pool, welcoming gifts, and other extras. Some seasonal discounts are available. Weekend guests must stay both Friday and Saturday nights during the summer, and a three-day minimum stay is required for in-season holidays. Wheelchair access is provided for all buildings on the property, and wheelchair-accessible rooms are available. The Sanderling Inn is open year-round.

Advice 5¢ $$$$
111 Scarborough La., Duck
(252) 255–1050, (800) 238–4235
www.advice5.com

Advice 5¢, in its seventh season, exudes an air of casual simplicity. Here, Nancy Caviness and Donna Black provide all their guests with private baths, rocking chairs, and decks. The suite also includes cable TV, a stereo, and whirlpool bath. Hardwood floors and juniper appointments, comfy Lexington cottage furniture, ceiling fans, quilts, colorful bath towels, linens, and greenery galore lend this idyllic beach getaway a crisp, unaffected atmosphere. Just .3 mile from the ocean, this sunny, spacious bed-and-breakfast has beautiful views of both sea and sound.

A common area with a fireplace for those chilly off-season evenings is a popular gathering spot for guests. A continental breakfast buffet of fresh fruit salad and just-baked breads and muffins is served daily in the common room. Afternoon tea tempts guests with more homemade delights as well as hot and cold beverages. At day's end, or when the weather doesn't cooperate, you can try your hand at a puzzle or round up some folks for an intense game of Scrabble. If quieter pursuits are what you crave, the den on the guest floor level is the perfect place to delve into one of a variety of good books available here.

Two outdoor showers allow beachgoers to wash off after a long day in the sun. A locking storage shed also provides protected shelter out of the elements for storing bicycles, boogie boards, golf clubs, and other gear. An in-ground pool across the street and tennis courts are available for guests.

All rooms at this establishment are nonsmoking. It is not accessible to the disabled, and young children cannot be accommodated here. Advice 5¢ closes in mid-November and reopens in March.

May's Landing Bed & Breakfast $$$
1158 Duck Rd., NC 12, Duck
(252) 261–2300
www.mayslandingduck.com

Nestled within the town of Duck is a true Insiders' find. Tom and Marianna of May's Landing Bed & Breakfast offer guests a perfect coastal getaway. Just relax and enjoy this picturesque inn.

A short walk or easy bicycle ride will get you to plenty of shopping, gourmet restaurants, and watersport activities. Bicycles and kayaks are available for guest use. If you're in a more reflective mood, just observe the birds on the sound. May's Landing is located on the Atlantic flyway—wild geese and ducks abound as they travel their centuries-old migration pathways. With the beautiful Currituck Sound located just yards from the back deck of May's Landing, guests can enjoy breathtaking sunsets from the decks or gazebo.

May's Landing offers three rooms. Each room has a private bath. A full breakfast buffet is served each day with the freshest fruit and an array of juices, cereals, and pastries. Hot entrees such as omelets, quiches, souffles, pancakes, and waffles accompanied with bacon, sausage,

or ham are served. Tea and coffee are available. At the end of a busy beach day, guests won't want to miss the snacks and beverages served in the family room.

May's Landing is open May 1 through October 31. The inn is pet free as well as smoke free. Children over 12 are welcome, and May's Landing is wheelchair accessible.

Kitty Hawk

The Summer Place Bed and Breakfast
$$$-$$$$
4424 Sea Scape Dr., MP 2, Kitty Hawk
(252) 255-1624

This bed-and-breakfast inn is full of good surprises. First there's the sweeping Tara-like staircase that greets you as you come in the door. Then there's the decor. You might be expecting a beachy pastel palette, but what you find is a refreshingly formal yet comfortable setting with rich hues and classic furniture. Another treat is the view of the ocean. Although the house is several blocks from the Atlantic, its high setting affords its occupants a sweeping view of the water. Owners Jean and Don Houston opened their vacation home as a bed-and-breakfast inn in 1999. Jean loves to entertain, and she treats every guest with the utmost care.

The house has the perfect layout for an inn. The Houstons live on the top floor, while the entire entry-level floor serves as guest quarters. Two guest rooms are available on this level: the Magnolia Room and the Rose Room. Both have queen-size beds and private baths. Egyptian linens and plush robes and towels are special touches. Separating the two rooms is a comfortable den with a TV, books, and a minifridge stocked with refreshments. Jean serves afternoon refreshments in the den. Both guest rooms open onto a long covered porch with a hammock swing and rockers. Downstairs is the sizable Cabana Room, with a queen-size bed, an efficiency kitchen, a billiards table, and a sliding glass door that opens onto the pool deck. On the south side of the house, the pool soaks up all-day sun. An arbor-covered hot tub and tranquil Japanese-style garden create an exceptional landscape. An outdoor shower is available for rinsing off after the beach.

Jean brings coffee and newspapers to the guest-room level at 7:30 A.M. At 9:00, she serves breakfast upstairs on the top floor, where the view of the ocean is superb. Breakfast is formal, with fine china and silver. The full gourmet meal includes juice, coffee, and fruit and something homemade and fancy, like eggs benedict, Belgian waffles with whipped cream and berries, baked French toast, sausage and cheese strata, or blueberry pancakes. Bikes, beach chairs, and umbrellas are available for guests to use. The Summer Place is open year-round, expect for a few weeks in the winter.

3 Seasons Bed & Breakfast   **$$$**
Sea Scape Dr., MP 2, Kitty Hawk
(252) 261-4791, (800) 847-3373
www.threeseasonsouterbanks.com

This bed-and-breakfast inn is tucked away from the ocean and highways at Seascape Golf Course on the west side of the Bypass. Golf enthusiasts find this location ideal: The putting green is in front of the property, and the ninth hole is behind it. You barely have to get out of bed before bellowing "Fore!"

Just 2½ blocks from the ocean, 3 Seasons sits on a high sandhill, so guests can

The Outer Banks is known for wide, sandy beaches with lots of room to play. PHOTO: COURTESY OF KAREN BACHMAN

enjoy views of the Atlantic. Even if you've never swung a nine iron, you'll enjoy unwinding and relaxing at this charming establishment. Susie and Tommy Gardner have been operating the bed-and-breakfast since 1992. It's a five-bedroom house, and four of the rooms are available for double occupancy. Each guestroom has a private bath and TV. The decor feels like home—comfortable and "beachy." Guests can gather around a fireplace in the common area or take in the ocean breezes off the canopied deck. The hot tub on the deck also creates a big splash. A tennis court and a swimming pool are available for guests to enjoy.

Complimentary cocktails are served afternoons on the enclosed patio. Guests can also enjoy a full breakfast cooked to order daily between 8:00 and 10:00 A.M. Bicycles are available for a ride to the beach or along trails nearby. The entire establishment is nonsmoking, although smoking on the outdoor deck is fine. Note that 3 Seasons is not equipped to accommodate children younger than 18 or the disabled. Two-night stays are required on summer weekends, and a three-day minimum is requested for holiday weekends. This quaint inn is open April through November.

Outer Banks International Hostel $
1004 W. Kitty Hawk Rd., Kitty Hawk
(252) 261–2294
www.hiayh.org

The Outer Banks International Hostel opened in April 1996 and has made it possible for travelers on a budget to enjoy their stay in comfortable, clean accommodations that won't break the bank. The former elementary school building is nestled on 10 acres in quiet Kitty Hawk Village, not far from where the Wright brothers stayed.

As part of Hostelling International American Youth Hostels, this facility is a year-round, inexpensive, no-frills operation—and there are no curfews or chores in the deal. You're just expected to clean up after yourself. All ages are welcome, and a friendly staff is on hand to help you plan your stay on the Outer Banks.

Amenities include shared kitchen facilities, a common lounge area with cable TV and books, a barbecue and campfire area, and a large front porch with Adirondack chairs. Guests can choose from sleeping in separate male and female dormitories or couple/private and family/group rooms. Private rooms with private baths are available. Sheets and towels can be rented here. Boogie Boards, fishing gear, and beach chairs are available for use. Guests are welcome to enjoy croquet and bocce ball in the spacious yard. Volleyball, badminton, and shuffleboard are other fun options. Tent-only camping is available at the hostel too.

As veteran international travelers already know, hostels are reputed to be safe, friendly places where it's easy to meet other adventurers. The Outer Banks International Hostel is as affordable as you get on the barrier islands, and you can have a pleasant, memorable stay to boot. Dormitory beds cost $15 a night for Hostelling International members and $18 for nonmembers; group rates are $13 per person. Reservations are required for groups, and there are group rates and discounts. There is an additional charge for a private room with a private bath. Children younger than 12 are charged half-price.

Sea Kove Motel $$$, no credit cards
NC 12, MP 3, Kitty Hawk
(252) 261–4722

This family-owned and -operated establishment rents 10 one-bedroom efficiency units, 10 two-bedroom units, and two cottages by the week only from April through November. It's across from the ocean and includes full-size kitchens and televisions in each apartment. A playground and outdoor pool also are available.

The Baldview Bed & Breakfast $$$–$$$$
3807 Elijah Baum Drive, Kitty Hawk
(252) 255–2829
www.baldview.com

You can view glorious sunrises and sunsets from The Baldview Bed & Breakfast on Kitty Hawk Bay with more than 1,000 feet of property on the sound. The inn houses four exclusive rooms with private baths; 11 acres of maritime forest with nature walks surround the properties, yet the main house is located only five minutes from the ocean.

The Baldview offers a quiet getaway for adults who enjoy tranquil, natural surroundings, and even has an authentic carriage house for the ultimate romantic experience. Smoking is restricted to a separate designated house on the property. A light breakfast is served each morning, and there's a weekly wine and cheese night. This is a perfect venue for larger party rentals, weddings, and corporate retreats. The Baldview is open year-round.

Beach Haven Motel $$$
NC 12, MP 4, Kitty Hawk
(252) 261–4785, (888) 559–0506
www.beachhavenmotel.com

This small motel sits across the road from its own private beach and includes two buildings with a total of six mini efficiency units. Owner Joe Verscharen makes sure his motel provides guests all they need for a peaceful and relaxing stay. A practical, homey atmosphere prevails at this motel, where each room has a refrigerator, microwave, hair dryer, cable TV, telephone, and porch chairs. Coffee is provided in each room at this uniquely groomed establishment, which Verscharen boasts has earned a Grade A cleanliness rating year after year from the Dare County Health Department. Beach Haven has also received AAA's Three-Diamond Rating.

Beach Haven is in uncrowded surroundings with natural beach landscaping that will remind visitors of a lovely oasis. Guests can loll on the elevated deck and enjoy the scenery. A grass-carpeted picnic area with tables and a gas grill are on the premises. Bike rentals are available, as are many beach accessories. You can practice your classic stroke on a putting green situated on the cashmere lawn, where you might also show off your talents in a game of croquet.

Economy rooms sleep two people, and deluxe rooms can accommodate up to four guests. Cribs are provided for infants. The decor throughout reflects a contemporary beach look with rattan and wicker furniture. Joe lives at the motel and promises to make your stay as pleasant as possible. Beach Haven is open mid-March through mid-November.

Holiday Inn Express $$$
US 158, MP 4¼, Kitty Hawk
(252) 261–4888, (800) 836–2753
www.hiexpress.com

Situated on the east side of US 158, Holiday Inn Express has an outdoor swimming pool and is a short walk to lifeguarded Kitty Hawk Beach, where guests can use the motel's private access and oceanfront deck. All the motel's 98 rooms are spacious and have cable TV, telephones, and refrigerators. Some also have couches, and half have microwaves. Most offer two double beds and some rooms have queen-size beds. All are attractively furnished in soft beach decor.

The inn provides a complimentary continental breakfast bar for guests each morning in the lobby. Nonsmoking and wheelchair-accessible rooms are available at this Holiday Inn Express. Children 17 and younger stay free if accompanied by an adult. Meeting rooms accommodate up to 10 people, and year-round group rates are available. This motel is within walking distance of shopping and several restaurants. It's open all year.

Cypress Moon Bed and Breakfast $$$$
1206 Harbor Court, Kitty Hawk
(252) 261–5060, (800) 905–5060
www.cypressmooninn.com

Nestled in the maritime forest with the sound just behind, you'll find Cypress Moon Bed and Breakfast. The owners are Linda and Greg Hamby, and they share quarters with their friendly Scottish terrier, Jock. This new home is furnished with antiques throughout the residence. Birdwatchers will enjoy the variety in bird sightings, and deer, foxes, and other wildlife frequently are spotted in the area.

Four rooms are available at the Cypress

Moon Bed and Breakfast. Each room is soundfront and has a semiprivate covered porch. All rooms have a queen-size bed—you can awaken each morning to a spectacular view of the Currituck Sound. Brunch is served each day, and you can choose to be served in the dining room, in your bedroom, or on your porch. Brunch consists of seafood, such as crab cakes or shrimp, breakfast meat, fresh bread, fruit, Cypress Moon specially blended coffee, and fresh-squeezed orange juice. Breakfast is served on pottery with silverware and fine linens.

If you choose to spend a day away from the beach, you may wish to use the kayaks or sailboards provided. There is a nice walkway to the water, and outdoor showers are available. At 3:00 P.M. each day, baked goods are served with tea and lemonade. If you return after 3:00, the afternoon snack is available on a self-serve basis until 5:00 P.M.. The inn welcomes people 18 and older, and smoking is not allowed on premise. Cypress Moon is closed for the month of December.

Buccaneer Motel and Beach Suites $$
NC 12, MP 5½, Kitty Hawk
(252) 261–2030, (800) 442–4412
www.outer-banks.nc.us/buccaneermotel
Repeat business is the name of the game at the Buccaneer, where folks who stayed here as teenagers are now bringing their grandkids for visits. Owners Sandy and Dave Briggman have fostered the authentic Outer Banks charm that's made the Buccaneer a place vacationers come back to year after year. Travelers have their choice of one- and two-bedroom units, and efficiency apartments with one to three bedrooms are available for those wishing to stay longer. Each unit has a refrigerator, cable TV, and a microwave.

While the Buccaneer is across the highway from the beach, there are no buildings between it and the ocean, and guests only have to cross a small sand dune to reach the surf. A dune-top deck and private beach access make enjoying the Atlantic from this establishment almost as easy as if the motel were right on the ocean. Other amenities provided include a large, outdoor swimming pool with adjoining deck, a children's playground, a basketball court, charcoal grills, and a fish-cleaning station. Discounts are offered on all weekly stays, and the Getaway Card is honored during the off-season. The motel is not wheelchair-accessible. The Buccaneer is open year-round.

Kill Devil Hills

Tan-a-Rama Motel Apartments $$$
NC 12, MP 6, Kill Devil Hills
(252) 441–7315, (800) 845–0903
www.tanarama.com
This family-oriented, oceanfront motel is smack on the beach, with no barrier dunes to obstruct your view of the water. Each of the 35 newly renovated efficiencies and apartments feature opening windows on two sides that allow for cross-ventilation of the sea breezes. Of course, all are air conditioned and heated too. One- or two-bedroom units are available, and you can get a room with or without a kitchen. All rooms have wall-to-wall carpet, cable TV, telephones, and daily maid service. Kitchen units have all the items you'll need for cooking, including stove tops, pots, and dishes. The upstairs oceanfront suites include a separate sitting room, two double beds, and a full kitchen. Oceanfront and courtside efficiencies have two double beds plus a sitting room and kitchen. Fax service, cot and crib rentals, and ice are available to guests.

Guests will enjoy the outdoor pool, playground, outdoor grills, outdoor showers, and fish-cleaning station. The Tan-a-Rama is next door to all the fishing and recreational action around the Avalon Pier and is close to popular restaurants and shops. There is a two-night minimum on all stays at this motel, and some holiday weekends have a minimum three-night stay. Kids five and younger stay free here. Complimentary beach blankets are provided for guests. The Tan-a-Rama is open April though October.

Days Inn Mariner Motel $$$
NC 12, MP 7, Kill Devil Hills
(252) 441–2021, (800) 325–2525
www.days-inn-mariner@outer-banks.com

A total of 70 units—58 of which are on the ocean—comprise the accommodations here: 33 offer two double beds in a single room, and 37 are one- and two-bedroom apartments with complete kitchens. Each room and apartment includes a telephone, refrigerator, and cable TV. All the rooms were refurbished recently with a fresh, contemporary beach look.

There's easy access to the Atlantic, and the units are spacious enough to offer flexible living arrangements for families or groups. This motel's recreation area has facilities for volleyball, and an outdoor swimming pool and showers are just off the ocean. Nonsmoking and wheelchair-accessible rooms are available. All Days Inn programs are honored, and AARP discounts are available. The Mariner is open mid-February through November, with rates discounted by 50 percent in the off-season.

Quality Inn Sea Ranch Hotel $$$$
NC 12, MP 7, Kill Devil Hills
(252) 441–7126, (800) 334–4737
www.searanchhotel.com

The Sea Ranch was one of the Outer Banks's first resort properties to include recreational amenities, a restaurant, lounge, and retail shops. This hotel is family-owned and -operated, with a five-story oceanfront tower and a two-story building that contains 50 motel-style rooms. Each unit has cable TV and free HBO, a refrigerator, microwave, coffeemaker, and telephone. The apartments have glass-enclosed oceanfront balconies, two bedrooms, and two baths. They typically rent weekly, but some can be rented nightly depending on occupancy. About 25 of the hotel rooms have oceanfront views. Nonsmoking rooms are available, and the hotel is wheelchair-accessible.

If you're in the mood for exercise, the Sea Ranch has a heated indoor pool that's open year-round on the premises, and across the road is a recently expanded Nautilus fitness center frequented by both locals and visitors. A women's boutique and hair salon also are on site. The Sea Ranch is closed from December through spring.

The Chart House Motel $$$
NC 12, MP 7, Kill Devil Hills
(252) 441–7418

With an eye-catching blue mural depicting dolphins dancing through the waves painted on the front of this building, you can't miss the Chart House Motel. David and Kristin Clark, the hosts of this 18-unit motel, live in the large oceanfront brick Colonial beside it, close enough to offer their personal touch. Built in 1966, the Chart House is a popular spot with six efficiency apartments and 12 motel rooms. Each unit has two double beds, a color TV, a telephone, refrigerator, microwave, and coffeemaker.

The one-room efficiencies also have fully equipped kitchens, and five of these units connect with regular motel rooms to accommodate larger groups and families. Nonsmoking rooms are available. This motel is not equipped for the disabled.

The Chart House sits perpendicular to the ocean, so direct ocean views are not available. A small pool and patio are away from the road. The Outer Banks Health Systems/Hammerheads Fitness Center (see our Recreation chapter) is across the street, and two local favorite restaurants are also in walking distance: the Jolly Roger and Goombays (see our Restaurants chapter).

The Chart House Motel is open mid-March through November.

Nettlewood Motel $–$$
NC 12, MP 7, Kill Devil Hills
(252) 441–5039
www.nettlewoodmotel.com

Locally owned and operated for 24 years, the Nettlewood is a favorite of the older set who like to come to the beach in small groups and who appreciate a small, clean motel. The Nettlewood has 22 rooms with one or two double beds and 16 efficiency units with two double beds and complete kitchens. All rooms have refrigerators, telephones, and color TVs with remote controls and cable. Rooms rent by the day during the week, but three-night minimum stays are required during summer weekends.

Across the street, four 1,500-square-foot apartments each offer three bedrooms and two baths and can accommodate up to eight people. These larger units rent weekly. There's also a large in-ground swimming pool on-site for guests. The Nettlewood is open year-round.

Insiders' Tip

If you can't bear to leave your pets at home, be aware that there are not many pet-friendly accommodations on the Outer Banks, nor are there many kennels. Try Salty Dog Grooming and Boarding, (252) 441-6501, in Kill Devil Hills or Salty Paws Bed and Biscuit, (252) 928-3093, on Ocracoke Island. Several veterinarians also provide boarding facilities. Ask your hotel proprietor or rental agent for a suggestion.

Nags Head Beach Hotel $$$
NC 12, MP 8, Kill Devil Hills
(252) 441–0411, (800) 338–7761

This 97-room, four-story hotel has exterior and interior corridors and was recently renovated inside and out. It's across the street from the ocean, so some guest rooms have views of the Atlantic, while others afford glimpses of the Wright Brothers National Memorial. Twelve of the first-floor guest rooms open directly onto the outdoor courtyard and pool.

Each room has a microwave, refrigerator, color TV (with remote control, cable, and free HBO), a telephone, and private balcony or patio, with nonsmoking and wheelchair-accessible rooms available. A complimentary continental breakfast featuring cereals, pastries, juices, coffee, tea, and fresh fruits is served daily in the lobby from 6:00 until 10:00 A.M. Discounts are available to AARP members. Children 18 and younger stay free in their parents' room, and pets are welcome for a $10 per day additional charge. During summer holidays, three-night minimum stays are required. The Nags Head Beach Hotel is open all year.

Comfort Inn North $$$$
NC 12, MP 8, Kill Devil Hills
(252) 480–2600, (800) 854–5286

Only 11 years old and one of the newer oceanfront motels on the Outer Banks, this three-story property includes 119 rooms that open along exterior corridors. They're filled with natural light and decorated tastefully. The building is T-shaped, so not all rooms have views of the Atlantic; however, oceanfront units also offer private balconies.

Some rooms at this Comfort Inn have refrigerators and microwaves, while most have full baths, cable TV and HBO, telephones, and coffeemakers. Nonsmoking and wheelchair-accessible rooms are available. Guests here can enjoy the hotel's oceanfront pool. Other amenities include a game room and coin-operated laundry facilities on-site. A complimentary breakfast is provided. Children 18 and younger stay free with an adult. A three-night minimum stay is required on summer holiday weekends. Managers honor AARP discounts. The Comfort Inn is open all year.

Cypress House Bed and Breakfast $$$$
NC 12, MP 8, Kill Devil Hills
(252) 441–6127, (800) 554–2764
www.cypresshouseinn.com

This historic bed-and-breakfast inn owned by Karen and Leon Faso was originally built as a private hunting and fishing lodge in the 1940s. Located 150 yards from the Atlantic Ocean, the inn, with its original tongue-and-groove cypress-paneled walls and ceilings, exudes a cozy, laid-back charm. Six guest rooms with queen beds and private shower baths are comfortably equipped with white ruffled curtains, ceiling fans, cable television, and central air. The wraparound porch is a perfect spot to enjoy the ocean breezes. In cold weather relax with a good book in front of a blazing fire in the common room. Early risers will find self-serve coffee and tea on the baker's rack outside the rooms, and a hearty home-baked breakfast is served each morning in the dining room. Afternoon refreshments are also served.

Bikes, beach towels, and chairs, along with an outdoor shower, enhance your enjoyment. Cypress House is smoke free and welcomes children 14 and older. The Inn does not allow pets.

The Cypress House is open year-round.

The Tanglewood $$$
NC 12, MP 8¼, Kill Devil Hills
(252) 441–7208

This family-oriented motel has an outdoor swimming pool, a boardwalk to the ocean with a deck for sunbathing, and an enclosed outdoor bathhouse with hot and cold water for a relaxing shower after a day at the beach. Other amenities include a fish-cleaning station, picnic tables, and grills. The Tanglewood is open year-round. There is a five-day minimum stay in summer.

Cavalier Motel $$$
NC 12, MP 8½, Kill Devil Hills
(252) 441-5584
www.thecavaliermotel.com

A variety of rooms is available at this courtyard motel on the oceanfront. Three one-story wings enclose the two swimming pools, a volleyball court, children's play area, and shuffleboard courts. The Cavalier has 54 rooms with double and single beds and six one-room efficiency units with two double beds and kitchenettes right on the beach. Some rooms have full baths, while others just have shower stalls. All are equipped with telephones, refrigerators, microwaves, cable TV, and free HBO.

Besides these units, the motel offers 13 cottages that rent by the week. Pets are allowed in the cottages only. There is some wheelchair access here, and ramps are on the premises.

Parking is available outside each room, and the covered porch with outdoor furniture is just right for relaxing with a free cup of coffee while watching the sunrise. An observation deck sits atop the oceanfront section. This is a well-maintained, family-oriented property and is reasonably priced for daily or weekend rentals. Children five and younger stay for free in their parents' rooms. The Cavalier Motel is open year-round.

Days Inn Oceanfront $$$-$$$$
Wilbur & Orville Wright
NC 12, MP 8½, Kill Devil Hills
(252) 441-7211, (800) 329-7466
www.outer-banks.com/days-oceanfront

An oceanfront property on a wide stretch of beach, this facility opened as an Outer Banks motel in 1948. It was built to resemble an old mountain lodge and offers an inviting lobby decorated in the nostalgia of Old Nags Head where guests can read the newspaper and sip a cup of free coffee. The room is further enhanced by Oriental rugs on polished hardwood floors and a fireplace large enough to take away the chill on cold beach evenings during the off-season.

Guests here enjoy balconies with old-fashioned furniture and nice views. All 52 rooms have been renovated and furnished with 1990s decor. There are singles, doubles, kings, king suites, and efficiency units that sleep six and include a living room, adjoining bedroom, and complete kitchen. All rooms have telephones, cable TV, and refrigerators. Oceanfront rooms also have microwaves. Nonsmoking and wheelchair-accessible rooms are available. The hotel has interior and exterior corridors, and suites have entrances to both.

A complimentary continental breakfast is available throughout the year. Hot apple cider and popcorn are served around the fireplace during the winter, and lemonade and cookies are served in the summer. Leisure amenities include a large outdoor pool, sun deck, volleyball court, barbecue pit for cookouts, and a boardwalk to the beach.

Children 12 and younger stay for free here. AARP discounts also are honored. There's a three-night minimum stay for summer holiday weekends, and Saturday check-ins aren't allowed unless you plan to stay for a week. Daily and weeklong rentals are available throughout the year.

Best Western Ocean Reef Suites $$$$
NC 12, MP 8½, Kill Devil Hills
(252) 441-1611, (800) 528-1234
www.bestwestern.com/oceanreefsuites

All 70 one-bedroom suites in this newer oceanfront hotel are decorated and arranged like luxury apartments with a contemporary beach decor. The views are great, and you'll find everything you need for a truly luxurious beach vacation. Each room has a telephone, cable TV, free coffee, and a fully equipped galley-style kitchen. The bath area has a double vanity.

Nonsmoking and wheelchair-accessible rooms are available. Upper-floor rooms have private balconies overlooking the ocean. Some first-floor units open onto the oceanfront pool and courtyard, while others offer a private patio. The Ocean Reef is one of the few facilities on the beach

to have a penthouse suite; this one boasts a private Jacuzzi and rooftop deck.

A heated, seasonal outdoor pool and a whirlpool are available to guests in the courtyard, and the exercise room features the latest equipment and a sauna. Other amenities include a laundry facility on the premises and year-round bar and food service available at Big Kahoona's. Children 13 and younger stay free with adults here. A two-day minimum stay is required on summer weekends. Ocean Reef is open all year.

Colony IV Motel $$$
NC 12, MP 8½, Kill Devil Hills
(252) 441–5581, (800) 848–3728

This modern family-owned and -operated oceanfront motel is well-maintained and offers lots of amenities. Manager Cindy Neal provides ample hospitality for moderate prices as well as an outdoor heated pool with a Jacuzzi and patio, a nine-hole miniature golf course, two picnic areas with grills, a children's playground, a dune-top gazebo, a video game room, horseshoe pits, a private beach with lifeguard, and other outdoor activities. A complimentary continental breakfast is served every morning. Laundry facilities are available on the premises.

The motel has 87 units, 14 of which are efficiencies. Most offer two double beds, but rooms with king-size beds are also available. Telephones, refrigerators, microwaves, TV with remote control and cable, and clock radios are provided in each unit. Some rooms have direct access to the beach, while others have a small balcony overlooking the ocean. The efficiencies have an eating area and, when combined with adjoining rooms, create a good arrangement for family vacationers. Nonsmoking units are available.

Children 12 and younger can stay for free here. Discounts of 10 percent are provided for AARP members. The motel is also handicapped-accessible. A three-night minimum stay is required on summer weekends. The Colony IV Motel is open February through October.

The White Egret Bed and Breakfast $$$$
1047 Colington Rd., Kill Devil Hills
(252) 441–7719, (888) 387–7719
www.whiteegret.com

The White Egret is tucked away from the busy beach life on the road that leads to Colington Island. The setting here is quiet and peaceful, and the inn is situated perfectly to offer expansive views of Colington Bay and the marvelous sunsets that sink into it. Three spacious guest rooms are furnished with antiques, queen-size beds, ceiling fans, and central air conditioning. Two of the rooms have gas log fireplaces. All three have private baths with Jacuzzis, TVs, phones, and Internet hookup. All rooms have a stunning view of the water. A full, homemade breakfast is served from 8:00 to 9:30 A.M. each morning, including fresh fruit, muffins, juice, coffee, and something homemade, like omelets, casseroles, or waffles. Continental breakfast is served to early risers by request, or the meal can be brought to your room if you desire.

The inn is along a bike trail that leads to the Wright Brothers National Memorial and the beach, and bikes are available for guests. Canoes and kayaks are also available for paddling around in the local creeks and bays. Beach towels and chairs are offered too—a nice touch for guests. One of the nicest things about this inn is its next-door proximity to the Colington Cafe, a favorite Outer Banks restaurant for dinner (see our Restaurants chapter).

Budget Host Inn $$$
US 158, MP 9, Kill Devil Hills
(252) 441–2503, (800) BUD–HOST
www.budgethost.com

This motel is on the Bypass, about two blocks from the ocean. All 40 rooms are tastefully furnished and well maintained, with either king-size beds or extra-length double beds. Each unit has a telephone, cable TV, and tub/shower combination. Refrigerators and microwaves are available upon request. The lobby also has a guest refrigerator, microwave, and a coin-operated laundry room.

The entire second floor of the inn has been made into a nonsmoking, no pets floor. Wheelchair-accessible rooms are also available here. The motel offers two family rooms that sleep six to eight people comfortably. The property maintains an indoor heated pool for year-round use, and a small picnic area is just south of the motel. Free coffee and tea are available in the lobby each day. Pets

are accepted. Cribs are provided free of charge, and children 16 and younger stay free with an adult. The Budget Host Inn is open year-round.

First Flight Inn $$
NC 12, MP 9, Kill Devil Hills
(252) 441–5007
www.netnc.com/firstflight

Of the 55 units at this oceanfront inn, 15 are efficiency apartments and one is a separate cottage. Most rooms have two double beds, and five have just one double bed. Rooms are equipped with small refrigerators, microwaves, and telephones. This is a family-oriented inn, with many return guests year after year. The inn has 256 feet of private beach, though when you're tired of sand and surf, there's a good-size outdoor pool and deck. A fish-cleaning station and outdoor showers are available. Children 12 and younger stay free with their parents. On summer holiday weekends, there's a three-day minimum stay required. Two fishing piers and several shops and restaurants are nearby. First Flight Inn is open from April through October.

See Sea Motel $$-$$$
NC 12, MP 9, Kill Devil Hills
(252) 441–7321
www.seeseamotel.com

A small, family-run motel across the street from the ocean, See Sea offers 20 rental units, including 11 motel rooms, five efficiencies, three two-bedroom apartments, and one three-bedroom cottage. The motel rooms and efficiencies rent by the day (the apartments and cottage require a one-week minimum stay in season). All units have a refrigerator, telephone, and cable television. There's also a pay phone on the premises. Laundry is on site and free coffee is provided.

Amenities here include an outdoor swimming pool, fish-cleaning facility, fish freezers, a picnic area, and gas grill. Nonsmoking rooms are offered, and children 14 and younger stay free. See Sea Motel is open March through November.

The Anchorage $$
NC 12, MP 9, Kill Devil Hills
(252) 441–7226

All 17 units at this oceanfront motel include full kitchens and cable TV. There are nine efficiencies that rent by the day or week all four seasons. Eight cottages rent only by the week during the summer. Pets are not accepted here. The Anchorage is open year-round.

Holiday Inn $$$$
NC 12, MP 9½, Kill Devil Hills
(252) 441–6333, (800) 843–1249

This oceanfront hotel has 105 rooms, many with spectacular ocean views. Banquet and conference facilities here can accommodate 10 to 300 people. An on-site restaurant and lounge provide room service, and guests can use the on-site video arcade game room and coin-operated laundry. An outdoor pool and Jacuzzi are other features.

All rooms include telephones, cable TV with remote, microwaves, and refriger-ators. This Holiday Inn has two nonsmoking floors and wheelchair-accessible rooms. Children 18 and younger stay free here, and AARP members receive a 10 percent discount. Weekends require three-night minimum stays during summer. Holiday Inn is open all year.

Ramada Inn at Nags Head Beach $$$$
NC 12, MP 9½, Kill Devil Hills
(252) 441–2151, (800) 635–1824
www.ramadainnnagshead.com

This five-story, 172-room oceanfront hotel was built in 1985. It's popular with tour groups and hosts many meetings throughout the year. All rooms have balconies or patios, cable TV with pay-per-view movies, small refrigerators, and microwaves. Bellhop and room service are available here. Nonsmoking, wheelchair-accessible, and pet rooms are offered. Meeting facilities are on the fourth floor overlooking the ocean. Several suites are available to fit a variety of conference and workshop needs.

For guests, an indoor swimming pool and Jacuzzi are just off the second floor atop the dunes and surrounded by a large sun deck. A flight of steps takes you onto the beach where volleyball is a popular pastime. Food and beverage services are available at the oceanfront Gazebo Deck bar adjacent to the pool. Peppercorns, the hotel's fine oceanview restaurant, serves breakfast and dinner year-round and offers lunch on the deck during the summer (see our Restaurants chapter). The Ramada Inn is open all year.

Tanya's Ocean House Motel $$$
NC 12, MP 9½, Kill Devil Hills
(252) 441-2900
www.oceanhousemotel.com

This seaside motel is an Outer Banks legend offering unique, individually designed accommodations the owners call Carolina Collection Rooms. Legend has it that original owner, Tanya Young, and a designer friend decided to do a theme room at the motel. Their ideas got a little out of hand, and they ended up selecting separate themes for each room. There's the Carolina Party Room, Jonathan Seagull's Nest, and dozens more. No two rooms at this motel are alike.

Tanya's has 43 rooms, including a few normal rooms that have been converted back from the original designs over the years. All units have refrigerators and cable TV with HBO. Oceanfront rooms also offer microwaves. Telephones are not provided.

Guests here can enjoy a 40-foot outdoor pool surrounded by umbrella-shaded picnic tables. Free coffee is provided throughout the day. During summer, there's a two-night minimum stay on weekends. The seventh night is free if you stay a week. Children younger than 13 stay free at this motel, and AARP discounts are honored. Tanya's is open April through mid-October.

Miller's Outer Banks Motor Lodge $$$
NC 12, MP 9½, Kill Devil Hills
(252) 441-7404

An oceanfront motel with 30 efficiency units and eight regular rooms, Miller's

Outer Banks Motor Lodge rents some units only by the week during the peak season. Other units, however, can be occupied by the day. Each room has cable TV, a refrigerator, and microwave. Wheelchair-accessible units are available. Also on-site are a washer and dryer, a playground, an outdoor swimming pool, and a restaurant. Children 9 and younger stay free here. Miller's is open from February through November.

Quality Inn John Yancey $$$$
NC 12, MP 10, Kill Devil Hills
(252) 441-7141, (800) 367-5941

This family hotel is on a wide beach that's lifeguarded during the summer. Shuffleboard courts, an outdoor heated pool, and a playground are on the premises.

The hotel has 107 rooms, most of them doubles, housed in three buildings. The oceanfront units each have balconies or patios so you can watch and hear the waves from your room. Cable TV with optional in-room movies, small refrigerators, and telephones are in each room. Ten units also offer microwaves, five have fully equipped kitchens, and three include hot tubs. Coffeemakers and coffee are provided in all rooms. About half of the rooms are nonsmoking, and there are wheelchair-accessible units.

Another feature here is a coin-operated laundry. VCRs, movies, and free coffee are available in the lobby. This Quality Inn has 24-hour front desk and maintenance service, a rare find on the Outer Banks. Children 18 and younger stay free, and you can rent rollaway beds to accommodate additional kids. A two-night minimum stay is required on summer weekends. AARP and other discounts are honored. The Quality Inn John Yancey is open all year.

The Ebb Tide $$
NC 12, MP 10½, Kill Devil Hills
(252) 441-4913

The ocean is just across the road from this family-run motel, which has 41 rooms with refrigerators, microwaves, and cable TV. Three seaside apartments across the street are right on the beach. Wheelchair-accessible rooms are available. Guests have full use of the outdoor pool, picnic table, and restaurant on the premises. Children younger than 13 stay free. The Ebb Tide is open from mid-March until the end of September.

Nags Head

Ocean Veranda Motel $$$–$$$$
NC 12, MP 10½, Nags Head
(252) 441–5858, (800) 58BEACH

A well-maintained oceanfront property, Ocean Veranda offers 16 standard rooms, 14 efficiencies, and one honeymoon suite with a king-size, canopy waterbed. Standard rooms are large and have two double beds, refrigerators, and cable TV. Nonsmoking rooms are available. Efficiencies have complete kitchens with microwaves and coffeemakers and can adjoin other rooms to accommodate larger families of up to five people. Roll-aways and cribs are available for a small charge. Some rooms on the second level offer partial ocean views.

Complimentary morning coffee is offered in the office. Other amenities include an outdoor pool and two gazebos, horseshoe pits, a children's playground, picnic area, and barbecue grill. Children younger than six stay free. A small charge for extra persons in the rooms is applicable. Ocean Veranda is open January through November.

Beacon Motor Lodge $$$
NC 12, MP 10¾, Nags Head
(252) 441–5501, (800) 441–4804

Visitors will find lots of options for seasonal and off-season stays at this family-oriented, comfortable oceanfront lodge. The James family has owned the 48-room Beacon Motor Lodge since 1970, offering one-, two-, and three-room combinations, including motel-type rooms and efficien-

cies, plus two cottages. Nonsmoking rooms are available. The attractive rooms, finished in mauve, turquoise, and peach, are all equipped with small refrigerators, phones, and cable TV with remote control. Most units also have microwaves.

Guests can gather on the oceanfront patio, a grand place for enjoying the beach scene from a comfy lounge chair. Oceanfront rooms open onto a large, walled terrace, affording wonderful views of the ocean from early morning until moonrise. Amenities include two children's pools; a large fenced-in, elevated outdoor pool with tables and umbrellas; a playground; patios with grills; an electronic game room, and laundry facilities. Some provisions have been made for disabled guests, including a ramp for beach access.

Inquire about discounts and weekly rentals (credit cards are not accepted for some discounts). The Beacon Motor Lodge is open late March through late October.

Colonial Inn Motel $$
NC 12, MP 11½, Nags Head
(252) 441-7308, (800) 345-9405
www.colonialinnmotel.com

The Colonial Inn sports oceanfront rooms, efficiencies with full kitchens, and nine apartments with separate bedrooms, kitchens, and full baths. All 38 rooms have televisions. While the inn is an oceanfront establishment, it also offers an outdoor pool. Colonial Inn is open from April through October. On the Web site, you can take a virtual tour of the property and rooms.

Sea Spray $$
NC 12, MP 12, Nags Head
(252) 441-7270

This down-to-earth beachfront establishment has a little bit of everything including eight rooms, 16 efficiencies, and four cottages. All rooms feature two double beds, and some efficiencies have queen-size beds. All units have TVs. Wheelchair-accessible rooms are available. The cottages with two and three bedrooms are across the street from the main establishment. Sea Spray is open March 15 through November.

Nags Head Inn $$$–$$$$
NC 12, MP 14, Nags Head
(252) 441-0454, (800) 327-8881
www.nagsheadinn.com

This sparkling white stucco building with blue accents and plush bermudagrass lawns is a tasteful contrast to the older Nags Head–style cottages nearby. Designed for family enjoyment, the oceanfront inn features a sunny lobby where greenery thrives. Also at ground level are offices and covered parking for guests.

Guest rooms begin on the second floor of this five-story building, and all oceanside rooms afford panoramic ocean views from private balconies. Rooms on the street side do not offer balconies, but the view of the Roanoke Sound from the fifth floor rooms is notable. All rooms have small refrigerators, cable TV with HBO, phones, and full baths. Nonsmoking rooms are available, and there are wheelchair-accessible rooms on each floor. The Nags Head Inn also features one suite with an adjoining sitting room, wet bar, and hot tub—a perfect honeymoon setting.

A small conference room with adjoining kitchen/sitting area can accommodate about 30 people comfortably. The heated, all-weather swimming pool is on the second floor with a deck overlooking the ocean. During the summer months, the glass doors are removed, providing a completely wide open lounging and sitting area for your enjoyment. Of course, it's nice and toasty in the pool area in the winter months, so don't forget to pack bathing suits; the kids will love you for it. Tour groups are welcome. The inn is closed from the Sunday after Thanksgiving until December 26.

Silver Sands Motel $$
NC 12, MP 14, Nags Head
(252) 441-7354, (888) 775-7354

Silver Sands, which sits across the road from a beach access, has 26 rooms that offer simple, basic decor (rustic pine walls and crate furniture) along with such amenities as refrigerators, microwaves, and cable TV with HBO. Guests are offered either two double beds or one queen-size bed. One wheelchair-accessible room is available.

A separate two-story building offers rooms on the upper level with balconies for ocean views. The main building offers 16 units near the outdoor swimming pool. For the location, you can't beat the price. It's open year-round.

Oceanside Court $$
NC 12, MP 15½, Nags Head
(252) 441–6167

There's nothing like an oceanside stay on the Outer Banks. That's what you'll get here, and you can choose from a room, efficiency, or cottage. This small establishment offers six efficiencies with cable TV and full kitchens; two rooms with microwaves, refrigerators, and cable TV; and seven cottages. Phones are not available in any of the units. The court is open from March 1 to November 30. Pets are not allowed.

Sandspur Motel and Cottage Court $$–$$$
NC 12, MP 15¾, Nags Head
(252) 441–6993, (800) 522–8486
www.outer-banks.com/sandspur

At the Sandspur you can choose from a room, efficiency, or cottage. All rooms feature two double beds, cable TV, ceiling fans, refrigerators, and microwaves. The efficiencies also have stoves. The rooms have no phones, but a pay phone is on the premises. The motel has a coin-operated washer and dryer. The Sandspur closes in December and reopens March 1.

Surf Side Motel $$$$
NC 12, MP 16, Nags Head
(252) 441–2105, (800) 552–7873
www.surfsideobx.com

This attractive five-story motel is situated on the oceanfront, and rooms face north, south, and east for ocean views. Some rooms have views of the Roanoke Sound as well. All rooms have private balconies and are decorated attractively in muted beach tones. Nonsmoking rooms are available. Refrigerators, cable TV, hairdryers, coffeemakers, microwaves, irons and ironing boards, and phones are standard

room features. The honeymoon suites feature king-size beds and private Jacuzzis. An elevator provides easy access, and wheelchair-accessible rooms are available. An adjacent three-story building offers rooms and efficiencies with either ocean or sound views.

A continental breakfast is provided each morning, and the staff hosts an afternoon wine and snacks social hour for guests. You can choose between an indoor pool and hot tub that are open all year and an outdoor pool for swimming in warm weather. The Surf Side is open all year.

First Colony Inn $$$$
US 158, MP 16, Nags Head
(252) 441–2343, (800) 368–9390
www.firstcolonyinn.com

Back in 1932, this gracious old structure was known as Leroy's Seaside Inn. Today, the landmark hotel has been moved and refurbished, but it's still a favorite for those who like the ambiance of a quiet inn. The old Nags Head–style architecture, resplendent under an overhanging roof and wide porches, has been preserved and now is listed in the National Register of Historic Places. This is as close as you'll come to what it must have been like 70-odd years ago when the little hotel first opened. The First Colony received a historic preservation award from the Historic Preservation Foundation of North Carolina.

The Lawrence family, with deep roots in the area, rescued the hotel from demolition in 1988. The building was sawed into three sections for the move from its oceanfront location to the present site 4 miles south between the highways. It took three years of rehabilitation to return the inn to its original appearance. The interior was completely renovated and now contains 26 rooms, all with traditional furnishings and modern comforts.

In the sunny breakfast room, you can enjoy a complimentary deluxe continental breakfast and afternoon tea. Upstairs, an elegant but cozy library with books, games, and an old pump organ is a favorite place to read the paper or meet other guests. A great selection of jazz as well as classical music wafts throughout the reception area.

Each room is appointed in English antique furniture. Special touches, such as tiled baths, heated towel bars, English toiletries, telephones, TVs, individual climate control, and refrigerators, are standard. Some rooms offer wet bars, kitchenettes, Jacuzzis, VCRs, and private balconies; some also include an additional trundle bed or day bed for an extra person. The first floor is wheelchair-accessible, and one room is designed for disabled guests. Smoking is not permitted in the inn.

Guests are invited to relax at the 55-foot swimming pool and sun deck behind the inn or to follow the private boardwalk across the street to the oceanfront gazebo. This magnificent year-round inn provides easy access to the ocean and is close to many shops and restaurants. The inn has a policy of one night free for stays of five weeknights or longer but must include consecutive Sunday, Monday, Tuesday, Wednesday, and Thursday stays.

Islander Motel $$$
NC 12, MP 16, Nags Head
(252) 441–6229
www.islandermotel.com

The Islander is a small, popular oceanfront property, due in part to its attractive landscape and well-maintained rooms. Most rooms have an ocean view, and all rooms have either a balcony or patio.

Some of the first-floor units do not offer ocean views because they are tucked behind the dunes. The motel has 24 rooms and two efficiency apartments. The rooms are large and frequently refurbished and feature either double or queen-size beds. One king is available. All have sitting areas, coffeemakers, and refrigerators. Some first-floor units offer kitchenettes.

Guests will enjoy the pool and private dune walk to the ocean. This property is convenient to all Nags Head restaurants, shops, recreational outlets, and attractions. You'll find the comforts of this attractive motel more than adequate. The

> **Insiders' Tip**
>
> If you can get away from the office, but not the work, Mail Boxes Etc. at the Marketplace in Southern Shores can help. They have weekly mailbox rentals plus such office services as copying, faxing, and overnight shipping.

Islander is open April through October. They can be reached on the Internet.

Blue Heron Motel $$$
NC 12, MP 16, Nags Head
(252) 441–7447

The Blue Heron Motel is considered one of the Outer Banks's best-kept secrets among the small motels in the area. The family-owned facility provides a year-round indoor swimming pool, a spa, and outdoor pools. The Gladden family lives on the premises and pays careful attention to the management of the property. It's in the midst of fine Nags Head restaurants and offers plenty of beach for those who come here to relax.

Nineteen rooms offer double or king-size beds, and 11 efficiencies sleep up to four people and provide full kitchens. All units have refrigerators, microwaves, coffeepots, cable TV, phones, and shower/tub combinations. Wheelchair-accessible rooms are available. Second- and third-floor rooms offer private balconies. The Blue Heron Motel is open all year and offers weekly rates.

Owens' Motel $$
NC 12, MP 16, Nags Head
(252) 441–6361
www.owensmotel.com

The Owens family has owned and operated this attractive motel, one of the first on the beach, for more than 44 years.

Outdoor showers are prevalent on the Outer Banks—make sure your accommodation has one! PHOTO: MOLLY HARRISON

Adjacent to the family's famous restaurant (see our Restaurants chapter), this property across the highway from the ocean is well maintained. You'll love the family atmosphere!

The Owens' three-story oceanfront addition includes efficiencies with large, private balconies. Each room has two double beds, a tile bath and shower, and a kitchen. Cable TV also is standard in the guest rooms.

The motel swimming pool on the west side of the property offers guests an alternative to the ocean. Easy access to Jennette's Fishing Pier and a comfortable oceanfront pavilion with rocking chairs also will entice you. Owens' Motel is open April through October.

Sea Foam Motel $$$
NC 12, MP 16½, Nags Head
(252) 441–7320

Twenty-nine rooms, 18 efficiencies, and three cottages make up this attractive oceanfront motel. Efficiencies accommodate two to four people, and cottages sleep up to six comfortably. The efficiencies and cottages rent weekly; inquire about rates. Rooms are tastefully decorated in mauve and green, and some have washed-oak furniture. All rooms have cable TV with HBO, refrigerators, microwaves, and phones. Some have king-size beds, and each has a balcony or porch with comfortable furniture. Some units in the one- and two-story buildings have ocean and poolside views.

Children are welcome, and they will enjoy the playground. Other features include a large outdoor pool, children's pool, sun deck, shuffleboard area, and a gazebo on the beach for guests' pleasure. Sea Foam Motel is within walking distance of restaurants and Jennette's Fishing Pier. Free coffee is provided until 11:00 A.M., and a special family plan allows children younger than 12 to stay free with parents. Sea Foam Motel is open March through mid-December.

Quality Inn Sea Hotel $$$$
NC 12, MP 16½, Nags Head
(252) 441–7191, (800) 440–4386
www.qualityinn.com/hotel/nc021

This year-round Quality Inn has an excellent oceanfront location near restaurants, recreation, shops, and Nags Head attractions. Each of the 113 rooms is tastefully furnished, and nonsmoking rooms are available.

This inn is one of the nicest places to stay on this end of Nags Head. Pets are allowed free-of-charge in the off-season from Labor Day to Memorial Day. The front desk is open 24 hours a day, and all rooms conform to Quality Inn's high standards. Each room has a coffeemaker, microwave and refrigerator, telephone, and cable TV with HBO. You'll also find a coin-operated laundry, snacks, and ice. A sheltered gazebo is on the beach. Inquire about Lost Colony and other package options. The inn is open all year.

Dolphin Motel $$
NC 12, MP 16½, Nags Head
(252) 441–7488

The Dolphin Motel features 46 rooms with 11 efficiencies. Some rooms have queen-size beds, but most have double beds. Two nice features are the breezeway to the beach and an outdoor pool. All rooms and efficiencies have cable TV. Nonsmoking rooms are not available. The Dolphin opens the last Friday in March and closes the last Saturday in October.

Comfort Inn South $$$$
NC 12, MP 17, Nags Head
(252) 441–6315, (800) 334–3302

The Comfort Inn South, a seven-story oceanfront hotel situated in a quiet residential neighborhood, is one of the few accommodations in this area and the tallest building on the Outer Banks. The light peach-and-teal exterior gives this hotel a clean, contemporary beach look. The 105-room hotel has deluxe oceanfront rooms with magnificent views from private balconies; oceanside and streetside rooms are available too. All rooms have remote cable TV, phones, refrigerators, and microwaves. Nonsmoking rooms are offered too. A honeymoon suite with a hot tub is popular, as are rooms with king-size beds. One wheel-

chair-accessible room is available. Corporate meeting rooms can accommodate groups of up to 350 people.

The oceanfront pool and deck are favorite gathering places. Other amenities include a children's pool, game room, and playground. These features make this hotel appealing to families and business groups alike. A deluxe complimentary continental breakfast is offered in the lobby. Jennette's Fishing Pier is only a block away. The Comfort Inn South is open all year.

Whalebone Motel $$$$
NC 12, MP 17, Nags Head
(252) 441–7423
www.whalebonemotel.com

The Whalebone Motel is open all year and has standard motel rooms and efficiencies divided among three buildings. One efficiency has a king, a double, and two single beds. Three have king-size beds, and others feature one double and two single beds. Some units have two double beds. All accommodations feature stoves, refrigerators, and cable TV with HBO. Pets are welcome at $5.00 a night.

Fin 'N Feather Motel $$–$$$
Nags Head-Manteo Causeway, Nags Head
(252) 441–5353, (888) 441–5353
www.finnfeather.com

A small motel along the water's edge, the Fin 'N Feather is popular with anglers and hunters. If you're planning to come in the fall or spring, call well in advance for reservations. This motel's proximity to Pirate's Cove Yacht Club is convenient for anyone headed out for a day on the open seas. There's a boat ramp here too.

Housekeeping units are available year-round at Fin 'N Feather, featuring double-bed efficiencies. Each efficiency has a stove and refrigerator and is equipped with cooking utensils. The renters take care of all their needs here. The rooms are clean and comfortable with blue and white decor. Large windows open onto the water from either side and offer stunning views of the sound.

Roanoke Island

Manteo

Island Motel & Guest House $$
US 64, Manteo
(252) 473-2434
www.theislandmotel.com

The Island Motel has been completely remodeled. In the heart of Manteo, convenience is a hallmark at this neat little motel. Most of the 14 rooms have their own microwave or full kitchen. The main building has a great room where you can meet and greet other guests. Each room has cable TV, air conditioning, and two double beds. Fold-away beds are available for children. Daily, weekly, and monthly rates are offered. Amenities include courtesy bikes, fishing poles, other sports equipment, and surfing lessons. Nonsmoking and smoking rooms are available, but smoking is not allowed in the main house. Dogs are allowed for a nominal pet fee. This motel is open all year.

The Island Motel also operates the Little Lifeboat House, an adorable honeymoon cottage that can accommodate two to four people. It offers a two-person whirlpool tub, a home theater, two full baths, and laundry facilities. It's off site at 706 Wingina Street. This puts you within walking distance of the charming Manteo neighborhoods and waterfront. In season, a two-night stay is required at this house.

The Elizabethan Inn $$$
US 64, Manteo
(252) 473-2101, (800) 346-2466
www.elizabethaninn.com

The Elizabethan Inn is a year-round resort facility with spacious shaded grounds, country manor charm, and Tudor architecture that reflects the area's heritage. Only 7 miles from the beach, the hotel consists of three buildings providing more than 80 rooms, efficiencies, and apartments, plus conference facilities, a health club, gift shop, and a dining room serving breakfast. Nonsmoking and wheelchair-accessible rooms are available. All rooms have cable TV with HBO, refrigerators, and direct-dial phones. Rooms are available with a king-size bed or two queen-size or double beds, and two rooms have whirlpool baths. Many rooms have coffeemakers. All rooms are comfortable and well suited for a quiet Roanoke Island vacation.

Breakfast in the on-site dining room is included in the room price. The lobby is filled with interesting antiques, and a friendly staff welcomes you. A small shop offers a selection of fine gifts, local books, souvenirs, and personal items.

The inn's Nautics Hall Fitness Center, one of the largest and most complete health clubs in the area, is available for guests (see our Recreation chapter). Guests may also use the outdoor pool and a heated, competition-size indoor pool. There's another nice touch: Guests have free use of bicycles to tour the nearby village or travel the paved bike path.

Inquire about special rate packages. The inn is open all year.

Roanoke Island Inn $$$$
305 Fernando St., Manteo
(252) 473-5511, (877) 473-5511

With the sparkling Roanoke Sound and quaint Manteo waterfront just a stroll away, you'll find yourself easing into the relaxed village pace the moment you step up to this attractive inn. The distinctive white clapboard building with dark green shutters offers the atmosphere of a gracious, restored residence with the comforts of a small, well-designed bed-and-breakfast. The furnishings are handsome, reflecting the meticulous care of the owner, designer-architect John Wilson IV. The ambiance is laid-back and friendly.

Each of the inn's eight rooms features a private entrance, private bath, TV, and phone. Guests can choose to stay in the quaint bungalow behind the inn, which is complete with an antique tub and furnishings, wet bar, and refrigerator. You'll enjoy browsing through a collection of Outer Banks-related books and artwork in the lobby, and a light breakfast is offered in the butler's pantry.

The private grounds are landscaped with gardenia, fig bushes, and other native plants. A picturesque pond complete with koi and sweet-smelling lotus plants is a great place to relax. Dip nets are provided so guests can experience netting crabs along the bay's edge. Bicycles are furnished for touring the town and nearby historic attractions, including the Elizabeth II and the Outer Banks History Center.

Roanoke Island Inn is open from April through October.

The White Doe Inn $$$$
Sir Walter Raleigh St., Manteo
(252) 473-9851, (800) 473-6091
www.whitedoeinn.com

In a restored 1898 home, The White Doe Inn retains its turn-of-the-century charm and offers guests an elegant escape in its rooms and hideaways. It is one of only two Dare County houses listed on the National Register of Historic Places. The inn offers eight guest rooms, each with its own personality. Each room has a private bath and fireplace. Honeymoon suites are available. The large, wrap-around porches are the perfect place to relax and be pampered. Guests have full use of the study-library, formal parlor, foyer, and dining room of this stately old home. Afternoon tea, coffee, and desserts are served, as is evening sherry. Bob and Bebe Woody work hard to fulfill their guests' every need.

The inn serves a full Southern-style, three-course breakfast every morning, a good time for guests to gather to read the newspapers, enjoy the fine food, and prepare for a day of exploring historic Manteo and Roanoke Island. This is a nonsmoking establishment, but smoking is allowed on the porch.

The White Doe is in a quiet neighborhood in downtown Manteo and is a perfect point of departure to explore the town on foot. Everything is within easy reach. The inn is truly beautiful, and guests won't be disappointed. Special events for up to 40 people can be accommodated. It's a perfect place for weddings,

anniversaries, reunions, or retreats. Check the Web site for special-interest weekend packages. The inn is open all year, and off-season rates are available.

The Cameron House Inn $$$$
300 Budleigh St., Manteo
(252) 473-6596, (800) 279-8178
www.cameronhouseinn.com

We love the look and feel of this place—dark colors typical of the Arts and Crafts period, original artwork on the walls, great music playing in the public areas, a large conference/living room that features an unusual but beautiful fireplace situated beside sink-into leather furniture, a well-appointed kitchen that's stocked with drinks and snacks for guests, and a big, shady side yard. One of our favorite things at this inn is the huge outdoor fireplace on the back porch. It all but calls you to sit down and relax for a while in front of it, and indeed that's the first thing many guests do. The guest rooms here are lovely, some with fireplaces, some with soaker tubs, some with down-stuffed sofas, and all offering luxurious tiled bathrooms. An added feature for travelers is that each room is wired for Internet access. And you should note that this is a nonsmoking inn. A big breakfast is set out each morning, and it usually offers homemade muffins and breads, fresh fruit, a Cameron House granola, juices, coffee, and tea. Afternoon treats help perk you up after a long day on the beach or visiting attractions, especially if you also take a moment to relax on the antique front porch swing or in the comfy wicker chairs. The inn is in historic downtown Manteo where restaurants, attractions, and shopping are all just a few minutes' walk away.

The Cameron House Inn also offers bikes for touring the island. You'll also get some of the best advice on what to see and do while you are on the Outer Banks—advice not easily matched, considering the owners of this inn masterminded and developed the Insiders' Guide series. The Cameron House is frequently the site for conferences, retreats, business meetings, and weddings.

Scarborough Inn $$
US 64, Manteo
(252) 473-3979

Across from the Christmas Shop, this small inn is a delightful and friendly place to stay. The two-story structure was modeled after a turn-of-the-century inn. Each of the guest rooms is filled with authentic Victorian and pre-Victorian antiques and other interesting furnishings, mostly family heirlooms.

Each room and piece of furniture has a story, and the Scarboroughs create a casual, comfortable atmosphere as they relate the history behind some of the pieces. The inn's nine rooms are set away from the street. The rooms offer king or double beds, cable TV, phone, microwave, private bath, small refrigerator, and coffeemaker. Tasty morning muffins are delivered the night before, an especially nice treat for early risers.

Rooms in the two-story inn have exterior entrances and open onto a covered porch. The annex has four units: two suites with queen bedrooms and sitting rooms and two regular queen rooms. The barn has two king rooms. All six units in the annex and barn are equipped with wet bars and small storage spaces for kitchen utensils and miscellaneous items. House-trained pets are allowed in some rooms at no extra charge, but they cannot be left alone in the rooms.

Complimentary bicycles are available for adult guests, and there's a glider swing in the backyard. Travelers will appreciate the owners' care and attention. We're sure your stay here will be most pleasant. It's open year-round.

Tranquil House Inn $$$$
405 Queen Elizabeth Ave., on The Waterfront
Manteo
(252) 473-1404, (800) 458-7069
www.tranquilinn.com

You will be charmed by this lovely 25-room country inn on Shallowbag Bay. The inn was modeled after an old hotel that stood on this site from just after the

Civil War until the 1950s. Although the inn looks authentically aged, it is only 12 years old, so all sorts of modern conveniences are included: TVs with HBO, telephones, and private baths. Two of the 25 rooms, on the second floor, are one-bedroom suites that feature a queen-size bed and a separate sitting room with sofa and two TVs. All are individually and delightfully decorated.

Large rooms on the third floor have high ceilings. Nonsmoking rooms are available, and the inn has one room equipped for disabled guests. A ramp to the first floor makes rooms on that level accessible to all. You're sure to enjoy the hospitality and fine surroundings.

The spacious second-floor deck faces east toward the bay. The Elizabeth II, the flagship attraction of Roanoke Island Festival Park, is docked across the water. Shops along the waterfront are just a few steps away, and the marina behind the inn is convenient for those arriving by boat.

The inn's restaurant, 1587, specializes in gourmet cuisine and offers an extensive selection of wines (see our Restaurants chapter). Guests have free use of bicycles. The inn is open all year.

Scarborough House Inn $$
Fernando and Uppowac Sts., Manteo
(252) 473-3849
www.bbonline.com/nc/scarborough

The Scarborough House, owned by Phil and Sally Scarborough, opened in 1995. Relax in one of four tasteful guest rooms, each with its own refrigerator, microwave, and private bath. Nonsmoking rooms are available. Queen- or king-size beds are available. A romantic loft room has a canopied king-size bed and a whirlpool bath. This inn is appointed with period antiques and other fine furnishings. A continental breakfast is served daily. Bicycles are available for guests' enjoyment and provide the best way, in our opinion, to discover downtown Manteo. Everything about these accommodations reflects the owners' care and personal touch. The Scarborough House is open year-round.

Duke of Dare Motor Lodge $
US 64, Manteo
(252) 473-2175

On the main street and only a few blocks from the Manteo waterfront, this 57-room family motel provides the basics in accommodations: clean rooms with full baths, cable TV, and phones. All rooms have queen-size beds. Wheelchair-accessible rooms are available. The lodge also has an outdoor pool.

The Creef family has owned and managed the motel for more than a quarter-century. The Duke of Dare is an inexpensive, family-oriented motel that's close to shopping, restaurants, and attractions. It is open all year.

Dare Haven Motel $
US 64, Manteo
(252) 473-2322

The Dare Haven, a family-run motel suited to the cost-conscious vacationer, is toward the north end of Roanoke Island and is a favorite place for families and fishing enthusiasts—there's enough room here to park your own boat and trailer. Visitors planning to attend *The Lost Colony* or visit any of the other Roanoke Island attractions and historic sites of Fort Raleigh will find this location convenient. The motel also is close to beaches and many other Outer Banks attractions.

The 26 motel-style rooms are basic, clean, and comfortable, and have cable TV and telephones. Most rooms are decorated in traditional Outer Banks–style, with paneled walls and wraparound porches. All rooms are on the ground level.

Call for special rates for groups and extended stays. The motel is open all year.

Wanchese

Island House of Wanchese Bed and Breakfast
$$$–$$$$
104 Old Wharf Rd., Wanchese
(252) 473-5619

This old home, built in 1902, was made a bed-and-breakfast several years ago. Furnished in period antiques with Oriental

rugs and cabana fans, the small but cozy establishment offers many comforts including private baths, cable TV, radios in every room, beach towels and chairs, and a hot tub for guests. Each of the four rooms and one suite has a double bed.

Of course, a bed-and-breakfast would not be complete without a hearty morning meal. Island House offers a breakfast buffet often including casseroles, grits, fresh fruit, sweets, and juice. Evening tea is served with snacks. This is a nonsmoking establishment, but smoking is allowed on the porch. This is an adults-only inn. Island House is open year-round.

Hatteras Island

Rodanthe

Hatteras Island Resort $$
NC 12, Rodanthe
(252) 987-2345, (800) 331-6541
www.hatterasislandresort.com

Plenty of leisure activities await guests at this large oceanfront resort next to the Hatteras Island Fishing Pier. The two-story building includes 24 motel-type rooms, each with two double beds, a dressing room, and shower, and eight efficiencies featuring queen beds and full kitchenettes. Each of the eight oceanfront rooms and efficiencies offers an ocean view. Each of the resort's rooms has a refrigerator and microwave oven.

The 25-acre oceanside property also has 35 two-, three-, and four-bedroom cottages, which are arranged in clusters. Cottages rent weekly; inquire about rates. All units are comfortably furnished and have cable TV. In-room phones are not available, but pay phones are on the premises. Pets are allowed in the cottages only. Inquire about the fee.

Families will enjoy the outdoor oceanfront swimming pool, kiddie pool, large patio area, and volleyball and basketball courts. The Hatteras Island Fishing Pier is right out front on the Atlantic and draws a lot of people to the resort. The motel is open April through December. AARP and AAA discounts offered.

Sea-Sound Motel $-$$
Sea Sound Rd., Rodanthe
(252) 987-2224

Sea-Sound is between NC 12 and the ocean and offers 11 efficiencies and regular motel-style rooms. The efficiencies have fully equipped kitchens including microwaves. Motel rooms feature either one double or two queen beds. All accommodations have heat and air conditioning, color TV, and phones, and most rooms have coffeemakers. There's an outdoor pool on the premises with a deck and hot tub. Sea-Sound also features an outdoor grill, picnic area with table, and small basketball court. It's open March through mid-December.

Avon

Avon Motel $$-$$$
NC 12, Avon
(252) 995-5774
www.avonmotel.com

This terrific 48-unit establishment has been in business for more than 40 years and offers a perfect starting point to enjoy everything Hatteras Island has to offer. The Avon has standard, oceanside motel rooms and a handful of efficiency apartments. Motel rooms come with either two double beds or one queen-size or one king-size bed, and they all have microwaves, compact refrigerators, and coffeemakers. The efficiencies have either two or three rooms with a variety of bed setups along with fully equipped kitchens. All rooms and efficiencies have air conditioning, cable TV with free HBO, and in-room phones (local calls are free). For the anglers in the group, there is a lighted fish-cleaning station at the motel, and there is a guest laundry.

The motel is in the neighborhood of tackle shops, a fishing pier, four-wheel-drive beach accesses, windsurfing and beach shops, restaurants, and gift stores. The Cape Hatteras Lighthouse is 6 miles away, and (listen up, windsurfers) the

famous Canadian Hole is within 4 miles. The Avon Motel is open March through December.

Buxton

Cape Hatteras Motel $$$$
NC 12, Buxton
(252) 995–5611, (800) 995–0711
www.capehatterasmotel.com

When you arrive in Buxton, you'll see the Cape Hatteras Motel situated on both sides of the road. Owners Carol and Dave Dawson maintain this motel, parts of which have been here for more than 34 years. The 30 efficiency units and 11 motel rooms are popular with anglers, surfers, and folks who just plain enjoy Hatteras Island's beaches. Windsurfers especially like this facility because it is near Canadian Hole, one of the best wind-surfing spots on the East Coast (see our Attractions chapter).

Efficiencies sleep up to six comfort-ably, offer double beds as well as queens and kings, and have full kitchens. The newer, more modern townhouses and effi-ciencies are on the ocean. The motel has an outdoor swimming pool and spa. The motel's position at the north end of Bux-ton is convenient not only to pristine, uncrowded beaches but also restaurants and services, making this a very popular place in the busy summer season. There are no nonsmoking rooms, but the motel does offer a ZonTech clean air machine.

Efficiencies rent weekly, but nightly rentals also may be available, depending on supply. Book reservations early. Cape Hatteras Motel is open year-round.

Outer Banks Motel $$
NC 12, Buxton
(252) 995–5601, (800) 995–1233
www.outerbanksmotel.com

Situated next to the Cape Hatteras Motel, this establishment offers 10 motel-style rooms, seven efficiency units, and 20 two-and three-bedroom cottages. Units accommodate from one to nine people

comfortably, and about 80 percent of the units provide an ocean view. Nonsmoking rooms are available. Rooms and efficiencies offer enclosed porches with sliding windows and screens, perfect for a relaxing evening listening to the ocean. The pine-paneled rooms have tiled baths, microwaves, toasters, and small refrigerators. Efficiencies have fully equipped kitchens. All units have cable TV and telephones.

The owners also have 14 additional cottages in Buxton Village, a mile from the ocean, near Connor's Market. Because these units are not oceanfront, rental rates are quite a bit lower. If you rent one of these cottages, you are welcome to use the motel pool and beach facilities. The cottages are clean and simply furnished and provide the basics for family vacationers, including cable television. The motel has a coin-operated laundry, fish-cleaning station, and a guest freezer to store your big catch. If you enjoy crabbing, or if you just want to paddle around on the Pamlico Sound, the motel has several rowboats that guests may use free of charge. There's even a library in the office in case you want a good book for the beach. This motel is open year-round.

Lighthouse View Motel $$$$
NC 12, Buxton
(252) 995–5680, (800) 225–7651
www.lighthouseview.com

Lighthouse View is easy to find on the big curve in Buxton, where the Hooper family has been serving vacationers for nearly 40 years. Located within 1 mile of the Hatteras Lighthouse, the 78 units include a choice of motel rooms, efficiencies, duplexes, villa units, and cottages. Most units are oceanfront, and all are oceanside. (The rate guideline above pertains to motel rooms.) The well-maintained complex has an outdoor pool and hot tub, and surfers, windsurfers, and anglers enjoy the proximity to ocean and sound.

Rooms have cable TV, phones, full baths, and daily maid service. Efficiencies accommodate two to six people and are equipped with complete kitchens. The oceanfront villas offer balconies on both the oceanside and soundside, so you can enjoy sunrises and sunsets. The six duplexes offer two decks and sleep up to six people each. Efficiencies and villas usually rent on a weekly basis, and there is a three-night minimum stay, but they can be rented nightly when available. Note that there is no daily maid service for the villas, efficiencies, and duplexes, but linens can

be exchanged. Cottages are rented by the week only. Efficiencies, duplexes, villas, and cottages are fully furnished. Wheelchair-accessible, one-room efficiencies are also available. It's open year-round.

Falcon Motel $$
NC 12, Buxton
(252) 995–5968, (800) 635–6911
www.falconmotel.com

The Falcon offers some of the best prices for accommodations on the Outer Banks. The traditional Outer Banks–style rooms here appeal to family-oriented guests who appreciate moderate prices, accommodations with character, and the peaceful environment of Hatteras Island. The Falcon, owned by Doug and Anne Meekins, is known for its attention to detail, which is apparent in the clean, well-maintained rooms and grounds. And it's only a short walk to the Hatteras Lighthouse.

This motel includes 35 units with 30 rooms and five fully equipped apartments, all at ground level. All rooms and apartments have daily maid service. Nonsmoking rooms are available. The spacious rooms have a light, airy feel and include cable TV with HBO. Many rooms have refrigerators and microwaves. All rooms have wooden deck chairs on a wide, covered porch. Park right outside your door.

If you like boating, staying at the Falcon offers you a big advantage. A boat ramp is available for use at no extra charge. Small boats, kayaks, or canoes can be launched easily into the sound here. The ramp is set among beautiful oak trees where wildlife and many varieties of birds abound. Guests have use of the swimming pool and complimentary bikes. You'll also find a shaded picnic area with barbecue grills amid mature oak trees, away from the road. The landscaping includes martin and bluebird houses, palm trees, and planted shrubs and flowers that attract the local bird population. Don't miss seeing the osprey platform on the soundside area beyond the trees. As you can tell, Anne and Doug Meekins are nature and bird lovers and they enjoy sharing their interests with guests.

The Falcon Motel is in the heart of Buxton, within an easy walk of several shops and restaurants, including Diamond Shoals Restaurant (see our Restaurants chapter) across the street. The beach and the lighthouse are a short walk away.

The rate guideline above pertains to the rooms only; apartments rent mostly on a weekly basis. The motel is open from March through mid-December.

Comfort Inn of Hatteras $$$$
NC 12, Buxton
(252) 995–6100, (800) 432–1441

The Comfort Inn is in the heart of Buxton, close to the beach and shops. The 60 units and one suite with exterior access are standard motel-style rooms with kings or dou-

ble beds. Rooms are decorated in attractive, soft beach colors; all have cable TV with HBO, refrigerators, and direct-dial phones and microwaves. Nonsmoking and wheelchair-accessible rooms are available.

Free ice and guest laundry are available. A complimentary continental breakfast is served in the lobby. Guests have use of the outdoor swimming pool, gazebo, and the three-story watch tower, the latter two providing panoramic views of the ocean, the sound, and nearby Cape Hatteras Lighthouse (see our Attractions chapter). AARP and AAA discounts are honored.

Comfort Inn of Hatteras Island has ample parking for both boats and campers and is open year-round.

Surf Motel $
Old Lighthouse Rd., Buxton
(252) 995–5785, (888) 295–8185

The ocean is only a 1-block walk from this motel managed by Bea and Jack Goldman,

which is one reason it's so popular with surfers, windsurfers, anglers, and family vacationers. Four motel-style rooms, eight efficiencies, and one apartment are available here. The rooms offer double or single beds; the efficiencies sleep two or four comfortably and have full kitchens; the apartments, featuring two separate bedrooms and one-and-a-half baths, are popular with families of up to five people. The decor features carpeting and traditional Outer Banks–style wood paneling. Amenities include an outdoor, enclosed hot and cold shower, barbecue grills, fish-cleaning stations, and a freezer for your daily catch. Daily maid service is provided. Weekly rates are available.

The Surf Motel is open late March through mid-December.

Cape Hatteras Bed and Breakfast $$–$$$
46223 Old Lighthouse Rd., Buxton
(252) 995–3002, (800) 252–3316
www.surforsound.com

A short walk to the beach makes this bed-and-breakfast inn popular with windsurfers, beach lovers, lighthouse enthusiasts, honeymooners, surfers, and couples who just want to get away. The two-story inn offers several styles of accommodations from which to choose. All nine units are nonsmoking, and six are on the first floor. Each has its own entrance opening onto a covered porch that runs the length of the building. Two of the rooms offer two double beds, and the rest have king- or queen-size beds. The inn has two efficiency units. A two-room unit features a bedroom with a queen-size bed, a living room with a queen sleeper sofa, and a full kitchen. The one-room unit has a queen-size bed and kitchenette. All units have cable TV and private baths. A large sun deck with comfortable chairs, a gas grill, and a table are available for guests' use.

Amenities include a common dining and living area upstairs where a complimentary full gourmet breakfast is served, color cable TV, VCR, and hot and cold outdoor showers. Beach gear, coolers, bicycles, and beach toys are available along with lockable storage for surf- and sailboards. Daily maid service is provided. Weekly rentals are available, with special accommodations available for honeymooners. It's open April through mid-December.

Tower Circle Motel $, no credit cards
Old Lighthouse Rd., Buxton
(252) 995–5353

This small motel, just off NC 12 oceanside, is one of the friendliest spots on the Outer Banks. The Gray family, which has owned

TOWER CIRCLE MOTEL
"On Cape Hatteras"
P.O. Box 88
Buxton, North Carolina 27920
252-995-5353

The 19 units, including eight duplexes, four two-room suites, and two efficiency apartments, all open onto the porch. All have cable TV and sleep two–six people comfortably in twin or queen-size beds. All suites and apartments have complete kitchens. No phones for optimum privacy although a pay phone is on-site. All linens are provided as well as daily maid service. A washer/dryer and fish-cleaning station is provided as well as a freezer to store your catch.

It's just a short walk to the beach, restaurants, and shops. Tower Circle is open April through November.

Tower Circle for some 30 years, treats guests like old friends, and many of them are. Guests sit on the porch, swap stories, and enjoy the atmosphere and salt air.

The 14 units, including eight duplexes, four two-room suites, and two efficiency apartments, all open onto the porch. All have cable TV and sleep from two to six people comfortably in twin to queen-size beds. All suites and apartments have complete kitchens. For optimum privacy, none of the units has a phone, although a pay phone is on site. All linens are provided as well as daily maid service. A washer and dryer are provided, and there's a fish-cleaning station and even a freezer where you can store your catch. A children's play area is on site.

It's just a short walk to the beach, restaurants, and stores. Tower Circle is open April through mid-December.

Cape Pines Motel $
NC 12, Buxton
(252) 995-5666

Cape Pines Motel, in the center of Buxton just a mile south of the Cape Hatteras Lighthouse, is a nicely maintained one-story facility with private exterior entry to each room. The inn has been owned by the same family since 1988.

Each of the 26 rooms offers cable TV and a full bath. Furnishings have a contemporary beach look. Some rooms have queen-size beds, and nonsmoking rooms are available. Guests will also find three apartments, each offering separate bedrooms, a living room, and a full kitchen. In the summer season, the apartments rent on a weekly basis only. Mini-efficiencies are available with microwaves, coffeemakers, and refrigerators.

Stretch out and relax around the pool and the lawn. The flowers and landscaping are some of our favorites on this end of the island—a splash of color along the main road through Buxton all summer. You'll also find picnic tables and charcoal grills. Fish-cleaning tables and a pay phone are on the premises. Cape Pines is close

> ## Insiders' Tip
> Stay off the beach dunes! The dunes are extremely fragile and a necessary barrier from erosion. Please use the walkways and accesses provided for you.

enough to walk or bike to shopping or attractions. The motel is open year-round.

Hatteras Village

Durant Station Motel $$$
NC 12, Hatteras Village
(252) 986-2244, (888) 550-2244
www.outerbanks.com/durantstation

The Durant Station Motel is oceanfront in Hatteras Village with one- to three-bedroom fully equipped apartments. Each unit has a well-equipped kitchen, separate bedroom(s), and a living/dining area. Towels and linens are provided. Amenities include an outdoor pool, easy beach access, and a fish-cleaning table. The apartments rent nightly or weekly, with a two-night minimum during peak season. The Durant Station Motel is open year-round.

Sea Gull Motel $$
NC 12, Hatteras Village
(252) 986-2550
www.seagullhatteras.com

Most nights at this motel, you can raise the window, catch the ocean breezes, and listen to the breaking waves about 125 yards away. The carefully maintained Sea Gull is at the northern end of scenic Hatteras Village, and patrons will enjoy the quaint, quiet charm and friendly ambiance of this popular establishment. Guests enjoy walking on the beach and along nearby Pamlico Sound or relaxing in the shade on a lazy

afternoon. Sea Gull Motel has spacious grounds and a walkway to the beach.

Other amenities include an outdoor pool, a wading pool for the kids, picnic tables, grills, and fish-cleaning tables. A few shops are within walking distance, and Fish Tails Restaurant, just across the street, serves three meals daily (see our Restaurants chapter).

Guests will find a variety of accommodations, including 35 motel-style rooms. Nine rooms offer ocean views. Rooms offer a combination of double beds or queen-size beds, and some rooms have refrigerators and microwaves. Six apartments and four efficiencies offer fully equipped kitchens. Wheelchair-accessible rooms are available. The large, comfortable rooms rent nightly, while the apartments and efficiencies require a three-day minimum stay. All rooms have cable TV and phones. Two cottages, one soundfront and one oceanside, rent by the week year-round.

The motel is open March through November.

General Mitchell Motel $$
NC 12, Hatteras Village
(252) 986–2444, (800) 832–0139
www.mitchellmotel.com

This oceanfront motel is named for Billy Mitchell, the aviation pioneer of the U.S. Army Air Service, who proved the value and power of airplanes against naval vessels by sinking two retired battleships off the coast of Cape Hatteras from his plane. The newly remodeled facility, on the left as you enter Hatteras Village from the north, is popular with anglers, divers, vacationers, and travelers alike. Two buildings house 33 motel-style rooms and 15 efficiencies with full kitchens. Some have ocean views. The rooms vary in size and offer double beds, king-size beds, or two doubles and one single bed. Efficiencies have a two-day minimum stay.

Microwaves and refrigerators are available in all rooms.

Amenities include an outdoor pool and hot tub, a lighted fish-cleaning pavilion, picnic area, freezer for storing the day's surf catch, and a wooden walkway to the beach. A horseshoe pit and volleyball court are provided. Last but not least, they serve a traditional continental breakfast. The motel is open year-round.

Seaside Inn Bed & Breakfast $$$
NC 12, Hatteras Village
(252) 986–2700
www.seasidebb.com

This inn is actually the site of the first motel built on the Outer Banks in 1928. It's been lovingly refurbished, and owner Cindy Foster offers guests something special here. On NC 12 in Hatteras Village, the Seaside features 10 guest rooms (three have separate sitting areas) with private bathroom facilities, and some have whirlpool baths. All rooms feature either king- or queen-size beds with fine linens. Each room has a distinct personality, size, and floor plan. The inn offers a full breakfast—served in a quaint dining room—that includes freshly squeezed juices, hot coffee and tea, and a menu that changes daily. Selections may include hot biscuits, ham and eggs, homemade granola, fresh fruit, or French toast. There are always choices to accommodate different tastes.

The inn requires a 50 percent deposit a week before your stay. It is not wheelchair-accessible, but the innkeeper is willing to work to accommodate disabled visitors. This is a nonsmoking establishment. One room is pet-friendly. Seaside Inn can handle small gatherings, weddings, and parties, and it is open all year long.

Hatteras Harbor Motel $$
NC 12, Hatteras Village
(252) 986–2565

This soundfront motel in the heart of Hatteras Village is convenient to restaurants,

shops, and services and is adjacent to the Hatteras charter boat fleet. Visitors can park their cars and walk or bike to most places in this quaint little community. We like this motel because of its location and cheerful staff.

Hatteras Harbor Motel has 15 rooms (each with a full bath), four two-bedroom efficiency apartments, and two studio efficiencies. All rooms have cable TV, microwaves, refrigerators, and telephones. Nonsmoking rooms are available. Daily maid service and fresh linens are provided. Guests will enjoy the in-ground pool (complete with a kiddie wading pool) and the long, shaded porches that are perfect for watching the daily village activities.

Some rooms allow pets for a $25 fee. The motel, a longtime favorite of anglers and budget-minded travelers, is open year-round. Inquire about off-season rates.

Hatteras Marlin Motel $
NC 12, Hatteras Village
(252) 986–2141

Hatteras Marlin Motel, owned and operated by the Midgett family, is in sight of the harbor fishing fleet, restaurants, and shops. The 40 units are divided among three buildings and consist of standard motel rooms with king- or double-size beds and one-bedroom efficiencies. A newer building near the back of the property away from the road offers a pair of two-bedroom suites with combined living, kitchen, and dining areas. From this building, located along a canal, you can often see ducks waddling around in the grassy areas of the yard.

The two older buildings near the road share parking with Midgett's Gas Station and convenience store. All rooms are well maintained and have cable TV and telephones. Accommodations sleep one to six people comfortably and rent weekly or nightly depending upon availability. The motel has an in-ground swimming pool and sun deck. Hatteras Marlin Motel is open all year, except for Christmas.

Holiday Inn Express $$$$
NC 12 at Marina Way, Hatteras Village
(252) 986–1110, (800) 361–1590

The Holiday Inn Express, opened in 1996, is at the tip of Hatteras Island and is open 24 hours a day. It offers 40 standard rooms with two double beds or king-size beds and 32 suites with two double beds or a king-size bed plus a separate living area with a fold-out double-bed sofa. All suites feature microwaves, refrigerators, and cable TV with HBO. Nonsmoking rooms are available. Wheelchair-accessible rooms and suites are available. A laundry facility is available to guests, as is free ice. Suites have additional amenities, such as coffeemakers, irons and boards, kitchen counter space with sink, and round kitchen tables with four chairs. The second-floor rooms have private balconies. Rooms with ocean and sound views are available, and first-floor rooms feature private patios. Guests are treated to a complimentary continental breakfast. There is also an outdoor pool. The inn is open year-round.

Ocracoke Island

The Anchorage Inn and Marina $$$–$$$$
NC 12, Ocracoke
(252) 928–1101
www.theanchorageinn.com

The Anchorage Inn, which resembles a small resort, overlooks Silver Lake and the village. Besides 39 motel-style rooms, the inn has a marina and fishing center, recreational amenities, an outdoor cafe, and gift shops nearby. The attractive five-story red brick building with white trim has elevator access to each floor.

Accommodations here offer some of the best bird's-eye views available of the harbor and Ocracoke Village, especially from upper-floor rooms. Most of the rooms have some view of Silver Lake Harbor. Each of the rooms has a king- or queen-size bed or two double beds, full bath, direct-dial phone, and cable TV with Showtime and Cinemax. The fourth-floor units are nonsmoking rooms, and wheelchair-accessible rooms are available. Pets are allowed in some rooms for a $10 fee.

The Anchorage Inn offers its guests a complimentary continental breakfast, a private pool with a sun deck situated on the harbor, and an on-premises boat dock and ramp. The gazebo at Silver Lake is a perfect place to watch an early evening sunset. Guests can walk to restaurants, shops, and the historical sites on Ocracoke Island. Bike rentals are available. Fishing charters, which depart from the dock across the street, can be booked with the marina's dockmaster. The motel is open year-round.

Berkley Manor B&B $$$$, no credit cards
NC 12, Ocracoke
(252) 928-5911, (800) 832-1223
www.berkleymanor.com

Two buildings situated on three acres house this 12-room bed-and-breakfast on Ocracoke Harbor. The Manor House, built in 1860, was remodeled in 1950. The Ranch House dates from the mid-1950s, and the architecture and cedar exterior create an impression of age and quality. Both buildings have been recently refurnished in Caribbean plantation style, making use of dark wood and lush colors. All interior walls, floors, and ceilings of the Manor House are made of hand-carved wood panels of redwood, pine, cypress, and cedar.

Berkley Manor is adjacent to the National Park Service offices and ferry dock but away from the congestion that one might anticipate from seasonal visitors. Lots of trees provide comfortable privacy. A complimentary continental breakfast is served daily in the breakfast room of the Manor House. There is also a guest lounge here, which offers the only television at the inn. Staying here is a real opportunity to get away from the hustle and bustle of everyday life. Guests also have the choice of relaxing on one of the porches overlooking the lovely lawn and enjoying the company of other guests. In addition to the porches, the top two stories of the four-story tower are now complete. The third and fourth stories house a lounge and observation floor with spectacular views of Silver Lake. This is the place to watch those legendary sunsets.

All rooms are spacious and have been furnished in classic fashion. Double sinks in the baths and large closets are among the nice features here. The inn has nine rooms, all with private baths. Phones are not provided in the rooms. Berkley Center is open year-round.

Blackbeard's Lodge $-$$$
Back Rd., Ocracoke
(252) 928-3421, (800) 892-5314
www.blackbeardslodge.com

Ocracoke's oldest hotel, Blackbeard's Lodge was once known as The Wahab Village Inn.

Built in 1936 by local entrepreneur, developer, and visionary Stanley Wahab, the building's first floor originally housed Ocracoke's only movie theater on one side and skating rink on the other. "Rooms for hire" occupied the second floor and often accommodated visiting dignitaries, movie stars, and well-heeled types who actually flew their planes to the island, landed on the barren sand flats, and taxied right up to the front door. Live oaks and cedar trees have long since obscured the beachfront view that guests once enjoyed, but you can actually "feel" the historic prominence this place has known.

A subsequent owner added some rooms to the gabled third floor and stretched the building out with additional rooms in the wing now called the annex. A Dynamo generator—salvaged from a

cruise ship that sank off the coast—once provided power for the inn. In fact, enough electricity was generated there to provide others on Ocracoke with their first community-wired source of power. While those days are past, you can still experience the high ceilings, wood plank floors, and tongue-and-groove pine paneling of the original building.

In 1999, Ann and Buffy Warner (owners of Ocracoke's popular Howard's Pub) purchased the 37-unit lodge. The inn is slated for an extensive and authentic renovation over the next 8 to 10 years. The building's various wings, nooks, and crannies will allow for the work to be done in stages, and during the off-season, so that most rooms will remain available to the public during the restoration.

This is a family-oriented property during the vacation season that changes focus to accommodate "outdoors and sporting types" and those just wanting to get away from it all during the fall, winter, and spring. Blackbeard's has 37 unique and affordable rooms and apartments ranging from a room with one double bed to a room that sleeps eight with a full kitchen and dining area. All rooms have cable TV with Showtime. Some rooms feature whirlpool baths, while others might include a kitchenette, king-size bed, refrigerator, or wet bar; there is a combination of amenities to suit just about any need. A game room complete with pool table and electronic games is available for those inclement days or for nights when friendly competition is in order. The Warners have acquired a brand-new fleet of bicycles for rent, and this year saw the addition of multi-passenger surrey bikes. The lodge has a heated swimming pool with sundeck, wrap-around porch with rockers, fish-cleaning table, and free water access for rinsing the salt and sand off your vehicle if surf-fishing or just beach driving is your passion. Blackbeard's Lodge is open all year long.

Boyette House $$–$$$$
NC 12 , Ocracoke
(252) 928–4261, (800) 928–4261
www.boyettehouse.com

Jon Wynn presides over this very pleasant motel that opened more than two decades ago. The Boyette House has more than doubled in size since 1994, and Boyette House II is now open. The addition offers wide porches and wicker furniture, all of which create a comfortable atmosphere.

Ceiling fans stir the air on warm summer evenings. Each of the rooms in the newer section is well appointed, with a queen-size bed, breakfast bar, microwave, refrigerator, and coffeemaker. Most rooms also have wet bars and steam baths; all rooms have phones and cable TVs with remotes. The two luxury suites on the third floor each have a private porch, picture windows on three sides, a whirlpool tub, and steam bath.

Boyette House I is a 12-unit, two-story wooden structure offering comfortable hotel-style rooms. Each room has a private bath, TV with remote, and a refrigerator. Ten of the rooms have two double beds, and the other two offer one double bed. The five units on the first floor have ramp access, and wheelchairs will fit through the doors into the rooms and bathrooms, but you can't turn around once in the bathroom. There is, however, one fully wheelchair-accessible room. Rocking chairs line the wide upper and lower decks fronting all rooms, which are nice places to read and relax. The lobby is a comfortable reading area as well, and visitors can borrow from the house selection of books. Guests will enjoy the complimentary coffee bar in the mornings.

Whether you're staying at Boyette House I or II, the sundeck in the back is perfect for sunbathing. You'll also find a hot tub here and hammocks under the trees out front.

Recently, the owner decided to create accommodations specifically for couples wanting to enjoy a romantic getaway on Ocracoke Island. A secluded duplex is available a short distance away from the Boyette House. These are luxurious accommodations decorated by Sally Newell, who also decorated the Boyette House II. Full kitchens, steam showers with separate Jacuzzis, and queen beds are some of the furnishings you'll find here. Also available nearby are three studio apartments. Spencer's Market, consisting of three separate retail shops, opened recently. The studio apartments are located above. Queen beds, a full kitchen, and a great room for dining and living are offered in these apartments. These newer additions are available to adults only, and no pets or smoking are allowed.

You can arrange to be picked up at the boat docks or the airport free of charge. Boyette House is within walking distance of Silver Lake and the restaurants in Ocracoke. The motel is open most of the year, but it's best to call ahead during the winter months just to make sure.

**The Castle Bed & Breakfast
on Silver Lake $$$$
155 Silver Lake Drive, Ocracoke
(252) 928–3505, (800) 471–8848
www.thecastlebb.com**

The Castle offers a bed-and-breakfast in a renovated historic Ocracoke structure that was originally built during the 1950s, '60s, and '70s by Sam Jones of Norfolk, Virginia. Mr. Jones contributed greatly to

Ocracoke's economy during the decades of construction and is considered a local legend, along with his favorite horse, Ikey D. Following Mr. Jones's death, The Castle sat vacant for 19 years before two local businessmen and longtime friends bought it along with a house known as the Whittler's Club. One partner undertook renovating the front half of the building and the other took the back half and the Whittler's Club. A rental duplex, The Castle Villas, has been recently built beside The Castle.

The Castle features 10 rooms, two with queen beds and whirlpool baths, one with a queen bed and double sofa bed, one with a queen and two twin beds, three with a double and a twin, and two with queen beds. A suite features a queen bed and a walk-in shower. All rooms have TVs. Two downstairs rooms are wheelchair-accessible. All rooms have private baths, and two have lakefront views.

The Castle Villas have six bedrooms total. Each side of the tastefully furnished duplex sleeps seven people, and large families or groups of friends can open doors that access each side. There's an entertainment center on each floor, complete with satellite television reception, and a sitting room occupies the second floor. The third floor of each side has a wet bar with a small refrigerator. The Villas offer outstanding views of Silver Lake and the summer sunsets over the Pamlico Sound. Guests can bring a boat and are provided a slip in front of the property (slip reservations are recommended).

New to The Castle are 16 courtyard villas, some with kitchenettes. A two-night stay is required on weekends. The Castle serves a full breakfast. Smoking is allowed only on the porches and decks. Children older than 12 years of age are welcome. The Castle is closed from January 2 to March 1.

The Cove Bed and Breakfast $$$$
21 Loop Road, Ocracoke
(252) 928-4192
www.thecovebb.com

The Cove is a beautiful new beach home located within walking distance of Ocra-coke's many shops and restaurants. This bed-and-breakfast is a large place—over 5,000 square feet—and it gives you a great view of the sound and Ocracoke's lighthouse. Andy Mason and Mel Powell run this establishment, where the rooms come equipped with cable TVs and hair dryers. Each room has its own balcony and bath. Full breakfasts are served each day in the large common area. An enormous screened porch beckons you to sit awhile and just absorb the wonderful, clean Ocracoke air at the end of a busy beach day.

Two suites are available with queen four-poster beds and Jacuzzis. Two rooms are available, each with a queen bed and one single bed. The outdoor shower is fun for rinsing off sand and salt after swimming in the ocean or sound.

The inn is a nonsmoking establishment and children age 12 and over are welcome. Pets are not allowed. A public boat dock is nearby for those who would like to launch a kayak or small craft. Bicycles are available for touring around town. Transportation is provided to and from the airstrip.

Crews Inn Bed and Breakfast
$, no credit cards
Back Rd., Ocracoke
(252) 928-7011

The Crews Inn is a great place to really get away from it all. No phones or TVs will disturb your privacy here. Three rooms have private baths, and two share a bath. All rooms have double beds. The wraparound porch is an especially nice spot for guests to gather, for the building is surrounded by large live oaks and is far enough away from traffic to make chatting easy. This is a nonsmoking establishment, but smoking is allowed on the porch. The inn serves mostly a continental but occasionally a full breakfast. Crews Inn is open year-round.

Edwards of Ocracoke $-$$
Pony Island Rd., Ocracoke
(252) 928-4801, (800) 254-1359
www.edwardsofocracoke.com

This refurbished motel, away from the center of Ocracoke and off the main route near The Back Porch Restaurant, consists of eight motel rooms, three efficiencies, five apartments, and three cottages. Most of the units have screened porches, and some open onto a veranda. Phones are available in most units, and there is cable TV. The cottages rent weekly during the summer, and the efficiencies require a three-day minimum stay. Some have refrigerators. The rate guideline above pertains to nightly rentals of the motel rooms only.

The motel offers inexpensive accommodations in a family setting with a carefully landscaped green lawn, flower beds, and pine trees. Pets are allowed in some of the cottages for an extra charge. The motel is open April through New Year's.

Harborside Motel $$
across from Silver Lake Harbor, Ocracoke
(252) 928-3111

This charming motel offers 18 rooms and four efficiencies, all well kept and comfortable. All rooms have cable TV, phones, and refrigerators. Most rooms offer two double beds; one has three double beds, and two have one double bed. Guests can use the waterfront sundeck, docks, and boat ramp across the street. Nonsmoking rooms are available.

Harborside has its own gift shop offering a wide selection of clothing, books, gourmet foods, and small gifts. Other shops and restaurants of Ocracoke Village are within walking distance. The Swan Quarter and Cedar Island ferry docks are nearby. The same family has owned this property since 1965, and their hospitality and service are firmly established. All rooms are refurbished on a regular basis.

A complimentary breakfast of homemade muffins, coffee, juice, and tea is provided. The motel is open Easter through mid-November.

The Island Inn $$$
NC 12, Ocracoke
(252) 928-4351
www.ocracoke-island-inn.com

The Island Inn, owned by Cee and Bob Touhey, provides a variety of accommodations suitable for single adults, couples, and families with children. Originally built as an Odd Fellows Lodge in 1901, the main building has served as a school, a private residence, and naval officers' quarters. It was restored by former owners and has been recognized in *Country Inns of the Old South, Southern Living, Cuisine,* and *The Saturday Evening Post.*

The owners had their first date on Ocracoke Island and vacationed here for many years; they have returned to live and work. The main building is a nonsmoking establishment. Many of the 35 rooms have been refurbished, reflecting the inherently romantic style of this country inn. The main building houses individual rooms and suites, all uniquely furnished with antiques and quilts, as if they were separate guest rooms in a private home, providing a restful ambiance. The adults-only rooms and suites accommodate a wide range of needs. If you're looking for a contemporary feel, ask for the Crow's Nest, which offers spectacular views of the postcard-pretty village.

Across the street, a much newer three-story structure includes two honeymoon rooms with king-size beds. Families with children will find these casual accommodations a welcome retreat. The third floor has brand-new one- and two-bedroom luxury villas overlooking the heated pool. Each beautifully furnished villa has a kitchen, living and dining area, washer and dryer, plenty of windows, and a whirlpool tub. They're a wonderful respite any time of the year. The inn also rents a number of cottages, some of which accommodate pets with no fee attached, and has a heated swimming pool that is kept open as long as weather permits. Cable TV with free Showtime is available in every room. The inn has an on-site restaurant (see our Restaurants chapter), a large lobby for lounging, and a covered porch with rocking chairs. The inn closes for a few weeks in January but otherwise is open year-round.

Joyce's of Ocracoke Waterfront Motel and Dockage $$$$
Silver Lake, Ocracoke Village
(252) 928–6461
www.joycesofocracoke.com

Joyce's offers water views of Silver Lake from a large deck. Four of the smaller efficiencies are larger than standard motel rooms. Each is set up with a queen bed and queen sofa bed. The two larger efficiencies have two queen beds and a queen sofa bed plus a full-size refrigerator, range, microwave, coffeemaker, toaster, and kitchen utensils. Daily housekeeping is offered; linens are furnished. Room amenities include phones, cable TV with HBO, heat, and air conditioning. Nonsmoking rooms are available. Boaters will love the location—you can pull your boat up at the establishment's 10-slip boat dock. Joyce's is open year-round.

Ocracoke Harbor Inn $$$
on Silver Lake Harbor, across from the Coast Guard Station, Ocracoke
(252) 928–5731, (888) 456–1998
www.ocracokeharborinn.com

This lovely new 16-room, seven-suite inn overlooks picturesque Silver Lake Harbor. Take advantage of the inn's private decks with Adirondack chairs—kick back, relax, and enjoy the view.

Each tastefully decorated room features either two queen beds or one king bed and includes a mini-fridge, cable TV, coffee pot, hair dryer, and climate control. The luxurious suites have two-person whirlpool tubs and kitchenettes. Suites are studio-style or one-bedroom.

Guests can enjoy a complimentary continental breakfast each morning. Also available are complimentary boat dock-

ing, outdoor showers, barbecue grills, bicycle rentals, and lots of outdoor decks. The Ocracoke Harbor Inn is open year-round. Pets are not allowed.

Ocracoke Island Wayfarer Hostel
$, no credit cards
125 Lighthouse Rd., Ocracoke
(252) 928-3411

Hostel accommodations are great for travelers on a budget who like the camaraderie of a communal lifestyle, and Ocracoke's Wayfarer Hostel is no exception. It's run by a friendly Ocracoke native, Amy Howard, whose surname reveals her family's rich heritage on this island. This is the house she grew up in, now renovated slightly to accommodate wayfaring souls. The house has two upstairs private rooms, each with a double bed; these rooms share a common bath at the bottom of the stairs. Two dorm rooms are available, one for men and one for women. Each dorm room can accommodate six people in three sets of bunk beds. The dorm rooms share one bath. The living room, piano room, dining room, and kitchen are open to everyone, so if you want to cook your own meals you can—as long as you clean up after yourself. A few bikes are available to use free of charge, but guests have to share. Smoking and pets are not allowed. The hostel stays full in summer, especially on weekends, so call in advance if you know you're coming. It's open March through October.

Oscar's House   **$$**
One block from Silver Lake Harbor, Ocracoke
(252) 928-1311

Oscar's House was built in 1940 by the keeper of the Ocracoke Lighthouse and was first occupied by the World War II commander of the Ocracoke Naval Base. Stories abound about Oscar, who lived and worked on the island for many years as a fisherman and hunting guide. This guesthouse has operated as a bed-and-breakfast since 1984. It is managed by Ann Ehringhaus, a massage therapist, local fine-art photographer, and the author of *Ocracoke Portrait*.

The house retains the original beaded-board walls, and all four guest rooms are delightfully furnished. One upstairs bedroom has a loft that creates a comfortable setting. You won't find private baths, but sharing is easily managed. Two baths, one upstairs and one down, accommodate guests, and there's also an outdoor shower (with dressing room) underneath the cedar tree. The house has central heating and air conditioning. The large kitchen with a big table is available to guests; however, the stove is off limits. Ann serves a complimentary full breakfast to all guests and will gladly adhere to special preferences for vegetarian or macrobiotic meals. Smoking is allowed on the back deck only. This is the perfect place for personal and spiritual renewal, and you can treat yourself to one of Ann's therapeutic massages. In spring and fall, Ann offers workshops in photography and therapeutic bodywork. Call for details.

Oscar's House has a deck area complete with barbecue grills. Meals can be eaten inside or outdoors. Oscar's House is within walking distance of all village shops and restaurants, and bicycles are free for guests. Ann will also gladly transport guests to and from the Ocracoke Airport, which is open to single- and twin-engine planes. This bed-and-breakfast is open from April to October.

Pelican Lodge   **$$–$$$**
across from fire station, Ocracoke
(252) 928-1661

Built as a lodge, the Pelican features a full sit-down breakfast. The four rooms, one with two double beds and the others with one double bed, are spacious and carpeted and have private baths. Nonsmoking rooms are available. Amenities include cable TV, a small pool, and free use of bicycles. The lodge is open year-round.

Pirate's Quay   **$$$$**
Silver Lake, Ocracoke
(252) 928-3002

This extraordinary hotel condominium directly across from the Coast Guard Station in Ocracoke Village opened in 1987 and provides some of the most luxurious accommodations available on a nightly basis anywhere on the Outer Banks. The hotel is made up of six individually owned condo suites, each with living room, dining room, full kitchen, two bedrooms, and one and one-half baths. Nonsmoking rooms are available. Linens and maid service are included. Units on the top floor have cathedral ceilings. Two decks off each suite, a waterfront gazebo, and docking facilities make the most of the harborfront location. Deepwater docking is available with each unit.

Each condo suite accommodates six (rentals are limited to two children) and has a whirlpool bath and cable TV with Showtime. All suites are beautifully furnished and have kitchens stocked with all the dishes, cookware, and gadgets you need. From Pirate's Quay (pronounced "key"), guests can walk or bike to quaint nearby shops, restaurants, and other attractions. Pets are not allowed. The hotel is open year-round.

Pony Island Motel $$
NC 12, Ocracoke
(252) 928-4411
www.ponyislandmotel.com

At the edge of Ocracoke Village, a short distance from Silver Lake Harbor, Pony Island Motel offers 50 rooms, efficiencies, and suites. The grounds are spacious and inviting. Family-owned for over 25 years, the inn hosts families and couples in search of peace and solitude on Ocracoke Island.

Most of the units have either single or double occupancy, but the motel offers some rooms that accommodate up to five people. Each room has a telephone, refrigerator, and color cable TV with Showtime, and the efficiencies provide fully equipped kitchens. Rooms are refurbished regularly but maintain a traditional decor with paneled walls. Nonsmoking rooms and one wheelchair-accessible room are available.

The motel has been recently remodeled and now has one- and two-bedroom suites on the third floor. Rooms on the first and second floors are spacious and have wet bars, refrigerators, coffeemakers, and microwave ovens.

The motel is within walking distance of the Ocracoke Lighthouse and other island attractions. Bike rentals and boat docking are available. The large, heated pool and spacious lawn with picnic tables and grills offer plenty of room for family activities. The Pony Island Restaurant, a local favorite, is right next door (see our Restaurants chapter). Pony Island Motel is open year-round.

Sand Dollar Motel $$
Sand Dollar La., Ocracoke
(252) 928-5571
www.ocracokeisland.com

This quaint establishment is in the heart of Ocracoke Village behind The Back Porch Restaurant (there are no street signs). Fresh flowers welcome guests to the lobby. You're likely to be greeted by Roger Garrish, the property's personable owner and an Ocracoke native, who is a great source of island information. The Sand Dollar has 12 rooms and a two-bedroom cottage. Two of the rooms are efficiencies, featuring small microwaves and coffeemakers; all rooms have refrigerators and cable TV. Bedding options include queen- and double-size beds. One special room is connected to the pool and has a private deck and a king-size bed. Nonsmoking rooms are available. Guests can enjoy a continental breakfast and a dip in the pool. Repeat visits are common at this neat little place, so book your stay early. The inn is open from April 1 to mid-November.

Silver Lake Inn & Motel $$-$$$
NC 12, Ocracoke
(252) 928-5721

Silver Lake Motel sits among a grove of trees along the main street of Ocracoke Village. The Wrobleski family built the two-story motel in 1983 and has added another three-story building since then for a total of 22 motel-style rooms and 12 suites. Featuring long porches and rooms paneled in California redwood, the motel rooms are well known for their rustic appeal and comfort; most of the furniture in the rooms was built by the owners. Wooden shutters, pine floors, and wallpapered baths create a cozy atmosphere.

The 12 suites in the newer building feature private porches with hammocks and wicker furniture, affording views of the lake. Rooms adjacent to these suites can be opened to provide for larger families. Suites, which offer living rooms and full kitchens, have wood floors, wallpapered baths, and Victorian-style furnishings and wall coverings. End units have their own 7-foot-wide hot tubs overlooking Silver Lake—a relaxing environment indeed. Rooms offer king, queen, or double beds. All the rooms have cable TV with Showtime. A common area in the older section of the motel serves as a lounge.

The Silver Lake Motel offers families comfortable and attractive rooms. A deepwater dock is provided for those arriving by boat. Wheelchair-accessible rooms are available. A suite and three rooms are pet friendly. It is open year-round.

Thurston House Inn   **$$**
NC 12, Ocracoke
(252) 928–6037
www.thurstonhouseinn.com

The Thurston House Inn is a relatively new accommodation on Ocracoke Island, but the structure itself was built in the 1920s. The former home of Capt. Tony Thurston Gaskill, it is now on the Register of Historic Places in North Carolina. It was renovated in 1996 by the captain's granddaughter Marlene Mathews and her husband, Randal.

Silver Lake Inn & Motel
Rooms & Suites overlooking
Silver Lake Harbor
252-928-5721

Enjoy our hospitality and spectacular sunsets from our Lounge.

The inn offers nine rooms, each with a private bath. A phone is available on the premises. All rooms are air conditioned and have private decks and porches. The rooms feature either king- or queen-size beds.

Guests will enjoy relaxing on the covered porches and deck, which connects the inn's two buildings. An expanded continental breakfast is part of the package. Children older than 12 are welcome. This is a nonsmoking establishment, but smoking is allowed on the porches. The inn is within walking distance of Silver Lake, Ocracoke Lighthouse, and various stores, restaurants, and historic sites. Local airport pickup is available. Reservations are recommended. The inn is open year-round.

Camping

North of Oregon Inlet
Roanoke Island
Hatteras Island
Ocracoke Island

Imagine drifting off to sleep on a bed of soft sand with the murmur of waves gently kissing the sandy shoreline. A gentle breeze ruffles your tent, ushering in the sounds of nocturnal creatures and the salt-laden air. Now imagine waking up to a spectacular sunrise over the ocean as gulls begin to wheel and turn above the waves looking for breakfast and dolphins play just off the beach. Welcome to an experience you won't soon forget—camping on the Outer Banks. From spring through autumn, lovers of the outdoors make their way to the numerous campgrounds that line these barrier islands to experience nature up-close and personal. Whether choosing to bed down with nothing more than a tent and a sleeping bag or deciding to "camp" in style in a recreational vehicle, opportunities abound for those seeking the solitude that only camping can offer.

When word first got out that the Outer Banks was a desirable location for a little rest and relaxation, campgrounds were a popular choice—and sometimes the only choice—for accommodations. Many of the visitors to the Outer Banks were hunters and anglers, people who relished the natural world and took pleasure in the outdoor experience of sleeping under the Carolina moon. For other tourists, camping was an alternative because motels and rental cottages were few and far between. Many of the older campgrounds have given way to change as development continues to encroach on former open areas, but today choices abound with campgrounds on Colington, Roanoke, Bodie, Hatteras, and Ocracoke Islands. Whether you desire a location right next to the ocean or tucked away in a wooded site, you have numerous spots to explore.

Most people think of summer as the best time to camp on the Outer Banks because of the warm temperatures, but be sure to arm yourself with lots of bug repellent. Many of the campgrounds listed are near the sound or in wooded areas where mosquitoes are always on the lookout for a nice juicy camper. Don't forget that the summer months are also a ripe time for thunderstorms and hurricanes. Be sure to read the chapter on Waves and Weather for additional information on how to stay safe while vacationing on the Outer Banks.

Some campers, many of them locals, prefer to get away from it all by camping during the off-season, or "shoulder seasons" as we call them. This includes the spring and fall when the temperatures are warm enough to enjoy all the outdoor activities. In the fall, the humidity has left, along with some of the crowds, and the evenings are crisp and clear, perfect for stargazing.

More than 100,000 people frequent the National Park Service campgrounds for their home away from home each year, while thousands of other nature lovers set up camp at privately owned campgrounds. Some of these private campgrounds are only open during the summer season, offering few creature comforts besides cold showers, but others are year-round establishments that have everything from electric and water hookups, sewage disposal, and laundry facilities to swimming pools, game rooms, bathhouses, and even cable television. There are also campgrounds that rent furnished RVs. All campgrounds have well-maintained roads and drive-up sites that will accommodate any type of vehicle.

All National Park Service campgrounds operate under the same rules and regulations and charge the same fees. Park Service campgrounds do not take reservations (the one exception is the Ocracoke Campground, which is on the National Park Reservation Service in the summer, between Memorial Day and Labor Day) and accept payment in cash or credit cards upon arrival. Sites operate on a first-come, first-served basis. The National Park Service provides lifeguards at Coquina Beach, the Cape Hatteras Lighthouse, south of the Frisco Pier at Sandy Bay, and on Ocracoke Island. For more information on any of the local National Park Service campgrounds, call (252) 473-2111, and be sure to check the Park Service's Web site for the most up-to-date information on the opening and closing dates of each campground: www.nps.gov/caha.

It is important to remember that camping on the beach is prohibited, as is wilderness camping in open areas, including Nags Head Woods, Kitty Hawk Woods, and Buxton Woods. But there is one spot where wilderness camping is allowed—Portsmouth Island. This now-uninhabited island is only accessible by boat. So if you really want to get away from it all, check out our Daytripping chapter for information on Portsmouth Island.

Nothing could be finah than to be in Carolina camping under the star-studded sky. Just remember, these islands are home to a variety of wildlife, locals included. Please respect their homes by not littering or disturbing the environment in any way. We want to keep it just the way it is so you can come back and enjoy the camping experience again next year.

North of Oregon Inlet

Adventure Bound Camping Center
1004 Kitty Hawk Rd., Kitty Hawk
(252) 255-1130

This tent-only campground is located at the edge of the beautiful Kitty Hawk Woods maritime forest, 1.5 miles from the Bypass. Campers can choose from wooded and open campsites. Hot showers, flush toilets, and gas and charcoal grills are available to visitors. Adventure Bound is affiliated with the Outer Banks International Hostel next door, so the hostel kitchen is open to campers. Rates are $15.00 for one or two people in one tent, with an additional $2.00 per adult and $1.00 per child per tent. Adventure Bound is open year-round.

Colington Park Campground
Colington Rd., Little Colington Island
(252) 441-6128

Less than 3 miles west of the Bypass, past the first Colington Road bridge, Colington Park Campground is situated on the quiet, calm waters of the sound—a stone's throw away from the best crabbing bridge on the Outer Banks (see our Kidstuff chapter). Fishing and boating opportunities also abound in the areas around this campground.

Heavily wooded, tucked beneath tall oak and pine trees, this campground originally was a tent-only area but has since been redesigned to accommodate recreational vehicles too. It's open year-round, and reservations are accepted. Tent campers, however, are limited to two-week stays at a time.

There are 55 sites at this campground, each with a picnic table. All RV sites have water and power hookups. Grills are not provided, and open fires are prohibited, so bring your own grill or camp stove if you plan to cook. Amenities for campers include hot showers, toilets, laundry facilities, and a swing set on the property. There's also an on-site general store.

Camping rates start at $15 per night for tents with two people and $20 a night for RVs with two people. The campground accepts personal checks. Pets are allowed on leashes as long as you clean up after them.

Joe & Kay's Campground
Colington Rd., Little Colington Island
(252) 441-5468

About a mile west on Colington Road, before you get to the first bridge, Joe & Kay's Campground has 70 full hookup sites that are rented on a yearly basis. An additional 15 tent sites are also available from April through November. Rates are

Camping is one of the best ways to get close to the Outer Banks elements. PHOTO: BRANT HARRISON

$14 a night for two people, with a $2 per night charge for each additional person. Reservations aren't accepted, so sites are secured on a first-come, first-served basis. Credit cards and personal checks are not accepted.

Oregon Inlet Campground (NPS)
NC 12, Bodie Island
(252) 473-2111

The northernmost National Park Service campground on the Outer Banks, this facility offers 120 sites along the windswept dunes just north of Oregon Inlet. If you're arriving from the north, look for the campground entrance on the east side of NC 12 just before you cross the Bonner Bridge. It is located on the ocean almost directly across from Oregon Inlet Fishing Center.

Water, cold showers, modern toilets, picnic tables, and charcoal grills are available here. There aren't any utility connections, but dumping stations are nearby.

Most of these sites are in sunny, open areas on the sand. Park rangers suggest that campers bring awnings, umbrellas, or other sources of shade. You also may need mosquito netting and long tent stakes here.

Oregon Inlet Campground is open from April through October. Campers are limited to a two-week stay. Reservations are not accepted, and sites are assigned on a first-come, first-served basis. Fees begin at $17 per night. Golden Age Passport holders receive a 50 percent discount. Note that this campground accepts cash, credit cards, and personal checks with Social Security numbers printed on them.

Roanoke Island

Cypress Cove Campground
US 64, Manteo
(252) 473-5231

Cypress Cove is a wooded, year-round, family vacation campground across from the Christmas Shop on Roanoke Island in Manteo. A total of 60 sites is available, including 20 tent sites with shade and 40 sites with hookups for RVs. Reservations are accepted, and pets are allowed on leashes.

Amenities at Cypress Cove include a playground, basketball court, batting cage, horseshoe pits, a nature trail with a wildlife lookout, and a fishing pond stocked with bass, bream, and catfish where no fishing license is required. Hot showers, restrooms, picnic tables, grills, and county drinking water also are on the premises. There's an on-site dump station here; six sites have sewer facilities. Laundry facilities are within walking distance at a nearby shopping center. The campground is within 15 miles of all major attractions.

Rates are seasonal, with fees going up in the summer and on holiday weekends. In season, tent sites begin at $20 a night and RV sites start at $24 a night. Additional charges apply for additional people and utilities.

Besides providing camping accommodations, Cypress Cove also rents 15 fully furnished trailers and air-conditioned "Kamper Kabins" that sleep one to six people. Rates run from $30 to $90 per night, depending on the cabin you rent, the number of guests, and the season. Some units have up to three bedrooms and efficiency-style kitchens. Weekly rentals also are available. Pets are not allowed in cabins.

Hatteras Island

Cape Hatteras KOA
NC 12, Rodanthe
(252) 987–2307, (800) 562–5268
www.koa.com/capehatteras

A large campground about 14 miles south of the Bonner Bridge across Oregon Inlet, Cape Hatteras KOA has about 300 sites, including one- and two-room "Kamping Kabins." These units feature locking doors, ceiling fans, electricity, and picnic tables, and each unit has a porch. Ask about

wheelchair-accessible units. Friendly, attentive staff greet campers as they arrive at this well-equipped campground. The campground is open March 15 through November and accepts reservations.

Besides hot showers, drinking water, and bathhouses, Cape Hatteras KOA offers campers a dump station, laundry facilities, two pools, a hot tub, a playground, a game room, a restaurant, and a well-stocked general store. Campers here can even take in a round or two of miniature golf or a whirl on the campground's "Fun Bike"—a low-slung three-wheeler to ride inside the park. The ocean is just beyond the dunes for fishing and swimming, and a 200-foot soundside pier is the perfect place to fish, crab, or just sit and watch spectacular sunsets. There's even a recreation program at this campground, offering varied activities in the summer. Rates for tent sites are $35 in summer and $30 in the off-season. Rates for RV sites range from $39 to $50, depending on the number of amenities and the location of the site; they are discounted in the off-season. Rates for Kamping Kabins are $60 for one room ($50 off-season) or $70 for two rooms ($60 off-season).

Rodanthe Watersports and Campground
NC 12, Rodanthe
(252) 987–1431

This soundfront campground is open year-round for recreational vehicles and tents. Wind- and kite-surfers especially enjoy this campground because they can sail right up to some of the sites. Other campers enjoy swimming, boating, and fishing in the sound. The watersports business next door rents kayaks, sailboats, Wave Runners, surfboards, and bicycles (see our Watersports chapter). But what really keeps campers coming back here are the spectacular, unobstructed sunset views.

Sites with electric and water hookups start at $14.50 per night. Tent sites include water and start at $10.00 a night. Hot showers, picnic tables, and a few grills are on site. If you'd rather not cook, you can grab a pizza from Lisa's Pizza right next door (see our Restaurants chapter). Pets are allowed. Reservations are accepted but not required. Personal checks and credit cards are accepted.

North Beach Campground
NC 12, Rodanthe
(252) 987-2378

In the village of Rodanthe, North Beach Campground sits alongside the ocean south of the Chicamacomico Lifesaving Station. Here, 110 sites, all with water and electric hookups, offer campers both tent and RV accommodations and a wide range of amenities. Bathhouse, hot showers, picnic tables, a laundry facility, an outdoor swimming pool, and a pump-out station are available. There aren't any grills here, and open fires aren't allowed, so bring your own grill or camp stove if you want to cook.

North Beach Campground also has a grocery store that sells LP gasoline, kerosene, regular gas, and virtually any convenience store item you might need. Pets are allowed on leashes. Reservations are accepted.

The campground is open from March through November. Rates begin at $14.50 a night for tents. Full hookups start at $19.50 a night.

Camp Hatteras
NC 12, Waves
(252) 987-2777
www.camphatteras.com

A 50-acre, world-class campground, Camp Hatteras is a complete facility that's open year-round and offers every amenity campers could desire. The site includes 1,000 feet of both ocean and sound frontage. Nightly and monthly reservations are accepted.

Most of Camp Hatteras's 320 sites have full hookups, concrete pads, and paved roads. There's also a natural area near the sound available for about 50 tents. Campers will find laundry facilities, hot showers, full bathhouses, and picnic tables on the premises.

For recreation, this campground provides three swimming pools, a clubhouse, a pavilion, a marina, fishing, two tennis courts, a nine-hole miniature golf course, volleyball, basketball, kayaks and windsurfers, and shuffleboard on-site. The grounds are extraordinarily well kept and more organized than most comparable facilities. Sports and camping areas are separate, so sleeping outdoors is still a quiet experience here—even if you're napping midday.

Rates for tent sites range from $23 to $35, and rates for full hookup sites range

from $28 to $52. Please call for details and be sure to ask about discounts. Personal checks and credit cards are accepted. Pets are allowed on leashes for an additional fee.

Ocean Waves Campground
NC 12, Waves
(252) 987–2556

Open March 15 through November 15, Ocean Waves Campground is a seaside resort with sites for RVs and tents. Of 68 spaces, 64 offer full hookups and concrete pads. Each site has its own picnic table. Three bathhouses, hot showers, and laundry facilities are available. Campers also enjoy the game room and outdoor pool. Asphalt roadways are well maintained.

Rates begin at $16.50 for a tent site or $19.00 for a tent site with electricity. A full hookup site begins at $22.00. Cable TV and 50-amp hookups are offered for $2.00 extra per night. Monthly rates in the off-season are $325.00 plus the cost of electricity.

Sands of Time Campground
North End Rd., Avon
(252) 995–5596

This year-round Avon campground has 51 full hookup sites and 15 tent sites, some with full shade. Hot showers, flush toilets, laundry facilities, a dump site, picnic tables, and a pay telephone also are offered to all Sands campers.

Visitors enjoy swimming, fishing, and sunbathing at the nearby beach and sound. Cable TV connections are available for $2.00 extra per night. Grills aren't provided, and open fires are not allowed, so bring your camp stove if you want to cook.

Pets are allowed on leashes. Reservations are accepted and recommended for summer and fall stays. Rates for tent sites are $17.50 a night in-season and $16 a night off-season. Rates for full hookups are $26 a night in-season and $24 a night off-season. Credit cards are not accepted.

Cape Woods Campground
Buxton Back Rd., Buxton
(252) 995–5850

Clean, quiet, and green best describe this campground. Scattered throughout the pine, live oak, and ash trees on the site are 125 sites, some for tents, some with water and electricity, and some with full hookups. Cape Woods is open year-round and gladly accepts reservations. Campers at this full-service campground will find fire pits, grills, picnic tables, and hot showers in two bathhouses, one of which is accessible to disabled visitors and one of which is heated for winter campers. They will also find an outdoor swimming pool, a playground, a small game room, a volleyball court, and a horseshoe pit. Children and grownups alike enjoy freshwater fishing in the canals that surround the campground. Laundry facilities are available, and ice and LP gas are for sale.

Rates for a family of four, including

two children age 16 or younger, are $26 a night for no hookups, $30 for a site with water and electricity, and $33 for a site with full hookups and cable TV. One-room cabins and camper rentals in a variety of sizes are available for $45 to $75. Good Sam discounts are honored, and credit cards are accepted.

Cape Point Campground (NPS)
Off NC 12, Buxton
(252) 473–2111

The largest National Park Service campground on the Outer Banks, Cape Point is about 2 miles south of the Cape Hatteras Lighthouse, across the dunes from the Atlantic. This campground has 202 sites—none with utility connections. It's open from Memorial Day through September but does not accept reservations.

Flush toilets, cold showers, drinking water, charcoal grills, and picnic tables are provided here. Each site has paved access. A wheelchair-accessible area is available, and a dumping station is nearby.

The campground is a short walk away from the ocean where world-class fishing and surfing abound. Most of these sites sit in the open, exposed to the sun and wind. Bring some shade, long tent stakes, lots of bug spray, and batteries. Cost is $17 a night; pets are allowed on leashes. Pay-

ment may be made with cash, credit cards, or personal checks with Social Security numbers printed on them.

Frisco Woods Campground
Frisco Woods, off NC 12, Frisco
(252) 995–5208, (800) 948–3942
www.outer-banks.com/friscowoods

This 30-acre campground in Frisco on Hatteras Island is one of the best privately owned facilities on the Outer Banks. Developed by Ward and Betty Barnett, the soundside property boasts abundant forest and marshland beauty and at least 150 sites in a wooded wonderland.

Electricity and water are available at 122 campsites. Full hookups are offered at 35 other sites, and there are 100 tent sites.

Amenities include an in-ground swimming pool, picnic tables, hot showers, a small country store, propane gas, and public phones. Windsurfers prefer this campground because you can sail right from the sites on the Pamlico Sound. Crabbing, fishing, kayaking, and wandering through the woods are also readily available to campers staying at Frisco Woods.

In-season rates for two people begin at $24 a night for tent sites, $28 a night for electric and water. Each additional adult is charged $6 per night. Cable TV, air conditioners, and heaters are included in the rate.

about 4 miles southwest of Buxton. Just off the beach, next to ramp 49, this is the area's most isolated campground. Its undulating roads twist over dunes and around small hills, providing privacy at almost every site. Some tent areas are so secluded in stands of scrubby trees that you can't even see them from the place you park your car. This campground is a welcome find for folks who like to camp away from civilization.

Frisco Campground has 127 no-frills sites, each with a charcoal grill and picnic table. Flush toilets, cold water showers in bathhouses, and drinking water are available. There aren't any hookups here, but RVs are certainly welcome. A wooden boardwalk crosses from the campground to the ocean.

Reservations aren't accepted, and payment may be made with cash or credit cards (or personal checks with Social Security numbers printed on them). Cost is $17 per night. Pets are allowed on leashes. Frisco Campground is open April through October. Golden Age discounts are honored.

Hatteras Sands Camping Resort
Eagle Pass Rd., Hatteras Village
(252) 986–2422, (888) 987–2225
www.hatterassands.com

A well-maintained campground near the Hatteras Village ferry docks, Hatteras Sands is about a 10-minute walk from the ocean and is open March through November. Reservations are accepted up to a year in advance. Pets are allowed on leashes.

This campground has 104 sites with water and electricity, 43 sites with full hookup that includes cable TV, and 25 tent sites. Pull-through sites for people who don't want to unhook their campers from their cars also are available. Each site has a picnic table. Grills aren't provided, and open fires are prohibited, so bring your own grill or camp stove if you plan to cook.

Hot showers, five-star bathhouses, laundry facilities, a hot tub, and a fitness center are on site here. There's also an

Camping Cabins are also available. The one-room cabins sleep up to four people and rates start at $50 per night. The two-room cabins sleep up to six people starting at $55 a night.

Frisco Woods is open March 1 through December 1, and reservations are accepted. Pets are allowed on leashes. Weekly, monthly, and seasonal rates are available on request, and special event and group rates are offered.

Frisco Campground (NPS)
NC 12, Frisco
(252) 473–2111

Our favorite spot for tent camping on the Outer Banks, Frisco Campground is operated by the National Park Service and sits

Olympic-size swimming pool, a game room, and a mini-mart that stocks all sorts of camping supplies. A canal winds through this campground, offering fishing and crabbing opportunities. Campers can also walk to village shops and restaurants from this Hatteras resort.

The following rates are based on 2002 prices for two people. Rates for tent sites run from $39.95 nightly in the off-season to $40.00 nightly in the summer. Sites with hookups range from $39.00 through $52.00 per night. Special rates and a 10 percent discount are available to Good Sam Park members.

Hatteras Sands rents six cabins, called "Camping Condos," that include beds and water. Electricity is available outside these units. Cost is $52.00 per night through $80.00 depending on time of year, and a $50 deposit is required.

There are also three "chalets," small single-wide units that include two bedrooms, a full kitchen and bathroom, and a fold-out couch that sleeps one adult or two small children. The chalets rent for $535 a week in the off-season and $995 per week in the summer. The minimum stay at a chalet is three nights, with a $110 security deposit required. All chalets are equipped with air conditioning units.

New to this campground are Teepees that sleep four people. Rates are based on two people and run from $37.00 during the off-season, to $45.00 in season. Also new are Villas with rates running between $678 a week to $995 a week. For more information on these new additions, call the campground.

Village Marina Motel & Campground
NC 12, Hatteras Village
(252) 986–2522

Open year-round, this soundside campground includes six tent sites as well as 30 hookups with electricity, water, and cable TV for recreational vehicles. A bathhouse with hot showers, a boat ramp, and full-service dockage are offered, as well as a new gift and tackle shop, boat slips, and picnic tables. Even tent sites, which cost $17.99 per day for two adults, include electrical outlets. Recreational vehicle sites cost $19.99 per day for two adults. Additional adults are charged $2.00 per person per site. Children younger than 12 get to stay free of charge. No open fires are allowed. Pets are welcome in the campground, but owners are responsible for their pet's behavior and must clean up after them (you bring the poopy scoop). Personal checks are accepted as well as Visa and MasterCard.

Motel rates are $69 for two people with one night deposit required in advance. For dock rates and yard rates or for any additional information, call the above telephone number.

Ocracoke Island

Teeter's Campground
British Cemetery Rd., Ocracoke Village
(252) 928–3135, (800) 705–5341

Near the heart of Ocracoke Village, tucked in a shady grove of trees, Teeter's Campground offers two full-hookup sites, 12 sites with electricity and water, and 10 tent sites. Rates for two people begin at $15 a night for tents, $18 a night for electric and water, and $20 a night for full hookups. Almost an anomaly on the Outer Banks, green grass lines this semi-wooded campground, creating a soft bed beneath thin tent floors.

Insiders' Tip
Even though it looks like an inviting spot, camping on the beach is not permitted. Local officers and National Park Service personnel patrol the areas regularly and will ask you to leave.

Camping near the ocean affords sights and smells and sounds that you'll experience nowhere else.
PHOTO: BOB REARDON

Hot showers are available. Six new charcoal grills were installed at tent sites in 1998, and a picnic table sits at every site. There aren't any public laundry facilities on Ocracoke, so don't plan to machine-wash any of your clothes while camping here.

Teeter's Campground is open March 1 through November. Reservations are recommended on holiday weekends. Credit cards are not accepted.

Beachcomber Campground and Convenience
NC 12, Ocracoke Village
(252) 928–4031

Less than a mile from Silver Lake and the nearest beach access, Beachcomber campground has 29 sites with electricity and water and seven tent sites. Rates for two

people begin at $20 a night for tents electric and water hookups. There's a $2.00 charge for each additional person.

Hot showers and fully equipped bathrooms are available here. Picnic tables and grills also are on the premises.

Pets are allowed at Beachcomber as long as they're leashed. The campground is open from late March through late November, depending on the weather. Reservations are recommended if you plan to camp here during the summer.

Ocracoke Campground (NPS)
NC 12, Ocracoke Island
(800) 365–CAMP (reservations)
reservations.nps.gov

An oceanfront campground 3 miles east of Ocracoke Village and just behind the dunes, this National Park Service campground maintains 136 campsites. No utility hookups or laundry facilities are available here, but there are cold showers, a dumping station, drinking water, charcoal grills, and flush toilets. As at all Park Service campgrounds, there's a 14-day limit on stays at Ocracoke Campground. The facility is open from May through September.

Since most of these sites sit directly in the sun, we suggest bringing awnings or some sort of shade. Long tent stakes also are helpful to hold down tents against the often fierce winds that whip through this campground. The constant breeze, however, is a welcome relief from summer heat. Bug spray is a must in the summer.

Ocracoke is the only National Park Service campground on the Outer Banks that operates on the National Park Reservation Service. Call (800) 365-CAMP or visit the Web site from mid-May through mid-September to make reservations. Major credit cards are accepted.

Sites are assigned on a first-come, first-served basis. All sites cost $17 per night.

Insiders' Tip

Take it from those of us who know...if you leave your shoes and other useful items on the beach when you take a shoreline stroll, look for a landmark and make sure that your stuff is well above the surf-line. You'd be surprised how easy it is to forget where you started, especially at Cape Hatteras National Seashore where there are no buildings to use as landmarks.

Shopping

Meandering through shops on the Outer Banks is an absorbing, relaxing pursuit—and apparently the first one to come to mind on rainy days! That's when the shops teem with activity, traffic crawls, and parking is at a premium in the little towns along these barrier islands. Still, rain or shine, there's so much to explore, and a lot of the truly unique shops can be found on side streets in quiet villages or between the Beach Road (NC 12) and the Bypass (US 158), not necessarily visible from the road. So take your time, please. Consider it a treasure hunt.

Outer Banks retailers make the vast majority of their income during the peak season, but as tourism during the quieter seasons increases, more shops are extending their schedules to remain open throughout more of the year. The holiday season is particularly strong in Manteo, which more and more seems to enjoy a steady flow of visitors even in the dead of winter. If you haven't visited Roanoke Island lately, you'll be amazed at the interesting new shops you'll find there.

The growth isn't just occurring on Roanoke Island, however; every year brings a sprinkling of new shops among the established favorites. Part of the fun of exploration is trying to remember what was there last year and what's brand new!

You'll find the obligatory souvenirs, such as seashells, inexpensive T-shirts, and lighthouses in every form imaginable, but there are a great many boutiques that offer one-of-a-kind gifts, fine arts, and crafts of exquisite quality. Young kids love the big beachy stores that offer aisle after aisle of colorful souvenirs, and the ubiquitous stores where nothing costs more (or less) than a dollar. Bring the little ones to one of these places and let them take plenty of time picking out a special memento (or several) of their vacation.

If your tastes are more sophisticated than that, you'll find plenty of places to indulge your material desires. Corolla and Duck shopping is upscale and contemporary, catering to the well-heeled, urban-dwelling tourists that visit the areas. Shop owners in these towns are used to seeing big spenders. Duck and Corolla are shopping destinations, where spending is recreation. Kitty Hawk, Kill Devil Hills, and Nags Head shopping is more modest, geared toward casual shoppers and vacation browsers. There are great shops here, but these are not considered the shopping meccas of the Outer Banks, with the exception of Tanger Outlet Center in Nags Head. Manteo shopping has gone full circle in recent years, and now it's a wonderful blend of antiques shops, art and craft galleries, and high-end shops. Many people cross the bridge to Manteo just to shop. Hatteras Island shopping is the most sporadic of all. The great little shops and galleries are spread out, and sometimes a few are clustered together. Most vacationers on Hatteras Island aren't die-hard shoppers—they're usually sporty types who are in or on the water.

Ocracoke shopping is quaint and wonderful, with shops dotted all over the village. People stroll or bike around the village and stop in the shops in a most casual way. The shops are not upscale or stuffy—the doors are always propped open, the shop owners are friendly, and the goods are unique and affordable.

If your shopping pursuits are more for nourishment than indulgence, you'll find a good variety of food stores. They run the gamut from those where you'll have difficulty finding whole-wheat products to a few that reserve shelf space for health food and imports. We have an abundance of seafood stores that carry fresh fish such as tuna, dolphin, wahoo, king mackerel, bluefish, snapper, croaker, and flounder, along with crabs, shrimp, mussels, clams, and oysters in season. The seafood at Seamark Foods—one is next to Wal-Mart in Kitty Hawk, another at the Outer Banks Mall in Nags Head—is reasonably priced, fresh, and diverse enough to compete with more traditional seafood stores. The Food Lion grocery chain has six stores spaced along the Outer Banks, so there's no need to carry perishables from home if you're coming for an extended stay.

Whatever you may have forgotten to bring along—film, sunscreen, or beach towels—you can find at large department stores and Wal-Mart and Kmart.

Many shops have seasonal hours, and some close down from December to March. During the height of the summer season, the majority are open seven days a week (some with extended evening hours). A good many shops in Southern Shores, Kitty Hawk, Kill Devil Hills, and Nags Head are open year-round, though not every day. Corolla and Hatteras shopping tends to be more seasonal, but don't discount those shops in both spots that keep their doors open through the fall and winter. During winter bluefin tuna season, some Hatteras shop doors will open to take advantage of the visitors.

Here are some of our favorite shopping spots on the Outer Banks, organized by community beginning at the northern reaches of Corolla and Duck and running south through Ocracoke Island. Please bear in mind that since we have a limited tourist shopping season, our shops generally can't offer discount prices. Still, they don't jack up prices as some resort areas do and are grateful for their visitors. When you purchase goods on the Outer Banks, you are helping the area extend its services to help handle the massive influx of visitors that flock to these shores in the summer. In gratitude, Outer Banks retailers offer terrific service, quality goods, variety, and a hometown greeting that's second to none. And just to show how much Bankers appreciate you, we'll share an Insiders' secret: There are unbeatable sales on the Outer Banks during our shoulder seasons. Spread the word!

Corolla

Corolla, about 10 miles north of Duck, offers convenient and novel shopping along NC 12. We begin at the northernmost point. Most Corolla shops close in the off-season, so always call ahead.

Austin Building
NC 12, Corolla

Winks of Corolla is the anchor of this shopping center near Historic Corolla Village. Winks is the oldest store in the area; it's been around since before NC 12 was opened to the public. Winks sells gas, sundries, groceries, snacks, drinks, toiletries, and any other convenience items you'll need. Next door is the **Corolla Post Office** and **Corolla Pizza** and an ice cream store. Nearby, across and down the street at the satellite building, is the ABC store, the only place you can buy packaged liquor.

Corolla Outback
NC 12, Corolla
(252) 453-3452

This tiny building is tucked away next to the post office. Corolla Outback deals primarily in wild horse safaris and kayak trips, but at their shop you can find clothes, sunglasses, sarongs, T-shirts, sweatshirts, hats, tote bags, conch shells, driftwood shell art, and more. There is some interesting local memorabilia here too, especially aerial photographs of the infamous Ash Wednesday storm.

Historic Corolla Village

This off-the-beaten-path section of town, which is really Corolla proper, was the original town center in the days of old Corolla. With the lighthouse, hunt clubs, lifesaving stations, post office, hunting, and fishing to support the local population, Corolla was a thriving village from the 1800s through the 1940s. Stores, a schoolhouse, a church, and many homes made up the village. Today, you can see remnants of old Corolla by walking down the dirt roads north of the lighthouse. The schoolhouse and chapel have been restored, as have a couple of the old homes that now house shops. New stores have been built here as well, but in an old style that gives visitors the feeling of how things looked in old Corolla. Shop owners are proud to bring vitality back to this historic area and will

gladly share the histories of their buildings with visitors. Ask for a walking-tour map, which also gives historic information. You can easily walk from The Whalehead Club to the lighthouse to the shops in Historic Corolla Village.

Outer Banks Style
NC 12, Corolla
(252) 453–4388

Outer Banks Style is housed in the old Kill Devil Hills lifesaving station, built in 1878. The Wright brothers walked on these floors, and some lifesavers from this station witnessed the world's first powered aircraft flight. Local lore also has it that a friendly ghost resides here. According to legend, a lifesaving crewmember lost his life during a rescue in a raging nor'easter. The ghost visits the station during big blows to try and complete his mission. Twiddy & Co. Realtors moved the lifesaving station north to Corolla in 1986.

Outer Banks Style offers a distinctive collection of fine art, decorative art, and handpainted furniture. Each item in this inviting shop is unique and handmade. You'll find the whimsical renderings and musings of artist Brian Andreas, known as StoryPeople. You'll be tempted by rugs, photography, artwork, furnishings, linens, and gifts.

Lighthouse Garden
Corolla Village Rd. and Schoolhouse Rd., Corolla
(252) 453–0171

Lighthouse Garden is located in the former Helen Parker House (c. 1920). The home has been restored to its turn-of-the-century look. The Lighthouse Garden is a unique shop offering must-have gifts and accessories for porches, gardens, and outdoor living. Silk flowers and topiaries, concrete statuary, botanical prints, locally crafted iron works, birdbaths, mosaic furniture, and candles are among the great finds.

Old Corolla Trading Company
Corolla Village Rd., Corolla
(252) 453–9942

Just north of Lighthouse Garden, this store occupies a new cedar-sided building that was made to look old. The shop has a nautical theme, with antiques, prints, pillows, lanterns, telescopes, and more. It's not just nautical though. There are frames, weather vanes, wicker furniture, vintage posters, gifts, and the wonderfully creative folk art of Troy Spencer. Upstairs is a Havana-inspired bamboo room with luxurious leather furniture, unique accessories, and masculine gifts.

Corolla Village Bar-b-que
Schoolhouse La., Corolla
(252) 457-0076

Corolla Village Bar-b-que is housed in the renovated Parker House garage. This great spot has mouthwatering take-out Carolina barbecue, pork, chicken, and ribs. Drinks and ice cream are available to enjoy under the shade of nearby live oaks.

Island Bookstore
Corolla Village Rd., Corolla
(252) 453-2292

This shop is built in the footprint of what was Callie Parker's general store. John Wilson IV (who has designed many of Manteo's historical reproductions) designed this building, which is reminiscent of a mercantile in the 1930s. Bill and Ursula, the owners

of Island Bookstore, bring 35 years of book-selling experience to Corolla. Best-sellers are discounted here, and books are available on just about any subject matter imaginable. Southern and regional books are well represented in this atmospheric bookshop.

The Village Bath House
Corolla Village Rd., Corolla
(252) 453-6525

Just behind the Island Bookstore, you'll find a breath of salt-air in the Village Bath House. This shop specializes in products that create a tranquil and rejuvenating spa experience in your own home. From bath gels and body lotions to massage oils and aromatherapy candles, all your needs for pampering are available here.

The Cottage Collection
Corolla Village Rd., Corolla
(252) 453-4291

Just north of the bookstore is The Cottage Collection. This establishment is housed in the former Lewark/Gray residence (ca. 1895), which was the home of Corolla's schoolteacher. The Cottage Collection has a wonderful array of home-decorating goods, including hand-painted furniture, bedding, fine art, Mackenzie-Childs pottery, linens, pillows, Riedel wine glasses, Susan Sargent rugs, lamps, and more.

Lightkeeper's Wife
Corolla Village Rd., Corolla
(252) 453-4190

This adorable building is the restored out-building of the Lewark/Gray home, which houses The Cottage Collection. This boutique is a wonderful find, with dresses, sportswear, and the best tiny T-shirts by BCBG, Three Dot, Max Studio, Michael Stars, and Chava. Jewelry, hats, bags and cool purses, scarves, and a few little girls' dresses round out the offerings.

Corolla Light Village Shops
NC 12, Corolla

Corolla Light Village Shops are clustered together outside the entrance to the Corolla Light development. Dining, shopping, and convenience items are found within, and there's plenty of parking. These are mostly seasonal shops, open from Easter through October.

Mustang Sally's offers ladies' and men's contemporary sportswear, hand-painted and embroidered one-of-a-kind articles of clothing, accessories, and jewelry such as rings and hand-cut stones and necklaces made of glass, iron, or wooden beads. You'll also find an assortment of handcrafted gifts like handpainted boxes, pottery, and ironworks. Gift certificates are available. Look for other Mustang Sally's locations in Village Square Shops in Duck and at TimBuck II in Corolla.

If you're looking for all things surfing, Gary can hook you up at the **Corolla Surf Shop**. This store and the new shop at TimBuck II carry a great selection of surfboards, plus clothing, shades, and shoes. Rentals and lessons are available. **Ocean Threads** specializes in swimwear for the entire family and features maternity, mastectomy, and long-torso suits. This shop is packed with lots of sportswear for men and women including a good selection of name brands such as Billabong, Airwalk, Rusty, Arnette, Oakley, Emeric, Janco, Roxy, Quicksilver, Rusty Girl, and more. The shop carries hats, stickers, and incense and is an authorized Beanie Babies dealership.

My Kid is a big store that sells everything for kids, including toys and clothing. **Mango's Tropical Boutique** sells women's clothing with a tropical, resort flair. Mango's has a second location in Scarborough Faire in Duck. **Ocean Atlantic Rentals** offers everything you'll need for vacation so you don't have to bring it from home—bikes, strollers, cribs, bedding, beach chairs, umbrellas, watersports gear, you name it. For fishermen, **Corolla Bait and Tackle** has it all, including rods and reels, live bait, tackle and lures, advice, charter booking, and a friendly dog sitting by the door.

Hungry? This center of shops houses the **Horseshoe Cafe,** which serves breakfast, lunch, and dinner and is family friendly, and **Nicoletta's** for a nice dinner (see our Restaurants chapter for both of these restaurants). **Corolla Bakery** is here, too, serving sandwiches, bagels, awesome cakes and pastries, and donuts. A branch of **Cosmo's Pizza** is here, serving up the yummiest pie on the Banks, plus a variety of Italian entrees. **Big Buck's Ice Cream and Convenience** serves ice cream and sells newspapers, beer and wine, sundries, snacks and grocery items, and over-the-counter medicines. This is also fireworks and hermit crab central.

Surf Source
NC 12, Corolla
(252) 453-0222

This shop, in the same building as the gas station across from Monteray Plaza, is a surf shop that offers lessons, rentals, gear, and clothing for men and women.

The Farmer's Daughter
NC 12, Corolla
(252) 453-9116

In the same building as Stan White Real Estate is a well-known Outer Banks store. The Farmer's Daughter has everything you need to add country charm to your home. You'll find home accessories, crafts, decoys, collectibles (such as Department 56, Boyd's Bears, and Byer's Choice babies), and a variety of gift items

Outer Banks boutiques are filled with take-home treasures. PHOTO: COURTESY OF ROANOKE ISLAND FESTIVAL PARK

such as T-shirts, lighthouses, statues, and Christmas decorations. Local artisans' work is for sale here, as is the world's first and only supply of saltwater fudge. This location is open year-round.

Monteray Shores Shopping Plaza
NC 12, Corolla

The plaza is anchored by **Food Lion** and speckled with several spots to buy ice cream or other goodies to nibble between stops on your north beach shopping excursion. The plaza has public restrooms and plenty of parking. This shopping center is the home of RC Theatres' Corolla location, which has two theaters and is open in season. There's a marquee in the parking lot that lists shows. For show-times, call (252) 441-5630.

Gray's Department Store is an Outer Banks clothing tradition for men and women. Celebrating over 50 years of business, Gray's offers name-brand swimwear and sportswear, a wide variety of top-qual-

ity T-shirts, sweatshirts, and everyday shoes.

Ocean Annie's sells handcrafted functional and decorative pottery, jewelry, wind chimes, and fine gifts and gourmet coffee.

Outer Banks Outdoors is an outfitter for hiking and climbing clothing and offers a variety of T-shirts, ladieswear, and children's clothing, plus jewelry and souvenirs. This sporting goods business is operated by Kitty Hawk Kites and features an outdoor climbing wall in the courtyard. Kayak tours and hang-gliding lessons are available.

Ocean Threads sells swimwear for the entire family plus name-brand sportswear for men and women. You'll also find stickers, sunglasses, sandals, and more. Labels include Roxy, Hurley, Volcom, Billabong, Quicksilver, and Rusty. **Donna Designs** sells handpainted clothing adorned with crabs, fish, turtles, flowers, frogs, and many other motifs. The baby clothes are adorable. The store also features gift items, jewelry, and painted furniture. **Soundfeet Shoes,** with several Outer Banks locations, is the most-trusted name in shoes on the Outer Banks. They offer name-brand shoes for the whole family, including Birkenstock, Naot, Dansko, Nike, Addidas, Reebok, Saucony, and more. **Ambrose Furniture** occupies an upstairs space here. This is an established Outer Banks business, with furniture for decorating homes and rental cottages and a knowledgeable, helpful staff. **TW's Bait & Tackle and Fishing Emporium** has everything the name implies and more for anglers. There are other great stores here as well; stop by and check them out for yourself.

Birthday Suits/OBX Gear is a beach-wear boutique that features casual sportswear and accessories for the entire family. The store is packed with an extensive line of swimwear for men, women, and children. Look for swimwear in bra sizes, long torso, maternity, mastectomy, and competition suits, and check out the selection of sunglasses, shoes, accessories, and swim goggles. Owners Greg and Jill Bennett keep up with the times.

Bacchus Wine & Cheese carries one of the most extensive selections of domestic and imported wines on the Outer Banks as well as wine accessories and delicious deli sandwiches. Boar's Head meats and a variety of imported and domestic cheeses are available, plus many gourmet food items. This shop also will put together special party platters and gift baskets.

Dockside Seafood Market, on the other end of the plaza from Bacchus, sells fresh fish, scallops, shrimp, clams, crabmeat, and oysters in season. A branch location of the Manteo-based **Weeping Radish Brewery and Bavarian Restaurant** is also in the plaza. It serves tasty German and American foods plus the wonderful Weeping Radish brews. **Smokey's Barbecue, Miriam's** fine dining, and **Whalehead Pizza** round out the dining options.

In front of Monteray Plaza is a new strip of shopping that opened in 2001. This strip includes many more dining options; see our Restaurants chapter. The **Corolla Cafe and Health Food** store sells a great variety of vitamins, herbs, beauty products, and organic and healthy groceries. In this same center, you'll find **Exotic Cargo and Furniture Outlet,** which has all sorts of imported goods and gifts, plus stunning teak furniture for indoors or out. **Surfside Casuals** sells swimwear, surfwear, sportswear, dresses, sandals, jewelry, sunglasses, and everything else you'll want to wear at the beach. They have thousands of swimsuits, including mix and match separates. **Outer Banks Video** has a large selection of movies and allows vacationers to rent.

Old Stoney's Beer and Wine
NC 12, Pine Island
(252) 457-1050

Right across from the Pine Island beach access, Old Stoney's specializes in adult libations: imports, domestics, microbrews, kegs, and wines of all kinds. If you're headed to the beach, you'll find coolers, ice, soda, mixers, boogie boards, chairs, and anything else you'll need. **The Pizza Guy** is right next door.

TimBuck II Shopping Center
785 Sunset Blvd., NC 12, Corolla
(252) 453-4343
www.timbuckii.com

TimBuck II is a shopping, dining, and entertainment village with more than 60 shops and restaurants. The entire family could spend a day here, with everyone happily entertained. Shops are geared to all interests, restaurants abound, and the entertainment factor is high. Due to space issues, we can't list every single store at TimBuck II. We'll give you a sampling of what's available and let you discover the rest of the wonderful stores on your own. While you shop, you can drop the kids off at the **Corolla Raceway** for go-carting and bumper boating, or the **Golf Links** for miniature golf. **Kitty Hawk Kites** offers kite-flying lessons, and **Kitty Hawk Sports** offers parasailing, kayaking, JetSkiing, and more. Everyone can meet back up for a great meal at one of many restaurants.

Ground-level parking, covered decks, public restrooms, a recreation area, and playground are features. The shopping center is open daily from Memorial Day to Labor Day from 10:00 A.M. to 9:00 P.M. During the rest of the year, individual shop schedules may vary, and only some shopkeepers stay open year-round. Operating hours in the shoulder seasons vary from store to store.

Joan's is a staple at TimBuck II. Owner Joan Estes offers complete interior design and furnishing services. Her boutique has home furnishings and accents including upholstery, dressers, nightstands, silk flower arrangements, lamps, pictures, and wall hangings. We've found exquisite glass decanters, mango soap, lotus flower candles, and hydrangea flower arrangements that took our breath away. Joan tries to keep her shop open all year. **Tar Heel Trading Company** carries American handcrafted decorator items, accessories, and serving pieces, puzzle boxes, pottery, wind chimes, and designer jewelry. This popular business has several locations. At the Corolla shop look for contemporary cottage decor, including art for the walls and exquisite blown glassware. **Wild Horses**

has a fun selection of Flax by Jeane Engelhart clothing, jewelry, handbags, hats, accessories, and more. The store has tons of sweaters in both classic and fun styles.

Looking for Beanie Babies? **Corolla Book, Card & Gift Gallery** has those popular little critters as well as beautiful gifts and items for the entire family—posters, candles, Corolla souvenirs, greeting cards, florals, Jelly Bellies, jewelry, and local T-shirts and hats. A large children's department sells hats, shirts, toys, books, and games. And the store offers a wide selection of local books and best-sellers in hardcover and paperback. It's open from Easter through Thanksgiving.

Island Tobacco has a nice selection of cigars, tobacco, pipes, and related items, plus fine art and prints. **Exotic Cargo** brings unique home accents to you from the world over. **Carolina Moon** is one of our favorite places on the Outer Banks to shop for gifts, ornaments, jewelry, cards, and New Age notions. **Michael's Gems and Glass** is a fun shop for kids of all ages. It offers rocks and minerals, fossils, marbles, and other toys plus sterling silver jewelry.

Cotton Gin offers quality clothing and gifts, including Department 56 collectibles and Tom Clark gnomes, decoys, and carvings. The store's primary location is a sprawling barn-red building on US 158 on the Currituck mainland. The Corolla shop features gifts, unique bedding, and bath and kitchen supplies.

Gourmet Kitchen Emporium and Confectionery features a full line of specialty foods including pasta, jams, jellies, and hot spicy stuff. You can also find unique culinary gadgets, kitchen accessories and appliances, gift baskets, linens, and cookbooks.

Try My Nuts Nut Company sells gourmet nuts and candies, Try My Nuts apparel, and Wall of Fire sauces and nuts, which are so hot the owners say they'll hurt your feelings. Free samples are offered daily. **The Glass Shop** sells wonderfully bright hand-painted glassware and accessories by local designer Renee Hilimire,

Here you can choose from 3,000 costumes and several settings to produce those wonderful, old-time photos that make a great souvenir. Once you select your costumes, whether it be a Civil War hero, a '20s flapper, or a cowgirl, it only takes three minutes to see the results. Antique-style frames are available.

If you're hungry after all that shopping and activity, you're already at the right place. Timbuck II has more than 10 places to eat, including ice cream shops, a pizza parlor, a deli, Subway, a fudge shop, and sit-down restaurants. See our Restaurants chapter for some of the options.

Be sure to stop by the **Seaside Farm Market** on your way in or out of Timbuck II. They sell a great variety of fresh fruits and vegetables, many of them grown on the Currituck mainland in season. This produce stand is open during the summer months only.

who can custom design everything from stemware to furniture to floorcloths. If you're worried about getting the glass home in one piece, they'll ship it to you.

Gray's Department store has a huge store here, selling the largest selection of Tommy Bahama and Fresh Produce sportswear on the Outer Banks. Gray's sells T-shirts, sweats, hats, sportswear, and swimwear for the whole family. **Halloran & Co. Jewelry** is a showcase for designer golf and silver jewelry. Diamonds, fine colored stones, estate jewelry, charms, watches, and exclusive Wright Flyer designs will tempt you. **... get the picture?** is a one-hour photo store that sells cameras, film, batteries, frames, photographs, and gift items. A northern location of **Nags Head Hammocks** sells handcrafted rope hammocks and swings. **Lighthouse Gifts and Gallery Row** is definitely for lighthouse-lovers only. Almost everything is adorned with a lighthouse, including dishes, pottery, artwork, and gift items, and there are some nautical pieces too.

A great way to spend some time is in **Miss Kitty's Olde Time Photo** studio.

Duck

Duck is a shopper's best friend—and a budget's nemesis. It is a definite shopping destination, and people from all over the Banks come here for intentional spending sprees. This small village is packed to the gills with shopping centers, and just when you think they couldn't possibly fit another one in, up pops another one, tucked into some small nook on the waterfront or in the trees.

Duck is perfectly walkable; in fact walking is preferable to maneuvering a vehicle around all the SUV-filled parking lots and on the crowded two-lane road. A paved bike path runs the length of the village, making it safe to walk from place to place. Plus, parking is at a premium in Duck so once you find a space, you'll want to hold on to it. Remember, the sound of rain is every shopper's battle cry, so if you want to avoid crowds, don't go on a rainy day.

Barrier Island Office Plaza
NC 12, Duck

This shopping center is on the north end

of the village, across from Sunset Grill and Raw Bar. In it you'll find **The Duck Duck Shop**, which houses the post office. The Duck Duck Shop also sells North Carolina decoys and duck-themed gifts, greeting cards and post cards, and prints. It is open year-round. Also here is an **Aginet Cybercade,** offering Internet access and vacation e-mail accounts, computer classes, and computer sales. **The B.I.G. Store** (Barrier Island Gifts) sells a variety of gifts, treasures, and souvenirs. **Eden Spa and Salon** is a full-service salon and day spa, where you can pamper yourself with massage therapy, manicures, pedicures, salt rubs, facials, and more.

Duck Waterfront Shops
NC 12, Duck

These cool shops—both in location and what they have to offer—provide all kinds of great shopping opportunities. **Sunset Ice Cream** is just the spot to sip or slurp your refreshments. The entertainment here is provided by dozens of mallards and other web-footed friends paddling around in the Currituck Sound shallows just below the railings. It's open Easter through Thanksgiving. At **Duck's General Store** you'll find a wide variety of unique gifts. Some of the most popular items include finely crafted sterling silver jewelry; a wide selection of T-shirts, sweatshirts, and hats; postcards and humorous greeting cards; books on North Carolina and the Outer Banks; ship models, picture frames, gourmet sauces, candy, weather instruments, and other unusual gifts, including B.D. Whort, the redneck frog fountain. It's open year-round.

Islands By Amity offers casually comfortable, lightweight women's clothing, and a designer clothing section for children. Islands has a large aromatherapy section with lotions, soaps, and candles. You'll also find lots of artistic gifts and jewelry, including sterling silver baby gifts and music, picture frames, and stuffed animals. It's open year-round.

Barr-Ee Station and Catalogue Outlet features unbelievably low prices on name-brand men's and women's clothing, shoes, and accessories—priced up to 50 percent off the regular retail price. And **Barr-Ee Station Swimwear Outlet**, inside the same shop, sells discounted namebrand swimwear at up to 50 percent off.

For one-of-a-kind clothing for women and children, visit **Donna Designs,** a unique shop featuring handpainted artwork—crabs, fish, turtles, flowers, and frogs, to name a few subjects—on cotton T-shirts including crop-top tees for adults and children, sweatshirts, sundresses, and French terry. A line of gifts and home decor items called "Out Of The Blue" was introduced recently, featuring lampshades and lamps, glassware, toy chests, and children's tables and chairs all handpainted in Donna's inimitable style. Her work is tasteful, colorful, and rendered in a meticulous fashion. Insiders know they always will find top quality, artistic goods here.

The **Kid's Store** has toys for kids of all ages. The selection includes stuff for the beach, craft kits, wildlife and museum replicas, and infants' and children's T-shirts in sizes ranging to preteens.

North Beach Outfitters sells outdoor clothing for men and women and adventure gear, including kayaks and all the accessories. High-end sunglasses, such as Oakley, Revo, and Costa del Mar, and rack sunglasses are available. Names you'll recognize include Patagonia, The North Face, Royal Robbins, Horny Toad, Columbia, Naot, Teva, Reef, Ocean Kayak, and Necky.

In a newer section of this building, you'll find several exciting shops. **Garden Alchemy** is a magical shop with mobiles, hanging glass lanterns, whimsical plant stakes, chimes, jewelry, unique cards, frames, doormats, candles, and many more gifty items. Yet another location of **Gray's** department stores sells clothing for men, women, and children, including a large selection of Tommy Bahama and Fresh Produce. **Sea Dragon** offers exquisite American-made crafts, with local, North Carolina, and national artists represented. Sea Dragon has wood carvings, soaps, pottery, whimsical dolls, pillows,

Grab a book and relax on the beach. PHOTO: COURTESY OF KAREN BACHMAN

purses, jewelry, ornaments, and gourmet sauces. The owner does beautiful bead-work and adorns many functional items with beads. **Ocean Threads** is a ubiqui-tous beach shop on the Outer Banks, sell-ing clothing, swimsuits, jewelry, sandals, sunglasses and all sorts of beachy items. **Cynthia's Lingerie and Home Decor** is a sensual shop, right on the waterfront. Inside this heavenly smelling store, you'll find sexy or sensible nightgowns and paja-mas, stuffed animals, baskets, soaps, can-dles, photos, and items for the home. **Life's a Beach, A Lily Pulitzer Shop** fea-tures fun, colorful dresses and clothing for women and girls plus shoes and acces-sories. Lily fans were happy to see this shop come to Duck.

Tommy's Village Market
NC 12, Duck
(252) 261–8990

Tommy's is a place to pick up delicious,

fresh-baked goods such as pastries, turnovers, breads, bagels, and doughnuts. You'll find a complete deli featuring roasted ham and chicken, ready-to-eat spiced shrimp, sandwiches, fresh salads, fresh-baked pies, and daily luncheon spe-cials. Tommy's is famous for its Angus beef steaks that are aged for 21 days. All steaks are cut to order. Tommy's main-tains an extensive wine selection and car-ries lots of imported beers in addition to a full range of groceries. It's open March through New Year's.

Wee Winks Square & Vicinity
NC 12, Duck

Wee Winks, across the street from Wee Winks Square, is a practical stop for a wide variety of needs. **Wee Winks** is the perfect quick stop for those last-minute food and gas purchases or for picking up a newspaper. If you're interested in fresh produce, **Green Acres Produce**, only open during the summer season, has fresh-from-the-farm vegetables and fruits. You'll also find an ABC package store in the vicinity.

We dare you to make it through the **Lucky Duck** without buying at least one remembrance of your visit. Every nook and cranny is filled with unique home acces-sories, local arts and crafts, pictures, shells, woven throws, bath items, books, and even fudge. This store, open from March through December, is a must-see in Duck. **Artisan's Boutique,** inside the Lucky Duck, offers an eclectic combination of ladies' apparel, T-shirts, women's hats, shoes, jewelry, and some gift items, all of which bring to mind the artist's touch.

Stop by **Beach Essentials,** open March through October, for virtually everything for a beach outing, including boogie boards, lotions, rafts, and lots more. Children are fascinated by the shop's hermit crabs. At **Lady Victorian** you'll find contemporary styles for today's woman. Outfits and suits are the empha-sis here, and you'll find lots of cotton, silk, and linen plus quality dresses, evening wear, intimate apparel, travel accessories, and personal items such as bath products, soaps, and powders. Lady Victorian is open year-round. **Dockside North Duck Seafood Market** sells all the fresh seafood you want to take home and cook yourself—crab, fish, clams, shrimp, scallops, and more.

Nags Head Hammocks
NC 12, Duck
(252) 261–1062
www.nagshead.com

This is another beautiful location of Nags Head Hammocks. Tucked into the trees on the waterfront, this shop is huge, with plenty of display space for all the hammocks, footstools, and porch swings made by this company. These are quality, handmade hammocks that are durable enough to last for years. Nags Head Hammocks has numerous Outer Banks locations, including one on US 158 on the way out of town in case you decide you want one at the last minute. Everything they make is available online.

Duck Common
NC 12, Duck

Confetti Clothing Company offers casual sportswear for the whole family. It stocks clothing made by small design firms—you won't find that mass-manufactured look here—but there's more to Confetti than designer threads. The shop carries novelty items and home accessories. Check out the home furnishings, including authentic, old Mexican furniture—one-of-a-kind items you won't want to miss. Also look for home accessories, silver, and ceramic gifts. This eclectic shop is open year-round.

Cravings, open year-round, is an appropriately named gourmet shop (see our Restaurants chapter). Just one sip of Northwest Market Spice Tea, and you'll be hooked. The shop features gourmet coffee and tea, cappuccino, blended ice drinks, and iced teas. You can buy your favorite beverage already made or take home your own special package. You'll find fresh coffee beans and fresh bagels and baked goods.

Searamics
Duck Village Sq., NC 12, Duck
(252) 261–2312

Searamics is a paint-your-own-pottery studio. Here you can pick out a piece of pottery, paint it, and then have it fired. You come back and get it in a couple of days. Pottery and craft classes are offered throughout the year.

Duck Trading Company
1194 NC 12, Duck
(252) 261–0491

This is a variety shop you won't want to miss. If you like North Carolina–made products, you'll love the selection of crafts and collectibles, Tar Heel specialty foods, cookbooks, peanuts, and other goodies. The staff will put everything together in a charming gift basket. It's open year-round. In the same shopping strip as Duck Trading Company is one of several locations of **Soundfeet Shoes,** which sells the biggest selection of shoes on the Outer Banks, including Birkenstock, Naot, Dansko, Nike, Reebok, and more. A branch of **Ocean Atlantic Rentals** is here, which rents any items you might have left behind, such as linens, towels, cribs, baby items, bikes, watersports gear, and more.

Loblolly Pines Shopping Center
NC 12, Duck

Loblolly Pines is a complex of shops and eateries where you can purchase anything from a postage stamp to precious gems. You can whet your appetite with an ice cream cone or sweet treat as well. **Yesterday's Jewels** carries an interesting collection of old and new jewelry, including gold and sterling silver. **Just for the Beach** sells just that—everything you'll need for a good day at the beach, including towels, chairs, coolers, sunglasses, buckets, and all the accessories. It also rents stuff for the beach, including chairs, umbrellas, Boogie Boards, and more. If it's T-shirts you're looking for, **T-Shirt World** has thousands with all sorts of decals and sayings and Outer Banks motifs. **Outer Banks Running Company** is the first of its kind on the Outer Banks. It sells running shoes in brands you'll recognize and trust, and the staff is very helpful with fittings. The shop also sells running wear and workout clothes and has all the information on local races. Stop in at **Rainbow Light Bookstore** for all your beach reading needs. Owner Jennifer Old is usually on hand to make a recommendation if you need one. This shopping center is also home to Pizzazz Pizza and I Scream Ice Cream.

Osprey Landing
NC 12, Duck

Osprey Landing is a smaller shopping area overlooking the sound. **Books & Things** offers all kinds of hardbacks and paperbacks, children's and local books plus a variety of cookbooks, collectibles, chimes, framed prints, and maps. It's open Easter through Thanksgiving. **Outer Barks** is a must stop for dog and cat lovers. Check out the terrific selection of jewelry, ceramics, art, clothing, and pet accessories. This shop even offers life preservers for your beloved pooch. Bring Fido along and he'll get his picture mounted on Outer Barks's wall of fame. Outer Barks is open March through the end of December.

Creative Wood is a unique shop specializing in furniture and home-decor items made of wood. Most everything is handmade in North Carolina. The owner has her own line of lawn and garden furniture that's made in Morehead City and sold here. She also sells a line of cedar furniture called Tomorrow's Antiques, with one-of-a-kind items such as chests. Painted furniture and hanging art by Louise O'Ham and the photography of Sarah Tyler are also sold here, as are Outer Banks Candle Company candles and Christmas items and ornaments.

Scarborough Lane Shoppes
NC 12, Duck

Scarborough Lane features amenities you won't find elsewhere in Duck village, including covered parking, sheltered walk-

ways, and public restrooms. Most of these shops are open part of the week March through December; during the summer season, they tend to stay open late, seven days a week. The popular **Fishbones Raw Bar & Restaurant** is located here; in the summer, plan to arrive early and get your name on the waiting list and then browse the shops while you wait for a table. (See our Restaurants and Nightlife chapters for more information on Fishbones.)

Look to the **Island Trader** for sterling silver jewelry and a variety of gifts, plus home and garden accessories. Here you'll find loads of baskets and candles, kitchen linens, and plenty of North Carolina food products with a flair—hot sauces, chutneys, and barbecue sauces. **Exotic Cargo** "brings the world to you," featuring handcrafted home accents, furniture, sterling silver jewelry, sundresses, sarongs, incense, and much more from India, Indonesia, Thailand, Mexico, and Guatemala. There are five other locations on the Outer Banks.

Also worth a stop is **Tar Heel Trading Co.,** where you'll find silver and gold jewelry and a wide variety of elegant items handcrafted in America by local and nationally known artists. Tar Heel is also known for its collection of wooden puzzle boxes and museum-quality wildlife art.

Different items are available at the store's other two locations, in Sea Holly Square in Kill Devil Hills and TimBuck II in Corolla.

Home Port Gifts, offers home furnishings with a nautical flair. Next door, **Toy-rific,** which recently moved from Scarborough Faire, features top-of-the-line playthings for infants, toddlers, and school-aged kids, including stuffed animals, puzzles, beach toys, and kites.

The Wooden Feather offers something really different in Duck. It's a store for decorators, decoy collectors, and wildlife enthusiasts. Even if you don't think you are one of those people, you should stop by this gallery and see what's in store. Handmade decoys, some of them antiques, make a rustic addition to any home. Shorebirds, wildlife sculptures, art furnishings, prints, fish carvings, birdhouses, and collectibles with a natural theme fill this charming shop. Some of the bird carvings are made by the owner's father, and these are fascinating, amazingly detailed works of art. Bird-watchers will find supplies here.

Birthday Suits is a favorite local store that specializes in bathing suits but also has hip clothes for men and women, sandals, jewelry, hats, and more. This is where to find the best selection of swimsuits on the Outer Banks—always the newest, most fashionable styles. Many visitors return to Birthday Suits every year for a new suit. There's a great selection of kids' suits too.

Diane Strehan, owner of **Diane's Lavish Linens,** will help you add just the right touch to your beach cottage or help you pick out a special gift, maybe for yourself. The shop has embroidered towels, face cloths, lace tablecloths, curtains, and body luxuries, like specialty soaps and lotions.

The Phoenix is a women's apparel boutique that's been a Duck mainstay for years. This Richmond, Virginia–based store offers high-quality fashions, jewelry, and accessories. The Phoenix has a huge selection of the perfect little T-shirts in all colors and styles, including those of Michael Stars. The fun and funky styles

here appeal to all ages. Shoes, purses, belts, accessories, scarves, and other accessories will help you put entire outfits together.

Scarborough Faire
NC 12, Duck

Scarborough Faire features a series of boutiques and businesses in a garden setting. The facade is reminiscent of the architecture of old-time lifesaving stations. The buildings are set into a grove of trees, and the shops are connected by a walkway through the woods, creating one of the shadiest spots in Duck in midsummer.

Rainbow Harvest is an eclectic gift boutique featuring crafts made in the USA. This colorful and fun-filled shop has delighted its customers with the creative and the unusual. Rainbow Harvest is known for its fabulous collection of handcrafted jewelry, including exclusive Outer Banks representations of world-renowned designer Ed Levin. Or, if you're looking for that perfect keepsake of your visit to the Outer Banks, Rainbow Harvest carries a wide range of Christmas ornaments that can be especially personalized just for you. Its enchanting collection of clocks and other home furnishings is simply delightful. Also, check out its unique toy collection. From the whimsical to the functional, you'll delight your senses and imagination with a visit to Rainbow Harvest.

Sara DeSpain has been in business nearly 30 years and offers a wide range of gold, gems, and diamond jewelry of her own creation. She features the original designs of 30 artisans in a special gallery section here. DeSpain accepts limited commissions.

Island Bookstore sells established works of fiction, discount hardcover best-sellers, a wide variety of nonfiction, children's books, and specialty selections. The collection of works by Southern authors is extensive, and you also can find audio books and jazz and blues on compact disc. Special orders are welcome. The shop is open year-round.

The Solitary Swan features cherry, pine, and walnut furniture and accessories such as porcelains, glassware, and pewter, plus traditional crafts and outdoor garden pieces, decoys, and folk art. The shop is open year-round.

Mango's is a women's boutique featuring artistic, funky-edged, comfortable clothing. There are many linen items, hand-knit sweaters, dresses, T-shirts, pants, and skirts, all with hip, trim cuts. You'll find many designer brands, including Cut Loose and Art Effects shoes. Many accessories and pieces of jewelry are sold to perfectly accompany the clothes.

Ocean Annie's, another ubiquitous Outer Banks store with a location in just about every town, is tucked under the trees at the back of this center. They sell lots of handmade pottery by a variety of artists. Some of it is functional, some decorative, and it's all beautiful. They also sell unique gift items, like wooden boxes, chimes, clocks, jewelry, and frames. The gourmet coffee beans smell so good you'll want a cup, but you'll have to get the beans to go and make yourself a cup at home. **The Culinary Duck** has everything for the kitchen—cookbooks, utensils, pots and pans, sauces, and more. A visit to **Rub A Dub Duck Bath Shop** will set you up with everything you need to pamper yourself, including soaps, bath oils, aromatherapy products, and more. One of three locations of **Morales Art Gallery** is located here, featuring fine art prints, originals, and sculptures.

The refreshing **Urban Cottage** offers cool home furnishings and gifts that you won't find anywhere else. It's a home-decor boutique with everything from sofas and beds to candles and glasses. Fabulous furniture pieces are handmade and can be custom ordered to suit your needs. You'll swoon over the Sandra Drennen bedding and pillows, which are handcrafted from antique and European linens and dish towels. Housewares, lamps, rugs, mirrors, wall art, candles, unique gifts, and hand-painted peppermills and glassware are just some of the other great things you'll find here. If you need help putting it all together, the friendly, talented ladies at this shop offer interior design services.

There are many other great stores at Scarborough Faire, and you'll find them all by wandering around a bit. Elizabeth's Cafe and Winery (see our Restaurants chapter), Beaker's Deli, and Tulio's Bakery provide edible options.

Duck Village Outfitters
NC 12, Duck
(252) 261–7222

This funky shop looks like it should be on a Caribbean island, but here it is in the heart of Duck, next to the Burger King and gas station. DVO sells surfwear for all four seasons, not just summer, including all the name-brand surf companies. They sell surfboards, wet suits, kayaks and kayaking gear, bikes and bike-related stuff, skateboards and the accompanying hard goods, shoes, and sunglasses. You can rent sports gear and bikes too.

Duck Soundside Shoppes
NC 12, Duck

For fine women's apparel, unique jewelry, and accessories, stop in at **La Rive Boutique.** The focus is on handpainted clothing featuring motifs such as fish, flowers, fruit, cats, and dogs. These are rendered in bold colors to give a contemporary feel. Many of the clothing lines come from California, so the fabric used is wearable year-round. Speaking of a great feel, check out their cotton cashmere clothing—it's the ultimate. The shop is open year-round.

Everything you need to add country charm to your home can be found at **The Farmer's Daughter,** including home accessories, crafts, decoys, collectibles (such as Department 56, Boyd's Bearstones, and Byer's Choice babies) and a variety of gift items such as lighthouses, statues, T-shirts, and Christmas decorations. Look for the Nags Head location at US 158, MP 16, and a Corolla location. All shops are open year-round.

Another location of **Surfside Casuals** is here offering thousands of swimsuits by names such as Roxy, Raisins, Jantzen, Quicksilver, Billabong, Rusty, Roxanne, and others. There are eight locations of this store on the Outer Banks and it has been in business for more than 25 years. **Bob's Bait and Tackle** is Duck's only tackle shop. Come here for live bait, lures, tackle, rods and reels, charter information, and advice.

Greenleaf Gallery
NC 12, Duck
(252) 261-2009

On the southern end of the village, Greenleaf Gallery is considered the most upscale of the galleries anywhere on the Outer Banks. You'll find the work of several accomplished local artists, including painter Rick Tupper, who owns the gallery with his wife, Didi. Didi sets a high mark for inclusion in her gallery, so everything here is finely crafted and one of a kind. Glass, wood, oil, watercolor, fiber, pottery, and sculpture are among the mediums featured. See our Arts and Culture chapter for more information.

Southern Shores

The Marketplace
US 158, MP 1, Southern Shores

The Marketplace in Southern Shores is the large shopping center on the north side of US 158 at MP 1. A Food Lion grocery store and a CVS pharmacy are its anchor stores. **Food Lion,** a large North Carolina–based chain, has six stores on the Outer Banks, and **CVS** has several additional locations as well. RC Theatres has a twin cinema here—a respite from too much time on the beach. The following are a list of the specialty shops that fill out the Marketplace selection:

You can't miss **Banks Cigar Store,** with its huge stained-glass fish in the window. This aromatic shop sells tobacco, premium cigars, pipes, and accessories, plus a well-chosen selection of wines you won't find elsewhere on the Outer Banks. **Professional Opticians,** with a second location in the Outer Banks Mall, is a good place for emergency eyeglass repair or replacement. The shop also has a nice selection of sunglasses—both prescription and nonprescription. **Robin's Fine Jewelry** has a loyal local following, and repeat vacationing customers as well. You'll find a stunning array of rings, bracelets, necklaces, and other jewelry items. They also offer stone replacement, remounting, and ring sizing services.

Capt. Party has a huge selection of necessities for your party or wedding, including decorations, balloons, invitations, imprinted napkins, and catering supplies. In addition, the store carries birthday and anniversary supplies, Beanie

Shoppers have a chance to add to their fine art glass collection during their Outer Banks excursions. PHOTO: COURTESY OF MARY ELLEN RIDDLE

Babies, candy, and every imaginable sort of party favor. The store is open year-round. **Total Communications** is an Outer Banks source for pagers, cellular phones, and two-way radios for individuals and businesses. Weekly rentals are available along with Internet access. For clothing, you'll find two stores at the Marketplace that carry clothes that will stay in your wardrobe for a long time to come. **Miss Lizzie's** carries clothes for women in size 4 to extra large. You'll find everything from formal wear to jeans to jackets, all in stylish cuts and fabrics that aren't trendy and won't go out of style next year. Jewelry, purses, belts, and more are also available. **The Mule Shed,** a longtime Outer Banks women's store, carries traditional women's clothing, sportswear, and acces-

sories. The Mule Shed has many loyal customers who return year after year to add new pieces to their wardrobe. This location of The Mule Shed is more casual, while the Nags Head location at Outer Banks Mall carries more formal items in addition to sportswear. The **Outer Banks Wellness Center** is the chiropractic office of Dan Goldberg, and vacationers are welcome if they need an adjustment or wellness care. **Dollar General** competes with Dollar Tree across the highway with a broad selection of inexpensive items. **Outer Banks Music** is your source for an eclectic mix of CDs. **Movie Gallery** is always a hopping place—in the winter, it's where the locals catch up on island happenings while procuring entertainment for the evening. Movie Gallery rents and sells newly released and old favorite films and has video games and DVD movies. **Southern Bean,** a fantastic little coffee shop with fresh bagel sandwiches, tempting desserts, and all those frothy, high-octane concoctions that'll make you say "au lait!" is tucked into The Marketplace as well (see Restaurants for more information). **Shun Xing** has great Chinese food at affordable prices. **Cosmo's Pizza** sells a variety of sandwiches and beer in addition to their hand-tossed pizza, considered by some to be the best on the Banks. **Carolina Blue** (see our Restaurants chapter) not only serves extraordinary fare, but it's a visual treat as well, with topiaries and other greenery gracing the entrance and storefront. Wines served at Carolina Blue are available at Banks Cigar, a few doors down. **Mail Boxes Etc.** provides 26 business communication and postal services all under one roof, including packaging, shipping, copying, faxing, and mailbox rental. If you've bought too much on vacation to easily cart home, owner Bart Smith will be glad to ship it for you.

Seabreeze Florist specializes in fresh flowers and arrangements by designers on staff. Dried arrangements incorporate shells and flowers to create tasteful beach mementos. Nautical baskets are very popular, and Seabreeze delivers balloons, plants, and flowers for all occasions. Weddings are a specialty. Seabreeze offers worldwide FTD and Telaflora services. The florist is open throughout the year.

Kitty Hawk

Central Garden & Nursery
US 158, MP¼, Kitty Hawk
(252) 261–7195

This is a family-owned and -operated business that's been serving the area for more than 40 years. The garden center sells indoor plants, shrubs, and trees plus annuals and perennials. Landscape services are also available, and you'll find Christmas trees and wreaths here at the holidays. It's open year-round.

Islander Flags
US 158, MP¼, Kitty Hawk
(252) 261–6266
www.flagfinder.com

Islander Flags specializes in custom flags, so figure out how you want to express yourself and wave it to the world. The professionals here can help you design a flag to suit your needs, or they can turn any logo or artwork into a flag. This is a big store, and you'll be surprised at all the flags they have in inventory. There are decorative flags, military flags, national and state flags, marine flags, and more. This shop is next to Coastal Auto Mart and is open year-round.

The Shoreside Center
US 158, MP 1, Kitty Hawk

This center features national chains including **Wal-Mart, Radio Shack, Subway, The Dollar Tree, Cato's,** and **McDonald's.** The shops are open year-round. **Natural Creations Jewelry** is a locally owned shop selling a variety of contemporary and traditional jewelry. **Seamark Foods** is an upscale grocery store with a terrific bakery, deli, and salad bar. Seamark has an extensive selection of cheeses and wines as well as other gourmet foods not always available in other supermarkets on the Outer Banks. Seamark carries a large selection of fresh fish, shellfish (including live lobsters), and everything else you need to fix a seafood feast. There's another location in Nags Head at the Outer Banks Mall, US 158, MP 15, (252) 441–4121. Both stores are open year-round.

Carawan Seafood
US 158, MP 1, Kitty Hawk
(252) 261–2120

Situated on the lot in front of The Shoreside Center, Carawan Seafood is locally owned and sells fresh local fish and shellfish in season plus flown-in fish, seafood, and live lobsters. We know quite a few Insiders who frequent this shop several times a week. The store also carries a growing selection of wines and beers, gourmet food items, seashells, lures, and tackle. An expanded area next to the seafood shop sells Southwestern crafts, including rugs, pottery, dolls, jewelry, and gift items. Carawan is open year-round.

Three Winks Shops
US 158, MP 1, Kitty Hawk

This modest strip of shops includes an ABC package store (liquor store), **North China** take-out, **Alternatives Salon,** and **Teed Off Discount Tennis and Golf** (see our Golf chapter for more information). Alternatives is a full-service salon that also offers massage therapy.

Bermuda Triangle Shops
US 158, MP 1³/₄, Kitty Hawk
(252) 261–4836

Just south of the NC 12 turnoff to Duck, this shopping center houses **Haynes Outer Banks,** a beach location of the Virginia-based fine-furniture retailer. There's also **Ocean Annie's,** which stocks functional and decorative pottery, gifts, jewelry, wind chimes, and gourmet coffee beans. The **Weeping Radish Brewhaus,** a branch of the main Manteo location, is a German restaurant that serves the famous handcrafted Weeping Radish beers.

Ocean Centre
NC 12, MP 1¹/₂, Kitty Hawk

This inviting band of shops is located across the road and south of Kitty Hawk Pier. **Bessie's Kitchen and Spirits** is the anchor restaurant here (see our Restaurants and Nightlife chapters), and there's also a coffee/smoothie shop-cum-art gallery called **Guru's Gallery Cafe. Surfside Casuals** has an amazing amount of name-brand swimsuits and beachwear that will wow your friends on the beach. **Books N Things** has best-sellers and books for the beach plus gifts and souvenirs. **Carolina Moon,** a legendary Outer Banks gift shop, has a location here. This location features the Moon's higher-end gifts, pottery, jewelry, ornaments, and celestial-inspired must-haves.

Ambrose Furniture
US 158, MP 2, Kitty Hawk
(252) 261–4836

Ambrose Furniture is a family-owned and -operated furniture showroom that has been in business in the area for more than 50 years. The store has a free design service and a qualified staff to assist you with your selection of furniture, blinds, and housewares. Check out the Corolla location at Monteray Shores Plaza. Both locations are open year-round.

Winks Grocery
NC 12, MP 2, Kitty Hawk
(252) 261–2555

Winks is what shopping is supposed to be like at a beach store—a sometimes-sandy floor, beach music filling the air, and a laid-back atmosphere. Winks has a deli, lots of edibles, plenty of beach supplies, beer, wine and deli sandwiches, plus sweatshirts and T-shirts, toys and gag gifts. The shop is open year-round.

Old Firehouse Gourmet Foods
NC 12, MP 2, Kitty Hawk
(252) 261–5125

Inside this red building you'll find gourmet foods, spices, cheese, chocolate, cooking utensils, and so much more. There's a great wine selection, with wine tastings held daily. Gift baskets are a specialty of this store. The proprietor is helpful and friendly and will be glad to help you make a decision.

Wave Riding Vehicles
US 158, MP 2¹/₂, Kitty Hawk
(252) 261–7952
www.waveridingvehicles.com

Wave Riding Vehicles is the largest surf shop on the Outer Banks. WRV has beach fashions, swimsuits, and gobs of T-shirts in all the way-cool brands (see our Watersports chapter for surfing equipment information). They also offer snowboarding equipment and apparel. It's open year-round.

Hotline Pink
US 158, MP 3¹/₂, Kitty Hawk
(252) 261–8164

In the hot pink building next to Ace Hardware is this community thrift shop that benefits the local women's shelter. You'll find books, furniture, clothes, and household items. Remember this place when you're spring cleaning—make a donation.

Bert's Surf Shop
US 158, MP 4, Kitty Hawk
(252) 261–7584

Bert's carries a full line of swimsuits, T-shirts, and other beachwear along with the obligatory surfing gear and souvenirs. Bert's has a second location at US 158, MP 10½, Nags Head. Both shops are open year-round.

Your Office by the Sea
US 158, MP 4, Kitty Hawk
(252) 261–2400

Your Office by the Sea is a complete office supply store featuring computer supplies, stationery, and other accessories. You can rent typewriters, and a fax service is available. It's open year-round.

Kitty Hawk Plaza
US 158, MP 4, Kitty Hawk
(252) 261–8200

Daniel's Homeport is the largest store in this complex. Daniel's specializes in housewares and accessories such as candle holders, dried flowers, picture frames, wine racks, rugs, bedding, lamps, wicker and outdoor furniture, and much more. There's also a full window-treatment department with curtains and shades, blinds, and shutters available (some on order). The knowledgeable staff can help you with any decorating need. In the same shopping center you'll find **Red's Army Navy,** a military surplus supply store, and the **Children's Hospital of the King's Daughters Thrift Shop,** where you'll find all sorts of used goods.

Crafter's Gallery
US 158, MP 4, Kitty Hawk
(252) 261–3036

Across from Daniels is Crafter's Gallery, a spacious, year-round marketplace featuring only handmade, one-of-a-kind crafts, pottery, and jewelry, much of it created by local artists. The shop has a large inventory of country crafts including cloth baskets, handpainted gourds and furniture, and more. It's open year-round.

Buccaneer's Walk
US 158, MP 4, Kitty Hawk

Right next to Capt'n Frank's hot dog restaurant is Buccaneer's Walk, a nice-looking shopping complex fashioned after 19th-century fishing and whaling villages and coastal places the owners have visited. Here you will find **Capt'n Frank's Peanut Shop,** which sells, of course, peanuts, in addition to candy, Carolina stuff, candles, linens, and gifts. **Beach Interiors** is the interior design service of Joan Henson, offering custom furniture, window treatments, lamps, home accessories, and decorating items. **The Toy Boat** toy store offers wonderful diversionary wares for kids of all ages. There are puzzles, games, dolls, baby toys, toddler toys, books, and more, all of it educational. Many of the quality brands of toys you'll recognize are stocked here. The owners are especially adept at helping you select the right toy for the right age group. **South Beach Traders** offers a variety of African, Indonesian, Indian, and Nepalese gifts, clothing, massage therapy products, Kama Sutra body products, and one-of-a-kind sterling silver jewelry. **Scentsations** smells like it sounds—heavenly. Crabtree and Evelyn products are featured, along with other brands of candles, body lotions, soaps, and luxury bath items. **Morales Village Art Gallery** sells fine-art prints and original artwork. This location often has guest artists around in the summer. **Voyage Books and Treasures** offers books and gifts and all sorts of treasures for everyone in the family. **Island Nautical** will supply you with a bounty of sea-inspired gifts, artifacts, and books. If you're worn out from all that shopping, let **Java Sweets** revive you with coffee drinks and ice cream.

Ocean Plaza
US 158, MP 4, Kitty Hawk

This is one of the newest shopping strips on the Outer Banks, and at this writing it was not yet full. A few great stores had set up shop, though, making it worth a visit. **Atlantic Music** sells all the latest and classic CDs for your listening pleasure. **Earth Art** is a neat gift store selling earthly trinkets and gifts, candles, jewelry, and more. **Cybercade USA** is a computer and gaming center, where you can rent computer time at reasonable prices. You can set up a vacation Internet account or year-round account if you don't have your own computer. At **Havana Sandwich, Wine and Cigar** you can indulge two favorite vices and have lunch. The wine selection is good, with unusual selections plus hard-to-find dessert wines and port. The cigars are stored in a humidor for preservation purposes. The deli makes a mean sandwich. Luxurious red velvet furniture awaits you if you need to sit down while you make a decision.

Kill Devil Hills

Hattie's Farm Market
US 158, MP 5½, Kill Devil Hills
(252) 449-0969

In an orange stand-alone building, Hattie's stocks a variety of fresh produce. You'll find locally grown produce in season, as well as a variety of all the fruits and vegetables you could need.

Shore Fit Sunwear
US 158 and E. Helga St., MP 5½, Kill Devil Hills
(252) 441-4560
www.yoursuit.com

You're sure to find a suit to fit at Shore Fit, where the mission is to find a suit for the hard-to-fit woman. This swimwear boutique stocks swimsuits in sizes from 8 to 28, many with features that will enhance or flatten your curves. There are maternity suits, suits for women who've had mastectomies, athletic suits, cover-ups, sarongs, swim dresses, and more. The

staff is very helpful with suit selection, and you can order suits from the Web site. The boutique closes in the off-season.

Seagate North Shopping Center
US 158, MP 6, Kill Devil Hills

At the north end of Kill Devil Hills, Seagate North offers a variety of shopping experiences. **T.J's Hobbies and Computer Rx** carries hobby and craft materials, model cars, airplanes, and boats, rockets, and kites plus radio control supplies for models and railroading equipment. The shop, open year-round, has metal detectors too. It also offers computer sales, service, and consultations.

Mom's Sweet Shop and Beach Emporium will remind you of an old-fashioned ice-cream parlor where you can choose from 24 flavors of ice cream and yogurt. They even make their own fudge. Browse around the emporium for souvenirs; it's open all year. **Movies, Movies** rents videos and provides all the services you would expect; it's open year-round.

The Coastal Cactus Southwestern Restaurant and General Store is much more than a tantalizing restaurant. Inside, there is a unique Southwest gift shop featuring collectibles from Peggy Karr Glass and Robert Shields Designs. They have wind chimes, nightlights, stuffed kokopellis and lizards, cooking apparel, salsas, and the largest selection of hot sauces available on the Outer Banks. There are numerous home accessories with Southwest designs and jewelry for both kids and adults.

Outer Banks Flag Shoppe offers more than 330 in-stock designs of decorative house flags, sports flags (including those popular NASCAR designs), state and county flags, and boat flags. There is also a custom flag-making service. Shop here for a variety of kites and hundreds of windsocks. A color catalog is available for mail orders. The shop is open year-round.

Hatteras Swimwear specializes in custom-made swimsuits for our custom-made bodies. At **I Love Country,** gifts, crafts, and woodworking are the focus plus teddy bears galore and the popular Beanie

Babies. The shop takes special orders and is open March through December.

Norm Martinus at **Nostalgia Gallery** specializes in antiques, vintage paper, antique advertisements, custom matting and framing. If you're looking for picture framing perfection, this is the place to go, and it's open year-round. Martinus is the co-author of *Warman's Paper,* an encyclopedia of antiques and collectibles. He's a real Insider on the subject and a local favorite. Stop and chat with him—he holds a warehouse of knowledge and is very personable.

Corner Stitch and Frame sells the area's largest selection of needlepoint and cross-stitching supplies, and **A Penny Saved Consignments** has a variety of used goods for sale.

In the parking lot of Seagate North is one of our favorite produce stands, **Tarheel Too**. You'll find a great variety of fruits and vegetables, locally grown when possible, as well as some of the best mesclun mix around. Homemade baked goods and jellies are delicious.

Cooke's Corner
US 158, MP 6, Kill Devil Hills
(252) 480–0519

Cooke's Corner features a surf shop, a children's clothing store, a women's apparel shop, a health food store, and a NASCAR sports paraphernalia shop. Anchoring Cooke's Corner is **Colington Speedway Sport Shop,** offering NASCAR hats, shirts, cars, mugs, and sunglasses year-round.

Daily Menu features organic foods including refrigerated, frozen, bulk, and fresh organic produce as well as herbs and spices, cleansing and beauty-care products, and free facials. It's open year-round. **Merle Norman Cosmetic Studio** sells that line of cosmetics plus has a professional cosmetics consultant on staff to help you with selection or even give you a full makeover. **Glazin' Go Nuts** is a paint-your-own pottery studio that everybody loves, especially on a rainy day. There are really cool things to paint, for kids and

adults, functional or fun (see our Kidstuff chapter). Glazin' Go Nuts shares a space with **Front Porch Cafe,** a coffee shop. Front Porch makes heavenly coffee drinks and baked goods and roasts its own coffee. You'll definitely want one of the freshly roasted Kill Devil Coffees once you get a whiff of this place. There are also coffee accessories and a bulletin board with community announcements.

Awful Arthur's Beach Shop
NC 12, MP 6, Kill Devil Hills
(252) 449–2220

This shop is a haven for Awful Arthur's paraphernalia inspired by the popular oyster bar next door. You'll find T-shirts, sweatshirts, golf shirts, hats, beach towels, and glassware bearing the eatery's infamous logo. Shop here for beach needs, including beer and groceries, beach chairs and umbrellas, fireworks, seashells, tackle, coolers, and hermit crabs. Bad Barracuda's merchandise is available here too. Awful Arthur's Beach Shop is open year-round.

The Dare Center
US 158, MP 7, Kill Devil Hills

This center is anchored by **Belk's** department store, which features clothing and shoes for men, women, children, and babies. There are also large shoe, accessory, jewelry, makeup, perfume, lingerie, and home decor departments. **Food Lion,** a national chain grocery store, is also here. Other stores include **Atlantic Dance and Boutique,** a dance studio but also a great little boutique selling dancewear for adults and children, plus tights, shoes, and bags. Next door is a thrift store, and next to that is **Hairoics,** one of the best hair salons on the Outer Banks. **Fashion Bug** offers discount fashions, and **Dollar Tree** has everything under the sun for $1.00. Kids love this store, but there are also good deals on toiletries and household items. **Pilpel** has everything you need for the beach—sunglasses, chairs, towels, clothing, and more. The **Outer Banks Sports Locker** specializes in sporting goods, sportswear, and fitness apparel and equipment by companies such as Nike, Starter, New-Era, Russell, Champion, Wilson, Spalding, and DeLong, to name a few. They handle uniform printing requests and have a full line of trophies. **Wizard of Odds** is a pet store and grooming facility. There are all sorts of pet supplies, plus you can view live bunnies, snakes, guinea pigs, fish, and more. **Good Vibes Video** is a rental shop that offers box-office hits and esoteric art films. This location is open all year. **The Blue Dolphin** is a wellness center that offers massage therapy and nutrition counseling, and, surprisingly, tanning beds.

You'll find plenty to eat at this shopping center. The **Good Life Gourmet** is open for breakfast, lunch, and dinner and has great coffee and some of the best homemade breads and desserts on the beach (see our Restaurants chapter). **New York Bagels** has fresh, yummy bagels every day for breakfast and lunch. **Little Caesar's Pizza** is here, as are Subway for sandwiches and **China King** for take-out Chinese.

North Carolina Books
US 158, MP 7½, Kill Devil Hills
(252) 441–2141

In the Times Printing building, North Carolina Books is chock-full of secondhand paperback books and a selection of reduced-price hardcover books. You can bring in your old paperbacks and use them as credit toward the purchase of other secondhand books from the store. The store also has new books and tapes and is open year-round.

Stop 'n' Shop
NC 12, MP 8½, Kill Devil Hills
(252) 441–6105

Insiders consider this little treasure trove a hidden gem that's well worth discovering. More than your average gas and goodies store, the Stop 'n' Shop offers an upscale convenience alternative. A 4,000-square-foot expansion means almost double the space of the original store and much more of all the good things on hand. The deli (which starts serving fresh bagels, hot coffee, and breakfast sandwiches at 6:30 A.M.

year-round) uses top-quality Boar's Head meats, and the store boasts a wide variety of gourmet food products and one of the best selections of wine and microbrewed beers on the beach. There are large selections of beach necessities and fishing stuff, and the store sells and rents beach equipment such as boogie boards, sand chairs, umbrellas, and rods and tackle. There's even an impressive variety of daily newspapers. During the summer season, the store is open until 1:00 A.M.

The Trading Post
NC 12, MP 8½, Kill Devil Hills
(252) 441–8205

Here's a good general store to buy things for the beach. It carries T-shirts, souvenirs, swimwear, and convenience grocery items and is also a branch post office. It's closed from late November through early March.

SunDaze
US 158, MP 8½, Kill Devil Hills
(252) 441–7272

Located just south of the Kill Devil Hills Post Office, SunDaze features islandwear, fine sterling silver jewelry, and a good selection of accessories such as sunglasses, hats, belts, and bags. If you're into all things reggae, this is the Outer Banks's best outlet for rasta-tinged CDs and accessories. Check out the shop's incense, aromatic oils, and candles. It's closed in January.

Kill Devil Hills Cooperative Gallery
US 158, MP 8½, Kill Devil Hills
(252) 441–9888

This gallery, a cooperative of numerous local artists, provides an eclectic mix of artworks that makes for a great shopping experience. Upstairs, you can see several artists at work in their studios. See our Arts and Culture chapter for more information.

The Bird Store
US 158, MP 9, Kill Devil Hills
(252) 480–2951

The Bird Store carries a complete line of antique and new decoys featuring local carvers. Antique fishing gear, fish prints, and original art are also on display. It's open Easter through Christmas.

The Pit
US 158, MP 9, Kill Devil Hills
(252) 480-3128

The Pit's surf shop is huge and stocks a great selection of surf and skate wear and gear, plus sunglasses, shoes, women's clothing, and more. See our Watersports chapter for more information.

Davis Everything to Wear
US 158, MP 9, Kill Devil Hills
(252) 441-2604

Davis is a long-standing Outer Banks clothing store, stocking clothes for men and women. They have the only formal wear department on the Outer Banks and stock wedding dresses, bridesmaid dresses, and wedding accessories. Davis is the only Outer Banks shop that rents tuxedos.

Charlotte's Web Pets and Supplies
US 158, MP 9, Kill Devil Hills
(252) 480-1799

Charlotte's is a well-stocked pet shop featuring fish, commercial and residential fish tank maintenance, birds, reptiles, small animals, pet food, and supplies. It's open year-round.

Compass Rose
US 158, MP 9, Kill Devil Hills
(252) 441-9449

Compass Rose sells a unique blend of gift items, including many imported by the traveling owners. You'll find candles, ornately carved furniture, fine paper, frames, jewelry, chimes, and much more.

Lifesaver Shops
NC 12, MP 9, Kill Devil Hills

Lifesaver Shops features practical stops. **Lifesaver Rentals** fills rental needs and offers thrifty bargains—these folks rent it all! Look for beach umbrellas, chairs, TVs, VCRs, baby equipment, cottage supplies, portable radios, microwaves, charcoal grills, and even blenders. They offer linen service complete with sheets, pillowcases, and bath towels. Look for surfboards, ocean kayaks, boogie boards, snorkel and fishing equipment, and bikes galore. It's open March through November. **Deb's Fine Consignments,** open year-round, is a consignment shop featuring men's, women's, and children's clothing, housewares, antiques, jewelry, and bedding.

Nags Head Hammocks
US 158, MP 9½, Kill Devil Hills
(252) 441-6115, (800) 344-6433
www.nagshead.com

You can't miss the setting, with its palm trees and lush landscaping. At the shop you'll find the famous, durable, high-quality handmade hammocks; single- and double-rope rockers, footstools, and bar stools; single and double porch swings; "slingshot" swings; captain's chairs; and double recliners. You can also purchase items via mail order year-round. Nags Head Hammocks has other showrooms at Timbuk II in Corolla, Duck village on NC 12, on NC 12 in Avon, and in Point Harbor (Currituck County) on US 158.

T-Tops Racing
US 158, MP 9½, Kill Devil Hills
(252) 441-8867

For everything NASCAR under the sun make a pit stop at T-Tops. This is a licensed

NASCAR store with merchandise for all of the NASCAR drivers. The main selling items here are die-cast cars, but there are also NASCAR-inspired jackets, sweatshirts, T-shirts, hats, clocks, wallets, jewelry, and more in this 4,000-square-foot store. It's one of the largest NASCAR stores in the nation. It's open year-round.

The Bike Barn
Wrightsville Ave., MP 9½, Kill Devil Hills
(252) 441-3786

The Bike Barn, located behind Taco Bell between the Beach Road and the Bypass, sells a wide variety of bikes and services all types. Skilled mechanics are on staff. It sells a full line of parts and accessories too. Serious bikers will appreciate name brands such as Caloi, Jamis, Diamondback Giant, Trek, and more. The shop rents 18-speeds and 21-speed hybrids, gear bikes, and beach cruisers. The shop is open year-round.

Sea Holly Square
NC 12, MP 9½, Kill Devil Hills

This shopping and dining complex was one of the early shopping venues in Kill Devil Hills. It's been refurbished and provides a central location where you can visit several shops by strolling along a little boardwalk-style deck. **Madison's Cafe,** on one end, serves lunch and dinner and has entertainment some evenings (see our Nightlife chapter). **Tar Heel Trading Company** is a favorite at this center and has been in business for more than 20 years. In the front central location, it stocks fine American handcrafts, artwork, and gift items. **Devi's** offers a wide variety of jewelry as well as jewelry repair service. They can handcraft custom jewelry for you as well. At **His Shells by Brenda** you can get beautiful souvenir shell arrangements or have them made to order out of your shells or theirs. **Outer Banks Posters, Prints, and Gifts** has a great selection of all of those items. The **Plantation Peanut Shop** sells peanuts and fine food items as well as gifts. Every pet's favorite store is the tiny **Salty Paws**

Homemade Biscuits retail outlet, featuring homemade, high-quality dog treats. You'll like that you recognize all the ingredients in these treats, and dogs love all the flavors. For human treats, **Sweet Melissa's Bakery** will tempt you with delicious baked goods and coffee. Other stores include **Big Daddy's Water Ice** for cool treats, **Hair Design,** and **Nails by Lori**. This is also the location of Sandbox Skate Park (see our Recreation chapter).

Island Dyes
NC 12, MP 9½, Kill Devil Hills
(252) 480-0076

Island Dyes offers T-shirts and a full line of women's clothing, reggae and Grateful Dead T-shirts, and tobacco accessories. You can get hairwraps and henna tattoos here too. Call for store hours or more information.

Beach Barn Shops
US 158, MP 10, Kill Devil Hills

On the west side of the Bypass, the Beach Barn Shops is a great place to stop. It houses **Birthday Suits/OBX Gear,** a popular swimsuit and sportswear shop. *Southern Living* magazine wrote, "Everybody goes to Birthday Suits for a new bathing suit," and it's true, they do. Locals and visitors return every year for a new, fashionable bathing suit. For women, there's an unbelievable selection of suits in all styles, including mix-and-match separates, bra-size tops, maternity and mastectomy, athletic, and long-torso suits. Women also love the contemporary sportswear and a fine selection of dressy dresses, including those by Betsey Johnson, and accessories, purses, shoes, hats, luggage, and pajamas. Men will find trunks and briefs and a whole selection of sportswear and Hawaiian surf shirts. Kids' and babies' suits are adorable, and there are even diaper suits. If you're looking for OBX gear, look no further. **Carolina Moon** is a great place for finding unusual gifts, scents, pottery, stationery, and greeting cards. The shop has an outstanding line of jewelry of all kinds—you'll find pieces you've never seen before. Be sure to see the delightful

Christmas ornaments, many with a whimsical touch. The shop has a New Age ambiance and a fine collection of esoteric gifts. You also can shop at their Corolla location in TimBuck II from Easter through Christmas. The Kill Devil Hills store is open year-round.

Roanoke Press and Croatoan Bookery
US 158, MP 10, Kill Devil Hills
(252) 480–1890

This shop is owned by the same folks who publish *The Coastland Times* newspaper and operate Burnside Books in Manteo. Here you'll discover secondhand and new books; both bookstores carry an extensive line of books about North Carolina and the Outer Banks. It's open year-round.

Wright Place Gourmet Market and Catering
US 158, MP 10, Kill Devil Hills
(252) 441–1497

If you don't feel like cooking, head to the Wright Place. This gourmet market and

deli sells a variety of deli items and sandwiches plus family dinners to go. Try a roasted chicken, eggplant parmesan, shepherd's pie, sausages, or macaroni and cheese with any of a number of sides. Salads, cheeses, sweets, and mean tapenade are also available. There's a modest wine selection and plenty of gourmet items. Fat Cat Ice Cream is right next door.

Nags Head

Nags Head is a shopper's mecca with its boutiques along the Beach Road, US 158, and the Nags Head/Manteo Causeway, and larger shopping destinations such as the Outer Banks Mall and the Tanger Outlet Stores on US 158.

Ben Franklin
US 158, MP 10, Nags Head
(252) 441–7571

Across the street from the Food Lion Plaza,

Ben Franklin carries clothing for all ages and everything you need for the beach. There are some great buys on ladies' dresses here. It is open Easter through mid-November.

Something Fishy
NC 12, MP 10½, Nags Head
(252) 441–9666

Here's a fun shop swimming with fish. You'll delight in the fish-print clothing made by owner Sherrie Lemnois, who has been creating these masterpieces for 14 years. Clothing, jewelry, toys, home decor, and gifts are available with a fishy theme. New to the shop are Asian-inspired items, prompting the owner to say she sells everything from "fish to Feng Shui." Lucky Bamboo home decor products are best-sellers here.

Gallery Row
Gallery Row and Driftwood St., Nags Head

Around MP 10 and thereabouts are numerous art galleries that are collectively referred to as "Gallery Row." If you're shopping in Nags Head, you'll want to see these wonderful art galleries that lie between the highways. See our Arts and Culture and Attractions chapter for a complete listing.

The Christmas Mouse
US 158, MP 10½, Nags Head
(252) 441–8111

This holiday-oriented shop is brimming with Christmas collectibles, Cairn Gnomes, papier-mâché Santas, Snow Babies, porcelain dolls, unique ornaments, and nautical- and midwestern-themed trees. There are 60 decorated trees to get you in the spirit. It is open year-round.

Gulf Stream Gifts
NC 12, MP 10½, Nags Head
(252) 441–0433

Gulf Stream features contemporary nautical gifts, jewelry, and lighthouse and dolphin memorabilia. The store is open from Easter until Thanksgiving.

Central Square
US 158, MP 11, Nags Head

This weathered cottage-style complex of shops has come to house a conglomeration of antiques shops. **Edith's Gallery** is owned by local artist Edith Deltgen, and some of her truly unique sculptures and creations are housed here. She also offers antiques, including furniture, estate jewelry, and household items. **Mike Post Antiques** sells a variety of true antiques, including furniture, dressers, and beds. These shops are right next door to one another and make for great browsing. **Antiques, Imports and Curiosities** is across the way. This store goes on forever with trinkets, treasures, knickknacks, and things of all kinds.

Pirate's Quay
US 158, MP 11½, Nags Head

You'll find an eclectic grouping of clever boutiques, stores, offices, and eateries here. Look for tobacco, jewelry, crafts, and clothing in these shops.

Cloud Nine is an adventure in clothing, accessories, and other discoveries from around the world. Owner Ginny Flowers has beads and lots of them. Other finds include recycled sea glass, Grateful Dead merchandise, T-shirts made by locals and visitors, beautiful batiks, and treasures from Africa and Nepal. Cloud Nine also carries gold and silver jewelry. Bring in your sea glass and have a custom necklace made. It's open Easter through Thanksgiving.

The **Quacker Connection,** open March through December, features decoys, country crafts, antiques, and a large selection of country collectibles. Doug, the resident carver, is often carving or painting a decoy, so take a moment to see this classic craft being performed. Need a one-stop shop for all your vacation gear? Check out **Wings,** where you'll find souvenirs, beach clothing, boogie boards, bathing suits, beach chairs, umbrellas, and fudge. There's another location in Kitty Hawk on US 158, MP 3, plus a new store in Corolla. The

This store was built to look like a lighthouse. PHOTO: COURTESY OF BRUCE ROBERTS

Nags Head and Kitty Hawk shops are open year-round.

Also here is **Beach Street Island Wear,** a contemporary shop with dressy and casual dresses, separates, and accessories for women. If you're into the latest looks, come here. **La Isla Bakery and Latin Market** sells fresh bread and pastries, cakes made to order, and Latin cooking supplies.

Austin Fish Company
US 158, MP 12½, Nags Head
(252) 441–7412

Austin's is a Nags Head fixture near Jockey's Ridge. It's a full-service seafood store that also serves as a gas station with some of the lowest prices on the beach. Austin Fish Company is open May through November.

Outer Banks Fly Shop
US 158, MP 12½, Nags Head
(252) 480–FISH
www.outerbanksflyshop.com

The Banks's only full-service fly-fishing shop opened in 1999 to serve the growing number of fly anglers who fish here. Owner Shawn Rollison is very knowledgeable about fly-fishing and can give you advice or help you find a guide. The shop is stocked to the gills with top-of-the-line rods (Sage, Orvis, St. Croix), Outer Banks-tested flies, line, and all the gear you'd ever need. Clothing especially suited to fly anglers is available, along with Costa del Mar sunglasses, hats, T-shirts, and gift items.

Jockey's Ridge Crossing
US 158, MP 13½, Nags Head

Jockey's Ridge Crossing is home to Kitty Hawk Kites and Kitty Hawk Sports, which are situated at opposite ends of the complex. **Kitty Hawk Kites/Carolina Outdoors** is one of the most colorful stops on the Outer Banks and sells just about any kite, windsock, or banner imaginable. It can supply everything you need for a great vacation on the Outer Banks, including quality men's and women's sportswear and outerwear, sandals, T-shirts, and sweatshirts. This shop also offers a large selection of toys. (See our Watersports chapter for exciting sporting opportunities offered by these folks.) Other locations are in Monteray Shores Plaza, NC 12, Corolla; TimBuck II, NC 12, Corolla; across from Wee Winks Square, NC 12, Duck; and Island Shops, NC 12, Avon. Look for a new shop in Ocracoke Village. The Nags Head location is open year-round. All other locations are open March through December.

Kitty Hawk Sports carries popular name-brand clothing, boogie boards, accessories, and sunglasses plus windsurfing and kayaking gear. It offers all sorts of sporting opportunities (see our Watersports chapter). Check out the other locations at Wee Winks Square, NC 12, Duck, and Timbuck II, NC 12, Corolla. The Nags Head shop is open all year. The northern beach shops are open March through December.

Also in the complex is **Salt Marsh** (other locations are in Corolla and Duck), a conservation-conscious shop filled with irresistible gifts, T-shirts, clothing, jewelry, books, and fun and educational toys. A portion of the profits from the store is donated to wildlife and environmental associations. **Donna Designs,** which also has locations in Duck and Corolla, sells the wonderful fish-print clothing created by the owner. It's not just fish, though; it's also crabs, turtles, flowers, frogs, and more, all printed on cotton T-shirts, sweatshirts, dresses, baby clothes, onesies, and other items. The goods here are tasteful, colorful, and rendered in a meticulous fashion. **How Sweet It Is** is the place to stop for homemade ice cream, tasty deli sandwiches, and delicious ice cream cakes. To satisfy a yearning for all types of fudge, stop by **The Fudgery**.

Surfside Plaza
US 158, MP 13, Nags Head

This is a great mix of shops you won't want to miss. You'll find everything from comic books to contemporary clothing and crafts. There are several food shops here (including a Subway) in case you get hungry.

Surfside Casuals has more swimsuits than just about any other store on the beach. This shop also carries an extensive line of casual wear for men and women. Look for other locations in just about every other town. All shops are open Easter through Thanksgiving.

Beach Peddler, open Easter through October, sells everything you'll need at the beach and also has jewelry, shells, postcards, souvenirs, gifts, hats, hermit crabs, and T-shirts. Darnell's offers hermit crabs, shells, fudge, and nautical gifts.

Adults and kids alike will love **Outer Banks Cards and Comics,** a collectors' paradise that features sport and nonsport cards and a massive collection of comic books, both foreign and domestic. It also sells action figures and T-shirts and holds Magic card tournaments during winter. It's open year-round. Art lovers will enjoy **We're Art** year-round for posters, prints, local artwork, and custom framing or ready-made frames. If you're hungry, there are two great eateries here. **The Country Deli** has delicious, huge, and inexpensive sandwiches for lunch, and **The Clove** offers yummy pizzas with a unique sweet-tinged crust.

Newman's Shell Shop
NC 12, MP 13½, Nags Head
(252) 441–5791

You can't miss Newman's, in the bright pink building on the oceanside of the Beach Road. It's an Outer Banks landmark, open since 1939! Newman's is a shell shop, tourist attraction, and local museum. Shells from all over world are displayed, from as far away as India and Peru. The owners are extremely knowledgeable about seashells and will be happy to educate you about them. A large variety of gifts, shell crafts and sculptures, wind chimes, T-shirts, and other items also fill this large store. Next to shells, though, Newman's is known for hermit crabs and its annual hermit crab race in July. See our Attractions and Annual Events chapter for more information.

Croatan Centre
US 158, MP 14, Nags Head

This is a fun group of shops featuring gifts from around the world, fine jewelry, CDs, and shoes. **Lion's Paw,** open year-round, features a variety of women's resort-wear clothing and accessories. **Halloran & Co.,** in the same shop as Lion's Paw, offers sterling silver jewelry, 14-karat gold and gemstones, and sterling silver watches. **Soundfeet Shoes,** open year-round, will fulfill your sole's desire in footwear. It offers a wide variety of men's, women's, and children's casual and fancy shoes and sandals, including popular sports shoes by Reebok and Nike. Explore the beautiful handcrafted home accents brought to you from the corners of the world by **Exotic Cargo,** which is open year-round.

If you're looking for new and used CDs, look no further than **Outer Banks Music,** which offers a wide variety of music for all tastes. It also sells music videos, T-shirts, posters, and accessories. If they don't have something in stock, ask Steve or Lisa to special order it for you; they can usually turn such requests around in a couple of days at no extra charge. It's open all year.

Riddick Jewelers sells a great selection of contemporary and traditional jewelry, including the popular "beach wave" his and hers wedding rings. They also sell crystal stemware and sterling silver gifts, making this a good place to come for a wedding present or special baby gift. **Island Tobacco** offers cigars, tobacco products, and smoking implements. **Rock-A-Bye Baby** is a baby store selling gently used goods such as clothes, cribs, toys, high chairs, and anything else you'd need for baby.

Outer Banks Mall
US 158, MP 15, Nags Head

The Outer Banks Mall is open year-round. **Seamark Foods** (see The Shoreside Center listing in our Kitty Hawk section) anchors the center of the complex, which is home to a mix of shopping, service, entertainment, and dining businesses. The north wing of Outer Banks Mall is predominantly food-oriented, but there are a few stores, including **GNC,** which stocks vitamins, herbs, health and beauty products (including the popular Burt's Bees line), and sports and nutritional supplements for healthy-minded people. **Video Andy** is our favorite video store, stocking a good selection of videos including an entire foreign film section, new releases, a cult classics section, a kids section, and a classics section, among others. Video Andy rents videos and players year-round. **Outer Banks Cleaners** is also here. The north wing has a true international flavor when it comes to food: Bacu Grill is Cuban inspired, New York Bagels tastes like a fresh bite of the city, Taiko offers Japanese cuisine and sushi, Carolina Pizza and Grits Grill are as American as you can get, and North China offers up more Asian cuisine.

On the south wing of Outer Banks Mall, recently remodeled from an enclosed mall to a strip center, you'll find several great stores.

The legions of Outer Banks boaters are excited about the recent opening of **West Marine,** a boating supply store, featuring boating hardware, gear, cleaning and repair supplies, Mercury engines, life jackets and safety equipment, marine electronics, and more. They also sell fishing equipment, including gear, coolers, rods, reels, tackle, and lures. **Outer Banks Furniture** is a huge home-furnishings store, with sofas, chairs, beds, dining tables, rugs, home accessories, and much more. You'll be surprised at how much furniture they have in stock, but you can special order if you'd like. Berkline, Bassett, Lane, Klassner, and Simmons Beautyrest are just a few of the companies they represent.

Mule Shed features ladies' apparel and lovely purses, gifts, and wedding, household, and outdoor garden items such as statuary and a sweet little brass bunny doorbell. It's open year-round. **Sea Witch Gifts** features sea motif gifts and pottery, shell vases, and fascinating birdhouses. At **T-Tops Trading Company,** you can choose from T-shirts, shorts, hats, mugs, and souvenirs. It's open year-round.

Habitat Earth carries groovy knit dresses, wild pants, couch throws with dancing bears, jewelry, CDs, and more; it's open year-round. **Lil Grass Shack** offers bathing suits for women in sizes 3 to 28 as well as children's swimwear. Look here for girls', women's, and men's sportswear. It's open year-round. You'll also find **Ocean Threads,** specializing in swimming. **Peggy's Hallmark** has a world of cards, wrapping paper, stuffed animals, and gifts, and **Outer Banks Books** is a huge warehouse-style bookstore where you'll find some great bargains.

Forbes
US 158, MP 15½, Nags Head
(252) 441-7293

You can't come to the beach without picking up a box of saltwater taffy. Forbes, an Outer Banks tradition, has it here. Stop in for a box or three of the company's famous homemade gooey goodies. The shop, which is open year-round, also features a gift and souvenir selection.

The Chalet Gift Shop
NC 12, MP 15½, Nags Head
(252) 441-6402

Celebrating more than 25 years at the same Beach Road location, The Chalet is one of the nicest stores on the beach. The gifts, collectibles, and souvenirs here are exquisite. Collectors will love the selection of David Winter Cottages, Harbour Lights, Lilliput Lane, Collectible Dolls, Legends, Michael Garman, Rick Cain, Iris Arc Crystal, and Madam Alexander dolls. The collection of 14-karat gold and sterling silver jewelry is gorgeous. The shop also carries fine home accessories and just about anything you'd need for the beach. Mail orders are welcome; it's open March through December.

Cahoon's
NC 12, MP 16½, Nags Head
(252) 441-5358

Cahoon's is a large, family-owned grocery and variety store that's been around for more than three decades. It's a nice change of pace from city-size supermarkets. Dorothy and Ray Cahoon bought the store shortly before the Ash Wednesday Storm of 1962 and, despite what must have been a rather wild start, continue to stock everything you'll need for your visit to the beach, including good meats that butcher Robert Heroux cuts to perfection. The store is near Jennette's Pier and is open March through Thanksgiving.

Tanger Outlet Center
US 158, MP 16½, Nags Head
(252) 441-5634

Tanger is a discount-outlet shopping center brimming with great buys in all sorts of merchandise, from clothes to dishes to shoes. These are nationally known names, so we don't give extensive store descriptions. We've listed some of our favorites below to get you started. Once you park, you'll wander for hours here. Bring plenty of cash! And when you get hungry, take a break at **Stone Oven Pizza.**

All shops in the Tanger complex are open year-round. **Pfaltzgraff** has dishes, glasses, and knickknacks. **London Fog** is very popular with locals and visitors alike who stop here for their yearly coat purchases. Check out the great buys on a vast selection of outerwear including casual jackets and rainwear. At **Rack Room Shoes** you can outfit the entire family with quality discounted tennis shoes and casual and dressy year-round footwear.

You'll adore the **Corning/Revere Store,** a great kitchen supply shop. Of course you'll find traditional Corningware with pretty designs, but the shop's also chock-full of gadgets that make your kitchen experiences easier. We've found fashionable short leather boots at **Nine West** that really last, plus lots of dressy and casual shoe selections for women only. **The Dress Barn** has great sweaters (dressy, sporty, and casual dressy) for women and some super tops for all occasions.

Claire's Accessories overflows with hair accessories, jewelry, fashionable clear plastic purses for kids, sunglasses, those little fuzzy cloth key chain books, and hats.

Kids love this shop. The prices are extraordinary. For a few dollars, the little ones feel like they've had a big shopping spree.

No visit to Tanger Outlet Center is complete without a stop at **Gap Outlet.** Bargains are abundant here, and many locals stop in every week to pick up fun fashions at great prices.

Other store names you'll recognize include **Polo/Ralph Lauren, Nautica, IZOD, Geoffrey Beene, Bass, Big Dogs, Coach, Leggs Hanes Bali,** as well as **Sunglass Hut.**

Whalebone Seafood
US 158, MP 16½, Nags Head
(252) 441-8808

Whalebone is run by the Daniels family, known locally for their commercial fishing roots. It's a full-service seafood market selling whatever's in season. It's open Easter through October.

Shipwreck
Nags Head/Manteo Causeway, Nags Head
(252) 441-5739

Shipwreck is another gift store with a nautical twist. Look here for local crafts, driftwood, nets, shells, and other sea treasures piled everywhere. It's open March through Thanksgiving.

Roanoke Island

The Town of Manteo is undergoing something of a renaissance. A variety of new retail shops has opened, and much more is in the planning stage. There is so much to see, do, and buy now in Manteo that parking can be a challenge, but that just means you'll need to park on a side street and walk a few blocks (hey, if you were in the city, you'd think nothing of walking a much greater distance!). Or you can park in the Roanoke Island Festival Park lot, where you'll find space almost any time of year, and take a pleasant stroll over the Cora Mae Basnight Bridge to great shopping and eating.

We start out with the shops along US 64, where you can find some great bargains as well as unusual gifts. Then we move on to downtown Manteo, where you'll find the bulk of the shops.

Manteo

Pirate's Cove Ship's Store
Pirate's Cove Yacht Club, Nags Head/Manteo
Causeway, Manteo
(252) 473-3906

This marina store has a nice selection of active sportswear, including Kahalas, a Hawaiian line of beautifully hand-screened and batiked clothing. The shop also carries gifts, picture frames, windup crabs, marina supplies, and groceries as well as a line of 14-karat gold jewelry with a fishy flair. It's open year-round.

Caimen Gardens
US 64/264, Manteo
(252) 473-6343

This shop sells a little bit of everything for your home and gardening needs. Look for lots of annuals, perennials, fruit trees, salt-tolerant plants, and a full line of vegetation that will thrive on the Outer Banks. They sell houseplants, blooming plants, seasonal plants, mulch, potting soils, and fertilizers. Shop in the year-round Christmas room or the home accents room. You'll also find planters, statuary, fountains, water garden supplies such as pond liners, pumps, and lily pads, and a selection of other aquatic plants and local art. It's open year-round.

Silver Bonsai Gallery
905 US 64/264, Manteo
(252) 475-1413

In a restored home on the main highway, Silver Bonsai is a great gallery owned by local artists Ben Stewart and Kathryn Holton-Stewart. The Stewarts are silver- and goldsmiths and bonsai artists, and their work is found in the gallery in addition to the work of many local artists. One of the artists is often at work in the studio. They have a miniature forest worth of bonsai, plus all the advice and supplies you'll need to keep the plants and trees alive. The artwork and gifts in Silver Bonsai are distinctive. You'll find paintings, sculpture, candles, soaps, exquisite jewelry, copper items, quilts, furniture, Japanese pottery and local pottery, and more. See our Arts and Culture chapter for more information.

Island Produce
US 64/264, Manteo
(252) 473-1303

Island Produce offers fresh seasonal vegetables and fruits. It also has flowering plants for the garden and home, including beautiful lilies, pumpkins, and Christmas trees in season. Statuary and fountains to adorn your garden are here too. They are open April until Christmas.

Jeanine's Cat House
US 64/264, Manteo
(252) 473-1499

Cat lovers will revel in this shop that abounds in delightful gifts and necessities ranging from "purr-ty" cat earrings to beds and carrying cases for the furry felines. Cat motif sculptures, wall art, clothing, collectibles, cards, and stationery fill this pussycat palace. Jeanine's is next to the Christmas Shop and is open daily year-round.

The Christmas Shop & The Island Gallery
US 64/264, Manteo
(252) 473-2838
www.outerbankschristmas.com

The Christmas Shop is such an Outer Banks legend that we've also included it in our Attractions and Arts and Culture chapters. Opened in 1967, this fabulous shop has expanded exponentially over the years, including a recent 4,000-square-foot addition. The main shop deals with Christmas, and there are more holiday decorations than you ever knew existed. Trees, sparkling lights, smells of cedar and cinnamon, and holiday music make the holidays come alive, even in the middle of the summer. There are 36 rooms in The Christmas Shop, and it's easy to get lost. As you sort through Christmas cards, peer into music boxes, sniff candles, select from thousands of ornaments, and play with toys, you may find that hours have passed and your shopping companions are nowhere to be found. You'll find Christopher Radko ornaments and Polonaise glass ornaments from Poland (available only at 43 places in the country), Byer's Choice Christmas figurines, collectibles of all kinds, an angel display, music, home decor, and more. An entire upstairs room is devoted to Halloween. Farther back into the store is The Island Gallery, with jewelry, oil and watercolor paintings, prints, frames, decoys, and other artwork by over 200 regional artists and craftspeople. Beyond that, the General Store has authentic, old-fashioned appeal and goods. The Candy Counter has an actual old-fashioned counter and penny sticks of candy plus all the modern candies in bulk and prepackaged varieties. Many visitors return to The Christmas Shop year after year. It's always packed and is open year-round. Parking is in front of the building and behind it, and there's a huge overflow parking lot across the street. Insiders know that The Christmas Shop has a super sale each December with holiday items greatly discounted.

Chesley Mall
US 64/264, Manteo

Food-A-Rama and **CVS** pharmacy hold down the fort here as well as a Family Dollar, a video store, film shop, and hometown pharmacy. Chesley Mall is a year-round shopping venue. **Island Pharmacy** is an old-fashioned store where you can buy prescription and over-the-counter medicines, sundries, film, and gifts, and take advantage of the UPS and Airborne Express services in the back of the store. Oddly enough, it's the only place on the Outer Banks to register your car, should you decide to move here. There are plenty of gift items, including glass and china knickknacks and some cute stuffed animals.

Qwik Shot serves your film and developing needs. They can provide a fast turn-around on your vacation film, with one-hour processing for 3½-by-5 and 8-by-10 prints. They offer a lovely selection of frames, as well as film and batteries. Custom printing is also available.

The Video Store has an array of first-rate drama, comedy, adventure, martial arts, horror, and children's movies. There are even some $1.00 videos. It also rents VCRs, Super Nintendo, Nintendo, and Sega Genesis games. **Susan's Hallmark** carries a wide variety of party supplies, religious products, candy (try the spicy jelly beans), cards, stationery, and photo albums. **Subway** and **Top China** offer options for quick meals.

Burnside Books
US 64/264, Manteo
(252) 473-3311

Burnside carries office and art supplies and a good selection of historical and children's books. Upstairs you'll find used hardback and paperback books and a North Carolina book section. It's open all year.

Hotline Thrift Shop
US 64/264, Manteo
(252) 473-3127

West of the Dare County Public Library, Hotline Thrift is a fund-raising shop for Outer Banks Hotline, a crisis intervention service that also operates a shelter for battered women and their children. Hotline is quite possibly the most popular second-hand store on the Outer Banks. The bargain-priced inventory includes furniture,

toys, books, knickknacks, and clothing for men, women, and children. It's open year-round. In addition to the Manteo location are stores in Kill Devil Hills, Rodanthe, Hatteras Village, and Kitty Hawk.

The Cloth Barn
Etheridge Rd., Manteo
(252) 473-2795

Returning to US 64, head north toward Manns Harbor and turn left onto Etheridge Road. Drive a short distance, and you'll be at a store packed nearly floor to ceiling with fabrics, notions, and patterns. The selection of woven tapestry cloth is unbelievably beautiful. You'll want to wear it, cover your walls in it, and just roll around in this eye-catching fabric. The Cloth Barn closes mid-December through mid-January.

Downtown Manteo

Wanchese Pottery
107 Fernando St., Manteo
(252) 473-2099

This artistic shop is a small business near The Waterfront on Fernando Street, where customers can watch local potters Bonnie and Bob Morrill at work (see our Arts and Culture chapter). The shop is known locally for its beautiful, useful art, and it also features handmade baskets and fresh cooking herbs. It's open year-round, but call for winter hours.

The Toy Boat
Corner of Sir Walter Raleigh and Old Tom Sts., Manteo
(252) 473-6171

This is a specialty toy store that makes playing educational and fun. The high-quality toys here are imaginative, and there's something for every age group. Most have a slant toward educational, developmental, or creative endeavors. But kids won't care about all that. They just like the toys. BRIO, Playmobil, Learning Curve, Gund, Gotz, Madame Alexander, and many other quality toys and dolls are sold here. Kids love the dolls, puppets, stuffed animals, musical instruments, art supplies and kits, blocks, train sets, models, games, puzzles, and so much more. This store is open year-round, and there's also a location in Kitty Hawk. If you like what you see, ask to receive copies of their catalog.

The Artful Dragon
110 Sir Walter Raleigh Rd., Manteo
(252) 473-6659

The Artful Dragon is a delightful shop offering medieval, renaissance, Celtic, and dragon-themed merchandise. Many of the items are historical re-creations of objects predating the 1600s. An outstanding array of wedding gifts and accessories are also available. This shop is quite unique and well worth stopping in. Thomas Gartman, Photographer, is located within the Artful Dragon. Thomas specializes in photographing weddings, portraits, and special events. Call (252) 473-1173 to arrange an appointment, or just stop in to enjoy examples of his work.

Manteo Furniture
Sir Walter Raleigh St., Manteo
(252) 473-2131

Manteo Furniture stocks a large selection of home and cottage furnishings ranging from traditional to contemporary. The store, which has been in operation for 55 years, offers down-home friendly service. Allow yourself plenty of time to browse through the many rooms of furnishings in this 48,000-square-foot showroom/warehouse. The company sells a full line of General Electric appliances and offers financing and free delivery. It's open year-round.

Outer Banks Quilts and Antiques
108 Sir Walter Raleigh St., Manteo
(252) 473-4183

This large store carries the goods of more than 10 antiques and collectibles dealers, so you'll find a lot to choose from. It's also the Outer Banks's only official quilt shop, with handmade quilts and quilting supplies.

Manteo Booksellers
105 Sir Walter Raleigh St., Manteo
(252) 473-1221

Housed in charming quarters dotted with wing chairs, cozy corners, and quaint antiques, Manteo Booksellers is a must-browse for every reader. Three rooms are packed with books ranging from literary classics to delightful children's stories. The Outer Banks and Latin American sections (they also have books in Spanish) are excellent, as are the historical, self-help, Civil War, and North Carolina fiction areas. The cookbook selection is extensive.

The bookstore has a busy calendar filled with book signings and free readings by authors, poets, and storytellers. This shop alone is definitely worth the trip to Manteo! Be sure to give the store cat, Stunt, a pat on the head (if he'll have it, that is). Manteo Booksellers is open year-round.

My Secret Garden
Sir Walter Raleigh St., Manteo
(252) 473-6880

Next door to Manteo Booksellers, My Secret Garden features Tiffany-style lamps, custom wreaths and swags, unique garden accessories and statuary, handmade birdhouses, and Mary Engelbreit cards and collectibles. This shop offers handpainted furniture, including mirrors, lamps, dressers and servers, plus indoor fountains, Muffy Vanderbears and Beanie Babies, the Lady Primrose bath line, and pottery. This is a charming shop with lots of gift ideas. It's open year-round.

Old Creef's Corner
Corner of Queen Elizabeth and Sir Walter Raleigh Sts., Manteo

In a slightly askew building on the corner, this former gas station houses **Water Street Station,** a women's apparel store. This shop offers casual resort wear and island wear for women and girls. Colorful dresses, linen clothing, fine accessories, luggage, handbags, hats, and babies' apparel are available. Next door, **Half Moon Junction** offers a place to get a snack, a drink, an ice-cream cone, or a cup of coffee. They also have T-shirts, inexpensive toys and candy for the kids, and small gift items.

Centennial Square
Sir Walter Raleigh, Queen Elizabeth, and Fernando Sts., Manteo

This beautiful square of buildings offers interesting shops on the first level with apartments above. On the Sir Walter Raleigh Street side, you'll find the delightful **Coffeehouse on Roanoke Island** serving coffee drinks, smoothies, milk shakes, and baked goods (see our Restaurants chapter). Next door is the Dare County Arts Council's **Sea and Sounds Gallery** (see our Arts and Culture chapter).

Around the corner on the Fernando Street side is the incomparable **John Silver Gallery.** This galley features the stunning oil and watercolor paintings of native John "Possum" Silver in addition to the work of many other artists not seen elsewhere on the Outer Banks. Silver and his wife, Sheila, have excellent taste in art, and they stock the gallery with wonderful paintings, sculpture, pottery, furniture, jewelry, glass, rugs, weavings, and more. This gallery is also in our Arts and Culture chapter. Next door is **Donetta Donetta Waterfront Salon and Day Spa,** a full-service salon and day spa with services like manicures and pedicures, massages, aromatherapy, and body wraps. **House of Celebrations,** next to Donetta's, is a bridal boutique and wedding consultant.

The Waterfront Shops
Queen Elizabeth Ave., Manteo

Along the Manteo Waterfront sits this four-story complex with businesses, restaurants, residential space, and covered parking.

Charlotte's is a quality women's boutique that features traditional and contemporary fine and casual clothing, accessories, and gifts. You must see the beautiful sweater collection, including ones by designers Lisa Nichols and Michael Simon. They carry Sak and Kaminski bags. The helpful staff is attentive and professional, and the store is open year-round.

Island Nautical is an Outer Banks headquarters for nautical gifts and decor. Owners Jack and Marilyn Hughes have devoted this shop exclusively to marine-related merchandise, including authentic maritime artifacts such as spinnakers, life rings, portholes, and authentic and reproduction lanterns; quality weather instruments; marine-style clocks; and an array of tide clocks, ship model kits, a ship-in-a-bottle collection, and much more. Authentic Greek fishermen's hats are available here, and it's the only place in the area to find out-of-print maritime books as well as current selections. It's open all year.

Ken Kelley and Eileen Alexanian are the owners of **Diamonds and Dunes,** a full-service jewelry shop. The "designing couple" produces fine handcrafted work, drawing on more than two decades of experience in the jewelry business. Services include everything from setting stones and sizing rings to creating one-of-a-kind keepsakes. They showcase their very own lighthouse bracelet that features the five Outer Banks lighthouses. They also offer Belgian diamonds and gold, silver, or gem-studded ear pins to give you the three-earring look without all the holes. Ken and Eileen are members of the American Gem Society. The store is open year-round.

Magnolia Market
Queen Elizabeth Ave., Manteo

This group of shops, which opened in 1999 across from The Tranquil House Inn, should be added to your list of shopping destinations. The stores are reminiscent of open-air market stalls, with rough-sawn wood plank walls and wide open doors. It's nice to wander from shop to shop, admiring items and chatting with the friendly merchants. Here you will find **Magnolia Market General Store,** where you can purchase drinks, snacks, sundries, and gourmet foods. **Manteo Blacksmith** is a purveyor of fine metalwork and other treasures. Among their handcrafted home and garden accessories and accents, you'll find some truly unique items.

The blacksmith is often working on the lawn outside the store. Stop for a while and watch the amazing process of hand-forging iron. **Outer Banks Nut Company** sells gourmet nuts, fresh-roasted peanuts, popcorn, candy, gift items and gift baskets, and T-shirts. The smells of fresh-roasting nuts will lure you inside. **Odds & Ends** is absolutely packed with antiques and collectibles, so much so that the owner has to move much of the merchandise out onto the deck each day. You'll find mirrors, frames, furniture, housewares, glassware, china, and collectible items. For lunch or dinner, stop at Magnolia Grille (see our Restaurants chapter).

Endless Possibilities is a store like no other. Here, local weaver Rabiah Hodges and a team of weavers create new items by recycling old ones. For instance, purses are woven from old T-shirts and fabrics, with an old belt used as a strap, creating a really cool conversation piece. Rugs and other items are also made here. All the recyclables come from Hotline Thrift Shop, a women's crisis intervention center thrift shop, and the proceeds benefit that organization.

Phoenix Shops
Between Budleigh and Ananias Dare Sts., Manteo

This strip of shops, facing an inner courtyard instead of the street, has an interesting blend of shops. **Joyce's of Manteo** is a gift/home accessory shop with home-decor items, dishes, linens, candles, costume jewelry, wood art, and more. You'll find Barbara Hardy jewelry, Raymond Waites wall plates, and accessories by Mary Engelbreit. Next door, **XYZ Gallerie** is a gift store with whimsical, zany, and eclectic items, like chimes, frames, mugs, toys, and ornaments. There are a lot of mobiles here too. **Sleeping In** sells everything for a comfortable bed and bath. With a pair of silky pajamas and a set of fine European linens from this store, you just might sleep in all weekend. Everything here is luxurious: lingerie, gowns, robes, bath items, body care products, candles, bedding, and home decor. **Once Upon a Tyme,** another great store in this

row of many, offers a mix of antiques and exquisite new items. The baby bedding and clothing, including christening dresses, is extraordinary. Gift items, cards, jewelry, gifts, and old furniture round out the offerings. **Always Cookin'** is just what it sounds like: a cooking store. As the owner says, if you're always cooking, this store has great products to make it simpler and more enjoyable. Cookbooks, aprons, cookware, gadgets, mixes, sauces, spices, and more fill this store.

Finally Mine
Across from Magnolia Market, Manteo
(252) 473-1387

For unique gifts for yourself or someone special, Finally Mine is the place to stop. There's quite a bit of sterling silver jewelry and earrings, including many pieces fashioned with sea glass. Home accessories, including old English stained-glass windows, blown glass, frames, pottery, and lamps, are unique. You'll also find teapots, weavings, mirrors, and more.

Muzzie's Antiques
Across from Magnolia Market, Manteo
(252) 473-4505

Muzzie's offers quite the assortment of antiques and treasures. Estate and heirloom jewelry, Shabby Chic and April Cornell linens, antique and rag dolls, vintage accessories, and wedding gowns are just a few of the items you'll find. There are also furnishings, mosaic tables, painted furniture, lamps, trinket boxes, pillows galore, cards, and bath products.

Nancy Ware Pottery
402 Queen Elizabeth St., Manteo
(252) 473-9400

In a great new building across from The Tranquil House Inn, this is the pottery studio of artist Nancy Ware. The potter's wheel is on display, and you can see her work from time to time. She also offers classes on the wheel. In this year-round shop you'll find Nancy's pottery, jewelry, and tile work. The pottery is high-fire functional stoneware that is dishwasher, microwave, and oven safe. There's a great variety of kitchen items, including deep-dish fluted pie plates, colanders, three-piece child dining sets that can be personalized, vases, dishes, and spoon rests.

The Museum Shop
Roanoke Island Festival Park, Manteo
(252) 475–1500

This Museum Shop at Roanoke Island Festival Park goes beyond what you'd expect at a museum store. This store is huge, packed to the gills with historically themed gifts and items for the home. Everything is inspired by Roanoke Island life and history. There are sections with Elizabethan, Civil War, nautical, and Native American themes. In the book section, the selection of books about the Outer Banks is extensive, and there are also handsome leather-bound blank journals and a wide range of music. In the Elizabethan section, you'll find teapots, tea, biscuits, and other English items. The nautical section has books, telescopes, tide clocks, old maps, models, and more. The toys here are great, including hats, swords, and capes for playing dress-up. Jewelry, candy, food items, games, gifts, and home decor items are all here. Don't miss it.

Clemons on Budleigh
406 Budleigh St., Manteo
(252) 473–9870

Clemons is a cute antiques shop housed in a little white cottage. It's a couple of blocks from the waterfront, but it's worth strolling up to. The shop stocks antiques and newer items for the home and garden. Three rooms are filled with china, furniture, linens, clothing, mirrors, frames, hats—you name it. On the porch are several garden statuary and yard ornaments.

Wanchese

After you cross Roanoke Sound westbound on the Nags Head–Manteo Causeway and pass Pirate's Cove, make a left at the next intersection onto NC 345, which will take you to Wanchese. Turning to the right onto Old Wharf Road (less than a

mile from the intersection with US 64/264), you'll find **Nick-E Stained Glass,** a studio and gallery, which is a veritable stained-glass wonderland featuring the original creations of Ellinor and Robert Nick (see our Arts and Culture chapter).

Dare County Mainland

Nature's Harmony
Shipyard Rd., Manns Harbor
(252) 473–3556

Nature's Harmony is a full-scale nursery with three greenhouses, specializing in herbs, perennials, and wildflowers. It offers a plant maintenance service for your office or home. This store sells pottery and garden-related accessories plus fertilizers and mulches. Landscaping services are available. It's a lovely, peaceful spot that's open from February through Christmas.

Rodanthe

Rodanthe has several general stores where you can find groceries, camping and fishing supplies, bait, and seafood—the vacation necessities. Read on for some additional arty shopping experiences.

The Waterfowl Shop
NC 12, Rodanthe
(252) 987–2626

The Waterfowl Shop offers a framing service and such gifts as crafts, new and used working decoys, tide clocks, and wind speed indicators. The shop also has a sports photography gallery featuring the work of Richard Darcey, an award-winning former photographer for *The Washington Post*. It's open March through January.

Olde Christmas at Rodanthe Gift Shop
NC 12, Rodanthe
(252) 987–2116

Stop here to browse one of the most complete cross-stitch departments on the Outer Banks. The shop has unusual gift items including statuary, lighthouse afghans, and a selection of nautical Christmas ornaments. There's also an expanded needlework department. It's open April though December.

Pamlico Station Shops
NC 12, Rodanthe
(252) 987–1080

This two-story shopping center is located on the east side of NC 12 in Rodanthe and houses a wide selection of shops and a restaurant. **Moon Over Hatteras Cafe** resides on the upper deck and offers breakfast, lunch, and dinner every day with a fine wine selection and imported beers on tap. The restaurant's atmosphere is a refreshing and welcome respite for daytrippers to the island, who can order their food to eat in or take out. **Village Video** offers a wide selection of rental movies as well as VCR and Nintendo system rentals. **Hatteras T-Shirts** offers a wide selection of T-shirts, hats, and accessories, and even hermit crabs! **Exotic Cargo** carries interesting and unique imported gift items not easily found elsewhere—plan enough time for some serious browsing. Bathing suits abound at the newly expanded **Surfside Casuals** shop located on the first level. This store offers a great selection of clothing to make your shopping quest on Hatteras Island a successful one. **Island Gift Shop** sells candles, lighthouse gifts, clothing, chimes, and sundries. For real relaxation, grab a seat on the deck and watch a magnificent Hatteras Island sunset over Pamlico Sound.

Bill Sawyer's Place
NC 12, Rodanthe
(252) 987–2214

Just a short distance south of Pamlico Station is Bill Sawyer's Place, which carries an assortment of gifts, a huge collection of shells, bait and tackle, and cold beer. Sawyer also rents boogie boards. It's open April through October.

The Island Convenience Store
NC 12, Rodanthe
(252) 987–2239

This is a one-stop shopping place for groceries, rod and reel rentals, bait and tackle, propane gas, gasoline, and an array of deli items, including breakfast biscuits, sandwiches, hand-dipped ice cream cones and sundaes, and fried chicken. You can take your food with you or eat at the tables. The store also carries souvenirs, gifts, and beach supplies and offers 24-hour AAA wrecker service and auto repair. Bike rentals are available too. It's open year-round.

Ocean Gourmet and Gifts
NC 12, Rodanthe
(252) 987–1166

This stand-alone store, just north of Camp Hatteras, is the place to come for fresh fudge, ice cream, and candy. Other vacation necessities are available too, such as hermit crabs, fireworks, bathing suits, beachwear, and nautical gifts and lighthouses.

Waves

Waves is home to just a few businesses including Hatteras Island Surf Shop (see our Watersports chapter) and Michael Halminski's Photography Gallery (see our Arts and Culture chapter for details).

Salvo

Salvo is a sleepy little village, so don't expect much in the way of shopping.

Fishin' Hole
NC 12, Salvo
(252) 987–2351

In 2002 the Fishin' Hole marked its 27th year as a general tackle shop. But the shop, open April through mid December, also sells plenty of beach supplies and groceries. If you need something they don't carry, they can tell you where to find it nearby.

Avon

Island Shoppes
NC 12, Avon

This small shopping center houses two of

the Outer Banks's most popular stores—
Ocean Annie's and **Kitty Hawk Kites/
Carolina Outdoors.** Ocean Annie's is a
craft gallery that sells pottery, wind chimes,
prints, artwork, wooden boxes, coffee, and
the like. Kitty Hawk Kites/Carolina Outdoors is a sports store selling kites and offering kayak eco-tours, kite-surfing lessons,
and parasailing. It's also an outfitter, selling sporty outdoor clothes and gear for all
your adventures.

The Fisherman's Daughter
NC 12, Avon
(252) 995–6148

The Fisherman's Daughter features pottery from all over the United States. Local
art and photography are available in the
upstairs room. Gift items include brass
nautical items and furnishings, Christmas ornaments, a large line from Dept. 56
Christmas, T-shirts with Outer Banks
themes, cotton afghans with various
designs including lighthouses, lots of
gold and silver jewelry, and Beanie Babies
and Yankee Candles. It's open Easter
through mid-December.

Avon Market
NC 12, Avon
(252) 995–5362

Avon Market, actually a general store, is a
local favorite for fresh-cut meats, plus
produce and groceries. They also have
most everything else you'd expect from an
all-purpose shop. Souvenirs, beachwear,
groceries, all kinds of fishing supplies,
beach chairs, quick-serve foods, gas, and
free air are all available. It's open April
through late December.

Hatteras Wind & Surf
NC 12, Avon
(252) 995–6275, (888) WND–SURF

Hatteras Wind & Surf has a full line of
skateboard gear, Tim Nolte surfboards,
windsurfing equipment sales and
rentals, and summer apparel with an
emphasis on shorts. They also operate
as a consignment shop for windsurfing

goods. (See our Watersports chapter for
further information specifically on
windsurfing and kite-surfing lessons
and kayak tours.)

Island Spice and Wine
NC 12, Avon
(252) 995–7750

Island Spice and Wine is a little bit of
wine heaven. Specializing in California,
Italian, and French wines, it has some
tasty accompaniments, including gourmet coffees, foods, and cheeses. How
about a gourmet gift basket? You can
sneak in some neat kitchen gadgets or
cute cookie cutters. There's also wine
racks, serving ware, barbecue tools,
Gourmet Kitchen cooking supplies, and
cookbooks. A selection of specialty beers
and Asian food products also includes
sushi-making supplies. There's an
expanded gift section that includes lots
of North Carolina food products, such
as delicious sauces and preserves and
organic North Carolina cooking wine
flavored with basil, tarragon, and rosemary. Check out the line of collectibles, a
huge mug selection, angel items, and
whimsical salt and pepper shakers. It is
open year-round.

Nags Head Hammocks
NC 12, Avon
(252) 995-3744
www.nagshead.com

Here's another branch location of the Outer Banks's legendary hammock shop. Nags Head Hammocks are known for their sturdiness, and you can select from traditional hammocks, hammock porch chairs, hammock tables, hammock swings, or hammock stools. Hammock pillows make them even more comfortable.

Country Elegance
Harbor Rd., Avon
(252) 995-6269

As you head south, if you turn right on Harbor Road at the only stoplight south of Whalebone Junction, you'll come across this store in Old Avon Village. Owned and operated by Lois and Dallas Miller, it features wearable art, birdhouses, aromatherapy oils, lighthouses, handpainted shirts, antique quilted heirlooms, whimsical art, designer dolls, and baskets. There are also wood crafts, cake candles, and lots and lots of lace. This shop is open Easter through mid-November.

Home Port Gifts
NC 12, Avon
(252) 995-4334

Home Port Gifts is one of the loveliest upscale gift shops on the Outer Banks. Here, original artwork, fine crafts, and exquisite jewelry in fine silver and 14-karat gold (much of it with a nautical theme) will tempt you. You'll also find quality accessories for the home and nautical antiques. We especially like the custom Tiffany-style stained-glass pieces, nautical sculptures, handcarved decoys, terra cotta sculptures, and sea candles by Sally Knuckles. The work of about 120 local artists is on display at Home Port, which enters its 14th year in 2002. You can spend anywhere from a nickel to about $2,500—there's something here for everyone.

Hatteras Plaza
NC 12, Avon

This Avon plaza is anchored by **Food**

Lion. Another **Ace Hardware** is here as well. **Beach Bites** is a well-rounded bakery/deli featuring fresh tuna salad, sliced meats, and cheeses and pizza kits. It's the home of the Outer Banks Elephant Ear (tasty sticky buns), Key lime pies, jumbo cookies, gourmet muffins, and homemade breads. It's open March through December.

Exotic Cargo features beautiful, handcrafted home accents brought to you from the world over. The owners bring enticing items from India, Indonesia, Thailand, Mexico, and other great locales. Be sure and reserve time for this shop—you'll make some distinctive finds here. **Ocean Threads** and **Surfside Casuals,** right next door to one another, have similar offerings—surfwear by Billabong, Roxy, and others plus bathing suits, T-shirts, sandals, sunglasses, stickers. This location of Surfside Casuals has more T-shirts than you can imagine and a similarly large selection of iron-on decals to put on them.

On the other end of the plaza is **Island Cycle,** which rents, repairs, and sells bicycles. **Beach Pharmacy** is here, along with **Sea Treasures,** which sells fudge, beachwear, and beachy knickknacks. For eats, Hatteras Plaza has a pizza restaurant, a Chinese restaurant, Bubba's Too BBQ, and Banditos on the Beach Mexican restaurant.

If you'd like to keep the rest of the family entertained while you shop, drop them off at **Hatteras Movies 4**. The theater has four showings daily of first-run films.

Buxton

A 5-mile drive south of Avon brings you to the village of Buxton, where you'll discover things are more spread out and range from a general store and bait and tackle shop to specialty boutiques. Buxton's supermarket, **Conner's Cape Hatteras Market,** offers groceries and basic supplies year-round.

Daydreams
NC 12, Buxton
(252) 995-5548

Daydreams has earned a reputation for having stylish clothing and a selection of top name brands such as Patagonia and Birkenstock. The shop, open March through Christmas, carries clothing for men, women, and children, plus accessories and jewelry.

Dillon's Corner
NC 12, Buxton
(252) 995-5083

Here's a terrific bait and tackle shop that carries all kinds of fishing rods, including custom-built ones. You'll find a charming little shop that features gifts, Yankee Candles, jewelry, pottery, lighthouse replicas, T-shirts, and a bevy of Beanie Babies. It's open year-round.

Hatteras Oaks
NC 12, Buxton

This new shopping center, situated behind some lovely oaks that the developer thoughtfully left behind, has a couple of shops plus **Angelo's Pizza** and a **Brew Thru,** home of world-famous T-shirts and convenience items brought to your car window.

T-Shirt Whirl has a mind-boggling array of T-shirts with all the Outer Banks town names and any crude, silly, or happy saying you can think of. There are also iron-on decals if you want to come up with something on your own.

Natural Art Surf Shop
NC 12, Buxton
(252) 995-5682

Natural Art is owned by Scott and Carol Busbey, two serious surfers who love the sport and the lifestyle. During the 25-plus years the shop has been in business, it has gained the reputation for being "the surfer's surf shop," meaning they specialize in surfing rather than all water-board sports. Surfers from everywhere and all walks of life have been coming here for years. Scott, who has his own line of boards called In The Eye, manufactures custom boards and does repairs. Carol makes clothing (her hand-sewn women's and men's tops and children's shirts and dresses are unique and colorful) and tries to find time to surf. The shop rents surf-

boards, boogie boards, swim fins, wetsuits, and surf videos, and sells all the necessary surfing gear and great T-shirts. It's open March through December. (See our Watersports chapter for more information.)

Osprey Shopping Center
NC 12, Buxton

Osprey is behind Natural Art Surf Shop and the Great Salt Marsh Restaurant and has an ABC package store. **Ocean Notions Gift Shop** has a nice selection of gifts including candles, bath products, and nautical gifts as well as women's and men's clothing and a small selection of children's apparel. Look no further for beach supplies and a selection of gold and silver jewelry. It's open March through mid-December. Turn toward the ocean on Light Plant Road to find **The Old Gray House** gift shop. Baskets, woodwork, stitchery, miniatures, dolls, shells, potpourri, and more fill the shelves in this old house, which looks much like it must have looked at the turn of the 20th century.

Buxton Village Books
NC 12, Buxton
(252) 995-4240

Comfortably nestled in what was once the summer kitchen of an island house, Buxton Village Books has been a village landmark since 1984. This charming space is packed with lots of good reads, including all the current best-sellers, sea stories, hard-to-find Southern fiction, kids' books, and saltwater fly-fishing titles. In a room overlooking Pamlico Sound, you can browse over a delightful selection of notecards and stationery. The shop has a public fax machine; ask about the shop's mail-order catalog. It's open year-round.

Cactus Flower Gallery
NC 12, Buxton

Right next door to Buxton Village Books is a big house with a big porch and a gallery inside. It's worth a stop here to see the architectural reproductions, including columns, pedestals, and wall hangings made to look like architectural renderings. Wall hangings, statues, and garden statuary are molded into Notre Dame–like gargoyles, gruff griffins, cherubic angels, and sensible seashells. There are also carved wall plaques, lamps, and a few pieces of furniture.

Frisco

Indian Town Gallery and Gifts
NC 12, Frisco

Nestled down in the woods in Frisco, Indian Town represents artists from the local villages. Many of the paintings have an Outer Banks theme, and the offshore-fishing theme paintings are stunning. The gallery also features pottery, chimes, cards, gifts, lighthouses, and jewelry. Artist Wayne Fulcher is often at work right in the store.

Red Drum Pottery
NC 12, Frisco
(252) 995–5757

Accomplished potters Rhonda Bates and Wes Lassiter moved their studio from Edenton, North Carolina, to Frisco in the summer of 2001. The artists are often at work in the studio, and you can watch them as they turn their wonderful creations at the wheel. These are well-crafted, artistic pieces, whether they are intended for functional or decorative use. It's definitely worth a stop to see their bowls, pitchers,

vases, vessels, platters, teakettles, miniatures, and their fabulous fish- and crab-imprinted hanging wall tiles. The gallery is open seven days a week year-round.

Scotch Bonnet Candies and Gifts
NC 12, Frisco
(252) 995-4242

The sweetest spot on Hatteras Island has homemade fudge (more than 20 varieties, including sugar-free), bulk taffy, Jelly Belly jelly beans, and many other sweet treats. Scotch Bonnet also carries T-shirts, sweatshirts, jewelry, gifts, hermit crabs, and accessories. Don't miss the hermit crab races every Friday during the summer.

Browning Artworks
NC 12, Frisco
(252) 995-5538

In addition to museum-quality clay, wood, fiber, metal, and glass by North Carolina's craftspeople, Browning Artworks offers an exclusive selection of original works by well-known Outer Banks watercolorist Russell Yerkes and photographers Michael Halminski and Ray Matthews. The ambiance, both inside and out, makes shopping—or browsing—at Browning's a real pleasure. Inside, knowledgeable staff members go out of their way to provide you with warm hospitality and friendly customer service. Outside, the shady deck invites you to sit for a while and enjoy the peace of the fountain pool and the beautifully landscaped grounds. Visiting artists, from woodturners and jewelry designers to potters and painters, provide demonstrations for parents and kids during the summer. Use Browning's convenient shipping service to get your purchases home, and if you're planning a wedding, Browning's bridal registry can accommodate both the resident and the visiting bride. Call ahead for hours of operation, which vary with the season.

Pirate's Chest of Frisco
NC 12, Frisco
(252) 995-5118

Pirate's Chest opened in 1953, making it the oldest gift shop on Hatteras Island. If you've been searching for a coconut pirate head, you'll find one here. The shop also has exotic shells and coral, jewelry, handmade Christmas shell ornaments, T-shirts, scrimshaw, children's books and learning tools, cookbooks, and lighthouse collectibles—a mountain of things for the whole family to enjoy, including hermit crabs. It closes for a few weeks after Christmas; otherwise it's open year-round.

All Decked Out
NC 12, Frisco
(252) 995-4319, (800) 321-2392

This is a furniture factory owned by Dale Cashman. He and his crew handcraft outdoor furniture such as picnic tables, Adirondack chairs, benches, wooden recliners, and hammocks, and they will ship anywhere in the United States. Stop by and have a seat. It's open year-round with the exception of two weeks at Christmas. Call for a free catalog.

The Frisco Market
NC 12, Frisco

The Frisco Market is directly across from the entrance road to Ramp 49 and Billy Mitchell Air Field. The market stocks all sorts of groceries, beer, wine, reading material, gas, and beach supplies. **Frisco**

Rod and Gun specializes in fishing and hunting equipment. You'll find everything you need for a hunting or fishing trip on the Outer Banks, including offshore and inshore fishing equipment, fly-fishing equipment, guns, ice, bait, tackle, and one of the best selections of knives we've seen anywhere. They also carry camping supplies, name-brand outdoor apparel, Sperry Topsiders, and T-shirts, and offer free air for your tires. They are open year-round.

Hatteras Village

Hatteras Village offers a mixture of services, including a pharmacy and grocery store, with shops mixed in. And don't overlook the ferry terminal's **Ship's Store,** located in the lobby—it offers a selection of T-shirts, coffee mugs, coloring books, and souvenirs.

Sandy Bay Gallery
NC 12, Hatteras Village
(252) 986–1338

At the north end of Hatteras Village, next to Village Video, this gallery puts an emphasis on showcasing Outer Banks artists. Sandy Bay is filled with original watercolor and acrylic paintings and local photography. Potters, jewelers, glass artisans, and paper, wood, stained glass, and fiber artists all have wares on display. Glass boxes with silver trim by Mary Anne feature a geometric collage of colored and clear glass—they are exquisite. If you're having a hard time making a decision in this shop, head out to the large porch and plop down into an Adirondack chair for a spell. Mull your quandary in shady comfort. Gift registry and shipping are available. The gallery is open March through Christmas Eve.

Village Rags
NC 12, Hatteras Village
(252) 986–6575

This is a great women's clothing boutique, one you wouldn't really expect to find in southern Hatteras Island. The Flax line of clothing is featured, though there are many other brands as well, including Kiko, Click, and April Cornell. Most of the clothing is loose-fitting and casual, and there is a lot of linen and a few dressier dresses. Separates include pants, skirts, tanks, tops, and light jackets. Upstairs are sundresses, workout wear, T-shirts, and swimsuits. Hats, jewelry, and bags round out the offerings. This shop is right next door to Sandy Bay Gallery.

Burrus' Red & White Supermarket
NC 12, Hatteras Village
(252) 986–2333

The Burrus' Red & White has been serving locals and visitors since 1866. They carry seafood and freshly cut meats, and they have a full-service deli and salad bar. You'll also find gourmet and Eight O'Clock coffee, fresh produce, frozen foods, dairy products, and health and beauty aids. It's open year-round.

Hatteras Hotline
NC 12, Hatteras Village
(252) 986–1332

Hotline is the local thrift store that benefits the local women's shelter. You can find some great deals on furniture, appliances, clothing, shoes, coats, bedding, books, toys, housewares, and many other things. This store is right in the heart of the village in a big white house.

Hatteras Harbor Marina Store Gift Shop
Hatteras Marina, NC 12, Hatteras Village
(252) 986–2166

The marina gift store has jewelry, name-brand sportswear, fishing supplies, unique gifts, deck shoes, and other items. It's open year-round.

Lee Robinson General Store
NC 12, Hatteras Village
(252) 986–2381
www.obag.com

The original Lee's opened in 1948 but was replaced by a replica several years ago. We're glad it kept the old look, including the wide front porch and the wooden floors. Owners Belinda and Virgil Willis carry everything you need for a vacation at the beach, plus something you wouldn't necessarily expect to find at a beach general store: a great selection of fine wines. The store also carries groceries (including gourmet items), chocolates, fudge, books and magazines, T-shirts, sweatshirts, jewelry and gifts, plus sundries such as film, lotions, boogie boards, and hats. Don't miss the upstairs gift gallery. You can rent bicycles here too. It's a good place to buy a Coke in a glass bottle and something to snack on for the ferry ride to Ocracoke. It's open year-round.

Hatteras Landing
NC 12, Hatteras Village
(252) 986–2205

Right next to the Hatteras-Ocracoke ferry docks at the southern end of Hatteras Village, this shopping center means you'll never again have a boring wait for the ferry. The only problem is people who get carried away with their shopping and are late for the boarding. When the ferry boards, inevitably you'll see someone dashing like a madman back to his vehicle. Hatteras Landing is also a marina.

There are some great shops here, which make it worth the risk of leaving the line. **Hatteras Landing Provision Company** stocks a large selection of sweatshirts, T-shirts, and other clothing with Outer Banks themes, but there are also jackets, windbreakers, hats, and other clothing. There are also necessities, like film and cigars. **Graveyard Deli and Market** opens into the Provision Company and offers deli sandwiches, snacks, candy bars, chips, gum, drinks, beer, wine, and many sundries that you'll need for a day on the boat or on the ferry.

Birthday Suits is an Outer Banks favorite for fashionable swimwear for the whole family. For hard-to-fit women, there are bra-sized tops that can be mixed with separate bottoms, plus long-torso suits and maternity suits. Men's sizes range from 28 to 4XL and include competition briefs and volleyball and surf trunks. Kids' swimwear ranges from size 2 to preteen, and there are even swim diapers. Birthday Suits has a huge selection of OBX gear and contemporary sportswear for women, men, and children.

Ocean Annie's is a craft gallery selling pottery, chimes, wooden boxes, frames, and many more gift items made by artists and artisans. They also sell coffee beans. Many people return here year after year for gifts and home accessories. **Surfside Casuals** is a surfwear store selling swimsuits for men, women, and children, plus casual beachy clothing, sandals, sunglasses, and T-shirts. Women love the fact that they can buy separates here, mixing and matching bottoms and tops. **Farmer's Daughter** has everything you need to bring a country-casual look to your home. Gifts and collectibles are the hallmarks of this store, which is a traditional Outer Banks favorite. There are also original artworks by Outer Banks artisans, and the world's first and only supply of saltwater fudge. Other locations are in Nags Head, Duck, and Corolla.

Lightkeeper Gallery features exclusive artwork by local artists. Photographs by Scott Geib are standouts, and there are numerous paintings with Outer Banks themes. Gift items are also available, including T-shirts, coffee mugs, coasters, and prints. **Kitty Hawk Kites/Carolina Outdoors** is an outdoor store selling kites, toys, outdoor apparel, sunglasses, sportswear, and more. This location has a rock-climbing wall right in the middle of the shopping center.

If you're here at the dinner hour, be sure to try the spectacular Austin Creek Grill, right on the docks (see our Restaurants chapter).

Ocracoke Island

Shopping in Ocracoke is casual, interesting, and easily managed on foot. Small shops are scattered throughout the village and along the main street, on sandy lanes, and in private homes. You'll also discover that some dockside stores have the feel of a general store and carry everything you need. Ocracoke Village shops offer a variety of local crafts, artwork, quality accessories for the home, antiques, beachwear,

books, music, and magazines as well as the ubiquitous T-shirts and even a few souvenir mugs. An ABC package store is adjacent to the Ocracoke Variety Store.

Ocracoke Variety Store
NC 12, Ocracoke
(252) 928-4911

Ocracoke Variety is on NC 12 before you enter the village from the north. Shop for groceries and fresh meat, beer, wine, T-shirts, beachwear and accessories, ice, gifts, books, magazines, camping and fishing supplies, household items, health and beauty aids, and even a few art supplies. True Value Hardware is conveniently located next door. There's a bulletin board posted at the front entrance featuring menus of the local restaurants and community information. They're open all year.

Pirate's Chest Gifts and T-shirts
NC 12, Ocracoke
(252) 928-4992

Pirate's Chest is a must-stop just to peruse

While waiting in line for the Ocracoke Ferry, many passengers run over to Hatteras Landing for snacks or to shop. Don't linger too long, or you'll miss the ferry! PHOTO: MOLLY HARRISON

the variety of merchandise sold here: T-shirts, souvenirs, jewelry, local shells, books, scrimshaw, coral, lighthouse prints, 14-karat gold jewelry, Joan Perry sculptures, and more. Look for the shell-filled boat in the parking lot. It's open March through November.

Island Ragpicker
NC 12, Ocracoke
(252) 928–7571

Island Ragpicker will catch your eye with an attractive mixture of bells, baskets, and hand-woven rugs displayed on the porch and everywhere inside. Owners Mickey Baker and Carmie Prete offer fine quality crafts (some by local craftspeople), handmade brooms, cards, decoys, pottery, dishes, jewelry, and casual cotton apparel. Look for local and nature books, short story collections, and self-help books along with an amazing assortment of easy-listening music. The Ragpicker has great cards. It's one of the few Ocracoke shops open all year.

Spencer's Market
School Rd. and NC 12, Ocracoke

This new shopping complex houses **Sally Newell Interiors,** with furniture, home-decor accessories, window treatments, and more for the home. Newell is a member of the American Society of Interior Designers and has designed many residential and commercial interiors. **Eleven Eleven Shades and Movies** offers just that—high-end sunglasses and video rentals. **Ocracoke Restoration Co.** is the newest shop of the owner of Roadhouse Stained Glass Co. The store is stocked with English stained glass, old and new furniture, architectural ornaments, old doorknobs and drawer pulls, and interesting salvaged materials. The same owner also recently opened the tiny **Sardine Gallery,** with the goal of promoting as many local artists as possible. You'll find sculpture, furniture, handmade stained-glass pieces, original paintings, and much more. Also in this center is **Thai Moon** carry-out restaurant (see

our Restaurants chapter). Stop by to see what else is new.

Deepwater Pottery & Books To Be Red
School Rd. and NC 12, Ocracoke
(252) 928–7472 (Deepwater Pottery)
(252) 928–3936 (Books to be Red)

On the corner of School Road and NC 12, a lovely historic home houses these two wonderful shops. This duo of stores is one of our favorite haunts on Ocracoke Island; in fact, we buy as many gifts for ourselves here as we do for others. Deepwater Pottery is a working pottery studio and gift shop, carrying handmade stoneware, candles, and glass, surprising home and garden accents, and a special bath section, which is filled with soaps and other great-smelling bath luxuries. The bath section carries Burt's Bees products as well. Books to Be Red has a wonderful selection of books by local authors, new-age journals, magazines, cards, and a paperback section of fiction, nonfiction, and children's books. There's a gently used section of books also. The shop is open March 1 through Christmas.

Natural Selections
School Road, Ocracoke
(252) 928–HEMP

Natural Selections, The Ocracoke Island Hemp Shop, offers a great selection of products made from hemp and other natural fibers. Natural Selections is a socially and environmentally conscious shop, committed to the belief that the use of hemp will save the planet from herbicides, pesticides, fertilizers, and deforestation. "Hemp is rope, not dope," they say at this store. Once you feel the natural fibers, you'll want to wear the pants, dresses, shirts, jackets, and hats they sell here. There are also bags, hemp home accessories, natural cosmetics, jewelry, and gifts.

Captain's Landing
NC 12 on Silver Lake, Ocracoke

Just past the Jolly Roger Pub and Marina is this little conglomeration of shops, not really connected in any way, but clustered together around the post office. Here you will find **Downpoint Decoys,** a small shop under an old oak tree. Inside it's rustic and antiquey, with decoys both old and new and the local carver/proprietor available to talk to. He also sells lures, painted oars, and wildlife art. **Sweet Tooth** tempts with candy, fudge, and ice cream. The **Island Christmas Shop** has gifts, accessories, trees, Santas, snowmen, ornaments, and fish, all with a holiday theme.

Ragpicker Too!
NC 12, Ocracoke
(252) 928–RAGS

A second location of the Ragpicker? Wonderful! This shop has been an Ocracoke mainstay since 1984, with this second location opening just down the road. You'll find finely crafted works of art from North Carolina artists and elsewhere. The clothing, T-shirts, hats, bags, and jewelry in this store are imaginative and casual, making it a fun place to shop. This shop also has furniture, trunks, lamps, and home accessories.

Island T-Shirt Shop
NC 12, Ocracoke
(252) 928–6781

In an old island home built in 1910, this shop offers stacks of T-shirts in every size and color. Look for children's wear, beach shoes, bathing suits, shorts, sweatshirts, and gift items, including frames, wind chimes, books, jewelry, and beach toys. There's a whole roomful of Christmas ornaments and decorations crafted by locals.

The Community Store
Ocracoke Waterfront, Ocracoke
(252) 928–3321

Operating since 1918, The Community Store is the place to shop for essential items in the heart of Ocracoke Village. It seems incongruous that you can rent videos here, for walking through the door is like stepping back in time. There's a cooler full of ice cream and frosty-cold sodas and beer.

The Gathering Place
NC 12, Ocracoke
(252) 928–7180

Across the parking lot on the harbor, The Gathering Place (located in a century-old building) boasts a front porch complete with an old swing. It's a great place to rest and view the boats on the harbor. Inside, the shop has a collection of local crafts, pottery from North Carolina, Margaret Furlong collectibles, Hanover lighthouse clocks, tide clocks, nautical gifts, coastal art, and lighthouse lamps. They've added a boutique featuring the April Cornell collection—an Outer Banks exclusive—as well as a variety of sundresses, hats, and sandals. Upstairs you'll find small antiques and art including English stained glass and the artwork of Frans Van Baars, Jim Wordsworth, and others. Shipping is available year-round. The shop is closed in January.

Joyce's of Ocracoke Gifts & Clothing
Ocracoke Waterfront, Ocracoke
(252) 928–6461

On the waterfront, Joyce's occupies the first floor space of Joyce's of Ocracoke Motel and Dockage. Owner Joyce L. Barnette offers well-made, comfortable men's and women's apparel, including a very nice collection of classic, sophisticated clothing for women in sportswear and dressier island styles. Joyce also offers an intimate apparel section. The shop carries lovely accessories for the home, such as collectors' items with frogs, cows, rabbits, fish, shells, and teddy bears. Other great finds here are hand-crafted fashion jewelry in all price ranges, mobiles, gifts, cards, stationery, wrapping paper, and T-shirts with unique designs. It's open March through Thanksgiving.

Harborside Gifts
NC 12, Ocracoke
(252) 928–3111

Harborside Gifts is one of the many pleasant surprises for visitors to Ocracoke. Quality sportswear for the family, a gourmet food section, gift basket service (some readymades are available), teas, cooking items, pottery, books, and magazines share the shop with an interesting collection of T-shirts and—look up!—a model train that chugs along overhead throughout most of the store. You'll also find domestic and imported wine and beer. It's open Easter through Thanksgiving.

Ocracoke Cigar and Wine
Ocracoke Waterfront, Ocracoke
(252) 928–1461

Formerly known as The Tobacco Shop, this store has a great selection of cigars, including Macanudo, Punch, and Fuente cigars, all enclosed in a humidor. The nice selection of wines is handled with care, stored in a temperature-controlled, walk-in cooler with each bottle stored on its side to prevent cork-drying. California dominates in the cellar, but there are also selections from France, Spain, Italy, Australia, and Virginia. This tiny shop somehow also squeezes in sunglasses, jewelry, gifts, candles, and artwork. The building is octagonal so you can't miss it.

Village Craftsmen
Howard St., Ocracoke
(252) 928–5541, (800) 648–9743

Village Craftsmen has become an Ocracoke landmark. It's been in business more than 30 years, but it isn't as easy to find as, say, the local lighthouse. The shop is on the narrow dirt lane known as Howard Street, a nice walk from the main street. Here you'll discover an abundance of North Carolina crafts, pottery, rugs, books, locally made soaps, candles, and jewelry. You can buy stoneware, tie-dyed dresses, and T-shirts here too.

Owner Philip Howard, a seven-generation Ocracoke Island resident, is an artist and his pen-and-ink and watercolor prints are in the shop. A fine selection of cassettes and CDs features Celtic, blues, jazz, and bluegrass music. Musical instruments, such as catpaws and strumsticks, help set a creative mood at this out-of-the-way place. The instruments are lightweight and simple to play. You can pick up a mail-order catalog at the shop or have one mailed to you. Village Craftsmen closes for the month of January.

Over the Moon
British Cemetery Rd., Ocracoke
(252) 928–3555

Over the Moon is a wonderful shop filled with handmade contemporary crafts. More than 100 artists and craftspeople provide work such as jewelry, porcelain, and Brian Andreas's Storypeople—books, prints, and sculptures with insights painted on the work. There are also pins and magnet cards, Metamorphicards, and hammock chairs. Pace yourself; this is a place to linger. It is open Easter through Thanksgiving.

Island Artworks
British Cemetery Rd., Ocracoke
(252) 928–3892

In a brightly colored little shop across from Over the Moon, Island Artworks is a fun place to browse and shop. It's a contemporary craft gallery, with colorful jewelry by local artist Kathleen O'Neal; fused glass and mosaics by Libby Hicks; photography, watercolors, pottery, woodworking, sculpture, mosaics, birdbaths, garden stakes, and so much more. Most of the art is original and one-of-a-kind.

Ocracoke Island Hammocks
British Cemetery Rd., Ocracoke
(252) 928–4387

These folks weave their own hammocks on the premises, and you are welcome to come and watch the process. The shop offers island mementos, lighthouse afghans, jewelry, and unique candles. You'll find a wide variety of bath and body and aromatherapy products and gourmet foods. In addition to the gift shop is **Candyland,** a place guaranteed to satisfy any sweet tooth. It's open Easter through Christmas.

Teach's Hole
Back Rd., Ocracoke
(252) 928–1718
www.teachshole.com

Come listen to the tales of the notorious Edward Teach—better known as Blackbeard the Pirate—at Teach's Hole. The "piratical pirate-phernalia," as George and Mickey Roberson call their collection, includes a gift shop and exhibit. More than 1,000 pirate items, including a life-size re-creation of Blackbeard in full battle dress and artifacts from the 17th and 18th centuries, form the exhibit. A new exhibit features "Blackbeard's Doom" on an eight-minute video. There is a fee to view it. Items in the gift shop include pirate toys, music boxes, movies, and more than 100 pirate book titles, plus maps, flags, hats, T-shirts, costumes, ship models, and treasure coins. For more information, see our Kidstuff chapter. It's open Easter though Thanksgiving from 10:00 A.M. to 6:00 P.M., Monday through Saturday.

Ocracoke Coffee Co.
Back Rd., Ocracoke
(252) 928–7473
www.ocracokecoffee.com

This aromatic shop is filled with bagels, baked goods, brewed coffee drinks, espresso, smoothies, shakes, more than 30 flavors of ground and whole bean coffee, and loose teas. You'll also find a selection of gift items, such as beautiful, hefty coffee mugs. Ocracoke Coffee is open daily from 7:00 A.M. until 9:30 P.M., and live music is offered during summer evenings on the deck.

Heart's Desire
Back Rd., Ocracoke
(252) 928–4104

Artist Mary Bassell combines her own creations of custom stained-glass windows, beach glass jewelry, papier-mâché, and folk art with fine crafts by other artists. There's also a nice selection of antique English stained glass and antique collectibles. The studio/gallery is open April through December.

Roadhouse Stained Glass Co. of Ocracoke
Back Rd., Ocracoke
(252) 928–3955

Recently expanded, Roadhouse Stained

Glass Co. of Ocracoke carries antique English stained glass, wrought iron gates, and other decorative items. Most of their glass decorates windows and doors, though smaller stained-glass pieces, many originally from porch lanterns, can be found here. You can find such imports as lamps and garden pieces, plus an occasional armoire or table. The store—operated by the same owner as The Gathering Place—is open from March through the end of January. Shipping is available anywhere.

Ride the Wind Surf & Kayak
NC 12 and Silver Lake, Ocracoke
(252)928–6311

Open April through Christmas, Ride the Wind Surf & Kayak offers complete surfing equipment and gear, swimsuits, ladies' and men's clothing, shoes, sandals, handbags, suntan lotions, sunglasses, watches, and jewelry. Obviously Ride the Wind is more than just a surf shop! See our Water-

sports chapter for surf and boogie board rental as well as kayak tour information.

Ocracoke Island Trading Company
NC 12, Ocracoke
(252) 928–7233

Right next to Ride the Wind, this store is an Aussie outfitter selling casual clothing. T-shirts range from size small to 3X, adorned with "Ocracoke" or funny sayings. There are also sportswear, hats, dresses, fish-print clothing, shorts, and more. If you're looking for gift items and souvenirs, look here.

Ocracoke Nautical Company
NC 12, Ocracoke
(252) 928–4192

An older home was renovated to house this new and charming shop in 2001. The beautiful wooden floors and vaulted ceiling are a nice backdrop to some wonderful merchandise. Most items here are related to ships and the sea. Ocracoke Nautical Company offers ships' clocks and wheels, original artwork, ship models and reproductions, model boats of both newer and classic designs, barometers, portholes, and tide clocks. Lamps made from buoys make great souvenirs. Wind chimes are sold here, and a selection of jewelry, including pearls, round out their selection.

Blue Door
Lighthouse Rd., Ocracoke
(252) 928–7216

What a creative place! This fun shop will lure you off Lighthouse Road to come inside and have a look around. It's in an old house surrounded by a picket fence. On the porch are a big spinning wheel and several antiques. Inside you'll find more antiques, unique gifts, art supplies, art, the weaving studio of the owner, and just plain cool stuff. Don't miss this shop. Just look for the sign made from—what else?—a blue door.

Pamlico Gifts
Lighthouse Rd., Ocracoke
No advertised phone listing

It's set back off the road, but if you can find it, this old-fashioned gift shop is worth the visit. Kids love the sharks' teeth they sell. They also have T-shirts, arts and crafts by local artists, stained glass, gifts, metal sculptures, lighthouses, and "schooners by order." Ask about that one. It's right down from the lighthouse across from Owen's Veggies stand.

Albert Styron's General Store
Lighthouse Rd., Ocracoke
(252) 928–6819

On the street as you approach the Ocracoke Lighthouse, you'll find Styron's, a store which dates back to 1920. Despite renovations, Styron's retains the appearance of an old general store and is in the National Registry of Historic Places. Make your purchases from a wide selection of cheeses, coffee beans, North Carolina foods, bulk spices and natural foods as well as beer,

wine, T-shirts, lighthouse gifts, and general merchandise. It's open March through January. For gourmet take-out items, **Cat Ridge Deli** is located in the store. Specializing in Thai food, wraps, and great meatball sandwiches, the deli also sells fine chocolates handmade on Ocracoke Island.

Silver Lake Trading Co.
58 Creek Rd., Ocracoke
(252) 928–3086
www.silverlaketradingcompany.com

Silver Lake Trading Co. is one of the best gift shops on Ocracoke Island, with goods that are eclectic and eccentric, fun and fashionable. You'll find great things for your home and garden, including Christopher Radko ornaments, Asian-inspired pottery, locally made pottery and wooden bowls, picture frames, funky lamps, Sandra Drennen linens, pillows, candles and soaps, garden statues, and even plants. Other cool things include off-the-wall refrigerator magnets and poetry kits, lunch boxes, unique toys, naughty but hilarious cards and cocktail napkins, Dirty Girl soap and bubble bath, and kitsch, like nun bottle openers. This store is in an old house right behind Styron's store.

Plan your activities over coffee and scones at a local coffee shop. PHOTO: J. AARON TROTMAN

Attractions

Corolla
Duck
Kitty Hawk
Kill Devil Hills
Nags Head
Roanoke Island
Bodie Island
Hatteras Island
Ocracoke Island

The Outer Banks's biggest attraction is, of course, the water. Nine hundred square miles of water surround these islands, providing a huge, liquid playground for swimmers, boaters, sailors, surfers, anglers, waders, and divers. For those who don't want to get wet, just being here on these narrow islands with 175 miles of Atlantic Ocean and views of blue from every angle is all the attraction they need.

Nature is so stark and apparent on the Outer Banks that no man-made attraction could ever compare with its glory, and it's the main attraction for many visitors. Sea birds and waterfowl, wildlife and sealife, wind-blown oaks and miles of undeveloped dunes, crashing waves and swirling tide pools, scattering ghost crabs and hungry fish, magenta sunsets and dark night skies full of stars—these are the things you can't find at home.

But don't think that means we don't have an abundance of stellar man-made attractions, many of them the sole reason people travel to the Outer Banks. There are attractions here to satisfy everyone—history buffs, nature lovers, arts aficionados, and thrill-seekers.

Some of the Outer Banks attractions were created by men and women out of pride for the significant historic events that took place here, namely the Wright brothers' first flight and the first attempted English settlement in the New World. Others, like *The Lost Colony* outdoor drama, are themselves as much a part of history as the events they portray.

If you're accustomed to metropolitan area prices, you're in for a real treat. Local attractions are affordable, with most everything costing less than $10 and many offerings open for free. The priciest attractions are worth every penny and still affordable compared to city prices. Most places offer special family, child, or senior discounts, so be sure to ask when you're there. While some of the attractions stay open year-round, many close in the winter months or strictly curtail their hours. Be sure to call ahead.

The Outer Banks is not just the home of two of the most significant events in the nation's history—the first English-speaking colony and the first powered flight—we're also gifted with an extraordinary coastline. Between lighthouses, lifesaving stations, wild horses, and shipwrecks, visitors can get lost in our long, lively barrier island history. In between, you can kick back, take off, or glide away. There's no better place to do virtually nothing but relax or to do every conceivable activity—barring mountain climbing and downhill skiing.

There are wide-open wildlife refuges across the islands and fluorescent-lighted fish tanks at the state aquarium. You can dive into history by boarding a reproduction of a 16th-century sailing ship or scuba dive beneath the Atlantic to explore a Civil War shipwreck. Whatever your interests, you'll find outlets for them here. There's never enough time to see everything the Outer Banks has to offer.

In this chapter, we have highlighted our favorite attractions. There are many others you'll discover on your own, and Insiders will gladly share their own secret spots. Many of these places have free admission or request nominal donations. We begin with the northernmost communities and work southward. Each area has its own section, so pick your pleasure.

Also, be sure to read our chapters on Recreation, Shopping, Arts and Culture, Watersports, Fishing, Kidstuff, Natural Wonders, and Nightlife for more exciting, educational, and unusual things to do and places to play on the Outer Banks.

Corolla

Historic Corolla Village
Schoolhouse and Corolla Village Lanes,
Corolla Village
(252) 453-3341

Though everyone refers to the whole Currituck Outer Banks as "Corolla," technically Corolla is the small village center on the unpaved road behind the lighthouse. Few people realize that Corolla was a thriving community that began to grow in 1875 after the lighthouse was built. In 1890, at the peak of the waterfowl hunting market in the area, there were as many as 200 residents living in the village. The village population declined during World War II and the following years, and there were only a few residents living in Corolla well into the 1980s, when a paved public road was opened to the area, and development of the Currituck Outer Banks began. The faces of the Currituck Outer Banks and Corolla Village have changed dramatically, but you can still get a sense of the old village by walking on the dirt road on the west side of NC 12 behind the lighthouse. In the shade of the oaks and pines, it is easy to imagine the life of the early residents.

A few of the historic buildings from the old village remain and have been restored to look as they did when they were built. A walking tour map is available at many of the shops in the area or at Twiddy & Company Realtors, whose owners took charge of restoring the buildings. The restored Corolla Schoolhouse is on the tour, though you can't go inside. The charming schoolhouse is on the corner of Schoolhouse Lane and Corolla Village Lane. The schoolhouse was built in the mid- to late 1890s and was finally closed in 1958. Also on the tour are several restored historic homes that have been converted into shops, so you can go inside. These include the Lewark and Parker residences. There is a new building that was built to look like Callie Parker's store. The walking tour will also take you past the 1878 U.S. Lifesaving Station that was moved to the village, the Currituck Beach Lighthouse and Lightkeeper's Residence, and the historic Whalehead Club.

Kill Devil Hills Lifesaving Station
Off NC 12, Corolla

Built in 1878, the Kill Devil Hills Lifesaving Station is now the setting for Outer Banks Style, Historic Village, (252) 453-4388, a specialty shop in Corolla. The interior doesn't look anything like the old outpost, but the exterior appearance, a peaked roof and crossed timber frame, remains relatively unchanged.

The U.S. Life-Saving Service was established in the late 19th century, and stations were built every 7 miles along the Outer Banks. Crews lived in the wooden structures throughout winter months, patrolling the beaches for shipwrecks and survivors. This station, which was moved almost 30 miles north of its original location, is especially significant because it was frequented by the Wright brothers during their several sojourns to the barrier islands. The Kill Devil Hills Lifesaving Station crew assisted Orville and Wilbur with their early experiments in flight, and some crew members witnessed the world's first powered airplane soar over the sand dunes.

This lifesaving station was brought from Kill Devil Hills to Corolla in 1986, where it was then restored and renovated. History buffs are welcome to visit Outer Banks Style and the lobby of Twiddy & Company Realtors (behind the station), where a collection of memorabilia used by the lifesaving service and the Wrights is on display. This unique, hand-wrought structure is at the foot of the Currituck

Lighthouse on the west side of NC 12 in historic Corolla Village.

The Whalehead Club
Currituck Heritage Park, NC 12, Corolla
(252) 453–9040
www.whaleheadclub.com

Overlooking the windswept wetlands of the Currituck Sound, this grand dame of days gone by was once the Outer Banks's biggest, most modern structure. Today, the Whalehead Club is one of the area's most magnificent attractions and affords a romantic trip back in time to an era of lavish accommodations and elaborate ornamentation.

The house was built as a hunt club between 1922 and 1925, when the Currituck Outer Banks was in its heyday as a waterfowl-hunting paradise. The owners, a wealthy northerner named Edward Collins Knight and his wife, Marie Louise LeBel Knight, originally called their club Corolla Island because the house was situated on

Corolla's Whalehead Club, built in 1925 and recently restored to look exactly as it did when it was first completed, is open for public tours.
PHOTO: HORSLEY/GARDNER

an islandlike mound that was created when a circular canal was dug around the lot. The Knights spend their winters and hunted at Corolla Island between 1925 and 1934.

The 23,000-square-foot house has seen many uses since then. It sat empty for years, as relatives of the Knights were not interested in the remote hunting lodge. In 1940 the house was sold to Ray Adams of Washington, D.C., for a reported $25,000. It was Adams who named the home the Whalehead Club. Adams rented the house to the Coast Guard during World War II, and it was used as a training base headquarters and barracks. From 1959 through 1961, the house was used as a private summer school for boys. Then, from 1963 through 1971, it was used by a rocket-fuel testing company. After that, this grand and beautiful home sat empty for nearly 25 years, often vandalized and pillaged of its furnishings and fixtures.

The house, on the National Register of Historic Places, is now owned by Currituck County and is almost completely restored to the way it looked in 1925 when it was owned by the Knights and called Corolla Island. The $5.6 million restoration project began in 1999, with the replacement of the copper roof. The exterior was painted its original canary yellow. The interior has been completely restored, down to the paint, cork floors, Tiffany glass, and Art Nouveau details. A team of researchers and restoration specialists has tracked down as much information as possible to make the restoration as accurate as possible.

Visitors are welcome and can take a guided tour of the house. The informative tour leads you through the 16-room basement, the main-floor living rooms and kitchen, the staff quarters, and the second-floor bedrooms and baths. A video is shown before the tour, and the guides are knowledgeable about the home and history of the area. The parklike grounds of the Whalehead Club, right alongside the sound, are perfect for a picnic or a rest. The Whalehead Club Museum Shop stocks an interesting array of tasteful Whalehead

Club souvenirs, including picture frames and Christmas ornaments made from the original copper roof.

The Whalehead Club is open from May 1 through October 31 and during the weeks of the Easter, Thanksgiving, and Christmas holidays (not on the actual holidays themselves). Tours of the house are offered daily from 10:30 A.M. until 6:30 P.M., with the last tour beginning at 5:45 P.M. The tours last 45 minutes. Cost is $5.00 for adults and free for children eight and younger.

In 2003 an exciting educational center and museum will open in Corolla: The Outer Banks Center for Wildlife Education. Just across the boat basin from the Whalehead Club, this free museum will inform visitors about waterfowl, ecology, hunting, and fishing.

Currituck Beach Lighthouse
Off NC 12, Corolla
(252) 453–4939
www.currituckbeachlight.com

Visitors can climb the 214 steps to the top of the lighthouse, coming eye-to-eye with the 50,000 candlepower lamp that still flashes every 20 seconds and can be seen for 18 nautical miles. The climb up the narrow, winding staircase is not for the faint of heart, but the trip is worth it. A panoramic view of the Currituck Outer Banks is your reward.

Inside, at the base and on the first two landings, are brand-new exhibits on lighthouses. The museum-quality exhibit panels were installed around Labor Day 2001. They cover the broad history of coastal lighthouses, including all of the North Carolina lighthouses, and give an in-depth history of the Currituck Beach Lighthouse and its buildings. An explanation of the Fresnel lenses is also offered, and a special exhibit on the former Currituck Beach Lighthouse keepers will be added by the summer of 2002.

The Outer Banks's northernmost lighthouse, this red brick beacon was the last lighthouse built on the Outer Banks. In 1872 Congress recognized the need "to

illuminate the dark space" between Bodie Island Lighthouse and Cape Henry, Virginia. In 1873 the U.S. government bought 36 acres next to the tiny village of Corolla, then called Currituck Beach by the locals. Almost a million bricks were laid in the tower, which reached 158 feet to the focal plane and 162 feet to the top. The lighthouse, left unpainted, was lit on December 1, 1875. The first keeper lived in the oil house until the double-sided keepers' house was completed on the site in 1876. The main keeper and his family lived in the south side of the house, and the two assistant keepers and their families lived in the north side of the house. Both the lighthouse and the Keepers' Residence have been restored.

The Lightkeepers' Residence, a beautiful Victorian dwelling, was constructed of pre-cut, labeled materials and was shipped for assembly on site by the U.S. Lighthouse Board. The house was abandoned when the lighthouse was automated in 1939 and keepers were no longer needed on-site. After automation, keepers were still needed to visit once a week to change batteries and perform maintenance. The residence, on the National Register of Historic Places, fell into serious disrepair but was restored by a group known as Outer Banks Conservationists starting in 1980. It is not open for tours, except by appointment during the first two weeks in November.

The current keeper, Ms. Lloyd Childers, has a much different job than her predecessors. Her main duties, among many others, are keeping the lighthouse open for tourists, overseeing preservation work, and hiring volunteers and staff. In 2000, the Currituck Beach Lighthouse celebrated its 125th anniversary as a working lighthouse. Be sure to visit the on-site Museum Shop.

Visitors can climb the lighthouse for a fee of $6.00. Children younger than eight climb for free. School groups and other large groups are offered a discounted rate. The lighthouse is open daily from Easter through Thanksgiving. Climbing hours are 10:00 A.M. to 6:00 P.M. during Eastern Standard Time (generally early April to

The restored Keepers Residence is part of the historic Currituck Beach Lighthouse complex. PHOTO: HORSLEY/
GARDNER

late October) and to 5:00 P.M. during Daylight Savings Time. If you're climbing, you must go up at least 15 minutes before closing time. During periods of lightning or high winds, the lighthouse tower may be closed to climbers.

Corolla Chapel
Old Corolla Village Rd., Corolla
(252) 453–4224

Over 100 years old, the Corolla Chapel, built in 1885, is one of Corolla's most-treasured historic structures. Snuggled into the soundside village, two and a half blocks behind the lighthouse, the chapel served generations of native Corollans in its small sanctuary. Today, there are big changes in store for the small chapel.

In its younger years, the church was used primarily by Missionary Baptists, although originally it was supposed to be interdenominational. Catholic masses were first said at the church in 1917 and continued to be offered on a sporadic basis through the world wars for Coast Guard personnel stationed nearby. In 1938, the Baptists dropped Corolla from their circuit, saying it was too remote, and the church become interdenominational. In the 1960s, as Corolla's population reached its all-time low, the church was no longer used, and it lay idle for 25 years.

The last living trustee of the chapel was John Austin, and when he died, the church passed to the hands of his son, Norris Austin, who still lives in the village. In 1987, as Corolla began to grow again, Austin invited Pastor John Strauss to be the minister of the chapel. Strauss led a restoration of the church, adding a vestibule, bathroom, and storage area in 1992. With regular interdenominational services, he also began to develop a following.

The church has outgrown its small chapel. In the summer months, the quaint village chapel that seats only 100 would have at least that many (or more) people standing outside. On Easter of 2001, Pastor Strauss offered communion to 2,000 people during four services. Therefore, a new church structure was constructed just

across the road from the original chapel location. In order to save the historic building, the Corolla Chapel was moved across the street and melded into the new sanctuary to form the shape of a cross. The new sanctuary has the same tongue-and-groove beaded-board paneling and details as the old one, so that the two blend seamlessly together, inside and out. All of this was under construction during this writing and was expected to be complete by Memorial Day 2002. The new facility will hold 200 to 250 worshippers.

The best way to see the Corolla Chapel, no doubt, would be to attend a service there. Interdenominational services are held year-round on Sunday mornings at 10:00 A.M. From Memorial Day through October, an additional Sunday service is held at 8:30 A.M. A local priest holds Catholic services at the chapel on Wednesday nights at 6:00 P.M., every week in the summer and the second and fourth weeks in the off-season. Four interdenominational services are held on Easter, one on the beach.

Pine Island Audubon Sanctuary
NC 12, between Duck and Corolla, Corolla

Ducks, geese, rabbits, deer, fox, and dozens of other animals make their home in this 5,400-acre wildlife refuge on the northern Outer Banks (between Duck and Corolla). Hundreds of other species fly through the skies during annual migrations. Set between remote villages of sprawling vacation rental cottages, Pine Island Audubon Sanctuary is a secluded outdoor enthusiast's paradise and a major resting area for birds along the great Atlantic flyway.

Live oaks, bayberry, inkberry, pine, yaupon, holly, and several species of marsh grass also grow naturally in this wild, remote wetland habitat. The Pine Island Clubhouse and grounds are privately owned, but if you're a member of the Audubon Society, tours are available.

Hikers, bikers, and strollers can park at Sanderling Inn to access a 2.5-mile clay trail through a portion of the sanctuary.

The path is maintained and is open year-round to the public.

Duck

U.S. Army Corps of Engineers Field Research Facility
NC 12, Duck
(252) 261–6840 ext. 401
frf.usace.army.mil

Set on a former Navy weapons test site, the Waterways Experiment Station of the U.S. Army Corps of Engineers has helped scientists study ocean processes since 1977. This 173-acre federally owned scientific mecca has gained a reputation as one of the premier coastal field research facilities in the world. Just north of Duck village, the site includes state-of-the-art equipment to monitor sand movement, wave forces and water currents, temperatures and sedimentation. Its 12 full-time employees regularly host dozens of scientists from around the globe to conduct experiments on sand movement, beach erosion, and coastal dynamics. In 1997, during the world's largest near-shore research experiment, billed Sandy Duck '97, 250 coastal engineers gathered at the research facility in the most ambitious effort ever undertaken to study the near-shore zone of breaking waves to determine the causes of beach erosion.

The public is invited to tour the research facility from mid-June through mid-August. One free tour is held each day, Monday through Friday, at 10:00 A.M. Reservations are not necessary, and the tour is held rain or shine, except in lightning. The educational tours last about an hour, sometimes longer, and include an eco-lecture about how the sound and ocean waters co-exist, barrier island environments, and ocean currents. Researchers lead the tours onto the beach, into the observation tower, and into the research facility. The public is not allowed on the pier because of the great amount of research equipment there. Since part of the tour is outside on a sandy trail and on the beach, participants should be prepared for a strenuous walk.

Besides the 1,840-foot pier, the U.S. Army Corps of Engineers' experiment station owns a 125-foot observation tower and a 35-foot-tall Coastal Research Amphibious Buggy, the CRAB, which carries people and equipment from the shore into the sea. The Corps works in cooperation with the U.S. Army and Navy and the National Oceanic and Atmospheric Administration, using the latest technically advanced equipment to improve the design of coastal navigation projects. Research conducted at the station could eventually alter the way engineers design bridges; help people pick sites for beach nourishment projects; improve projections about where the shoreline might erode; determine how and why sandbars move; and predict what effect rock jetties might have on Oregon Inlet.

NOTE: Because of the events of September 11, 2001, tours at the research pier were temporarily suspended. Call to find out if tours are available during your visit.

Kitty Hawk

Kitty Hawk Public Beach & Bathhouse
NC 12, MP 4, Kitty Hawk

Across the road from the ocean, a bathhouse and small, free parking area offer visitors access to the beach as soon as they arrive on the Outer Banks at Kitty Hawk. If you arrive too early for check-in, you can change into bathing suits here and enjoy a few hours at the ocean until it's time to head to your hotel or beach cottage. Public showers also are available to rinse off after one last stop in the sand on the way home. Another parking lot is available close by, right off Byrd Street.

Kitty Hawk Village
Along Kitty Hawk Rd., west of US 158, Kitty Hawk

If you want to check out one of the islands' oldest neighborhoods and see where the Wright brothers stayed when they first visited the Outer Banks, head west on Kitty Hawk Road, turning just north of the 7-Eleven in Kitty Hawk. This winding, two-lane street dead-ends after about 3 miles at Kitty Hawk Bay. Drivers pass through at least two centuries in the process.

The old post office for this isolated village still stands on the north side of the road and has been restored to become the town's police station. Several two-story farmhouses still stand along the shady streets and shallow canals. Boats on blocks and fishing nets tied to trees are strewn along backyards. On warm weekend afternoons, families still ride horses down lanes lined with live oaks, waving to neighbors sitting on their covered porches. You can forget you're at the beach in this quaint, quiet community on the western shores of the Outer Banks.

Kill Devil Hills

Wright Brothers National Memorial
**US 158, MP 8, Kill Devil Hills
(252) 441-7430
www.nps.gov/wrbr**

Set atop a steep, grassy sand hill in the center of Kill Devil Hills, the trapezoidal granite monument to Orville and Wilbur Wright is within easy walking distance of the site of the world's first powered airplane flight. Below where this lighthouse-style tower now stands, on the blustery afternoon of December 17, 1903, the two bicycle-building brothers from Dayton, Ohio, changed history by soaring over a distance of more than 852 feet and staying airborne for an unheard-of 59 seconds in their homemade flying machine. The monument was erected in Orville and Wilbur Wright's honor in 1932.

In the low, domed building on the right side of the main drive off US 158, the National Park Service operates a visitor center, gift shop, and museum. Here, you can view interpretive exhibits of humankind's first flight and see displays on later aviation advancements. Exhibits about the Wright brothers' struggles to fly include parts of their planes, engines, and research notes. Reproductions of their gliders are displayed in the flight room, and rangers offer free guided historical tours year-round.

The visitor center is itself an attraction. Opened in 1960, the visitor center is recognized as a significant example of modernist architecture. It's one of only a handful of examples of modernist architecture built in eastern North Carolina during the 20th century, mainly because the National Park Service was one of a few groups in the region that had the financial resources to hire architects from outside the region.

The Philadelphia architectural firm of Ehrman Mitchell and Romaldo Giurgola designed the building to reflect the natural environment of the Outer Banks and symbolically portray flight in static form. The horizontal roof with a shallow concrete dome reflects the surrounding landscape of beach and dunes, while the overhang of the dome represents the soaring possibilities of flight. The National Historic Register-listed structure is considered a key work in the Philadelphia School of expressive modernist architects. At this writing, the visitor center was closed due to roof leaks, and a temporary visitor center, museum, and gift shop was set up on-site. The National Park Service hopes to have the repairs completed by Memorial Day of 2002.

Outside the exhibit center, four markers set along a sandy runway commemorate the takeoff and landing sites of each of Orville and Wilbur's December 17 flights. Reconstructed wooden sheds replicating those used at the Wrights' 1903 camp and hangar also are on the grounds and open to visitors. These sheds are furnished with tools, equipment, and even cans of milk like the brothers used.

A short hike takes you from the visitor center to the monument hill, but if you'd rather drive or ride, parking is available closer to the base of the hill. Paved walkways make access easy. Cacti and sand spurs abound in the grass, so you're advised to stay on the paths. Also, be wary that the walk up the monument hill is longer and more strenuous than it looks, so it's best to go at a leisurely pace. On a hot summer day, consider visiting the site in the morning or late afternoon, when the sun is not as strong. This seemingly simple structure is most powerful when you can really contemplate the immensity of the brothers' accomplishment.

Besides tours, the Exhibit Center at the Wright Brothers National Memorial offers a variety of summer programs. Grounds and buildings are open to vehicles from 9:00 A.M. until 5:00 P.M. Labor Day through Memorial Day. Hours are from 9:00 A.M. to 6:00 P.M. in the summer. Thirty-minute flight-room talks are given by rangers every hour on the hour, year-round. Expect it to take about an hour to two hours to tour the visitor center and bookstore, walk the grounds, and climb up to the monument.

Cost for entry at the guard gate is $2.00 per person or $4.00 per vehicle, and admission is good for seven days. Persons age 16 and younger get in free, as do seniors with Golden Age Passports and other passports, which are available at the gate.

On the centennial of the first flight, December 17, 2003, the world will focus on the Outer Banks and the Wright Brothers National Memorial, as thousands of people are expected to visit the site. The First Flight Centennial Foundation is already planning a variety of events for the celebration. For more information, see our Close-up in the History chapter.

Kitty Hawk Aero Tours
Behind the Wright Memorial,
off Colington Rd., Kill Devil Hills
(252) 441–4460

For a bird's-eye view of the Outer Banks and a unique perspective on how fragile the barrier islands really are, take a 30-minute air tour over the land and ocean in a small plane.

A short runway and parking lot sit behind the Wright Brothers monument. In front of a tiny ticket booth, blue and yellow airplanes beckon adventurers to fly the same skies that hosted the world's first flight. Pilots will gear tours to passengers' wishes but usually head south to Bodie Island Lighthouse and back. Views are breathtaking, and the experience is one that's not to be missed. Bring your camera for this high-flying cruise.

Rates are $29 per person for parties of three to six and $39 per person for parties of two.

Biplane flights in an open-air-cockpit authentic 1941 Waco are also available from the same site starting at $68 per person. These 15-minute trips take you back in time, complete with goggled leather helmets. Pilots fly south to Bodie Island Lighthouse and back to the Wright Brothers monument.

Air tours are offered year-round, weather permitting. Advance reservations are accepted.

Nags Head Woods Ecological Preserve
Ocean Acres Dr., Kill Devil Hills
(252) 441–2525
www.nature.org

If you've had a little too much sun, or if you'd just like to spend time in a secluded forest on a part of the Outer Banks few people get to see, allocate an afternoon for The Nature Conservancy's Nags Head Woods Preserve, west of US 158. The maritime forest itself is well hidden, and many rare plant and animal species abound within this protected landscape. It's one of the most tranquil settings on the Outer Banks.

The Nature Conservancy, an international, nonprofit conservation organization, oversees this maritime forest. Nags Head Woods is not a park—it is an example of a successful private-public partnership between The Nature Conservancy, the Towns of Nags Head and Kill Devil Hills, and private landowners.

More than 5 miles of trails and footbridges wind through forest, dune, swamp, and pond habitats as well as graveyards and farm sites from the 19th and 20th centuries. Trails are open to visitors on weekdays from 10:00 A.M. to 3:00 P.M., while members of The Nature Conservancy are welcome during any daylight hours. There is a small visitor center and gift shop near the parking lot. Staff members offer a variety of field excursions, including guided walks, day camps for children, and kayaking during warm months. No camping, firearms, picnicking, or alcoholic beverages are allowed in the preserve. Bicycling, pets on leashes, and other activities that might damage the trails are restricted to the Old Nags Head Woods Road, which winds from north to south through the woods.

Write to The Nature Conservancy at 701 West Ocean Acres Drive, Kill Devil Hills, North Carolina 27948. All donations are welcome, and memberships start at $25. Monies support the preserve's environmental education and research programs.

Nags Head

Jockey's Ridge State Park
US 158, MP 12, Nags Head
(252) 441-7132
www.jockeysridgestatepark.com

The East Coast's tallest sand dune and one of the Outer Banks's most phenomenal natural attractions, Jockey's Ridge has been a favorite stop for tourists for more than 150 years. In the early 1970s, bulldozers began flattening the surrounding dunes to make way for a housing subdivision. A Nags Head woman, Carolista Baum, single-handedly stopped the destruction and formed a committee that saved Jockey's Ridge.

The top of a castle is all that remains of this miniature golf attraction that was slowly swallowed up by the Jockey's Ridge sand dune. PHOTO: COURTESY OF BOB REARDON

Insiders' Tip

Save your soles! The sand on the dunes at Jockey's Ridge State Park can be 30 degrees hotter than the air on summer days. Wear shoes. By the way, flips flops are worthless in the soft sand.

State officials made the sand hill a protected park in 1975, but the dunes are unruly subjects. The sand mountains have migrated southwest in fits and starts over the decades. In the past 25 years, the steepest side of the hill has shifted more than 1,500 feet to the southwest. Jockey's Ridge is also getting shorter. At the turn of the century, the highest mound was estimated at 140 feet tall. In 1971, it was about 110 feet tall. Development has blocked replenishment of the sand, and nearby grasses have caught the blowing sand before it reaches the ridge.

Today, the 1.5-mile-long, 420-acre-plus dune—which varies from 90 feet to 110 feet in height—is open to the public year-round until sunset. It's a popular spot for hang gliders, summer hikers, small children who like to roll down the steep slopes, and teenagers who delight in sand-boarding or flinging and flipping themselves dramatically down the sandy hills. Sand-boarding is allowed only from October 31 through March 31. In 1999, over one million people visited Jockey's Ridge.

Park headquarters is near the northern end of a parking lot off the west side of US 158. You'll notice an entrance sign at MP 12, Carolista Drive, in Nags Head.

A visitor center, museum, and gift shop are near park headquarters. Centered around the theme of wind and how it affects Jockey's Ridge, the free museum features photo displays of the history and recreation at the dune and a diorama of the animals that inhabit the area. Information panels of plants and animals and an auditorium where slide shows and videos are shown is also at the facility. Maps available from the park ranger indicate walking areas. Two trails—the Soundside Nature Trail, a very easy 45-minute walk, and Tracks in the Sand, a 1.5-mile trek—are on-site for hikers looking for a change of scenery. Jockey's Ridge State Park offers natural history programs throughout the summer, including stargazing and wildlife discovery evening hikes and early-morning bird-watching and natural history discovery adventures. Fantastic educational programs for kids are also offered, but rangers warn that they fill up fast and many require advance registration. Call for program schedules. Sheltered picnic areas also are available for leisurely lunches.

It's a long, hot hike to the top of the ridge, but it's well worth the work. Bring shoes or boots. Don't try it barefoot in summer; you'll burn your feet. Also, some lower areas around the dune are covered with broken glass. From the top of Jockey's Ridge, you can see both ocean and sound. Cottages along the beach look like tiny huts from a miniature train set. Kite-flying and hang-gliding enthusiasts catch the breezes that flow constantly around the steep summit, shifting the sand in all directions. Kitty Hawk Kites, a large store just across the street from Jockey's Ridge, has the largest selection of kites you'll probably ever see. Many people buy a kite and then head over to Jockey's Ridge, where they're always able to find an open space of their own to fly it. Kitty Hawk Kites is also an on-site hang-gliding concessionaire within the park, offering lessons and rentals to experienced fliers. See our Recreation chapter for information on hang-gliding. The desert-like appearance of the sand dunes reveals strange but artistic patterns of winds and of footprints made by people climbing the hills.

If your mobility is impaired, there's a 360-foot boardwalk that affords wheelchairs and baby strollers a slightly sloping incline onto a wooden platform overlooking the center of the dune. For the visually impaired, audio guides are available at the park office. Park rangers can also provide a ride on a four-wheeler to the top of the dune if you call in advance.

The park opens at 8:00 A.M. every day except Christmas. Closing time depends on the season: November through February, 6:00 P.M.; March and October, 7:00 P.M.; April, May, and September, 8:00 P.M.; and June through August, 9:00 P.M.

This is sunset-watching central, especially in the summer months. Literally hundreds of people climb the dunes to watch the sun sink into the Roanoke Sound. There's also a soundside access on the southwest side of Jockey's Ridge. This provides access to a great beach on the gentle sound waters.

Newman's Shell Shop
NC 12, MP 13½, Nags Head
(252) 441-5791

This bright pink establishment on the ocean side of the Beach Road is an Outer Banks shell shop, tourist attraction, and local museum. Newman's was the first store on the beach, opening in 1939. It has remained a family-owned business throughout the years and stocks shells from all over the world. The owners display a labeled collection of shells from as far away as India and Peru. A large variety of gifts, local and imported crafts, and accessories also are arranged in attractive displays.

Wind chimes, shell sculptures, and jewelry made from ocean artifacts abound at this charming seaside shop. There's even a display of antique guns, pistols, and swords that have been in the family for many years. After being in business for more than a half-century, Newman's has supplied thousands of Outer Banks visitors with reminders of their summer sojourns to the beautiful barrier island beaches.

Besides shells and crafts, many of which are made on the premises, Newman's is known for its hermit crabs. On the last Saturday in July, the shop hosts a Hermit Crab Race that has become increasingly popular with the younger set

(see our Annual Events chapter). So select your crustacean critter early and start training for the big event.

Newman's Shell Shop is open seven days a week in season. See our Shopping chapter for related information.

Nags Head Beach Cottage Row Historic District
NC 12, MP 12–13 , Nags Head

The long row of rustic, weather-worn cottages on the ocean in Nags Head around mileposts 12 and 13 are famously known as the "Unpainted Aristocracy," a moniker given them by a writer. The row of homes has been on the National Register of Historic Places since 1977. These homes are what people think of when they think of "Nags Head style"—cedar siding that has grayed in the wind and salt, wrap-around porches, propped-open shutters, dormers, gabled roofs, and obviously added-on rooms to accommodate growing families. Although Nags Head was a vacation destination earlier, it wasn't until 1855 that an Elizabeth City doctor built the first house on the oceanfront at Nags Head. He was lonely on the oceanfront, so he sold the land around him to other people who vacationed in the wooded area by the sound. By 1885 there were 13 homes at the ocean's edge. Many of the cottages are still in the original families. Nine of the original 13 are still standing. Two were replaced with similar structures, one was destroyed by fire, and one was razed. Several of the other cottages in the mile-long row between mileposts 12 and 13, though not of the original 13 homes, are historic in their own rights, having survived since the early 1900s. The land around these homes is private, and the homes are occupied. Feel free to drive by and admire, or walk by and admire from the beach, but please respect the owners' privacy and don't trespass on their property.

Gallery Row
Between US 158 and NC 12, MP 10½, Nags Head

Nags Head has its own cultural corner in a grouping of galleries known as Gallery

Row. Tucked between the highways around milepost 10½ are 10 galleries within walking distance of one another. You'll find Glenn Eure's Ghost Fleet Gallery, Ann's Beach Crafts, Sally Huss Gallery, The Lighthouse Gallery, Jewelry By Gail, Gallery Row Consignment Gallery, Morales Art Gallery, Anna Gatrell's Gallery By the Sea, and Ipso Facto Gallery, which also houses the John de la Vega Gallery. Nearby are two more galleries, Seaside Art Gallery and Something Fishy. That's a whole day's worth of browsing and shopping. Park the car and walk around. You'll enjoy meeting all the friendly gallery owners, often the artists themselves. Most of these shops are open year-round. For more information about galleries, see our Arts and Culture chapter. A green sign on the east side of US 158 will direct you to Gallery Row. Look for streets named Driftwood and Gallery Row.

Roanoke Island

Roanoke Island is brimming with attractions. Anyone visiting the Outer Banks should definitely come over for the day, though with many new bed-and-breakfasts, restaurants, and shops in town, it's becoming more of an overnight destination in its own right. There are more attractions here than you can see in one day, so overnighting here is a good way to see it all.

If you're planning to visit many of the attractions on Roanoke Island, a Roanoke Island Attractions Pass or Queen's Pass will save you up to 25 percent of the admission fees. The Attractions Pass combines admission to the North Carolina Aquarium, The Elizabethan Gardens, and Roanoke Island Festival Park for $14 for adults and $8 for children ages five and older. The Queen's Pass allows admission to the same three attractions, plus *The Lost Colony*, for $28 for adults and $14 for ages five and older. Children younger than five can visit all of these attractions except *The Lost Colony* for free. The passes are good for one calendar year and are available at the local attractions and the Outer Banks Visitor Bureau.

The Elizabethan Gardens
Off US 64, Roanoke Island
(252) 473-3234

Created by the Garden Club of North Carolina Inc. in 1960 to commemorate the efforts of Raleigh's colonists at establishing an English settlement, these magnificent botanical gardens offer an exquisite, aromatic environment year-round. They include 10½ acres of the state's most colorful, dazzling flora. The flower-filled walkways are the perfect contrast to the windblown, barren Outer Banks beaches.

Six full-time gardeners tend more than 1,000 varieties of immaculately manicured trees, shrubs, and flowers in the Elizabethan Gardens, which you'll find north of Manteo. The tree-lined landscape is divided into a dozen gardens, where translucent emerald grass fringes marble fountains, and beauty blooms from every crevice.

Visitors enter at the Great Gate into formal gardens along curving walkways carefully crafted from brick and sand. The bricks were handmade at the Silas Lucas Kiln, in operation during the late 1800s in Wilson, North Carolina.

Although this botanical refuge is breathtakingly beautiful all year, offering different colors and fragrances depending on the season, it is perhaps the most striking in spring. Azaleas, dogwood, pansies, wisteria, and tulips bloom around every bend. Rhododendron, roses, lacecap, and other hydrangea appear in May. Summer brings fragrant gardenias, colorful annuals and perennials, magnolia, crape myrtle, Oriental lilies, and herbs. Chrysanthemums and the changing colors of leaves signal the beginning of fall and camellias bloom from late fall all the way through the winter.

In the center of the paths, six marble steps down from the rest of the greenery, the crown jewel of the Elizabethan Gardens awaits discovery. A sunken garden, complete with Roman statuary, tiered fountains, and low shrubs pruned into geometric flower frames springs from the sandy soil. The famous Virginia Dare

Take a peaceful stroll through the Elizabethan Gardens. PHOTO: COURTESY OF ROANOKE ISLAND FESTIVAL PARK

statue nearby is based on an Indian legend that says Virginia, the first English child born in America, grew up among Native Americans (see the Roanoke Island section of our Area Overviews chapter).

A wonderful treat is to see a performance of *Elizabeth R* in the gardens. This one-woman, hour-long show features Queen Elizabeth I in her full regalia and is held on summer Tuesdays at 5:00 P.M. (See more about *Elizabeth R* later in this chapter.)

The gardens are closed Thanksgiving Day, Christmas Eve, Christmas Day, and New Year's Day. From March through November, the gardens open at 9:00 A.M., and closing time varies depending on the season (between 5 and 7:00 P.M.). The gardens are open daily from 10:00 A.M. to 4:00 P.M. in December, January, and February. When *The Lost Colony* is running, the gardens stay open until 8:00 P.M. so that visitors can tour the gardens then head next door to see the outdoor drama. Admission is $5.00 for adults, $1.00 for youths 6 through 18, $4.50 for adults aged 62 and older, and free for children younger than 5 when accompanied by an adult. Season passes are available for $15.00.

Wheelchairs are provided. Most paths are wheelchair-accessible. Some plants are for sale in the garden gift shop. A meeting room is available for a fee to community groups up to 100 people. The gardens also are a favorite wedding locale (see our Weddings chapter).

Fort Raleigh National Historic Site
Off US 64, Roanoke Island
(252) 473-5772
www.nps.gov/fora

When you visit Fort Raleigh, don't expect to see a fort. What exists on the site is a small earthworks fortification. It is not a daunting barricade, but a lovely spot drenched in American history. On the north end of Roanoke Island, near the Roanoke Sound's shores, Fort Raleigh marks the beginning of English settlement in North America. Since this attraction is next to the Elizabethan Gardens and *The Lost Colony*'s Waterside Theatre, many people combine a trip to all three.

Designated as a National Historic Site in 1941, this more than 500-acre expanse of woods includes the "outerwork"—an area built intentionally away from living space, a soundside beach, the National Park Service's Cape Hatteras National Seashore headquarters, the Fort Raleigh Visitor Center, and nature trails.

The Fort Raleigh Visitor Center offers interpretive exhibits in a small museum. The museum is not particularly interesting to children, though adults will be fascinated by the story of the colonists who attempted the first English settlements in the New World. A 17-minute video provides an introduction to the historic site. Also, a 400-year-old Elizabethan room from Heronden Hall in Kent, England, is on display. It was removed from an authentic 16th-century home. The room gives visitors a feel for the type of living accommodations the aristocratic English were used to living in at the time of the attempted settlements. The furnishings, carved mantelpiece, paneling, stone fireplace, and blown glass offer a glimpse of America's origins across the ocean. There's also a gallery inside, with artifacts excavated from the site and copies of watercolors by John White, governor of the Roanoke colony.

Outside, Fort Raleigh has a variety of options for experiencing the history of Roanoke Island. Behind the visitor center is the earthworks, which is not very impressive, but gives you an idea of the original. The Thomas Hariot Nature Trail, named for the scientist who accompanied one of the voyages, winds through the woods behind the visitor center. Hariot's descriptions of the New World are quoted on interpretive signs along the trail. The pine-needle path leads to the sandy shores of the Roanoke Sound.

Self-guided tours and tours led by Park Service personnel are available at this archaeologically significant site. Interpretive programs on African-American history, European colonial history, Native American history, and Civil War history are offered in the summer. Fort Raleigh National Historic Site is open year-round from 9:00 A.M. to 5:00 P.M. seven days a week. Hours are extended in the summer. The grounds of Fort Raleigh provide an excellent place for a picnic, especially under the huge live oaks on the grass median of the parking lot. Restrooms are on-site.

Freedmen's Colony Site, Weirs Point, and Fort Huger
North end of Roanoke Island, Roanoke Island
(252) 473-5772

At the northernmost end of Roanoke Island, on the east side of the Manns Harbor bridge, are several historic landmarks that are part of the Fort Raleigh National Historic Site. You can access these sites by the Freedmen's Trail, a 2-mile, self-guided trail that starts near The Elizabethan Gardens entrance. You can get there by car and park in the sizable lot, or ride a bike along the Manteo Bike Path, which ends at this site. Weirs Point is an attractive public beach on the Croatan Sound. The beach here is wide enough to allow for a picnic or game of Frisbee, and the sound water is warm and shallow. Picnic benches, a Dare County information kiosk, and restrooms are provided at Weirs Point. Watch for stumps and broken stakes in the water. The tide creeps up quickly, so keep blankets out of its encroaching flow.

Next to the beach is an exhibit about the Freedmen's Colony, a community for runaway slaves between 1862 and 1867. During the Civil War, Roanoke Island was seized by Union soldiers in 1862. After that, runaway slaves were welcomed on the island, and were even given food and allowed to settle in the Union camp. Slaves from all over northeastern North Carolina flocked to the safe haven. The freed slaves worked for the Union forces for $10.00 a month plus rations and clothing. Women and children were paid $4.00 a month. In 1863 the colony was officially established, and the freed slaves were given land and agricultural tools. Many of the freed slaves joined the Union effort, but the ones who remained behind were given health and education services. By 1866, however, most of the freedmen were forced to leave. Exhibits at the site explain the story.

In 1901, from a hut on Weirs Point beach, one of the unsung geniuses of the electronic age began investigating what was then called "wireless telegraphy." Reginald Fessenden held hundreds of patents on radiotelepathy and electronics, but he died without any credit for many of them. In a letter dated "April 3, 1902, Manteo," Fessenden tells his patent attorney that "I can now telephone as far as I can telegraph . . . I have sent varying musical notes from Hatteras and received them here with but 3 watts of energy." Thus, the world's first musical radio broadcasts were completed on this soundside sand of the Outer Banks.

About 300 yards north of Weirs Point, in 6 feet of water, lay the remains of Fort Huger. This was the largest Confederate fort on the island when Union troops advanced in 1862. The island has migrated quite a bit in the last 130 years; the fort used to sit securely on solid land.

The Lost Colony
Off US 64, Waterside Theatre, Roanoke Island
(252) 473-3414, (800) 488-5012
www.thelostcolony.org

The nation's longest running outdoor drama, this historical account of the first English settlement in North America is a must-see for Outer Banks visitors. It's almost as legendary as the story it depicts. Pulitzer Prize–winning author Paul Green brought the history of English colonization to life through an impressive combination of Elizabethan music, Native American dances, colorful costumes, and vivid drama on a soundside stage in 1937. His play continues to enchant audiences today at Waterside Theatre, near Fort Raleigh, on Roanoke Island.

The Lost Colony is a theatrical account of Sir Walter Raleigh's early explorers who first settled on the shores near the present-day theater in 1585. (Andy Griffith got his start playing Sir Walter Raleigh for several seasons.) Children and adults are equally captivated by the performers, staging, and music; many locals see the show every year and always find it spellbinding. If you have youngsters, come early and have them sit in the very front row by the stage. They'll

Elizabeth R, a one-woman drama starring Miss Barbara Hird, is performed in the Elizabethan Gardens on Tuesdays in mid-summer. PHOTO: MIKE BOOHER

never stop talking about it! The closer you sit to the stage, the more you'll enjoy the show.

In 2001, *The Lost Colony* got a boon when Tony Award–nominated Broadway actor Terrance Mann agreed to direct the show. Mann, who has held principal roles in *Cats, Les Miserables, Beauty and the Beast,* and *The Scarlet Pimpernel*, performed in *The Lost Colony* as a dancer and in the role of Old Tom before making it big on Broadway. Mann made many changes to the play, returning many of the nostalgic nuances of the glory days of the show. Mann will return as director for the 2002 season. Another famous name associated with the show is William Ivey Long, who won a second Tony Award in 2001 for his costume design work on *The Producers*. Long has been the costume designer for *The Lost Colony* for 15 years and has been associated with the show since a young boy when his parents worked on the show. Mann and Long are joined by a cast and crew of 125, some of them locals but most of them imported to Roanoke Island for the summer.

It can get chilly in the evenings when the wind blows off the sound, so we recommend sweaters, even in July and August. Mosquitoes at this outdoor drama also can be vicious, especially after a rain, so bring plenty of bug repellent. The theater is wheelchair-accessible and the staff is glad to accommodate special customers.

Once you arrive, settle back and enjoy a thoroughly professional, well-rehearsed, technically outstanding show. The leads are played by professional actors. Most of the backstage personnel are pros too—and it shows. Supporting actors are often locals, with some island residents passing from part to part as they grow up. On August 18, four local infants are chosen to participate in the play in honor of Virginia Dare's birthday.

The drama has changed its pricing structure and is now charging slightly more for the best seats in the house (though the theater is so well designed they're all pretty good). All seats in The Producer's Circle, Rows O through T, which offer the most panoramic view of the show, are $20.00. General Admission seats are $16.00 for adults, $15.00 for seniors 62 and older, and $8.00 for children 11 and younger. Family night is held on Monday night, and children are admitted at half price ($4.00). Groups of 20 or more may reserve seats for $14.00 each. Group reservations must be made in advance.

The show begins at 8:30 P.M. and runs each night of the week (except for Sundays) from May 31 through August 23.

This is probably the most popular summertime event on the Outer Banks, and we recommend you make reservations, though you can try your luck at the door if you wish. You can make paid mail reservations by writing *The Lost Colony*, 1409 U.S. Highway 64/264, Manteo, North Carolina 27954; or you can reserve tickets by phone. Tickets can also be purchased at 70 outlets across the Outer Banks. Call for locations. If a production is rained out, ticket holders can come back any other night any other week, month, or year.

North Carolina Aquarium on Roanoke Island
374 Airport Rd., Roanoke Island
(252) 473-3494
www.ncaquariums.com

After a $16 million expansion completed in May 2000, the North Carolina Aquarium on Roanoke Island is better than ever! If you haven't been lately, you need to go back. If you've never been, what are you waiting for? It took two years to complete this extraordinary expansion, with the aquarium closed for an entire year, but all visitors agree it was worth the wait. Close to 437,000 people toured the facility in the first year after the re-opening.

The theme of the 68,000-square-foot aquarium is Waters of the Outer Banks, and visitors get to see a variety of marine communities: coastal freshwaters, wetlands, estuaries, roadside ditches, the Gulf Stream, and the Graveyard of the Atlantic on the ocean floor.

A major attraction here is the Graveyard of the Atlantic tank, holding 285,000 gallons of salt water, or about 2.35 million pounds. It takes 209 pilings sunk about 35 feet into the ground to support the weight of this enormous tank. The tank's highlight is a 53-foot-long replica of a Civil War Ironclad, the USS *Monitor*. The wreck is so realistic that the exhibit's reef fish try to find a meal amongst the fabricated corals and sponges. Expert scuba divers who have seen the real *Monitor* wreck say the replica is extremely accurate. Scuba divers give educational presentations from the tank and answer spectators' questions while inside the tank. Also in the tank are sea turtles and nearly 1,000 other sea creatures, including sharks, cobia, tarpon, jack crevalle, bluefish, and black and red drum.

Wetlands on the Edge is one of the favorite exhibits. In this tree-filled atrium, two adorable river otters swim and play in a clear pool of river water, and visitors can watch them through a glass screen. The male river otter is about four years old, and his female counterpart is over a year old and was brought to the aquarium in 2001. It is hoped they will mate and produce some more river otters for the exhibit. Also here are several American alligators, who like to bask in the sunlight near their pond. You'll also see turtles here.

There are exciting things to see around every corner. The Coastal Freshwaters exhibit explores freshwater marine animals and habitats. From ponds and lakes to the Albemarle Sound, this exhibit displays turtles, sunfish, gars, and bowfins. The Croatan Sound tank showcases the fishes that local anglers catch. Marine Communities features nine tanks representing environments from grass flats to the Gulf Stream. You will see blue crabs, summer flounder, puppy drum, lobster, a porcupine puffer, and much more. Close Encounters is the touch tank area, where kids can touch horseshoe crabs and other creatures. Staff is on hand to answer questions. We love the area where you can watch a live video of an osprey family in its nest. The ospreys have nested at the aquarium for over 20 years, and there's video camera installed above their nest site.

Walk outside, behind the aquarium, and you're right on the banks of the Roanoke Sound. There are benches for resting, or you can walk along a path through the trees. Bleached-white whale bones on display form a natural sculpture garden. Along the short path, interactive exhibits will teach you about the birds and plant life of the area.

The aquarium offers educational films, lectures, and classes year-round. Field trips to nearby salt marshes and fishing areas are available with a fee. For information about daily programs or special activities, such as crabbing classes, call (252) 473–3494, ext. 242. The gift shop is a real treasure, with a multitude of toys that teach children to think and become environmentally aware. Posters, stuffed animals, gifts, souvenirs, puzzles, games, T-shirts, and more are top-quality and based on a natural theme.

The North Carolina Aquarium on Roanoke Island is open year-round from 9:00 A.M. to 5:00 P.M. daily, except Christmas and New Year's Days. Prices are $5.00 for adults, $4.00 for seniors and active military personnel, and $3.00 for children under age six. Preregistered school groups are granted free admission.

Old Swimming Hole
Airport Rd., Roanoke Island
(252) 473–1101 ext. 313

Right next door to the aquarium is a great soundside beach with lots of amenities. This is a great place to go for a swim after a visit to the aquarium. The county facility has a nice beach, picnic tables, grills, a picnic shelter, a kids' playground, a sand volleyball court, and restrooms. The beach is lifeguarded from 10:00 A.M. to 6:00 P.M. between Memorial and Labor Days. Families with small kids love the calm sound waters.

Elizabeth R / Bloody Mary and the Virgin Queen
The Elizabethan Gardens and the Pioneer
Theatre, Roanoke Island and downtown Manteo
(252) 473–1061

Adding to the cultural delights of Roanoke Island are the finely crafted short plays

Elizabeth R and *Bloody Mary and the Virgin Queen*. Performed by the acclaimed Miss Barbara Hird, these two dramatic performances offer insight into the life of Queen Elizabeth I. *Elizabeth R* is an internationally acclaimed one-woman show that examines the private life of Elizabeth Tudor, or Queen Elizabeth I. During the hour-long performance, the queen, dressed in her full regalia, gives the private details of her life, including her likes and dislikes, the basis behind her decisions, and information about the people around her. *Elizabeth R* is a tasteful production set in the tranquil atmosphere of The Elizabethan Gardens. Performances are held at 5:00 p.m. on Tuesdays from June through August. Seating is on the lawn, and you'll need your own blankets or beach chairs. The performance is moved indoors in hot or rainy weather. Tickets are $8.00 and include the gardens tour.

Bloody Mary and the Virgin Queen is a humorous musical farce based on the relationship between Queen Elizabeth I and her half-sister Mary Tudor. The two absolutely loathed one another, yet they're buried in the same tomb in London's Westminster Abbey. This drama takes place in the tomb in the present day, after all the tourists have gone home. Through fast-paced dialogue of bantering, arguing, cajoling, singing, crying, and laughing, the two actors will teach you a history lesson in a most entertaining way. Barbara Hird plays Elizabeth, and Marsha Warren plays Mary. *Bloody Mary* is held at the Pioneer Theatre on Budleigh Street in downtown Manteo during July and August. Performances are on Wednesday afternoons at 3:30 P.M. Tickets cost $8.00, and the performance is about an hour long. Neither of these performances is suitable for young children. While the dialogue is witty and interesting for adults, there really isn't enough action for short attention spans.

Mother Vineyard
Off Mother Vineyard Rd., Roanoke Island

The oldest-known grapevine in the United States grows on Roanoke Island. When the first settlers arrived here, the Outer Banks were covered with wild grapes. Arthur Barlowe wrote to Sir Walter Raleigh in 1584:

"... Being where we first landed very sandy and low toward the water side, but so full of grapes as the very beating and surge of the sea overflowed them, of which we found such plenty, as well there as in all places else, both on the sand and on the green soil, on the hills as in the plains, as well on every little shrub, as also climbing toward the tops of high cedars, that I think in all the world the like abundance is not to be found."

The Mother Vine is one of those ancient grapevines, so old that it may have been planted even before Europeans arrived in the New World. Certainly it was already old in the 1750s, as records attest, and scuppernong grape vines do not grow swiftly. Another story is that this vine was transplanted to Roanoke Island by some of the Fort Raleigh settlers. Whichever story is true, the Mother Vine is more than 400 years old, and it's still producing fine fat, tasty grapes. In fact, for many years, a small winery owned by the Etheridge family cultivated the vine on Baum's Point, making the original Mother Vineyard wine until the late 1950s.

Mother Vineyard Scuppernong, the Original American Wine, is still produced by a company in Petersburg, Virginia. It is a pink wine, quite sweet, similar to a white port or Mogen David.

The Mother Vine is on private property and a bit out of the way. To find it, drive north from Manteo on US 64. About .75 miles past the city limits, turn right on Mother Vineyard Road. Go less than a half-mile, where the road makes a sharp turn to the right at the sound. About 300 feet past the turn, on the left, the patient old vine crouches beneath a canopy of leaves, twisted and gnarled, ancient and enduring. Please stay on the road if you're sneaking a peek.

Downtown Manteo
Off US 64, Queen Elizabeth Ave., Budleigh and Sir Walter Raleigh Sts., Manteo

Named for a Roanoke Island Native American who accompanied English explorers back to Great Britain in the 16th century, Manteo is one of the oldest Outer Banks communities and has long been a commercial and governmental hub for the area.

When Dare County was formed in 1870, this area along Shallowbag Bay became the county seat. Roanoke Island provided a central location that everyone could reach by boat. It wasn't until 1873, when a post office was established here, that the county seat became known as Manteo. In 1899 Manteo incorporated and became the Town of Manteo. Today hundreds of permanent residents make this Roanoke Island town their home, and many more county residents commute here from other towns to work. On Budleigh Street, many of the county and town offices are scattered in older office buildings up and down the street. Restaurants, shops, and bed-and-breakfast inns beckon tourists, and thousands of visitors arrive each summer to explore this historic waterfront village. (See the Roanoke Island section of our Area Overviews chapter.)

On the docks of Manteo's waterfront, 53 modern dockside slips with 110- and 220-volt electrical hookups offer boaters overnight or long-term anchorage. A comfort station with restrooms, showers, washers, and dryers also serves vessel crews and captains. There's plenty of shopping and dining within walking distance in Manteo—or better yet, break out the bikes. This is the perfect town to enjoy on your two-wheeler.

Across the street from the waterfront, in the center of the downtown area, independently owned shops, eateries, and businesses offer everything from handmade pottery to books to clothing, all in a four-square-block area.

Around the southeast point of the waterfront, the town's American Bicentennial Park is tucked in between the courthouse and a four-story brick building that houses shops and condominiums. There's an emotionally moving inscription under the cross. Picnic benches afford a comfortable place to rest and enjoy the view across the bay to Roanoke Island Festival Park, where the state's 16th-century representative sailing ship *Elizabeth II* rocks gently on small sound waves. A wood-plank boardwalk leads along the town's waterfront. One end is bustling, with kayak and boat tours coming and going, boaters docking up in the harbor, and tourists strolling along the docks or ducking in and out of shops and restaurants. Around the corner, there's a gazebo for resting and a long pier for fishing or crabbing. A children's playground with lots of equipment is on the corner, as are picnic tables. Down at the far end of the docks, you'll find a bit of serenity, where the activity dies down and the only company you'll have is a few cattails.

If, as most visitors do, you reach the Banks via US 158, you can get to Manteo by continuing south until you reach Whalebone Junction. Bear right onto US 64 at the traffic light near RV's restaurant. Continue across the causeway and high-rise bridge past Pirate's Cove, then bear right at the Y-intersection, staying on US 64. Turn right at either of the town's first two stoplights to go downtown.

Roanoke Island Festival Park and the *Elizabeth II*
1 Festival Park, Manteo
(252) 475-1500, (252) 475-1506 24-hour events line
www.roanokeisland.com

An expansion of the *Elizabeth II* Historic Site, Roanoke Island Festival Park is one of the largest attractions on the Outer Banks. This vibrant new history, educational, and cultural arts complex opened completely in 1998, with top-quality facilities that add a tremendous variety to the year-round offerings on Roanoke Island. It remains lively almost year-round, rain or shine, day and night, with a dazzling array of programs that seem to come at you from everywhere once you cross the little bridge from the Manteo waterfront.

Visitors can explore the evolution of Roanoke Island and the Outer Banks from the late 16th century through the early 1900s through living history interpretation, exhibits, film, and visual and performing arts programs.

The site includes the 8,500-square-foot Roanoke Adventure Museum where interactive displays allow you to touch, see, and hear the history of the Outer Banks. In the Film Theater, *The Legend of Two Path,* a 45-minute film developed especially for the site by the North Carolina School of the Arts, tells the story of the first English landing on Roanoke Island from the Native American point of view. There's an outdoor performance pavilion that offers classical and popular concerts on lush pastoral lawns; a gallery, with art shows that change monthly; a small theater where special films and plays are held in an intimate setting; and a museum store bursting with treasures. The porches, lawns, and boardwalks add to the laid-back charm of the site, and you're just as likely to encounter an Elizabethan settler there as you are inside! The Children's Performances, held daily in the summer months in the Film Theater, are excellent. Many special events are held at Festival Park year-round, from fishing rodeos to beach music festivals to a Civil War encampment. See the Web site or call for details, and also see our Annual Events chapter.

The *Elizabeth II*, designed as the centerpiece for the 400th anniversary of the first English settlement in America, is a representative sailing ship similar to the one that carried Sir Walter Raleigh's colonists across the Atlantic in 1585. Interpreters clad in Elizabethan costumes conduct tours of the colorful 69-foot ship.

Although it was built in 1983, the *Elizabeth II*'s story really began four centuries earlier, when Thomas Cavendish mortgaged his estates to build the *Elizabeth* for England's second expedition to Roanoke Island. With six other vessels, the original *Elizabeth* made the first colonization voyage to the New World in 1585 and landed on the Outer Banks.

There wasn't enough information available about the original vessels to reconstruct an exact replica, so shipbuilders used the designs of vessels from 1585 to build the *Elizabeth II*. Constructed entirely in a wooden structure on the Manteo waterfront, the completed ship slid down hand-greased rails into Shallowbag Bay in front of a crowd of enthusiastic dignitaries and locals in 1983.

Stretching 69 feet long and 17 feet wide and drawing 8 feet of water, *Elizabeth II* was funded entirely through private donations. Her decks are hand-hewn from juniper timbers. Her frames, keel, planking, and decks are fastened with 7,000 locust wood pegs.

Every baulk, spar, block, and lift of the state ship are as close to authentic as possible, with only three exceptions: a wider upper-deck hatch for easier visitor access; a vertical hatch in the afterdeck to make steering easier for the helmsman; and a controversial pair of diesel engines that were installed in the *Elizabeth II* in 1993. The 115-horsepower motors help the grand sailing ship move under her own power, instead of relying on expensive tug boats that had to tow her before. Now, the vessel can cruise up to 8 knots per hour with no wind and travel for up to 40 hours without refueling its two 150-gallon tanks. The state ship stays on the Outer Banks most of the year, but during

Featuring the impressive Elizabeth II, *Roanoke Island Festival Park is a must-visit.* PHOTO: COURTESY OF ROANOKE ISLAND FESTIVAL PARK

the off-seasons, it sometimes travels to other North Carolina ports, acting as an emissary for her Roanoke Island home and serving as the state's only moving historic site.

Roanoke Island Festival Park is open year-round. Hours vary according to season. Admission is $8.00 for adults, $5.00 for students, and free for children under five. Group rates are available. Call ahead for a schedule of events.

Illuminations Summer Arts Festival
Roanoke Island Festival Park Pavilion
1 Festival Park, Manteo
(252) 475–1500
www.roanokeisland.com

The outdoor Pavilion at Roanoke Island Festival Park provides an idyllic setting for the cultural arts performances of the North Carolina School of the Arts. Visitors are invited to spread out blankets or set up folding chairs on the expansive, lush lawn that faces the Pavilion. Performances include dance, classical music, drama, film, and jazz. Picnics are welcome. The Pavilion has an open back, so if there's not a set, you can see the waters of the Roanoke Sound flowing behind the performers, making for an especially tranquil setting. Performances are held Tuesday through Saturday evenings at 8:00 P.M. from June 25 through August 10. A $5.00 donation is requested.

Outer Banks History Center
Roanoke Island Festival Park
1 Festival Park, Manteo
(252) 473–2655

Adjacent to the Visitor Center at Roanoke Island Festival Park, the Outer Banks History Center is a remarkable repository of North Carolina state and regional history. The North Carolina State Archives, Division of Archives and History, Department of Cultural Resources, administers this Outer Banks treasure.

Opened in 1988, the history center collection includes 100,000 manuscript items, 35,000 books, 35,000 photographs, 1,500 periodical titles, a large collection of important maps, hundreds of audio and video recordings, microfilm, and ephemera. Some of the more than 700 maps in the collection are more than 400 years old. The David Stick Library and Archives was the founding collection. Stick is a local author and historian who has written many books about the area. The collection also includes items relating to lighthouses and other Outer Banks architecture, local history about towns, shipwrecks, the U.S. Life-Saving Service, Civil War artwork, and *The Lost Colony* outdoor drama records and memorabilia.

Materials are housed in closed stacks to ensure security and the climate control needed for preservation. However, staffers at the history center are knowledgeable and happy to help anyone access the facility's vast resources. Journalists, authors, history buffs, students, scientists, genealogists, and even casual tourists will find the stop well worth their time.

New at the Outer Banks History Center is a gallery featuring exhibits of materials and photographs found in the archives. The debut exhibit focused on The Pirates Jamboree, a lively festival that helped promote tourism in the early days on the Outer Banks. Traveling exhibits will be featured from time to time.

The reading room and gallery are open year-round from 9:00 A.M. to 5:00 P.M. Monday through Friday and 10:00 A.M. to 3:00 P.M. on Saturday. The Outer Banks History Center is a public facility and is open free of charge.

Pioneer Theatre
113 Budleigh St., Manteo
(252) 473-2216

This nostalgic movie house is the best place to see movies on the Outer Banks. It's the oldest theater continuously operated by one family in the United States. The original Pioneer Theatre, opened in 1918 by George Washington Creef, was located 1 block over and showed silent films accompanied by a local pianist. The current Pioneer Theatre opened in 1934 and is now run by Creef's grandson, H.A. Creef. The 1947 carbon-arc projector, a rare find for movie buffs, was used until 1997. Even with new equipment, the Pioneer has the best old-fashioned feel you'll find anywhere.

This movie house is a family gathering place for Manteo locals. All of the movies are first-run and usually family-oriented (G, PG, or PG-13), and people come whether or not they're interested in the show. Friday nights the place is overrun with school kids, so it's best to avoid that night unless you're one of them. This place is definitely old-fashioned in its prices: $4.00 for all tickets. You won't get gouged at the candy counter either. A bag of Goobers might cost you 65 cents and a bag of fresh-buttered popcorn $1.00. One movie is shown every night at 8:00 P.M., as long as there are at least three people in the theater. Listings change weekly, without fail, on Fridays. Check the billboard on the highway in Manteo, or call the theater for the current listing and a brief synopsis of the movie.

North Carolina Maritime Museum on Roanoke Island
104 Fernando St., Manteo waterfront
(252) 475-1750

In 1998 the vintage George Washington Creef Boathouse in downtown Manteo was revitalized as an outpost of the North Carolina Maritime Museum in Beaufort. This effort breathed new life into the old boathouse that has stood on the Manteo waterfront since 1940.

The museum is dedicated to North Carolina's place in boatbuilding history. The crew at the museum, many of them volunteers, stay busy refurbishing and rebuilding wooden boats. Inside you'll see a number of craft that represent the region's maritime history. There's an 1883 original Creef shadboat, a variety of sailing skiffs, and a Davis Runabout speedboat. There's a multimedia presentation on the construction of the Elizabeth II, which was built on this site. This is also a working boat shop, and visitors will see staff and volunteers working on a variety of repair and building projects. If you're interested in becoming a volunteer, talk to the curator.

Before the boathouse, this site was home to much of Manteo's extensive boatbuilding history. A boatyard and repair railway were here from the 1880s until 1939, when just about everything on the Manteo waterfront burned in a devastating fire. George Washington Creef Jr. built this boathouse in 1940 to build shallow-draft freight boats and to repair the shadboats invented and built by his father, George Washington Creef Sr. The shadboat is now the North Carolina state boat. The boathouse was later used to build rescue craft for the military and world-record-holding speedboats.

The museum is well worth the trip to Manteo for those interested in boats and boatbuilding of the past and present. It is open Tuesday through Saturday. Hours

The Elizabeth II, *built in 1983, was funded entirely by private donations.* PHOTO: COURTESY OF ROANOKE ISLAND FESTIVAL PARK

are 10:00 A.M. to 6:00 P.M. during the summer months and 9:00 A.M. to 5:00 P.M. during the fall, winter, and spring.

The Christmas Shop and The Island Gallery
US 64, Manteo
(252) 473-2838, (800) 470-2838

The original Outer Banks ornament shop and a perfect excuse for celebrating Santa year-round, the Christmas Shop and Island Gallery offer an exquisite world of fantasy and festive delights. Edward Greene opened this unique store on June 1, 1967. It remains the only one of its kind, although others have tried to emulate its wide array of holiday statues, decorations, and unusual collectibles. In 1998 Greene added 4,000 square feet to the building.

This shaded shopping complex includes seven rambling, multilevel buildings, all connected. Each room is furnished with well-restored antique furniture (that's not for sale). The trip will fill visitors with wonder.

The Christmas Shop stocks about 60,000 items from 500 companies and cottage industries. Creations from more than 100 artists and craftspeople from across the country are included in the inventory, says Greene, a former New York City actor who decorated Christmas trees for area department stores. Whole walls are filled with toys, pottery, and handcrafts. Others overflow with baskets, carvings, miniatures, handmade jewelry, ornaments, seashells, candles, and Christmas cards. The shop's 125 switches control innumerable atmospheric lights that give everything a magical glow. There's even a year-round Halloween room, an old-fashioned candy store, a card and stationery area, sun-catchers, and fun things for the kids.

The Christmas Shop is open Memorial Day through mid-September, Monday through Saturday from 9:30 A.M. to 9:00 P.M. and Sunday from 9:30 A.M. to 6:00 P.M.. From mid-September through Christmas, hours are Monday through Saturday from 9:30 A.M. to 6:00 P.M. and Sunday from 9:30

A.M. to 5:30 P.M.. The shop is open from 9:30 A.M. to 5:30 P.M. daily January 1 through March 1. It's closed Christmas Day.

Weeping Radish Brewery
US 64, Manteo
(252) 473-1157

Historians say the first beer made in America was brewed on Roanoke Island. In 1585, they write, English colonists made a batch to befriend the Native Americans—or maybe to calm their own nerves. Roanoke Island today boasts its own brewery at a Bavarian-style eatery called The Weeping Radish, 1 mile south of downtown Manteo.

On the shaded grounds, a full-time brewmaster makes both light and dark lager beers, which can be sipped on-site at the restaurant or taken to go in 1-liter refillable bottles and six-packs of their Fest brew. Weeping Radish beer in 22-ounce bottles is sold at area retailers. Notice the artistic labels that depict local landmarks.

Half-hour brewery tours are given in season (June, July, and August) at 1:00 and 4:00 P.M. The rest of the year, call for the schedule. Free samples are given on the tour for tasting in the pub or at outdoor patio tables.

An annual Oktoberfest is held the weekend after Labor Day. Events and activities include oompah bands and German folk dancers (see our Annual Events chapter for details). Locals find this a favorite evening spot in the off-season. Visitors will feel at home too. There's even a colorful playground for the kids.

Historically Speaking's Customized Evening Entertainments
(252) 473-5783
nikndug@aol.com

Nicholas Hodsdon and Douglas L. Barger, both seasoned actors and performers, offer made-to-order programs for tour groups, conferences, or conventions. They'll either come to the group or have the group meet them at a local venue. Each program can be adapted to meet any situation, and both are delightful alternatives to pub-hopping. The entertainment is available year-round on an as-requested basis.

Call for additional information. Two popular presentations offered by Historically Speaking are "A Sea Song Sing-Along," featuring Outer Banks folk music with entertaining commentary on 400 years of coastal Carolina history, and *The Troubadour*, a staged and costumed "living history" visit with a costumed gentleman of Queen Elizabeth's court. Meet a 400-year-old standup comic who leads songs and weaves in the history of Roanoke Island's colonization while playing seven Renaissance instruments. Other programs are designed on request. Historically Speaking also offers step-on guides and receptive services for motor coach groups. See our Getting Here, Getting Around chapter for more information.

Mill Landing
NC 345, Wanchese

Near the end of a winding 5-mile road, past a long expanse of wide, waving marshlands overflowing with waterfowl, Wanchese is well off the beaten path of most visitors (see the section on Roanoke Island in our Area Overviews chapter) and remains one of the most unspoiled areas on the barrier islands. At the very end of NC 345, one of the most picturesque and unchanged areas of the Outer Banks is often overlooked: Mill Landing, which embodies the heritage of the Outer Banks. Here, active fishing trawlers anchor at the fish scale–strewn docks, their mesh still dripping seaweed from the wide roller wheels. Watermen in yellow chest waders and white rubber boots (known locally as Wanchese wing-tips) sling shark, tuna, and dolphin onto cutting room carts. Pieces of the island's past float silently in the harbor, mingling with remade boats that are still afloat and sunken ships that have long since disappeared.

The fish houses at Mill Landing include Wanchese Fish Company, Etheridge's, Jaws Seafood, Quality Seafood, and Moon Tillett's. These houses ship seafood to restaurants in Hampton Roads, Baltimore, New York, Boston, and Tokyo. Scallops, shrimp, fish, and crabs are available here in season.

Wanchese Seafood Industrial Park
615 Harbor Rd., Wanchese
(252) 473-5867

A 69-acre industrial park on a deep harbor at Wanchese, this state-supported facility was built in 1980 with $8.1 million in state and federal funds. It was designed to attract large-scale seafood processing companies to set up shop on the secluded Roanoke Island waterfront. After federal promises about stabilizing Oregon Inlet failed to materialize, few deep-draw fishing trawlers could afford to keep risking the trip through the East Coast's most dangerous inlet.

Oregon Inlet continued to shoal terribly through the 1980s, and the seafood park remained largely vacant until 1994, when some smaller area businesses and fish processing plants began establishing themselves there. Unpredictable weather patterns still affect the channel's navigability.

Today the 30-lot industrial area is almost 100 percent full with marine-related industries. Outer Banks Marine Maintenance, Harbor Welding, Wanchese Trawl and Supply, Bay Country Industrial Supply (fish-box manufacturer), Davis Boatworks, Wanchese Boat Builders, O'Neal's Sea Harvest, Gregory Poole Power Systems, and the Division of Marine Fisheries are just a few of the companies here. The industrial park is an educational attraction for anyone interested in the maritime world of boatbuilding and sea harvesting. Visitors are welcome to drive or walk through and visit the boat docks. Stop by the office if you have questions.

Pirate's Cove Yacht Club
Nags Head–Manteo Causeway, Manteo
(252) 473-3906, (800) 367-4728
www.piratescove.com

If you're interested in what the boats were

catching in the Gulf Stream someday, head over to Pirate's Cove Yacht Club between 4:00 and 5:00 P.M. When the charter boats return to their slips, the catches of the day are thrown out on the docks to be picked up by the fish cleaners. Visitors are welcome to stroll along the boardwalk and watch. You might see tuna, wahoo, dolphin (the fish, not the mammal), cobia, or any of a number of fish. This is especially exciting for kids, who may not have seen such big fish before. If you would rather see the fish on the end of your own line, charter opportunities are available at Pirate's Cove. See our Fishing chapter for more information.

Dare County Mainland

Wolf Howls
Alligator River National Wildlife Refuge
Dare County Mainland
(252) 473–1131 ext. 243
www.alligatorriver.fws.gov

Here's something you don't do every night. At least once, you must go to the Alligator River National Wildlife Refuge to listen to the red wolves howl. After sunset, you meet a refuge staff person at Creef Cut Wildlife Trail at the intersection of US 64 and Milltail Road on the Dare County mainland. After a brief talk about the red wolves, you are led (in vehicles) about 6 miles back into the dark refuge. On the way back, you might even see some bears. Back in the dark woods, you get out of your car and listen as the staffperson howls to elicit howls from the wolves. They almost always respond with eerie howls that are so wild they'll give you goosebumps. You can't see the wolves, which makes them seem even more wild and exotic and adds to the allure of this experience. The two-hour howl tours are held every Wednesday night at 8:00 P.M. from late June through mid-August. Howls are also held on Earth Day, April 22, at 7:00 P.M., on the Friday of Memorial Day weekend at 7:30 P.M., in mid-October for National Wolf Awareness Week, and on Halloween. Call to double-check the starting times and alter-nate dates. This is a free program and one that you won't soon forget.

A threatened species, red wolves have made a great comeback in northeastern North Carolina due to careful manage-ment since the early 1980s. There are 10 wolves in captivity at the Alligator River National Wildlife Refuge and nearly 100 roaming free over about one million acres in northeastern North Carolina, including the refuge. For more information, see our Natural Wonders chapter.

Bodie Island

Cape Hatteras National Seashore
Bodie, Hatteras, and Ocracoke Islands
(252) 473–3111
www.nps.gov/caha

Cape Hatteras National Seashore is a tremendous treasure for the residents and visitors of the Outer Banks. Here you will find the Outer Banks's most captivating open spaces, where long reaches of rugged dunes, wind-blown brush, wide beaches, and soundside wet-lands are forever protected from devel-opment. Established in 1953 by the National Park Service and dedicated in 1958, the National Seashore includes part of Bodie Island and most of Hat-teras and Ocracoke Islands, except for the village centers and Pea Island National Wildlife Refuge. The northern boundary is just south of Whalebone Junction in Nags Head, and the southern boundary is on Ocracoke Island. This was the very first National Seashore in the nation. It consists of some of the nar-rowest landmasses inhabitable by humans—skinny stretches of sand often less than a half-mile wide. The National Seashore provides miles-long stretches where there is not even a simple struc-ture to obscure the view. Wildlife, water-fowl, and seabirds are abundant in the National Seashore, including the Ameri-can oystercatcher and the threatened piper plover. Sea turtles can be spotted as well, as they often come ashore to lay eggs on the beaches in summer. Designated shorebird and sea turtle sanctuaries are well marked for protection on the beaches.

The Cape Hatteras National Seashore beaches are some of the cleanest and least crowded beaches on the East Coast. If you're looking for solitary recreational space or just simple peace and quiet, you'll find it here. Most of the beaches do not have lifeguards, however, so make sure you know swimming safety precautions before going in. Lifeguards are stationed at Coquina Beach on Bodie Island, at the beach near the Cape Hatteras Lighthouse, and at the Ocracoke Guarded Beach in the summer. Numerous access points are offered all along NC 12, the highway that runs directly through the heart of the Seashore. Three of the Outer Banks's four lighthouses are located within the Cape Hatteras National Seashore, and there are four primitively exquisite campgrounds in the Cape Hatteras National Seashore (see our Camping chapter). Camping is not allowed on the beach.

Three visitor centers are established in the National Seashore. The Bodie Island Visitor Center, (252) 441–5711, is on NC 12, in Nags Head heading south. The Cape Hatteras Visitor Center, (252) 995–4474, is in Buxton next to the Cape Hatteras Lighthouse. The Ocracoke Island Visitor Center, (252) 928–4531, is near the Cedar Island ferry dock. All provide extensive information on camping and activities in the National Seashore.

The Cape Hatteras National Seashore is dedicated to community outreach and has a great variety of summer programs to help visitors learn more about the natural surroundings here. There are guided beach walks, bird walks, campfires, fishing trips, history tours, dozens of kids programs, snorkeling trips, turtle talks, and many more. The schedules are lengthy, so the best way to find out about programs is to pick up the information at one of the visitor centers, or call ahead and have them mail it to you.

Driving on the beach is allowed in the Cape Hatteras National Seashore at certain access points. Four-wheel-drive vehicles may enter only at designated ramps. Soundside off-road travel is permitted on established roads or trails. Off-road access ramps are available at the visitor centers. Beach bonfires are permitted with a permit. Several day-use areas are available throughout the area, and nature trails provide visitors with an upclose look at the seashore environments. Personal watercraft like Jet-Skis and Wave Runners are prohibited in Cape Hatteras National Seashore.

Bodie Island Lighthouse and Keepers' Quarters
West of NC 12, Bodie Island
(252) 441–5711

This black-and-white beacon with horizontal bands is one of four lighthouses standing along the Outer Banks. It sits more than a half-mile from the sea, in a field of green grass, closer to the sound than the ocean. This site, 6 miles south of Whalebone Junction, is one of the most picturesque on the Outer Banks. Photographers are drawn to the immaculately kept, spacious lawns, the charming double keepers' quarters and oil house, and the proud tower. The lighthouse itself is not open for climbing, but the setting alone makes it worth the trip. The keepers' quarters has nice exhibits about the lighthouse and a small bookshop. The grounds are the perfect place for a picnic, and there are nature trails that lead into the wide expanses of marshland behind the tower, through cattails, yaupon, and wax myrtle. The trails end up at the Roanoke Sound, offering a view of the private camp on Off Island. The slough that rushes through the water between Bodie and Off Islands is a lucrative fishing hole, and anglers often line the banks.

The current Bodie Island Lighthouse is the third lighthouse to stand near Oregon Inlet, which opened during a hurricane in 1846. The first lighthouse was built south of Oregon Inlet in 1847 and 1848 and was the only lighthouse in the 140 miles between Cape Hatteras and Cape Henry, Virginia. The lighthouse developed cracks and structural damage within 10 years and had to be removed and rebuilt. The second light was also

Bodie Island Lighthouse is one of four lighthouses still standing along the Outer Banks. PHOTO: COURTESY OF JACKIE THOMAS

built south of Oregon Inlet. It was complete and lighted in 1859. Confederate forces destroyed the second tower during the Civil War so that it wouldn't fall into Union hands. The 170-foot lighthouse that stands today was built in 1872, this time north of Oregon Inlet because the inlet was moving south at a steady pace. Wanchese resident Vernon Gaskill served as the last civilian lightkeeper of the Bodie Island Lighthouse. The U.S. Coast Guard operated the light for many years, and it was transferred to the National Park Service in 2000. The National Park Service hopes to restore the lighthouse so that it will one day be open to the public, but the price tag on the restoration work is $1 million. The First-Order Fresnel lens will be of particular interest to visitors. Grounds-touring hours at Bodie Island Lighthouse are 9:00 A.M. to 6:00 P.M. daily, except after Labor Day when it closes at 5:00 P.M.

Coquina Beach
NC 12, Bodie Island

Though not as broad as it once was due to storms, Coquina Beach is still one of the widest beaches on the Outer Banks and is a favorite getaway beach. Just 6 miles south of Whalebone Junction, this beach has half the crowd but all the amenities you need: a lifeguard in the summer, a bathhouse, restrooms, outdoor showers, and lots of parking. Part of the allure of this remote area is that it's miles away from any business or rental cottage, making it a superb spot to sunbathe, swim, fish, or surf. The sand is almost white, and the beach is relatively flat.

Drawing its name from the tiny butterfly-shaped coquina clams that burrow into the beach, at times almost every inch of this portion of the federally protected Cape Hatteras National Seashore harbors hundreds of recently washed-up shells and several species of rare shorebirds. Coquinas are edible and can be collected and cleaned from their shells to make a fishy-tasting chowder. Local brick makers also have used the shells as temper in buildings.

The *Laura A. Barnes*
Coquina Beach, NC 12, Bodie Island

One of the last coastal schooners built in America, the *Laura A. Barnes* was completed in Camden, Maine, in 1918. This 120-foot ship was under sail on the Atlantic during a trip from New York to South Carolina when a nor'easter drove it onto the Outer Banks in 1921. The *Laura A. Barnes* ran aground just north of where it now rests at Coquina Beach. The entire crew survived. In 1973 the National Park Service moved the shipwreck to its present location, where visitors can view the remains of the ship behind a roped-off area that includes placards with information about the *Laura A. Barnes* and the history of lifesaving.

Oregon Inlet Fishing Center
NC 12, Bodie Island
(252) 441-6301, (800) 272-5199

Sportfishing enthusiasts, or anyone remotely interested in offshore angling, must stop by this bustling charter boat harbor on the north shore of Oregon Inlet. Set beside the U.S. Coast Guard station on land leased from the National Park Service, Oregon Inlet Fishing Center is owned by a group of 18 stockholders, most of them local fishermen. All vessels charge the same rate. A day on the Atlantic with one of these captains may give rise to a marlin, sailfish, wahoo, tuna, or dolphin on the end of the line. See our Fishing chapter for details. An exciting afternoon activity is to head to the boat docks at Oregon Inlet Fishing Center between 4:00 and 5:00 P.M. When the charter boats return to the docks, you'll have an opportunity to see a variety of Gulf Stream creatures as the mates unload the boats and hurl the huge fish on the docks. In the summer, the docks are quite crowded with spectators. Next to the fishing center store is a display case housing a 1,030-pound blue marlin, caught in 1973 and brought back to this fishing center. The store stocks bait and tackle, supplies, hot dogs and snacks, T-shirts and hats galore, and more. The fishing center has an air-fill tank for

Oregon Inlet Fishing Center is home to many locally made sportfishing boats. PHOTO: HORSLEY/GARDNER

putting air back into your tires after driving on the beach (there's a 4WD access across the street). The boat ramp at the fishing center provides easy access to the some of the best fishing grounds on the East Coast. There is plenty of parking, and restrooms are on-site.

Oregon Inlet Coast Guard Station
NC 12, Bodie Island

In the last century, the federal government operated two lifesaving stations at Oregon Inlet. The Bodie Island station was on the north side of the inlet. The Oregon Inlet station was on the south. Both of these original facilities are now closed. The Oregon Inlet station sits perilously close to the migrating inlet, the victim of hurricanes and decades of neglect. It is weather-worn and bedraggled, a testament to the ravages of salty winds and storms. Yet this building is a picturesque reminder of the history of the Outer Banks and how quickly changes occur. There is plenty of parking next to the station, and you can walk around the grounds and out to the jetties, but you can't go inside the building. The old station

is now in the hands of the State of North Carolina, and there may be plans to restore it in the future. This is also a popular and lucrative fishing spot. You can fish from the rock jetties, wade out into the deep cove, or walk the catwalk on the south end of the Bonner Bridge. The Bodie Island station has been replaced by the current Coast Guard facility behind the Oregon Inlet Fishing Center.

Opened in 1991 with wide boat docks and an ample parking area, the newer Oregon Inlet Coast Guard station includes a 10,000–square-foot building, a state-of-the-art communications center, maintenance shops, an administrative center, and accommodations for the staff. Coast Guard crews have rescued dozens of watermen off the Outer Banks. They also aid sea turtles and stranded seals by helping the animals get back safely to warmer parts of the ocean.

Oregon Inlet and the Bonner Bridge
NC 12, Oregon Inlet

The view from the crest of the Herbert C. Bonner Bridge has got to be the most beautiful vista on the Outer Banks. If only there was a place to pull over and enjoy it longer. As you drive over, you get a sweeping glimpse of this infamous inlet and all its surrounding shoals, sandbars, and spoil islands. Sea captains call this the most dangerous inlet on the East Coast—and with good reason. Since 1960 at least 30 lives and an equal number of boats have been lost at Oregon Inlet. The current through the inlet is dangerously swift and reckless, and shoals form alarmingly fast, causing boats to run aground.

The only outlet to the sea in the 140 miles between Cape Henry, in Virginia Beach, and Hatteras Inlet south of Hatteras Island, Oregon Inlet lies between Bodie Island and Pea Island National Wildlife Refuge. It is the primary passage for commercial and recreational fishing boats based along the northern Outer Banks. Even though it's often dredged, the inlet is sometimes impassable by deep-draft vessels.

Though a safe inlet is crucial to the commercial and recreational fishing industries, federal officials have refused to authorize or fund construction of jetties, rock walls that some scientists say would stabilize the ever-shallowing inlet. Environmentalists and other scientists oppose the proposed $100 million jetties project, saying it would cause increased erosion on beaches to the south. The debate continues and the sand keeps building up in the area's only outlet to the Atlantic.

Oregon Inlet was created during a hurricane in September 1846, the same storm that opened Hatteras Inlet between Hatteras Village and Ocracoke Island. It was named for the side-wheeler *Oregon*, the first ship to pass through the inlet.

In 1964 the Herbert C. Bonner Bridge was built across the inlet. This two-lane span finally connected Hatteras Island and the Cape Hatteras National Seashore with the northern Outer Banks beaches. Before the bridge was built, travelers relied on ferry boats to carry them across Oregon Inlet.

Hurricane-force winds blew a dredge barge into the bridge in 1990, knocking out a center section of the span. No one

was hurt, but the more than 5,000 permanent residents of Hatteras Island were cut off from the rest of the world for four months before workers could completely repair the bridge.

Four-wheel-drive vehicles can exit NC 12 on the northeast side of the inlet and drive along the beach, even beneath the Bonner Bridge, around the inlet. Fishing is permitted along the catwalks of the bridge and on the beach. Free parking and bathrooms are available at the Oregon Inlet Fishing Center. There are also parking and portable toilets on the southern end of the bridge. This trip is especially beautiful at sunset or sunrise.

Hatteras Island

Pea Island National Wildlife Refuge
NC 12, Pea Island
(252) 987-2394

Pea Island National Wildlife Refuge begins at the southern base of the Herbert C. Bonner Bridge and is the first place you'll come to if you enter Hatteras Island from the north. The beach along this undeveloped stretch of sand is popular with anglers, surfers, sunbathers, and shell seekers. On the right side of the road, heading south, salt marshes surround Pamlico Sound, and birds seem to flutter from every grove of cattails.

Founded on April 12, 1938, Pea Island refuge was federally funded as a winter preserve for snow geese. President Franklin D. Roosevelt put his Civilian Conservation Corps to work stabilizing the slightly sloping dunes, building them up with bulldozers, erecting long expanses of sand fencing, and securing the sand with sea oats and grasses. Workers built dikes near the sound to form ponds and freshwater marshes. They planted fields to provide food for the waterfowl.

With 5,915 acres that attract nearly 400 observed species of birds, Pea Island is an outdoor aviary well worth venturing off the road, and into the wilderness, to visit. Few tourists visited this refuge when Hatteras Island was only accessible by ferry. After the Oregon Inlet bridge opened in 1964, motorists began driving through this once isolated outpost.

Today, Pea Island is one of the barrier islands' most popular havens for bird-watchers, naturalists, and sea-turtle savers. Endangered species, from the loggerhead sea turtle to the tiny piping plover shore-birds, inhabit this enchanted area. Pea Island's name comes from the "dune peas" that grow all along the now grassy sand dunes. The tiny plant with pink and laven-der flowers is a favorite food of migrating geese.

Four miles south of the Bonner Bridge's southern base, the Pea Island Visi-tor Center offers free parking and easy access to the beach. If you walk directly across the highway to the top of the dunes, you'll see the remains of the more than century-old federal transport *Oriental*. Her steel boiler is the black mass, all that remains since the ship sank in May 1862.

On the sound side of the highway, in the marshes, ponds, and endless wetlands, whistling swans, snow geese, Canada geese, and 25 species of ducks make winter sojourns through the refuge. Savannah sparrows, migrant warblers, gulls, terns, herons, and egrets also alight in this area from fall through early spring. In summer, American avocets, willets, black-necked stilts, and several species of ducks nest here.

Bug repellent is a must on Pea Island from March through October. Besides insects, ticks may also cause problems. Check your clothing before getting in the car, and shower as soon as possible if you hike through any underbrush. See the next two entries for trail and visitor center information

North Pond Trail
NC 12, Pea Island

A bird-watcher's favorite, this wheelchair-accessible nature trail begins at the visitor center parking area and is about a mile long, a 30-minute brisk walk to the sound and back. The trail runs along the top of a dike between two man-made ponds that were begun in the late 19th century and completed by the Civilian Conservation

Insiders' Tip

The shipwreck site of the USS *Monitor* was the first site in the United States to be designated a National Underwater Marine Sanctuary. The *Monitor*, a Civil War ironclad, sank in 230 feet of water about 17 miles off Cape Hatteras in a storm on New Year's Eve of 1862. The sanctuary is federally protected, and divers can visit only if they have a federal permit.

Corps. The walkway includes three view-ing platforms, marshland overlooks, and mounted binoculars.

Wax myrtles and live oaks stabilize the dike and provide shelter for scores of songbirds. Warblers, yellowthroats, cardi-nals, and seaside sparrows stop here dur-ing biannual migrations. If you whistle the correct calls into the brush and wait quietly, the bird collective will answer in a symphony. The quarter-mile Salt Flats Trail starts at the north end of the North Pond Trail.

The U.S. Fish & Wildlife Service man-ages Pea Island refuge's ecosystem carefully. Workers plant fields with fescue and rye grass to keep the waterfowl coming back. Besides migrating birds, which don't occupy the island during summer, pheas-ants, muskrats, and nutria live along these ponds year-round. This short journey through a virtually unspoiled area will enhance any stay on the Outer Banks. If you crave quiet, fresh air, isolation and, above all, an opportunity to commune with wildlife, you'll want to walk these trails.

They are open to foot traffic only. This area is about 4 miles south of Oregon Inlet.

Pea Island Visitor Center
NC 12, Pea Island
(252) 987-2394

A paved parking area, free public restrooms, and the Pea Island Refuge Headquarters are 4 miles south of the Oregon Inlet bridge on the sound side of NC 12. Refuge volunteers staff this small welcome station year-round and are available to answer questions. Visitors can see exhibits on wildlife, waterfowl, and bird life. There is also a small gift shop. In the summer, the facility is open seven days a week from 9:00 A.M. to 4:00 P.M.. In the off-season, the center is open Thursday through Sunday from 9:00 A.M. to 4:00 P.M.. It's closed Christmas Day. Free nature trail maps are available, and in summer months, special nature programs are offered, such as bird walks, turtle talks, and guided canoe tours.

Hunting, camping, and driving are not allowed in the refuge. Open fires are also prohibited. Dogs must be kept on leashes on the east side of the highway. Firearms are not allowed in the refuge; shotguns and rifles must be stowed out of sight even if you're just driving straight through Hatteras Island. Fishing, crabbing, boating, and other activities are allowed in the ocean and sound but are prohibited in refuge ponds.

About 3 miles south down NC 12, a kiosk just beyond the Refuge Headquarters marks the site of the remains of the nation's only African-American lifesaving station. Pea Island was established with the rest of the U.S. Life-Saving outposts in 1879 and was originally manned by mostly white crews. Black men were confined to tasks like caring for the horses that dragged surfboats through the sand.

The year after the station was set up, however, federal officials fired Pea Island's white crew members for mishandling the Henderson shipwreck disaster. Black personnel from other stations were placed under the charge of Richard Etheridge, who was of Native American and African-American descent. The new crew carried out their duties honorably.

Pea Island's surfmen rescued countless crews and passengers of ships that washed ashore in storms or sank in the seething seas. Etheridge became known as one of the best-prepared, most professional and most daring leaders in the service. One of the crew's most famous rescues was in 1896 when the captain of the E.S. Newman sounded an SOS off Hatteras Island's treacherous shores, an area also known as The Graveyard of the Atlantic.

In 1992 the U.S. Coast Guard Service, a latter-day version of the Life-Saving Service, dedicated a cutter to the Pea Island crew. About a dozen of the African-American surfmen's descendants witnessed the moving ceremony. A plaque on board the big ship commemorates the lifesaving crew's heroism.

Chicamacomico Lifesaving Station
NC 12, Rodanthe
(252) 987-1552
www.chicamacomico.org

With volunteer labor and long years of dedication, this once-decrepit lifesaving station is beautifully restored and open for tours. Its weathered, silvery-shingled buildings sparkle on the sandy lawn, which is surrounded by a perfect picket fence. Even the outbuildings have been brought back to their former uses.

Chicamacomico was one of the Outer Banks's original seven lifesaving stations, opening in 1874 at its current site. The present boathouse building was the original station but was retained as a storage shed when the bigger facility was built in 1911. Under three keepers with the last name of Midgett, Chicamacomico crews guarded the sea along Hatteras Island's northern coast for 70 years. Between 1876 and the time the station closed in 1954, seven Midgetts were awarded the Gold Life Saving Award; three won the silver; and six others worked or lived at Chicamacomico. Perhaps the station's most famous rescue was when surfmen pulled crew members from the British tanker *Mirlo* off their burning ship and into safety.

Today the nonprofit Chicamacomico Historical Association oversees and operates the lifesaving station. Volunteers set up a museum of area lifesaving awards and artifacts in the main building and have recovered some of the lifesaving equipment for the boathouse. Volunteers take school groups on tours of the station, showing them how the britches buoy helped rescue shipwreck victims and explaining the precise maneuvers surfmen had to follow on shore (see our History chapter for more about the britches buoy).

The station is open from Easter weekend through the Saturday after Thanksgiving, Tuesday through Saturday from 9:00 A.M. to 5:00 P.M. Various interesting programs have been added to the program roster and are offered every open day in the summer and on Wednesday, Thursday, and Friday in the off-season. Every Thursday at 2:00 P.M. there are fascinating costumed re-enactments of the beach apparatus drills. This is your chance to get a feel for what the lifesaving crews had to do to rescue sinking ships. The drill lasts about an hour. On other days at 2:00 P.M., other programs might include a guided tour, a knot-tying class, or a storytelling hour. Bonfires are held one evening a week in the summer at 8:00 P.M. All programs are suitable for all ages. The guided tour gives more details of the site and the lifesaving service and the equipment used. Group tours can be accommodated with advance notice. Admission to this treasure is free, though donations are welcome and are greatly needed to further the restoration and expand the programs at this site. Call for additional program information.

Salvo Post Office
NC 12, Salvo

If you're heading south on NC 12 through Hatteras Island, slow down as you leave Salvo, and try to spot a tiny whitewashed building with blue and red trim on the right side of the road. That's the old Salvo Post Office, which was the country's smallest post office until an arsonist burned about half of it down in 1992. It sat atop low rails in the postmaster's front yard. Over the years, villagers moved it to the front yard of each new postmaster's house.

The wooden structure had beautiful gilt post boxes surrounding the small glass service window, but it didn't have a bathroom, air conditioning, or a wheelchair-accessible ramp. Although community volunteers rallied and rebuilt their little post office quickly, the federal government refused to reopen the outpost, which was originally erected in 1901. Today, Salvo residents drive to Rodanthe to pick up their mail, and this tiny charmer sits empty by the road.

Canadian Hole
NC 12, Avon

If a breeze is blowing, pull off the west side of the road between Avon and Buxton (1.5 miles south of Avon) into the big parking lot on the sound. Known as Canadian Hole, this is one of America's hottest windsurfing spots—and a magnet for visitors from the great white North. Whether you ride a sailboard or not, this sight is not to be missed. On windy afternoons, more than 100 windsurfers and kite-boarders spread out along the shallow sound, their brightly colored butterfly sails gently skimming into the sunset. There's a nice bathing beach here, so bring chairs and coolers and plan to watch the silent wave riders, some of whom are famous in windsurfing circles. The state recently expanded the parking area here. See our Watersports chapter for more details.

Cape Hatteras Lighthouse
Off NC 12, Buxton
(252) 995-4474
www.nps.gov/caha

The Cape Hatteras Lighthouse is one of the most adored lighthouses in the nation, especially after it survived a move of more than 1,600 feet in 1999. The nation's tallest brick lighthouse at about

210 feet, this black-and-white striped beacon was seen the world over as it was precariously jacked up and moved along roll beams to its new location, away from the encroaching sea. The relocation project was named the 2000 Outstanding Civil Engineering Achievement by the American Society of Civil Engineers. The lighthouse now stands the same distance from the Atlantic Ocean as it did when it was first built in 1870.

The original Cape Hatteras Lighthouse was built in 1803. The tower sat near Cape Point and was only 90 feet tall. Lit with whale oil, it was barely bright enough to be seen offshore. Erosion weakened the structure, and in 1861 Confederate soldiers removed the light's lens. The current Cape Hatteras Lighthouse was erected in 1870 with more than one million bricks and 257 steps. A special Fresnel lens that refracts light increased its visibility. The lighthouse was 1,600 feet from the ocean when it was built, but by 1987, it was only 120 feet from the crashing waves. After years of study, the National Park Service came to the conclusion that they had to "move it or lose it." The lighthouse was moved 1,600 feet back from the shore in just a few weeks, from June 17 to July 9, 1999. About 20,000 visitors a day watched. It reopened to the public on May 26, 2000. Its 800,000-candlepower beacon, rotating every seven-and-a-half seconds, can be seen about 20 miles out to sea.

Visitors are allowed to climb the Cape Hatteras Lighthouse. At the top, the view of Hatteras Island and the Atlantic Ocean is surreal and unforgettable. The fee is $3.00 for adults and $1.50 for children younger than 12, seniors, and the blind or disabled. The lighthouse is open from the Friday before Easter through Columbus Day. Summer hours are 10:00 A.M. to 6:00 P.M., and spring and fall hours are 10:00 A.M. to 2:00 P.M. Children must be taller than 38 inches, and they cannot be carried to the top.

The visitor center, called the Museum of the Sea, and the bookstore, both housed in the historic former keepers'

quarters, were moved to this location before the lighthouse was moved. Restrooms are located here. If you continue past the parking area, you'll pass the picnic area and the Buxton Woods Nature Trail. If you continue on, you'll come to the Cape Point Campground and off-road vehicle ramps. The beach here is great for swimming, sunbathing, surfing, and fishing, and you can take four-wheel-drive vehicles along many sections of the beach year-round. Park rangers and volunteers are willing to answer questions and can be found in the visitor center and on the historic district grounds. Visitor center and bookstore hours are 9:00 A.M. to 5:00 P.M. daily, except for Christmas Day.

In Buxton, signs lead you to the lighthouse site. To the left, you can visit the original lighthouse location, marked by a circle of granite stones that are etched with the names of 83 former lighthouse keepers. To the right is a parking area and the lighthouse's new location.

NOTE: The Cape Hatteras Lighthouse is closed for climbing in 2002, while repairs are being made to the interior stairway. At this writing, the National Park Service does not expect to open the lighthouse to climbers until April 2003. Even without the climb, it is worth your while to visit this interesting site.

The Altoona Wreck
Cape Point, Buxton

Four-wheel-drive motorists should enter the beach at the end of Cape Point Way on Ramp 44. Here, the Outer Banks juts out into the Atlantic in a wide elbow-shaped curve near the Cape Hatteras Lighthouse. The beaches in this area offer some of the barrier islands' best surf fishing. Two rules of the beach: do not try to drive on the beach in anything but a four-wheel-drive vehicle, and be sure to let the proper amount of air out of your tires before traversing sand (see our Getting Here, Getting Around chapter for more information).

For those not driving on the beach, park on solid ground near the road and walk over the ramp to a foot trail. The path begins at the base of the dune and veers off at a 45-degree angle. At the edge of a seawater pond, about a 10-minute walk from the parking area, you'll catch a glimpse of the remains of the ancient shipwreck *Altoona*.

Built in Maine in 1869, the *Altoona* was a two-masted, 100-foot-long cargo schooner based in Boston. It left Haiti in 1878 with a load of dyewood bound for New York. On October 22, a storm drove it ashore near Cape Point. Lifesavers rescued its seven crew members and salvaged some of the cargo, but the ship was buried beneath the sand until a storm uncovered it in 1962. The sea has broken the big boat apart since then, but you can still see part of the bow and hull beneath the waves.

Diamond Shoals Light
In the Atlantic Ocean, off Cape Point, Buxton

You can't really visit this attraction, except in private boats, but you can see this unusual light tower from the eastern shore of Cape Point and from the top of the Cape Hatteras Lighthouse. Its bright beacon blinks every two seconds from a steel structure set 12 miles out in the sea.

Diamond Shoals once held a lighthouse, but waves beat the offshore rocks that held the lighthouse so badly that federal officials gave up the project. Three lightships have been stationed on the shoals since 1824. The first sank in an 1827 gale. The second held its ground from 1897 until German submarines sank it in 1918. The third beamed until 1967 when it was replaced by the current light tower.

Diamond Shoals, the rocks around the tower, are the southern end of the treacherous near-shore sandbars off Hatteras Island.

Buxton Woods Nature Trail
Cape Point, Buxton

Leading from the Cape Point Campground road about .75 mile through the woods, the Buxton nature trail takes walkers through thick vine jungles, across tall sand dunes, and into freshwater marshes (see also our Natural Wonders chapter). Small plaques along the fairly level walkway explain the area's fragile ecosystems. People who hike this trail will learn about the Outer Banks's water table, the role of beach grass and sea oats in stabilizing sand dunes, and the effects salt, storms, and visitors have on the ever-changing environment.

Cottonmouths seem to like this trail too, so beware of these unmistakable snakes. They are fat, rough-scaled, and stubby-looking in brown, yellow, gray, or almost black. If you see a cottonmouth, let it get away—don't chase it. If it stands its ground, retreat.

This hike is not recommended for disabled visitors or young children, but picnic tables and charcoal grills just south of the nature trail provide a welcome respite for everyone. The walk is well worth it for hardy nature lovers who don't mind mingling with the outdoor elements.

Frisco Native American Museum
NC 12, Frisco
(252) 995-4440
www.nativeamericanmuseum.org

This enchanting museum on the sound side of NC 12 in Frisco is stocked with unusual collections of Native American artifacts gathered over the last 65 years, plus numerous other fascinating collections. Opened 13 years ago by Carl and Joyce Bornfriend, the museum boasts one of the most significant collections of artifacts from the Chiricahua Apache people and has displays of other Native American tribes' works from across the country, ranging from the days of early humans to modern time. Hopi drums, pottery, kachina dolls, baskets, weapons, and jewelry abound in homemade display cases. Many visitors are astonished at the variety, amount, and eclectic appeal of the displays in the museum. A souvenir gift shop offers Native American art, crafts, jewelry, educational materials, toys, and books. Native craft items made by about 40 artisans from across the country are also available for sale.

The book section and natural history center have recently been expanded. With advance notice, the Bornfriends will give guided tours of their museum and lectures for school and youth groups. Call for prices. The museum property also includes outdoor nature trails through three acres of woods, with a screened-in pavilion, a large pond, and three bridges on the land. Hours are 11:00 A.M. to 5:00 P.M. Tuesdays through Sundays, year-round. Admission is $2.00 per person or $5.00 per family. Seniors are charged $1.50.

Hatteras–Ocracoke Ferry
NC 12, Hatteras Village
NC 12, Ocracoke Island
(252) 986–2353, (800) BY FERRY

The only link between Hatteras and Ocracoke Islands, this free state-run ferry carries passengers and vehicles across Hatteras Inlet daily, year-round, with trips every hour from 5:00 A.M. to midnight. A fleet of 10 ferry boats, some 150 feet long, carry up to 30 cars and trucks each on the 40-minute ride. (See also our Getting Here, Getting Around chapter for the schedule.)

You can get out of your vehicle and walk around the open decks or stay inside the car if it's cold. A passenger lounge a short flight of steps above the deck offers cushioned seats and wide windows. On the lower deck, telescopes give people a chance to see sea gulls and passing shorelines up close for a quarter. Free, always clean restrooms also are on the deck; however, there's no food or drink to be found on this 5-mile crossing, so pack your own picnic. Beware if you decide to break bread with the dozens of birds that fly overhead. After they eat, they, too, look for free bathrooms. And they'll follow—overhead—all the way to Ocracoke.

A souvenir shop is located at the Hatteras ferry docks selling everything from coloring books and Frisbees to sweatshirts and coffee mugs. Drink and snack machines also are on-site.

A daytrip to Ocracoke is a must for every Outer Banks visitor, whether you're staying in Corolla or Kill Devil Hills. (See the Ocracoke section of our Area Overviews chapter for more about Ocracoke.) The free ferry is the only way to get there besides by private boat or airplane. On summer days, more than 1,000 passengers ride the flat boats.

If you arrive at Ocracoke Island on the ferry, there's a 12-mile drive through open marshlands and pine forests before you get to the village. NC 12 picks up at the ferry docks and continues, two lanes, to the end of the island. On the left, some wide-open beaches await avid four-wheelers and those who like to have a piece of the seaside to themselves.

A National Park Service oceanfront campground will be on your left before you get to the village. Ocracoke itself is a quaint fishing village that has recently grown into a popular tourist destination. About 800 people live on Ocracoke Island year-round. Boutiques, seafood restaurants, craft shops and other retailers line the quiet, twisting lanes, but most are open only during the summer season. We recommend you park your car somewhere near the waterfront and rent a bicycle to tour this picturesque, isolated island.

Graveyard of the Atlantic Museum
NC 12, Hatteras Village
(252) 986–2995

This is a coming attraction, read: Not Yet Open. But it's so exciting we think it's worth mentioning while we wait for it to open in 2003. Plus, you'll surely notice this exotic-looking building while you wait in line at the Hatteras ferry docks and want to know what it is. This will be the Graveyard of the Atlantic Museum, a 19,000-square-foot museum with exhibits on Outer Banks geology, history, lighthouses, shipwrecks, recreational and commercial fishing, wars, pirates, and more. The museum will also host exhibits of recently discovered shipwreck artifacts. The unusual building was designed to look like a ship, with ships' curves and naval architectural elements. The building is also hurricane proof, able to withstand winds of 135 miles per hour and gusts over 200 miles per hour.

The Graveyard of the Atlantic

The ocean waters off the Outer Banks are considered some of the most dangerous waters in the world. From the 16th century to the present, historians say there have been close to 1,000 shipwrecks off the coast of North Carolina, predominantly on the Outer Banks. That number is debatable—some say more, some say less—but nevertheless, the waters here do have the nasty reputation that earned them the moniker "Graveyard of the Atlantic."

The first recorded Outer Banks shipwreck was in 1585, when John White's English flagship *Tyger* ran aground near Ocracoke Inlet. Thereafter, shipwrecks were a common occurrence, prompting the establishment of lighthouses and the lifesaving stations on the Outer Banks in the 1800s. Two notable 1877–78 wrecks were the USS *Huron* in Nags Head and *Metropolis* in Corolla. The *Huron* sank in November of 1877 at a cost of 98 lives. The *Metropolis* sank on January 31, 1878, at a cost of 85 lives. These wrecks prompted the building of additional lifesaving stations on the Outer Banks.

One of the most treacherous places on the Outer Banks and the site of numerous shipwrecks is Diamond Shoals, where the northbound Gulf Stream and the southbound Labrador Current meet at Cape Hatteras. This meeting of currents creates shoals that extend almost 20 miles out to sea, causing unwary vessels to run aground several miles from shore. Today there is a light on the shoals to warn off ships.

To tell the story of these shipwrecks and of North Carolina maritime history, the Graveyard of the Atlantic Museum is under construction in Hatteras Village. This 19,000-square-foot museum will showcase 400 years of coastal history. It will not be open in 2002, but it has been built and plans to open as soon as more money is raised and exhibits are complete. For information, visit www.graveyardoftheatlantic.com.

If you're a certified diver, several dive companies take trips to local wrecks. Many divers consider the Outer Banks as the premiere wreck-diving location in the nation. If you're a landlubber, look for shipwreck remnants at these sites:

Schooner *Francis E. Waters* is on display at the Nags Head Town Hall. The boat sank in October 1889, and its remnants make an interesting sculpture on the Town Hall lawn.

The USS *Huron* can sometimes be seen at the Nags Head Fishing Pier at low tide. The *Huron* sank in 1877.

Schooner *Laura A. Barnes* is on display at the Coquina Beach bathhouse in the Cape Hatteras National Seashore. She sank in June 1921.

Trawler *Lois Joyce* is visible in the surf at Oregon Inlet. The trawler sank in December 1981.

Oriental, a federal transport ship, sank in May 1862. Her boiler stack is visible at low tide from the second beach access after Oregon Inlet.

The propeller from the USS *Dionysus* is on display at Oregon Inlet Fishing Center. An interpretive sign gives the details of the shipwreck.

An unknown barge is visible at low tide just north of Rodanthe, across from the Pea Island U.S. Fish and Wildlife Station.

Schooner *G.A. Kohler* is visible on the beach at ramp 27 north of Avon. The ship sank in August 1933.

Schooner *Altoona* is visible north of the pond at Cape Point in Buxton. The *Altoona* sank in 1878.

Although not yet open, the Graveyard of the Atlantic Museum has been built next to the ferry docks in Hatteras Village and promises to be a popular Outer Banks attraction. PHOTO: MOLLY HARRISON

Donations are needed for this independently run museum. Call the number above to help out.

Ocracoke Island

Ocracoke Pony Pens
NC 12, Ocracoke Island

The Ocracoke Pony Pens are one of the most popular attractions on Ocracoke Island. The National Park Service maintains a herd of about 30 horses in a 180-acre pasture that's located on NC 12, about 6 miles south of the Hatteras–Ocracoke ferry docks. Visitors can walk up to the pens to view these once-wild horses. There's an observation platform that allows a good view of the ponies. A few of the ponies are always in the front pen for visitors to see.

The Ocracoke ponies have played a large role in the history of the island. At times the herd's population ranged from 200 to 500, all of the animals roaming free on the island.

No one is really certain how the horses arrived at the island, but legend says they swam ashore from Spanish shipwrecks off the coast. The horses adapted well to a diet of marsh grasses and rainwater. The locals used this natural resource of ponies for work and for recreation, and even the Coast Guard and U.S. Life-Saving Service employed the ponies. In the 1950s the local Boy Scout troop rode them.

When NC 12 was paved along the island in 1957, horse-car accidents became a problem. The herd was also causing extensive damage to dune vegetation, contributing to beach erosion. The National Park Service wanted to get rid of the entire herd, but the islanders protested so strongly that the Park Service agreed to keep some of the ponies contained on the island. They were penned in 1960, and they're still there today. Their shelters, food, and veterinary care are funded partly by donations. It's free to visit, but donations are certainly welcome. Though not running wild, the ponies are not tame, and they may try to kick or bite if you try to climb into the pen or feed or pet them.

The Ocracoke ponies have distinctive physical characteristics: five lumbar vertebrae instead of the six found in other horses, 17 ribs instead of the 18 found in other horses, and a unique shape, posture, color, size, and weight. For more information see the Ocracoke Island section of our Area Overviews chapter.

Hammock Hills Nature Trail
NC 12, Ocracoke Island

A .75-mile nature trail north of Ocracoke Village, Hammock Hills covers a cross-section of the island. The 30-minute walk begins near the sand dunes, traverses a maritime forest, and winds through a salt marsh. Hikers can learn how plants adapt to Ocracoke's unusual elements and the harsh barrier island weather.

Bring your camera on this scenic stroll. We highly recommend bug repellent in spring and summer months. Watch out for snakes in the underbrush. The well-marked trailhead is on NC 12 just across the road from the National Park Service campground.

Ocracoke Island Visitor Center
NC 12, Ocracoke Village
(252) 928-4531

The National Park Service's Ocracoke Island Visitor Center, at the southern end of NC 12, is a clearinghouse of information about the island. It's in a small building with a large lawn next to the Cedar Island ferry docks. If you're arriving on the island from the Hatteras ferry, stay on the main road, turn right at Silver Lake, and continue around the lake counterclockwise until you see the low brown building on your right. Free parking is available at the visitor center.

Inside, there's an information desk, helpful staff, a small bookshop, and exhibits about Ocracoke. You can arrange to use the Park Service's docks here and pick up maps of the winding back roads that make great bicycle paths.

The visitor center is open March through December from 9:00 A.M. to 5:00 P.M.. Hours are extended in the summer. Rangers offer a variety of free summer programs, including a beach walk, a walk through the village, turtle talks, a pirate play, snorkeling, an evening campfire, kids programs, and more. Programs last from 30 to 90 minutes and offer a fun way to learn more about the history and ecology of the island. Check at the front desk for changing weekly schedules. Restrooms are open to the public in season.

Ocracoke Island Museum and
Preservation Society
Silver Lake, Ocracoke Village
(252) 928-7375

A visit to the Ocracoke Island Museum provides a wonderful peek into Ocracoke as it once was. The home of Coast Guard Capt. David Williams, the historic, two-story house was moved to this location in 1989 and restored to its former early 19th-century glory by the Ocracoke Preservation Society. The original wainscotting, floors, staircases, and wood-burning stove are still intact. Inside, a bedroom, living room, and kitchen are set up with period furnishings donated by local families. Original photographs of island natives can be found throughout. Exhibits about fishing and seafaring are especially interesting, as is the exhibit on the island's traditional brogue, including a short video of some old-timers talking. Special exhibits are set up and can vary. The Fort Ocracoke exhibit, including artifacts found at the fort, will likely be held through 2002. Upstairs, the museum has a small research library that the public can use with the museum personnel's permission. It's free to visit this museum. It's open from Easter through the end of November. In summer, hours are 10:00 A.M. to 5:00 P.M. Monday through Friday and 11:00 A.M. to 4:00 P.M. Saturday and Sunday. Off-season hours are 11:00 A.M. to 4:00 P.M. Monday through Saturday.

Ocracoke Village Walking Tour
West end of NC 12, around Ocracoke Village

The easiest ways to explore Ocracoke are by bicycle and on foot. The narrow, winding back lanes weren't meant for cars. And you miss little landmarks and interesting areas of the island if you try to drive through too quickly. People on Ocracoke are generally very friendly, and you'll get a chance to chat with more locals if you slow down your touring pace through this picturesque fishing village.

Ocracoke Village is one big canvas for all sorts of spontaneous walking tours. No matter where you are, just start walking and you'll find something interesting. One nice tour of the northeast side of the village starts at the Ocracoke Island Visitor Center. Park in the lot opposite the visitor center. Turn left out of the lot and walk down NC 12 around the shores of Silver Lake, past the sleepy village waterfront. You'll pass many small shops, boutiques, and some large hotels. Keep walking until you see a small brick post office on your right.

Opposite the post office, a sandy, narrow street angles to the left. This is Howard Street. It winds through one of the oldest and least-changed parts of the village. Note the humble old homes, the attached cisterns for collecting rainwater, and the detached kitchens behind these historic structures.

Continue walking past or stop in Village Craftsman, a great gallery. After about 400 yards, Howard Street empties onto School Street. Turn left, and you'll see the Methodist church and K–12 public school that serves all the children on Ocracoke. With graduating classes of fewer than a dozen students, this is the state's smallest public school.

The church is usually open for visitors, but use discretion if services are in progress. And please wipe your feet as you go in. On entering, note the cross displayed behind the altar. It was carved from the wooden spar of an American freighter, the *Caribsea,* sunk offshore by German U-boats in the early months of 1942. By strange coincidence, the *Caribsea*'s engineer was Ocracoke native James Baugham Gaskill, who was killed when the boat sank. Local residents say that several days later a display case holding Gaskill's mate license, among other things, washed ashore not far from his family home.

Ocracoke has had a Methodist Church since 1828. The current one was built in 1943 from lumber and pews salvaged from older buildings. A historical-sketch pamphlet is available in the vestibule for visitors.

On leaving the church, walk around the north corner of the school, past the playground, onto a narrow boardwalk. This wooden path leads to a paved road beyond it. Turn left. This was the first paved road on the island and was constructed by Seabees during World War II.

After walking less than a mile down this road, turn right at the first stop sign. A few minutes' walk along this narrow, tree-shaded street will bring you to the British Cemetery where victims of World War II are buried far away from their English soil. (See the subsequent listing in this section.) It's on your right, set back a bit from the road and shaded by live oak and yaupon. The big British flag makes it easy to spot.

To return to the visitor center, walk west until you reach Silver Lake, then turn right. You'll pass craft shops and several boutiques along the way. (See our Shopping chapter for details.) If the weather's nice, we suggest a stop for an outdoor drink at the waterfront Jolly Roger, the Creekside Cafe upstairs above the bicycle stand, or Howard's Pub on the highway before heading back to the ferry docks. See the Ocracoke Island section of our Area Overviews chapter for additional information.

Ocracoke Lighthouse
Southwest corner of Ocracoke Village

The southernmost of the Outer Banks's four lighthouses, this whitewashed tower is the oldest and shortest. It is the second-oldest lighthouse in the nation. It stands $77\frac{1}{2}$ feet tall, and has an askew iron-railed tower set on the top. The lighthouse is not open for tours or climbing, but volunteers occasionally staff its broad base, offering historical talks and answering visitors' questions. Inquire about possible staffing times at the visitor center or National Park Service offices.

Ocracoke's lighthouse is still operating, emitting one long flash every few seconds from a half-hour before sunset to a half-hour after sunrise. It was built in 1823 to replace Shell Castle Rock lighthouse, which was set offshore closer to the dangerous shoals in Ocracoke Inlet. Shell Castle light was abandoned in 1798 when the inlet shifted south.

The beam from Ocracoke's beacon rotates 360 degrees and can be seen as far as 14 miles out to sea. The tower itself is brick, covered by hand-spread, textured white mortar. The walls are 5 feet thick at the base.

On the right side of the wooden boardwalk leading to the lighthouse, a two-story white cottage once served as quarters for the tower's keeper. The National Park Service renovated this structure in the 1980s. It now serves as the home of Ocracoke's rangers and the structure's maintenance supervisor.

To reach the light, turn left off NC 12 at the Island Inn and go about 800 yards down the two-lane street. You can park near a white picketed turnoff on the right. Visitors must walk the last few yards down the boardwalk to the lighthouse.

Styron's General Store
Point Rd., Ocracoke Village
(252) 928–6819

One of the oldest establishments on Ocracoke Island, Styron's General Store opened in its present location in 1920. Former owner Al Styron tore down his family's store on Hog Island, near Cedar Island, and loaded the cypress walls into his boat. He carted Styron's Store to Ocracoke and rebuilt the business there. Today, Styron's great-granddaughter, Candy Gaskill, runs the family business.

Styron's stocks a variety of items ranging from ordinary to fascinating. The simpler things like whole wheat flour are still sold here, but there's also an amazing mix of virtually everything anyone would need.

Wooden milk crates and apple boxes hold gourmet wines imported from Australia and France. Metal fish baskets are filled with fresh onions and red potatoes. Shelves along the sides are stacked with Chinese roast duck mix and Thai sesame oil.

The store has been expanded over the years, but the front room retains some of its past, proudly displayed amidst the newfangled fodder: Burgundy leather-bound ledgers contain records of every transaction made in the store since 1925. The antique, gilt cash register that Al Styron installed is now on display in the store. The former feed scale holds storeroom keys. The original safe and a multi-drawer roll-top desk all are displayed and used, as they have been for nearly a half-century.

Besides food, wine, and general merchandise, Styron's offers two wooden tables and a dozen ladder-backed chairs for customers to sit a spell or sip one of Candy's locally famous fresh milk shakes. Excellent sandwiches and take-out items are available. Styron's store sits on the Point Road, about two blocks before the lighthouse. It's open from 8:00 A.M. to 5:00 P.M. Monday through Saturday, and from 10:00 A.M. to 5:00 P.M. on Sunday. The store stays open later during summer months. Styron's is closed January through March.

British Cemetery
British Cemetery Rd., Ocracoke Village

Beneath a stand of trees, on the edge of a community cemetery, four granite gravestones commemorate the crew of the British vessel HMS *Bedfordshire*. This 170-foot trawler was one of a fleet of 24 anti-submarine ships that Prime Minister Winston Churchill loaned the United States in April 1942 to stave off German U-boats. On May 11 of that year, a German submarine torpedoed and sank the British ship about 40 miles south of Ocracoke.

All four officers and 33 enlisted men aboard the *Bedfordshire* drowned. U.S. Coast Guard officers stationed on Ocracoke found four of the bodies washed ashore three days later. They were able to identify two of the sailors. Townspeople gave Britain a 12-by-14-foot plot of land

The Wild Horses of Corolla

Corolla's wild horses are part of the mystique of the Outer Banks: a symbol of the roots, endurance, and resilience of an isolated land and its tough inhabitants. They are also the symbol of the toll taken by breathtaking growth in Corolla.

Visitors to the northernmost stretches of barrier beach no longer see pastoral views of horses grazing on golf courses or newly planted lawns. They no longer see the majestic beasts loping on oceanside sands. They won't even see close-ups of the few that, until recently, were corralled at the Currituck Beach Lighthouse.

There are no horses left in Corolla. They are now fenced in the nearby Currituck National Wildlife Refuge and on the nearby Dews Island.

Believed by many to be descendants of Spanish mustangs, the wild horses have the compact, stocky confirmation and, according to one scientist, the genetic markers of the Barb horses that were brought to the Outer Banks as early as 1523 by Spanish explorers. One native Outer Banker who has studied the "Banker ponies" said they may be the oldest breed of horse in North America. Though the horses have Spanish origins, they are of a breed all their own, due to nearly 400 years as an isolated species. The horses are recognized as a significant cultural and historical resource by the state of North Carolina.

Before development in Corolla took off like a shot in the mid- and late 1980s, wild horses ranged freely among the sea grasses and dunes of the northern barrier islands. A late discovery for developers, the area didn't have electricity until 1968,

Wild horses are no longer free to roam in Corolla. PHOTO: COURTESY OF LINDA LAUBY

telephone service until 1974, or a public paved road until 1984. Tourists driving on the new road were charmed that undomesticated horses milled freely in plain view. Less than 10 years later, horses were lounging in shade under rental cottage decks, nosing through garbage cans, and strolling nonchalantly through the grocery store's automatic door. Tourists took to feeding and petting them—or attempting to. Close calls with horse bites and kicks became part of the local lore.

Tragically, in the past many horses were struck by vehicles on NC 12. After the road between Duck and Corolla was made public in 1984, 17 horses were killed in vehicle accidents in just four years.

A group of local citizens established the Corolla Wild Horse Fund in 1989 to protect the animals after three pregnant mares were killed. The group rallied public support, managing to have the county pass an ordinance to help protect the horses from harm. Signs were posted along the road: Wild Horse Crossing; You Are Entering A Wild Horse Sanctuary; Do Not Feed Horses. Bumper stickers proclaiming "I brake for wild horses" began materializing on cars. Horse souvenirs from the lighthouse gift shop became some of the most popular Corolla memorabilia. The wild horses, in fact, quickly established themselves as the area's most popular attraction.

Still, horse fund volunteers and staffers were unable to protect their charges. After a poll revealed that most people wanted to preserve the horses in their own environment instead of relocating them, the fund erected a mile-and-a-half-long fence, stretching from sound-to-sea near where the pavement ends in Corolla. The idea was not to enclose the wild animals but to allow them to roam freely—but safely—in the more than 1,600 acres of public and private land north of the fence. On March 24, 1995, the horses were herded behind the fence. But the Corolla wild horse story was not yet over.

Like clever children, some of the herd, which numbered 100 by then, strayed around the fence up to Virginia, where they were not welcome. Other horses, led by a particularly stubborn stallion, began sneaking back into Corolla village. They were always herded back home, but the few recalcitrant horses always found a way out. In 1999, the Corolla Wild Horse Fund took the wandering horses to the private Dews Island in Currituck Sound, where they have 400 acres to graze. There are now 10 horses on Dews Island, including two foals born in the spring of 2001. The other 50 horses stay behind the fence and roam the vast area between the off-road ramp and Carova.

The horses are seeing better protection than ever, now that the Corolla Wild Horse Fund has its first set of paid directors. Gene and Donna Snow are the new part-time codirectors, responsible for overseeing the health and safety of the herd. Volunteers are needed to help with activities such as a census, marking the horses, and taking health samples. The new Corolla Wild Horse Fund Office is at the Currituck County Satellite Building at 1123 Ocean Trail in Corolla proper. The Snows are in the office two to three days a week, usually Monday, Wednesday, and/or Friday from 10:00 A.M. until around 1:30 P.M., and they're often out in the field. The office phone number is (252) 453–8002, and there is an answering machine. The mailing address is P.O. Box 361, Corolla, North Carolina 27927, or you can e-mail them at info@corolla wildhorses.com.

Insiders' Tip

The Outer Banks is no longer a ghost town in the winter months. You'll find museums, galleries, restaurants, shops, and other sites open year-round. If businesses do close for the winter, they usually stay open at least through the holidays because many visitors come for Thanksgiving and Christmas.

and buried the seamen in a site adjacent to the island's cemetery.

Since then, Coast Guard officers have maintained the grassy area within a white picket fence. They fly a British flag above the graves, and each year, on the anniversary of the sailors' deaths, the local military establishment sponsors a ceremony to honor the men who died so far from their own shores.

Deepwater Theater
School Rd., Ocracoke
www.molassescreek.com

Deepwater Theater is home theater of Ocracoke's most famous band, Molasses Creek. This high-energy acoustic folk-fusion band plays bluegrass and ballads and rolls everything together with a wacky sense of humor. Gary Mitchell, Kitty Mitchell, and fiddler Dave Tweedie make up the band that has formed a loyal following in the United States and abroad. Based on the island, they play here all summer and at other times of the year. Molasses Creek also performs all over the nation, and they were recently featured on National Public Radio's *Prairie Home Companion* with Garrison Keillor.

Molasses Creek plays here on Tuesdays and Thursdays in summer. The screened-in-porch–style Deepwater Theater hosts other musicians as well, including singer-songwriter Noah Paley. Ocrafolk Opry is held on Wednesday nights. There's no phone number, so when you get to the island just ask around. Any local will be able to fill you in on times and prices.

Portsmouth Village
South of Ocracoke Island, by private boat access, Portsmouth Island
(252) 728–2250
www.nps.gov/calo

The only ghost town on the Eastern Seaboard, Portsmouth Village is about a 20-minute boat ride south of Ocracoke Island and was once the biggest town on the Outer Banks. Today, the 23-mile-long, 1.5-mile-wide island is owned and managed by the National Park Service as part of Cape Lookout National Seashore. Wilderness camping, hiking, shelling, fishing, and other activities are available on the wide beach. Free, self-guided walking tours of the village are a great way to see how islanders lived in the 19th century.

Visiting Portsmouth Village is utterly surreal. Many of the former homes and village buildings are intact and restored, but they sit hollow, yet hopeful, as if waiting to come to life. Peeking into the windows of some of the unrestored buildings, you'll see remnants of the families who once lived there—curtains, unmade beds, upturned old chairs, broken frames—as if they left in a hurry and never came back.

Portsmouth Village was established in 1753 and grew to become one of the largest settlements on the Outer Banks. Situated along the banks of a major trade route, Ocracoke Inlet, Portsmouth became known as a "lightering" village. Large ships could not pass through the inlet with a full load of cargo, so the Portsmouth villagers would unload the cargo onto small flatboats while the ships passed through the inlet. On the other side, they'd put all the cargo back onboard and send the big ships off to the

Portsmouth Island's abandoned Coast Guard station has been lovingly restored, yet it sits eerily empty.
PHOTO: MOLLY HARRISON

mainland. When the more navigable Hatteras Inlet opened in 1846, lightering at Portsmouth was no longer needed. The Civil War and hurricanes drove Portsmouth residents inland over the next century, until only three residents remained on the island in 1970, two women and one man. When the man died in 1971, the two aging women reluctantly left the island. The National Park Service began restoring the village in 1976. It is listed on the National Register of Historic Places.

There is a visitor center on-site, staffed by volunteers who commit to living on the island for extended periods of time. You can see the old post office, the church, the old Coast Guard station, and other buildings. Some of the homes are private, their owners granted extended leases in exchange for restoration work. Portsmouth Island is a rugged adventure, and there are few conveniences. Restrooms are provided in the visitor center, and there's a comfort station (toilets only) on the other side of the village. You must bring your own water, food, insect repellent, and sunscreen. Mosquitoes are notorious in the summer and fall.

You can get to the island by private boat or with a charter service. Capt. Rudy Austin runs round-trip boat trips to the island, daily in summer and by appointment in the off-season. Call at least one day in advance for reservations, (252) 928-4361 or (252) 928-5431. Portsmouth Island ATV Excursions, (252) 928-4484, leads guided tours of the village and island on ATVs from April through November. Call for reservations and information.

Kidstuff

The beach is always a popular lure for children where they can play tag with the waves, build whimsical sandcastles, fly a kite, play volleyball, or dig for treasure they just know has been left in that exact spot by a pirate of long ago.

Think of the Outer Banks as a large sandy playground, with opportunities for exploration that are only limited by your imagination. For kids, this means the possibilities are infinite, especially on sunny days at the beach. Be sure to check out our Waves and Weather chapter so your children have a safe vacation at the beach. If the skies are overcast or the temperature too cold to play by the shore, they'll need a little more help from you (and us!) to know how to entertain themselves.

You'll want to read the chapters on Recreation, Attractions, and Watersports for a more complete listing of activities that children will enjoy. This chapter takes a look at the not-so-obvious as well as some hands-down favorites.

In compiling this chapter, we asked the experts themselves—kids from 5 to 15, both "locals" and veteran visitors—to recommend their favorite sunny- and rainy-day activities. Here's what they told us when we asked, "What are your favorite things to do on the Outer Banks?"

Kids' Favorite Things to Do

The Beach

They'll dig for coquinas, those tiny crab-like creatures that burrow frantically into the wet sand when the surf pulls away from the beach. They'll chase sand crabs and sandpipers and poke at jellyfish with sticks. They'll draw pictures and letters in the sand, construct structures both simple and intricate, and cover themselves and selected victims with sand, making you grateful so many Outer Banks accommodations have outdoor showers so you can wash off the gritty crust at the end of the day. (As a convenience to visitors, each township offers public restroom and shower facilities at one or more beach access areas.)

Little kids who aren't old enough or confident enough to immerse themselves in the ocean still find an endless variety of ways to enjoy the beach. Your job is to keep them safe (more on that in a minute), keep them fed and watered, and then get out of the way of their creativity unless they make you the object of it.

An inflatable baby pool will make a day shoreside more pleasant if you have infants and toddlers in tow. Set it up under a big umbrella and toss in some floating toys. Buckets and shovels and boogie boards are essential equipment for slightly older kids. Even if they're not old enough to ride the waves, little kids like to sit or lie on boogie boards at the very edge of the water. Older kids tend to gravitate to more expensive props such as body boards and surf boards.

At the risk of stating the obvious, here are a few things to remember about kids on the beach: Keep your young ones slathered in sunscreen, reapplying it frequently. Never take your eyes off of them at the ocean or the sound. The surf, even where it is most shallow, can be rough; undertows and currents are insidious. There are sudden drop-offs and deep holes in both the ocean and the sound. Stay away from the water when the red warning flags are flying.

The surfing bug takes hold! PHOTO: COURTESY OF J. AARON TROTMAN

Please read carefully about beach safety, and for good measure, choose a section of the beach that is served by our excellent lifeguards. A list of guarded beaches is provided in the Waves and Weather chapter.

If you have very small children, try one of the soundside beaches for a more tranquil alternative to the ocean. The gentle waters are perfect for children who are intimidated by the wave action at the ocean, enabling them to build their confidence and their swimming skills.

Fishing or Crabbing

Soundside Beaches, Docks, and Piers

Many a grown-up's most cherished childhood memories involve fishing at the Outer Banks as a child. It's a wonderful way for you and your kids to share some special time together.

You can rent or buy equipment at a tackle shop (see our Fishing chapter) or at a pier. Along with your equipment, get some advice on what's biting, what to use to catch it, and where to find it. Stake out a spot at the surf or head out to one of the piers.

For a truly unique experience, treat the family to an excursion on a headboat, which offers per-person rates for half-day charters. Rookie anglers can get plenty of help with their rods and reels, which are supplied, from experienced mates. Many passengers just go along for the ride and spectacular scenery. Either way, it's a comfortable and affordable way to experience the Outer Banks from the water, which Insiders consider an essential part of the

Sometimes kids like the soundside beaches better because the water is calmer than the ocean. PHOTO: KAREN BACHMAN

Outer Banks experience. Check the Fishing chapter for more information on the head-boats that operate in the area: the *Crystal Dawn* out of Pirate's Cove in Manteo, the *Miss Oregon Inlet* out of Oregon Inlet Fishing Center, and the *Miss Hatteras* out of Oden's Dock in Hatteras Village. Also refer to our Recreation chapter for information on sunset and moonlight cruises.

Crabbing excursions can be particularly memorable. If you head out in the early morning or late afternoon, you'll probably have more crabs to steam up at the end of the day. Head west to the calm waters of the sounds. Try the soundside beaches closest to you or the soundside piers in Kitty Hawk on Kitty Hawk Bay (off West Tateway and Windgrass Circle) and in Kill Devil Hills (on Orville Beach between Durham and Avalon streets). In Corolla, there are some good crabbing spots near the Whalehead Club. One of the most popular locations is on Big Colington Island, below the second bridge on Colington Road near the firehouse.

Part of the fun of crabbing is rigging up the simple equipment. You don't need to invest in crab traps or special bait. Some fishing line, chicken necks, a net, and a deep bucket or cooler will do just fine. Tie a chicken neck to the end of your string, dangle it in the water, and wait for the crabs to come. Then scoop them up (quickly now!) with the net. It'll take a few tries, but you'll get the hang of it. Grown-ups or older kids can wield the net for the little ones. To free the crab from the net, don't use your hands; simply dangle the net over the cooler and wiggle it free. Make sure to tell the kids to keep their fingers out of the bucket!

If your catch measures less than 5 inches at the widest part of the shell, you need to throw it back. (Not only is this the law, but it will ensure another batch of crabs for next year's visit.) Try for the real "keepers," the ones that measure more than 6 inches.

The best part of crabbing, like fishing, is feasting on what you've caught. Steam the crabs with your favorite spice, pile the steamed crabs on a picnic table spread with newspaper, and serve with melted butter and lemon.

Hunt for Buried Treasure

Anywhere

What could be more exciting than finding a pirate's map leading to a treasure chest full of gold and silver and jewels? After all, some of history's most famous and feared pirates, including the notorious Blackbeard, visited these shores. Surely they left something behind.

This adventure doesn't leave it to chance. You're going to create the treasure and map for the little kids to find. Recruit the older kids to help set up the treasure hunt—but make sure they can keep a secret. This adventure requires some advance planning and preparation, but it's well worth it; in fact, it's a big part of the fun. For maximum excitement, talk about pirates and tell pirate stories—or, better yet, schedule a trip to Teach's Hole (see subsequent entry)—a day or two before the big event.

What you'll need:

- A book about pirates (geared to the appropriate age for your children: *Blackbeard the Pirate*, by Robert E. Lee, is packed with information, or buy one of the many coloring books on the subject, which you'll find at many drug stores and gifts shops as well as bookstores)
- A bag full of bright and colorful baubles (fake gold coins, plastic jewelry)
- Silver and gold spray paint
- A lot of small rocks and pebbles
- A wooden box to serve as a treasure chest
- Parchment paper
- Pretty shells

Turn the rocks and pebbles into precious metals by spraying them with the gold and silver paint. When they're dry, heap them into the treasure chest along with the baubles, leaving a few handfuls to scatter around the burial site. Depending upon the type of wooden box you use for your treasure chest, you might want to beat it up a little to make it look old and authentic. Stake out a likely spot to bury your treasure. Don't make it too difficult to find, but don't make it too easy, either! Somewhere close to your cottage will do. Draw the treasure map. Be creative with your route and clues. You can crumple the paper, smudge it, rub it in the dirt, and char the edges to make it look old. Remember "X" marks the spot. Okay. Now somehow you've got to have the good fortune to "accidentally" stumble upon this authentic pirate treasure map, preferably when the little ones are in tow. Help them find their way to the buried treasure, and enjoy their excitement. How

many times do you suppose a three- or four-year-old will want you to bury the treasure for them to find again? Wrong. Way low.

Take in a Show

Summer Children's Series
Roanoke Island Festival Park, Manteo
(252) 475-1506

Roanoke Island Festival Park offers excellent children's programming in the summer months with its Summer Children's Series. From late June through early August, programs are held Tuesday through Friday at 10:30 A.M. and change weekly. Past performances have included puppet and marionette shows, storytellers, and plays. Christmas programs, such as *The Littlest Angel*, are also held. There is usually a fee, though it is waived if you have paid for park admission. Programs are held in the Film Theater, which seats about 200 people.

Professional Theater Workshop
(252) 473-2127

Performers and technicians with *The Lost Colony* stage at least one show for children every summer. Expect to see these talented dramatists putting on hilarious and imaginative interpretations of popular fairy tales, fables, and legends. The show usually plays once or twice a week from mid-July to early August. A small admission fee is charged. Locations vary so call ahead for details.

Race a Hermit Crab

Newman's Shell Shop
NC 12, MP 13½, Nags Head
(252) 441-5791

One of the most anticipated events for kids is the annual hermit crab race held at Newman's Shell Shop each July for over 25 years. If you think your crab has the crawling power to win the race, bring it along and compete for prizes. Not only is this *the* place to go for a day of racing, Newman's is one of the oldest and most

Children's theater is great fun for both the young and the old. PHOTO: COURTESY OF ROANOKE ISLAND FESTIVAL PARK

fascinating shops on the Outer Banks—complete with a museum of shells sure to entertain kids of all ages. Look for the bright pink building, and be sure to check the listing on Newman's, the first store built on the beach, in our Attractions chapter. Call Newman's for information on this year's race. (See also the listing in our Annual Events chapter under "July.")

Scotch Bonnet Candies and Gifts
NC 12, Frisco
(252) 995-4242

And they're off! Every Friday in season, hermit crabs race to the finish line at Scotch Bonnet Candies and Gifts. For lots of family fun, bring your crab or rent one at the store and get set to race. Large, medium, and small crabs take off in separate contests to win prizes for their sponsors. Join the Scotch Bonnet Candies and Gifts crowd under the tent on Friday afternoon for free soft drinks and prizes. After the races, remember to pick up some homemade fudge (they even have sugar free) from inside the shop.

Curl up with a Good Book

Manteo Booksellers
105 Sir Walter Raleigh St., Manteo
(252) 473–1221

Forget those mega-stores in your hometown, and if you've been browsing the stacks only in the virtual realm, come rediscover the deep pleasures of a bookstore that exists because its proprietor loves books. And bring the kids, because they are made to feel welcome here.

The charming small-town appearance of Manteo Booksellers will draw you right inside, where you might be surprised at the size of the selection. You'll find modern literature and the classics, as well as stacks arranged by subject. While you're here, check out the section on local topics of interest and local authors and feel free to ask for recommendations.

Little readers can plant themselves in little chairs in the children's section and browse an extensive selection of the very best books for kids. If you haven't already discovered the Crabby and Nabby series by author Suzanne Tate and artist/illustrator James Melvin, do yourself and your child a favor and start collecting. They introduce children to a variety of friendly indigenous creatures whose adventures afford a perfect opportunity to learn a little something about the Outer Banks.

The place stays lively throughout the year with author signings, readings, children's storytelling, and other special events. Check calendar listings in local newspapers or call the number listed for more information.

Summer Stories for Kids
Corolla Library, 1123 Ocean Trail, Corolla
(252) 453–0496

The neat thing about this library is the storytelling hour every Wednesday at 10:30 A.M. from late June through early August. The story sessions are held on the grounds of the Whalehead Club, at the picnic area.

If you need to check out a book, the library is open year-round, Monday through Wednesday from 10:00 A.M. to 3:00 P.M. and Thursday from 3:00 to 7:00 P.M. You'll need a picture ID to check out books.

StoryTime at the Dare County Library
Manteo (252) 473–2372
Kill Devil Hills (252) 441–4331
Buxton (252) 986–2385

Preschool story hours are held at the libraries to aquaint young kids with the library and get them to enjoy books at an early age. The story hours include games, songs, puppets, stories, and plays, and sometimes there are guest storytellers. Programs last 30 minutes to an hour. Programs are held once a week at each of the library locations: Tuesdays in Buxton, Wednesdays in Manteo, and Thursdays in Kill Devil Hills. Separate programs are held for two-year-olds, three-year-olds, and four- to five-year-olds.

Kids' Favorite Places to Go

Miniature golf, waterslides, "dollar stores," movie theaters, and more attractions and gifts from nature than you could explore in two weeks' time—there's an abundance of places to delight the most discriminating kid visitor. We're hard-pressed to cull from the list, but here are some favorites. See our Recreation and Attractions chapters for more ideas.

Jockey's Ridge State Park
US 158, MP 12, Nags Head
(252) 441–7132

Talk about a sandbox! Jockey's Ridge is the tallest sand dune on the East Coast. There's no better location for kite flying. The kids will have plenty of room to run without worrying about getting their lines

A trip to the beach can be both exciting and relaxing. PHOTO: COURTESY OF JACKIE THOMAS

crossed or caught in a tree. See the Kite-Flying section of our Recreation chapter.

Scrabbling around in the sand is a joy unto itself. Clamber up to the top of the dune (it's great exercise) and enjoy the expansive ocean-to-sound views. If you make arrangements in advance, a park ranger will drive a physically challenged visitor up the dune in a four-wheel-drive vehicle. From October through May, you can pick up a free permit at the park's offices for sand boarding, but you don't need any equipment to enjoy a good old-fashioned roll down the huge sandy hill. Don't let the kids have all the fun; there's something about the environment that encourages cutting loose!

Check local newspapers and at the park office for a current schedule of programs offered by the state park rangers. These are wonderful opportunities to stimulate and satisfy curious young minds. What could be more enchanting to a young child than to climb the ridge at night and gaze at constellations or learn

about animal tracks in the sand or net-fishing in the sound?

Don't worry too much about all that sand and sweat on a hot summer day: Rinse off at the great soundside beach at the park's southwest corner, which also has picnic tables and parking. Be sue to wear shoes.

The park headquarters is north of the dune and west of US 158 on Carolista Drive.

The Promenade
US 158, MP 0
Kitty Hawk
(252) 261-4400

The Promenade is one huge family fun center, where everyone in the family can find something fun to do. There's an outdoor play park for kids, an indoor arcade with everybody's favorite games, an 18-hole miniature golf course, a chip and putt, an ice-cream parlor, and a driving range. Then there's the watersports division, with parasailing, sailing, boating, and personal watercraft. This is a place where you could spend the whole day. There are a restaurant, snack bar, and picnic tables on-site. It's open every day in the summer and closes from October through March.

Diamond Shoals Family Fun Park
US 158, MP 9½, Kill Devil Hills
(252) 480–3553

Diamond Shoals is another place the kids could spend a whole day. First, there's the wild waterslides, where kids can slip and slide all day long. Paddle boats, batting stations, miniature golf, an arcade, a tot lot, and a snack bar and picnic area round out the offerings. See our Recreation chapter for more details.

Glazin' Go Nuts
US 158, MP 6, Kill Devil Hills
(252) 449–2134

This paint-your-own-pottery studio is a favorite place for kids and adults to spend a creative afternoon. Studio time costs $6.00 per painter for the day. You buy the pieces you want to paint for an additional charge, from $3.00 to $35.00, with most pieces averaging around $15.00. After you've painted, leave your masterpiece to be fired. It takes about three or four days for the turnover. They will ship your works to you if you go home before then.

Sandbox Skate Park
Sea Holly Sq., NC 12, MP 9½, Kill Devil Hills
(252) 480–0542

Kids who like skateboarding love riding the ramps at the Sandbox. For $5.00, any age kid can go all day. Helmets and kneepads are required and are available to rent for $1.00 each. For everyone under age 18, a parent must sign a waiver. You can bring in a notarized waiver also. The waiver stays on file so kids can come back again and again. The Sandbox is open from 10:00 A.M. to dark every day. Snacks and drinks are available in Sea Holly Square.

Kitty Hawk Kites
US 158, MP 13½, Nags Head
(252) 441–4124

Just across the street from Jockey's Ridge State Park, Kitty Hawk Kites is a fun store for kids to visit. There are all sorts of kites, a rock-climbing wall, and toys galore. Kitty Hawk Kites leads kayak tours that kids are welcome to join. They also have a Family Fun Day every summer Saturday from noon to 4:30 P.M., with activities for children and adults. Call to inquire about kite-making workshops, where kids make their own kites and fly them. Kitty Hawk Kites sponsors many family-friendly events on Jockey's Ridge and at other locations. See our Annual Events chapter or call for information.

Nags Head Bowling
US 158, MP 10, Nags Head
(252) 441–7077

Yes, Nags Head Bowling offers fun for kids, but we also notice that parents can bowl peacefully here too while little ones are totally enthralled. This facility sports kiddie bumpers that run the length of the lane, so even barely walking tykes can knock down pins every time. We watched one toddler bowl for an hour while the adults carried on a serious game unhindered at the lane beside him. There are light, six-pound balls available for the toddlers. Turn them toward the pins, and away they go.

Games cost $3.50 each; shoes rent for $2.25. Nags Head Bowling is open from noon until midnight daily. If you're sensitive to smoke, try bowling early in the afternoon. See our Recreation chapter for evening specials.

There's a great selection of video games in the entrance including Tekken 2, Ultimate Mortal Kombat, Ms. Pac-Man, Stargate pinball, and air hockey. Games run from 25 cents to 75 cents. You must be 21 to play pool in the on-site bar unless you're accompanied by an adult. Yes, there is a snack bar!

The Playhouse Family Fun Center
Mall Dr., between the highways, MP 14, Nags Head
(252) 441–3277

Once they know about The Playhouse, your kids will beg you to take them here again and again. An indoor arcade has Skee-Ball, video games, basketball, and other games you can play to win prizes. There are also air hockey, Foosball, and pool tables. For toddlers, there's a soft-play area and a climbing area. As you might imagine, this is a popular place for birthday parties. The food court serves pizza, hot dogs, ice cream, soft drinks, and other snacks. A teen dance is held here on Friday and Saturday nights from 7:00 to 11:00 P.M., with a DJ and a dance floor. The Playhouse is open every day in the summer, and on weekends in the off-season.

Outer Banks Daredevils Baseball Games
Manteo High School's Tillett Field,
Wingina Ave., Manteo
(252) 441–4889

A summer-league team, the Outer Banks Daredevils play their home games at Manteo High School. We're hoping to see their return in 2002, but you should call first to make sure funding was available to play another season. This is an exciting outing for children, who love to sit on the bleachers, eat hot dogs, and yell for their team. The players are college athletes so the games can get pretty exciting. Games start at 7:05 P.M. Admission in 2001 was $4.00 for adults and $3.00 for kids and seniors.

Wolf Howls
Alligator River National Wildlife Refuge
Dare County Mainland
(252) 473–1131 ext. 243

Kids love the eerie experience of going to the refuge at night to hear the red wolves howl. The refuge staff leads a guided trip deep into the refuge, and a leader can usually get the wolves to start howling. Sometimes kids get to howl to see if the wolves will respond. Howls are held once a week in the summer and at other times during the year. It's free! See our Attractions chapter for more information.

The Roanoke Island Festival Park offers children's programming throughout the year. PHOTO: COURTESY OF ROANOKE ISLAND FESTIVAL PARK

The Fishing Docks

At the end of the day, kids love to go to the fishing docks to see all the fish that were caught on the charter boats that day. Take the kids down to the docks between 3:00 and 5:00 P.M., and you're sure to see some big tuna, dolphin, wahoo, and more. This is a spectator event only. Head to Pirate's Cove Yacht Club in Manteo, Oregon Inlet Fishing Center south of Nags Head, or Hatteras Harbor Yacht Club or Oden's Dock in Hatteras Village.

Playgrounds

If you're looking for a place to let the kids burn off some energy, head to one of these playgrounds.

Behind Outer Banks Style,
Schoolhouse Lane, Corolla

County Family Recreation Park
Mustian Street, Kill Devil Hills

Nags Head Park
W. Barnes Street, Nags Head

Manteo Tot Lot
Waterfront, Manteo

Old Swimming Hole
Airport Road next to the Aquarium,
Roanoke Island

Rodanthe/Waves/Salvo Community Center,
NC 12, Rodanthe

Fessenden Center
NC 12, Buxton

Double L Bird Ranch and Petting Zoo
Back Rd., Buxton
(252) 995-5494
Here's a golden opportunity to experience the exotic on Hatteras Island. At the Double L you'll see anything from a small zebra finch to a blue-and-gold macaw. You can interact with these feathered friends in the aviary by handfeeding them or even offering them a little affection by scratching their heads. The larger birds put on a show at 10:30 A.M. and noon. The ranch is open year-round, Tuesday through Saturday from 10:00 A.M. until 2:00 P.M. Adults pay $5.00, and kids $3.00 (this admission includes the bird show). Groups larger than 20 persons are eligible for reduced rates.

While you're on Hatteras Island, check out the Frisco Native American Museum and the Cape Hatteras Lighthouse, two stops sure to interest kids. (See our Attractions chapter for more information on these sites.)

Teach's Hole
Back Rd., Ocracoke
(252) 928-1718
This Ocracoke stop is sure to fascinate the younger crowd. All you have to do is mention pirates, and they'll be begging you to take them to Teach's Hole. The pirate shop features a historical exhibit about Edward Teach (a.k.a. Blackbeard) that includes a short video, weapons of the pirates, old bottles, Blackbeard in full battle-dress, and dioramas for the kids. There is a small fee to view the exhibit, but children under six get in free. The gift shop, a must for all ages, is filled with everything you can think of that is related to pirates

and piracy. Teach's Hole is open Easter through Thanksgiving.

Kids' Camps

EcoCamps at Nags Head Woods Preserve
Nags Head
(252) 441-2525
Each summer, children come to Nags Head Woods to take part in weeklong day camps in which they can learn about the world around them. Activities include hiking, canoeing, kayaking, games, drawing, and other fun things. These camps fill up early, so reserve your spot well in advance. Since the programs vary from year to year, call for dates and costs. Nags Head Woods also hosts two-hour marsh tours daily during the summer. A trained naturalist leads families on an adventure through the marshes of Nags Head Woods Preserve, teaching about the creatures and plants found within. You must register a day in advance. You'll need to bring old shoes, sunscreen, and bug spray and plan to get wet.

North Carolina Aquarium at Roanoke Island
Roanoke Island
(252) 473-3493
The Aquarium leads the Aquatic Adventures Summer Camp for students who have completed the fourth and fifth grades. The camps last for five half-days, with children learning about the Outer Banks waters and habitats with many hands-on activities and field trips. Each weeklong camp concludes with a sleepover at the Aquarium. Also, the Aquarium can be rented for sleepover parties among the fishes and sharks. Many kids do this for their birthday parties.

Outer Banks Family YMCA
US 158, MP 11, Nags Head
(252) 449-8897
The YMCA has weeklong day camps for all ages. Half-day Kindercamps are for ages 3 to 6, and full-day camps are for ages 7 to 12. Each week has a special theme, and kids do activities related to the theme in

addition to going to the pool and ocean and on field trips. The YMCA also hosts several sports camps in beach volleyball, girls field hockey, soccer, basketball, and junior ocean rescue. Call for information.

Summer Art Camps
KDH Cooperative Gallery
502 US 158, MP 8½, Kill Devil Hills
(252) 441-9888

The KDH Cooperative Gallery offers arts camps for kids in the summer. Each session rewards kids with art and craft projects that they can take home at the end of the week. Painting, drawing, sculpting, and printmaking are some of the classes taught by professional artists. Camps are held from 9:00 to 11:00 A.M. for five days. The gallery also offers candle-making workshops for ages 6 to 12 and a pottery class for teens.

It's not really a camp, but if the kids want something great to do on a summer night while parents go out to dinner, KDH Coop offers Kids Night Out programs from 6:00 to 9:00 P.M. on weeknights in the summer. Kids must be ages 6 to 12. Activities include soap making, painting picture frames and switchplates, and more. Call for information.

Dare County Parks and Recreation
(252) 473-1101 ext. 313

Parks and Rec offers weeklong sports camps in basketball, soccer, cheerleading, gymnastics, triathlon training, fishing, and possibly others. These are weeklong camps, held Monday through Friday, and they are usually about five hours long per day. There's also an Adventure Camp, where participants go on a weeklong camping trip. Toddler Camps for ages three to five last about two hours. Call for information.

4H Camps
Dare County Cooperative Extension
(252) 473-1101 ext. 442

In the summer, 4H offers weeklong day camps for elementary school children at four sites in the county: Kitty Hawk Ele-

Another happy Outer Banks visitor. PHOTO: COURTESY OF KAREN BACHMAN

mentary, First Flight Elementary, Manteo Elementary, and Munchkin Academy in Buxton. Camps last from 7:30 A.M. to 5:30 P.M. and include educational and fun activities and a field trip based on a particular theme. The Support Our Students is for middle school students and alternates between Manteo Middle and First Flight Middle Schools. This is more like a daytripper's program, with off-site educational field trips. One-week camps away from home, in which campers travel to one of five 4H camps in the state, are also held. You must preregister for all these camps. Call for information.

Kitty Hawk Sports Kayaking Kids Clinic
(252) 441-4800

Kitty Hawk Sports holds kayaking clinics for kids in the summer. For $25, kids get a two-hour lesson in kayaking safety and paddling. There are lots of games, and kids say it's really fun. Clinics are held five days a week from mid-June through mid-August. Call to register.

Weddings

The wedding industry is booming on North Carolina's Outer Banks. For decades, the area has been a haven for honeymooners, though in recent years, couples of all ages have opted to have their ceremonies here as well. In the year 2000, there were 1,190 marriage licenses issued in Dare and Currituck Counties, according to the Outer Banks Visitors Bureau, and the Outer Banks Wedding Association (OBWA) estimates there were more than 1,200 weddings in Dare, Currituck, and Hyde Counties. The OBWA expects that number to double for 2002. While many still hold traditional church ceremonies, a growing number of couples plan outdoor weddings, either on the beach or in such historic settings as an old hunt club or the Elizabethan Gardens. Wedding receptions are often far from traditional, and many are held in the palatial three-story oceanfront rental homes that line the 90-plus miles of beaches from Corolla to Ocracoke.

In this chapter, we'll help guide you through the intricacies of planning a wedding on the Outer Banks, from applying for a license and choosing a magistrate or minister to hiring a caterer and photographer. We'll also provide you with information on locations, rental companies, musicians, florists, formal wear, transportation, gifts, and lodging. And for those of you who would rather pay someone else to handle all the headaches, we'll let you know about some excellent wedding consultants. Planning a wedding far away from home should be a thrilling adventure; our goal is to make it as easy as possible.

Tying the Knot

When asked their idea of the perfect place for romance, most everyone will say the beach. Maybe it's the melodic rhythm of the waves upon the sand or the gentle breezes that caress a bare shoulder. Perhaps it's a strong gust of wind laced with the smell of salt on a clear autumn day that infuses you with energy and renewal. One thing's for sure, the Outer Banks is becoming more and more popular as a place for brides and grooms to pledge their love to each other for eternity. It's so popular, in fact, that service providers (caterers, photographers, musicians, ministers, etc.) are having trouble keeping up with the demand. Everyone recommends that you start planning your wedding at the very least a year in advance.

The main wedding season on the Outer Banks is from April through October, though May and October are the most popular wedding months thanks to nice weather, fewer visitors, and off-peak accommodations rates. Remember that hurricane season is from July through early November, so be sure to inquire with all your service providers about their policy concerning hurricane evacuations or other causes for cancellation.

North Carolina law requires that a wedding ceremony be conducted by an ordained minister or by a magistrate. Sorry, it doesn't appear that a boat captain can do the trick any more.

The state has replaced its former justice of the peace system with court-appointed magistrates. These officials may perform wedding services but are often severely

An outdoor seaside wedding will be as memorable for your guests as it will be for you. PHOTO: COURTESY OF
LINDA LAUBY

limited as to the times and places they can accommodate. A magistrate's fee for performing a ceremony is $10. Magistrates are, however, required to marry any people who show up with a marriage license and two witnesses.

Most major Christian denominations are represented on the Outer Banks. Many do require a special counseling period, and some have specific requirements regarding remarrying divorced persons. If you wish to be married in the Outer Banks Catholic Parish, you must meet with the pastor at least six months before the wedding. There is no Jewish congregation on the Outer Banks; the nearest temple is in Norfolk, Virginia. Most Jewish couples bring a rabbi from their home temple. For more information on local churches, see our Worship chapter or visit www.outer banks.org/locations for a list of churches.

Marriage Licenses

You must obtain a marriage license in order to be wed in North Carolina. Licenses are issued by the register of deeds in any North Carolina county, not just the county you plan to get married in. Both applicants must bring a photo ID and a Social Security card or proof of Social Security number. If you have been divorced, you must bring your legal divorce papers. The license costs $50 and is good for 60 days after it is issued. There is no waiting period. A blood test is not required in North Carolina.

Bring your marriage license to the wedding. After the wedding ceremony, whoever performs the ceremony is required to give the couple a marriage certificate. This certificate includes the couple's names and address, the date of the marriage, the county that issued the license, and the date of the license. The minister or magistrate must sign the license. The license must be returned to the register of deeds in the county in which the couple was married.

Dare County
Register of Deeds (252) 473–3438
Magistrate's Office (252) 473–2010

Currituck County (Corolla)
Register of Deeds (252) 232–3297
Magistrate's Office (252) 232–3404

Hyde County (Ocracoke)
Register of Deeds (252) 926–3011
Magistrate's Office (252) 926–4101

Locations

In addition to the numerous churches on the Outer Banks, you might consider an outdoor wedding, perhaps an informal affair on the beach where everyone can go barefoot. The trend in Outer Banks weddings is to rent a large oceanfront house, or several in a row, and house all the family and friends together for the weekend or up to a week. The wedding takes place on the beach in front of one of the houses, and the reception takes place either in one of the homes or at a nearby location. More and more vacation rental companies are equipped to handle this, and some even allow an unlimited number of guests for a reception in a few of their rental properties. If this is appealing to you, call several of the companies in our Weekly and Long-term Rentals chapter to start looking for a suitable home or homes. If you have trouble finding something, ask your wedding planner or caterer to recommend a company or contact the Outer Banks Wedding Association at (252) 473–4800.

Church Weddings

A traditional wedding often requires that you have some affiliation with the church itself if you are planning to use its facilities.

The best thing to do is to contact the minister of the church you would like to use, and he or she can give you the specifics. You also have the option of bringing a minister from home to perform the ceremony in a local church.

Prepare to pay a fee for the use of the church sanctuary as well as to compensate the minister for his services. It is customary to pay the minister between $50 and $150 for his professional services, and don't forget to add something for travel and accommodations if the wedding is taking place away from the minister's usual church.

Beach Weddings

Getting married on the beach is romantic and special—if you're one of those people who won't be upset if everything isn't perfect. You can't predict the elements, you know. Wind is a major factor, something that brides with major hairdos may want to consider. The width and condition of the beach will depend on the tides and the wind direction on your wedding day. Lighting is also difficult on the beach. Talk with your photographer about having the wedding at the proper time of day. You don't want everyone squinting in the wedding photographs. While sunset is a romantic time to be married, remember that the light will be very low, making it difficult for the photographer and videographer to get vivid shots.

The National Park Service charges a fee of $100 for gatherings within its boundaries, and that includes the beach. You cannot bring in chairs, arbors, flowers, balloons, ribbons, or anything else that is not natural to the area. For information, contact the National Park Service at (252) 473–2111.

Outdoor Weddings

Many people choose to have their ceremony on the Outer Banks because of the magnificent outdoor settings that can be found here. With more than 100 miles of pristine beaches from Corolla to Ocra-coke, weddings on the shore are quite appealing. But remember that Outer Banks weather can be unpredictable, so have an indoor alternative available.

There is no guarantee as to what the weather will be like on any given day on the Outer Banks, but generally the summer is sunny, hot, and humid; spring can be a bit rainy and cool; winter is cold and raw, but occasionally warm days make an appearance; and autumn offers warm clear days and crisp cool nights, perfect for an outdoor wedding.

The Whalehead Club
NC 12, Corolla
(252) 453–9040
www.whaleheadclub.com

Corolla's historic Whalehead Club (see our Attractions chapter) is a popular choice for an outdoor wedding. With many acres situated on the Currituck Sound, waterfowl abounds in this location, and the sunsets are spectacular. An old arched wooden bridge spans a channel that leads to the club's marina and boathouse; instead of a walk down the aisle, many brides instead walk across the bridge. A long pier on the premises leads to a gazebo where some couples exchange vows over the water. For added ambiance, the Currituck Light-house is visible over the treeline. The cost to use the grounds is $350. The Whalehead Club does not allow alcohol to be served on the grounds, so many people hold their receptions elsewhere.

Currituck Beach Lighthouse
NC 12, Corolla
(252) 453–8152

The Currituck Beach Lighthouse allows weddings and receptions on its charming, well-kept property. The Keeper's Quarters, lighthouse, and outbuildings make a beautiful setting. Cost for weddings is $350, and the cost for receptions is an additional $350. If you plan to have alcohol at your reception, there's an additional $250 fee for the alcohol license. All weddings are held on the southwest corner of the grounds. Some people choose to get married at the Whalehead Club and then have everyone walk over to the light-house for the reception.

Jockey's Ridge State Park
US 158, Nags Head
(252) 441–7132

The East Coast's largest sand dune provides amazing views of the ocean and sound as the backdrop for your wedding ceremony. Of course, all your guests will have to trek up the East Coast's largest sand dune as well. The park also has a soundside beach that makes a great site for a small ceremony, especially at sunset. This state park charges only $25 to use the site for wedding ceremonies. There are no accommodations for receptions.

The Elizabethan Gardens
Off US 64, Roanoke Island
(252) 473–3234

This is one of the most romantic spots to exchange vows on the Outer Banks, and it's also one of the most popular. On some Saturdays, there are as many as four weddings here in one day. These gardens provide an outstanding location for weddings year-round. Besides offering large, grassy lawns that are ideal for the ceremony, the setting offers many backgrounds for picture poses after the wedding. For more intimate gatherings, you may wish to investigate the rose garden or thatch-roofed gazebo that overlooks the sound. To hold a wedding ceremony in the gardens costs $200 for up to 50 guests and $400 for up to 100 guests. For weddings with more than 100 guests, additional charges apply. The first 100 chairs must be rented from The Elizabethan Gardens for $3.00 each. Receptions may be held in the Meeting Hall for an additional fee of $200 to $400, depending on the number of guests (up to 100). The Meeting Hall has a kitchen, tables, and chairs. Alcohol may be served in the Meeting Hall.

**Hatteras Island Soundfront
Recreation Center, Rodanthe
(252) 987–2777**

Camp Hatteras, a premier camping resort in the historic village of Rodanthe, provides a wonderful alternative for a reception site. Their 3,000-square-foot building has a fully equipped kitchen and two restrooms, plus a window-lined reception hall with views of the Pamlico Sound. They've even installed a corner stage for your cake-cutting ceremony. If your guests decide to stay at Camp Hatteras, they'll also enjoy one of the finest outdoor recreation facilities found anywhere.

Hatteras Island Soundfront Recreation Center

P.O. Box 10 • Waves, NC 27968
252-987-2777
www.camphatteras.com
E-mail: camphatteras@interpath.com

**National Park Service Lighthouses
Bodie Island, Buxton, Ocracoke
(252) 473–2111 ext. 121**

The Bodie Island, Cape Hatteras, and Ocracoke Lighthouses make beautiful backdrops for a wedding ceremony. The National Park Service charges a $100 fee for gatherings. Weddings at these sites are very simple because the NPS does not allow anyone to bring in chairs, altars, flowers, birdseed, or any of the usual wedding items. Receptions are not allowed on-site because there are no facilities, but there are places nearby to have receptions.

Boat Weddings

***Downeast Rover*
Manteo waterfront
(252) 473–4866**

If you really want to do something unique, get married on a boat. The *Downeast Rover* is a 55-foot topsail schooner based in Manteo. It can accommodate up to 29 people for a two-and-a-half-hour sail in the Roanoke Sound in the afternoon or at sunset. The cost to charter the boat ranges from $400 to $700, depending on the time of day and the season. You can bring your own food and drinks and have a party on the boat, or just have your ceremony on the boat and then have your reception at one of several possible locations in downtown Manteo. Call Capt. Brad Gunn for information.

***Crystal Dawn*
Pirate's Cove Yacht Club, Manteo
(252) 473–5577**

The *Crystal Dawn* is a huge headboat that can accommodate up to 97 passengers. You can have your ceremony and reception on the boat, floating through the scenic waters of the Roanoke Sound. Cost to rent the boat is $250 an hour, with a minimum of two hours. Alcohol is allowed on the boat. Boarding location is at Pirate's Cove Yacht Club.

Accommodations

On the Outer Banks, you may discover that your accommodations are the perfect place to host your rehearsal dinner or wedding. We've only included a few suggestions here. Please see our Accommodations chapter and Weekly and Long-Term Rentals chapter for more options.

Seaside Inn Bed & Breakfast
NC 12, Hatteras Village
(252) 986–2700
www.seasidebb.com
Seaside Inn is a charming location for small gatherings, weddings, and parties. On NC 12 in Hatteras Village, the Seaside features 10 guest rooms (five have separate sitting areas) with fully modernized bathroom facilities and some with whirlpool baths. All rooms feature either king- or queen-size beds with fine linens. A full breakfast is served daily.

This inn is actually the site of the first motel built on the Outer Banks in 1928. It's been lovingly refurbished, and owner Cindy Foster offers guests something special here. See our Accommodations chapter for more information.

Midgett Realty
P.O. Box 250, US 12
Hatteras; Offices also in Avon and Rodanthe
(252) 986–2841, (800) 527-2903
www.midgettrealty.com
Host your family for the big event or find the perfect honeymoon spot in one of Midgett Realty's 460 rental cottages and condos. You can choose from a soundfront hideaway to an oceanfront slice of paradise. Accommodations are available all the way from Rodanthe through Hatteras. Online secure bookings are available. Call (800) 527-2903 to receive a free rental brochure or to find out more information.

R&R Resort Rental Properties, Inc.
1184 NC 12, Duck
(800) 433–8805
www.rr-udeservit@outer-banks.com

R&R represents more than 350 fine family vacation rental homes situated along some of the most pristine beaches and sounds on the East Coast. Many selections are oceanfront or soundfront and feature private pools and romantic hot tubs and fireplaces—perfect for an Outer Banks wedding. R&R has a number of spacious homes that welcome small wedding parties. Any of these homes would be an ideal choice for an intimate, one-of-a-kind seaside event.

Stan White Realty & Construction,
Inc./Duck's Real Estate
US 158, MP 10½, Nags Head
(252) 441–1515, (800) 338–3233
Duck Rd., Duck
(252) 261–4614, (800) 992–2976 in Duck
www.outerbanksrentals.com

If you're looking for a rental house at which to host your wedding by the sea, Stan White Realty & Construction, Inc./Duck's Real Estate offers 400 legacy vacation rental homes on the northern Outer Banks. They offer oceanfront and

soundfront homes and the romantic settings of private pools, hot tubs, and fireplaces. Call (800) 338–3233 or (800) 992–2976 for more information and a rental brochure.

The Inn at Corolla Light
1066 Ocean Trail, Corolla
(252) 453–3340, (800) 215–0772
www.corolla-inn.com

Quiet, undiscovered, and romantic best describe the Inn at Corolla Light, with its luxurious soundfront rooms, pool, and hot tub deck overlooking the Currituck Sound. Rooms are beautifully decorated and have king beds with custom pillow-top mattresses, TVs, VCRs (with complimentary tapes), radios, refrigerators, complimentary in-room coffees and teas, and private baths. Some rooms have whirlpool tubs and fireplaces. The inn has an on-site consultant to assist with your wedding, catering, and limousine service. Honeymoon packages with special pricing that include dinner and champagne are available all seasons of the year. The inn also offers receptions or rehearsal dinners in their intimate dining room or ceremonies in the pier gazebo on the sound.

Have a beautiful wedding on the beach. PHOTO: COURTESY OF TOM MARINO

Surf Side Motel
NC 12, MP 16, Nags Head
(252) 441–2105, (800) 552–7873
www.surfsideobx.com

The Surf Side Motel in Nags Head is a great place to accommodate a large wedding party, especially when the wedding events are in Nags Head or on Roanoke Island. The motel is on the oceanfront, with rooms that face the ocean and have private balconies. Refrigerators, cable TV, hair dryers, coffeemakers, microwaves, irons and ironing boards, and phones will make your guests feel truly comfortable. For the bride and groom, the honeymoon suites have king-size beds and Jacuzzis. The Surf Side has an indoor pool and hot tub and an outdoor pool. The Surf Side is open year-round.

The White Doe Inn
319 Sir Walter Raleigh St., Manteo
(252) 473–4708, (800) 473–6091
www.whitedoeinn.com

The White Doe Inn is a picturesque turn-of-the-twentieth-century inn located in historic Manteo. The inn provides special yet comfortable surroundings decorated with antiques and reproductions—perfect for gathering the members of your wedding party. Small weddings of up to 40 people are handled in the inn and lovely outdoor garden. All-inclusive wedding packages with every last detail covered are available.

The Cameron House Inn
300 Budleigh St., Manteo
(252) 473–6596, (800) 279–8178
www.cameronhouseinn.com

The Cameron House Inn is a restored 1919 Arts & Crafts bungalow in the heart of historic Manteo. The inn offers five guest rooms, a comfortable sitting area, and a cozy back porch, making a wonderful place for the special members of your wedding party to stay together. For small weddings, both ceremonies and receptions, Cameron House has a spacious lawn covered by trees. The yard accommodates a wedding tent easily.

The Tranquil House Inn
405 Queen Elizabeth St., Manteo
(252) 473–1404
www.tranquilhouseinn.com

The Tranquil House, right on the waterfront in Manteo, offers 25 rooms, making it an excellent lodging choice for wedding parties. And the on-site 1587 Restaurant provides an exquisite waterfront reception location, including catering.

Wedding Planners

Any out-of-town wedding requires early preparations and an established budget. Since visits to the area and long-distance phone calls can add up, you may wish to hire a local contact. That's where a wedding planner comes in. A local contact can save you time and money by making phone calls, setting up appointments, and booking blocks of discounted hotel rooms.

Since a wedding planner is already familiar with area musicians, florists, caterers, and everyone else necessary to make your day successful, he or she can really ease your mind and may even suggest options that you haven't yet considered.

Avery Little Detail
(252) 441–1880
www.outerbanksweddings.com/avery

From your first phone call to the final "I do," Avery Hesford Harrison will orchestrate personal and stress-free planning. This is a unique company that specializes in coordinating Outer Banks weddings. Many out-of-town couples find that long-distance planning is costly, stressful, and time-consuming. Specializing in budget management, Avery can alleviate the burden on your time and finances by helping you plan the wedding of your dreams. She will confirm arrangements with vendors, make deliveries, and handle your last-minute tasks, allowing you to arrive relaxed, so you can properly welcome your guests—and most important—savor your wedding weekend.

House of Celebrations
105 Fernando St., Manteo
(252) 473–9398, (888) 280–4819
www.houseofcelebrations.com

House of Celebrations can help with all of your wedding planning needs. Certified wedding consultant Beth Pallett works on an hourly basis to help brides and grooms make their day go off without a hitch. She can plan the entire event from start to finish or just help you find vendors. Pallett works out of the House of Celebrations boutique, which sells fine gifts and accessories geared toward weddings, such as toasting glasses, gift books, bridesmaid and groomsmen gifts, etc.

Above House of Celebrations in the beautiful Centennial Square are three romantic honeymoon suites known as Whispering Bay. Each suite has a gas fireplace, a Jacuzzi tub, and a marvelous view of Shallowbag Bay.

Insiders' Tip

If you're planning an Outer Banks wedding, seek help on the Web. Several Web sites provide all the information you'll need. The Outer Banks Wedding Association Web site, www.outerbanks weddingassoc.org, is the most comprehensive. You can also try www.outerbankswedding guild.com. The Outer Banks Visitors Bureau also has wedding planning information on its Web site, www.outer-banks.org.

Wedding Bells
Ann Bell
121 Garden Dr., Manteo
(252) 473–2635
www.annsweddingbells.com

A successful wedding involves many details, and a reliable wedding consultant can smooth the way and avoid last-minute complications. In 25 years of Outer Banks wedding planning, Ann has assisted hundreds of brides and grooms and knows the answers to almost any questions that could arise. She is thoroughly familiar with the Outer Banks from Corolla to Ocracoke. If you desire a small, private affair, Ann offers the Chapel in the Woods in her lovely garden in Roanoke Island Gardens. Ann is a nondenominational minister and can perform your wedding ceremony with your own special vows.

Flowers

What's a wedding without flowers? The Outer Banks has a fine collection of talented florists that can create and customize anything you can dream up. There are florists in almost every town up and down the beach. Here are a few samplings of what is offered.

Brooks at Vista
US 64/264, Kill Devil Hills
(252) 449–4080, (888) 449–4080
www.brookstheflorist.com
Brooks has 26 years' experience and specializes in weddings, offering silk and fresh-cut flowers. Not only will he supply the flowers, but he also rents items like candelabras and arches to give that extra something special to the ceremony. Each wedding is a custom affair with Brooks, and he strives for perfection in each presentation. The busiest season is May through October though he says the off-season is becoming quite popular because of low rates. His advice is to set your date early.

Every Blooming Thing
NC 12 Piney Ridge Road, Hatteras
(252) 995–5486, (800) 515–1510
Jenny McBride has been in business for over 15 years and prides herself on going the extra mile for her customers. She is a full-service florist who serves all of Hatteras Island. Not only can she supply your wedding with beautiful flowers, she has tuxedos available for rent. If you would like plants at your big event, you can rent or purchase them from Every Blooming Thing. Jenny can also supply your wedding with candelabras, kneeling benches, and even jewelry. As an added bonus, Jenny will act as a bridal consultant at no additional charge.

Holiday House
US 158, MP 9, Kill Devil Hills
(252) 441–5959, (800) 628–6553
www.holidayhouseobx.com
Holiday House offers daily deliveries from Manteo to Corolla, and the staff works in fresh, dried, or silk flowers. Weddings are a specialty for these award-winning designers, who tout themselves as the "Outer Banks Wedding Specialists." Holiday House also creates balloon bouquets and carries gourmet baskets, candles, and bath products.

Seabreeze Florist and Gifts
US 158, MP 1, Kitty Hawk,
The Marketplace in Southern Shores
(252) 261–4274, (800) 435–5881
Formerly at MP 3 in Kitty Hawk, owners Gail James and Tori Ferebee have 17 years' experience offering flowers and gifts "from the heart and soul." Because of the personal touch given to each customer, Gail and Tori have a large following of repeat customers. These designers create artistic floral sculptures using fresh flowers or silk. The silk creations look so real you have to touch them to be sure they're not. Besides wedding flowers, Seabreeze has a line of gifts for the bride or bridal party. Their mood-enhancing oil candles, firelights, are so popular that customers keep coming

back for more. Tori feels the trend for the new century is toward more informal weddings, "more open and garden-like." Stop in at Seabreeze for a fun time where the customers are treated like guests.

Music

Music sets the mood of a wedding, adding to the beauty of the ceremony and the enjoyment of the reception. The Outer Banks abounds with musicians to suit any taste and situation. The following is a small sampling of the varied choices for your special day.

Phil Chestnutt
P.O. Box 262, Nags Head
(252) 441–4174
Acoustic guitarist and singer Phil Chestnutt has been providing music for brides and grooms for nearly 15 years. His selections range from music of the 1930s to modern melodies.

John Harper
(252) 473–4528
Disc jockey John Harper, known for his music column in *The Coast,* is available for spinning tunes at receptions and other events.

Nick Hodsdon
(252) 473–5783, (704) 372–9372
Nick Hodsdon offers classical, acoustic, vocal, and instrumental music for weddings. Solo, duet, and trio performances are available. Instruments include psaltery, guitar, cello, bass, flute, file, and the mandolin. Hodsdon offers selections from the Middle Ages through contemporary times, including Elizabethan, baroque, Celtic, folk, and contemporary music. He will even learn and perform your favorite piece of music.

The Laura Martier Band
(252) 261–6773
The Laura Martier Band is committed to making sure everyone has a good time.

This band is well known on the Outer Banks—they've played at fund-raisers for Sen. Marc Basnight and Gov. Jim Hunt, the Chrysler Museum and Town Pointe Park in Norfolk, as well as private parties and events. Jazz, blues, and rock are among the styles they offer, but special requests, such as bagpipe, classical guitar, or string quartet, can be accommodated too. One thing is for sure, they will bring lots of spirit and good energy to your reception.

Live Oak Trio
P.O. Box 902, Ocracoke
(252) 928–7143
The Live Oak Trio (Cheryl Roberts, violin; Leslie Gilbert, flute; Nancy Hartlaub, piano) is Ocracoke's premier classical music ensemble. They are available for weddings, receptions, anniversaries, or other special occasions. Please contact Cheryl at the above number.

Roy Murray Jr.
(252) 480–1532
Roy Murray has been the music director for more than 700 weddings on the Outer Banks since 1992. He knows the area well and is able to advise on a musical presentation for all styles, situations, and locations. Trumpets, violins, flutes, and many other instruments and musicians are used according to your specifications. Flute duos and trios, chamber music, brass ensembles, acoustic piano, or church organ are some of the selections he offers.

Outer Banks Chamber Players
(252) 473–5860
For classical melodies before, during, and after the ceremony, contact the Outer Banks Chamber Players, a trio consisting of Elsie Brill (flute), Cathey Clawson (clarinet), and Jane Brown (viola).

Carolyn Price
(252) 441–4375
Carolyn specializes in piano, organ, and keyboard and offers a selection of musical styles including classical, elegant, or modern.

You may wish to invite your own minister to officiate at your Outer Banks wedding.

Carolyn can arrange for a variety of instruments for your wedding or reception.

Formal Wear

Since Outer Banks locals are generally a casual lot, there are not a lot of options for dress wear on this strip of vacationland. For non-traditional bridal wear, anything goes. A number of boutiques offer lovely garb appropriate for an island wedding. If you're a traditionalist, read on.

Davis Bridal Formals and Tuxedos
US 158, MP 8, Kill Devil Hills
(252) 441–2604
www.outerbankstuxedo.com
For everything from the bride's and bridesmaids' gowns to rental tuxedos, call Roy Parker at Davis Bridal. You'll get big-city selections at hometown prices, and Roy can deliver the gown to the church steamed and

ready for the big day. Davis's wedding consultants are available to help you select your gown, the bridesmaids' dresses, tuxedoes for the groom and the groomsmen, and they will coordinate dresses for your mother and mother-in-law. Their selection of accessories provides just the right touch.

Bridal Works
Food Lion Shopping Center, US 158, Grandy
(252) 457–0200
On the Currituck mainland in Grandy, Bridal Works is a full-service bridal shop. For the bride, they sell and fit bridal gowns, along with jewelry, shoes, garters, and headpieces, even custom, made-to-order headpieces. Bridal Works offers dresses for bridesmaids, mothers, and flower girls, and they dye shoes in-house. For the men, Bridal Works rents tuxedoes. They also rent any equipment you may need, such as arches, candelabras, unity candles, catering equipment, and linens. Bridal accessories, like cake toppers, glasses, and guest books, are sold in the store. Other services include wedding invitations, silk floral arrangements, and party favors.

Keeping Up Appearances

You're going to be under enough stress on your wedding day; let someone else do your hair for you. While you're at it, you can have your nails done, enjoy a massage, and get a facial as well. You may even want to consider massages or manicures and pedicures as bridesmaids' gifts. Go ahead, indulge.

Eden Spa/Di Dario Concept Salon
Barrier Island Shoppes, NC 12, Duck
(252) 255–0711
For your wedding and pre-wedding day, the women at Eden Spa will make you feel like a new person. They offer a full spectrum of services to help you with all your beauty needs. Hair, makeup, facial, and nail services are provided, as are massages and a wide range of relaxing and beautifying spa services. Our suggestion is to make two days of it: On day one get a full-body massage, a manicure, and a pedicure with

a foot massage; on day two, the wedding day, come in for makeup and a hairstyle.

Donetta Donetta Waterfront Salon
Manteo Waterfront, Manteo
(252) 473–5323
The salon and boutique provide cuts and color, facials, spa treatments, waxing, acid peels, manicures, and pedicures—everything you need to feel beautiful on your wedding day. They also offer massage, La Stone therapy, and other wonderful nurturing therapies to make you feel more relaxed than ever.

Hairoics
US 158, MP 6, The Dare Center, Kill Devil Hills
(252) 441–7983
This large, contemporary salon offers complete wedding packages for the bride, groom, and attendants, including formal, modern, or classic hairstyles, waxing, manicures, acrylic nails, and pedicures. Hairoics' staff includes five wedding specialists trained to create beautiful looks; brides receive a free wedding consultation. They recommend a demonstration of your selected style prior to your wedding day to be sure that it perfectly fulfills your expectations.

Food for Thought

The reception is usually the most expensive and most fun part of a wedding with as many choices as you can imagine. Your options include choosing a hotel or restaurant that provides all the necessary food and beverage services, or you can engage a caterer. Our Restaurants chapter lists a number of excellent places to host either a rehearsal dinner or a full-blown reception. Sanderling Inn in Duck and Penguin Isle in Nags Head are two of the larger facilities on the Outer Banks at which to host an extravagant fete. For more intimate gatherings, consider Miriam's in Corolla, Blue Point in Duck, Ocean Boulevard in Kitty Hawk, 1587 in Manteo, or The Island Inn in Ocracoke. The Sanderling Inn, The Island Inn, and

1587 (at The Tranquil House Inn) provide accommodations as well.

If you have your reception at a beach house, a caterer can take complete charge while you enjoy the company of your guests. The caterer will clean up afterward, too. Expect to spend between $20 and $55 per guest, depending upon your choice of menu and type of bar service.

Wright Place Gourmet Market Catering
US 158, MP 10, Kill Devil Hills
(252) 441–1497
www.wrightplacemarket.com/catering
Wright Place Gourmet offers a variety of wedding planning services and catering. Food ranges from contemporary to traditional, and they can offer anything you want, from continuous appetizers to a casual barbecue, though elegant sit-down dinners for any number of people are their specialty. The chefs are happy to create custom menus that reflect your personal preferences.

Catering by Cabbages & Kings
200 Budleigh St., Manteo
(252) 475–1110, (888) 280–4819
www.cabbagesandkingscatering.com
Catering by Cabbages & Kings is an off-premises event management and catering company. Chef Ron Kneasel creates

Insiders' Tip

You may want to attend the bridal show held on the Outer Banks each January. You can plan your wedding from A to Z at this event— caterers, florists, musicians, ministers, and more will be in attendance. Bridal fashions are modeled throughout the show. Call Deborah Sawyer at (252) 473-4800 or visit www.outerbankswedding assoc.org for more information.

Katering by Kim
Kill Devil Hills
(252) 441–7010
www.kateringbykim.com

Katering by Kim offers everything from a casual beach clambake to an elegant sit-down meal. For buffets, a food station can be simply planned, with individual tables for seafood, hand-carved roasts, pastas, salads, and desserts. In addition to your meal, Katering by Kim can supply you with a cake that serves as a focal point of the day, whether it's one with fresh flowers, something exceptionally decadent, or an impressive, simply decorated white cake. Katering by Kim has self-contained kitchen trailers that they can pull up to any site, even outside, and provide the most elegant of meals without the need for a standard kitchen. This catering company can also provide exquisite floral arrangements by Lynn James.

Seamark Foods
US 158, MP 1, Kitty Hawk
(252) 261–2220
US 158, MP 14½, Nags Head
(252) 441–4121

Seamark Foods offers deli treats, hot and cold foods, and wedding cakes for small and large groups at reasonable prices. Delivery available.

incredible, bountiful buffets and sit-down dinners, and his appetizers are to die for. The entire team of professionals will ensure that your special day is worry-free.

Kelly's Outer Banks Restaurant and Tavern
US 158, MP 10½, Nags Head
(252) 441–4116

Kelly's has self-contained trailers and a trained staff to provide hot and cold food for groups of 10 to 1,000 throughout eastern North Carolina. Mike Kelly and his staff have a lot of experience serving everything from casual hors d'oeuvres to elegant buffets and banquets.

Duncan's Bar-B-Q
US 64, Manteo
(252) 473–6464

If you're looking for an informal, Southern-style pig-pickin', Doug has a pig cooker and will travel. This is authentic North Carolina barbecue, and these people sure know how to put on a spread. For more information, see our Restaurants chapter.

Let Them Eat Cake

No wedding is complete without a wedding cake. And since this is the South, it's customary to have a groom's cake as well. If you need to make separate arrangements for your wedding cake, call well in advance because decorated wedding cakes take a lot of preparation. Also, if you're planning an out-of-doors midsummer wedding, bear in mind that the heat and humidity can cause some icings to melt. Be sure to advise the caterer or cake-baker just where the cake will be kept.

Tullio's Pastry Shop
Scarborough Faire Shops, NC 12, Duck
(252) 261–7111
www.tulliospastry.com

Pastry chef Walter Tullio will bake you a beautiful wonder of a wedding cake, plus any other desserts, rolls, breads, or pastries you may desire. Walter learned his craft at the Culinary Institute of America in Hyde Park, New York; he'll provide you with a delicious and memorable addition to your day and will prepare cakes for any occasion. Tullio's cinnamon buns will make the morning of the wedding even more special.

Just Desserts
Melinda Gregory
(252) 441–2931
justdesserts@outerbanksweddings.com

Just Desserts can create an original wedding cake design for you using an array of flavors, colors, and custom artwork unmatched on the Outer Banks of North Carolina.

They will customize your wedding cake with a variety of cake flavors and fillings and will even make each tier of your cake different if you choose. These delicious cakes are available in assorted shapes and sizes and can be ordered on relatively short notice. We think they're the most beautiful cakes we've ever seen. Unusual decorative options include white chocolate seashells, pearl strands, gum-paste ribbon, flowers, and satin ribbon—all edible. Just Desserts also makes grooms' cakes specifically for that special man, with an array of flowers, colors, and designs. Custom artwork is available, and any concept can be reproduced in edible form. Call or e-mail for a free, no obligation consultation.

Photographers and Videographers

Silver Light Studio
JoEllen Willis, P.O. Box 4, Hatteras
(252) 986–2641

Have your precious memories captured forever with Silver Light Studio's professional photographic coverage. With more than 15 years of experience, JoEllen Willis can offer you complete, friendly, and affordable service. Covering only Hatteras and Ocracoke Islands, she can photograph a variety of special events. Whether it's a small, intimate beach wedding, a full-scale traditional church wedding with reception, or a special event such as a 50th wedding anniversary party, JoEllen offers a range of services to meet your needs. If you're thinking about gathering the clan together for a portrait on the beach or at a cottage, she will be happy to assist you in selecting the best spot for your outdoor portraits. She can accommodate large extended families, individuals, or special groups. JoEllen uses the services of professional photofinishers for her color work, but custom prints her black-and-white work in her own darkroom.

Deborah Sawyer Photography
107-A Budleigh Street, Manteo
(252) 473–4800
www.beachportraits.com

Deborah Sawyer Photography offers 25 years of experience in portraiture, specializing in weddings, beach portraits, engagement photos, and special portrait gifts. In addition to color photos, you can choose from black-and-whites or sepia-toned prints as well. Brides-to-be: A wonderful groom's gift would be a special portrait of you. Deborah shines in the creativity department and can suggest some truly wonderful options. Deborah is president of a new Outer Banks wedding vendor group, the Outer Banks Wedding Guild. See their Web site at www.outerbanksweddingguild.com.

J. Aaron Trotman Photographs
US 158, MP 9½, Kill Devil Hills
(252) 480–1070, (877) 764–5378
www.jaarontrotman.com

J. Aaron Trotman refers to his style of photojournalistic wedding photography as "storybook." Paying particular attention to your own special touches and your own circle of family and friends, he takes minimally posed shots, instead focusing on the people and events most important to you in a candid, unobtrusive manner and offering guidance where needed. All wedding options include a finished full-size album and various extras. Call for a personal consultation.

Thomas Gartman, Photographer
(252) 491–8566, (866) 275–6679
www.gartmanbeachpix.com

Thomas Gartman, Photographer specializes in weddings, family portraits, and special events. Using high-quality medium format equipment, Thomas captures your special day with a combination of relaxed candid shots and formal posed portraits. Since each couple is distinctive, every wedding is approached with a fresh creative eye. Thomas prides himself with wedding photographs that exude warmth and individuality.

Walter V. Gresham III Photography
Kill Devil Hills
(252) 441–5091, (800) 887–1415
www.gresham-photography.com

When the dress has been folded and put away, the cake has been eaten, and the flowers have withered and died, only the photographs will remain. Walter Gresham promises the highest quality photography available anywhere, with a series of portraits that tell the story of your wedding day.

Shooters at the Beach
Central Square Shopping Center, MP 11, Nags Head
(252) 480–2395
www.shootersphotos.com

Shooters' professional photo services promises fun photos that capture great memories. Owner Biff Jennings specializes in weddings, anniversaries, reunions, and birthdays and will work with groups of all sizes.

Memories in Motion, KTM Productions
P.O. Box 1676, Nags Head
(252) 480–0543, (888) 538–5832

You can capture your day forever with a professional wedding video. Memories in Motion by KTM Productions is an affordable way to preserve your Outer Banks wedding in brilliant sound and color. KTM offers complete wedding and reception coverage by a professional, premier video photographer with state-of-the-art equipment and 14 years' experience with video production. KTM has packages to fit all budgets.

Rental Equipment

Metro Rental
US 158 and Colington Rd., Kill Devil Hills
(252) 480–3535
www.metrorental@obx.com

Metro Rental is *the* rental source on the Outer Banks for wedding and party supplies. They have a complete line of tents, tables, chairs, linens, fountains, china, glassware, chafing dishes, wedding arches, flower stands, and guest book stands. You can even rent a portable bar and dance floor. Metro Rental offers the services of a certified wedding consultant too. Delivery is available, and quality and dependability are guaranteed.

Transportation

If you can't borrow Cinderella's coach, what better way to arrive at a wedding than in a limousine? The following limousine services are just a phone call away.

Island Limousine
Kill Devil Hills
(252) 441–5466, (800) 828–5466
www.islandlimo.com

Island Limousine rolls out the red carpet for a new bride. They also offer shuttle connections to the Norfolk Airport.

Karat Limo Service
Manteo
(252) 473–9827
www.karatlimo.com

Karat Limo Service offers VIP service in a stretch limousine. The vehicle can hold up to 10 people, and the company offers service to Norfolk Airport.

Outer Banks Limo and Jimmy G's Auto Detailing
(252) 449–2WAX
www.outerbankslimo.com

Outer Banks Limo and Jimmy G's Auto Detailing offers wedding services and airport delivery and pickup. If you'd rather not hire transportation, you can have them detail your car and have it looking like new for the big day.

Gifts

Jewelry By Gail, Inc.
207 East Driftwood Street, Nags Head
(252) 441–5387
www.jbgjewel@interpath.com

Jewelry By Gail features jewelry uniquely crafted in precious metals and high-quality gemstones. At this award-winning studio, you can get advice on diamond selection and find extraordinary engagement and wedding rings and anniversary gifts, as well as gifts for the bride, groom, and members of the wedding party.

Diane's Lavish Linens
Scarborough Lane Shoppes, NC 12, Duck
(252) 255–0555

Diane's offers luxury linens, sheets, blankets, and towels, plus fabulous nightgowns of cotton and silk. You can register your choices of patterns with Diane Strehan so that friends and family can purchase matching items for your new home.

Riddick Jewelers
The Croatan Center, US 158, MP 14, Nags Head
(252) 441–3653

Riddick Jewelers offers hand-crafted wed-

ding bands among its many other lovely jewelry items. The bands are a blend of traditional and contemporary designs, with styles reminiscent of the sea and dunes. Riddick Jewelers also carries classic cultured pearls, diamond engagement rings, bridal accessories, and gifts for the entire wedding party.

Outer Banks Honeymoons!

People don't just come here to get married. The Outer Banks has traditionally been a hot spot for honeymooners, especially off-season, when the crowds are scarce, the prices low, and the island feels like a private paradise. Consult our Accommodations and Weekly & Long-Term Cottage Rental chapters for information on lodging. Then, think about all the wonderful diversions that the Outer Banks has to offer that will make your honeymoon even more memorable. Depending upon the time of year and the amount of physical activity you're up for, you can do everything from visiting art galleries to trying your hand at hang gliding. We can assure you that there are copious couple-conducive amusements. Outdoor activities include bicycling, swimming, diving, playing golf, fly-fishing,

The Outer Banks is a hot spot for honeymooners.

deep-sea fishing, kayaking, sailing, or just lying on the beach. Together, you could take an aero tour, a dolphin tour, a walk through the Elizabethan Gardens, or have an off-road adventure. You may wish to have a beach portrait taken, or spend the day at a full-service spa. Numerous fine restaurants, rustic eateries, and establishments that provide outdoor entertainment abound in this area. Leaf through this guide; you'll find suggestions for each of the aforementioned activities and then some. We're convinced that anyone who decides to honeymoon on this stretch of barrier islands will enjoy it so much that they'll want to keep coming back for each anniversary.

Arts and Culture

The Outer Banks is the kind of place where many artists envision spending their days while painting the beauty that surrounds them or sculpting forms wrought by visions brought forth by the ocean. For many, this dream has come to fruition, and the beach has become a welcoming haven for artists of all kinds, from the painter to the sculptor, the potter to the bird carver, the writer to the actor. The area is a haven for anyone with an artistic bent. The powerful influence of the ocean and wetlands appears in many works of art, as do the abundant wildlife and spirit of the locals as they work and play. Even our historic landmarks all provide fodder for an artistic appetite. The relative isolation of our barrier islands, though seen by some as a drawback to year-round living, is a real plus to the artist, especially in the off-season. This is the time to contemplate and study, then call up the muse and put your feelings into a tangible piece of art. When a nor'easter blows on a gray February day, the muse may be an artist's only visitor! Take the time to visit our many galleries and talk with some of our local artists and writers: through their eyes you are sure to gain even more appreciation of this special area.

You can get a feel for this fascinating visual arts arena, which runs the gamut from conceptual art to classical painting, by attending several annual events. One of the longest running of these is the Dare County Arts Council's Frank Stick Art Show, which was started back in 1978. The show is held at the Ghost Fleet Gallery in Nags Head every February and features more than 150 artworks. (Frank Stick, 1884–1966, was a legendary illustrator and wildlife artist who moved to the Outer Banks in the 1940s.) The reception that marks its opening is always packed, and scores of local artists exhibit recent work during the event that lasts a little more than three weeks (see our Annual Events chapter for more information).

For some family fun of the artistic kind, set aside the first weekend in October for the arts council's annual Artrageous Art Extravaganza, which features hands-on creative booths with cookie decorating, hat creations, weaving, face painting, and much more. Fashion shows, food, live music, art collaborations, and local art and craft booths highlight the two-day event. During an elegant Sunday auction, fine art by adults and children is put on the block. Dedicated volunteers who coordinate the weekend event seem to outdo themselves year after year. It's never the same old thing! (See our Annual Events chapter for more information.)

Another must-see is the New World Festival of the Arts each August on downtown Manteo's waterfront, an ideal site for showcasing the talents of approximately 80 local and national artists and artisans. Look for painting, photography, jewelry, pottery, and an assortment of handcrafted items. The two-day event was first held in 1982. If you would like to show your work or need more information about the festival, see our

Annual Events chapter for contact information. The literature for this show usually comes out in January.

Private visual art studios scattered from Corolla to Ocracoke are another option for the art-seeker. Many of these local artists offer lessons, mostly in watercolor and other painting techniques. We do have a large concentration of landscape painters here, but our 50 or more commercial art/craft galleries are packed with expressions as individualistic as grains of sand. Galleries offer art ranging from the hand-hewn decoy to the delicately painted Russian black lacquer box.

The Outer Banks has become a bona fide art community. Artists living here and in the surrounding areas are a close-knit group, sharing tips and encouraging each other in their endeavors. Perhaps because of the lifestyle here, our artists are some of the friendliest people around and are always eager to meet visitors and welcome newcomers and to offer help and direction about the arts community when asked. The Town of Nags Head has certainly done its part in supporting local artists by setting aside up to $20,000 a year in surplus revenues to purchase artwork for its Town Hall. Since 1997, the town has spent over $50,000 on more than 50 pieces of art by local and regional artists. The collection, selected by the town's Artwork Selection committee, includes paintings, sculpture, photographs, wood carvings, etchings, mobiles, found-object art, and more. The public is invited to view this collection during Town Hall operating hours, and there is a directory with artist bios and other information.

The performing arts flourish on the Outer Banks. Local theater groups present plays, comedies, and dramas both seasonally and year-round. Music streams from our nightclubs, and standup comics performing summer stints tickle our funny bones. Symphonies, vocal groups, and individual classical, folk, and pop artists enliven our local auditoriums all year. What we can't generate ourselves in the way of cultural experiences, we import with the help of volunteer-based nonprofit organizations. Thanks to the efforts of the Dare County Arts Council, Outer Banks Forum, The Theater of Dare, the Roanoke Island Historical Association (producers of *The Lost Colony*), the North Carolina School of the Arts, and Roanoke Island Festival Park, Insiders on the Outer Banks enjoy exposure to local, regional, and national cultural opportunities.

We begin our pilgrimage with a description of the area's major arts organizations and follow with a north-to-south excursion through the Outer Banks's eclectic galleries and other creative venues. We promise the journey will be as ever-changing and fresh as our climate. See our Annual Events chapter for arts events.

Organizations

Dare County Arts Council
104 Sir Walter Raleigh St., Manteo
(252) 473–5558
www.darearts.org

Celebrating its 27th year in 2002, the Dare County Arts Council supplies the Outer Banks with a wide variety of creative opportunities with the help of countless volunteers, generous patrons and members, and some state and county support. This nonprofit group has a permanent office/gallery in downtown Manteo at the address above. The gallery, called Sea and Sounds Gallery, hosts about monthly visual arts shows, and visitors are encouraged to stop by to view these shows or to gather information on arts and cultural events in the area. Office hours are 10:00 A.M. to 5:00 P.M. Monday through Friday and occasional weekends when volunteer staff is available.

The council is affiliated with the North Carolina Arts Council as the local distributing agency of the state's Grassroots funds. The DCAC also subsidizes other area arts organizations such as International Icarus, a nonprofit art exhibition honoring humankind's first powered flight, held each December at three Nags Head galleries (see our Annual Events chapter), Theater of Dare, The Writers' Group, and the Outer Banks Forum.

DCAC sponsors several cultural programs in the community and local schools every year. In 2001, for example, DCAC brought nationally known poet Luis Rodriguez into the community to work with at-risk students and brought Cajun-zydeco master Terrance Simien from New Orleans to do a five-day residency in the Dare County schools and give a performance at the DCAC annual fund-raising gala. They brought North Carolina Poet Laureate Fred Chappell to do readings at the Dare County Alternative High School and in the community. In addition, DCAC put on its 23rd Annual Frank Stick Memorial Art Show, a photography competition, a watercolor competition, the Mollie Fearing Memorial Art Show, *The Beach Book* Cover Competition, eight visual arts exhibitions in its gallery, and the annual Artrageous Art Extravaganza weekend for kids and families.

In addition, DCAC publishes its quarterly newsletter, *Art Throb*, full of events listings, feature articles, profiles of local artists, poetry, and more. The publication is distributed to members and at events. It's a way for artists to voice their concerns and share their news as well as keep the community up to date on all the happenings in the arts community. DCAC's regularly updated Web site also offers a wealth of information on the arts.

DCAC operates on funds from grants, fund-raisers, and annual memberships. Memberships generally range from $10 for students to $25 for artists to $100 for businesses. This is a great way to support the arts in the community. To join, visit the Web site or call the number above.

Elizabeth R & Company
(252) 473-1061

Elizabeth R & Company is a professional producing organization that sponsors

Don't miss the hilarious farce Bloody Mary and the Virgin Queen, *performed in the summer at The Pioneer Theater in Manteo.* PHOTO: WALTER GRESHAM

scholarly research projects centered on North Carolina history and professional films, audios, and performances that interpret history. Two of its most popular interpretive performances are staged on Roanoke Island every summer—*Elizabeth R* and *Bloody Mary and the Virgin Queen*. *Elizabeth R*, celebrating its 10th anniversary in 2002, stars Barbara Hird and portrays the personal life of Queen Elizabeth I. It is held in The Elizabethan Gardens on Tuesday afternoons at 5:00 P.M. from early June through mid-August. *Elizabeth R* tours internationally the rest of the year; it was part of the 1995 Edinburgh Festival and has been performed in London, New York City, and across the mid-Atlantic United States. *Bloody Mary*, also starring Barbara Hird and Marsha Warren, tells the story of Queen Elizabeth I and her half-sister Mary Queen of Scots in a hilarious farce. It is performed mid-July through mid-August at The Pioneer Theatre in downtown Manteo on Wednesdays at 3:30 P.M. For more information, see our Attractions chapter.

Outer Banks Forum for the Lively Arts
(252) 202–9732
www.outerbanksforum.org

The Outer Banks Forum organizes six lively arts performances a year, bringing world-class performers to this remote stretch of the world. Since 1983 the forum has scheduled these performances from October through April, making the off-season months a little brighter for many folks. The forum seasons are filled with interesting and varied selections, ranging from bluegrass to opera to folk tales. For example, the 2001–2002 season featured the Grammy-nominated Eroica Trio; the acoustic western swing/jazz music of Hot Club of Cowtown; Le Trio Gershwin from Paris; the cowboy/folk music and comedy of Riders in the Sky; the Irish group Kila; and the Virginia Beach Symphony, who return every year.

All performances are held at Kitty Hawk Elementary School. Starting times vary. Season subscriptions cost $40.00, and individual tickets cost $12.00 to $18.00 for adults, $5.00 for students, and free for children under age 12. If you come early, 45 minutes before each performance, you can attend a lively and informative lecture series to enhance your appreciation of the performance.

Roanoke Island Festival Park
1 Festival Park, Manteo
(252) 475–1500,
(252) 475–1506 24-hour events line
www.roanokeisland.com

Roanoke Island Festival Park blends art, history, and education in celebration of Roanoke Island's role as birthplace of English-speaking America. The state park is on its own small island across from the Manteo waterfront, also the home berth of the *Elizabeth II*. Completed in 1998, the park features a variety of cultural opportunities

The North Carolina School of the Arts conducts a summer institute for about 50 students and offers a variety of cultural programs in music, dance, and drama. PHOTO: COURTESY OF ROANOKE ISLAND FESTIVAL PARK

year-round. The park's Art Gallery is a beautiful space that holds month-long art shows. Receptions for these shows on Sunday afternoons are great ways to meet fellow arts-minded folk. The Film Theater's house film is *The Legend of Two Path*, a 45-minute film depicting the English landing on Roanoke Island from the Native Americans' point of view, but other top-notch cultural arts performances and films are also staged in the theater year-round.

The outdoor Pavilion, which can seat up to 3,500 people on the lawn, is a marvelous place to watch cultural arts performances. North Carolina School of the Arts students perform here five nights a week in the summer, offering dance, drama, music, and film. Visiting symphonies and musicians often perform here as well. Also on-site are an 8,500-square-foot Adventure Museum where kids can learn about history, a museum store, and the Outer Banks History Center. For more information about Roanoke Island Festival Park, see our Attractions chapter.

Roanoke Island Historical Association
1409 US 64/264, Manteo
(252) 473–2127
www.thelostcolony.org

The dramatic arts have a unique outlet on the Outer Banks in *The Lost Colony* outdoor drama, staged throughout the summer in a waterside theater on Roanoke Island (see our Attractions chapter). Perpetuated by the Roanoke Island Historical Association, *The Lost Colony* entices 125 actors and crew across the nation to answer the casting call for the symphonic drama that chronicles the fate of the first English settlement in America.

In 2001, *The Lost Colony* got a boon when Tony Award–nominated Broadway actor Terrance Mann agreed to direct the show. Mann, who has held principal roles in *Cats, Les Miserables, Beauty and the Beast,* and *The Scarlet Pimpernel*, performed in *The Lost Colony* as a dancer and in the role of Old Tom before making it big on Broadway. Mann made many changes to the play, returning many of the nostalgic

nuances of the glory days of the show. Mann will return as director for the 2002 season. Another famous name associated with the show is William Ivey Long, who won a second Tony Award in 2001 for his costume design work on *The Producers*. Long has been the costume designer for *The Lost Colony* for 15 years and has been associated with the show since a young boy when his parents worked on the show. He is also responsible for much of the updated set design.

Many of *The Lost Colony* thespians also try out for the Lost Colony's Children's Theater that wows junior audiences during the summer months with classics such as *The Princess and the Pea* (see our Kidstuff chapter). Others take on roles as time-warped sailors for hilarious and educational interpretive tours of the *Elizabeth II*.

A full day of special events, including free children's theater selections, interpretive park tours, and special performances, takes place on Virginia Dare's birthday, August 18. Call the Lindsey Warren Visitor Center at Fort Raleigh, (252) 473–5772, for a schedule.

If you're interested in joining the Roanoke Island Historical Association and supporting *The Lost Colony*, write to them at 1409 Highway 64/264, Manteo, North Carolina 27954 or call the previously listed number. Contribution details vary. You may become a member and/or contribute to the annual fund or their endowment fund.

The Theatre of Dare
(252) 441–3088
www.theatreofdare.org

The Theatre of Dare was established in 1992 with a grant from the Outer Banks Forum. Its members bring quality live theater to the Outer Banks by taking part in all phases of production, from directing and set design to performing. The Theatre of Dare produces three main stage productions a year from fall to spring. TOD embodies the true spirit of community theater by welcoming amateur and professional thespians alike. The

The Lost Colony *outdoor drama re-enacts Roanoke Island's 16th-century history nightly during the summer.*
PHOTO: COURTESY OF ROANOKE ISLAND HISTORICAL ASSOCIATION

organization thus far has produced hits such as *Arsenic and Old Lace, Steel Magnolias, The Odd Couple,* and *South Pacific.*

The Theatre of Dare lacks a permanent rehearsal space, but most of its performances are held at Manteo Middle School. Season tickets cost $25. Different levels of membership are available. The minimum category calls for a $25 donation or active participation in two productions per year. For more information about membership, volunteering, auditions, or production dates, call Kathy Morrison at the number above.

Icarus International
(252) 441–6584
www.icarusinternational.com

Icarus International was founded in 1993, purposely a decade before the centennial of flight in 2003, with the goal of celebrating flight through the arts. The organization has been widely successful in its efforts to raise the awareness of the history,

beauty, and mystery of flight. Each year, Icarus International holds an international visual arts competition and a literary competition based on a flight-related theme. Literary entries are published annually in a chapbook. Icarus International also sponsors an annual portrait commission for inductees into the First Flight Shrine at the Wright Brothers National Memorial. They are currently raising funds for their biggest project, the construction of the $1 million Icarus Monument celebrating 100 years of flight. The monument, to be complete in 2003, will be located at MP 1 in Kitty Hawk next to the Aycock Brown Welcome Center. Icarus International is also in the process of creating a book called *Pioneer Aviators of the World.* The book will be finished by the 2003 centennial celebration of flight and will tell the story of the first pilots from 100 countries. For information about the visual or literary competitions or any Icarus' projects, visit the Web site or call the number above.

Galleries

Corolla

Outer Banks Style
1122 Ocean Trail, Corolla
(252) 453–4388, (800) 261–0176

Outer Banks Style offers viewers a taste of local art, crafts, furniture, and home accessories in its Corolla shop. Owner Gary Springer has stocked the gallery with works by popular Outer Banks painter James Melvin and photographer Ray Matthews. Check out Troy Spencer's reproduction signs. Outer Banks Style recently acquired Story People by Brian Andreas, artist and storyteller. This line of fanciful art includes prints, sculptures, books, and furniture decorated with short prose. The shop is open year-round seven days a week. Hours vary, so call ahead.

Dolphin Watch Gallery
TimBuck II Shopping Village, Ocean Trail, Corolla
(252) 453–2592
www.dolphinwatchgallery.org

Dolphin Watch Gallery features the works of owner/artist Mary Kaye Umberger. This artist creates hand-colored etchings on handmade paper drawn from scenes indigenous to the Corolla area including wildlife, ducks and other waterfowl, seascapes, and lighthouses. Other art pieces here include pottery, stoneware, carvings of marine life, and wax sculptures (candles shaped by hand, with flower petals molded by the artist's fingertips). The gallery is open year-round; call for off-season hours.

Duck

Greenleaf Art Gallery
1169 NC 12, Duck
(252) 261–2009
US 158, MP 16, Nags Head
(252) 480–3555
www.outer-banks.com/greenleaf

Greenleaf galleries offer their guests a chance to experience exquisite fine crafts and paintings from nationally, regionally, and locally known American artists at their gallery locations in Duck and Nags Head (see separate listing).

Approximately 300 artists and artisans are represented by Greenleaf galleries, affording a good geographic variation. Featured are one-of-a-kind handcrafted jewelry, ceramics, wood, glass, and furnishings, plus sculpture, acrylic, and watercolor paintings, etchings, lithographs, and mixed-media pieces. Expect to find both the delightful and the serious at Greenleaf, anything from a huge, whimsical praying mantis to the works of some of the nation's finest glass artisans. One of the best things about visiting Greenleaf is seeing the sublime paintings of Outer Banks artist Rick Tupper, who owns the galleries with his wife.

Often there are special exhibitions of an artist's work; call for an exhibition schedule. Both galleries are closed on Sundays and closed from January through mid-March.

The Wooden Feather
Scarborough Lane, NC 12, Duck
(252) 261–2808

The Wooden Feather presents award-winning handcarved decoys and shorebirds as well as driftwood sculptures. The gallery features an outstanding collection of antique decoys. It's open seven days a week from March through December, with longer hours during the summer season.

Morales Art Gallery
Scarborough Faire Shoppes, NC 12, Duck
(252) 261–7190, (800) 635–6035

This is one of three locations of the Morales Art Gallery (the others are in Kitty Hawk and Nags Head, see separate listings). Featured here are a large selection of Outer Banks–themed prints and original paintings by local and regional artists as well as prints by nationally recognized artists like Steve Hanks, Barbara Woods, James Christensen, and others.

knickknacks. The scene changes as the artists who show here change, but usually the emphasis is on handmade crafts. (See our Shopping chapter for details.) The gallery is open all year.

Morales Art Gallery
Buccaneers Walk, US 158, MP 4, Kitty Hawk
(252) 255-2306

This gallery, which opened in May 2000, offers all the quality art that can be found in the other Morales Art Gallery locations (in Duck and Nags Head), including prints by nationally recognized artists as well as local and regional artists. The main focus of this gallery, however, is sculpture. Some original art is featured as well as giftware. And guest artists may make appearances at this location too for an evening of lively conversation and art demonstrations.

Kill Devil Hills

Nostalgia Gallery
Seagate North Shopping Center, US 158,
MP 5½, Kill Devil Hills
(252) 441-1881
www.obxgallery.com

Norm Martinus specializes in paper memorabilia that deserves mention in any art chapter. He has to know his stuff as the coauthor of *Warmon's Paper*, an encyclopedia of antiques and collectibles. You'll find oodles of advertising art at Nostalgia as well as the original art of Matinus's daughter, Lee. Revel in old prints of Maxfield Parrish and Norman Rockwell. Martinus offers full-service custom framing and matting. Insiders know that he's one of the Outer Banks's finest framers. See our Shopping chapter for more tips of what Nostalgia has in store for you. The shop is open year-round.

This gallery also offers a wide selection of original art along with custom framing. One of the things that keeps customers returning to the Morales Gallery is the knowledgeable and helpful sales staff. Call for weekly show and exhibit information and for hours of operation.

During the summer season, this location offers guest artist receptions that are crowd-pleasers.

Kitty Hawk

Crafter's Gallery
US 158, MP 4, Kitty Hawk
(252) 261-3036

You are entering a handmade one-of-a-kind craft haven here. Crafter's features mostly country crafts coupled with some contemporary styles. The gallery offers cloth and wicker basketry, handmade dolls, cards, and handpainted wooden

First Flight Shrine
Wright Brothers National Memorial Visitor Center, US 158, MP 8, Kill Devil Hills
(252) 441-7430
www.nps.gov/wrbr

While the First Flight Shrine is not a commercial art gallery, it has a body of portraiture that deserves recognition in any Arts and Culture chapter. Every year for more than 30 years, the First Flight Society has inducted into the shrine one or more individuals who have accomplished an outstanding "first" that has enhanced the development of aviation. Hanging in the same room as a replica of Wilbur and Orville Wright's first flyer are more than 55 faces of great aviators, such as Amelia Earhart, Adm. Richard E. Byrd, Neil Armstrong, and Col. Edwin Aldrin. The portraits, which are donated by International Icarus, are produced annually and exhibited through a partnership with the National Park Service at the Wright Brothers National Memorial Visitor Center (see our Attractions chapter for more about the Memorial).

KDH Cooperative Gallery and Studios
US 158, MP 8½, Kill Devil Hills
(252) 441–9888
www.kdhcooperative.tripod.com

This is an artist-operated cooperative, the dream and now reality of artist and owner Julie Moye. It's a centralized place where you can see the work of 29 local artists. The juried members of this cooperative show their work and assist in running the gallery. Oil, acrylic, watercolor, pastels, pen and ink, ceramics, jewelry, fiber, furniture, candles, pottery, glass, and metal are featured in the three-room gallery. Each member serves on panels to hang and display art, jury, organize shows, and assist customers during daily business hours. Upstairs is the Artists Attic, a lively studio space and classrooms. Several artists have set up studios upstairs and are often at work during business hours. Visitors are welcome to come upstairs and talk with the artists and watch them work. The other half of the upstairs is classroom space, where a great variety of classes are held year-round for children and adults. Pottery, drawing, photography, stained glass, mosaic, candle making, and basket making are just some of the classes

offered, or you can design your own class and pitch it to the staff. KDH Cooperative offers art classes for kids, including creative writing, drawing, and comic strip drawing, and even offers summer art camps and classes on school holidays.

Nags Head

A treasure trove of art galleries is tucked into an unlikely nook of Nags Head known as Gallery Row. There are seven galleries and a consignment shop within a block of each other and three more galleries in the vicinity. This little art mecca is a great place to spend an entire afternoon, poking in and out of each gallery and chatting with the owners. Gallery Row is at about MP 10, and the streets to look for are Gallery Row and Driftwood Street. Park at any one of the galleries and walk to the others. This is a low-traffic, laid-back area so you won't feel rushed to get out of your parking space. The galleries considered a part of Gallery Row are Glenn Eure's Ghost Fleet Gallery, Lighthouse Gallery and Gifts, Sally Huss Gallery, Jewelry by Gail, Morales Art Gallery, Ipso Facto Gallery, and John de la Vega Gallery. During the summer months on Wednesday nights from 6:00 to 9:00 P.M. the Gallery Row galleries host a wine-and-cheese gallery stroll. Nearby on the Beach Road are Seaside Art Gallery, Anna Gartell's Gallery by the Sea, and The Yellowhouse Gallery.

Lighthouse Gallery and Gifts
Gallery Row, 301 E. Driftwood St., Nags Head
(252) 441–4232, (800) 579–2827
www.seabeacons.com

Owners Woody and Cindy Woodall have put together a shop dedicated to the "Keepers of the Light." They've built their gallery as a replica of an original Victorian-style lighthouse that represents the U.S. Lighthouse Service in its prime at the turn of the 20th century.

Open every day of the year except Christmas, this shop features lighthouse art and artifacts including hundreds of

Locals and visitors can experience art of all genres on the Outer Banks. PHOTO: COURTESY OF ROANOKE ISLAND FESTIVAL PARK

impressionistic paintings done in bold colors and featuring childlike scenes. Her designs, which are coupled with cheerful sayings, are transferred onto mugs, gift wrap, T-shirts, cards, and key chains. Adults and kids alike will get a kick out of her lighthearted creations that are dotted with toucans, mermaids, elephants, hearts, and sailboats. You'll also want to see the original ceramics created by Bob Martin. Because of the popularity of the Sally Huss Gallery, the owners recently expanded their store. In addition to Huss's art, this gallery now also features unique home décor, gifts, and work from local potters. The gallery is open all year.

Ipso Facto Gallery
206 Gallery Row, Nags Head
(252) 480–2793

The merchandise at Ipso Facto—antiques, curios, and objects of art from all over the world—is eclectic, and it's reasonably priced too. Look for furniture, ethnic trinkets such as Mexican holiday candle-holders, and original paintings. Ipso is really more of an antiques shop than a gift shop. It's a great place to browse, ooh and aah, and, of course, find a treasure to take home. Ipso Facto Gallery is open year-round; it's closed Sunday.

John de la Vega Gallery
206 Gallery Row, Nags Head
(252) 441–9699
www.portraitartist.com/delavega

This gallery features the paintings and portraiture of artist John de la Vega, a nationally recognized artist and Renaissance man. After establishing himself on the Outer Banks several years ago, de la Vega left for New York City, spending three years studying with master painters Burt Silverman and Nelson Shanks. He recently returned to the Outer Banks and opened this gallery in the heart of Gallery Row. His gallery is atypical of Outer Banks galleries in that it is sparse, giving the viewer space to appreciate each of de la Vega's fine portraits, figure drawings, seascapes, nature scenes, and floral stud-

lighthouse models, collectibles, brass nautical memorabilia (such as compasses, sextants and octants, both authentic and reproduction), books, jewelry, prints, paintings from all over the United States, and local artwork. You must see the special collection of lighthouse books with photography by Bruce Roberts, who offers unique and breathtaking views of these beloved sentinels.

Add your name to the Outer Banks Lighthouse Society newsletter mailing list at the gallery, or call for information about joining the society, which boasts 600 members.

Sally Huss Gallery
Gallery Row, 300 E. Driftwood St., Nags Head
(252) 441–8098
www.ceramicsbythesea.com

Sally Huss Gallery features the upbeat original art and prints of the California artist of the same name. Huss creates

ies. The artist is often at work in the gallery, which, he says, should not make people uncomfortable. He encourages visitors to come in to see his works. De la Vega accepts portrait commissions.

Morales Art Gallery
107 E. Gallery Row, Nags Head
(252) 441-6484, (800) 635-6035

Mitchell and Christine Lively at the Morales Art Galleries have made financial success a personal reality for many struggling artists by showcasing their work and producing fine-art prints that are shown at their three gallery locations on the Outer Banks.

Morales Art Gallery is the oldest art venue on Gallery Row; the late Jesse Morales first opened the doors in 1971. Today, the Morales galleries and their Fine Art Print Shop carry fine original local, regional, and nationally known art. Showcased here are the works of Larry Johnson, Pat Williams, Dennis Lighthart, Pat Troiani, Tony Feathers, and Anda Styler. Expect to find limited-edition prints by the Greenwich Workshop, Mill Pond Press, Hadley House, Somerset Publishing, and Wild Wings. If you want to view a major collection of original seascapes, this is the place to come.

Mitchell has been framing and publishing art for more than two decades. The couple's dedication to the arts has been felt community-wide, especially in their generosity to the Dare County schools. A member of the Professional Picture Framers Association, Morales Gallery offers a wide variety of choices in custom framing.

The Nags Head Gallery is open year-round. And don't forget the Morales Gallery location in Duck and their newest location at Buccaneers Walk in Kitty Hawk (see separate listings).

Glenn Eure's Ghost Fleet Gallery of Fine Art
Gallery Row, 210 E. Driftwood St., Nags Head
(252) 441-6584

Glenn and Pat Eure, owners of the Ghost Fleet Gallery, run an original art establishment that primarily features Glenn's work. A printmaker, Glenn creates in a variety of forms including etching, woodcutting, collagraphy, serigraphy, and relief carving in addition to drawing, oil, acrylic, and watercolor painting, and woodcarving. He's recently completed a series of collagraphs (thin collages run through a printing press) honoring Wilbur and Orville Wright's first flight. The fine-art prints, each hand-pulled by the artist, contain flight imagery ranging from da Vinci's time to the present. Glenn also specializes in large canvases that bulge out from their frames—irregular shapes that are painted in a nonobjective style. He produces lighthearted watercolors that feature boat scenes. Most have two small skiffs lying in a sandy cove and romantically tied together by one anchor. He personalizes these with names and special dates. Many have the Cape Hatteras, Ocracoke, or Currituck lighthouses in the background.

The Eures rotate other artists' work in the West Wing Gallery and the Second Dimension gallery located a flight up. In the off-season Eure hosts several community shows: The International Icarus Show in December commemorates the Wright Brothers' first flight; the Frank Stick Memorial Art Show each February sponsored by the Dare County Arts Council; and a county public school art show. The first two shows draw more than 400 artists into the exhibition arena, and opening nights attract more than 1,000 art lovers to the gallery. Poetry readings also are held year-round at the gallery (see our Annual Events chapter). The Ghost Fleet Gallery is open year-round. Hours are cut back some in January and February.

Jewelry by Gail
Gallery Row, 207 Driftwood St., Nags Head
(252) 441-5387
www.jewelrybygail.com

Gail Kowalski is a designer-goldsmith who has won national recognition for her creations in precious metals and stones. Most of the jewelry designed and made

A sampling of art from one of the many shows held at Roanoke Island Festival Park. PHOTO: COURTESY OF ROANOKE ISLAND FESTIVAL PARK

here falls into the "wearable art" category. Check out Selections by Gail, a department of very high-quality but moderately priced handmade jewelry from all over the world. Kowalski personally selects each piece exhibited here. The "Charming Lights" sterling and gold lighthouse jewelry collection is a favorite. Images of the four local lighthouses are fashioned into earrings, pendants, and charms. The gallery is open Monday through Saturday and is closed in January.

Seaside Art Gallery
NC 12, MP 11, Nags Head
(252) 441-5418
www.seasideart.com

Original etchings and lithographs by Picasso, Whistler, Rembrandt, and Renoir are among the thousands of original works of art on display at Seaside Art Gallery. Sculptures, paintings, drawings, Indian pottery, fine porcelains, Mexican silver jewelry including the work of William Spratling, seascapes, and animation art from Disney and Warner Brothers are spread throughout numerous rooms in this sprawling gallery. Seaside is a Gold Circle dealer for Disney Classic Figurines. Prints by David Hunter are meticulously

rendered and range from biblical portraiture to peaceful coastal scenes.

The gallery hosts several competitions annually, including an International Miniature Art Show (see the May listings in our Annual Events chapter) and the Icarus International Art Show. Printmaking workshops are held here each year by David Hunter. The gallery is open year-round.

Anna Gartrell's Art & Photography By the Sea
NC 12, MP 10, Nags Head
(252) 480-0578

Gartrell's artistry is evident in her expressive watercolors and photography. Her work seems to brighten every darkened recess in your being. Original is the key word here. A deeply spiritual woman, Gartrell said she revels in "God's explosive beauty frozen forever for you." Examine her series of jeweled and crystal wave photos, depictions of wild storms, sunrises and sunsets, ducks, dunes, wild stallions and lighthouses, crystal flounders, and amazing sea angels. Take a bit of Outer Banks brightness home with you. A photo of a skyscape that Gartrell shot recently has been accepted into the National Aeronautics & Space Museum art collection for special art shows.

The gallery is open daily, but hours are flexible. The owner posts a note on the door every day with the day's operating hours.

Yellowhouse Gallery and Annex
NC 12, MP 11, Nags Head
(252) 441-6928
www.yellowhousegallery.com

Yellowhouse Gallery houses one of North Carolina's largest collections of antique prints and maps. Thousands of original old etchings, lithographs, and engravings are organized for browsing in several rooms of one of Nags Head's older beach cottages. Established in 1969, the gallery features Civil War prints and maps; prints of botanicals, fish, shells and birds; and old views and antique maps and charts of the Outer Banks. Yellowhouse Gallery also offers a huge selection of decorative and fine-art prints and posters as well as souvenir pictures and maps of the Outer Banks. If the picture you want is not in stock, Uncle Jack, the proprietor, will order it for you.

Greenleaf Art Gallery
US 158, MP 16, Nags Head
(252) 480-3555
www.outer-banks.com/greenleaf
Greenleaf Gallery features fine art and crafts from national, regional, and local artists. You can expect only top-quality arts in this gallery, including oil paintings, watercolors, handcrafted jewelry, ceramics, wood, glass, furniture, sculpture, fiber, etchings, lithographs, and mixed-media works. Greenleaf represents more than 300 artists in its Nags Head and Duck galleries. For more information, see the write-up in the Duck section. The Nags Head location is open from late March through the end of December.

Roanoke Island

Silver Bonsai Gallery
905 US 64/264, Manteo
(252) 475-1413
Silver Bonsai Gallery, nestled in one of the island's original homes, is a distinctive art gallery. Owners Ben and Kathryn Stewart, both metalsmiths and bonsai artists, sell their own creations here, as well as the works of other artists, and can often be seen at work in the studio at the back of the gallery. The Stewarts create simple yet elegant silver and gold jewelry and sculpture and can design special pieces upon request. The gallery sells a broad range of fine art by local artists, including paintings, wood, glass, sculpture, quilts, and more. If you're looking for a unique gift, you're sure to find it here. We like the Asian-inspired pottery and gifts, candles, wind chimes, fine paper, and locally made soaps. Bonsai trees make great gifts. Silver Bonsai's recently expanded bonsai garden includes trees that range from very young to specimen level bonsai. Each tree comes

with information on how to care for it. Silver Bonsai is open seven days a week, but closes for the month of January.

Island Art Gallery
The Christmas Shop, US 64, Manteo
(252) 473-2838
The work of more than 100 artists is displayed in this adjunct to the popular Christmas Shop. The gallery, which has been operating for 33 years, is open daily year-round. It consists of several large rooms of paintings, sculptures, and works in other media ranging from decoys and lighthouse art to photographs and paintings of Outer Banks landscapes. Look for works by Patricia Breen and Christopher Radko as well as the well-known P. Buckley Moss. Check out the jewelry nook that's filled with locally handcrafted work and a touch of the international too, including fascinating Russian brooches.

The shop has a 4,000-square-foot addition that fronts US 64. It's like an old-fashioned general store featuring collectibles and an expanded candy, candle, and stationery department. The addition has Christmas dinner all set in a model dining room—complete with full-size fireplace, dining table, and a crystal chandelier that's displayed in conjunction with the glass ornament shop that's also part of the new space. Another windfall of the expansion is more art gallery space. Ask shop personnel for information on the New World Festival of the Arts held each August under the guidance of Christmas Shop owner Edward Greene.

Wanchese Pottery
107 Fernando St., Manteo
(252) 473-2099
Customers can watch local potters Bonnie and Bob Morrill at work in their studio in downtown Manteo. This shop is known locally for its beautiful, useful art graced with delicate, lead-free glazes. One savvy Insider bought a handsome mug here that holds a generous amount of coffee, sits easily without wobbling, and has an exquisite glaze that turns a morning

This Event Isn't Just Good—It's Artrageous!

Every October, hundreds of Insiders gather in Kill Devil Hills at the Dare County Family Recreational Park on Mustian Street to celebrate the arts. The Dare County Arts Council, a local nonprofit organization, sponsors the two-day Artrageous Art Extravaganza the first weekend in October. It includes an all-day cultural arts festival on Saturday and finishes off the weekend with an evening art auction on Sunday. The festival, celebrating its 12th year in 2001, is designed to stimulate creativity and generate an artsy kind of fun.

Multiple booths are set up where children can enjoy face painting, hair wrapping, or hat making; learn to fashion a musical instrument; paint a flower pot; or work on a collaborative piece with their peers. The youth groups have turned out some unique creations including a mammoth papier-mâchè rock or a large mural with an outer-space theme. There's no admission fee on Saturday but some activities charge a fee.

You'll enjoy diverse entertainment. Each year's line-up is different, but past festivals have included local musical groups, a balloon-tying clown, vintage-wear fashion shows, and even educational workshops such as recycling with an art twist. Area artists and artisans set up booths to sell their creations. You can purchase a hand-painted wine glass, a dog-hair hat, a watercolor painting, or beach-glass jewelry. The surprises are endless but none can compare with the intent looks on the children's faces as they move from booth to booth creating their own works of art. Adults have a chance to kick back on Sunday evening and enjoy cocktails and hors d'oeuvres while bidding on local art and exciting golf, dinner, and getaway packages. Things get hot and heavy when people from all walks of life start bidding, and everyone enjoys the friendly competition. There are lots of laughs as everyone struggles to keep hold of his or her favorite painting, photograph, drawing, hand-woven hat, or one-of-a-kind necklace. The adult auction also includes children's art that was created during Saturday's festival, and sometimes these pieces summon the highest prices. Money

"I can outpaint you with my eyes closed!" PHOTO: COURTESY OF DARE COUNTY ARTS COUNCIL

sure can't buy you love, but there are plenty of parents in the audience who grab up these works and prove that love surely can earn some cash for a worthy cause!

Proceeds from both days directly benefit the local arts council, which disperses profits to needy artistic causes in the community. A scholarship fund was set up last year so local kids could pursue extracurricular art experiences like music camp or art classes, and for years, money has also been put into a fund for a future Outer Banks youth center.

Artrageous is open to the public. You don't have to be a local to enjoy the entire weekend or take a piece of local art home with you. That special painting of a Nags Head landscape or ocean cottage may be just the thing to keep you from pining away for the Outer Banks until you return, once again, to our sandy haven. The adult auction is usually held at the Village at Nags Head Beach Club at MP 15 on the Beach Road. Call the Dare County Arts Council at (252) 473–5558 for an update on times, location, and ticket information for the Sunday auction. This is one of our biggest off-season events. Join us Insiders on the first weekend in October. We promise it will be Artrageous!

routine into an artistic awakening. Choose dinnerware, oil lamps, hummingbird feeders, mugs, bowls, and pitchers among other items. The shop also features some handmade baskets and fresh cooking herbs.

Wanchese Pottery is open year-round. Winter hours are 1:00 to 5:00 P.M. Thursday, Friday, and Saturday.

John Silver Gallery
101-A Fernando St., Manteo
(252) 475–9764
www.johnsilvergallery.com

This is a fabulous gallery, owned and operated by local painter John Silver and his wife, Sheila. It's a large gallery, with a portion of the space devoted to John's bold and stunning oil paintings and watercolors. The Silvers also have a special exhibition wall featuring the works of a different artist every month. The rest of the gallery is filled with creative, lively, and inimitable works of art. You'll find jewelry, ceramics, sculpture, furniture, weavings, rugs, glass, mixed media works, iron works, and paintings—some serious, some whimsical and all amazing. The Silvers pride themselves on featuring many

artists whose works are not normally seen in Outer Banks galleries.

Sea and Sounds Gallery
104 Sir Walter Raleigh St., Manteo
(252) 473–5558
www.darearts.org

Sea and Sounds Gallery is the gallery space for the Dare County Arts Council. The council holds monthly shows in this space, including group shows, competitions, and individual shows. Receptions for each show, held on Sunday afternoons, offer a chance to meet the artists. The gallery has a bin of unframed works of art for sale. This is also the DCAC office so stop by if you want any arts-related information.

Nancy Ware Pottery
402 Queen Elizabeth St., Manteo
(252) 473–9400

This is the pottery studio of artist Nancy Ware. The potter's wheel is on display and you can see her work from time to time. She also offers classes on the wheel. In this year-round shop you'll find Nancy's pottery, jewelry, and tile work. The pottery is high-fire functional stoneware that is dishwasher, microwave, and oven safe. There's a great variety of kitchen items, including deep-dish fluted pie plates, colanders, three-piece child dining sets that can be personalized, vases, dishes, and spoon rests.

Roanoke Island Festival Park Art Gallery
Across from the Manteo waterfront, Manteo
(252) 475–1506
www.roanokeisland.com

Roanoke Island Festival Park's Art Gallery is the finest arts-exhibition space on the Outer Banks. The gallery is vast and uncluttered, allowing much room for appreciating the works of art that hang in the exhibitions. Gallery shows change monthly, featuring the works of an individual artist or sometimes groups of artists. The prestigious North Carolina Watercolor Society Show was held here in 2000. The Priceless Pieces Past & Present Quilt Extravaganza is a popular show, hung every year in March with dozens of quilts made or owned by locals. The Dare County Arts Council's Mollie Fearing Art Show is another popular show that's held here. Each monthly show has an opening reception on a Sunday afternoon. Roanoke Island Festival Park is closed in January.

Hubby Bliven, Wildlife Art
543 Ananias Dare St., Roanoke Island
(252) 473–2632

Bliven runs a full-service frame shop and wildlife art gallery that features his own work. He also operates a museum on the premises that includes Civil War, World War I, World War II, and Native American artifacts. Bliven's shop is the place to go if you're looking for lighthouse photos that include all eight North Carolina sentinels framed together or as individual prints. This group includes the Prices's Creek lighthouse in Southport, a rare find. Bliven is very fortunate to have been given access to photograph this structure that's on private property. His shop is open year-round.

Nick-E Stained Glass
813 Old Wharf Rd., Wanchese
(252) 473–5036

This is the stained-glass studio of Ellinor and Robert Nick. The Nicks create their works of art here as well as hold demonstrations and classes in stained glass. The Nicks also sell stained-glass supplies and tools in this shop. If you want to see how the work is done, commission a piece, or talk with the artists, stop by this location. If you want to buy their stained-glass creations, go to their gallery at the Dare Shops in Nags Head. The Dare Shops are at MP 16½. Call them at (252) 441–1112.

Hatteras Island

Gaskins Gallery
NC 12, Avon
(252) 995–6617
www.gaskinsgallery.com

The focus at Gaskins Gallery is on original local art and custom framing. Artists and owners Denise and Elizabeth Gaskins feature exclusively original family art, including their own watercolors and those of their octogenarian grandmother, who began painting several years ago. The paintings generally are coastal scenes or florals. You'll also find pottery, decorator prints, and posters. It is open year-round.

Browning Artworks
NC 12, Frisco
(252) 995–5538

This fine-art and craft gallery, which opened in 1984, has a reputation for showcasing top-notch North Carolina crafters, including many local artists. Browning now also carries the work of 12 to 15 out-of-state artists who are considered exceptional exceptions to the "North Carolina only" rule. The collection includes the creations of 200 artisans who make stained and blown glass, weavings, porcelains, pottery, copper work, forged wrought-iron work, and stoneware. Wood turners, many of whom use North Carolina woods, have a variety of crafts showcased here. Browning's jewelry selections are breathtaking, incorporating a variety of colorful semiprecious stones to form necklaces, rings, pins, bracelets, and earrings. Several dozen jewelry designers are featured, including the innovative and colorful creations of Outer Banker Austin Cake.

The gallery also exhibits paintings and prints, such as the exclusive collection of Linda Browning's watercolor skyscapes as well as the color photography of Ray Matthews and Michael Halminski. Both photographers have a passion for the coastal scene. Antique tribal weavings by Majid are a beautiful attraction. Art and craft demonstrations are held on their deck by the artists whose work is featured. Call for a schedule. Proprietors Linda and Lou Browning also maintain a bridal and gift registry for residents and visitors and will ship your selections.

Browning Artworks is open March through December.

Indian Town Gallery and Gifts
NC 12, Frisco
(252) 995-5181

Nestled down in the woods in Frisco, Indian Town represents artists from the local villages. Many of the paintings have an Outer Banks theme, and the offshore-fishing theme paintings are stunning. The gallery also features pottery, jewelry, chimes, cards, gifts, lighthouses, and jewelry. Artist Wayne Fulcher is often at work in the store.

Red Drum Pottery
NC 12, Frisco
(252) 995-5757

Accomplished potters Rhonda Bates and Wes Lassiter moved their studio from Edenton, North Carolina, to Frisco in the summer of 2001. The artists are often at work in the studio, and you can watch them as they turn their wonderful creations at the wheel. These are well-crafted, artistic pieces, whether they are intended for functional or decorative use. It's definitely worth a stop to see their bowls, pitchers, vases, vessels, platters, teakettles, miniatures, and fabulous fish- and crab-imprinted hanging wall tiles. The gallery is open seven days a week year-round.

Sandy Bay Gallery
NC 12, Hatteras Village
(252) 986-1338

This casual yet upscale gallery features

original fine art and crafts with an emphasis on Outer Banks artists. Located in a 1940s-era Hatteras Island house, Sandy Bay is filled with original watercolor and acrylic paintings and photography by local artists. You'll also find regional and national fine-art crafts by potters, jewelers, glass artisans, and paper, wood, stained glass, and fiber artists. The handcarved decorative waterfowl, including egrets, blue herons, sandpipers, and dowitchers, have grace and personality. The wood's grain is masterfully employed in the carving process to lend movement to curving necks, wings, and feathers. Glass boxes with silver trim by Mary Anne feature a geometric collage of colored and clear glass reminiscent of Mondrian's paintings. You also can choose from a nice selection of prints. It's open March through Christmas Eve.

Ocracoke Island

Sunflower Center
Back Rd., Ocracoke Village
(252) 928–6211

If you take the road that runs in front of the Back Porch Restaurant and drive around the loop, you'll find this shop. Sunflower Center combines contemporary and traditional East Coast arts and crafts, but most of the artists featured here are from Ocracoke. Only original art is exhibited. Other items here include fused glass, stained glass, art glass, pottery, and handcrafted jewelry.

Owner Carol O'Brien offers weekly winter workshops in oil and acrylic painting, plus pastels and drawing. A school of arts and crafts is provided October through Easter for adults. O'Brien features one medium (such as oil paintings, acrylic works, pen-and-ink, or mixed media) biweekly in an upstairs gallery. A recent addition to the gallery includes aromatherapy products, Long Life herbal teas, Nature's Way herbs, and other health products. The gallery is open daily Easter through September or by appointment.

Deepwater Pottery
School Rd., Ocracoke Village
(252) 928–7004

Artistic and functional stoneware and raku pottery are made here. You can choose from functional dining and kitchenware and decorative raku pottery with copper glazes. The shop carries an assortment of gifts. See our Shopping chapter for more details. It's open seasonally, so call ahead.

Village Craftsmen
Howard St., Ocracoke Village
(252) 928–5541

The artwork in this well-known gallery includes North Carolina pottery, handmade wooden boxes, jewelry, and other original items. The focus is on excellent craftsmanship and variety. Owner Philip Howard also sells his pen-and-ink and watercolor prints here. See our Shopping chapter for more about this local landmark, open year-round except the month of January and possibly half of February.

Island Artworks
British Cemetery Rd., Ocracoke Village
(252) 928–3892

Owner-artist Kathleen O'Neal has lived on Ocracoke for more than 25 years. "Art jewelry" aptly describes most of the finds here. O'Neal does all the copper enameling and silver- and goldsmithing work herself. The gallery also features local and North Carolina artwork such as large, contemporary-style watercolors of island scenes by Debbie Wells and the fused glass work of Libby Hicks. Local photography, sculptural assemblages created by O'Neal, glass art, hand-carved wooden boxes, and mixed-media art are just some of the exciting discoveries at Island Artworks. It's a real fine-art experience. You won't find any mass-produced items here. The shop is open from mid-March until Christmas.

Over The Moon
British Cemetery Rd., Ocracoke Village
(252) 928–3555

Over The Moon features handmade contemporary crafts from 150 artists across the nation. Shop here for jewelry, porcelain, and Brian Andreas's Story People—books, prints, and sculptures adorned with insightful sayings. See our Shopping chapter for other items found here. The shop is open from Easter through Thanksgiving.

The Gathering Place
NC 12, Ocracoke Village
(252) 928–7180

This turn-of-the-20th-century building is chock-full of interesting finds, including a collection of local crafts and pottery from across North Carolina. Look here for artwork by Frans Van Baars, Jim Wordsworth, and other creative folk. See our Shopping chapter for more on this artsy hot spot. It's open year-round except for January and February.

Heart's Desire
Back Rd., Ocracoke Village
(252) 928–4104

This shop features a variety of fine crafts including pottery, glass works, jewelry, folk art, copper works, and beach glass creations. Heart's Desire is open April through December.

Studios

These are private studios that can be approached by appointment only.

Southern Shores and Kitty Hawk

Russell Yerkes
(252) 261–6947

One of the Outer Banks most popular artists is Russell Yerkes, probably best known for his vibrant "fish" paintings, though his subject matter encompasses much more than fins. This nationally recognized watercolorist, always in high demand, creates imaginative images of aquatic scenes and will accept commissions.

Both locations of the Greenleaf Gallery in Duck and Nags Head (see separate listings under Galleries) carry a nice selection of Yerkes's work. Yerkes also serves as president of the Watercolor Society of North Carolina and is a real plus to the arts community, eager to help others in any way he can.

A visit to Yerkes' studio to view his work is a real treat. Those wishing to contact the artist may do so at the above telephone number.

Pat Troiani
(252) 261–4659

Pat Troiani is one of the Outer Banks's top watercolorists. She teaches her craft at her Kitty Hawk studio and primarily works in a realistic style. She's produced some gorgeous renditions of the Whalehead Club in the winter, beautiful florals, and various coastal scenes. Her work is sold at Indian Town Art Gallery in Frisco and the Island Art Gallery at the Christmas Shop in Manteo (see separate listings under "Galleries"). She offers classes twice weekly. Class size is limited to seven students. Troiani emphasizes color, composition, and drawing instruction. Call for an appointment.

W.E. (Ellie) Grumiaux, Jr.
120 S. Dogwood Trail, Southern Shores
(252) 255–0402

One of the most recognized artists on the Outer Banks, Grumiaux, who works in watercolor, specializes in portraying the buildings, boats, and landscapes that typify this resort area, as well as the lesser-known places in the surrounding towns. Grumiaux is also the one to call for that portrait of your cottage or boat. His work can be found in local churches, homes, and galleries such as Greenleaf Gallery in Duck, Seaside Gallery in Nags Head, and the John Silver Gallery in Manteo (see separate entries under Galleries). For additional information, you may reach the artist at the above number.

Kill Devil Hills

Marsh Ridge Studio
115 Ridge Rd., Kill Devil Hills
(252) 441–6581

Award-winning watercolorist Chris Haltigan offers lessons and original art for sale in her private studio. She describes her work as impressionism and contemporary realism featuring scenes from the Outer Banks and general locale. The word "radiant" well describes her work, which is characterized by iridescent sound waters and atmospheric early morning boat scenes. The passage of light gets special attention in her pieces. Haltigan's work appeared on the 1998–99 and 2000–01 editions of *The Beach Book*, the local phone book.

Call for an appointment to see Haltigan's work. The studio is open year-round.

E.M. (Liz) Corsa
(252) 480–0303

Think Beatrix Potter. Now throw in some sophistication and humor, and you have an idea of the depth and delight of E.M. Corsa's work. Referred to as a "watercolor wordsmith," her original watercolors and prints feature both wild and domestic animals with an attitude, presented in an anthropomorphic style. Corsa's inspiration comes from nature and family and is coupled with her unique sense of humor. She's a published writer of humorous magazine essays who combines images and titles in a thought-provoking and fresh manner. Her work can be viewed at Greenleaf Gallery in Duck and Nags Head, The Island Gallery at The Christmas Shop in Manteo, and Browning Artworks in Frisco. To view her work or find out where her next showing is, call the artist. Corsa's work appeared on the 1999–2000 edition of *The Beach Book* telephone directory.

Carol Trotman
(252) 441–3590

Painter Carol Trotman specializes in floral watercolors. Her work is so spectacular

Outer Banks galleries are chock-full of a variety of fine arts and crafts. PHOTO: COURTESY OF MARY ELLEN RIDDLE

that she was invited to show her watercolors at the American Horticultural Society in the spring of 1996 as a one-woman exhibition. Trotman's complicated garden scenes as well as poetic profiles of single blossoms are exceptional. You can purchase reproductions of her work on cards or original full-size work by calling the artist for an appointment or by visiting Greenleaf Gallery in Duck and Sandy Bay Gallery in Hatteras Village.

Susan Vaughan
(252) 480–3301
www.wellsvaughan.byregion.net

This is a working studio where Vaughan paints in a folk-art style. She produces town portraits in acrylics that are very popular on the Outer Banks. Available prints include her representations of Manteo, Kill Devil Hills, Duck, Elizabeth City, and Corolla. Vaughan also paints local scenes, and she welcomes commissions. Her work is on display at the Island Gallery at the Christmas Shop in Manteo. Call for commission information.

Nags Head

Marcia Cline
(252) 441–5167

Marcia Cline, a longtime resident of the

Outer Banks, is well known for her dedication and versatility. Her medium is constantly changing and expanding, yet her style remains distinctive. People have come to recognize the vivid color and warm spirit in Cline's work. A passion for painting and love of life is evident in her local Outer Banks scenes, travel-inspired works, and latest passion to be captured on the canvas. You may be familiar with her work because it is on display in many popular local restaurants such as the Rundown Cafe, Southern Bean, Quagmires, and Tortuga's Lie. Her work is also on display at the John Silver Gallery, at the KDH Cooperative Gallery, in area businesses, and in homes from coast to coast. She paints also by commission and welcomes contact by appointment at her home studio in Nags Head.

Ray Matthews Photographer
(252) 441-7941
www.raymatthews.com

Ray Matthews has been living on the Outer Banks for more than 25 years during which time he has developed a love for nature that is presented masterfully in his prints. While the Outer Banks is a real haven for the photographic arts, the height of excellence is represented in Matthews's work. He is a consummate custom-slide printer as well as a commercial photographer. His work is shown at Browning Artworks in Buxton, The Christmas Shop in Manteo, Greenleaf Galleries in Duck and Nags Head, and Outer Banks Style in Corolla. Call for an appointment. He is available year-round. Look for his Outer Banks calendar in finer retail stores.

Roanoke Island

The Hat Lady
(252) 473-1850

This is the working studio of Genna Miles, who creates fine-art wearable hats in one-of-a-kind designs. Miles employs spinning and crochet techniques with natural, hand-dyed fibers and trinkets to set off these artistic creations that will warm your head and your heart. Her baby bonnets crafted in 100 percent cotton are precious. The Hat Lady specializes in spinning animal hair into yarn. Bring in your dog or cat's shedded hair, and she'll make it into a hat for you! Miles accepts commissions, or you can see her work in many of the annual Outer Banks art exhibitions where she has been known to break away from headwear and create fiber and mixed-media sculptures that reflect her love for nostalgic items and thrift-store treasures.

Nick Sapone
292 The Lane, Wanchese
(252) 473-3136

Local decoy carver Nick Sapone produces hand-carved, hunting-style decoys. He makes both wooden decoys and the traditional Outer Banks–canvas style. He welcomes visitors to his home studio by appointment.

Hatteras Island

Michael Halminski Studio
Midgett Way, Waves
(252) 987-2401

Outer Banks seascapes and landscapes dominate the photography collection displayed at this studio. The bird photos are inspiring, especially his egret pictures. Call for an appointment. Halminski also has a fine collection of cards that features his work.

Juried Art Exhibitions

The Outer Banks offers several juried art exhibitions each year. While the traditional definition of juried implies that work is selected for showing by judges, most shows here have an open-entry policy, and the work is judged for excellence and originality. Most shows have an entry fee that averages $10 to $15.

Here we've listed the major shows in the area; for detailed information, call either the galleries mentioned or the Dare

County Arts Council, (252) 473-5558. New shows are always cropping up, so keep in touch with the arts council. See also our Annual Events chapter for more art activities.

Nags Head

Frank Stick Memorial Art Show
Glenn Eure's Ghost Fleet Gallery,
Gallery Row, 210 E. Driftwood St., Nags Head
(252) 473-5558

This February show is open to Dare County residents and Dare County Arts Council members. All genres of art are welcome; some restrictions (including the size of the work) apply. See our Annual Events chapter for more information.

International Miniature Art Show
Seaside Art Gallery, NC 12, MP 11, Nags Head
(252) 441-5418

Any artist may enter this May show held at Seaside Art Gallery. Work entered cannot exceed 40 inches. The show features mini-paintings, drawings, sculpture, wood-turned bowls, collages, and more.

Mollie Fearing Memorial Art Show
Roanoke Island Festival Park, Manteo
(252) 473-5558
www.darearts.org

The Dare County Arts Council puts on this annual art show, held at the beautiful Festival Park Art Gallery. Dare County Arts Council members and Dare County residents are invited to enter this show, which is held in May. Call DCAC at the number above for information.

International Icarus Art Show
Various locations, Nags Head
(252) 441-6584

Open to any artist, the International Icarus Art Show is held in December at Glenn Eure's Ghost Fleet Gallery and the Seaside Art Gallery. The show's theme always revolves around flight, as the show was created to pay annual homage to the Wrights' first powered flight. See our Annual Events chapter.

***The Beach Book* Cover Competition**
Sea and Sounds Gallery
104 Sir Walter Raleigh St., Manteo
(252) 473-5558
www.darearts.org

Open to all artists, both locals and visitors alike, this annual competition selects one entry to be featured on the cover of *The Beach Book*, the Outer Banks's telephone directory. Not only will the winning artist have her or his image on the cover of the book, but the painting will also appear on a billboard on US 158, welcoming visitors to the Outer Banks. And if that's not enough, the image will be reproduced as a limited-edition print. This show is held at the Dare County Arts Council gallery each October. Capture your vacation memories in a drawing or painting and your work could be featured on the next cover. (Hints: Keep your entry colorful and representative of the area. A vertical format works best.) Past winners include a beach scene of a young girl painting, Cape Hatteras lighthouse, a sandcastle, and a fisherman on the beach. For additional information, call the DCAC or the Beach Book at (252) 480-2787.

Dance Studios

Atlantic Dance Studio
Dare Center, US 158, MP 7, Kill Devil Hills
(252) 441–9009

The Atlantic Dance Studio, run by Victoria Toms, is a fantastic addition to the Outer Banks creative scene. Toms brings with her an outstanding history of professional experience. In fact, she studied under the Martha Graham School of Contemporary Dance and the Joffrey Ballet. Atlantic Dance Studio offers lessons for adults and children in genres of tap, ballet, jazz, gymnastics, and modeling. Both locals and visitors are welcome—from the beginner to the professional.

A boutique carries garments, shoes, bags, and dance paraphernalia—items needed to keep dancers on their toes.

Island Dance Studio
3017 Virginia Dare Trail, Nags Head
(252) 441–6789

Sophia Sharp has been teaching dance on the Outer Banks for two decades. She offers classes in ballet, jazz, tap, and preschool movement. Sharp's studio closes during the summer, so she caters mostly to local folks. She teaches children and adults in the atmospheric setting of an old Nags Head cottage just off the ocean.

Young ballerinas get their first on-stage experience in a local dance studio recital. PHOTO: KAREN BACHMAN

Annual Events

Keep in mind the beach isn't just for summer any-
more. The Outer Banks has become a favorite destination for visitors year-round, providing those vacationing during less crowded times with an ongoing selection of
activities to enjoy. You'll find it easy to fit in with the natives when life slows up a bit and
everyone gets to kick back and have some fun.

The opening of Roanoke Island Festival Park has provided a much-needed venue for
large events, something the area sorely lacked in previous years. Very often, our public
buildings double as cultural centers, hosting plays, concerts, and even symphony performances. Most local organizations prefer to host fund-raising events in the off-season,
when it's easier to get the attention of locals who are too busy during the summer to play
themselves, which means the area calendar remains chock-full all year. In fact, the quiet
seasons bring out the real character of the area, with hometown parades, a pig pickin' or
two, oyster roasts, fishing tournaments, watersports events—you name it.

When it comes to annual events on the Outer Banks, the environment and history
are on our side. We have our time-honored cornerstones that draw national audiences:
the festivities scheduled each December that surround the anniversary of humankind's
first powered flight and the annual celebrations that revolve around Virginia Dare's
birthday. Our environment is the calling card for national surfing championships, hang-
gliding events, and world-class fishing tournaments.

Our restaurants offer the annual Taste of the Beach, featuring talented chefs with
awe-inspiring credentials. Our St. Patrick's Day Parade that promenades down the Beach
Road in Nags Head each March is said to be the largest in the state. Retail stores, art galleries, the Outer Banks Chamber of Commerce, and state sites also sponsor happenings
such as dramatic vignettes, printmaking workshops, nature films, luncheons, lectures,
and book signings.

Manteo Booksellers in downtown Manteo holds a signing every week from mid-
June through Labor Day. These generally begin at 1:00 or 2:00 P.M. and last two hours.
Authors of local and national repute have participated, including National Book Award
winner Bob Shacochis and Pen Hemingway Award winner Mark Richard. Book subjects
include both serious and humorous nonfiction and fiction works. Occasionally they
schedule an evening reading by an author; call (252) 473-1221 for more information on
these free happenings.

Check out our Arts and Culture chapter for other options. The Outer Banks Forum,
(252) 261-1998, offers a variety of musical performances, drama, and comedy plays in
the off-season. Look to the Theatre of Dare, (252) 441-6726, for comedy and drama performances in the off-season. The Dare County Arts Council (DCAC), (252) 473-5558,
sponsors a variety of performing and visual arts events throughout the year.

January

Dare County Schools Annual Art Show
Glenn Eure's Ghost Fleet Gallery
210 E. Driftwood St., Gallery Row, Nags Head
(252) 441–6584

For one week in mid-January, the Dare County Schools put together an art show that showcases works by kids from seven public schools, grades K–12. If you like children's art, this is the show for you. It's not surprising that the work is exceptional, what with the large population of adult artists living on the Outer Banks. Artist or not, parents here are very supportive, and many kids have taken years of private art lessons.

The works range from delightful watercolors to wild chairs crafted after the student's favorite artist. The Georgia O'Keeffe and Picasso chairs were awesome at a recent exhibition. This show is primarily for viewing—it's difficult to wrestle work away from parents. Don't expect to make any purchases, although some high school students may be more inclined to sell for some pocket money. The show's reception is on a Sunday, generally at 2:00 P.M. Call for more information. Admission is free, and you can't beat the brownies and other goodies they serve.

February

Frank Stick Memorial Art Show
Glenn Eure's Ghost Fleet Gallery
210 E. Driftwood St., Gallery Row, Nags Head
(252) 473–5558

This art show has been held in early February every year since 1978 and features the work of more than 160 artists. If you want to submit work, you must be at least 18 years old and a Dare County resident or a member of the Dare County Arts Council, which sponsors the show. The evening reception is eagerly looked forward to, and local artists and patrons flock to the gallery to view the newest offerings from the art world. But don't be shy; the event welcomes visitors to partake of the sights, sounds, and tastes of the evening. If you can't make the reception, be sure to stop by during the month of February and view this always exciting and innovative exhibit.

This is the best venue to see what area artists have been producing of late. Many artists go out on a limb introducing new styles (at least new for them!). It's a fun show, and the reception becomes an annual get-together for locals and visitors alike.

A Literary Evening
Glenn Eure's Ghost Fleet Gallery
210 E. Driftwood St., Gallery Row, Nags Head
(252) 441–6584

This free event is held in mid-February as part of the month-long Frank Stick Memorial Art Show. Members of the Dare County Writers Group and other guests read original recent works. Poetry as well as humorous essays have a forum here. We even have witnessed barking dogs as part of one off-the-wall performance (but that's not the norm). The group, sponsored by the Dare County Arts Council, meets monthly at the Kill Devil Hills branch of the Dare County Library. It's open to all writers, and meetings are informal. Admission to A Literary Evening is free.

Civil War on the Outer Banks
Roanoke Island Festival Park, Manteo
(252) 475-1500

This two-day festival explores the Civil War era and its effects on the Outer Banks. Re-enactors and living history encampments bring the era to life, and there are also crafters, demonstrations, presentations, kids activities, and more. It's held on President's Day weekend and is free.

Priceless Pieces Past & Present Quilt Extravaganza
Roanoke Island Festival Park Art Gallery, Manteo
(252) 475-1500

If you love quilts and the fabric arts, you'll love this popular annual show, celebrating its fifth year in 2002. The show features old and new quilts made by or belonging to Dare County residents. There are also demonstrations. It's held throughout the month of March.

St. Patrick's Day Parade
NC 12, Nags Head
(252) 441-4116

The St. Patrick's Day Parade is held the Sunday before St. Patrick's Day every year. The parade begins at the Nags Head Fishing Pier at MP 12 on the Beach Road and proceeds north to about MP 10. Reputed to be one of the largest parades of its kind in North Carolina, the event is always fun for the whole family. Float participants throw candy, so wear something with pockets! Kelly's serves free hot dogs and sodas after the parade, and there's an evening of live entertainment at Kelly's under a tent. All events are free.

Pirate's Cove Inshore/Offshore Fishing School
Pirate's Cove Yacht Club
Manteo/Nags Head Causeway, Manteo
(252) 473-1451, (800) 762-0245

Going strong since 1993, this one-day, mid-March program features North Carolina fishing experts conducting hands-on round-table sessions at Pirate's Cove Yacht Club. The three-session program is held at the club's restaurant, clubhouse, and fitness center. Pick up an entry form at Pirate's Cove Yacht Club. The day is rounded out with a pig pickin' and beer social. The fee is $85 per person. Anglers of all skill levels are welcome. Offshore fishing and bait-rigging are demonstrated.

Kitty Hawk Kites
Annual Easter Egg Hunt
US 158, MP 12, Nags Head
(252) 441-4124, (800) FLY-THIS

This event is held at Kitty Hawk Kites in Nags Head, with the specific date dependent on when Easter falls. Kids will enjoy the chalk coloring contests, a variety of games, and, of course, an Easter egg hunt on the premises. Small fries will get a kick out of meeting KHK's fuzzy brown mascot Wil-Bear Wright. All activities are free.

Outer Banks Folk Festival
Roanoke Island Festival Park, Manteo
(252) 473-2197

The popular Outer Banks Folk Festival is moving to Festival Park for its fifth annual show in 2002. The Folk Festival is brought to Dare County by people who love music. They then give all the proceeds to local charities. Some of the best musicians from around the country perform at this event. The headliner for 2002 is Arlo Guthrie. Other performers include Kim O'Brien, Darryl Scott, Celtic Thunder, Camille West, and Jack Williams. It's held on a Saturday in early April starting in the early afternoon and running through late evening. Tickets are $20 each; libations and food are available from vendors. Bring blankets and chairs to sit on the lawn. Call Debbie Russo at the number above for information.

Outer Banks Home Show
(252) 449-8232

This year's Outer Banks Home Show is

The largest St. Patrick's Day parade in eastern North Carolina is held in Nags Head. PHOTO: COURTESY OF JEANNE REILLY

held the weekend before Easter. Builders, products, lending agencies, and other services will be exhibited to consumers. Expect about 75 exhibits of home improvement items from hot tubs to tiles. A nominal fee gets you in, and the proceeds are donated to local charity. Call for location.

Kelly's Midnight Easter Egg Hunt
Kelly's Outer Banks Restaurant
US 158, MP 10½, Nags Head
(252) 441-4116

Adults enjoy searching for treats by flashlight. It's lots of fun, and it's free. Anyone 21 or older may participate in this late-night egg hunt on the restaurant premises. The event's exact date depends on when Easter falls. Participants find eggs that may be empty or contain prizes such as gift certificates, free drink coupons, or free T-shirt coupons. Stop in the tavern prior to the event for a drink or some great light fare at reasonable prices.

Antiques Show and Auction
Roanoke Island Festival Park, Manteo
(252) 475-1500

This antiques fair is a new event at Roanoke Island Festival Park, held to benefit the Friends of *Elizabeth II*. Antiques dealers from around the region will gather on the Pavilion lawn, and there will be an antiques auction. There will be an admission charge. Call for more information.

The Outer Banks Senior Games
Thomas A. Baum Senior Center
300 Mustian St., Kill Devil Hills
(252) 441-1181

Dare County seniors 55 and older are eligible to compete in the Outer Banks Senior Games, a competition that features shuffleboard, billiards, spin casting, golf, bowling, horseshoes, table tennis, and much more. All ages are welcome to watch and cheer for the competitors in this mid-April event, which has been happening every year since 1988.

A modified version of the games is offered for disabled seniors. Volunteers work with each individual needing assistance. Games for this group can include door basketball and rubber horseshoes.

The local group of seniors sends hundreds of competitors to state competitions every year. Some even have gone on to the national contest. The festivities include dinner at a local restaurant. The registration fee is $10 to participate in four events including the arts competition (see next listing) and includes lunch on opening day and on track and field day.

The Outer Banks Silver Arts Competition
Thomas A. Baum Senior Center
300 Mustian St., Kill Devil Hills
(252) 441–1181

This is the art component of the Outer Banks Senior Games, featuring an exhibition of talent and craftsmanship in the visual, literary, heritage, and performing arts. The events last for several days, culminating in a free evening performance at the Kitty Hawk Elementary School. The $10 games registration fee covers entry into the arts competition.

Inner-Tribal Powwow "Journey Home"
Cape Hatteras School, Buxton
(252) 995–4440
www.nativeamericanmuseum.org

For something truly special come to the Inner-Tribal Powwow put on by the folks at the Frisco Native American Museum and Natural History Center. In its fourth year in 2002, this is a popular annual event on Hatteras Island. The Inner-Tribal Powwow gathers from 75 to 100 members of many different tribes for a weekend of celebration on the ancestral grounds of Hatteras Island. Tribal representatives come from all over North Carolina and the East Coast and from as far away as Canada, Ohio, Washington State, and Arizona. It's a family event, where the emphasis is on the sharing of cultures. Many of the Native Americans dress in full regalia. Storytelling, drumming, and dancing are all part of the celebration. You'll get to sample Native American food, buy Native American wares, and watch Native craftspeople at work, as vendors often craft their wares on-site. Demonstration dances and Friendship Dances, where even the public gets to join in, make this an exciting cultural event. There is a bonfire on Saturday night. Small admission fees are charged either by the day or for the entire weekend, and children, seniors, and families get a discount. The public is invited to this event, which is held in mid-April.

Tour de Cure
Roanoke Island Festival Park, Manteo
(757) 455–6335 ext. 3281, (919) 743–5400 ext. 3254

If you're into serious cycling, consider putting your legs to work for the American Diabetes Association. This mid-April event has two cycling events, both of which end up at Roanoke Island Festival Park in Manteo. The Saturday event starts in Virginia Beach, Virginia. As if that weren't far enough, the Sunday event starts in Raleigh, North Carolina. All proceeds go to a good cause, and there are fun celebrations at Festival Park after the rides. Call the (757) number if you're interested in starting from Virginia, and the (919) number if you want to start from Raleigh.

Windfest
Frisco Woods Campground, NC 12, Frisco
(252) 995–5208, (800) 948–3942

Wind lovers will enjoy this event, which also benefits charity. All donations go to the Cape Hatteras Meals on Wheels program. Bed down at the campground for a fee (see our Camping chapter) and enjoy the rest of the event for a donation. Wind- and kite-surfing reps offer free demos; join in the regatta, and end each evening of the three-day festival with a cookout. The folks at Frisco Woods promise lots of wind and good company. Bring your own wind rider or use one of theirs. The donation covers your meals. As part of Windfest, Kitty Hawk Kites offers a Kite Surfing Fun Ride at the campground. The event offers wind lovers the opportunity to take part in kiting clinics, watch demos, and meet the pros. The fun ride takes place from Frisco to Hatteras or Avon, depending on wind direction.

Relay for Life
Whalehead Club, Corolla
(252) 261–1023

Held the last weekend in April, Relay for Life is a 20-hour relay walk that benefits the American Cancer Society. Competitors form teams and raise money prior to the event, which is held on the beautiful grounds of the Whalehead Club in Corolla. During the relay, one person from each team is on the track at all times from 3:00 P.M. on Saturday until 10:00 A.M. on Sunday. All during the day there are events on the lawn, including food vendors and music. It's a fun event that benefits a great cause.

May

Hatteras Village Offshore Open Billfish Tournament
Hatteras Harbor Marina, NC 12,
Hatteras Village
(252) 986–2555, (888) 544–8115
www.hatterasoffshoreopen.com

Anglers contend for prizes as they fish to catch and release the biggest billfish. A meat fish category is included for the largest tuna, dolphin, and wahoo caught daily. The three-day fishing tournament is held in early May and sponsored by the Hatteras Village Civic Association. This is a Governor's Cup–sanctioned event, and it's the kickoff tournament in the Governor's Cup challenge. All competitors must enter Level 1 for $500; two additional levels—Level 2 at $700 and Level 3 at $300—are not mandatory. Fishing begins at 8:00 A.M., and lines come out of the water promptly at 3:00 P.M. Festivities with food and drink are usually held each evening. The event closes with an awards banquet. The tournament is open to the public. Over 55 boats entered in 2001 so the purse was high. More boats are expected in 2002.

Mollie Fearing Memorial Art Show
Roanoke Island Festival Park, Manteo
(252) 473–5558

This exhibition replaces the annual spring art show sponsored by the Dare County Arts Council. Mollie Fearing, one of the founders of the local cultural arts group, The Sea and Sounds Arts Council, which was the precursor of the current DCAC, died in 1997. To honor this former mayor of Manteo's efforts to promote the arts, the council voted to name their spring fling after Fearing. The show is open to all artists, and $2,000 in cash awards are given. It is held in May and is open for public viewing. Call for membership, reception, and entry information.

Hang Gliding Spectacular and Air Games
Jockey's Ridge State Park, US 158, MP 12, Nags Head
(252) 441–4124, (800) FLY–THIS
Currituck County Airport
US 158, Barco
(800) FLY–THIS

Spectators and participants cover the dunes at the park every year to attend the longest-running hang-gliding competition in the country. Pilots from all over the world compete in a variety of flying maneuvers including an aerotow competition. Beginning hang-gliding lessons are given. The event is sponsored by Kitty Hawk Kites, and a complimentary street dance and an awards ceremony add icing to the cake! Annual inductions to the Rogallo Hall of Fame (Francis Rogallo is the father of the Flexible Wing Flyer—the prototype for the modern hang glider) close the ceremony. Hang-glider pilots who have achieved their Hang One are welcome to compete. The public is invited to view the event for free. Participants pay an entry fee.

British Cemetery Ceremony
British Cemetery Rd., Ocracoke Island
(252) 928–3711

The event commemorates the 1942 sinking of the British trawler HMS *Bedfordshire*. A British official is sent to Ocracoke each year to attend this U.S. Coast Guard service. Four bodies of British naval seamen are buried in the British Cemetery. Their ship was stationed off Ocracoke to protect our shores during the beginning of World War II. The armed trawler was torpedoed and sunk by a German submarine on May 11. (The ceremony is held on May 7.) All perished, and the four bodies were the only ones recovered; they were buried by island residents. A plaque at the cemetery memorializes the men: "If I should die think only this of me that there's some forever corner of a foreign field that is forever England." This event is free. (See our Attractions chapter for more historic information.)

Outer Banks Walk America
Roanoke Island Festival Park, Manteo
(800) 732–7097

This fund-raising walk benefits the March of Dimes. The walk starts at Festival Park, winds through downtown Manteo, and ends at Festival Park. Music and refreshments are offered after the walk. This event is held in mid-May.

Nags Head Woods 5K Run and Post-Run Beach Party
Nags Head Woods Preserve
Ocean Acres Dr., Kill Devil Hills
(252) 441–2525

Folks from all walks of life run side by side through Nags Head Woods in this annual event that is held on a Saturday in May. The run is limited to the first 400 runners to register. To participate, write Nags Head Woods 5K Run, 701 W. Ocean Acres Drive, Kill Devil Hills, North Carolina 27948. The post-run party at Quagmire's on the Beach features music, food, and drinks. Proceeds benefit Nags Head Woods. For entry fees and tickets, call the preserve.

International Miniature Art Show
Seaside Art Gallery, NC 12, MP 11, Nags Head
(252) 441–5418, (800) 828–2444

Artists from all over the world compete for cash prizes in this exhibition of miniature art. Past shows have seen more than 450 works from 38 states and 12 countries. The work includes paintings, sculpture, and drawings of all styles. The art is available for viewing for about two weeks. The reception occurs in late May. Call the above number for a prospectus for this annual event, which is celebrating its 10th year in 2002.

OBX Jaycees Beach Music Festival
Roanoke Island Festival Park, Manteo
(252) 480–2227

Ready for some fun in the sun? The Jaycees put on this annual festival that celebrates beach music and the coming summer season. Big crowds gather for this event, which is held on the spacious

The annual Hang Gliding Spectacular on Jockey's Ridge is the longest-running hang-gliding competition in the country. PHOTO: HORSLEY/GARDNER

lawn of the Pavilion. Beach music bands and local bands play all day long. Kick off your shoes and dance on the lawn. Bring plenty of sunscreen and blankets or folding chairs. Food and beverages, including beer, are available on-site. Tickets can be purchased in advance or on-site the day of the event. Proceeds benefit the Cystic Fibrosis Foundation and the Outer Banks YMCA. It's held on the Saturday of Memorial Day weekend.

Pirate's Cove Memorial Weekend Tournament
Pirate's Cove Yacht Club
Nags Head–Manteo Causeway, Manteo
(252) 473–3700, (800) 537–7245
www.fishpiratescove.com

This tournament is for pure fun only. No money prizes are awarded, but contenders can go home with a trophy. There is a $150 team entry fee. Anglers head offshore to fish for billfish, tuna, dolphin, and wahoo. All billfish are released, and there is a prize for the largest release and

the combined weight of the three largest meat fish caught per team. Call for entry dates and more information.

June

Dare Day Festival
Downtown Manteo
(252) 473–1101 ext. 319

This is the quintessential small-town family event. Dare Day is a much-loved local tradition that celebrates the wonderful county of Dare. It's always held the first Saturday of June, and you'll find locals, visitors, politicians, children, and just about everybody you can think of coming out to enjoy the day in downtown Manteo. Dare Day features arts and crafts booths, lots of food (including in-season soft-shell crabs), national and local musical entertainment, kids activities, games, rides, and much more. A free concert (in 2001 it was the legendary Doc Watson) is held over at

Roanoke Island Festival Park in the Pavilion. All of Festival Park's sites, including the *Elizabeth II*, are free on this day. For a taste of real local culture, don't miss this event.

Rogallo Kite Festival
Jockey's Ridge State Park, US 158, MP 12,
Nags Head
(800) 334-4777
This two-day, free, family fun fly in early June celebrates the beauty of kite flying and honors the father of hang gliding, NASA scientist Francis Rogallo. It is open to kite enthusiasts of all ages and features stunt kites, home-builts, kids' kite making and flying competitions, and an auction where you can bid on display and demo stunt kites. Rogallo, the inventor of the flexible wing, generally makes an appearance. The event, sponsored by Kitty Hawk Kites, celebrates its 21st year in 2002.

The Lost Colony Outdoor Drama
Fort Raleigh National Historic Site
(800) 488-5012
America's longest-running outdoor drama opens its 65th season in June 2002. The show runs nightly except Saturdays through August. Call for performance dates and times. For more information, see our Attractions chapter.

Illuminations Summer Arts Festival
and Children's Performances
Roanoke Island Festival Park, Manteo
(252) 475-1506
Starting in late June and running through mid-August, Roanoke Island Festival Park stages wonderful cultural activities almost every day of the week. Illuminations is the performance series of the North Carolina School of the Arts, and the students perform Tuesday through Saturday nights in the outdoor Pavilion amphitheater. You'll see dance, jazz, classical music, film, and drama. See our Attractions and Arts and Culture chapters for more about this series. The Children's Performances are held Tuesday through Friday in the Film Theater. Performances are geared to all ages of children and include things like storytelling, puppets, and singers. See our Kidstuff chapter for more information.

Hatteras Marlin Club Billfish Tournament
Hatteras Marlin Club, off NC 12, Hatteras
Village
(252) 986-2454
The Hatteras Marlin Club Billfish Tournament, going strong since 1959, offers a week of competition fishing and entertainment to participants and their guests. Teams head for offshore waters looking to catch the biggest billfish or meat fish including blue marlin, tuna, dolphin, and wahoo. Evenings are filled with socials that include entertainment, cocktails, appetizers, and dinner. The tournament is for members and anglers invited by the tournament committee. Write to the Hatteras Marlin Club for membership and tournament information, Box 218, Hatteras, North Carolina 27943. Registration costs $2,000.

Youth Fishing Tournament
Piers from Kitty Hawk to Nags Head
(252) 441-5464
This tournament is a low-key pier-fishing competition for kids ages 4 to 16. The cost is 50 cents per person, and you register at all oceanfront fishing piers from Kitty Hawk to Nags Head. It's sponsored by the Nags Head Surf Fishing Club, North Carolina Beach Buggy Association, and the North Carolina Sea Hags. The event is held in late June. It lasts from 8:00 A.M. until 1:00 P.M., ending with an awards ceremony.

July

Sand Sculpture Contest
On the beach north of Ocracoke Village
(252) 928-7689
This artistic endeavor kicks off Fourth of July festivities on the island. Kids and adults are welcome to participate in the early morning event. You can work alone or in groups. Past events have seen sand transformed into turtles, jumping dolphin,

pirates, and ships. There's no entry fee for the contest. Call for times and location.

Independence Day Parade and Fireworks Display
Ocracoke Village
(252) 928–7689

This festive parade featuring a half-dozen floats makes its way through the streets starting around 3:00 P.M. on July 4. Local shopkeepers and residents get creative making floats for what's dubbed the village's biggest annual event. The parade moves down NC 12 from Captain Ben's Restaurant through Ocracoke Village. The evening ends with a gala fireworks display at Lifeguard Beach. Ocracokers say it's the best Fourth of July celebration on the Outer Banks.

Manteo Independence Day Celebration
Manteo Waterfront
(252) 473–1101

Activities run from 1:00 to 9:00 P.M. and include a Wacky Tacky Hat Contest, children's games, food and other concessions, musical entertainment, and a street dance

from 6:00 to 9:00 P.M., when a fireworks display begins. The event is free.

Fireworks in Hatteras Village
Hatteras Village
(252) 986–2719

The fireworks sponsored by the Hatteras Village Civic Association and the Volunteer Fire Department start at 8:30 P.M. at ramp 55 in the village. There is no admission fee.

Fireworks Festival and Fair
Whalehead Club, NC 12, Corolla
(252) 453–9040

The historic hunt club is the backdrop for the fireworks and fair that begin at 6:00 and run to 11:00 P.M. The Currituck County Board of Commissioners and the Corolla Business Association host this event. Expect fun, food, live musical entertainment, and, of course, pyrotechnics galore. Admission is free.

Annual Wright Kite Festival
Wright Brothers National Memorial,
MP 8, Kill Devil Hills
(252) 441–4124, (800) 334–4777

This Bud's for the creator of these amazing sand sculptures. PHOTO: COURTESY OF BOB REARDON

This mid-July family event involves kite flying for all ages and also includes free kite-making workshops, stunt kite demos, and children's games. The event, sponsored by Kitty Hawk Kites and the National Park Service, has been held every year since 1978. You can watch for free. Adults are invited to participate in kite contests. Call for fees.

Hermit Crab Race
Newman's Shell Shop, NC 12 , Nags Head
(252) 441–5791

Kids of all ages love this fun—and funny—event featuring hermit crabs. Seventy-five to 100 contestants vie for prizes on the last Saturday in July. Kids bring their own pet crabs or purchase one at the shell shop. There is no entry fee.

August

Annual Watermelon Regatta and Race
Kitty Hawk Connection and Kitty Hawk Sports
US 158, MP 12, Nags Head
(252) 441–6800

This watermelon-centered event begins with a parade led by the state's Watermelon Queen and includes an Olympic watermelon toss, big league watermelon bowling and carving, long-distance seed spitting, and watermelon consumption. The most energized event of the day is the Kamikaze Watermelon Drop—kids join in the on-premises tower and drop watermelons. Register at Kitty Hawk Sports's Nags Head store. The event is free.

Annual Herbert Hoover Birthday Celebration
Manteo Booksellers
Sir Walter Raleigh St., Manteo
(252) 473–1221

On August 10, browse through this superb bookstore, munch on three cakes (each one inscribed with "Happy," "Birthday," or "Herbie"), sip some famous "Herbert Sherbert" punch, and chat with Hoover fans at this tongue-in-cheek free event, now in its 16th year. The reason for

the fun? It's all done purely for the sake of having a celebration. The day includes an author signing. Look for a special display of Hoover memorabilia. Come eat, drink, and think Herbert Hoover!

Annual Senior Adults Craft Fair
Thomas A. Baum Center
300 Mustian St., Kill Devil Hills
(252) 441–9388

Local senior citizens provide the crafts for this community project sponsored by the Outer Banks Women's Club. It's been a tradition for more than 25 years. Admission is $1.00.

Alice Kelly Memorial Ladies Only Billfish Tournament
Pirate's Cove Yacht Club
Manteo–Nags Head Causeway, Manteo
(252) 473–6800, (800) 367–4728
www.fishpiratescove.com

The tournament, sponsored by Pirate's Cove since 1989, honors the memory of local fishing enthusiast Alice Kelly, who died in her 30s from Hodgkin's disease. Kelly was a high-spirited woman whose love for fishing inspired many local women to try (and fall in love with) the sport. Women form teams and arrange for charter boats to carry them out to sea. The tournament occurs in early August. Call for entry fee information.

Pirate's Cove Billfish Tournament
Pirate's Cove Yacht Club,
Manteo–Nags Head Causeway, Manteo
(252) 473–6800, (800) 367–4728
www.fishpiratescove.com

Pirate's Cove Yacht Club has hosted a billfish release tournament every August since 1983. Contenders fish for several days trying to catch and release the largest billfish. A meat fish (tuna, dolphin, and wahoo) category, in which a prize is awarded for the largest catch, adds to the fun. The tournament is an official part of the N.C. Governor's Cup Billfish Series and occurs mid-month. Call for entry fee information.

New World Festival of the Arts
Manteo Waterfront
(252) 473-2838
Coordinated by The Christmas Shop, this mid-August event makes downtown Manteo come alive with art every year. The outdoor two-day show features more than 80 artists showcasing fine art and crafts including pottery, jewelry, paintings, and more. Outdoor booths and tents line the historic waterfront, attracting visitors who return each year looking for their favorite artists. There is no admission fee. Call for booth registration fees. It's held mid-week, on Wednesday and Thursday.

Virginia Dare Birthday Celebration
Fort Raleigh National Historic Site Visitor Center
US 64/264, Roanoke Island
(252) 473-2127
This event, held August 18, commemorates the birth of Virginia Dare, the first English child born in the New World. The celebration features a daylong series of special happenings. Past events have featured members of the cast of *The Lost Colony* singing and dancing and demonstrations of arms from that period in history. Call the National Park Service for details. This event is free. The Elizabethan Gardens, right next to Fort Raleigh, honor Virginia Dare's Birthday by offering free admission to the gardens on this day. They also offer special gardening workshops throughout the day.

Virginia Dare Night Performance of *The Lost Colony*
Waterside Theatre
US 64/264, Roanoke Island
(252) 473-3414, (800) 488-5012
www.thelostcolony.org
On August 18, *The Lost Colony* celebrates Virginia Dare's 1587 birth by casting local infants in the role of the baby Virginia Dare. This makes for a special and spontaneous performance, as usually baby Virginia is played by a doll. (For details on the famous outdoor drama, see our Attractions chapter.)

National Aviation Day
Wright Brothers National Memorial
US 158, MP 8, Kill Devil Hills
(252) 441-7430
www.nps.gov/wrbr/wright
Explore planes galore at this free mid-month event, held on August 19. Aviation enthusiasts will enjoy viewing about 25 different types of single-engine aircraft ranging from the antique to modern-day models. The schedule is not firmed up until a few days before the event so that weather conditions can be taken into consideration. Past events have included a flyover with Air Force and Navy planes, jets from Langley Field, and the Blue Angels. The day's festivities include free admission to the memorial.

September

"The Allison" Crippled Children's White Marlin Release Tournament
Pirate's Cove Yacht Club
Manteo–Nags Head Causeway, Manteo
(252) 473-6800, (800) 537-7245
Since 1992, The Allison has raised funds for disabled kids. Travel offshore to the infamous Outer Banks fishing grounds and search for billfish and other pelagic species. All billfish caught are released. Bait and tackle are provided. The event takes place the first weekend in September. There are four categories; entry in category 1 ($1,000) is mandatory. Costs for the other categories are $400 for category 2, $500 for category 3 (which is the pool for the daily prize) and $500 for category 4 (the prize for the largest meat fish). Call for more information.

Weeping Radish Restaurant and Brewery Oktoberfest
US 64/264, Manteo
(252) 473-1157
www.weepingradish.com
The Weeping Radish hosts its 17th Oktoberfest in 2002 during the second week in September. Expect a family-oriented out-

door celebration featuring Bavarian-style food, an oompah band, children's games, specially brewed German beer, and a chance to win a trip to Germany. There is no admission fee.

Outer Banks Triathlon
Roanoke Island
(252) 480–0500

An Outer Banks tradition since 1984, the triathlon is held in early September. Entrants swim .6 mile, run 3.1 miles, and bike 15 miles. The swimming segment is held at the Old Swimming Hole at the north end of Roanoke Island; the running and biking thirds are done on the island. Individuals can participate in all three events, or a team of three can split up the events. The entry fee for individuals is around $45 for Triathlon USA members; $55 for nonmembers. Team entries are $120 for Triathlon USA members; $150 for nonmembers. The event is limited to 300 participants.

Labor Day Arts and Crafts Show
Cape Hatteras School
NC 12, Buxton
(252) 986–2879

This traditional arts and crafts fair is sponsored by the Hatteras Island Arts and Crafts Guild and features pottery, dolls, clockmaking, shellwork, and countless other goodies. No admission fee.

Kitty Hawk Kites Annual
Boomerang Competition
First Flight Middle School, Kill Devil Hills
(252) 441–2124, (877) FLY–THIS
www.kittyhawk.com

Boomers from across the nation flock to the Outer Banks for this competition of the U.S. Boomerang Association. Novice throwers are welcome to compete, or you can just come and watch the competition and fun. Boomerang workshops are held on Sunday.

Outer Banks Surf Kayak Festival
Ramada Inn, NC 12, Kill Devil Hills
(252) 441–6800

Sponsored by Kitty Hawk Sports, this event is fun to watch or participate in. Expect surf kayak events for paddlers with intermediate and advanced skills. There are men's, women's, high-performance and sit-on-top categories as well as a junior division. Included are cash prizes, demonstrations, used kayaks for sale, mini clinics, food, and reduced rates if you stay at the Ramada Inn. Call for entry fee information.

NOWR Annual Outer Banks
Surf Kayak Rodeo
Rodanthe Pier, NC 12, Rodanthe
(252) 441–6800, (800) 948–0759

This is a mid- to late September event, held by the National Organization of Whitewater Rodeos since 1995. It features rodeo and traditional kayak surfing for the experienced and the novice kayaker. There are men's, women's, and junior divisions. The two-day festivities include a silent auction, boat raffle, boat demos, food, and music. Profits help promote recreational boating and to protect our rivers. Call Kitty Hawk Kayaks for fees and dates.

Hatteras Village Civic Association Surf
Fishing Tournament
Hatteras Village Civic Center
NC 12, Hatteras Village
(252) 986–2579

Since 1982, surf-fishing fans have met the third week in September for this tournament. Anglers fish for a wide variety of eligible species including drum, bluefish, trout, and more. Call for registration fees and information.

North Carolina Big Sweep
Dare County beaches
(800) 27–SWEEP
www.ncbigsweep.org

This is a local waterway cleanup that's hooked into a statewide and national event. Trash picking runs from 9:00 A.M. to 1:00 P.M. on the third Saturday in September. Folks have cleaned the waterways since 1986 to do their civic duty. Obviously, it's free. Call the above number for more information.

Ocean Fest
Ramada Inn
NC 12, Kill Devil Hills
(252) 441–6800, (800) 948–0759
www.khsports.com

Participate in surf kayak and rodeo clinics and watch boat demos at this late September event. The five-day program features paddle races, surf ski sprints, an outrigger race, contests, raffles, music, food, and parties. Call Kitty Hawk Kayaks for prices and dates.

ESA Eastern Surfing Championships
Location varies
(800) 937–4733
www.surfesa.org

Competition is open to Eastern Surfing Association members only, but it's a fun and free spectator event. Watch as surfers grab their boards and head to the ocean to pit their skills against the waves and their fellow competitors. For more information, write to Box 400, Buxton, North Carolina 27920.

East Coast Kite Surfing Championships
Frisco Woods Campground, Frisco
(252) 441–4124, (877) FLY–THIS
www.kittyhawk.com

Kitty Hawk Kites sponsors this annual kite-surfing competition on the sound and ocean waters of Hatteras Island, considered one of the best kite-surfing locations in the country. Join or watch the best kite surfers in the world as they vie for the title of East Coast Kite Surfing Champion. Vendors are on hand with all their gear. If you're really into this, camp at Frisco Woods Campground over the weekend so you won't have to miss a minute of the action.

Quagmire's Annual Sandcastle Contest
Quagmire's Restaurant
NC 12, Kill Devil Hills
(252) 441–9188

Quagmire's Restaurant sponsors this annual sandcastle-building contest, now in its sixth year. The event is held on the beach right in front of the restaurant. Individuals or group teams get three and a half hours to concoct whatever sculpture or creature they can conjure up with wet sand. Many families enter this contest year after year. It's held in late September.

Kitty Hawk Heritage Day Celebration
The Promenade
US 158, MP ¼, Kitty Hawk
(252) 261–3552

This daylong festival at the end of September is great fun for kids of all ages. Numerous food vendors, 30 crafters, children's events and games, local entertainers and singers, and a heritage display about Kitty Hawk are just some of the fun festival fare you'll find here. All of The Promenade's activity facilities are open throughout the day. Kids of all ages will have a lot of fun here. It's sponsored by the town of Kitty Hawk, so call the town office at the number above for dates, rain dates, and times. Parking is limited, so a shuttle bus runs from the Wal-Mart parking lot to The Promenade.

October

OBX Paddle Race
Roanoke Sound
(252) 441–6800, (800) 948–0759

This two-day event is sponsored by Kitty Hawk Kayaks and features a race to benefit clean water. The 12-mile professional race and the 5-mile recreational races are held in Roanoke Sound. The mid- to late October benefit includes a raffle, silent auction, demos, and clinics. Cash awards are given to the top six finishers in each class competing in the pro race. Some cash (but mostly prizes) is awarded in the recreational race. Entry fees for the pro race range from $30 to $40. Recreation race fees range between $15 and $25. The lower fees apply in each category for early entries. Call the above number for more information.

Nags Head Surf Fishing Club Invitational Tournament
Nags Head
(252) 441–5464

The Nags Head Surf Fishing Club's tournament celebrates its 52nd year in 2002. Team fishing, held on a Thursday and Friday in early October, is usually booked solid for years to come. But participants are welcome to fish the individual tournament on Saturday from 8:00 A.M. to noon. Register at George's Junction Restaurant in Nags Head. Good luck!

Outer Banks Homebuilders Association's Parade of Homes
Homes from Corolla to South Nags Head and Manteo
(252) 449–8232
www.obhomebuilders.org

The OBHA opens new and remodeled homes to the public for this early October event. There's a $7.00 fee to tour about 20 participating homes. Proceeds are donated to local charities.

Artrageous Art Extravaganza Weekend
Dare County Arts Council
Dare County Recreation Park
Mustian St., Kill Devil Hills
(252) 473–5558
www.darearts.org

Artrageous, started in 1990, is a community art festival and auction sponsored by the Dare County Arts Council (see our Close-up in the Arts and Culture chapter) the first weekend in October. Children and adults are invited to spend Saturday painting, weaving, and creating various arts and crafts. All art supplies are provided. Listen to local musicians young and old, eat tasty food, and witness art in the making by professionals. Artists sell their wares. Collaborative paintings by children are auctioned on Saturday; a more formal adult auction, complete with hors d'oeuvres and cocktails, takes place on Sunday. There is no admission fee to Saturday's events. Average price for booth activities is $1.00. The Sunday evening auction event is held at varying locations; call for details. It's a lively event, where you can get some great deals on art by local artists and catch up with the locals.

Beach Book Cover Art Competition
Sea and Sounds Gallery
Sir Walter Raleigh St., Manteo
(252) 473–5558
www.darearts.org

The Dare County Arts Council and *The Beach Book* hold this annual art show and competition in order to select the cover art for the local phone directory. Local judges select the winning piece, but visitors can vote on the People's Choice award. The winner gets his or her work of art on thousands of copies of the phone book plus on a billboard in Currituck. Call the Dare County Arts Council for entry information. The show hangs in the gallery throughout the month of October.

Outer Banks Stunt Kite Competition
Jockey's Ridge State Park
Nags Head
(252) 441–4124, (800) FLY–THIS
www.kittyhawk.com

Entrants compete on the Eastern League Circuit of the American Kiting Association. The program features novice, intermediate, and expert challenges, as well as workshops and demos. Kids enjoy making kites. Ballet competitions, music, and team train competitions highlight the sanctioned event. Registration and competition fees are charged to competitors. Contact Kitty Hawk Kites for more information on this annual competition.

Red Drum Tournament
Frank and Fran's Fisherman's Friend
NC 12, Avon
(252) 995-4171

Two hundred anglers fish the surf and try to catch the largest red drum during this late October event, sponsored by this popular Avon tackle shop. Fees range from $30 to $85 per person. Limited space is available for this three-day tournament.

Kelly's–Penguin Isle Charity Golf Tournament
Village of Nags Head
US 158, MP 15, Nags Head
Currituck Club, Corolla
(252) 441-4116

Six-person teams play 18 holes for charity during late October. Proceeds benefit the Outer Banks Community Foundation. Fees per team generally run around $400.

Teach's Lair Shootout King Mackerel Tournament
Teach's Lair Marina, NC 12, Hatteras Village
(252) 986-2460

In this tournament, anglers try their luck in capturing the largest king mackerel. It's held in Hatteras Village at the end of October or early November. Entry fees range from $200 to $300. The tournament is open to the public.

Octoberfest at Frisco Woods Campground
Frisco Woods Campground
NC 12, Frisco
(252) 995-5208

Here's a great way to enjoy autumn on the Outer Banks and help out the commu-

nity's Meals On Wheels program. Octoberfest events include a pig pickin' with all the trimmings, live music, crafts, a bake sale, and a rummage sale. It's a free, late-October event. Donations to the charitable cause are welcome.

The Knights' Ball
Pine Island Racquet Club, Corolla
(252) 453-9040
www.whaleheadclub.com

The Knights' Ball is an elegant fund-raising ball that benefits the Whalehead Preservation Trust. Proceeds are used in the restoration efforts at Corolla's historic Whalehead Club (see our Attractions chapter). Tickets for the ball are $100 each and must be purchased in advance. The evening features a live band, dinner buffet, and silent auction—and a lot of preservation-minded guests looking to have a good time for a good cause. The ball lasts from 6:00 P.M. to midnight. Call for more details.

November

Wings Over Water Festival
Many Outer Banks locations
(252) 441-8144
www.northeast-nc.com/wings/

In its sixth year in 2002, Wings Over Water is a celebration of the Outer Banks's wonderful wildlife and wildlands. It is an amazing three-day event that includes something for everyone who enjoys the outdoors—birders, wildlife enthusiasts, individuals, couples, families, whoever. It offers an unbelievable number of activities for those who want to learn more about this enchanted natural area. You select the field trips, programs, and seminars that interest you the most and then get an inside look at the various ecological settings and wildlife of the Outer Banks. You can, for example, go on guided bird-watching trips at Pea Island National Wildlife Refuge, one of the most popular fall birding sites in the southeast. You can check out shore birds at Cape Hatteras

Lighthouse or visit Buxton Woods and Nags Head Woods with a naturalist. You can kayak or canoe into a salt marsh, motor out to the waters of the Gulf Stream to look at pelagic birds, or travel to Mattamuskeet National Wildlife Refuge, where eagles and raptors and wintering birds are common. You can explore the swamp of Alligator River National Wildlife Refuge looking for bears or listen to red wolves howl. You can climb Jockey's Ridge at night to look at the stars or paddle Milltail Creek by moonlight. You can take a photography seminar, learn about coastal geography, or hear about the plight of the snow goose. Theirs is such an enormous list of activities that this is only the tip of the iceberg. All programs charge a moderate fee. For information or to register for the event, call the number above or visit the Web site, where there's an online registration form. This event is held the first weekend in November.

Wildfest
Manteo Middle School
US 64/264, Manteo
(252) 441–8144
www.northeast-nc.com/wings

Held in conjunction with Wings Over Water, Wildfest is an exciting family event held on a Saturday in early November. Wildfest is for all ages, but especially kids, who will get to learn about wildlife and wildlands in a fun way. Kids can build birdhouses, make kites, compete in a critter-calling contest, identify animal tracks, see a live alligator, study bird beaks, make leaf prints, and participate in an environmental scavenger hunt. There's also face painting, games, photos with Smokey Bear and other animals, and a chance to see live animals. There's no fee to enter, but some activities may have a small charge. It's held from 9:00 A.M. to 4:00 P.M.

Mt. Olivet United Methodist Church Bazaar & Auction
300 Ananias Dare St., Manteo
(252) 473–2089

For this event, the church is filled with all sorts of goodies including books, kitchenware, antiques, and baked treats. Get there early—this is a very popular event. Browse table after table covered with exciting finds—something old, something new. The day features a late afternoon/early evening auction. There's no charge.

Surf and Sand Triathlon
Kitty Hawk Sports
US 158, MP 12, Nags Head
(252) 441–4124, (800) 948–0759

Paddle a boat up the coast, run down the beach, then paddle a surfboard out and back (hands only). The water's still warm, so it's a great way to kick off the winter. Activities include a paddle sports fashion show and a party. Call for reservation information.

Manteo Rotary Rockfish Rodeo
Roanoke Island Festival Park, Manteo
(252) 473–4268

Whether you call them rockfish, striped bass, or stripers, the fish can win you big money and help a good cause in this tournament. Participants fish in the sound or ocean from 6:00 A.M. to 3:00 P.M. and bring one fish back to the weigh station to be weighed. Trophies are given to the top four winners in the ocean and sound categories, and the top winner can win up to $9,000. All nonfishing events and the weigh-in are held at Roanoke Island Festival Park. Registration, a social hour, and an anglers' rule meeting are held Friday night. Saturday it's fishing, the weigh-in, and an awards dinner. Manteo Rotary, the sponsor of this event, uses the profits to give college scholarships to local youth, and over the last four years they have granted over $50,000 to students because of this tournament.

Cape Hatteras Anglers Club Individual Surf Fishing Tournament, Buxton
(252) 995–4253

The Cape Hatteras Anglers Club sponsors a one-day individual surf-fishing tournament in mid-November. Registration is held at the Cape Hatteras Anglers Club in

Rockfish, also known as striped bass or stripers, are the featured fish in the annual Rockfish Rodeo tournament held each year. PHOTO: MOLLY HARRISON

Buxton, and fishing takes place from 8:00 A.M. to noon. Prizes are awarded.

Chowder Cookoff and Oyster Roast
Seagate North Shopping Center
US 158, MP 5½, Kill Devil Hills
(252) 441–6600

Skip breakfast and get your appetite working. This annual event is all about eating. Local amateur cooks and professional chefs compete for the prizes for best seafood chowder and best nonseafood chowder, but you get all the rewards by getting to taste them all for just $10. Standard chowders are offered, but some cooks can get pretty creative. In 2001, winners included Mediterranean shrimp chowder, a Cajun lobster-shrimp chowder, and a hickory-smoked duck chowder. Yum! There's also an oyster roast and hamburgers and hot dogs for the less adventurous. Beer, wine, soda, and water are available. The 2002 edition is the eighth year of this event, and it's quite popular with hungry locals. It's always held in mid-November on a Sunday afternoon, usually the second

or third weekend. Tickets are $10 to eat. To enter as a competitor you must register early, pay a $25 entry fee, and bring at least six gallons of chowder. All proceeds benefit local charities.

Elizabethan Tymes: A Country Faire
Roanoke Island Festival Park, Manteo
(252) 475–1500

This free event celebrates the Renaissance era. It's a country-fair–style event, with a variety of demonstrations, kids games, hands-on activities, music, dancing, and games. Kids love this one-day festival, which takes place in early November on Veteran's Day weekend. All events are held on the Pavilion lawn.

Kitty Hawk Fire Department Turkey Shoot
& Pig Pickin'
The Promenade, US 158, MP 1, Kitty Hawk
(252) 261–2666

This Kitty Hawk Fire Department–sponsored event, first held in 1980, usually happens in mid-November but dates may vary so call ahead. It's a major fund-

Learn more about the area's wildlife, including black bears, at Wildfest, an annual wildlife festival held in early November. PHOTO: KAREN BACHMAN

Crafts include pottery, dolls, shellwork, and woodworking. Admission is free.

Christmas Arts & Crafts Show
Kitty Hawk Elementary School, Kitty Hawk
(252) 261-3196

The two-day show, held in late November, is sponsored by the Outer Banks Women's Club. Expect to find a wide variety of crafts, including woodworking, pottery, dolls, and more. Admission is $1.00.

Town of Nags Head Festival of Thanksgiving
Various locations
Nags Head
(252) 441-5508
www.townofnagshead.com

The town of Nags Head holds a weeklong festival during the week of Thanksgiving, with fun activities for town residents, visitors, and families. Opening ceremonies are held on Monday at Town Hall, with the proclamation of the Town Lightkeeper, music, and an open house of the town's extensive artwork collection. Also during the week the town gives out free beach-friendly plants to Nags Head residents and holds a Thanksgiving Sunset celebration on Jockey's Ridge. On the Friday following Thanksgiving, there's an art show, a dance recital, safety activities, and kids' activities galore at Outer Banks Mall. That evening, there's a youth dance under the tent. Saturday brings another big day of activities, with a 5K run through the village of Nags Head at 8:30 A.M., a junior fishing tournament, an all-day festival, a pig pickin', and a free concert. All this takes place at Outer Banks Mall. On Sunday, there's a tour of several of the historic cottages in Nags Head. What a fun week! Activities may vary for 2002, but expect to see many of the same and new ones too. For information about the run or any other events, call the town or e-mail them through the Web site.

Advice 5K Annual Turkey Trot
Duck
(252) 255-1050
www.advice5.com

raiser for the firefighters. The fee includes the turkey shoot, annual auction and dinner, and pig pickin'. Fire department personnel also have fun events for kids. Call closer to the event date for more information.

Christmas Arts and Crafts Show
Cape Hatteras School
NC 12, Buxton
(252) 986-2879

This late-November show is sponsored by the Hatteras Island Arts and Crafts Guild.

Pump up your Thanksgiving Day appetite with an early morning 5K run. This annual, nonsanctioned 3.1-mile run starts at Advice 5 Cents behind Scarborough Lane Shops in Duck and ends up at the Red Sky Cafe/Village Wine Shop, where everyone gathers for a raffle and to see the winners. The top male and female runners win a cake from Village Wine Shop. This is a fun and lively event, a great way to kick off your holiday. Walkers and runners are welcome, and no one is expected to take it too seriously. Register early by calling the number above, or register in person at the Red Sky Cafe on the Wednesday before Thanksgiving Day. There is no race-day registration. Entry fee is $20 early, or $22 the day before.

Kites with Lights
Jockey's Ridge State Park, Nags Head
(252) 441-4124

Stunt kites are strung with lights to create a magical, multicolored nighttime scene. The kites are sent sky high to dance to traditional Christmas carols. Climbing up Jockey's Ridge at night is fun, especially when you're treated with a show like this at the top. Christmas carols, hot apple cider, and cookies make it even more fun. This event is held in late November. It's free and begins at sunset.

Chicamacomico Lifesaving Station Christmas Lighting
Rodanthe
(252) 987-1552

This classic lifesaving station looks absolutely stunning when it's decorated for the holidays with lights, greenery, and ribbons. In late November when the building is decorated in its finery, the folks at Chicamacomico have a daylong celebration and open house. In 2001, there were storytellers, free tours, strolling musicians playing sea chanteys, a lifesaving drill, and an art show, and at 5:00 P.M. everything was lit up with much ado. A barbecue fund-raiser followed. Expect similar events in 2002.

December

Lighting of the Town Tree and Christmas Parade
Manteo waterfront
(252) 473-1101 ext. 319, (252) 473-2774

Manteo and Dare County get ready for the holidays over the first weekend in December with events that are fun for the whole family. On Friday evening, the big town tree, right on the waterfront next to The Tranquil House Inn, is lit about 6:30 P.M. The event is accompanied by carols, a yule log, cake, and hot chocolate. It's a good place to gather to get in the holiday spirit.

On Saturday morning, there's a hometown parade through the streets of downtown Manteo. Kids love watching the floats, bands, dancers, local organizations, and, of course, Santa, cruising along through the streets. Afterward, there's a celebration with food, holiday crafts, entertainment, and a chance to visit with Santa at the waterfront. We like to go to the parade then do some early Christmas shopping in downtown Manteo.

Christmas at Roanoke Island Festival Park
Manteo
(252) 475-1506 24-hour events line

This beautiful cultural center is alive in December with plenty of good cheer. Expect concerts, sing-alongs, children's performances, and a sale in the Museum Store. Call the events line for the holiday offerings.

Outer Banks Hotline's Festival of Trees
(252) 473-5121

Since 1988, this popular auction and fund-raiser has taken place in early December. Businesses and individuals donate fully decorated Christmas trees and other holiday items to be auctioned and delivered to buyers. Proceeds benefit Hotline's crisis intervention program and needy families in the area. Past trees have been decorated with collectible Beanie Babies, handwoven tapestry wear and accessories, and CDs. The festive event includes several days of celebrations. Call the Hotline office for location and ticket information.

Swan Days
Lake Mattamuskeet National Wildlife Refuge
Hyde County
(252) 926–4021, (888) 493–3826
www.albemarle-nc.com/hyde/events

Swan Days celebrates the annual return of thousands of tundra swan to the Lake Mattamuskeet National Wildlife Refuge. It's a two-day event that joyfully welcomes the swans and at the same time commemorates the natural beauty of the refuge. Lake Mattamuskeet is about an hour's drive from Dare County on US 264, but the drive is absolutely beautiful and worth it for this early December event. During the weekend there are guided tours of the refuge; arts and crafts demonstrations and sales; children's activities galore; guided wildlife tours where you'll see tundra swan, ducks, geese, and maybe even a deer or black bear; photography workshops; a 10K walk through the refuge; slide shows; book signings; raffles; and more. Vendors selling food and drinks are on hand. All activities center or begin at the Lake Mattamuskeet Lodge. This is a great way to get out and experience nature in peaceful Hyde County.

Man Will Never Fly Memorial Society International Annual Seminar and Awards Program
Comfort Inn South
NC 12, MP 17, Nags Head
(800) 334–4777

This tongue-in-cheek organization tries to prove every year that man never really flew and abides by the motto "Birds Fly, Men Drink." The banquet is held annually in conjunction with the anniversary of the first flight and is open to the public. The food is prepared buffet-style and features meat as well as seafood. Call for ticket and reservation information.

Wright Brothers Anniversary of First Flight
Wright Brothers National Memorial
US 158, MP 8, Kill Devil Hills
(252) 441–7430, (800) 334–4777

On December 17, 1903, Wilbur and Orville Wright made their first successful flights before a handful of local residents. This event is celebrated every year on December 17, in the exact same place where those flights occurred. Bands play and planes fly as the monumental events of the Wright brothers are recalled. Speakers generally include military personnel, local dignitaries, and individuals who have dedicated their lives to the advancement of flight technology. A portrait of the year's induction to the First Flight Society is unveiled. There is no charge. In 2003 this event will really take off for the centennial celebration of flight. Plans are still in the works for the event that is expected to draw thousands of people and media attention from all over the world. See our Close-up in the History chapter.

International Icarus
Glenn Eure's Ghost Fleet Gallery
210 E. Driftwood St., Gallery Row, Nags Head
(252) 441–6584
Seaside Art Gallery
NC 12, MP 11, Nags Head
(252) 441–5418

This international art show, started in 1992, is a theme show that celebrates the mystery and beauty of flight. Each year a flight-related theme is chosen, and artists submit original art in all genres to compete for a multitude of top-dollar prizes. The art is displayed through the month of December at two Nags Head galleries. A children's component is included at another location. Call the listed numbers to get on the mailing list. The art is part of the countdown to the year 2003, when the world celebrates the 100th anniversary of Wilbur and Orville Wright's first flight achievement in Kill Devil Hills. Children enter for free. Adult entries run between

These Boy Scouts are ready to march in a local parade. PHOTO: COURTESY OF BOB REARDON

$10 and $15. A commission is taken for sold work by International Icarus, a non-profit group. A literary competition is held on the same theme as the visual arts competition every year. The chapbook of juried entries is published in December.

Unofficial Beach Road 5K
Don Gatos Restaurant
NC 12, MP 11, Nags Head
(252) 441-9330

This 5K fun run is held every New Year's Eve at 11:00 P.M. In its 13th year in 2002, it's become a traditional way for many folks to ring in the New Year. The run begins at Don Gatos and winds through the back roads of Nags Head, ending up at the restaurant. There's a big party afterward. You don't need to preregister. Just show up, pay the $15 entry fee, and have fun!

Sand and sea create a wonderland for us to explore.

Natural Wonders

To reach the status of a true Outer Banks Insider, you must develop a relaxed attitude and a healthy respect for nature, especially the weather. Outer Bankers' lives are ruled by Mother Nature's temperaments and the first rule of order is: Respect her or else! From the clear, calm, and sunny days of early summer to the windy days of autumn and the raw days of nor'easters that arrive each fall, you'll marvel at the variable weather conditions.

The interplay of sand, land, water, and wind is the primal force that drives life on these barrier islands. Some time during your visit, even if you're not inclined toward contemplation, slow down and spend some time getting acquainted with your temporary habitat and with what makes it unique.

"Without an inherent ability to move as sea level rises, the Outer Banks would not be a complex ecological system of beaches, dunes, hammocks, and marshes. They would be one of the world's most spectacular underwater sand parks," write John Alexander and James Lazell in *Ribbon of Sand: The Amazing Convergence of the Ocean and the Outer Banks* (now out of print but well worth combing the bookstores to find).

Bounded by the Atlantic Ocean on the east and a vast expanse of sound waters to the west, and connected in between by waterways and wetlands, the Outer Banks is among the most fascinating and complex habitats in North America. The Gulf Stream and the Continental Shelf's edge influence us from a mere 37 miles away. Cradled within our boundaries are several unusual maritime forests, and Cape Hatteras marks the dividing line for northern and southern animal and plant species presenting variety that drives nature lovers wild.

Because of our geographic location and environmental offerings, animal lovers from the world over come to the Outer Banks to sight rare pelagic birds, breaching humpbacks, and nesting waterfowl. Even manatees and harbor seals have visited our shores. Anglers can ply the waters for anything from the humble flounder to the majestic blue marlin. Botanists study our ancient live oaks. Writers hole up in wooden beach cottages and ponder how poetically the wind howls. Families return year after year, generation after generation, to dash among the waves, explore tidal zones for sealife, and canvass the shores for colorful shells.

While the old-timers will rightfully argue that things have changed dramatically here during the last 25 years, there's always been a constant: We are at the mercy of the forces of nature. Our dependency is clear: Nature feeds us, creates and crumbles livelihoods, offers unlimited free entertainment, is the muse to the artist, and sends us scurrying for shelter at a whim.

In this chapter we'll introduce you to the land and its wonders, our bountiful waters, and our crazy Outer Banks weather.

Our roles as environmental stewards are an essential part of Outer Banks life. This stewardship is manifested in efforts to protect our waters, marine life, and beaches by stopping huge conglomerates from drilling for natural gas off the coast. You can join our efforts (the Outer Banks is your vacationland, after all) by learning more about LegaSea, an environmental group that was instrumental in stopping Mobil Oil from drilling for natural gas off the coast years back. LegaSea and many Outer Banks residents wish to preserve this wonderland to share with their descendants and the many visitors who come to this non-polluted haven. Visit the group's Web site at www.LegaSea.org.

Insiders also have self-imposed, state, and national restrictions on game fish. We support tag and release programs and escort infant loggerhead sea turtles off the sand and into the water. Young and old alike participate annually in a nationwide coastal cleanup. All we ask of our visitors is that you treat the area's fragile ecosystem with care. This vacation paradise is home not only for us, but also for our less vocal friends who thrive on the air, sea, and land.

The Land

It doesn't take long to realize that the Outer Banks's barrier island system—a small stretch of sand—contains vast variety in topography. Geologists refer to the Outer Banks and similar land forms as "barrier islands" because they block the high-energy ocean waves and storm surges, protecting the coastal mainland. Winds, weather, and waves create the personality of the slender strips of sand. Inlets from the sounds to the sea are ever shifting, opening new channels to the ocean one century, and closing off primary passageways the next.

Sand forms a partnership with the sea to create a wonderland that sweeps from Carova down through the Cape Hatteras National Seashore to Ocracoke Island. At Jockey's Ridge State Park in Nags Head, huge migrating dunes heralded as the largest sand hills on the East Coast create one of the most popular attractions on the Outer Banks (see our Attractions chapter). It is an amazing sight to see the sand moving ribbonlike as the wind whips across the dunes. Human forms dot the landscape, insignificant against the towering backdrop as they climb the dunes to fly kites, hang glide, or simply view the sound and ocean from atop an 85-foot-high ridgetop.

At sunset, the visual drama intensifies. The forms coming and going become stark silhouettes. Come nightfall, the dunes are silent, but wildlife is there. Foxes roam the area as do deer and opossum, and vegetation thrives in the sand. Wild grapes and bayberry, along with black cherry and Virginia Creeper, are found along the park trail.

Sand is a challenge and a blessing. It thwarts seaside gardeners who replace their sandy land with mainland soil to grow vegetables. Outer Bankers have a long-standing love/hate relationship with the gritty stuff: We play in it, pour it out of our shoes daily, and constantly suck it into vacuums, but we know that this movable earth has played a vital role in the formation of our natural habitat.

The next time you stroll along the shore, notice the vegetation such as sea oats and spartina climbing the sloping dunes. Windblown sand collects behind these pioneer plants, which often grow in otherwise barren soil. With the right combination of currents and breezes, a dune can grow large enough to protect areas that lie behind them, forming tall barriers against the salty sea spray, hence allowing the birth of maritime forests. Our habitat has generated several such phenomena that interest the naturalist and layperson alike. Nags Head Woods and Buxton Woods are good examples of gifts of the dune.

Nags Head Woods

Lo and behold! There's a maritime forest flourishing on the Outer Banks that

A drive near any Outer Banks body of water is likely to provide glimpses of birds like this egret. PHOTO: COURTESY OF BOB REARDON

seems to defy the rules of nature. Normally, vegetation that is constantly battered by salt and wind is stunted and minimal. In the Nags Head Woods preserve, 1,400 acres of maritime forest contain a diversity of flora and fauna that's nearly unheard of in a harsh barrier island climate. This forest has been able to thrive due to a ridge of ancient sand dunes, some 90 feet high, that has shielded the land from the effects of the sea. The woods also owe their diversity to the freshwater supplied by the high dunes that absorb and slowly release rainwater into the underlying aquifer, swamps, and dozens of year-round and seasonal ponds.

Botanists have identified more than 300 plant species in the forest with a mixture of northern and southern varieties. This combination is rare, existing in only four places in the world. In fact, Nags Head Woods is classified as globally rare. The oldest tree in the woods is thought to be a 500-year-old Live Oak, but woody plants have been growing in this area for thousands of years.

Plant lovers will appreciate the woods year-round. The forest is lush with ferns, pines, oaks, red bay, blueberry, grasses, bamboo, sassafras, gums, and hundreds more species. Several species rare to North Carolina thrive in the forest, including the wooly beach heather, water violet, southern twayblade, and mosquito fern.

Arguably, the most diverse population of reptiles and amphibians on the Outer Banks has found a permanent home in Nags Head Woods. These include 5 species of salamanders, 14 species of frogs and toads, more than 20 species of snakes, and multiple species of lizards and turtles. This unusual forest provides nesting spots for more than 50 species of birds and is home to a wide variety of mammals including raccoons, river otters, gray fox, white-tailed deer, and opossum.

Insiders like to enter the forest in the fall and spring. Cooler weather and fewer mosquitoes make the trek more appealing, and you have plenty of visiting birds and waterfowl to look for. The great blue heron and green heron are common to the woods. Several species of songbirds may serenade you as you walk: Carolina chickadee, great crested flycatcher, many thrushes, and numerous warblers.

Hikers can traipse over 5 miles of trails. **The Center Trail** is a quarter-mile long and features scenic pond overlooks. The **Sweetgrass Swamp Trail** takes over an hour to hike through rolling hills of forests, dunes, and ponds. The **Blueberry Ridge Trail** connects to the **Sweetgum Swamp Trail** for a total length of 3.5 miles. To head toward the sound, take the Roanoke Trail past the farm site and cemetery of the Tillett clan—allow about an hour for a 1.5 mile round-trip. And the **Discovery Trail** provides a quick quarter-mile view of the ponds, swamps, and dune ridges found on the longer trails.

Dogs on leashes, four-wheel-drive vehicles, and bikes are allowed on the road that runs through Nags Head Woods, but they are not allowed in other parts of the preserve. Visitation hours are 10:00 A.M. to 3:00 P.M. Monday through Friday during the off-season and Monday through Saturday during the summer. Members of the Nature Conservancy can tour the preserve during any daylight hours. These limitations help preserve the natural habitats of this rare ecosystem. There is no fee to enter, but a donation is requested. Call the information line at (252) 441-3481 for field excursion schedules and more information.

The Nags Head Woods Preserve, (252) 441-2525, is overseen by The Nature Conservancy, an international nonprofit conservation organization. If you wish to contribute to The Nature Conservancy, you can send a donation to 701 West Ocean Acres Drive, Kill Devil Hills, North Carolina 27948 or call (252) 441-2525 for membership information.

Buxton Woods

Buxton Woods on Hatteras Island is the largest maritime forest in North Carolina. The 3,000-acre forest sits on the sole source of drinking water for the inhabitants of the area from Avon to Hatteras Village. Mea-suring 3 miles wide and 50 feet high at the tallest ridge, this landmass has the capacity to act as a storage area for freshwater. Only 900 of the 3,000 acres are owned by the National Park Service. The state of North Carolina bought an additional 800 acres to protect as the North Carolina Coastal Reserve. The county also designates Buxton Woods as a special environmental district.

Buxton Woods is a much simpler ecosystem than Nags Head Woods because it sticks out 30 miles farther into the ocean and doesn't have the protection that the Nags Head forest has; however, compared to the surrounding land at the Cape Hatteras National Seashore, Buxton Woods holds incredible diversity. A bird's-eye view shows an overall ridge and lowlands throughout the area.

The woods lie at the meeting place for several Northern and Southern species and have a viable population of dwarf palmetto and laurel cherry. There's a mix of wetlands and forests that are a combination of both Northern deciduous maritime forests and Southern evergreen maritime forests. Nowhere else on Hatteras Island will you find the diversity in mammal population as in Buxton Woods. The woods are home to white-tailed deer, gray squirrels, eastern cottontail rabbits, raccoons, and opossum. In the woods is Jennette's Sedge, one of the largest, most highly developed and diverse freshwater marsh systems found on a barrier island in North Carolina (see our Attractions chapter for more information on Buxton Woods).

Alligator River National Wildlife Refuge

On the mainland to the west of Roanoke Island is the Alligator National Wildlife Refuge, covering parts of Dare, Hyde, and Tyrrell Counties. The refuge encompasses 150,000 acres of wetlands, wooded fields, and pocosin habitat. Pocosin is the Native American word for "swamp on a hill." These swamps are characterized by high organic content soils with deep peat deposits that hold vast quantities of water. In dry weather, pocosins are highly susceptible to wildfire.

The refuge is home to black bears, white-tailed deer, gray fox, bobcats, raccoons, mink, beaver, squirrels, possum, river otter, nutria, alligators, and its most-talked-about residents—red wolves.

Red wolves are a critically endangered species because of hybridization and because of a lack of public acceptance of large carnivores in most habitats. In the early 1970s the U.S. Fish and Wildlife Service declared the species extinct in the wild because they had been eradicated in nearly every segment of their southeastern United States range. Fish and Wildlife captured the remaining red wolves and bred them until a location was found to bring them back into the wild. The location they found was Alligator River National Wildlife Refuge, chosen because it is within the red wolf's historical range, the human population is of moderate size and density, prey species are abundant, the area is surrounded by water on three sides (which, it was hoped, would restrict some movement by the wolves), and the area had very few coyotes, which would lessen the chance that the wolves would hybridize.

In 1986 a five-year experiment to rebuild a self-sustaining red wolf population in the wild began. During this experiment, red wolves proved that they could adapt to life in the wild, find food, and avoid people, thus proving themselves successful. Today, close to 100 red wolves roam free in Alligator River National Wildlife Refuge. There are also free-ranging wolves on three islands on the coasts of South Carolina and Florida. The refuge staff offers a unique program called a "Wolf Howling" during which you can go into the refuge at night with a ranger and listen to the wolves howl. See our Kidstuff chapter or call (252) 473-1131 for information.

Mackay Island National Wildlife Refuge

On Knotts Island in both North Carolina and Virginia, Mackay Island contains 8,646 acres of important wildlife habitat and wintering grounds for waterfowl. Mackay Island offers both walking and driving trails that provide wildlife obser-

vation opportunities. Hunting and fishing are allowed at Mackay Island Refuge. To get there, take the free, short ferry ride from the Currituck mainland to Knotts Island and follow the signs. You'll see signs for the ferry as you drive on US 158.

Currituck National Wildlife Refuge

Just north of Corolla on the Currituck Outer Banks, this refuge was established in 1984. The refuge consists of 3,213 acres managed by the Mackay Island staff. There are no public facilities in the refuge, but it is open to the public during daylight hours. Visitors mostly look for wildlife and take photographs. The wild horses that used to roam in Corolla now roam here, along with deer, wild boar, and a variety of wildlife.

Audubon Wildlife Sanctuary at Pine Island

Audubon is a northern Outer Banks, 5,000-acre wildlife sanctuary at Pine Island, and is a protected habitat for deer, birds, rabbits, and a huge variety of plant life. There is an unmarked 2-mile trail you can walk, but the sanctuary is not really a park for people. While you are allowed to wander down the path, there is no planned parking. The land is primarily soundside marshland with lots of pine trees and waterfowl. The sanctuary runs 3 miles long north to south and is approximately 200 yards wide from east to west.

Cape Hatteras National Seashore

The Outer Banks should get a medal for firsts. Not only do we claim First Flight and the first English pioneers to colonize in the New World, but Cape Hatteras was the first seashore in the United States to become a national seashore (in 1953). The park covers 85 percent of Hatteras Island, which stretches south of the Bonner Bridge for 33 miles to Hatteras Inlet.

The beaches are clean and uncrowded. Subtle beauty abounds in the park. The swaying sea grasses, shifting sands, and tenacious vegetation appear monochromatic at first glance. A closer study reveals pleasant surprises. Lush purple flowers and

A fiddler crab scurries along the sand, hoping to get out of sight—fast! PHOTO: HORSLEY/GARDNER

delicate white-petaled flowers with scarlet centers grow entwined in the roadside brambles. In the marshes, sea lavender, morning glories, and marsh aster add color. In the early morning or late afternoon, you can usually see dozens of brown marsh rabbits nibbling grasses along the roadside. All along the seashore, ghost crabs burrow in the sand and can be seen scurrying about by day and night—a pure delight for children. One of the more spectacular sights is the occasional glow of phosphorous visible in the waves breaking on shore on a dark night. Sometimes even the crabs glow eerily.

The park offers visitors a respite from the frenzy of living in a resort community. It's a peaceful ride down NC 12 and always a welcome one except when the ocean washes away the dune and claims the road. There are several attractions within the park borders that appeal to the nature lover, including the **Pea Island National Wildlife Refuge** featuring more than 5,000 acres of wildlife refuge. The refuge is both a year-round and seasonal home for nearly 400 species, including the snow goose, Canada goose, and whistling swan. During the fall you can watch large flocks of snow geese ascend from their watery

resting places. Their flight is breathtaking. This section of the park may be one of the most poetic spots on the Outer Banks. The waterfowl are just far enough away to appear untouched by the human element. You can get up-close views of them through binoculars and a camera's lens. Photographers also enjoy this stretch for the interesting tree lines and sunsets on the salt marsh. Plan to stop and bird-watch at the platform available just off the road.

The **North Pond Trail**, on Pea Island, is another bird-watcher's option. The **Ocracoke pony pens** and **Hammock Hills Nature Trail** across from the Ocracoke Campground are two more hot spots in the Cape Hatteras National Seashore. See our Hatteras Island section in the Attractions chapter for more information on these sites; our How to Stay Safe: Waves and Weather chapter for lifeguard information within park boundaries; and our Getting Here, Getting Around chapter for more about off-road driving.

In Buxton, at the tip of Cape Hatteras, is an area of beach only approachable by four-wheel-drive vehicles. Locals call this "The Point," and it serves as a well-used haven for surf-casters. The sea is powerful at this spot, marked by strong currents, deep holes, shoals, and opposing waves crashing into each other. Wildlife writers and anglers alike call it heaven. The bottom topography—created by strong shoaling and The Point's proximity to the Gulf Stream and its spinoff eddies—justifies calling this wet and sandy spot a real Outer Banks natural wonder. (See our Fishing chapter for more about The Point.)

Whale watching is an exciting option for park visitors, though sightings are not restricted to the park boundaries. There are more species of whales passing by the coast of North Carolina than anywhere in eastern North America. Mostly groups of small- to medium-toothed whales make passage both far offshore and in sight of the beach. Deeper offshore is the migration path for killer and blue whales.

The three largest species are the sperm whale, humpback, and fin whale. The sperm whales make their way past our coast in the springtime. In the winter you can see both humpback and fin whales. The humpbacks are particularly visible from the shore. They can be seen breaching and lunge feeding. In the latter action, the whale blows a bubble net to corral fish, then leaps through it open-mouthed to gulp in everything.

Pilot whales can be seen offshore year-round. Even the most endangered species, the Northern right whale, was identified while scratching its head on an Outer Banks sandbar. We've also had rare washups of the dense beaked whale. Offshore sightings have been made of the Cuvier's beaked whale, and the first live sighting of the True's beaked whale was made 33 nautical miles southeast of Hatteras Inlet.

Whether you're sitting on the beach with binoculars or viewing the creatures from an offshore charter boat, whale watching is an awe-inspiring pastime.

Whales are a hard act to follow, but let's face it—it is a rare visitor who comes to the park who does not delight in filling all available pockets and pails with shells. Hatteras Island doglegs to the west, making it one of the farthest points out on the Eastern Seaboard. Its steep beaches cause high-energy wave action, so unbroken shells rarely make it to the shore. But the sea tosses up lovely blue mussels, quahog, jackknife clams, slipper shells, baby's ears, jingle shells, and oysters. A good time to search for shells is at changing tides, after high tide, or following a storm. If you are seeking whole shells, continue south to Ocracoke Island, where the beaches have gentle slopes.

The Water

Estuary, Sound, and Salt Marsh

Fly over the Outer Banks in a small plane, and it will become clear that this string of islands is more an offspring of the sea than the land. With more than 2.2 million acres of sounds and bays between its barrier islands and mainland, North Carolina ranks behind only Alaska and Louisiana in the amount of estuarine acreage. With 2 million acres covered by the vast Currituck-Albemarle-Pamlico sound system, the Outer Banks region ranks second in size only to the Chesapeake Bay in terms of water surface area. Each day, more than 15 billion gallons of water pass into the barrier islands' estuaries. The bulk of it flows into the Pamlico Sound and then into the Atlantic through four major Outer Banks inlets.

The Albemarle Sound, the mouth of which sits west of Kitty Hawk, is fed by seven major rivers and is the largest fresh-water sound on the East Coast. The Currituck Sound, also freshwater, lies northeast of the Albemarle. Due south of these bodies of water are two brackish sounds, the Roanoke and the Croatan. Farther south is the saltwater Pamlico Sound. Nestled in the crook of this sound, where Cape Hatteras indents toward the sea, is the famous Canadian Hole, one of the nation's top windsurfing spots (see our Watersports chapter).

The Outer Banks landscape is also defined by its salt marshes. The marshes shelter the barrier islands from the sounds, and cordgrass and other vegetation break much of the wave action and act as safe havens for marine life. The wetlands are nursery grounds for many of the fish we enjoy dining on. Ninety percent of all commercial seafood species must spend at least part of their life cycle in the salt marsh. They spawn offshore and then release their eggs into the inlets, where currents carry them into the marsh. Oysters, crabs, shrimp, and flounder flourish in the calmer waters of the marsh, which offer places to hide and lots of food. The salt marsh is also attractive to waterfowl and other bird species, which find food here.

The Sea

Perhaps the sea in its entirety is too huge for the human mind to comprehend, but it is only through trying to understand her that you come to appreciate the Outer Banks fully. The ocean dominates the islands, influencing their weather, land,

The marshy banks of the sounds are important breeding grounds for a variety of sea life and should be protected from litter and contaminants. PHOTO: MOLLY HARRISON

flora, fauna, and the lifestyle of the people. Scientists work daily at the U.S. Army Corps of Engineers Field Research Facility in Duck studying currents to understand erosion. Outer Banks's history is steeped in harrowing accounts of lifesaving efforts, and the economy is heavily based in sea-oriented tourism, the commercial seafood industry, and recreational fishing. Newcomers who arrive here to work in these livelihoods and those who come merely to visit the sandy, windswept edge of a continent are affected by the Atlantic Ocean.

The position of Cape Hatteras, jutting into the Atlantic, puts us near the Continental Shelf's edge, which is approximately 37 miles southeast of Oregon Inlet and near the junction of three ocean currents, the Deep Western Boundary Current, Gulf Stream, and Shelf Current. These physical combinations create a nutrient-rich habitat for sea life, resulting in a world-renowned offshore fishing hot spot and a wonderland for pelagic birds. Our proximity to the toasty Gulf Stream current is one of our most prestigious calling cards.

Gulf Stream

A forceful flow of water in the Atlantic Ocean passes off the Outer Banks's shores every day. The Gulf Stream is a swift ribbon of blue sea that has been flowing by since time immemorial. Powered by forces arising from the earth's rotation and the influence of the winds, the energy and warmth it emits has had a profound effect on humankind. While the stream's course is influenced somewhat by gales, barometric pressure, and seasonal changes, the general flow remains fairly constant, creating a dichotomy: While the stream is ever-present, its contents are ever-changing. Millions upon millions of tons of water per second are carried along this ancient path. Swept along are fish, microscopic plants and animals, and gulfweed that originates in the Sargasso Sea.

Gulfweed lines the edge of the stream, creating a habitat for baitfish. You can easily pull up a handful of vegetation and find it teeming with life. The weed offers protection to infant fish, turtles, crabs, sea horses, and the most peculiar sargassumfish. Endangered loggerhead sea turtles less than two weeks old, their egg beaks still intact, have been spotted in the weed.

Flying fish are always fun to watch, although what we see as antics is actually the fish's sprint for life as it glides about 200 to 300 yards to escape a predator. The offshore life cycle is fascinating, and nowhere is it more evident than at the Gulf Stream.

Bird-watching

With ocean beaches, sand dunes, scrub thickets, marsh, pocosins, black-water swamps, and maritime and inland forests, the Outer Banks and surrounding inland regions are rich in waterfowl and other birds. Nearly 400 species of birds have been sighted within Cape Hatteras National Seashore and its surrounding waters. Many birds choose the area because of the diverse habitats and because it's a convenient stop along the eastern flyway. But occasionally a vagrant will blow in with strong winds or storms. Accidental species spotted on the Outer Banks are numerous, including the pacific loon, western grebe, white-winged dove, snowy owl, western tanager, cerulean warbler, sandhill crane, and many others.

Though birding is always exciting on the Outer Banks, the greatest variety of species occurs during the spring and fall migrations. Good numbers of migratory shorebirds can be seen on inlet tidal flats, the ponds at Pea Island and Bodie Island, and the salt ponds at Cape Hatteras Point. Land-bird observations occur in the shrub thickets along the dikes at Pea Island and in the maritime woods. Herons, egrets, terns, skimmers, and other birds that breed locally are best seen in the warmer months. These birds frequent both salt-

and freshwater areas. Winter ducks, geese, and swans usually concentrate on ponds at Pea Island and Bodie Island and on Lake Mattamuskeet.

In the marshes you will see herons, egrets, ibises, waterfowl, rails, and shorebirds. These birds can be seen in the marshes all over the Outer Banks, but an easy access point into the marsh is via the trails behind the Bodie Island Lighthouse.

Pea Island National Wildlife Refuge is one of the top birding sites on the whole East Coast. Impoundments, salt flats, and ponds house snow geese, Canada geese, willets, tundra swan, and several species of ducks. The live oaks here house songbirds during the fall migration. On the beaches you can see shorebirds, gulls, terns, and pelicans. Nesting birds may include piping plover, American oystercatcher, terns, and skimmers.

Other great birding spots to visit include Nags Head Woods, Buxton Woods, Alligator River National Wildlife Refuge, Currituck National Wildlife Refuge, Jockey's Ridge State Park, and Ocracoke Island.

Pelagic Bird-watching

You don't have to be a bird lover to realize you have entered a unique bird-watching area as you tool down NC 12 through the National Seashore. Off in the distance, in the wetlands, a variety of species feed and sun. What is not so obvious is the goldmine of pelagic species offshore, where bird-watchers can witness both common and rare birds that never come to shore.

Local fishing headboats have been taking bird-watchers to the deep water for years. In fact, the sightings are so fruitful, a good part of Capt. Allan Foreman's charter boat business involves these trips. Foreman's *Country Girl*, (252) 473-5577, which fishes out of Pirate's Cove Yacht Club on Roanoke Island, is a 57-foot headboat built to carry large parties offshore. Down in Hatteras, Capt. Spurgeon Stowe runs birdwatching excursions aboard the 72-foot *Miss Hatteras*, (252) 986-2365, from Oden's Dock (see our Fishing chapter for more

Bird-watching made easy: A great blue heron makes a rare landing on a rooftop. PHOTO: MOLLY HARRISON

information on these boats). Bird enthusiasts spend the day searching for more than two dozen species that live on the water.

The petrel and shearwater families are the largest groups of birds available to bird-watchers here. Traveling from the Caribbean and the coast of Africa, these species leave their winter climate to spend summer off the Outer Banks.

Among the petrels, the black-capped petrel is probably one of the most common to North Carolina waters. Twenty-five years ago this species was believed to be on the verge of extinction. No one knew where the birds were. Scientists now say that the world's population hangs out in the Gulf Stream off the Outer Banks area. For comparison's sake, Florida bird-watchers may see one or two black-capped petrels per trip, whereas trips departing from the Outer Banks can yield as many as 100 sightings on a good day.

What's exciting about these trips is that you have the chance to view species that only come to land to breed, but when we speak of land, we refer to oceanic islands, not any place you can easily bump into these creatures. These birds are highly adapted for life on the sea. They could be mistaken for gulls or ducks, but as a group they are quite unique. Their tubular nostrils allow them to drink salt water and then expel the salt.

A much rarer bird sighted off North Carolina is the white-faced storm petrel. In a good year, one or two sightings are recorded. This bird shows up in the late summer or early fall and is very difficult to spot anywhere else in the world.

While bird-watching off the Outer Banks, Mike Tove, a biologist from Cary, North Carolina, discovered two species of petrel that were rarely seen near North America. One of them, called the herald petrel, up until 10 years ago was known from only a handful of recordings going back to the 1920s.

"In 1991 boats started venturing offshore farther than usual," Tove said. "We started finding them. It's now a bird we see a half-dozen times a year. People come great distances looking for them."

Tove officially presented to discovery another rare species in May 1991. "I had a bird that was identified as a Cape Verde petrel," he said. Prior to Tove's sighting, resurrected field notes revealed only three other recorded sightings of the bird.

This species was entirely unknown in the United States and is extraordinarily rare anywhere in the world. "And we're seeing them with almost predictable regularity in late spring in very deep offshore waters past the edge of the Continental Shelf," he said. Tove's sightings form the baseline data for research. All the birds have been well documented with photographs.

You don't have to have a doctorate, as Tove does, to enjoy bird-watching. If you want to get a glimpse of these offshore species here are a few tips:

• Bring fairly low-power, waterproof binoculars (Zeiss or Leitz 7X or 8X are excellent).

• Don't bother to bring your spotting scope; if you're a photographer, bring a telephoto lens to help document rarities.

• Constantly scan the horizon and wave tops for birdlife, and call out your sighting with the boat as reference; for example, six o'clock is directly off the stern.

• Don't wait to try and identify the bird before calling it out; many eyes on the bird will aid in that. Identification is often very difficult, and to do it accurately you must have a great deal of field experience and ability to interpret flight and molt patterns, which can be even more difficult during heavy seas.

• Expect long periods where no birds are seen, but be prepared for the appearance of a good number and variety. Always take good notes on any unusual species before consulting your field guide. Describe and sketch exactly what you saw without allowing outside influences to color your recollection.

• Offshore bird-watching can be an exciting new adventure. If you haven't spent any time on the water, don't allow your fears to get the best of you. Captains won't take

you out if the weather is too risky, and you can follow our tips on preventing sea sickness (see our Fishing chapter).

Happy bird-watching!

Weather

By the end of this guidebook, you may well be tired of the word "variety." It aptly describes not only the above-mentioned natural wonders but our weather as well. We find the weather to be more changeable on the Outer Banks than our inland counterparts. Business owners who specialize in outdoor attractions are plagued by phone calls when the skies turn dark:

"Is the cruise going to be canceled? Can you fish in the rain?"

We tell our visitors that because the weather is so mercurial, wait 10 minutes and those dark clouds very possibly may be gone. There's variation from town to town. It may be pouring in Corolla, but it's sunny skies in Manteo. Torrential rains could send beachgoers scattering at noon, but 20 minutes later the heavens are beaming. Get the picture?

It seems to rain less in the winter, while late summer evenings hold their share of window-rattling thundershowers. The good part is that the skies are usually clear during the day. The bad part is that unless you are a heavy sleeper, you may awaken from the booms on and off between midnight and 3:00 A.M.

The Atlantic Ocean, which is slow to warm and cool and heats to a maximum of about 80 degrees in the summer, affects the air temperatures. Our nearness to the sea keeps summer air temperatures about 10 degrees cooler than our mainland counterparts. In the winter, disregarding the wind chill factor, our air temperatures do just the opposite. Air flowing over the Gulf Stream toward us warms the winter air.

Nor'easters, occurring most often in the fall and winter, plague homeowners and fishermen alike. The high winds keep boats at the docks, sometimes knocking out three to seven workdays. These same

Moving the Cape Hatteras Lighthouse

They said it couldn't be done, that it would topple into the sea as surely as if it was hit by a hurricane. But in June of 1999, the 4,800-ton sentinel began its historic move, reaching its final resting point in early July without losing even one of its bricks.

Perhaps the most recognizable of all the nation's lighthouses, and certainly among the most beloved, the Cape Hatteras Lighthouse has been at the center of a bitter debate for more than a decade. The tallest brick lighthouse in the United States, the Cape Hatteras Lighthouse was built in 1870, 1,500 feet from the shoreline, replacing a lighthouse built near the present site in 1803. Its rotating beacon beams out to a range of 15.8 nautical miles when viewed from exact sea level, providing a landmark for local boat traffic and confirmation of modern navigational methods. It is thought to have survived some 40 hurricanes since it was first constructed, not to mention a series of earthquakes in 1886 with shocks of up to 7.7 on the Richter scale; but over the years, it has grown increasingly vulnerable to the encroaching ocean.

Situated on a picturesque corner of sand that juts into the most dangerous waters of the Atlantic, the handsome spiral-striped tower had lost all but 120 feet of sand as a buffer between it and the sea. As powerful currents and storms eroded the east-facing shorelines and threatened to undermine the 200-foot tall structure and send it toppling over into the ocean, the debate raged just as forcefully over whether to move the historic landmark to a safer location or to shore up the lighthouse at its present location.

Government officials have tried frantically to prevent disaster—certain to occur if they failed to act. The National Park Service has spent at least $3 million studying options to save the structure, piling sandbags at its base and reinforcing rock jetties to deflect threatening waves. A committee formed in 1987 to study options for preserving the lighthouse concluded that the only way to preserve the structure for the enjoyment of future generations would be to relocate it.

A group of prominent citizens lobbied strenuously in favor of shoring up the lighthouse at the present location, expressing concern that the 4,800-ton lighthouse would not survive the move and that, even if it did, the move would damage its historical integrity.

It has been clear to both sides that, without action, this cherished icon would soon become a pile of black-and-white rubble. Engineers have said that there is an 80 percent chance that, in its original location, the lighthouse would topple in a category four hurricane or in a string of three nor'easters hitting one right after another. Finally, after a $9.8 million appropriation from Congress, plans were finalized to begin relocation of the lighthouse in the spring of 1999.

Thousands of visitors flocked to the site to witness the snail-like move, which was accomplished in only 23 days. It was estimated that over half a million tourists and locals visited the site. The Cape Hatteras Lighthouse now sits at a safe distance from the sea. The lighthouse's beacon, which was extinguished on March 4, 1999, in preparation for the move, was relit at a ceremony in November 1999. The September ceremony was postponed due to hurricanes. This permanent light is actually rotating back-to-back spotlights with 1,000-watt bulbs. In clear weather, the beam can be seen 20 miles out to sea. The lighthouse reopened at its new location in May of 2000.

Cape Hatteras Lighthouse Trivia
Here are some fun and interesting facts about the Outer Banks's favorite landmark:

The move of the Cape Hatteras Lighthouse has sparked considerable debate. PHOTO: COURTESY OF DREW WILSON

- To reach the balcony from the sidewalk, you'd have to climb 257 steps up, plus one down, making about seven revolutions.

- 1,250,000 bricks were ordered for the structure.

- The tower rests upon Vermont rose granite blocks, set in mortar and resting on a double mat of yellow pine timbers about 7 feet below ground on naturally compacted sand—what is called a "floating" foundation.

- The famous spiral stripes distinguished the Cape Hatteras light from its neighbors and serve as an important daytime identification aid, or daymark.

- Two black and two white stripes on the lighthouse circle the tower; all are wider at the bottom than at the top.

- When it was first built, the cost of construction was $167,500. Laborers received $1.50 a day.

- Three keepers were employed to staff the tower, working shifts of 24 hours on and 48 hours off and standing watches every three days. They were paid $800 a year, plus housing, staple foods, and medicines.

- The lighthouse is one of 406 historic lighthouses, more than 50 years old, still in active use as navigational aids. The Coast Guard intends to retire many lighthouses early in the 21st century.

The beach is deserted as a storm gathers energy over Nags Head. PHOTO: MOLLY HARRISON

winds wreak havoc on precariously perched oceanfront property. If the high winds coincide with the high tide and—heaven forbid—the full moon, powerful storm waves cover the land and cause beach erosion, structural damage, and both ocean and soundside flooding.

March has seen a few nasty storms too, including the infamous Ash Wednesday Storm that struck on March 7, 1962, and the more recent March Storm in 1993 when winds were clocked at 92 MPH. The sound waters rose 8 to 10 feet, causing great damage. Year-round residents see all this nasty weather as a trade-off for living in such a paradise. While we tend to highlight the more extreme weather patterns here, there are far more absolutely gorgeous days occurring year-round.

The wind blows most of the time at an average of 8 to 10 MPH. Occasional gale force winds range from 30 to 35 MPH. In summer the wind blows predominantly out of the southwest, almost always picking up speed in the late afternoon. Southwest winds are warm, and if you're on a beach facing east, they create a generally flat ocean but stir up the sound. The wind often switches to come out of the northeast, which is a colder wind. Old-timers say that the wind always blows out of the northeast for an odd number of days—one, three, or five—before switching around again. Count it to see for yourself if it's true. Northeast winds create a rough ocean on east-facing beaches. Northeast winds are more predominant in fall and winter, and it seems as if everyone is always asking when the wind is supposed to switch back to the southwest. Northwest and southeast winds are less common, but of course they do occur, usually as the wind is about to switch to northeast or southwest. The weather is endlessly fascinating on the Outer Banks, something that almost every resident watches with vigilance. Surfers and anglers and anyone else who works or plays outside watch The Weather Channel (channel 16) for entertainment. Many restaurants and bars even keep a TV tuned into The Weather Channel. Hurricanes, of course, are a whole different ballgame. See our chapter on Waves and Weather: How to Stay Safe for additional information on what to do in case a hurricane threatens.

Waves and Weather: How to Stay Safe

The Outer Banks is known for its sparkling, clean beaches. Sun worshippers of all kinds and from all parts of the world come to the Outer Banks to play in the usually gentle surf. But remember, the ocean is a fickle being and can change her mood in the blink of an eye. Each beach is different and to stay safe you need to follow a few rules. Store these tips along with your seashells to help make your stay a comfortable and safe one.

The Ocean

Most of the time, you don't even notice the bare flagpoles dotting the dunes up and down our coast. But when the ocean is too rough for swimming, there's no way you can miss the red flags hoisted all along the beach. *If red flags are flying, do not go into the water at all.* Not only will the ocean be too dangerous for swimming or wading, it is against the law to swim during a red-flag warning. You will be fined for going into the water.

The flags signify not only dangerous waves, but deadly rip currents as well. Churning water can easily knock you down, and reports of broken bones are not uncommon. Rough water also produces

Better safe than sorry: Never take your eyes off the kids as they play in the surf. PHOTO: MOLLY HARRISON

421

floating debris—such as ships' timbers—that seems to come from nowhere. We've seen adult men wading in knee-deep water knocked down by powerful waves and dragged by rip currents on red-flag days. In short, even if you see surfers in the water, stay out while the flags are flying, and caution children to keep well away from the tide line. Keep in mind, too, that if you go into the water while the flags are flying and need rescuing, you are jeopardizing not only your life but also the lifeguard's life when he or she has to come in after you.

Water Sense

- Never swim alone.
- Never swim at night.
- Observe the surf before going in the water, looking for potentially dangerous currents.
- Nonswimmers should stay out of the water and wear life jackets if they're going to be near the water.

- Swim in areas with on-duty lifeguards, or use extreme care.
- Keep nonswimming children well above the marks of the highest waves.
- Keep an eye on children at all times; teach them never to turn their backs on the waves while they play at water's edge.
- Don't swim near anglers or deployed fishing lines.
- Stay 300 feet away from fishing piers.
- Watch out for surfers and give them plenty of room.

Losing Control in the Waves

If a wave crashes down on you while you are surfing or swimming, and you find yourself being tumbled in bubbles and sand like a sheet in a washing machine, don't try to struggle to the surface against it. Curl into a ball, or just go limp and float. The wave will take you to the beach, or you can just swim to the surface when it passes.

Soundside beaches are calmer—and therefore safer—for young children. PHOTO: KAREN BACHMAN

Backwash Current

A backwash current on a steeply sloping beach can pull you toward deeper water, but its power is swiftly checked by incoming waves. To escape this current, swim straight toward shore if you're a strong swimmer. If you're not, don't panic; wait and float until the current stops, then swim in.

Littoral Current

The littoral current is a "river of water" moving up or down the shoreline parallel to the beach. It is created by the angled approach of the waves. In stormy conditions, this current can be very powerful due to high wave energy.

Rip Currents

Rip currents often occur where there's a break in a submerged sandbar (see the diagrams in this chapter). Water trapped between the sandbar and the beach rushes out through the breach, sometimes sweeping swimmers out with it. You can see a rip; it's choppy, turbulent, often discolored water that looks deeper than the water around it. If you are caught in a rip, don't try to swim against the current. Instead, swim across the current, parallel to the shore, and slowly work your way back to the beach at an angle. Try to remain calm. Panic will only sap the energy you need to swim out of the rip.

Undertow

When a wave comes up on the beach and breaks, the water must run back down to the sea. This is undertow. It sucks at your ankles from small waves, but in heavy surf the undertow can knock you off your feet and carry you offshore. If you're carried out, don't resist. Let the undertow take you out until it subsides. It will only be a few yards. The next wave will help push you shoreward again.

Sharks

In the summer of 2001 shark attacks got a lot of media attention, including a shark attack resulting in a fatality at Avon on Hatteras Island and one in nearby Virginia Beach. Remember, though, that shark attacks are extremely rare, less likely than fatal bee stings, fatal auto accidents, or lightning strikes. Before the 2001 incident, the last shark fatality in North Carolina was in 1957. There have only been 18 shark attack reports in North Carolina since 1670.

To reduce your risk of shark bites, take the following precautions:

• Do not swim alone since sharks are more likely to attack a solitary individual.
• Do not wander too far from shore.
• Avoid being in the water at dawn or during twilight hours when sharks are most active and have a competitive sensory advantage.
• Don't wear bright clothing and reflective jewelry that can attract the attention of sharks and other fish.
• Be especially wary if you're bleeding or menstruating, since shark's olfactory senses are acute.
• Avoid thrashing about wildly—excessive splash can appear to be shark prey. For this reason, it is advised that you not swim with pets.
• Do not swim near people who are fishing.
• Stay away from inlets, fishing piers, and if possible, steep drop-offs and the areas between sandbars—these are favorite hangouts for sharks.

- If you see a shark, calmly leave the water as quickly and as quietly as possible.

Jellyfish

Watch for jellyfish floating on the surface or in the water. While some can give little more than an annoying stinging sensation, others can produce severe discomfort. The Portuguese man-of-war is sometimes blown onto Outer Banks beaches and can be recognized by its distinctive balloon-like air bladder, often exhibiting a bluish tint. Man-of-war stings can be serious. Anyone who is stung by the tentacles and develops breathing difficulties or generalized body swelling should be transported to the nearest emergency facility for treatment. In extreme cases, death can result from anaphylactic shock associated with man-of-war toxin exposure.

If you're stung by a jellyfish, apply vinegar or meat tenderizer to the affected area. Don't rub the wound site, since rubbing can force toxins deeper into the skin.

Pain relievers can also allay some discomfort. Infections can occur, so it's also a good idea to see a doctor.

Beach Services

Emergency Assistance

Some areas of the Outer Banks don't have lifeguards or flag systems warning you to stay out of the water. Keep in mind that help can be a long way off, and an emergency is not the time to learn about ocean safety. As you've learned after reading about the ocean currents listed above, water conditions here call for unusual vigilance. We are vigilant about hanging red warning flags, but sometimes they are stolen by souvenir-seeking scavengers. It's always best to listen to local radio stations or call municipal headquarters for daily water conditions anytime you plan to enter the ocean, despite the season. Accidents can and do occur. If you have an emergency and need the rescue squad, dial 911 for help. Please remember that this number is for emergencies only.

Lifeguards

Lifeguard services are at fixed sites throughout Dare and Currituck Counties.

Corolla Ocean Rescue, (252) 453–3242, provides guards from 9:30 A.M. to 5:30 P.M. from Memorial Day weekend through Labor Day at the following Corolla beaches: Ocean Hill, Corolla Light, Bonito Street (Whalehead), Ocean Sands at Buck Island and Sections P, O, F, and D, and Pine Island at the South County Beach Access. Lifeguards also patrol the beaches on 4WD vehicles from Pine Island to the Penny's Hill area of the off-road area.

Kitty Hawk Ocean Rescue, (252) 261–2666, www.kittyhawkfd.com/ocean-rescue, operates two stands, one at Byrd Street and one at the Kitty Hawk Bathhouse. The stands are staffed from Memorial Day to Labor Day from 10:00 A.M. to 6:00 P.M. Roving lifeguards also patrol the beaches of the town. From Labor Day through mid-October there is a supervisor on the beach.

In **Kill Devil Hills,** (252) 480–4066, lifeguard stands are at the following beaches: Helga Street, Hayman Boulevard, Fifth Street, Fourth Street, Second Street, First Street, Asheville Street, Woodmere Street, Carlow Street, Ocean Bay Boulevard, Oregon Street, Clark Street, Martin Street, Atlantic Street, Calvin Street, Ocean Acres Beach Access, and Lake Drive. There are also patrolling guards on 4WD vehicles. Guards are on duty from 9:30 A.M. to 5:30 P.M. in the summer.

Surf Rescue places guards on the beaches in Duck and on Roanoke Island from Memorial Day weekend through Labor Day weekend. Hours are 9:30 A.M. until 5:30 P.M. The Duck lifeguard locations change according to where the greatest population of swimmers is in any given year. Duck has four fixed but movable stands and two roaming lifeguards. On Roanoke Island a guard is at the Old Swimming Hole on the sound between the airport and the aquarium.

Nags Head Ocean Rescue Services, (252) 441–5909, are provided by the town of Nags Head to that town's beaches. This service is also provided to Southern Shores through a contracted arrangement. Guarded beaches are available daily beginning Memorial Day weekend through Labor Day, 10:00 A.M. until 6:00 P.M. Nags Head Ocean Rescue stands will be located at the following beaches:

• In Southern Shores: Hillcrest and Chicahauk plus two roving ATVs.

• In Nags Head: Albatross Street, Bonnet Street, Enterprise Street, Espstein Street, Forrest Street, Gray Eagle Street, Hargrove Street, and Juncos Street. There are also seven roving ATVs and two trucks. Nags Head's lifeguard stations may change slightly in 2002, so call ahead if you need that information.

Within the **Cape Hatteras National Seashore,** lifeguards are on duty from

If the red flags are flying over the beach, it means conditions are too dangerous for swimming. Stay out of the water! PHOTO: HORSLEY/GARDNER

Memorial Day through Labor Day at Coquina Beach on Bodie Island, at the Cape Hatteras Lighthouse beach, and at the Ocracoke Lifeguard Beach (use the first access road past the airport).

Always use caution before entering and/or swimming in the ocean, and be alert for red warning flags and red-and-white warning posters.

Alcohol

The effects of alcohol can be amplified by the heat and sun of a summer afternoon, so be aware. It's illegal to operate boats or motor vehicles if you've had too much to drink, and enforcement officers keep an eye out for violators, so practice moderation. Alcohol and swimming can be a potentially deadly combination. Even small amounts of alcohol can give you a false sense of security.

Safety in the Sun

It's amazing how many red-bodied people we see lying on the beach, limping into restaurants or, worse yet, waiting in medical centers while visiting the Outer Banks. Yes, we know. The sun feels so good. Combined with the sea air, it seems to have a rejuvenating effect. Actually any form of tan or burn is now considered damaged skin. While we can't stop visitors and Insiders alike from toasting themselves, these tips will help keep you comfortable.

• Start out with short periods of sun exposure when you first arrive. It seems as if most visitors initially overdo it and have to be careful for the rest of their stay. The summer sun is pretty intense, and you'd be surprised how much of a burn your skin can get in 20 or 30 minutes on an afternoon in July. We always take our umbrella to the beach to keep our exposure within reasonable levels. You might want to do the same.

• Use ample sunscreen (SPF 15 or higher) whenever you're in the sun for any length of time. We always put an extra coat on our noses, cheeks, lips and any other high-exposure spots. We also apply sunscreen at least 20 minutes before we go out, since it can take a while for it to become fully effective.

• Avoid the hottest parts of the day, from 10:00 A.M. until 2:00 P.M., when the sun's rays are the strongest. It's a great time to take a break from the beach and explore some of the other fun things listed in this guide.

• Don't be afraid to cover up on the beach. Just remember: healthy, protected skin is a sign of good sense.

Pets

Dogs must be on a leash unless they are in the water. Park Service rangers and lifeguards do patrol the beaches regularly, and they will approach you if your dog is running free. Voice command control is not enough. Save yourself some money and leash up; fines range around $50. Some communities do not allow pets on the beach at all from mid-May through mid-September. Heed local signs. Not only are unleashed pets a nuisance to non-pet owners, but also they can damage turtle and bird nests and the fragile dune systems.

Insiders' Tip

Hot summer days can be hard on dogs, who don't have sweat glands to cool themselves down. Try to avoid having your dog on the beach in the hottest part of the day, and make sure your dog has plenty of freshwater to drink on the beach so that he won't be tempted to drink salt water. Signs of heat stroke and exhaustion in dogs are excessive panting, vomiting, diarrhea, purple gums, weakness, and disorientation. If your dog shows these signs, cool him down by spraying him with cool water, especially on the belly, and call a vet.

Don't forget sunscreen when heading out on the sea. The reflection of the sun on the water increases the chance of sunburn. PHOTO: COURTESY OF ROANOKE ISLAND FESTIVAL PARK

Litter

We shouldn't even have to say it, but, believe it or not, there are people who leave trash behind when they leave the beach. If you're getting ready to throw down a soda bottle or candy wrapper, remember that while you may only be visiting the Outer Banks, you are littering in a year-round community, not to mention destroying natural beauty. Inevitably what is tossed in one backyard winds up gracing the lawn of another due to the wind factor. With that in mind, you'll want to secure all trash and trash bags carefully so the wind can't make mischief. Feel free to pick up any stray trash. It's not uncommon to see locals doing just this. Don't be shy—after all, we've already established that the ocean is yours too!

If you can't find a trash can that isn't already overflowing, please find another appropriate spot to dispose of potential litter. A good idea is to look into our recycling efforts when you first get to the Outer Banks.

Hurricanes

June through November marks our hurricane season. Basically, the whole shoreline of the East Coast is threatened when a hurricane blows in, but because of our low elevation, lack of shelter, and our situation in the ocean, the barrier islands known as the Outer Banks are especially vulnerable to storms. Forecasters and almanac writers state that a hurricane strikes the Outer Banks approximately once every nine years.

After the active hurricane season of 1999, visitors and locals alike were reminded of the dangers these huge storms can bring. It's wise to be prepared by packing a hurricane kit in advance. See the gray box below for a list of items to include in such a kit.

When Dare County officials order an evacuation, everyone must leave the Outer Banks. This includes everyone from vacationers who have already paid for their week's stay to permanent residents who are sometimes hesitant to leave their homes. Newspapers and radio

Hurricane Kit

Be sure to include these items in your hurricane kit:
- AM/FM radio with extra batteries
- Baby supplies, if necessary
- Bar soap
- Can opener
- Cash
- Change of clothing for each member of the family
- Eating utensils
- First-aid kit
- Flashlights and extra batteries
- Food (nonperishable) and water, enough for three days for the entire family
- Hygiene items: toilet paper, toothpaste, etc.
- Ice chest or cooler
- Important documents: birth certificates, medical records, insurance papers, etc.
- Matches
- Plastic bags for waste
- Plywood for windows
- Prescription medications, glasses, etc.
- Sleeping bags and blankets
- Spare key for home and vehicles

And don't forget your pets during a storm. They need special attention since they can't take care of themselves. Animals are barred from public shelters for health reasons, so make plans for evacuating your pet before the storm strikes by finding out which hotels and motels in safe areas allow pets. Have an up-to-date identification tag on your pet's collar, a current photograph, and current medical/vaccination records with you. Make sure your pet is properly restrained with a carrier or leash, since even the calmest animals become frightened in a storm. Be sure to bring a week's worth of food as well as any medications your pet might need, and don't forget a litter pan and litter if you have a cat.

and television stations keep the public notified about evacuations as well as re-entry information. Make plans early especially if you have pets or elderly people with you. The Weather Channel (channel 16 in the local cable listing) will issue early warnings or signs of an approaching storm. By all means, stay off the beaches and out of the water especially during an electrical storm. More information about our emergency procedures can be gleaned by calling Dare County at (252) 473-3355, Currituck County at (252) 232-2115, or Ocracoke at (252) 928-1071.

Tornadoes spawned by hurricanes are among the worst weather-related killers. When a hurricane approaches, listen for tornado watches and warnings. (A tornado watch means conditions are favorable for tornadoes to develop. A warning means a tornado has been sighted.) When a warning is issued, seek shelter immediately, preferably in an inside room away from any windows. If you are outside at the time and a tornado is headed your way, move away from its path at a right angle. If you feel you don't have time to escape, lie flat in a ditch or ravine.

Hurricane watches mean a hurricane could threaten the area within 24 hours, but evacuation is not necessary at this point. If a warning is issued, however, visitors should leave the islands and head inland using US 64/264 or US 158 following the green and white Hurricane Evacuation Route signs.

Here are some guidelines to help you stay safe if a hurricane threatens.

• By late May, recheck your supply of boards, tools, batteries, nonperishable foods and other items you may need during a hurricane.

• Listen to the latest weather reports and official notices. This will give you advance notice, sometimes before watches and warnings are issued. Keep a battery-powered radio on hand in case the power goes out.

• If your area comes under a hurricane watch, continue normal activities but stay tuned to the Weather Channel or to a local radio station and ignore rumors.

• If your area receives a hurricane warning, stay calm. Leave low-lying areas that may be swept by high tides or storm waves. If there's time, secure mobile homes before leaving for more substantial shelter. Move automobiles to high ground as both sound and sea can flood even central spots on the Outer Banks.

• Moor boats securely or haul them out of the water to a safe place.

• Board up windows or protect them with storm shutters. (Though some people recommend using tape on windows, many experts and most locals will tell you tape isn't strong enough to work and it's very difficult to remove.) Secure outdoor objects that might blow away such as garbage cans, outdoor furniture, tools, etc. that may become dangerous missiles in

high winds. If the items can't be tied down, bring them inside.

• Store drinking water in clean bathtubs, jugs, or bottles because water supplies can become contaminated by hurricane floods.

• Be sure you have lots of flashlights, batteries, a battery-operated radio, and perhaps emergency cooking facilities.

• Keep your car fueled since service stations may be inoperable for several days following a storm.

• Stay indoors during a storm, and keep your pets inside too. Do not attempt to travel by foot or car. Monitor weather conditions and don't be fooled by the calm of the hurricane's eye—the storm isn't over yet!

• Stay out of disaster areas unless you are qualified to help. Your presence might hamper rescue work.

• If necessary, seek medical attention at the nearest Red Cross disaster station or health center.

• Do not travel except in an emergency such as transporting someone who is injured. Be careful along debris-filled streets and highways. Roads may be undermined and could collapse under the weight of the car. Floodwater could hide dangerous holes in the road.

• Avoid loose and dangling wires. Report them to North Carolina Power or the police.

• Report broken sewer or water mains to the county or town water department.

• Be careful not to start fires. Lowered water pressure may make fire fighting difficult.

• Stay away from rivers and streams.

• Check roofs, windows, and outdoor storage areas for wind or water damage.

• Do not let young children or your pets outside immediately after a storm. There are numerous dangers like fallen power lines and wild animals that have been disoriented because of the storm.

Remember, you already possess the most important safety tool there is—common sense. Use it often and you're sure to have a safe and enjoyable vacation.

Recreation

If you're visiting the Outer Banks for the first time, you'll soon discover what Insiders already know and love about this area: Play is a priority. From early on, these barrier islands have lured sunbathers, swimmers, surfers, and outdoor enthusiasts in search of excellent sportfishing and waterfowl hunting. The appeal has since widened to include even more outdoor activities: windsurfing, hang gliding, parasailing, scuba diving, biking, playing golf, playing tennis, and in-line skating, just to name a few. And for a respite from these more strenuous workouts, you can choose among sightseeing cruises, ATV excursions, and beach combing.

Since the Outer Banks offers such a diverse—and plentiful—array of activities, we've divided up these diversions, and have devoted entire chapters to such pastimes as fishing, golf, and watersports. We've tried to shed light upon all the other recreational activities and adventures in this chapter: tennis, biking and in-line skating, athletic clubs, miniature golf, horseback riding, and go-carts, plus hang gliding, parasailing, and airplane tours. If you want to get in or on the water, try slipping down a twisting waterslide, seeking a school of dolphin on a boat trip, or enjoying a pirate tour while cruising around the Pamlico Sound. Not all activities involve a fee. You can spend an afternoon walking the wide beaches searching for shells and pieces of sea glass or buy the kids a kite and help them send it soaring atop the wafting winds. Bird-watching opportunities abound in the wildlife refuges along the Outer Banks; see our Bird-watching section of the Natural Wonders chapter. Nags Head Woods offers both a shady respite during the heat of summer and a great place to take secluded hikes through one of the most marvelous preserved maritime forests on the Atlantic seaboard. Bike paths line roads along the sounds and the sea, through towns, and even along the Wright Brothers National Monument. If you just need to get to sea for a while and enjoy the Outer Banks from a different vantage point, riding the state ferry to Ocracoke Island is one of our favorite year-round pastimes. Best of all, each of these activities is free!

When you've had a little too much fun in the sun, there are sections on indoor activities such as bowling alleys, movie theaters, roller rinks, and noisy, state-of-the-art video arcades. Don't forget to check out our Kidstuff chapter for additional activities geared toward the children.

If you're looking for parks, Dare County Parks and Recreation Department has several throughout the county, some with playgrounds, tennis courts, picnicking sites, and ball fields. Call them at (252) 473-1101 ext. 313 to find the one nearest you. See the Playgrounds section of our Kidstuff chapter for the best kids' playgrounds.

If Bingo is your bag, several fire stations and civic clubs along the barrier islands host regularly scheduled sessions in the early evenings throughout the summer. Colington Island's Volunteer Fire Department off Colington Road, (252) 441-6234, and Nags Head's Fire Department on US 158 just south of the Outer Banks Mall, (252) 441-5909, are home to two of the area's more popular part-time Bingo parlors. Outer Banks Beach Bingo on Colington Road in Kill Devil Hills, (252) 449-8332, has games year-round several nights a week until 2:00 A.M., and the First Flight Lions Club at MP $5\frac{1}{2}$ on US 158 in Kill Devil Hills, (252) 441-8308, hosts Bingo nightly at 7:00 P.M.

For home entertainment, video sales and rental stores are scattered from Corolla to Ocracoke. The stores are set up to accommodate our transient tourist population, so don't worry about memberships. Try Good Vibes Video, (252) 453-3503, in Corolla; Movie Gallery, (252) 261-0179 in Southern Shores; Good Vibes, (252) 441-2244 in Kill Devil Hills; Video Andy (252) 441-2666 in Nags Head; Village Video, (252) 995-5138, with several locations on Hatteras Island; and Eleven Eleven Shades and Movies on Ocracoke, (252) 928-9000. Many stores also rent out Play Stations and Nintendo. You'll find at least one videocassette recorder in every rental cottage on the Outer Banks, but if you're staying in a hotel or motel that doesn't have one in the room, most stores do rent VCRs.

It's nearly impossible to experience all the recreational opportunities the Outer Banks has to offer. We're sure you'll have fun trying, though.

Airplane Tours

Even people who have lived on the Outer Banks for years are awestruck when they first view this stretch of islands from the air. Small planes offer tours daily most of the year from Corolla through Ocracoke. Pilots are always pleased to dip their passengers over a school of dolphins frolicking in the Atlantic, circle one of the four lighthouses beaming from these beaches, or cruise around the Wright Brothers National Monument where Wilbur and Orville flew the world's first successful heavier-than-air craft. Bring your camera, for these adventures provide great photo opportunities of both sea and sound shores and otherwise inaccessible wetlands. Trips can be catered to fit any desire and are well worth the reasonable rates to obtain a bird's-eye view of these narrow strands of sandy terrain.

Reservations are strongly recommended at least a day in advance of takeoff. All flights depend on the wind and the weather. For information on charter flights to Norfolk and other destinations off the Outer Banks, please refer to our air service section in our Getting Here, Getting Around chapter. Several services offer flight instruction to obtain a pilot's license and certification.

Kill Devil Hills

Kitty Hawk Aero Tours
Wright Brothers Airstrip, Kill Devil Hills
(252) 441-4460

Based just behind the Wright Brothers National Monument, off Colington Road, these air tours offer half-hour flights in Cessna aircraft year-round. Trips take you soaring south over Oregon Inlet, flying above the waves to see shipwrecks, over Jockey's Ridge and Roanoke Island and back to circle the monument. It costs $39 per person for parties of two and $29 per person for three- to six-person parties. Tours are offered from 10:00 A.M. to 5:00 P.M. in the off-season, and from 9:00 A.M. to sunset during the summer.

If you're up for more high-flying excitement, try a trip in a 1941 Waco biplane, where the cockpit is open and your head is literally in the clouds. Twenty-minute trips take two passengers around the central

Outer Banks for a total of $136. Leather helmets and old-fashioned Red Baron–style goggles are included in the price. Biplane tours are offered from May through September from 9:00 A.M. until sunset. Reservations are preferred for both types of flights.

Roanoke Island

Outer Banks Seaplanes
Wanchese Seafood Industrial Park, Wanchese
(252) 475–1007

This company offers air tours via seaplane, taking off and landing on the Roanoke Sound. You board the Cessna seaplane at their dock at the Wanchese Seafood Industrial Park, then take a half-hour tour above Jockey's Ridge, the Wright Brothers Memorial, Roanoke Island, the beach, and Oregon Inlet. Two passengers can go at a time, each paying $45. To get to the industrial park, take NC 345 off US 64/264 on the south end of Roanoke Island. Once you're in Wanchese, a brown state sign will direct you to the park.

Hatteras Island

Burris Flying Service
Frisco Shopping Center, NC 12, Frisco
(252) 986–2679

Burrus Flying Service offers sightseeing tours of Hatteras Island and the surrounding areas. The short tour, about 30 minutes, takes you around Cape Hatteras and the lighthouse, while the longer tour, about an hour, can go either north to Rodanthe or south to Ocracoke Island. Short tours cost $30 each for two people or $25 each for three people. Long tours cost $45 each for two people or $40 each for three people. Additional trips are available, including a summer sunset tour. This is a great opportunity for aerial photography. Tours are offered daily from May 1 through October 31. Advance reservations are recommended.

Ocracoke Island

Pelican Airways
Ocracoke Airstrip, Ocracoke
(252) 928–1661

Half-hour trips above Ocracoke and Portsmouth Islands are available any time of year in this Aero-Commander plane. Trips can be tailored to suit individual interests or narrated to explain interesting aspects of the southern Outer Banks area. A trip costs a total of $70 for two people and $100 for three people. Flight instruction is offered by appointment. Charter service is also available—see our Getting Here, Getting Around chapter.

All-terrain Vehicle, 4WD, and Horse Tours

One of the most exhilarating ways to see the off-road areas of the Outer Banks is on an all-terrain vehicle (ATV). Whether you're cruising along the beach or chasing a sunset up the marshy sounds, you get closer to nature on one of these sturdy vehicles. Keep in mind you're limited to 15 mph, and you can't play on the dunes. These tours are available only on the northern Outer Banks north of Corolla.

Corolla

Corolla Outback Adventures
Wee Winks Shopping Center, NC 12, Corolla
(252) 453–4484

This outpost on the northernmost area of the Outer Banks has been operating for 20 years and conducts guided tours with ATVs. You will be transported by truck north of where the pavement ends to the four-wheel-drive area, where a Corolla Outback guide will take you by ATV along the beaches and through protected wildlife refuges. Even though the area has becoming more populated, you can still catch a glimpse of wild horses, rare waterfowl, and even wild boars. There are feral hogs too; however, there is no mistaking the now-rare black boars with their visible tusks.

During the summer season, two-hour guided tours are available for $109 a vehicle; the ATVs seat two people. Off-season rates are available. Corolla Outback's Wild Horse Safari Tour heads up to Carova, near the North Carolina/Virginia border, to look for the famous wild horses—and they find them every time. The two-hour tours are led in Chevy Suburbans that hold up to 10 people. After the 15-mile drive up the beach to the horses' stomping grounds, passengers unload from the vehicle and take a few photos, while the guide educates everyone about the horses. This tour costs $44 for adults and is half-price for kids ages 4 to 11. Children age 3 and under ride for free. Along the tour you'll see other wildlife, plus all the elements of the Outer Banks ecosystem. This is a great tour that anyone in the family can go on. These tours are offered year-round. Corolla Outback Adventures also offers four-wheel-drive/kayak expeditions. Further information is available in the Kayaking section of the Watersports chapter. All tours and rentals are weather-dependent.

Corolla Adventure Tours
NC 12, Corolla
(252) 453–6899
www.obxwaterworks.com

With two locations on NC 12 in Corolla, one next to the Inn at Corolla Light and one north of the post office, Corolla Adventure Tours offers ATV and four-wheel-drive truck tours on the beaches north of Corolla, plus ocean and sound kayak tours (see our Watersports chapter for information about kayak tours). ATV tours cover about 20 miles of territory and last about two hours. Truck tours (in Chevy Suburbans) are about the same length, covering the entire stretch of beach north of Corolla up to the Virginia line, where there are no paved roads. You may get a glimpse of the wild horses. Corolla Adventure Tours is open March through January.

Ocracoke Island

Portsmouth Island ATV Excursions
NC 12, Ocracoke Village
(252) 928–4484
www.portsmouthislandatvs.com

In Ocracoke Village, this tour service offers guided tours of Portsmouth Island and historic Portsmouth Village. A Portsmouth Island ATV Excursion allows you to ride the shoreline of one of the most beautiful and remote beaches in the world on an island famous for its shorebirds, sea turtles, and seashells. Excursions begin with a 20-minute boat ride from Silver Lake Harbor in Ocracoke Village. Once on the island, you will discover the historic deserted village of Portsmouth, a settlement that in 1860 was a thriving port town with more than 685 residents. Now owned by the National Park Service, Portsmouth Island is home to the only ghost town on the East Coast (see our Day Trips and Attractions chapters for more details). The 23-mile-long island is part of Cape Lookout National Seashore and is listed on the National Register of Historic Places. As part of the tour, you will be guided through the village's U.S. Life-Saving Station, the Methodist church, the post office and general store, and the village visitor center.

Two trips a day are offered, from 8:00 A.M. to noon, and from 2:00 P.M. to 6:00 P.M., weather permitting. The season runs from April 1 through November 30. The cost is $75 per person, and ATVs accommodate two persons per vehicle, with a six-person maximum. Reservations are required. For more information, visit the Web site.

Athletic Clubs

Despite all the outdoor activities the Outer Banks has to offer, many locals and visitors still crave vigorous indoor workouts at traditional gyms and health clubs. During the heat of the summer and the cold winds of winter, they're your best choice for strenuous exercise. These fitness centers are open year-round and include locker room and shower facilities. They are open to the public for annual, monthly, weekly, and walk-in daily membership rates.

Sanderling

The Spa at The Sanderling Inn
NC 12, Sanderling
(252) 261–4111, ext. SPA (772)
www.thesanderling.com

The Spa is an integral part of The Sanderling Inn Resort and Conference Center, a 12-acre luxury resort located 5 miles north of Duck. Here guests can select from a lengthy menu of massage therapies, plus body, skin, or nail care treatments. Many of these treatments have been created uniquely for The Spa, and utilize sea mud and minerals indigenous to the area. Treatment rooms overlook the scenic Currituck Sound. In addition, The Spa includes a complete Fitness Center with state-of-the-art Cybex™ exercise equipment and the latest in cardiovascular training machines. Steam rooms, sports showers, a whirlpool, heated lap pool, and other hydrotherapy options are also offered. Call for Spa appointments and Fitness Center membership rates. Walk-in charges are $20 a day and $80 a week.

The Sanderling Inn Eco-Center offers kayak tours through Pine Island National Audubon Sanctuary, along with rentals of bicycles, in-line skates, and outdoor adventure equipment.

Kitty Hawk

Barrier Island Fitness Center
US 158, MP 1, Kitty Hawk
(252) 261–0100

Barrier Island Fitness Center (located behind Wal-Mart) is a complete, full-service health club. It has a full line of Trotter free weights, circuit-training equipment, and an assortment of cardiovascular equipment including elliptical trainers, treadmills, stair-steppers, recumbent cycles, and Airdynes. Certified aerobics classes, including aquafit, are offered.

The staff includes fitness instructors, two ACSM-certified personal trainers, and two massage therapists. The new heated, dry, hydrotherapy massage tables by Thermapulse are a welcome addition.

Other amenities at the center include tennis courts, saunas, steam rooms, tanning beds, and an indoor pool. Parents rejoice: There is on-site baby-sitting and a cybercade with computer games for the kids. The cybercade is complete with high-speed Internet and e-mail access.

The facility is open to the public (ages 18 and older) Monday through Friday from 6:00 A.M. to 9:00 P.M.; Saturday, 9:00 A.M. to 7:00 P.M., and Sunday, 9:00 A.M. to 5:00 P.M. The pool is open until 10:00 P.M. daily. Drop-in rates are $15 a day or $45 a week.

Kill Devil Hills

Outer Banks Health Systems/Hammerheads Fitness Center
NC 12 and Third St., MP 7, Kill Devil Hills
(252) 441–7001

Outer Banks Health Systems/Hammerheads Fitness Center has the most serious gym atmosphere and is one of the most popular exercise facilities on the Outer Banks. The facility is well equipped with top-of-the-line resistance equipment, Bodymasters selectorized machines, Icarian and Hammerstrength benches, cables, and plate-loaded equipment. Hammerheads offers the largest selection of free weights and equipment in the area. The in-house aerobics program offers more than 20 classes weekly, in addition to hatha yoga classes with certified instructors and Tae Kwan-Do. For cardio workouts, Hammerheads offers treadmills, upright and recumbent bikes, lifesteps, and elliptical trainers.

Outer Banks Health Systems provides one-on-one instruction and personal training by appointment only. Private sessions may be scheduled in the area's only private personal-training studio. Outer Banks Health Systems uses the Tri-Fit 600 computer-enhanced fitness assessment system, which measures flexibility, strength, aerobic capacity, blood pressure, and percentage of body fat. Information from the assessment is then used to structure a program for your individual needs, expectations, and time availability.

Vacationers are welcome to drop in on a daily or weekly basis. Memberships are available on a seasonal or annual basis. Hours are Monday through Friday 6:00 A.M. to 9:00 P.M., Saturday 8:00 A.M. to 5:00 P.M. The gym will relocate in late 2002 so call in advance.

Nags Head

Outer Banks Family YMCA
US 158, MP 11, Nags Head
(252) 449–8897

A brand-new facility, just opened in December 2001, the Outer Banks Family YMCA is centrally located in Nags Head. The 28,000-square-foot facility includes a fitness room with weight and cardiovascular equipment. A wood-floored exercise room is available for such activities as aerobics, yoga, Pilates, and karate. The 7,000-square-foot gymnasium is marked for both basketball and volleyball and has indoor soccer capabilities. An 8,000-square-foot pool, 25 meters long with six lanes, is the highlight of the YMCA, since it is the only public pool in the beach communities. Swim lessons, water aerobics, and lap times are available. A hot tub can accommodate 8 to 10 people. Wellness programs and family programs, such as Parents Night Out, are available, as is a nursery where children are actively stimulated while parents work out. Children and youth sports leagues include soccer, hockey, basketball, volleyball, and wrestling, and there are adult basketball and volleyball leagues. Call for membership rates. No day passes are issued, except to members of other YMCAs who have their membership card with them. Other YMCA members are charged a fee, and there is limited access in summer.

Roanoke Island

Nautics Hall Health & Fitness Complex
US 64, Manteo
(252) 473–1191

A competition-size, indoor heated pool is the centerpiece of this health club at the Elizabethan Inn, where water aerobics, swimming lessons, and lap times are offered throughout the year. There's also a workout room with Nautilus and Paramount equipment, free weights, Stairmasters, treadmills, and an aerobicycle. Low-impact and step aerobics instruction is available daily.

Other amenities include an outdoor pool, a hot tub, a racquetball court, sun decks, a sauna, and massage therapy on the

Insiders' Tip

The Sandbox Skate Park at Sea Holly Square in Kill Devil Hills has the only skateboard ramp on the Outer Banks. Call (252) 480-0542 for details.

The waters of the Outer Banks allow for a great number of recreational activities. PHOTO: COURTESY OF KITTY HAWK KITES

premises. Nautics Hall is open from 6:30 A.M. to 9:00 P.M., Monday through Friday, and from 9:00 A.M. to 9:00 P.M. on summer weekends. On Sundays during the off-season, their hours change to 9:00 A.M. to 5:00 P.M. Monthly memberships cost $50.00 per person. Daily passes cost $5.00 each for 18 years and younger, $7.00 for 19 years and older, and $5.00 for seniors.

Biking and Skating

With NC 12 stretching along more than 100 miles of the Outer Banks from Corolla to Ocracoke and hugging the seaside almost all the way, cyclists can cruise the Outer Banks and get almost anywhere they want to go. The flat terrain on these barrier islands is quite a treat for cyclists used to hills. (The only hills you'll find for cycling over are man-made bridges.) But be forewarned that the roads here are especially crowded, and NC 12 is quite narrow. Cyclists need to be skilled enough to ride without swerving too much and to anticipate the actions of car drivers, who, as many bikers know, often don't even see bicycles on the road or yield any sort of right-of-way to cyclists. It is unwise to allow children to ride their bikes on NC 12, and especially on US 158, where drivers often swerve out of their lanes as they're scoping the sights or looking for a business. It's best to restrict children to side streets or to the designated bicycle paths. These side streets and paths are also the best places to in-line skate.

Bicycle Paths

• Corolla: extended shoulder along NC 12 on the Currituck Outer Banks, some separate paths in private developments
• Duck: separate bike path along NC 12, from Southern Shores town line to Sanderling
• Southern Shores: separate bike path along NC 12 from Town Hall to Duck
• Kitty Hawk: separate bike path starting at Kitty Hawk Elementary School on US 158 south to Kitty Hawk Road

• Kill Devil Hills: separate bike path from the end of West First Street, along Colington Road, ending at NC 12
• Nags Head: separate bike path along NC 12 from MP 11½ to MP 21
• Roanoke Island: separate bike path running the entire length of the island along US 64/264 from the base of the Washington Baum Bridge at Pirate's Cove to the Manns Harbor Bridge
• Hatteras Island: extended shoulder along NC 12
• Ocracoke Island: extended shoulder along NC 12

While there is little crime on the Outer Banks, bicycles do disappear. Lock up carefully, and never leave your bike parked overnight in a front yard or in an easily accessed spot. If your bike is stolen, call the local police. Sometimes bikes are taken on nocturnal "joy rides" and then found by the local police department, so call them before you panic. It's also a good idea to record your bike's serial number for identification purposes.

Since vehicular traffic is very heavy during the summer months, and many of the drivers are unaccustomed to the roads, arm yourself with the following safety tips. If you have children who will be biking, make sure that they understand the rules of the road before they even leave the driveway.

• Use designated bike paths when available
• Wear safety helmets
• Ride on the right side of the road with the flow of traffic
• Always maintain a single file
• Obey all traffic rules
• Cross US 158 at a stoplight whenever possible
• Use hand signals for stops and turns
• Don't double up unless the bike is designed for more than one rider
• Keep your hands on the handlebars
• Observe pedestrians' right of way on walks, paths, and streets
• Be alert for off-road areas with tire-puncturing cacti and sandspurs
• Look out for soft sand that can cause a wipeout

• Use a front-lighted white lamp and a rear red reflector when riding at night

Corolla

Ocean Atlantic Rentals
Corolla Light Village Shops
NC 12, Corolla
(252) 453–2440
NC 12, Duck
(252) 261–4346
NC 12, MP 10, Nags Head
(252) 441–7823
NC 12, Avon
(252) 995–5868
www.oceanatlanticrentals.com

In-line skates and bicycles, kiddy karts, and pull-behind bikes (for kids) can be rented by the day, weekend, and week from each location of Ocean Atlantic Rentals, now in its 23rd year of business. These rental outfits also lease kayaks, baby equipment, videos, and various recreational equipment. Most Ocean Atlantic outposts are open seven days a week year-round, from 10:00 A.M. to 6:00 P.M. in the off-season (call ahead for the Avon location) and 10:00 A.M. to 9:00 P.M. throughout the summer. Delivery is available from Corolla through Hatteras Island.

Kitty Hawk

Moneysworth Rental Services
947 W. Kitty Hawk Rd., Kitty Hawk
(252) 261–6999, (800) 833–5233

Moneysworth offers free delivery and pickup of all types of beach and sports rental equipment, including items such as adults' and children's bikes, baby seats and bicycle helmets, volleyball and horseshoe game sets, and beach utility carts. They deliver from Corolla to Ocracoke.

Kill Devil Hills

The Bike Barn
1312 Wrightsville Blvd., MP 9½, Kill Devil Hills
(252) 441–3786

For 18 years the locally owned and operated Bike Barn has sold top-of-the-line bikes and biking accessories on the Outer Banks, including quality brand names such as Giant, Caloi, Jamis, and Diamond Back. The Bike Barn is well trusted by locals for bicycle repairs on various makes and models. The shop also rents bikes (hybrids and Beach Cruisers) for $30 a week or $10 a day, helmets and locks included. Kiddie carts and strollers are available as well. The Bike Barn gives free maps of the area to all renters, and the helpful staff can assist with touring information. The Bike Barn is located directly behind Taco Bell.

KDH Cycle
203 NC 12, MP 8½, Kill Devil Hills
(252) 480–3399

Open year-round, this full-service bicycle shop rents excellent equipment at competitive prices. Owner Chip Cowan says his store has the best rental fleet on the beach, offering all types of bikes (including cruisers, hybrids, roadbikes, and mountain bikes). A 24-speed Cannondale with suspension rents for $15 per day or $50 per week. Cruisers rent for $10 per day or $35 per week. All safety equipment is included in the rental cost. KDH Cycle offers full-service repair on all makes and models of bicycles and sells a wide selection of parts, clothing, and bicycles, including Trek, Cannondale, and Specialized.

In business since 1993, KDH Cycle is open daily from 8:00 A.M. to 8:00 P.M. in summer and 9:00 A.M. to 6:00 P.M. in the off-season.

Sandbox Skate Park and Skateboard Store
Sea Holly Sq., NC 12, MP 8 , Kill Devil Hills
(252) 480–0542

New in May 1998, Sandbox Skate Park welcomes in-line skaters, BMX bike riders, and skateboarders. The Park features a 24-foot-wide half-pipe and a street course with pyramids, wedge ramps, and quarter-pipes. Parents: Your children under 18 must be accompanied by a legal guardian, and the guardian must sign a release form or the youngsters will not be permitted to use the Park. The store sells a full range of equipment and supplies. Concessions are also sold at the Park. The hours for both the Park and Store are from 9:00 A.M. to 10:00 P.M. in the summer and from 11:00 A.M. to 5:00 P.M. in the off-season.

Nags Head

Family Life Center
US 158, MP 11½, Nags Head
(252) 441–4941

A recreational facility for the Outer Banks Worship Center, this Christian-affiliated roller-skating rink behind the ark-shaped church is open to the public on Friday and Saturday evenings from 7:00 to 9:30 P.M. year-round. Here, kids can rent regular, old-fashioned roller skates for $3.00 and cruise around the slick floor. Table tennis and video games also are available, as are special event and birthday bookings.

Manteo

Kitty Hawk Kites/Carolina Outdoors
The Waterfront, Manteo
(252) 473–2357, (800) FLY–THIS

Bicycle tours of Roanoke Island—in which you rent your own cycle or a beach cruiser—are offered by Kitty Hawk Kites. Quaint Manteo is the perfect town to tour by bicycle. Two-hour tours are offered on varied days and times during the summer. Bike rentals are $5.00 for two hours, $15.00 for four hours, $20.00 per day, or $50.00 for the entire week. Child seats are available free of charge.

Hatteras Island

Island Cycles
NC 12, Avon
(252) 995–4336, (800) 229–7810

This all-encompassing bicycle shop is north of the only stoplight in Avon, right next to the Subway sandwich shop. Sales, repairs, advice, and bicycle rentals are offered. Mopeds and scooters are also available for sale or rent. Cyclists can lease seven-speed beach cruisers, single-speed beach cruisers, mountain bikes, and road bikes or higher-end bikes, recumbent bicycles, and tandems. Group and off-season

rates are available. Island Cycle is open year-round. Summer hours are 9:00 A.M. to 6:00 P.M. Off-season hours will vary, so call ahead.

Hatteras Wind N Surf
NC 12, Avon
(252) 995–4525, (888) WND–SURF
www.windnsurf.com

Besides catering to your watersports needs, this shop, across from the pier, rents bikes and in-line skates, both for $10 a day or $35 a week. Rental fees include pads and helmets. It closes during the winter months.

Lee Robinson's General Store
NC 12, Hatteras Village
(252) 986–2381

Here, well-maintained Beach Cruisers, some with baby seats, can be rented year-round, seven days a week for cycling tours around the southern end of Hatteras Island. Lee Robinson's is open until 11:00 P.M. in the summer, with abbreviated hours during the off-season.

Ocracoke Island

Slushy Stand
NC 12, Ocracoke Village
(252) 928–1878

Take a breather and rock a spell in a chair on the wraparound porch before renting a two-wheeler here. You can't miss the bike racks spread out in front of this juniper-sided building just across from Silver Lake Harbor. Traditional coaster and kids' bikes rent by the hour, day, or week from April through November. Daily rates are $13, and weekly rates are $36. Special tandem bicycles and tricycles also can be leased. Call for rental rates. After a long ride through Ocracoke Island, be sure to sample a hand-dipped ice cream cone or an old-fashioned slushy at the snack bar.

Island Rentals
Silver Lake Rd., Ocracoke Village
(252) 928–5480

It should be against the law for tourists to drive cars on Ocracoke, for the island is the perfect size for exploration on foot or by bicycle. This Ocracoke Island outpost rents adult bicycles for $10 a day. It's next to the Ocracoke Harbor Inn and is open Easter through Thanksgiving.

Beach Outfitters
NC 12, Ocracoke Village
(252) 928–6261, (252) 928–7411

Beach Outfitters, in the Ocracoke Island Realty office, is open all year and accepts reservations. You can rent bikes for $13 a day or $36 a week. See our Cottages and Long-term Rentals chapter for more information.

Bowling

Sometimes even the most dedicated sun-worshippers need an afternoon or evening in air-conditioned comfort. When you've caught too many rays or if the weather just won't cooperate, bowling is an alternative way to while away the hours on the Outer Banks.

Nags Head Bowling Center
US 158, MP 10, Nags Head
(252) 441–7077

Open for year-round league and recreational excitement, this is the Outer Banks's only bowling center. Here, 24 lanes are available for unlimited members of a party. There is also a billiards room, pro shop, video arcade, and a cafe serving light meals, sandwiches, wine, beer, and hamburgers. Laser light and glow-in-the-dark bowling is offered at 10:00 P.M. on Friday and Saturday nights. Bowling costs $3.75 per game, and shoes rent for $2.50. Nags Head Bowling is open from noon to midnight Sunday through Friday and from 10:00 A.M. to midnight on Tuesday and Saturday. Call for league information.

Climbing

Rock-climbing walls are available for all ages at the following locations.

Kitty Hawk Kites/Carolina Outdoors
Monteray Plaza, NC 12, Corolla
(252) 453–3685, (800) FLY–THIS
Across from Jockey's Ridge, US 158, MP 13,
Nags Head
(252) 441–4124
Hatteras Landing, NC 12 , Hatteras Village
(252) 986–1446

If you're tired of our flat Outer Banks landscape and are itching for more than scaling lighthouse steps, try one of Kitty Hawk Kites/Carolina Outdoors's climbing walls. Two climbs and basic instruction cost $7.00 per person. Rappelling equipment, climbing shoes, and ropes are all part of the package.

At the Nags Head location, an hour training class is available for $19. The cost of the lesson includes equipment and climbs. Scale the 22-foot-high wall with four main routes and an overhang for extra challenges. At Monteray Plaza, there's a 25-foot climbing wall with four main routes and an overhang. Only the Nags Head location is open year-round, but only on the weekend in winter. The climbing wall in the Nags Head location is indoors, while the walls at Corolla and Hatteras are outside. You may want to consider the weather when you are choosing the wall you'll climb. Call for hours at other locations.

Dolphin Tours, Boat Rides, and Pirate Trips

Most Outer Banks boat cruises are included in our Watersports and Fishing chapters. However, a few unusual offerings are worth mentioning here as well. These trips, of course, are weather-dependent and available only during warmer spring and summer months. Reservations are recommended for each of these tours. Unlike sailing and more participatory water adventures, you don't have to be able to swim to enjoy these activities and you probably won't even get wet on board these boats as they slip along the shallow sounds.

Nags Head

Bodie Island Adventures
Nags Head–Manteo Causeway, Nags Head
(252) 441–6682
www.bodieislandadventures.com

If you'd like to get an up-close glimpse of bottlenose dolphins playing in the Roanoke Sound, this company has daily trips throughout the summer. Dolphin trips are led on a 40-foot pontoon boat that can accommodate up to 44 passengers. Along the way, you'll see the Bodie Island marshes, the Bodie Island lighthouse, Pelican Island, osprey nests, and a variety of other wildlife, including dolphin. This company also offers thrill-a-minute airboat rides along the same area south of Nags Head. Airboats, which can accommodate 14 people, are noisy and fast, so think twice about bringing very young children. Both trips cost $20 for adults and $10 for kids.

Nags Head Dolphin Watch
Willett's Wetsports, Nags Head–Manteo
Causeway, Nags Head
(252) 449–8999
www.dolphin-watch.com

If you're interested in bottlenose dolphins, this is the best way to get to know more about them. Now in its fifth year, the Nags Head Dolphin Watch is run by a team of independent dolphin researchers who conduct the trips in order to pay for their ongoing research. The team of expert naturalists leads dolphin watches through the Roanoke Sound three times a day, six days a week from the week before Memorial Day through the end of September. The two-hour tours are given on a new, speedy pontoon boat that holds 36 people. Along the way you'll see bottlenose dolphins and learn about their fascinating feeding and social behavior and also about local ecology, history, and wildlife. Cost is $20 for adults and $15 kids age 12 and under. The researchers take photos of the dolphins' dorsal fins on every trip, and they can call the dolphins they see by name.

Roanoke Island

The Crystal Dawn
Pirate's Cove Marina, Manteo
(252) 473-5577

Sunset cruises around Roanoke Island are offered every evening except Sunday throughout the summer on this sturdy, two-story 65-foot vessel that accommodates 95 passengers. Trips include commentary about the Outer Banks, while the boat cruises past Andy Griffith's house, Roanoke Island Festival Park, and Jockey's Ridge. The boat departs at 6:30 P.M., returning about 90 minutes later. Adult admission is $8.00 per person, and children 10 and younger pay $4.00 each. This is also a fishing headboat; for additional information see our Fishing chapter.

Outer Banks Cruises
Queen Elizabeth Ave., Manteo
(252) 473-1475
www.outerbankscruises.com

Outer Banks Cruises offers dolphin tours, sightseeing tours, and evening cruises aboard the 53-foot covered pontoon boat *Capt. Johnny*, which can accommodate 49 passengers. The dolphin-watch tours are offered in the Roanoke Sound from June through October, and ninth-generation native Capt. Stuart Wescott has a knack for finding the playful mammals. He even recognizes many of them by their fins and knows the names given them by local researchers. Dolphin sightings are guaranteed: If you don't see any on your trip, you are given a rain check for a free ride another time. The two-hour cruises cost $20 for adults and $15 for children age 12 and under. Evening cruises are available by charter; call for schedules and rates. The *Capt. Johnny* is docked on the Manteo waterfront next to the little bridge that heads to Roanoke Island Festival Park.

Downeast Rover
Manteo Waterfront Marina, Manteo
(252) 473-4866

A 55-foot topsail schooner, the *Downeast Rover* tall ship is a modern reproduction of a traditional 19th-century sailing vessel. Two-hour cruises onto the placid waters of Roanoke Sound delight passengers with views of dolphin, osprey, heron, and seabirds. A hands-on adventure is also possible on this lovely boat: Passengers can help trim the sails and take a turn at the wheel. Tickets can be purchased on the *Downeast Rover*, which also has a ship's store and restroom on board. Deck seating and a below-deck lounge are available. Daytime cruises are $12 for children age 2 to 12 and $20 for adults. Sunset cruises are $25 per person. Daytime cruises depart at 11:00 A.M. and 2:00 P.M. daily. Sunset cruises depart at 6:30 P.M. in the summer, and earlier in the spring and fall. Call for updates and off-season schedules. Reservations are recommended but not required. Private charters for wedding, parties, and other special occasions are available. The *Downeast Rover* sails from early spring to late fall.

Outer Banks Jet Boats
Manteo Waterfront Marina, Manteo
(252) 441-4124
www.outerbanksjetboats.com

Take an adventure-packed ride with a Coast Guard licensed captain on Outer Banks Jet Boats. The 34-foot boat, named *The Yellow Bird* and holding up to 24 passengers, departs on one-and-a-half-hour trips from Manteo's scenic waterfront. The first 30 minutes of your adventure take you on a search in the sound for dolphin, and they are usually pretty easy to find. Along your journey, you'll see osprey, pelicans, cormorants, gulls, ducks, and other wildlife. During the next 30 minutes, you tour Wanchese by water and explore a working fishing harbor and see old wrecks and large and small fishing boats. After viewing uninhabited islands and navigating natural waterways, the custom-built twin engine 700 HP boat will give you a final 30-minute thrill with its full jet-boat power. It's a fun ride for all ages. Trips depart between 9:00 A.M. and 5:30 P.M. and cost $20 for adults and $15 for children under 12. Call for reservations or purchase tickets at Carolina Outdoors at Manteo Waterfront.

Hatteras Island

Captain Clam
Oden's Dock, NC 12, Hatteras Village
(252) 986–2365

The *Captain Clam* is a fishing headboat (see our Fishing chapter), but it also offers family-style pirate cruises that are a hit with the kids. The pirate cruise is offered Wednesday, Thursday, and Friday in summer from 6:00 to 7:00 P.M. The crew dresses as pirates and tells tales about Blackbeard and the area's pirate history as you cruise around the Pamlico Sound. Complimentary swords and eye patches are given to every passenger. Cruises cost $15 per person and are available June through September. The boat can hold 40 people.

Miss Hatteras
Oden's Dock, NC 12, Hatteras Village
(252) 986–2365

The headboat *Miss Hatteras*, which ties up at Oden's Dock, offers dolphin tours on Wednesday, Thursday, and Friday evenings from 6:30 to 8:00 P.M. in summer. Bird-watching cruises are available; call Brian at 986–1363. Call for more information.

Ocracoke

The Windfall
The Community Store Docks, NC 12
Ocracoke Village
(252) 928–7245

You can sail around Blackbeard's former haunts aboard this traditional gaff-rigged schooner that seats up to 30 passengers. One-hour cruises depart from The Community Store docks several times daily during the summer months, and cost $15 per person, and $10 for kids. The longer sunset cruise is $20 per person. Call the number listed for the schedule.

Go-carts

If you're looking for a way to race around the Outer Banks without fear of getting a speeding ticket, several go-cart rental outlets offer riders a thrill a minute on exciting, curving tracks. Drivers have to be at least 12 years old to take the wheel at most of these places, but younger children are often allowed to strap themselves in beside adults to experience the fast-paced action.

Corolla

Corolla Raceway
TimBuck II Shopping Village
NC 12, Corolla
(252) 453–9100

Entering its sixth season in 2002, Corolla Raceway is the sister track of Nags Head Raceway. It is in TimBuck II Shopping Center and features one large track with 16 Indy cars. The go-cart raceway is open Easter through November. Corolla Raceway also has free-standing, gas-powered bumper cars. There's also a family arcade on-site. Summer hours are 10:00 A.M. until 11:00 P.M. daily.

Kill Devil Hills

Colington Speedway
1064 Colington Rd., Kill Devil Hills
(252) 480–9144

Colington Speedway features three tracks and about 40 Indy-style two-seaters or NASCAR-style 5.5 horsepower cars. Riders choose between a kiddie track, a family road course, or a slick track. The facility's gift shop features NASCAR items, Outer Banks souvenirs, and children's toys. Colington Speedway is open daily from Memorial Day through Labor Day until 10:00 P.M. The track is also open on weekends until 10:00 P.M. in the spring. Call for opening hours and more information.

Nags Head

Dowdy's Go-Karts
NC 12, MP 11, Nags Head
(252) 441–5122

This is one of the area's oldest go-cart tracks, across from the ocean next to Tortuga's Lie Shellfish Bar & Grill. All the cars are only a few years old and can take tight turns around the oval track. Outdoor bleachers provide a perfect place for parents to watch this noisy sport. These motorized carts can be ridden daily throughout the summer from midmorning until 11:00 P.M.

Dowdy's Amusement Park
US 158, MP 11, Nags Head
(252) 441–5122

A second go-cart track, also owned by the Dowdy's, awaits riders at this amusement park. This long, oval track is open evenings only from May through early September. There's also an indoor video arcade and snack bar here.

Speed-n-Spray Action Park
US 158, MP 15½, Nags Head
(252) 480–2877

This racetrack treats drivers to wild rides around quick curves that twist back toward the blacktop just as you think you might slip off into the sound. It's open from early May through September daily. Call for prices.

Nags Head Raceway
US 158, MP 16, Nags Head
(252) 480–4639

Speed demons and thrill seekers will revel in this chock-full-of-fun roadway, complete with two-seater carts and slick new racers. Drivers can time themselves trying to beat the clock or sprinting against their friends in hurried heats. Nags Head Raceway is open from April through Thanksgiving. Calmer pursuits can be had at the family arcade on the premises. Summer hours are from 10:00 A.M. until 11:00 P.M., seven days a week.

Hatteras Island

Waterfall Action Park
NC 12, Rodanthe
(252) 987–2213

This sound-to-sea amusement area offers the biggest selection of go-cart tracks on the Outer Banks—and more recreational opportunities in a single spot than anywhere else on Hatteras Island. Here, kids of all ages will enjoy eight separate race car tracks where drivers can test their skills on a different style vehicle at each pit stop. Wet racers are great for hot afternoon sprints against the wind—and other boaters. Bumper boats, two mini–golf courses, and a snack bar also are open from 11:00 A.M. to 10:00 P.M. daily from May through October.

Hang Gliding

The closest any human being will ever get to feeling like a bird is by flying beneath the brightly colored wings of a hang glider, with arms outstretched and only the wind all around. Lessons are available for fliers of all ages. Just watching these winged creatures soaring atop Jockey's Ridge or catching air lifts above breakers along the Atlantic is enough to make bystanders want to test their wings.

Kitty Hawk Kites/Carolina Outdoors
US 158, MP 13, Nags Head
(252) 441–4124, (800) FLY–THIS

Kitty Hawk Kites, the country's most popular hang-gliding school, offers a variety of ways to learn how to fly. The company's headquarters, in Nags Head across from Jockey's Ridge State Park, faces the main training site on the largest sand dune in the East. Here you can learn to fly solo 5 to 15 feet over the soft, forgiving sand, or you can soar through the clouds at altitudes up to 2,000 feet with an instructor. Either method, offered at various locations along the Outer Banks, is an exhilarating experience you'll never forget and undoubtedly will return home to brag about.

If hang gliding has kindled your desire to fly, Kitty Hawk Kites can also help you train to become a certified pilot. There are a number of packages designed to help you achieve your goal.

This school, the world's largest, has taught more than 250,000 students to fly since 1974. Beginning lessons on the dune are probably the most common method of learning to hang glide. In these classes, you will learn to launch and land the glider by

Soar over the fragile barrier islands for a view that's literally tops! PHOTO: COURTESY OF KITTY HAWK KITES

foot, and control the glider through the air approximately 5 to 15 feet above the sand and 35 to 40 feet in distance. You are alone in the glider to experience the thrill of flight, while your certified instructor runs alongside. No experience is necessary, and there are no age limitations. As long as you weigh within the parameters, you can fly! Dune lessons begin at $85 for beginners and $75 for advanced lessons, but these are 2001 prices and they may go up.

Tandem hang gliding instruction is offered at three locations along the Outer Banks. This lesson begins with you hooking into the glider with your instructor, who stays with you in the glider throughout the duration of your flight. Then you are towed up to 2,000 feet and released from the tow line, leaving you to soar freely through the clouds over breathtakingly beautiful terrain. There are no age restrictions, and no minimum weight requirement for tandem instruction, which is also accessible to the disabled. Kitty Hawk Kites offers two methods of tandem instruction: by plane or by boat. Aerotow instruction, offered at the Currituck County Airport in Maple, tows you behind an ultralight airplane and you land back where you launched, rolling in softly on wheels. Boat tow instruction, offered on both the northern and southern beaches, tows you behind a motorized boat and you glide smoothly back onto the water on pontoons. Rates for tandem lessons begin at around $110.

Reservations are required for most recreation, so be sure to call ahead. Discount packages are available. Ask about fun and exciting events for adventure enthusiasts of all ages offered throughout the season!

Horseback Riding

At one time, descendants of Spanish mustangs roamed much of the northern Outer Banks. Unfortunately, due to continued development and an increase in vehicular traffic, we've had to confine the last of these magnificent wild animals to the four-wheel-drive area north of Corolla

for their protection. If you have a four-wheel-drive vehicle and also possess some local knowledge, you might be able to find some of these horses on your own. Better yet, a couple of adventure tours are available that will deliver you and your family or friends right to these wild horses. The trip in itself is an experience not to be missed: the four-wheel-drive area has its share of spectacular scenery and engaging lore. An excursion into these parts with someone possessing local knowledge will make your trip all the more memorable. See the ATV Tours section of this chapter for horse-tour companies.

If you're seeking a place for horseback riding, Buxton Stables on Hatteras Island is the only venue on the Outer Banks. We can think of no finer way to experience the beach, especially in the cooler temperatures of spring or fall.

Hatteras Island

Buxton Stables
NC 12, Buxton
(252) 995–4659
Mild-mannered horses take riders on unforgettable tours from these wooden stables year-round. No experience is necessary for one-hour trail rides through the maritime forest of Buxton Woods, but you have to be an experienced rider who can sit at all gaits to enjoy the three-hour beach ride that winds through the woods, onto the wide sand, and into the surf. The horses are ridden with English saddles. Riders must be older than age 10 and weigh less than 200 pounds and not be pregnant. One-hour rides through the woods are offered in the afternoons and cost $40 per person. The three-hour trip costs $75 each and departs in the morning. The stables are open every day except Sunday. Call for reservations.

Kite Flying

Kite flying is not what it used to be. Thanks to modern technology, today it's an adventurous, interactive activity, even a competitive sport. And the Outer Banks is the perfect place to try your hand at it, since one of the top kite stores in the world, Kitty Hawk Kites, is here. There are plenty of open spaces to fly kites on the Outer Banks, though Jockey's Ridge State Park in Nags Head is the absolute best because it offers acres of space unobstructed by power lines and trees.

Kitty Hawk Kites/Carolina Outdoors
US 158, MP 13, Nags Head
(252) 441-4124
www.kittyhawk.com

This is the only dedicated kite store in the area, and it offers an enormous range of kites, from the backyard variety to the competition style, which come with an instructional video. The staff is knowledgeable about what they sell, and they can help you pick out just the right kite for your skill level. In addition to lessons and repairs, they offer kite-making workshops in the summer. There are several locations of Kitty Hawk Kites on the Outer Banks, but the Nags Head location across from Jockey's Ridge has the largest selection of kites. This company hosts several kite-flying events throughout the year, including the annual Outer Banks Stunt Kite Competition and Festival at Jockey's Ridge in October. See our Annual Events chapter for more kite events.

Miniature Golf Courses

No beach vacation is complete without the timeless activity of miniature golf. More than a dozen mini-golf courses adorn the Outer Banks from Corolla through Hatteras Island. Themed fairways featuring African animals, circus clowns, and strange obstacles await even the most amateur club-swinging families. Small children will enjoy the ease of some of these holes, and even skilled golfers can get into the par 3 grass courses that have been growing in numbers over recent years.

You can tee off at most places by 10:00 A.M. Many courses stay open past midnight for night owls to enjoy. Several of these attractions offer play-all-day packages for a single price. Almost all mini-golf courses operate seasonally, and since they are all outside, their openings are weather-dependent.

Corolla

The Grass Course
NC 12, Corolla
(252) 453-4198

Offering the Outer Banks's first natural grass course, these soundside greens are open seven days a week throughout the summer season from 10:00 A.M. to 11:00 P.M. The 18-hole course includes par 3s, 4s, and 5s. The undulating hills winding around natural dunes will provide intriguing challenges for beginning and better golfers. The course is open from April to October and at Thanksgiving and Christmas. Make sure to try The Grass Course's hot dogs and barbecue.

Kitty Hawk

The Promenade
US 158, MP¼, Kitty Hawk
(252) 261-4900

This family fun park includes Victorian-style buildings, turn-of-the-century streetlights, waterside recreation, a children's playground, and an 18-hole themed mini-golf course called Waterfall Greens. There's also a nine-hole, par 3, natural grass putting course, complete with separate putting greens; a target driving range; a par 3 chip-and-putt nine-hole course; and an 18-hole course. A restaurant, snack bar, and picnic tables are on-site. The Promenade is open Easter weekend through early October. Summer hours are from 8:30 A.M. to midnight, seven days a week.

Paradise Golf
US 158, MP 5½, Kitty Hawk
(252) 441-7626

More challenging than the usual mini-golf fairways, this natural grass course includes two 18-hole, par 56 courses. Most holes are 110 feet from the tees. The courses are open from 10:00 A.M. until midnight daily during summer. For one price ($7.00) you can play all day.

Kill Devil Hills

Lost Treasure Golf
US 158, MP 7¼, Kill Devil Hills
(252) 480–0142

One of the barrier islands' newer—and most attention-getting—mini–golf parks, Lost Treasure Golf features two 18-hole courses situated among five waterfalls that are illuminated with different colors at night. Kids will love the little train that carts them up to the first hole and through a series of caves and mines. Professor Hacker, a fictional adventurer, tells his story about gold and diamond expeditions that the kids can read about as they play. Lost Treasure Golf is open April through November. Hours are 9:00 A.M. to 11:00 P.M. daily in the summer and are decreased accordingly in the off-season.

Diamond Shoals Family Fun Park
US 158, MP 9¾, Kill Devil Hills
(252) 480–3553

Two 18-hole miniature golf courses await putters here from Easter through October. All the grass is natural. Also, enjoy a video arcade, a batting stadium where you can slam a softball or baseball up to 250 feet, paddleboats, waterslides, and a snack bar. Diamond Shoals is open from 10:00 A.M. to midnight during the summer. See the Waterslides section in this chapter for information on Diamond Shoals Family Fun Park's incredible waterslides.

Nags Head

Galaxy Golf
NC 12, MP 11, Nags Head
(252) 441–5875

Aliens, flying saucers, and outer space objects surround 36 lighted holes of mini–golf at this popular Outer Banks course on the Beach Road. Galaxy Golf is open on weekends in April, early May, Sep-

tember, and October and daily throughout the summer. In-season hours are 9:00 A.M. to midnight. Children younger than four with a paying adult play free. The price doesn't change after dark as it does on many mini–golf courses. You can play all day for $7.00.

Blackbeard's Golf and Arcade
US 158, MP 16, Nags Head
(252) 441–4541

The Outer Banks's most infamous pirate wields his 6-foot sword above these greens. Open daily, summers only, until at least 10:00 P.M., Blackbeard's includes a video arcade if you're tired of putting around.

Jurassic Putt
US 158, MP 16, Nags Head
(252) 441–6841

Life-size models of dinosaurs from the Jurassic period hover over and among Jurassic Putt's greens, delighting kids and adults alike. Two 18-hole courses wind through caves and streams and around the dinosaur models. Jurassic Putt is open daily from mid-March until November. Hours are 9:00 A.M. until midnight. Call or stop by for rates. You can play all day for $7.00.

Hatteras Island

Avon Golf
NC 12, Avon
(252) 995–5480

Adjacent to the Avon Pier, this 18-hole, natural grass course is open from 11:00 A.M. to 11:00 P.M., seven days a week all summer. You can play as many games as you can squeeze in from noon until 6:00 P.M. for only $7.00. In the off-season, you can play all day for $7.00. Avon Golf is open from Easter through the week after Thanksgiving, depending on business.

Cool Wave Ice Cream Shop and Miniature Golf
NC 12, Buxton
(252) 995–6366

Located in the neighborhood of the Cape Hatteras Lighthouse, this nine-hole course is open from Easter through Thanksgiving. Summer hours are noon until 10:00 P.M., seven days a week. Call for prices. If you play one round of nine holes, the second time around is free. Ice cream, milk shakes, and the best banana splits on Hatteras provide extra incentive to play a good game.

Frisco Mini Golf and Go-Karts
NC 12, Frisco
(252) 995–6325
The 18-hole championship miniature golf course here is a little more challenging than your average miniature golf game, though all levels of players will enjoy the experience. Waterfalls splash amidst the well-manicured course, and there are goldfish for the children to feed. For $6.00 you can play as many games as you want during the day, but after 6:00 P.M., it's $6.00 per game. There are also two go-cart tracks, a concession stand, and an arcade on the premises.

Movie Theaters

On some steamy summer afternoons or rainy Saturday nights, there's no better place to be than inside a dark, air-conditioned movie theater catching the latest flick with a friend. First-run movies are offered at most Outer Banks theaters. Popcorn, candy, and sodas are, of course, sold at all movie houses.

Corolla

RC Theaters Corolla Movies 4
Monteray Plaza, NC 12, Corolla
(252) 453–2999
This seasonal establishment in Monteray Plaza includes four wide screens and is open from May through Labor Day. The theater reopens for shows again from Thanksgiving through New Year's Day. Movies are shown seven days a week from 2:00 P.M. to midnight. Tickets cost $7.00 for adults, and $5.00 for children younger than 11. Matinees cost $5.50 for children and adults.

Southern Shores

RC Theaters Marketplace Twin Cinema
The Marketplace
US 158, MP 1, Southern Shores
(252) 261–7866
Two screens feature first-run movies in this theater year-round, seven days a week. Matinee prices before 6:00 P.M. are $5.50 for adults. Tickets for children and seniors cost $5.00 in the evening. Evening-only shows are offered during the off-season weekdays. Movies begin at 2:00 P.M. on weekends and throughout the summer. Evening shows cost $7.00 for adults.

Kitty Hawk

RC Theaters Kitty Hawk
US 158, MP 4, Kitty Hawk
(252) 441–5630
Open in the summer only, this movie house has two screens that show films seven days a week, from 2:00 P.M. until midnight. Tickets are $7.00 for adults and $5.50 for children.

Nags Head

RC Theatres Cineplex 4
US 158, MP 10½, Nags Head
(252) 441–1808
Offering four screens and first-run movies year-round, this large movie house shows films all day on weekends and throughout the summer, and on evenings only in the off-season. Admission is $7.00 for adults and $5.00 for children. Matinee shows are $5.50 for everyone.

Roanoke Island

Pioneer Theatre
113 Budleigh St., Manteo
(252) 473–2216
The nation's oldest theater operated continuously by one family, the Pioneer is filled with nostalgia and smells of just-buttered popcorn. And it's been showing great

flicks since 1934. For the $4.00 admission price—and the old-fashioned feel of the place—it can't be beat. Even the popcorn, sodas, and candy are a great deal. The Pioneer is open year-round, and all movies start at 8:00 P.M. daily. Listings change weekly on Fridays; call the above number for a synopsis of the current show's plot. See Attractions for more information.

Hatteras Island

RC Theatres Hatteras Cineplex 4
Hatteras Island Plaza, NC 12, Avon
(252) 995-9060

Offering four screens and first-run movies year-round, this large movie house shows films all day on weekends and throughout the summer, and on evenings only in the off-season. Admission is $7.00 for adults and $5.00 for children. Matinee shows are $5.50 for everyone.

Nature Trail Hikes

The Outer Banks is home to several diverse ecosystems that house a wide variety of wildlife. If you love nature, you'll love heading out on one of many self-guided nature trails that allow you to see the diversity of the Outer Banks up close. You can hike in wildlife refuges, across sand dunes, and through maritime forests. The National Park Service offers some guided walks; call (252) 473–2111 or visit www.nps.gov/caha for more information.

Corolla

Audubon Wildlife Sanctuary at Pine Island

An unmarked trail leads through this 5,000-acre wildlife sanctuary, a protected habitat for birds, deer, rabbits and a variety of plants. Park at The Sanderling Inn to access the 2.5-mile soundside path through a portion of the sanctuary.

Nags Head

Nags Head Woods Preserve

Part of The Nature Conservancy, Nags Head Woods is a preserved maritime forest with a diversity of flora and fauna. There are more than 5 miles of trails through forest, dunes, swamp, and pond habitats. You'll also see 19th-century cemeteries. For maps and start locations, go to the visitor center at 701 West Ocean Acres Drive in Kill Devil Hills or call (252) 441–2525.

Jockey's Ridge State Park

Climbing up the tallest sand dune on the East Coast is a hike in itself, but there are also two nature trails that wind through the lower regions of the dune. The Soundside Nature Trail is an easy 45-minute walk, and the Tracks in the Sand Trail is a 1.5-mile walk. Start at the state park visitor center at MP 12 in Nags Head.

Roanoke Island

Thomas Hariot Nature Trail at Fort Raleigh

This trail winds through a heavily wooded area from the Fort Raleigh National Historic Site to the Roanoke Sound. Along the way are several interpretive markers with Hariot's descriptions of Roanoke Island in the 16th century. Call the Fort Raleigh National Historic Site at (252) 473–5772 for information.

Freedmen's Trail

This 2-mile trail commemorates the history of the Freedmen's Colony, a Roanoke Island community that provided a safe haven for freed slaves during the Civil War. Access to the trail is near The Elizabethan Gardens entrance, and exhibits are at the end of the trail on the Roanoke Sound. Call the National Park Service for information at (252) 473-5772.

Mainland

Alligator River National Wildlife Refuge

Two trails lead through this refuge. Sandy Ridge Wildlife Trail starts at the south end of the dirt Buffalo City Road. The trail, a half-mile out and a half-mile back, has footpaths and a boardwalk. Creef Cut Wildlife Trail starts on US 64 at the intersection of Milltail Road. A kiosk with parking marks the trailhead. It's also a half-mile out and back. It has a fishing dock, an overlook, and a boardwalk. Both trails are wheelchair-accessible. Call (252) 473-1131 for information.

Bodie Island

Bodie Island Dike Trail and Pond Trail

Starting at the Bodie Island Lighthouse, there are two trails that wind through marsh and wetlands to the sound. Call the light station at (252) 441-5711 for information.

Pea Island

Pea Island National Wildlife Refuge

North Pond Trail starts behind the Pea Island Visitor Center and leads hikers on a half-mile, 30-minute brisk walk around the refuge. The quarter-mile Salt Flats Trail starts at the north end of the North Pond Trail. These are favorite walks for bird-watchers year-round, but especially in late fall and winter when migrating swans, ducks, and geese winter here. Call (252) 987-2394 for information.

Buxton

Buxton Woods Nature Trail

Starting at Cape Point Campground, this .75-mile trail leads through maritime forest, across dunes, and into freshwater marshes. Small plaques along the way explain the fragile maritime forest ecosystem.

Ocracoke

Hammock Hills Trail

This .75-mile trail, about a 30-minute walk, leads through the salt marsh and forest. The trailhead is north of the village on NC 12; signs will direct you to it. Call the Ocracoke Island Visitor Center at (252) 928-4531 for information.

Portsmouth Island

This ghost-town island is accessible only by boat, but once you get there you'll find numerous trails that lead on a fascinating exploration of this island. The self-guided trails lead you past abandoned but restored buildings. A 2-mile-long trail leads from the village to the beach through the heart of the island. Call Cape Lookout National Seashore for information at (252) 728-2250.

Parasailing

If you've always wanted to float high above the water beneath a colorful parachute, opportunities for such peaceful adventures await you at a variety of locations along the Outer Banks. Although a boat pulls you from below, allowing the wind to lift you toward the clouds, you don't get wet on these outdoor adventures over the sounds unless you want to. You take off and land on the back of the boat. Riders don't even have to know how to swim to soar with the sea gulls above whitecaps and beach cottages. People of any age, without any athletic ability at all, will enjoy parasailing and find it one of their most memorable experiences. And it's safe too; unbreakable ropes are standard.

Corolla

Kitty Hawk Watersports
TimBuck II, NC 12, Corolla
(252) 453–6900

Parasail flights are offered daily throughout the summer at this shop, owned by Kitty Hawk Sports. Rates are set according to the height you choose to soar at—call for rates and schedules.

Duck

North Duck Watersports
NC 12, Duck
(252) 261–4200

This watersports center is 3 miles north of Duck, on the border of Duck and Sanderling. Parasailing trips are offered at heights from 400 to 1,400 feet above the Currituck Sound. Call ahead for reservations and rates. Parasailing is offered in the spring, summer, and fall only. This company also rents Wave Runners, boats, windsurfing gear, and kayaks.

Sunset Watersports
NC 12, Duck
(252) 261–7100
www.barrierislandboats.com

Specializing in single, tandem, and triple flights, this was one of the original parasailing locations on the Outer Banks. All vessels that give you your ride are Coast Guard–inspected and are able to take passengers up 400 to 1,400 feet. Parasailing is available from May through October. Prices start at $59 and go up to $257 for a three-person flight at 1,400 feet.

Kitty Hawk

Promenade Watersports
US 158, MP ¼, Kitty Hawk
(252) 261–4400

Promenade offers parasailing with an experienced captain in the Currituck Sound. Persons of any age can take off for a single, tandem, or triple ride up to 1,400 feet. Prices start at $49 for a single-person ride.

Nags Head

The Waterworks
US 158, MP 17, Nags Head
(252) 441–8875

Whatever height you wish to reach, parasailing captains from The Waterworks can take you there. Uplifting experiences are offered daily from April through November. These 8- to 15-minute flights allow you to float at 400 to 1,400 feet; cost depends on how high you want to fly.

Nags Head Watersports & Kawasaki
Nags Head–Manteo Causeway, Nags Head
(252) 480–2236

Nags Head Water Sports & Kawasaki offers parasailing in addition to its complete line of watersports retail and rental equipment. Solo and tandem flights to a variety of heights are piloted by a U.S.C.G.–certified/licensed captain. And for those left waiting while you're soaring with the osprey and pelicans, there's a small picnic area, a boat dock, and a sandy beach for the kids on the premises. Rental operations run from mid-May through October, though the shop is open year-round. Call for parasail prices and rental reservations in season.

Hatteras Island

Hatteras Watersports
NC 12, Salvo
(252) 987–2306

Hatteras Watersports offers parasailing trips from June through September. You can take single or tandem flights without ever getting wet. Flight height ranges from 700 to 1,300 feet, and prices range from $49 for a single, 700-foot flight to $139 for a tandem 1,300-foot flight. Reservations are required.

Island Parasail
NC 12, Avon
(252) 995–0177

All summer long, you can soar over the Pamlico Sound beneath a rainbow-colored

Parasail and soar with the gulls over the Outer Banks. PHOTO: COURTESY OF GEORGIA BEACH

parachute based at this Avon outpost. Ten-minute flights are offered from 9:30 A.M. to 6:30 P.M. daily at heights of 700 feet or 1,200 feet. Single rates range from $45 to $65, and tandem flights are available. As long as you're strapped in and sitting on air, go ahead and take it to the top. You'll be glad you saw everything you can see from high above the salty marshes and shallow sound. Island Parasail is closed from December 1 through March 1.

Races

Nags Head Woods Annual 5K Run
Nags Head Woods Preserve, Kill Devil Hills
(252) 441-2525
The Nags Head Woods Run is a well-loved spring tradition on the Outer Banks.

Close to 400 runners, from ages 6 to 60 and beyond, gather to run (or walk) the soft dirt road that winds through this rare maritime forest. Afterwards, there's an awards ceremony, then a big party at Quagmire's oceanfront restaurant. There is no race-day registration and it fills up fast, so you must register early. Call the preserve to enter. The 2002 date is May 18.

Outer Banks Triathlon
Roanoke Island
(252) 480-0050
The Dare Voluntary Action Center (DVAC) sponsors this annual sanctioned sprint-distance triathlon each September. The .6-mile swim, 15-mile bicycle ride, and 3.1-mile run are held on Roanoke Island, starting at the Old Swimming Hole on Airport Road next to the North Carolina

Aquarium. Contact DVAC at the number above or register at www.active.com.

Advice 5K Turkey Trot
Duck
(252) 255-1050

The annual Turkey Trot is a Thanksgiving Day tradition in the village of Duck. The race starts at Advice 5¢, a bed-and-breakfast in the village, and ends at the Red Sky Cafe, where there is a fun post-race party. It's the perfect way to work up a Turkey Day appetite. There is no race-day registration. You must register in advance at the Red Sky Cafe at 1197 Duck Road or by mail: Advice 5K, c/o Advice 5¢, P.O. Box 8278, Duck, North Carolina 27949. Entry fee for walkers and runners is $20. The race is limited to 350 people.

Nags Head Festival of Thanksgiving 5K Run
Nags Head
(252) 441-5508
www.townofnagshead.com

Burn off those Thanksgiving calories. On the Saturday after Thanksgiving, the town of Nags Head sponsors a 5K run on a certified course through the neighborhood streets of The Village at Nags Head. This is a family event, and walkers are welcome. The race starts at 8:30 A.M., and there are fun events to follow during the town festival. Call the number above to register.

Unofficial Beach Road 5K
Nags Head
(252) 441-9330

Looking for a different way to spend New Year's Eve? Try running 3.1 miles in the dark on a freezing cold night. This Unofficial 5K Run, now in its 13th year, is held at 11:00 P.M. on December 31, starting at Don Gatos restaurant at MP 11 on the Beach Road. The run winds through the roads between the highways and ends up back at the restaurant. It's purely fun, not for the certification crowd. No registration is required. Just show up, pay the $15 entry fee and get your T-shirt, and run. Everyone is finished running by midnight and there's a big celebration at Don Gatos. Running with a flashlight is a good idea because there are some dark places along the way.

Tennis

Many cottage rental developments throughout the Outer Banks have private tennis courts for their guests. Outdoor public tennis courts include the following free courts:

• Kill Devil Hills—two hard-surface courts are located near the Kill Devil Hills Fire Department at MP 6 on US 158 and four hard-surface courts are beside the Kill Devil Hills Water Plant on Mustian Street.

• Nags Head—a public court is behind Kelly's Restaurant, off US 158 at MP 10½.

• Roanoke Island—courts are available at Manteo High School on Wingina Avenue and at Manteo Middle School on US 64/264 after school hours.

• Hatteras Island—courts are available at Cape Hatteras School on NC 12 in Buxton after school hours.

If you don't own a racquet or left yours back on the mainland, you can lease one by the day or week from Ocean Atlantic Rentals in Corolla, (252) 453-2440; Duck, (252) 261-4346; Nags Head, (252) 441-7823; or Avon, (252) 995-5868.

Corolla

Pine Island Racquet Club
NC 12, between Corolla and Duck
(252) 453-8525

Offering the Outer Banks's only indoor tennis courts, Pine Island is 2.5 miles north of The Sanderling Inn. It is open to the public year-round for recreational play, and several tournaments are held here each season.

Three hard-surface courts are under a vaulted roof for air-conditioned or heated comfort, while two clay courts and two platform tennis courts are outdoors. There are two platform tennis courts and indoor squash and racquetball courts as well as an upper-level observation deck overlooking all indoor courts. Restroom, locker, and shower facilities are included.

Pine Island also has two ball machines, a radar gun to time your serves, and a videotape analysis machine to help improve your game. U.S. P.T.R. professional Rick Ostlund and his assistant Betty Wright teach clinics for adults and children and offer individualized instruction at any skill level. The pro shop sells racquets, clothes, and tennis accessories and provides stringing services.

Reservations are suggested for indoor and outdoor courts. It costs $20 an hour in the off-season and $24 an hour in the summer months for outdoor facilities. Indoor courts cost $24 an hour September through May and $28 an hour June through August. Racquetball and squash courts cost $14 per hour. Pine Island is open every day except Christmas from at least 9:00 A.M. in the off-season and from 8:00 A.M. in season.

Waterslides, Arcades, and Other Amusements

On those hot afternoons when you're ready for a break from sand and salt water, slip on down to a water park, and splash into one of its big pools. Most of these parks are open daily during the summer—some well into the evening. Waterslides generally close on rainy days.

Among the recreational outposts, many include video arcades in their offerings, but the Outer Banks's amusement centers also offer brightly lit computerized games and other unusual activities. We can't list everything the owners of these establishments include, so you'll have to experience these places for yourself to discover all the surprises in store.

Nags Head

Diamond Shoals Family Fun Park
US 158, MP 9³/₄, Kill Devil Hills
(252) 480–3553

Parents and kids alike will enjoy this enormous wet playground that includes three waterslides, two tubular slides that you ride down on an inner tube, and one open body slide. You are dropped with the other frolicking bathers into a wide, 48-inch-deep catch pool.

Diamond Shoals is open from 10:00 A.M. until midnight daily, but the waterslide closes at 8:00 P.M. The waterslide is open Memorial Day to Labor Day. There's also a kiddie pool for little tykes. All-day passes are available for sliders and spectators or for the kiddie pool only. Season passes are also available. Call for prices.

Paddleboats, a video arcade, batting stadium, snack bar, sunbathing deck with lounge chairs, and mini–golf courses also are on the premises.

Playhouse Family Fun Center
105 Mall Dr., Nags Head
(252) 441–3277

The Playhouse Family Fun Center is nestled into a small shopping area between US 158 and the Beach Road at MP 14. This indoor amusement park is a great place for kids when the weather acts up or when they're beach-worn—offering paintball, moonwalk, video arcade, food court, and more.

Hatteras Island

Waterfall Action Park
NC 12, Rodanthe
(252) 987–2213

You can't miss this palm-tree-lined playground, geared for hours of fun for both adults and kids. An Outer Banks fixture for more than 20 years, this amusement park has more than 20 rides and the area's only bungee jumping outlet for those dyed-in-the-wool daredevils. Two waterslides, the Corkscrew and the Cyclone, give heart-thumping, thrill-filled rides.

But this wonderland has a multitude of other offerings: two mini–golf courses, scale-model Grand Prix race cars, Winston Cup stock cars, Outlaw sprint cars, NASCAR super trucks, and free-fall go-karts—not to mention speedboats and bumper cars. Children have to be at least 12 years old to ride the adult rides. Kiddie Land features rides for the age 3 to 9 set. There's no admission charge to get into the park; individual tickets for rides start at $6. Your best deal can be had with one of the 40 combination tickets, which save you more money the more you ride. Waterfall Action Park is open daily 10:00 A.M. to 9:00 P.M. from Memorial Day through Labor Day.

Frisco Mini Golf and Go-Karts
NC 12, Frisco
(252) 995–6325

This miniature golf and go-cart establishment also has an arcade that can keep the kids entertained on a rainy day. In the 1,800-square-foot arcade are pool tables, air hockey, video games, and other games. A concession booth sells ice cream, snow cones, cotton candy, hot dogs, and drinks.

Yoga

Islands Yoga
Phoenix Shops, 107 Budleigh St., Manteo
(252) 202–YOGA
www.islandsyoga.com

Islands Yoga, based in the Phoenix Fitness Studio in downtown Manteo, offers hatha yoga classes several times a week. Workshops are offered occasionally, and private lessons are available. Class schedules and workshop information can be found on the Web site or by calling the above number. Drop-in students are welcome.

Yoga Teachers Association of the Outer Banks
P.O. Box 801, Nags Head, NC 27959
(252) 480–1331

The Yoga Teachers Association represents several hatha yoga teachers and can offer information about classes in Manteo, Nags Head, Kill Devil Hills, Kitty Hawk, Hatteras Island, and Corolla. Call for class descriptions, locations, and schedules. Private yoga sessions are popular with vacationers, and the Association can find an instructor to come to you. Workshops are occasionally offered; call or write if you'd like to be on the mailing list.

Watersports

Water is the Outer Banks's biggest draw. Everywhere you look on the Outer Banks there's wet, wonderful H_2O—the deep, blue Atlantic Ocean; the wide, shallow Currituck, Croatan, Roanoke, and Pamlico Sounds; brackish bays and estuaries teeming with wildlife; thick, sopping marshes; and dark, man-made canals sluicing through the islands. And everywhere you look there are people trying to get on or in the water. Whether it's on a surfboard, a kite surfer, a JetSki, a kayak, or just in a pair of swimming trunks, everyone eventually finds their way into or on the water. Numerous watersports establishments are more than happy to accommodate anyone's wish to get wet.

Surfing, windsurfing, and kite-surfing, or kite-boarding, are among the area's most popular watersports, next to fishing, which we cover in a chapter of its own. Each year, thousands of novice to expert athletes flock to the Outer Banks to whet their appetites for these outdoor adventures. The Outer Banks is renowned as having the best surf breaks on the East Coast, and the constant wind and wide sounds make for perfect kite-surfing conditions. Be forewarned: You too may become addicted and find yourself, like many other watersports enthusiasts, moving to these barrier islands to be closer to the waves and shallow sounds year-round. All of the gear you'll need is available at local surf shops and outfitters. Some Outer Banks surf shops lease body boards and skimboards to daredevils who like to skirt the shoreline breakers.

The use of personal watercraft, including JetSkis, Sea Doos, and Wave Runners, has exploded in popularity. Rental outposts are established on the sound shores all along the Outer Banks to satisfy people's need for speed. The less-invasive sports of kayaking, canoeing, and sailing also are available, with ecotours and sunset cruises becoming increasingly popular pastimes. For more unusual endeavors, the National Park Service offers occasional snorkeling expeditions for families, and local dive shops will take you out wreck-diving in the Graveyard of the Atlantic. Divers from the world over come to the Outer Banks to explore the numerous shipwrecks on the ocean floor. Several outfitters along the barrier islands rent powerboats for near-shore fishing and water-skiing.

Weather, of course, plays a big factor in whether a particular watersport is currently desirable or even advisable. Many area surf shops offer surfing hotlines and wave or wind updates so you can check the conditions before you get geared up. The waters are generally warm enough to get in from late May through late September. Even in the off-season months, waters can stay warm enough for bathers to enjoy a quick frolic. In the winter, real watersport devotees take the plunge with a wetsuit. Local boaters and paddlers get out on the water every month of the year and relish the smattering of warm days that we usually get in the dead of winter.

Some water workouts require special training and equipment, and shops and sports schools in almost every area of the Outer Banks rent and teach whatever you need to know. (Also, see our Waves and Weather chapter for information about riptides and other hazards.)

Whether you're an athletic adventurer or a couch potato, you should be able to find exactly what you want in the way of watersports. Kayaking, for example, requires neither physical prowess nor extraordinary skill if you take a few minutes to learn to do it properly. On the flip side, scuba diving in these waters is dangerous without proper training and experience. Generally, you'll have fun sharing the wet wonderlands with the fish and birds—and scores of other water lovers who are just as thrilled as you are to be part of the Outer Banks water scene.

In this chapter we give you the rundown of the watersports and a list of places to rent and buy equipment and take lessons. We list prices to give you a general idea of how much things cost, but be aware that many of the prices may change slightly by the time this book is printed.

Surfing

Warmer than New England waters and wielding more consistent waves than most Florida beaches, the Outer Banks's surf is reputed to have the best breaks on the East Coast. Local surfing experts explain that since we are set out farther into the ocean in deeper waters than other coastal regions, our beaches pick up more swells and wind patterns than any place around. Piers, shipwrecks, and offshore sandbars also create unusual wave patterns. Along with those swells, the Outer Banks has the added bonus of sharp drop-offs and troughs right off shore, which make the waves break with more power and force.

The beaches from Corolla through Ocracoke are some of the only spots left that don't have strict surfing regulations:

Surfing along the Outer Banks dates back to the 1930s. PHOTO: COURTESY OF J. AARON TROTMAN

As long as you keep yourself leashed to your board and stay at least 300 feet away from public piers, you won't get a surfing citation.

Outer Banks historian David Stick said he saw the first local surfboard in the 1930s, when native Tommy Fearing built one after hearing about guys riding waves on big boards in Hawaii. He said it took six men to handle the board, a clumsy 9-foot giant made of juniper. Whether anyone caught waves on this board may be information lost to history, but wouldn't present-day surfers love to get a look at that board!

By the late 1960s, station wagons loaded with teenagers and their surfboards began arriving on the sparsely populated Outer Banks. Surfers skirted the soft sands each weekend, traveling from Virginia Beach, Virginia, and Ocean City, Maryland, to hang 10 in the Outer Banks's huge waves. Hatteras Island native Johnny Connor Jr. said boys sold their boards when they ran out of money. He bought several. He then turned around and rented those surfboards to local friends and newcomers who also wanted to ride the waves.

Cape Hatteras's black-and-white striped lighthouse, at the elbow of the barrier islands, had become known as a magnet for East Coast swell seekers by the early 1970s.

In the late 1970s, the East Coast Surfing Championships started here, and they're still held here. The U.S. Championships were held on the Outer Banks in 1978 and 1982. Each summer, and during winter storms, famous surfers can be seen riding the competition circuit along the Atlantic or just catching waves.

The Outer Banks surfing subculture, those surfers who live here year-round, is a far cry from the young, sun-bleached stereotype. Lawyers, engineers, middle-aged parents, waiters, doctors, construction workers, architects, and restaurateurs all have been known to rearrange busy schedules to catch a few waves. In this region, a company "board meeting" usually refers to a surf break for co-workers. When there are waves, almost all surfers, young and old alike, make the necessary excuses to get in the water. If your house-construction crew doesn't show up one day or the grocery store is short on bag-boys, assume there are waves.

Shapers along the barrier islands design, shape, and sell their own boards, with prices ranging from $100 for used models to $600 for custom styles. Some stores offer lessons for beginning surfers, and many rent boards for as little as $10 a day plus a deposit. Don't forget board wax, or you won't be riding very long.

The best surfing is from late August through November in hurricane season, when swells from storms are likely to come rolling toward shore. Mid-summer is traditionally the worst time for surfing. On small summer waves it's more fun to surf on a longboard.

Surfing is a strenuous sport, and you need a good amount of upper-body strength to be able to swim well in wicked waves. But with a variety of board lengths—and more than 90 miles of ocean-front to choose from—there are usually breaks to accommodate almost every surfer's style and stamina.

Since the beaches are getting increasingly crowded with summer surfers, some folks understandably don't want to reveal their favorite spots to catch waves. Plus, breaks, which are affected by shifting sandbars, change every year. After fall hurricane season and a winter's worth of nor'easters, no one really knows which breaks will fade or where they'll reappear. It takes some looking around in the spring to find new breaks and say goodbye to old ones.

We'll share some of the best-known haunts with you here, but remember there may be better ones by the time this book is printed. Piers always make for good breaks because of the sandbars that form around them. In Corolla, there is a good break on the beach in front of the Corolla Light swimming pool. You can't park there unless you're staying in the resort, so park at the south ramp road next to the lighthouse and walk up the beach. Swan Beach in the four-wheel-drive area is also good to try. Kitty Hawk Pier in Kitty Hawk and Avalon Pier in Kill Devil Hills each boast ample parking and pretty good waves. Also check out the area around First and Second Streets in Kill Devil Hills. Nags Head Pier is a good spot, but also check out the beaches north and south of there, especially around Milepost 13.

When the swells are coming from the south, the Hatteras Island beaches have the best waves. If you don't mind hiking across the dunes with a board under your arm, Pea Island and Coquina Beach both have waves worth the walk. Rodanthe has always been a popular destination, and its name sparks fond recognition with surfers all over the world. Just north of Rodanthe, the "S-turns" are renowned for surf breaks. The name refers to the old S curves on NC 12, which are no longer there since the road was straightened out. If there are waves, you'll have no trouble spotting the area because you'll see hundreds of surfers squeezing into wetsuits along the roadside. The surf is just a short hop over the dunes from the road. The ramps north and south of Salvo are also worth a try. Ramp 34, just north of Avon, is another location, as are the turnout north of Buxton, ramp 49 in Frisco, Frisco Pier, and the public beach access area between Frisco and Hatteras Village.

The best and biggest waves by far roll in around the original site of Cape Hatteras Lighthouse. Here at Cape Point, the beaches jut closest to the Gulf Stream and face in two directions, doubling the chances for good conditions. Concrete and steel groins jut out into the Atlantic though, so beware of being tossed toward one of these head-bashing barriers.

Surf jargon measures waves in reference to body parts. In the summer, waves along the Outer Banks average knee to waist high, meaning 2 to 3 feet. Fall and winter swells can be head high or double overhead (6 to 8 feet). Many areas along the barrier islands also have strong rip currents, strange sandbars, and shipwrecks—so always surf with a friend and stay alert of water, weather, and beach conditions. You'll need a wetsuit for surfing in the spring, fall, and winter. If you can stand that first frigid shock of jumping in, winter rides are well worth it.

With hurricanes and other summer storms often skirting off the coast, swells here can usually keep surfers plenty happy. Bear in mind that Atlantic waves are far less predictable than West Coast waves. One day Mother Ocean will serve up perfectly curled waves and prime conditions for great rides. The very next day, however, the fickle Atlantic may offer only a few ripples lapping meekly at the shoreline.

How to Surf

If you've never tried to surf, you might want to begin on a body board. Area surf shops rent these short, light boards that will allow you to get the feel of the waves without having to stand up. You ride a body board lying on your belly, and they're easier to maneuver than surfboards. Once you get the feel of riding waves, progress to a surfboard. Longboards are easier to surf on so try one of those first. Shortboards are for high-performance shredding—they're lighter so they go faster and perform quicker turns.

Strong swimming skills are a prerequisite for any surfer. Like most sports, the younger you start, the easier it is to learn. If you feel confident braving waves 100 yards off the beach and are patient enough to learn to work with, rather than

Before you get in the water, you have to find the spot with the best wave breaks. PHOTO: MOLLY HARRISON

against, the Atlantic, you can learn to ride waves on the Outer Banks.

Start off in small swells that break cleanly and evenly. You'll probably want to work in uncrowded areas at first because it's difficult to maneuver surfboards around other people—and good surfers won't want you getting in their way.

Paddling is the first step. Lie on your stomach, with your chest across the thickest part of the surfboard. Paddle your arms in a freestyle stroke, practicing until you can really control the board and find a good balance spot. Paddle around just beyond shore break, and when you're comfortable, stroke on out into the real waves.

To ride a swell, you have to get slightly ahead of it and travel at almost the same speed as it's moving. Paddle out past the breaking waves, then turn around until you're facing the beach. Watch your back until you see a swell forming. Waves are cyclical, so once you've watched a few, it will be easier to gauge the timing you'll need to paddle with the wave and let it crest beneath you. You'll know when the wave

begins to carry you. Just as in body surfing, you can feel it carry you forward fast.

When you're positioned in the breaking wave, use your arms, as if you're doing a push-up, to stand up on the speeding board. Don't try to get to your knees first. Just pop up on your feet and keep your arms outstretched for balance. Place one foot in front of the other, about shoulder-length apart, and enjoy the ride.

Surf only until you've had enough, and don't exhaust yourself. This sport takes incredible stamina and strength and can get the best of you if you've been out in the Atlantic too long. Once you've gotten good enough to hang with other surfers, respect their space. Do your best to stay out of others' way and never cut in on a wave that someone else is riding

Surf Reports

A couple of local radio stations offer daily surf reports in season. The COAST 93.7 airs its report at 8:35 A.M.; WOBR 95.3 runs its update at 12:20 P.M.

Most surf shops have an even more up-to-the-minute pulse on the surf, but not all provide a formal "surf line" service. Following is a list of numbers to call for the daily wave report. Most shops give the scoop only on the portion of the beach in their geographical area.

Corolla Surf Shop, Corolla, (252) 453–WAVE

Wave Riding Vehicles, Kitty Hawk, (252) 261–3332

Whalebone Surf Shop, Nags Head, (252) 441–6747

The Pit, Kill Devil Hills, (252) 480–3128

Rodanthe Surf Shop, Rodanthe, (252) 987–2435

Natural Art Surf Shop, Buxton, (252) 995–4646

Hatteras Wind N Surf, Avon, (888) WND–SURF

Besides calling for a surf report, you may want to see the conditions for yourself. The Internet has made it so you don't even have to leave your house to check on waves. For an on-line surf report, log on to surf chex.com or www.outer-banks.nc.us/surf, or check out surf cams for the following locations:

Kitty Hawk Pier: surfchex.com
Avalon Pier: avalonpier.com
Avon Pier: windnsurf.com

Surf Shops

Ranging from sublime to specialized to hip, the Outer Banks is inundated with surf shops. And the shops are the hot spots for wave riders of all ages and skill levels. Each summer, surf shop managers post competition schedules for beginners through surfing-circuit riders near the storefronts. Most shops stock gear, and many offer instruction during the season. The following list highlights some favorites of Outer Banks surfers.

Corolla

Corolla Surf Shop
Corolla Light Village Shops
110-A Austin Dr., Corolla
(252) 453–WAVE
TimBuck II Shopping Village, NC 12, Corolla
(252) 453–9273
www.corollasurfshop.com

Corolla Surf Shop is a full-service shop with boards, lessons, sales, repairs, and rentals. Its second store—in the TimBuck II shopping center—has all the goodies of the first store, including a portion of the surfer's museum. The store also has a full line of new surfboards for sale (more than 100 boards are in stock). A good stock of used boards is available for purchase, along with new skateboards, skimboards, and body boards. The store also carries a full skateboard department, clothing, shoes, shades, and jewelry.

Surf lessons, including all equipment, are $40 per student for a two-hour lesson. Up to six people can takes lessons together. Rentals are available on a daily and weekly basis. Call for rates. The shop is the home of the Nalu Kai Surf Museum, a free exhibit of 15 collectible surfboards and other surfer memorabilia. Corolla Surf Shop is open year-round. Winter hours vary. Listen for surf reports by Gary, the Corolla Surf Shop owner, on 93.7 The Coast and on WOBR-95.3 FM. Log on to their Web site for a daily surf report with pictures, or click and buy directly from the Web site.

Whalebone Surf Shop
TimBuck II Shopping Village
NC 12, Corolla
(252) 453–2667
www.whalebonesurfshop.com

This is the newest location of this Outer Banks classic surf shop (see the Nags Head section for the other shop). Whalebone is one of the oldest surf shops on the Outer Banks; owner Jim Vaughn opened it at Whalebone Junction in the 1960s. The Corolla location is right on the sound. The shop sells all major brands of surfboards and the best of the smaller brands. The owners and staff are surfers themselves and, therefore, very helpful. The store is well stocked with surfwear and bathing suits for all ages. The Corolla location rents surfboards.

Duck

Duck Village Outfitters
1207 Duck Rd., Duck
(252) 261–7222
www.duckvillageoutfitters.homestead.com

With surfboards and body boards, Duck Village Outfitters (DVO) is surf shop central for Duck. Surfing lessons are offered daily during the summer season. The shop conducts kayak tours daily in the summer and has a large assortment of rentals and retail items, including bikes, wetsuits, fishing equipment, kayaks, and ocean toys.

Kitty Hawk

Wave Riding Vehicles
US 158, MP 2, Kitty Hawk
(252) 261–7952
www.waveridingvehicles.com

Carrying top-of-the-line surfboards, apparel, and accessories since 1967, WRV puts its emphasis on what the owner calls "the godfather of watersports"—surfing. Although this year-round shop also sells skateboards and snowboards, it's one of the largest full-service surf shops on the barrier islands. WRV is also the biggest surfboard manufacturing company under one label on the East Coast. The company produces in-house, private-label surfwear, which is sold wholesale from Maine to Florida and overseas. Surfboards can be rented for $25 daily.

Kill Devil Hills

Vitamin Sea Surf Shop
US 158, MP 6, Kill Devil Hills
(252) 441–7512

A landmark since 1978, Vitamin Sea offers a large variety of every imaginable item a surfer could want. New and used surfboards, boogie boards, wetsuits, and beach goods are available. Vitamin Sea

also offers ladies', junior's, and misses' clothing, and other surfwear. A great selection of surfing stickers lines the walls and racks of this fascinating store. Sunglasses, T-shirts, and swimwear are reasonably priced, and there's a large selection of jewelry, plus watches and footwear. Skateboards, gravity boards, and all the accessories can also be purchased at Vitamin Sea.

Surfboards can be rented here for $15 to $25 a day. The store is open year-round.

The Pit Surf Shop, Bar and Grill
US 158, MP 9, Kill Devil Hills
(252) 480–3128
www.pitsurf.com

The Pit bills itself as a "surf hangout." The setup includes a 3,000-square-foot surf shop that covers all the board sports—surfing, body boarding, skimming, and skate boarding. The store is stocked with all the gear and accessories you need for any of those sports. Owners Steve Pauls and Ben Sproul, both devout surfers, sell a large selection of new, used, and custom boards, including the locally made Gale Force boards, plus they stock a selection of wetsuits and related accessories. All boards—skim, body, skate, and surf—are all available for sale or rent. Surf boards rent for $10.00 a day or $50.00 a week, while body boards rent for $5.00 a day, and skim boards rent for $5.00 to $15.00 per day. Surf lessons and camps are offered in the summer months for groups or individuals. Lessons run about two hours and include board rental and a T-shirt. While the store's primary focus is the sports themselves, they also sell the latest apparel and fashions for men and women.

Nags Head

Whalebone Surf Shop
US 158, MP 10, Nags Head
(252) 441–6747
www.whalebonesurfshop.com

Surfer-owned and -operated, Whalebone boasts that it has been in business since the 1960s. All major brands of surfboards, and the best of the smaller brands, are available at this well-stocked store. Both popular and hard-to-find surfwear and bathing suits can also be found. Surfboard rentals are available for trials. The store is open year-round, but hours vary so call ahead.

Secret Spot Surf Shop
US 158, MP 11, Nags Head
(252) 441–4030
www.secretspotsurfshop.com

No secret to surf enthusiasts, Secret Spot is one of the old-timers of the barrier islands' surf scene and claims to have the most boards available. Packed with the best of contemporary and classic boards and favorite surfwear, the store prides itself in catering to both younger and older surfers without the corporate or highly commercialized underpinnings. In other words, quality is emphasized over trendiness. The business has been manufacturing its own surfboards since 1977; the shop was opened five years later. A full line of shortboards, longboards, custom, and used boards is available, along with a selection of wetsuits.

Surfboards can be rented for $15 daily. Lessons are available and you can call the shop or visit the Web site for surf reports. Secret Spot has recently expanded its offerings for women and girls; look for sundresses, Ts, bathing suits, shorts, shoes, and accessories. The skate store was also expanded, and now there is a full selection of skateboard paraphernalia, including decks, trucks, wheels, and accessories. Secret Spot's new exterior, airbrush painted with tropical murals, will inspire you to take that surf trip you've been thinking about.

Cavalier Surf Shop
NC 12, MP 13½, Nags Head
(252) 441–7349
www.cavaliersurfshop@beachaccess.com

This classic shop, the only one on the Beach Road, has been in business since the 1960s. It's a family-run operation dedicated to the surfing lifestyle. Cavalier

Insiders' Tip

When you're surfing or kayaking in the ocean waves, look out for your fellow surfers and for swimmers. Do not cut across the path of someone actively riding a wave. Ask swimmers to move down the beach a bit if they're swimming in the best breaks.

rents a variety of surfboards, boogie boards, and skim boards, plus gloves, booties, and wetsuits. They also rent umbrellas, chairs, and rafts for long beach days. Surfboard rentals start at $15 a day. Surf videos are available for rent. New and used boards are for sale, and Cavalier also does a consignment business on boards. You'll also find a huge collection of stickers and sunglasses, watches, name-brand clothing for men and women, Reef sandals, and a too-cool-for-school selection of book bags.

Wave Shack
Nags Head–Manteo Causeway, Nags Head
(252) 449–2600
www.waveshack.com

Wave Shack opened in June 2001 next to RV's Restaurant in Nags Head. The shop caters to local surfers and skateboarders, with all the necessary equipment for those sports. Surfboards, boogie boards, and wetsuits are available. There's an in-house shaping room where you can watch local surfboard shaper Steve Head in action. Men's and women's clothing, shoes, sunglasses, jewelry, bathing suits, T-shirts, you name it, it's all here. Surfboards rent for $15 a day and $75 a week.

Hatteras Island

Rodanthe Surf Shop
NC 12, Rodanthe
(252) 987–2412

Rodanthe Surf Shop owners Randy Hall and Debbie Bell moved to the southern Outer Banks to surf, and the shop evolved naturally from their lifestyle. A hands-on, no-frills operation, the shop sells only the boards it makes, Hatteras Glass Surfboards, along with surfing equipment and surfer lifestyle clothing. Surfboards rent for $20 per day or $60 per week, and body boards rent for $8 per day or $25 per week. The shop is closed Thanksgiving through March.

Hatteras Island Surf Shop
NC 12, Waves
(252) 987–2296
www.HISS-waves.com

Veteran surfers Barton and Chris Decker have operated Hatteras Island Surf Shop since 1971. In recent years, they've expanded their ventures to a nearby windsurfing business, Hatteras Island Sail Shop. The surf shop offers new and used equipment, rentals, and lessons. It sells surfboards, balsa boards, longboards, body boards, ocean toys, kayaks, and some in-line skates. Wetsuits, surfwear, beach clothing, and bathing suits are also for sale in this no-nonsense surf shop for the dedicated surfer. The shop closes in January and February.

Natural Art Surf Shop
NC 12, Buxton
(252) 995–5682

Natural Art specializes in both custom-made surfboards and a full line of hand-made surfwear for men, women, and kids. The shop also carries shoes, wetsuits, skatewear, and videos. The surfboards are shaped by owner Scott Busbey in a shop right in the storefront's back yard. After 25 years in the Buxton shop, Busbey has gained a national reputation for his beautiful craftsmanship and reasonably priced boards. Surfboards can be rented for $10.00 a day or $50.00 a week, boogie boards for $5.00 day or $25.00 a week, and wetsuits for $10.00 a day with a board or $5.00 daily without a board. Videos rent for $2.00 daily.

Hatteras Wind N Surf
NC 12, Avon
(252) 995–4525, (888) WND–SURF
www.windnsurf.com

Specializing in rentals and lessons, this fully equipped surf shop keeps 200 surfboards in stock. Boards are available to rent for $15.00 a day, and weekly rates are also offered. Custom boards can be rented for $25.00 a day. Daily surf lessons are offered at the cost of $45.00 for beginner lessons, including equipment. Body boards and skim boards rent for $8.00 a day. Accessories are also available for rent or sale. Log onto the daily surf report at their Web site. Surf camps for all ages are offered in spring, summer, and fall. The shop is open year-round.

Ocracoke

Ride the Wind Surf Shop
NC 12, Ocracoke
(252) 928–6311
www.surfocracoke.com

In business since 1985, Ride the Wind features two floors of merchandise, ranging from the latest contemporary surf gear to casual, comfortable clothing and footwear for men and women non-surfers. Ride the Wind rents surfboards, body boards, wetsuits, and practically all watersports equipment, except windsurfing items. Surf boards rent for $16 a day. The shop is open seven days a week from March through December and is closed for the winter. Ride the Wind also offers outfitting trips to Portsmouth Island and a surf and kayak day camp for kids and adults. The shop's surf camp is the only one of its kind on the East Coast. Beginner surf lessons are available.

Windsurfing

Springtime on the Outer Banks brings a specific annual migration, mostly from Canada and northern United States. From a distance, we know where these migrating flocks are from and why they're here, for their vehicles give them away. Their luggage racks are laden with windsurfing equipment, and some even tow trailers stacked with boards and sails for every imaginable wind condition. In spring and fall, tourism officials estimate that as many as 500 windsurfers a week arrive at the Outer Banks. Dozens of other visitors try the sport for the first time while vacationing in Dare County.

Owing to our position in the Atlantic, plus the area's prevailing winds, shallow sounds, and temperate weather, windsurfing aficionados call this area the "Windsurfing Capital of the East Coast." When the wind is whipping just right, you can see hundreds of neon-striped sails soaring along the sound and ocean shores, silently skimming over the salty water like bright butterflies flitting near the beach.

Windsurfing is not an easy sport, although once you get the hang of it, it is one of the most intoxicating experiences imaginable. It's clean and quiet and just as easily lends itself to solitary excursions as it does to group outings. With the proper equipment, sailboarders can control their speeds, sliding slowly into a sunset or cruising more than 40 mph across choppy breaks. On the Outer Banks, sailboarders can usually find some wind to ride year-round. Windsurfing is permitted any place you can set your sails, except lifeguarded beaches. This sport truly lets you feel like a part of the natural surroundings—and it's an incredible rush to be able to maneuver with the wind.

Canadian Hole and Other Places to Windsurf

By the thousands the sailboarders come, and they remain until the winter cold sets in. Many swear that the Outer Banks is one of the top three locations in the country. Hatteras Island's Canadian Hole, so named for all of our visitors from the far north, has often been touted in international windsurfing circles as one of the continent's best sailboarding spots. Some of our perennial windsurfing visitors drive as many as 30 hours or more to catch the warm breezes in their Mylar sails.

Canadian Hole, on the west side of NC 12 between Avon and Buxton, is undoubtedly the most popular windsurfing spot on the Outer Banks and the East Coast. Formed in the early 1960s, it was created after a storm cut an inlet across Hatteras Island, just north of Buxton, and workers dredged sand from the sound to rebuild the roadway. Dredging activities carved troughs just offshore in the Pamlico Sound. The deep depressions, which extend to about 5 feet, help create ideal conditions for sailboarders. Additionally, Canadian Hole flanks one of the barrier islands' narrowest land masses. The walk from ocean to sound is under five minutes, enabling sailboarders to easily switch between the two bodies of water. Besides the sound and the Atlantic, Canadian Hole's amenities include a 100-space paved lot in which to park big vans and trailers, four portable toilets, a phone booth, and a half-dozen metal trash cans. Even the beach at Canadian Hole is much wider than other soundside stretches of sand—it's about 50 yards wide and able to accommodate sunbathers, coolers, and plenty of spectators.

The wide and flat sound here allows sailboarders to sail for miles without turning. Better still, no signs or buildings obstruct the sailors' views of the natural beauty surrounding them. During spring breaks and then again from October through Christmas, scores of Canadians arrive at the Hole, turning Hatteras Island into a temporary French-speaking haven.

Nags Head's soundside beaches also provide areas that are great for sailboarding. The sounds are shallower than at Canadian Hole, thus safer for beginners.

Windsurfing is a favorite pastime for watersports enthusiasts, and boy, do we have wind! PHOTO: COURTESY
OF J. AARON TROTMAN

The town of Nags Head has a soundside access at Milepost 16 that's perfect for windsurfers, and there's plenty of parking. Jockey's Ridge State Park's soundside access area also provides parking and a small beach for launching sailboards. In Duck, most people launch on the sound. There are dozens of launch areas on the soundside all along the Outer Banks; just look for an access and a parking spot. This is not to say people don't windsurf in the ocean; it's just that we don't need to tell you that you can launch anywhere you want to in the Atlantic.

Learning to Windsurf

From Corolla through Ocracoke Island, there are more than a dozen outposts that sell windsurfing gear and sailboards. Many of those shops offer windsurfing lessons for less than $40. We recommend receiving professional instruction if you're just starting out. It's also better to decide whether you like this sport or not on rented equipment, as even beginning rigs cost about $500. Windsurfing is free once you're outfitted, but the initial investment for equipment can be quite expensive.

Anyone who's patient enough to learn to understand wind and wave patterns can eventually learn to ride a sailboard. People of all ages (except young children) who are in good health can learn to windsurf. With a good instructor, few will fail. Most beginners are able to gain enough skill to at least have fun within two hours; however, even some sailboarders who have been skimming the seas for 20 years say they still haven't mastered all the complexities windsurfing offers.

In a nutshell, windsurfing is based on a system of manipulating a mast, boom, and sail with a device that swivels and pivots in every direction while balancing on a board. To sail crosswind, make sure the mast is vertical. To sail downwind, tip the mast toward the front of the board, which will turn the front of the board downwind. Lean the mast toward the back of the board, and it turns in the opposide direction, upwind.

Some sailboard instructors let their students start out on land, on specially made boards that let you feel how to balance and move before ever getting wet. Learning how to work with the wind is the toughest part, but you also need some arm and back strength to hold up the sail.

Sailboarders are strapped onto their masts in a sling-like contraption similar to those used in rappelling or rock climbing. You control the board with your feet and the sail with your hands. You have to learn to upright yourself in case you fall, and standing the sail up again is difficult when it fills with water.

If you're just starting out, don't sail too far from shore at first. If your rig breaks, or the wind dies down, you won't have as far to walk back through the shallow sound with your board. One of the best ways to learn windsurfing maneuvers is to watch the good sailboarders who make this challenging sport seem so effortless.

Along the Outer Banks, several windsurfing competitions and speed trials are held each year, including the Hatteras Wave Classic in October and the Pro-Am each spring.

Kite-surfing

Kite-surfing, or kite-boarding, is a relatively new sport, only a few years old, and it's the latest watersports craze among windsurfers, wake boarders, and surfers alike. Some say it has taken off faster than windsurfing did 20 years ago, and it definitely seems to be taking over as the top choice among wind-driven sports fanatics. The Outer Banks is widely recognized as one of the top places in the world to kitesurf because of the ever-present wind and shallow sounds. Kite-surfers favor the Pamlico Sound off Hatteras Island because it is so wide and has few obstructions to the kite lines. Some daredevil types also kite-surf in the ocean.

Kite-surfing does offer significant advantages over windsurfing: The gear is much more portable, you can do it in a wider range of winds (even low winds), and most people say it's much easier to

learn. However, windsurfing is safer. Kitesurfing is a dangerous sport, though it's hard to perceive that danger when you're watching from the shore. The amount of wind power behind the kite is enormous.

For this reason, you cannot simply rent a kite and board at the local outfitters and go on your merry way. You must attain a basic level of certification before you are allowed to rent or buy kite-surfing equipment, and some outfitters don't rent the gear at all, saying the risks are just too great.

Two types of kites are used in kitesurfing: an inflatable kite and a foil kite. The inflatable kite is crescent-shaped, with an inflatable leading edge that allows it to float. This kite is easier to use, is more stable and predictable, and can be used in a broader wind range. The foil kite is flatter and it fills with wind for a high-performance, more powerful ride. The foil kites are a little more unpredictable and are subject to unexpected gusts. You guide the kites with a control bar, hook into a harness, and stand on a kiteboard. You steer with the kite while using the board as a rudder. Steering techniques allow you to travel across and even upwind.

Many sailing shops on the Outer Banks offer kite-surfing lessons, but you should definitely look for responsible retailers who encourage proper training. Windsurfing Hatteras does not rent equipment at all because they feel it is too dangerous for both ill-trained users and any innocent bystanders. They do offer lessons, from beginner to advanced, but after that they encourage kite-surfers to buy their own equipment.

Kitty Hawk Kites Kite Surfing School does rent equipment, but only to people who have completed their Professional Air Sports Association–certified training courses at Carolina Outdoors at MP 16 in Nags Head. It takes about four hours of training to become certified, and then you are able to rent gear. The amount of training time depends upon your previous kiting skills. If you're not familiar with kite physics, trainers suggest that you practice with a trainer kite until kite steering techniques become ingrained in you. In the summer of 2001, Kitty Hawk Kites trained close to 400 people in the sport.

If you want to buy kite-surfing gear, the whole setup will cost you $1,500 or more. If you want to watch or compete in kite-surfing, check out Kitty Hawk Kites Kite Surfing Expo at Frisco Woods Campground the last week in September.

Wind- and Kite-surfing Shops and Lessons

Whether you're looking for a lesson, need a sail or a fin of a different size, or want to ask for advice about sailboarding, more than a dozen shops stock windsurfing and kite-surfing supplies, and many provide instructors in season.

Nags Head
Kitty Hawk Watersports
US 158, MP 16, Nags Head
(252) 441-2756
www.khsports.com

Dealing in windsurfing on the Outer Banks for more than 20 years, Kitty Hawk Watersports was one of the first windsurfing operations on the barrier islands. At its site on Roanoke Sound, the watersports center is open almost all year-round and offers windsurfing instruction in spring, summer, and fall. With a $49, three-hour lesson, instructors guarantee you'll be skimming the Roanoke Sound on your own. Call the number listed for rates. Kite-surfing lessons are available, but rentals are not. Wind- and kite-surfing equipment is also available for sale.

Carolina Outdoors
US 158, MP 16, Nags Head
(252) 449-2210
www.kittyhawk.com

Kitty Hawk Kites Kite Surfing School at Carolina Outdoors offers kite-surfing lessons with highly qualified instructors at this location on the Roanoke Sound in Nags Head, right next to Windmill Point restaurant. Two-hour intro lessons, in which you learn to properly control kites, cost $99. More advanced, in-water lessons cost an additional $148 for two hours. This school offers Level I, II, and III certification that is recognized by the Professional Air Sports Association. Once you have achieved a certain level of certification, you can rent kite-surfing gear at this location. Call for rental prices.

Hatteras Island
Windsurfing Hatteras
NC 12, Avon
(252) 995-5000
www.windsurfinghatteras.com

With private access to the Pamlico Sound, this widely respected store was opened in 1988 by a group of dedicated local windsurfers. The operation offers windsurfing and kite-surfing lessons and clinics every year for both beginners and advanced students. The clinics are staffed by some of the best kite- and wind-surfing talent around.

Lessons come with guaranteed success for beginners. Windsurfing lessons start at $45 for beginners, including all equipment and on-water instruction. Windsurfing boards and rigs can be rented at the site for $20 to $35 for two hours, depending on the level of equipment. Kite-surfing lessons, starting at $75 for a 90-minute beginner lesson, are offered by highly qualified instructors. Kite-surfing gear is not available for rent. Call for rates on renting surfboards, body boards, kayaks, Hobie Cats, and other fun-inspired items. Windsurfing Hatteras stocks everything you could possibly need for wind- or kite-surfing.

Hatteras Island Sail Shop
NC 12, Waves
(252) 987-2292
www.HISS-waves.com

On the soundfront, this windsurfing shop was opened in 1996 by the owners of Hatteras Island Surf Shop, which is 250 yards south. They offer sales, rentals, and lessons. Owner Barton Decker says the sailing site here is the largest on the Outer Banks, with a grassy rigging area and a sandy beach launch. With about 150 new and used boards in stock, the store has all necessary accessories in its complete inventory. A beginner windsurfing lesson costs $55 for about three hours. Rentals are available for $15 an hour, $35 a half-day, and $55 a day. The Sail Shop sells kites and kite boards and offers lessons. Kite-surfing lessons cost $75 an hour; no rentals are available. The store closes in January and February.

REAL Kiteboarding
Cape Hatteras
(252) 995–4740, (866) REAL–KITE
www.realkiteboarding.com

REAL Kiteboarding is a full-service kiteboarding center that offers gear and instruction. With home bases on Hatteras Island and Puerto Rico, they offer instruction in many areas of the East Coast. Three-day Kite Camps ($495) are offered on Hatteras Island in the spring, summer, and fall, and after one of these intense camps, you're guaranteed to be ripping. Less expensive instruction involving less of a time commitment will teach you the basic skills.

Hatteras Wind N Surf
NC 12, Avon
(252) 995–4525, (888) WND–SURF
www.windnsurf.com

Whether you're a novice or a pro, you'll find something to suit your windsurfing and kite-surfing needs at Hatteras Wind N Surf. Qualified staff offers private and special lessons daily for all skill levels. You can take a three-hour beginner lesson, including equipment rental, for $45. Perfect your board handling during a two-hour board speed and handling course for $65. Practice beach starts, pivot jibes, and upwind sailing during a one-hour private intermediate class for $55. Advanced lessons are also available at $65 an hour. If you're looking to rent equipment, you can choose from body boards, boogie boards, skim boards, and windsurfing gear. For kite-

surfing, Hatteras Wind N Surf has everything you need, including traditional, stunt, and paper kite gear and lessons. An introductory lesson to kite-surfing costs $45. Private lessons are $75. High-performance kite and board rentals are $50 for a half-day or $95 for a whole day.

Hatteras Adventures
NC 12, Buxton
(252) 995–7000
www.hatterasadventures.com

This outfitter specializes in watersports gear and beach and water toys. Daily, weekend, and weekly camps are offered in windsurfing, kite-surfing, kayaking, and surf kayaking. Call for rates and camp information.

Kayaking and Canoeing

The easiest, most adaptable and accessible watersports available on the Outer Banks—kayaking and canoeing—are activities people of any age or physical ability can enjoy. These lightweight paddlecraft are extremely maneuverable, can glide almost anywhere along the seas or sounds, and afford adventurous activity as well as silent solitude. They're also relatively inexpensive ways to tour uncharted waterways and see sights you'd miss if you stayed on shore.

In recent years, more than a dozen ecotour outlets have opened on the barrier islands. Stores offer everything from rent-your-own kayaks for less than $40 a day to guided, daylong, and even overnight tours around uninhabited islands. With no fuel to foul the estuaries, no noise to frighten wildlife, and no need for a demanding skill level, kayaks and canoes offer a sport as strenuous or as relaxing as you want it to be—an outdoor activity that will make a splash with the entire family.

Unlike the closed-cockpit kayaks used in whitewater river runs, most kayaks on the Outer Banks are a sit-on-top style and stretch from 7 to 10 feet long. They're molded in bright colored plastic, are light

Kayaking and canoeing are activities people of almost any age or physical ability can enjoy.
PHOTO: COURTESY OF KITTY HAWK KITES

enough for even adolescents to carry to a launch site, and come in one- and two-seat models. A double-blade paddle and a life jacket are the only other pieces of equipment you'll need, and these are included with all rentals and lessons.

Canoes are heavier and harder to get into the water but slightly more stable than kayaks. They seat two or three people and include a more sheltered hull to haul gear or picnic lunches inside. Single-blade paddles, usually two per boat, are needed to maneuver this traditional watercraft.

Perhaps the best aspect of kayaking and canoeing is versatility. You can perform these paddle sports in any weather, with or without wind, in calm or rough seas, and in shallow sounds and narrow creeks. These sports lend themselves to solitary enjoyment just as easily as group fun.

Thrill-seekers can splash kayaks through frothy surf in the Atlantic or paddle past the breakers and float alongside schools of dolphin. For more tranquil times, kayakers and canoeists can slip slowly through mysterious, marshy creeks at the isolated Alligator

River National Wildlife Refuge, explore narrow canals that bigger boats can't access, or slip alongside an uninhabited island in the middle of the shallow sound. There are historical tours around Roanoke Island, nature tours through maritime forests, and self-guided trails with markers winding through a former logging town called Buffalo City on the Dare County mainland. Virtually anywhere there's 2 feet of water or more, you can take a kayak or canoe.

Learning to Paddle

Unlike other watersports, little to no instruction is needed to paddle a kayak or canoe. It helps to know how to swim, in case you capsize, but since most of the sounds are only a few feet deep, you can walk your way back to shore if you stay in the estuaries—or, at least, jump back in your boat from a standing position.

Different strokes are required for each type of craft. For kayaks, double-blade paddles are designed to be used by one person. The blades are positioned at opposing angles so you can work across your body with a sweeping motion and minimal rotation and still paddle on both sides of the boat. The trick is to get into a rhythm and not dig too deeply beneath the water's surface. Canoeing is done with one person paddling on each side of the boat, if there are two passengers, or a single operator alternating sides with paddle strokes.

Most kayak- and canoe-rental outfits also offer lessons. Even if you prefer to be on your own, rather than with a guided group trip, people renting these watercraft are happy to share advice and expertise with you. If you have any questions or need directions around the intricate waterways, just ask.

Paddling Places

All the sounds around the Outer Banks are ideal for kayaking and canoeing, because they are shallow, warm, and filled with flora and fauna. There are marked trails at Alligator River National Wildlife Refuge;

tours through Nags Head Woods; buoys around Wanchese, Manteo, and Colington; and plenty of uncharted areas to explore around Pine Island, Pea Island, Kitty Hawk, Corolla, the Cape Hatteras National Seashore, and Portsmouth Island. Unlike other types of boats, you don't even need a special launching site to set a kayak or canoe in the water and take off.

Corolla

Corolla Outback Adventures
Wee Winks Shopping Center
NC 12, Corolla
(252) 453–0877
www.corollaoutback.com

Corolla Outback Adventures is a time-honored name in adventuring on the northern beaches. Started by the Bender family in the 1960s, this guide service is still in the family—now run by the second generation. Besides Wild Horse Safaris (see our Recreation chapter), this company offers a most unusual and fascinating tour called the 4WD/Kayak Expedition. On this tour, up to 10 people load into an old-school Chevy Suburban for a 4WD trip—kayaks in tow—up the off-road area north of Corolla to Carova at the Virginia/North Carolina line. Along the trip you'll see beaches, dunes, the site of a buried town, maritime forest, an old life-saving station, a shipwreck, and a petrified forest. Once you get to Carova, the kayaks are unloaded and everyone boards the boats for a tour of the pristine upper recesses of the Currituck Sound. Knowledgeable guides point out all the sites along the way, and you're likely to see the wild horses, dolphin, a variety of birds, and sometimes even fox or wild boar. This is the Outer Banks's most pristine country—there are no paved roads and very little development. On this tour, you'll see and learn about all seven Outer Banks ecosystems—ocean, beach, dunes, maritime forest, marsh, sound, and freshwater lakes. The 4WD/Kayak Expedition lasts three-and-a-half to four hours. It costs $64 for adults and is half-price for children ages 3 to 11, with discounts in the off-season.

Tours run twice a day in the summer and daily in spring and fall as long as the weather is nice. Reservations are required.

Corolla Adventure Tours
NC 12, Corolla
(252) 453–6899
www.obxwaterworks.com

For kayak ecotours on the north beaches, look to Corolla Adventure Tours. Experienced guides lead the two-hour tours through the Currituck Sound and marsh, where you'll see a variety of birds and wildlife. For those interested in dolphin-watching, this company leads two-hour ocean tours on calm days. To find the dolphin, you spend part of the time riding along the beach in a truck with your kayaks on top. When you spot dolphin, you unload the kayaks and paddle directly out to them to get a better look. Make reservations in advance. This company has two locations on NC 12, one next to the Inn at Corolla Light and the other north of the post office. Kayak tours are offered March through January.

Carolina Outdoors
Monteray Shores Plaza, NC 12, Corolla
(252) 453–3685
www.kittyhawk.com

Carolina Outdoors, a division of Kitty Hawk Kites, offers kayak rentals for paddlers who want to get out on the sound. This company also rents kayaks and takes out kayak ecotours from the Inn at Corolla Light. Kayak ecotours, $35 for a two-and-a-half-hour tour, are in the sound waters in view of the Whalehead club and the Currituck Beach Lighthouse.

Kitty Hawk Watersports
NC 12, Corolla
(252) 453–6900
www.khsports.com

Kitty Hawk Watersports, behind Tim-Buck II Shopping Village, offers kayak rentals and kayak ecotours in the Currituck Sound. Call for details. The Corolla store is open Memorial Day to Labor Day.

Duck

Carolina Outdoors Watersports Center
NC 12, Duck
(252) 261–4450
www.kittyhawk.com

Next to the Kitty Hawk Kites retail store in Duck is the Carolina Outdoors Watersports Center, complete with a pier and a canal. This location rents kayaks for the ocean and the sound. The Carolina Outdoors retail store is across the street. Carolina Outdoors offers kayak ecotours through the Pine Island Audubon Sanctuary, but these tours leave from the Sanderling Inn; call (252) 441-2144 for further information.

Sunset Watersports
NC 12, Duck
(252) 261–7100
www.barrierislandboats.com

Single as well as tandem kayaks are available for sale or rent here on the pier behind Sunset Grille & Raw Bar. Prices range from around $10 an hour for a single kayak to $75 a week for a tandem kayak. They're open from May through October.

Duck Village Outfitters
1207 Duck Road, Duck
(252) 261–7222
www.duckvillageoutfitters.homestead.com

DVO will take you wherever you want to go in a kayak. Their two preplanned tours are ocean kayak dolphin tours and scenic tours through the estuaries of Kitty Hawk Nature Preserve, Kitty Hawk Bay, and Ginguite Creek. The two-hour soundside tours cost $29 for a single kayak or $44 for a tandem. The ocean tour is $33 for about two hours, and you can rent a spring suit or wetsuit if need be. Kayak rentals cost around $12 an hour or $59 a week, more for tandem models. Tours are conducted daily in the warm seasons, but call in the off-season and one of the enthusiastic guides will take you out. The shop is open year-round, with abbreviated hours through the winter. DVO has a large assortment of rentals and retail items, including bikes, wetsuits, beach attire, kayaks, and ocean toys.

Nags Head

Carolina Outdoors
US 158, Nags Head
(252) 441-4124, (800) 334-4777
www.kittyhawk.com

Carolina Outdoors, Kitty Hawk Kites's watersports operation, offers a selection of flat-water tours from Corolla to Hatteras, in addition to sea and surf kayak lessons. No experience is necessary, and tours include all necessary equipment, including single and tandem kayaks, paddles, and life jackets. Guides meet you onsite with all of the necessary items. Tours are offered around soundside Duck and Corolla, in Kitty Hawk Woods, around Manteo and Roanoke Island, at the Alligator River, and at Pea Island and Hatteras Island. Sunset tours, dolphin tours, lighthouse tours, and tours with historical narration are offered. Tours range from one hour to over two hours and cost from $25 to $40. Long, specialty tours are available; see the Web site for more information. A full line of sea, surf, and touring kayaks as well as a selection of personal sailboats are available for sale, including Escape boats and the Wind Rider trimarans. Special programs for kids are available in the summer months. Surf kayaking lessons are offered along the Outer Banks's miles of beaches for about $35 an hour. Rent equipment by the hour, day, or week.

Kitty Hawk Watersports
US 158, MP 13, Nags Head
(252) 441-6800
www.khsports.com

A division of Kitty Hawk Sports, the kayak service offers tours ranging from two hours to extended expeditions and covers the soundside areas from Corolla to Portsmouth Island, including Pea Island and Alligator River. Launch sites are in Corolla, Kitty Hawk, Nags Head, and Avon. Sales and rentals are available. Lessons for any experience level, from beginner to advanced, are available. Two-and-a half-hour tours are $35 for adults, $19 for children. Alligator River tours

cost $39 for adults and $19 per child. Kayaks start at $10 an hour, depending upon the craft.

Bodie Island Adventures
Nags Head-Manteo Causeway, Nags Head
(252) 441-6822
www.bodieislandadventures.com

Bodie Island Adventures offers kayak tours beginning on the Nags Head-Manteo Causeway. The tours lead through the protected sound waters around Bodie Island, where you'll see a variety of wildlife and islands. Tours are also offered in the canals at Kitty Hawk Woods. Two-hour tours cost $35 for adults and $17 for kids age 12 and younger. If you want to go solo, you can rent single or tandem kayaks for two hours, a half-day, or a full day. Call for prices. Bodie Island Adventures is open from April through October.

The Waterworks
US 158, MP 16½, Nags Head
(252) 441-8875
www.obxwaterworks.com

Right on the sound in Nags Head, The Waterworks offers kayak and canoe rentals for those who want to go it alone. Rent surf and flat-water variety kayaks for your own adventures in the sound behind the shop or at your own location. For guided kayak tours, Bodie Island Adventures (see previous entry), an affiliate of The Waterworks, will take you out for spectacular viewing.

Roanoke Island

Wilderness Canoeing Inc.
P.O. Box 789, Manteo, NC 27954
(252) 473-1960

An Outer Banks native, Melvin T. Twiddy Jr. conducts wilderness adventure tours by canoe around Alligator River National Wildlife Refuge and through the former frontier town Buffalo City and Milltail Creek. All equipment is provided, and the tours last a leisurely three-and-a-half to four hours. Tours depart from Manns Harbor, usually around 9:00 A.M., but the times can vary according to the group. Be sure to bring water and lunch or snacks to eat on the tour. Wilderness Canoeing is one of the few tour operations open year-round, and its trip through the Alligator River area is the longest guided tour available. Along the way, Twiddy will steer you past blooming waterlilies and tell you about local history and folklore. Advance reservations are recommended. Call for rates and more information.

Carolina Outdoors
Queen Elizabeth St., Manteo
(252) 473-2357, (800) 334-4777
www.kittyhawk.com

Carolina Outdoors rents kayaks from its location, which is right on Shallowbag Bay in downtown Manteo. Ecotours through Shallow-bag Bay and surrounding canals are given at 9:00 A.M., 2:00 P.M., and 5:00 P.M. for $30 per person. The tours last about two-and-a-half hours. Sunset and moonlight tours are available.

Hatteras Island

Hatteras Island Sail Shop
NC 12, Waves
(252) 987-2292
www.HISS-waves.com

Kayak rentals and sales are offered at this soundfront shop, located behind Getaway's Restaurant. The site includes a large, grassy area and a sandy beach launch. The shop also rents Hobie Cats and day sailers. Kayak rentals cost $25 or $30 a day, with discounts for a half-day.

Hatteras Watersports
NC 12, Salvo
(252) 987-2306

On the soundside across from the Salvo Volunteer Fire Department, Hatteras Watersports rents and sells canoes and flat-water and surf kayaks. One-and-a-half-hour soundside kayak tours are offered for $30 per person. Call for rental prices.

Hatteras Wind N Surf
NC 12, Avon
(252) 995-4525, (888) WND-SURF
www.windnsurf.com

A complete kayak outfitter, Hatteras Wind N Surf has a full line of kayaks and paddling gear. Guided, three-hour wildlife tours are offered daily from March 15 through December 15 to Hatteras, Pea, Ocracoke, Bird, and Portsmouth Islands, ranging from $29 to $59. Group discount rates are available. All-day tours from Ocracoke to Portsmouth Islands and sunset tours can be arranged. Rentals of surf,

All the sounds around the Outer Banks are ideal for kayaking and canoeing. PHOTO: COURTESY OF KITTY HAWK KITES

touring, sit-on-top, and two- and three-person kayaks and canoes are available by the day or week, and they will deliver anywhere on Hatteras Island.

Carolina Outdoors
Island Shops, NC 12, Avon
(252) 995–6060, (800) 334–4777
www.kittyhawk.com
Hatteras Landing
NC 12, Hatteras Village
(252) 986–1446, (800) 334–4777
www.kittyhawk.com

These locations of Carolina Outdoors offer kayak rentals for the sound as well as the ocean. They also offer kayak ecotours on the sound. A two-hour sunset tour costs around $25 per person. A two-and-a-half-hour soundside tour in Hatteras Village costs around $35 per person.

Hatteras Adventures
NC 12, Buxton
(252) 995–7000

In addition to daily kayak ecotours, this outfitter offers camps in kayaking and surf kayaking. You can rent kayaks for use in the surf, the sound, or the tidal creeks behind the store. The store also rents a variety of beach and water toys.

Ocracoke Island

Ocracoke Adventures
NC 12 and Silver Lake Rd., Ocracoke Village
(252) 928–7873
www.ocracoke-nc.com/ocracokeadventures

Kayak ecotours in the Pamlico Sound and around Ocracoke Island give paddlers the opportunity to learn about the fragile plant and animal life that inhabits these remote islands. Daily ecotours include Early Bird Catches the Worm, Blackbeard's Domain, Ocean Excursions, Horsepen Point, Sunset, and Full Moon tours. Clamming tours, snorkeling trips, and late-night tours are available too. Tours are often guided by native Michael O'Neal and biologist Shirley Schoelkopf, owners of Ocracoke Adventures, and last two to two-and-a-half hours. The owners

also oversee several Ocracoke natives who take out paddlers.

Fees include kayak, paddle, backrest, life jacket, dry bag, and instructions. Any size group can be accommodated, and customized tours are available. Kayaks can be rented on an hourly, daily, or weekly basis, with free delivery on Ocracoke. Hourly rates are $10 for singles and $15 for doubles. Reservations are recommended in the summer. Surfish sailboats are also available for rent. Kids age 10 and younger ride free, and daily programs for children are available.

Ocracoke Adventures hosts Wave Cave Summer Surf Camp, Ocracoke's first and finest surf camp for anyone who can swim. The camp operates during the summer on Tuesdays, Wednesdays, and Thursdays from 10:00 A.M. until noon and includes surfing, body boarding, skim boarding, and surf kayaking. Ocracoke Adventures proudly hosts school groups on educational walking and kayak tours around Ocracoke Island; call for details. The store sells surfboards, body boards, T-shirts, boardshorts, rash guards, exotic novelties, and shells, shells, shells. Used kayaks and surfboards are sold at certain times of the year. The store closes in January and February, but call and leave a message and the owners will get back to you if you'd like a tour.

Ride the Wind Surf Shop
NC 12, Ocracoke
(252) 928–6311
www.surfocracoke.com

Ride the Wind offers four two-and-a-half-hour kayak tours (The Sunrise, The Midday, The Sunset, The Full Moon) of the Pamlico Sound and the surrounding estuarine waters every day in spring, summer, and fall, weather permitting.

Naturalist/ecologist Terrilyn West is charged with guiding the tours or overseeing the several ecology interns who take out paddlers. Terns, pelicans, egrets, herons, many species of fish, and porpoises are just some of the species that paddlers may see on their tour through the waterways. Any size group can be accommodated with advance notice. The fee includes kayak, life jackets, and a four-page plastic field guide to area fish, shellfish, and fauna. Call for prices. Reservations are strongly suggested during the summer.

Scuba Diving

Cloudier and cooler than waters off the Florida Keys and the Caribbean Islands, offshore areas along the Outer Banks offer unique scuba-diving experiences in "The Graveyard of the Atlantic." The area owes its moniker to the more than 1,500 shipwrecks (at least 200 named and identified) whose remains inhabit the ocean floor from Corolla to Ocracoke. Experienced divers enjoy the challenge of unpredictable currents and always seem to find something new to explore beneath the ocean's surface. From 17th-century schooners to World War II submarines, wreckage lies at a variety of depths, in almost every imaginable condition. After each storm, it seems, a new shipwreck is unearthed somewhere near the barrier island shores, but most of these wrecks are sunk well beneath the sea.

Some underwater archaeological shipwreck sites are federally protected and can be visited but not touched. Others offer incredible souvenirs for deepwater divers: bits of china plates and teacups, old medicine and liquor bottles, even brass-rimmed porthole covers and thick, hand-blown glass that's been buried beneath the ocean for more than a century. If you prefer to leave history as you find it, waterproof cameras are sure to bring back even more memorable treasures from the mostly unexplored underwater world.

Sharks, whales, dolphins, and hundreds of varieties of colorful fish also frequent deep waters around these barrier islands. There's even a coral reef off Avon—the northernmost one in the world. Submerged Civil War forts are also scattered along the banks of Roanoke Island in much more shallow sound waters.

While dive-boat captains will carry charter parties to places of their choosing, some shipwrecks have become popular with scuba divers and are among the most frequently selected sites. The freighter *Metropolis,* also called the "Horsehead Wreck," lies about 3 miles south of the Currituck Beach Lighthouse off Whalehead Beach in Corolla, 100 yards offshore and in about 15 feet of water. This ship was carrying 500 tons of iron rails and 200 tons of stones when it sank in 1878, taking 85 crewmen with it to a watery grave. Formerly the federal gunboat *Stars and Stripes* that worked in the Civil War, this is a good wreck to explore in the off-season. If you have a four-wheel-drive vehicle, you can drive up the beach and swim out to this shipwreck site.

Off the shores of Kill Devil Hills, an unidentified tugboat rests about 300 yards south of Avalon Pier, about 75 yards off the beach, in 20 feet of water. Two miles south, the Triangle Wrecks—*Josephine, Kyzickes,* and *Carl Gerhard*—sit about 100 yards offshore, about 200 yards south of the Sea Ranch Motel, in about 20 feet of water. These vessels sank in 1915, 1927, and 1929, respectively. You can access these wrecks by boat or swim from the beach.

Nags Head's most famous dive site is the USS *Huron,* a federal gunship that sank in 1877, taking 95 crewmen to the bottom with it. This wreck is about 200 yards off the beach at MP 11, resting in about 26 feet of water and including many salvageable artifacts. The tugboat *Explorer* is nearby.

Long known as the East Coast's most treacherous inlet, Oregon Inlet rages between Nags Head and Hatteras Island. It's infamous for the hundreds of ships—and scores of lives—that it has claimed through the ages. The liberty ship *Zane Grey* lies about a mile south of this inlet in 80 feet of water. A German sub U-85 sank northeast of the inlet in 100 feet of water in 1942. The *Oriental* has been sitting about 4 miles south of Oregon Inlet since sinking there in 1862; its boiler is visible above the surf. Most of these dive sites can be accessed only from boats.

About a mile north of Rodanthe Fishing Pier, 100 yards offshore, the *LST 471* lies in about 15 feet of water. This ship sank in 1949 and is accessible by swimming out from shore. Nearby off Rodanthe, about 22 miles southeast of Oregon Inlet, the tanker *Marore* is about 12 miles offshore. It sank after being torpedoed in 1942 and lies in about 100 feet of water.

Experienced deepwater divers enjoy the *Empire Gem,* a British carrier that sank in January 1942 after being torpedoed by a German U-boat. This shipwreck sits about 17 miles off Cape Hatteras in 140 feet of water and was one of the first vessels to go down in World War II. It, too, must be reached by boat.

Learning to Dive

Unlike other watersports, scuba diving isn't something you can learn on your own. You have to be certified to do deep dives. This takes special training by certified instructors—and, sometimes, weeks of practice in a pool. Average recreational dives are 80 to 100 feet deep, while extreme divers reach depths of more than 300 feet. There are dangers associated with such deep dives, however. Every seasoned diver knows the perils associated with the sport: the potential for death in underwater caves, shark attacks, and the hazards of surfacing too fast and being afflicted with "the bends." Divers universally agree, however, that the thrill and tranquillity of deep-wreck diving are well worth the risks.

Several Outer Banks dive shops offer lessons, advanced instruction, and all the equipment you'll need to get started. This is a relatively expensive sport. Divers say it takes at least $1,500 just to get the necessary tanks, hoses, wetsuits, and other paraphernalia to take that first plunge. Dive boat charters, which all dive-shop workers will help arrange, begin at about $550 per day, depending on how far offshore you want to go.

Some dive shops can also recommend shallow dive spots that you don't need a boat to get to, as well as nearby-shore or sound areas that you can explore with just a face mask and snorkel. Ocean Atlantic Rentals in Corolla, (252) 453–2440, and Avon, (252) 995–5868, rents fins, masks, and snorkels. And the National Park Service has sporadic snorkeling adventures along the Cape Hatteras National Seashore in the summer. Call (252) 473–2111 for tour times and information.

Dive Shops

Nags Head

Sea Scan Dive Centre
NC 12, MP 10½, Nags Head
(252) 480–3467
www.wreckdive.com

Sea Scan is a full-service NAUI Pro facility offering scuba equipment sales, rentals, repairs, tank refills, charters, and instruction. Sea Scan specializes in charters and

Before You Dive

If you're going scuba diving, you might want to jot down these important numbers.

Emergency Numbers:
    U.S. Coast Guard
    24-Hour Search and Rescue,
    and all boating/diving emergencies,
    (252) 995–6411

    U.S. Coast Guard Aids to Navigation Team
    (252) 986–2177

    Divers Alert Network (DAN)
    (919) 684–2948, 8:30 A.M. to 5:00 P.M. daily
    (919) 684–8111 after hours

    Ocean Rescue Squad
    (helicopter available) 911

U.S. Coast Guard Stations:
    Oregon Inlet
    (252) 441–1685

    Hatteras Inlet
    (252) 986–2175

    Ocracoke Inlet
    (252) 928–3711

beach dives to the many offshore shipwrecks fringing the Outer Banks. Certification classes through Dive-master are also available. Sea Scan is open year-round.

Outer Banks Dive Center
US 158, MP 12½, Nags Head
(252) 449–8349
www.obxdive.com

This center in Nags Head meets the needs of all divers onboard its 46-foot crew boat named the *Pelican*. Guided beach dives are offered at the wreck of the *Huron* in Nags Head. Dive trips are offered to the offshore wrecks of the *Advance*, the *Jackson*, *U-85*, and others. The shop offers all levels of diving instruction, rentals, equipment, sup-

plies, repairs, and tank fills. It's open year-round. Visit the Web site for information about trips, dives, and equipment.

Roanoke Island

Cape Hatteras Nautical Institute
406 Uppowac Ave., Manteo
(252) 473–6211

Here's your chance to get certified for scuba diving. This instructional dive school offers everything from introductory courses to instructor-level certifications. Instructor Pam Malec is very enthusiastic about her love for Outer Banks diving and shares this with her students. Instruction is offered in a pool for ages 12 and older. There's a one-day resort course that will have you diving in one day with an instructor. Several course packages are available to become a certified scuba diver, including a two-month course, a one-month course, and even a one-week intensive course. Courses include class time, pool work, and, best of all, open-water schooling. Basic certification costs $350. Cape Hatteras Nautical also offers NAUI instruction for dive masters and search and rescue teams.

Hatteras Island

Outer Banks Diving and Charters
57540 NC 12, Hatteras Village
(252) 986–1056
www.outerbanksdiving.com

Offering daily dives on Gulf Stream wrecks for individuals and groups, Outer Banks Diving and Charters specializes in family and group outings. Dive trips are made on *Bayou Runner*, a 42-foot U.S.C.G.–certified vessel, which is docked at Teach's Lair Marina, 1 mile from the dive shop. This full-service PADI facility is open year-round and has equipment sales, full rental gear, tank fills, and Nitrox.

Atlantic Wreck Diving
Teach's Lair Marina, Hatteras Village
(252) 986–2835

Through Atlantic Wreck Diving, friendly Capt. Art Kirchner takes scuba divers out on his 36-foot custom dive boat, the *Margie II*. The boat, which is certified to carry 20 passengers, leaves from Teach's Lair Marina from May through the end of August. Sport and technical divers can explore any of about 30 wrecks in depths ranging from 40 feet all the way to 360 feet. Capt. Art is an experienced diver and captain; he has been diving since 1971 and has run this boat on the Outer Banks for the last 13 years. Call the number listed for reservations.

Sailing

With wide, shallow sounds and more than 90 miles of easily accessible oceanfront, the Outer Banks has been a haven for sailors since Sir Walter Raleigh's explorers first slid along these shores more than four centuries ago. Private sailboat owners have long enjoyed the barrier islands as a stopover while en route along the Intracoastal Waterway. Many sailors have also dropped anchor beside Roanoke or Hatteras Islands—only to tie up at the docks permanently and make Dare County their year-round home.

Until recently, you had to have your own sailboat to cruise the area waterways. Now, dozens of shops from Corolla through Ocracoke rent sailboats, Hobie Cats, and catamarans to weekend water enthusiasts. Others offer introductory and advanced sailing lessons. Some even take people who have no desire to learn to sail on excursions across the sounds aboard multi-passenger sailing ships. Ecotours, luncheon swim-and-sails, and sunset cruises have become increasingly popular with vacationers who want to glide across the waterways but not necessarily steer their own vessels. From 40-passenger catamarans sailed by experienced captains to pirate-like schooners carrying up to six passengers to single-person Sunfish sailboats, you can find almost any type of sailing vessel you desire on these barrier islands.

Unlike motorized craft, which pollute the water with gasoline and cause passengers to shout over the whirr of engines, sailing is a clean, environmentally friendly sport that people of all ages can enjoy. You can sail slowly by marshlands without disturbing the waterfowl or cruise at 15 mph clips in stiff southern breezes. It all depends on your whim—and the wind.

If you've never sailed before, don't rent a boat and try to wing it. Winds in this area are trickier than elsewhere and either increase in intensity or shift direction without a moment's notice. If you get caught in a gale, you could end up miles from land if you don't know how to maneuver the vessel. A two-hour introductory lesson is well worth the minimal investment to learn basic sailing skills such as knot tying, sail rigging, and steering.

Dozens of Outer Banks outfitters lease sailboats by the hour, day, or week. PHOTO: COURTESY OF ROANOKE ISLAND FESTIVAL PARK

Sailors with basic on-water experience can usually manage to navigate their way around the shallow sounds. All boats come with life jackets, and it's best to wear the life jacket in case you capsize.

Sailboat Cruises, Courses, and Rentals

Prices for sailboat cruises depend on the amenities, length of voyage, and time of day. Midday trips sometimes include boxed lunches or at least drinks for passengers. Some sunset tours offer wine, beer, and appetizers. Almost all of the excursions let people bring their own food and drink aboard, and some even accept dogs on leashes. Special arrangements can also be made for disabled passengers. Prices generally range from $30 to $60 per person. If you'd like to book a boat for a private charter for you and your friends, some captains will also offer their services along with the sailboats, beginning at $50 per hour per vessel.

Lesson costs, too, span a range, depending on how in-depth the course is, what type of craft you're learning on, and whether you prefer group or individualized instruction. Costs can be from $10 to $50 per person. Call ahead for group rates if you've got more than four people in your party.

If you'd rather rent a craft and sail it yourself, dozens of Outer Banks outfitters lease sailboats by the hour, day, or week. Deposits generally are required. Costs range from $25 to $60 per hour and $50 to $110 per day. Most shops accept major credit cards.

Corolla

Kitty Hawk Watersports
NC 12, Corolla
(252) 453–6900
www.khsports.com

On the sound behind TimBuck II shopping village, Kitty Hawk Watersports rents day sailors and catamarans. Call for rates.

Duck

Sunset Watersports
NC 12, Duck
(252) 261–7100
www.barrierislandboats.com

In recent years, Duck has become one of the Outer Banks's busiest sailing hubs and is among the easiest places in the area to learn to sail or take a calm cruise. Sunset Watersports rents day sailers and catamarans hourly, by the half-day, or daily. It is open May through October.

Carolina Outdoors
1215 Duck Road, Duck
(252) 261–4450, (800) 334–4777
www.kittyhawk.com

A division of Kitty Hawk Kites, Carolina Outdoors rents the WindRider trimaran, a near foolproof and extraordinarily stable sailing vessel for hourly and day rates. The lightweight Escape, a less destructible and more portable version of the Sunfish, is also available for rent or sale. The Escape is equipped with a Windicator, which sets the sail by measuring wind speed and direction. Carolina Outdoors is on the south side of the big green water tank in Duck. WindRider trimarans are also available to rent in Corolla; call (252) 453–3685.

Kitty Hawk

Promenade Watersports
US 158, MP¹⁄₄, Kitty Hawk
(252) 261–4400

At the foot of the Wright Memorial Bridge, the Promenade is the only full-service watersports center in Kitty Hawk. Of its multitude of services, it offers sailboat lessons and rentals. Try out a Precision 13, an 18-foot day sailer, Hobie Cats, or a 20-foot trimaran in the wide stretches of sound behind the Promenade. Call for prices. Reservations are recommended.

Nags Head

The Waterworks
US 158, MP 16¹⁄₂, Nags Head
(252) 441–8875
www.obxwaterworks.com

Sailboat rentals are offered at this complete watersports center from March through November. Try out a 14- or 18-foot American Day-sailer or a Sunfish. This area of the Roanoke Sound is shallow, making for safe day sailing. There are several small islands to stop and explore, if you want a break.

Kitty Hawk Watersports
US 158, MP 16, Nags Head
(252) 441–2756
www.khsports.com

Kitty Hawk Watersports, a division of Kitty Hawk Sports, rents day sailers and catamarans from its soundside Nags Head location. This is a great place to learn to sail on a not-too-windy day. The sound is wide, and there aren't too many hazards to look out for—except for Jet-Skiers and other watersports enthusiasts. Personal watercraft and kayaks are also available here.

Hatteras Island

Hatteras Wind N Surf - Avon Boathouse
NC 12, Avon
(252) 995–4525
www.windnsurf.com

Rent a Hobie Cat, Prindle, or Escape sailboat by the hour, day, or week at this soundside boat ramp and marina. Rates start at $45 an hour. Lessons begin at $45 for a one-hour private lesson. For the ultimate convenience, the company will even deliver a sailboat to your waterfront rental cottage.

Hatteras Island Sail Shop
NC 12, Waves
(252) 987–2292
www.HISS-waves.com

Catamarans, day sailers, and Hobie Cats are available for rent by the hour at this extension of the respected Hatteras Island Surf Shop. Kayaks and other ocean toys are also available to rent. Sound access is on-site. Lessons are also offered. Call for more information. The sail shop is closed in January and February.

Carolina Outdoors
Island Shops, NC 12, Avon
(252) 995–6060
www.kittyhawk.com

The Avon location of Carolina Outdoors rents WindRider trimaran sailboats, which have to be the easiest boats to learn to sail on. Carolina Outdoors also offers kayak rentals.

Boating

From small skiffs to luxurious pleasure boats, there is dock space for almost every type of boat on the Outer Banks. Most marinas require advance reservations. Space is extremely limited on summer weekends, so call as soon as you make plans to visit the area. Prices vary greatly, depending on the dock location amenities, and type of vessel you're operating.

If you don't own your own boat, you can still access the sounds, inlets, and ocean around the Outer Banks by renting powerboats from area outfitters. Most store owners don't require previous boating experience. If you leave a deposit and driver's license, they'll include a brief boating lesson in the rental price. Whether you're looking to lease a craft to catch this evening's fish dinner or just want to take the kids on an afternoon cruise, you can find a vessel to suit your needs at a variety of marinas. Slow-going pontoon boats are popular with vacationers because they're easy to handle and can accommodate a crowd of boaters. Prices range from $15 an hour to more than $100 per day, depending on the type of boat. Some places require a two-hour or more minimum. Most accept major credit cards. See our Fishing chapter for charter information. If you're interested in simply taking a boat tour, see our Recreation chapter.

Public Boat Launch Ramps

Free public launch ramps are located at:
- Whalehead Club in Corolla
- Soundside end of Wampum Drive in Duck
- Bob Perry Road on Kitty Hawk Bay in Kitty Hawk
- Avalon Beach off Bay Drive in Kill Devil Hills (small boats only)
- Washington Baum Bridge on Nags Head–Manteo Causeway, opposite Pirate's Cove
- Thicket Lump Marina near Thicket Lump Lane in Wanchese
- Foot of the bridge leading to Roanoke Island Festival Park in Manteo
- Oregon Inlet Fishing Center
- Avon Boathouse, Hatteras Wind N Surf, Avon
- Oceanside end of Lighthouse Road in Buxton
- Frisco Cove in Frisco
- Between Cedar Island/Swan Quarter ferry docks on Ocracoke Island

Marinas and Dock Space

There are numerous marinas on the Outer Banks that offer services to boaters, such as fuel, bait and tackle, ice, supplies, and weighing stations. If you're interested in dockage at a marina, see our Getting Here, Getting Around chapter. If you're interested in chartering a boat at one of these marinas, see our Fishing chapter.

Kitty Hawk

Dock of the Bay
Bob Perry Rd., Kitty Hawk
(252) 255-5578

This fuel dock and conveniences shop is a welcome service to boaters on the northern beaches. Dock of the Bay is easily accessed by boat from Kitty Hawk Bay. It offers ice, gas and diesel fuel, snacks and drinks, and fishing tackle and bait. Fishing and crabbing are allowed on the docks here as well. It's located at the end of Bob Perry Road, on the Loving Canal at Hog Island, past the Dare County boat landing.

Roanoke Island

Pirate's Cove Yacht Club
Nags Head–Manteo Causeway, Manteo
(252) 473-3906, (800) 367-4728
www.fishpiratescove.com

This full-service marina is known for its good service and many amenities. It offers a fuel dock with gas and diesel fuel, and diesel is now available at every slip. An on-site restaurant, Hurricane Mo's (see our Restaurants chapter), serves lunch and dinner. Professional fish-cleaning staff is on-hand at the dock, or you can do it yourself at the facilities. The dock master's office monitors channels 16 and 78. Pirate's Cove is open year-round. For boat-ramp access, head across the street to the site just under the west side of the Washington Baum Bridge. This site has two concrete ramps and plenty of parking for vehicles with trailers.

Manteo Waterfront Marina
207 Queen Elizabeth Ave., Manteo
(252) 473-3320

Located within walking distance of restaurants, a movie theater, a bookstore, and various retail shops, this marina has 53 slips and can accommodate boats up to 130 feet.

Air-conditioned heads and showers are available here as well as laundry facilities, a picnic area with gas grills, e-mail access, and rental cars. Fuel is not available. Both 30-amp and 50-amp power is on-site. Block and cube ice are sold on site.

Rates are $1.00 per foot during the off-season and for long stays. Otherwise, expect to pay about $1.25 a foot. During special events like Fourth of July weekend, rates may be higher. Ask about weekend packages, plus sailing charters and fishing charters. Manteo Waterfront Marina is open year-round.

Salty Dawg Marina
US 64, Manteo
(252) 473-3405
www.saltydawgmarina.com

Salty Dawg has 55 slips, all with power and water, and an air-conditioned/heated bathhouse. Light repairs can be done on-site. Boats up to 150 feet can be docked at Salty Dawg, which is on Shallowbag Bay near downtown Manteo. Rates are $1.15 per foot per day for transient boats, plus electricity; $7.35 per foot per month; and $56 per foot per year, with a minimum of 30 feet. A ship's store and dry storage for boats up to 26 feet are also on the premises. Commercial towing and courtesy cars are available. Salty Dawg monitors Channel 16, the hailing and distress frequency on marine radios. A lift has been installed to accommodate larger boats. The marina is open year-round, 8:00 A.M. to 6:00 P.M. in season. It closes at 5:00 P.M. November through February.

Thicket Lump Marina
Thicket Lump Rd., Wanchese
(252) 473-4500

This family-owned and -operated, 28-slip marina rents dock space to pleasure and fishing vessels up to 45 feet by the day, week, month, or year. Yearly dockage is $5.50 a foot, monthly dockage is $7.00 per foot, and the daily slip fee is $7.00 per day with a minimum of three days. A ship's store and tackle shop are at the marina, and both gas and diesel fuel. Thicket Lump offers inshore and offshore char-

ters; call for information. The marina is
open year-round.

Mainland Dare County

**Manns Harbor Marina, US 64, Manns Harbor
(252) 453–5150**

The Manns Harbor Marina serves boaters
with a boat ramp that's the perfect put-in
spot for those fishing for striped bass on
the Manns Harbor and Croatan Sound
bridges. Gas and diesel fuel are available.
A bar/lounge and a small motel are also
on-site.

Bodie Island

**Oregon Inlet Fishing Center
NC 12, Bodie Island
(252) 441–6301**

The closest marina and fuel dock to Oregon Inlet, Oregon Inlet Fishing Center is
on the north side of the Herbert C. Bonner
Bridge, about 10 miles from Nags Head.
The fishing center accommodates anglers
with gas and diesel fuel and a well-stocked
bait and tackle shop that opens at 5:00
A.M. The tackle shop carries a complete
line of surf, inshore, and deep-sea fishing
equipment, plus drinks, snacks, coffee,
hot dogs, T-shirts, ice, sunscreen, sunglasses, and anything else you'd need. The
boat ramp at Oregon Inlet Fishing Center,
with five concrete ramps, is one of the
nicest in the area, with plenty of parking
for vehicles and trailers. Restroom and
trash facilities are on-site.

Hatteras Island

**Frisco Cove Marina
NC 12, Frisco
(252) 995–4242**

On the Pamlico Sound, about nine miles
from Hatteras Inlet, this full-service
marina has 30 slips available to rent for
boats up to 35 feet long for $20 a day, $120
a week, or $950 a year. Seasonal dry storage
costs $40 a month. The on-site boat ramp
costs $10. The facility sells marine sup-
plies, including Sea Value products, and
fishing supplies. The marina also sells and

services all major brands of outboard motors, including Suzuki, Nissan, and Yamaha. Regular fuel and bait and tackle are available.

A bathhouse with sinks and men's and women's showers, a convenience store, a large gift shop, and a fuel island are also located at Frisco Cove. The marina is open year-round. See our listings in the Boat Rental section of this chapter and our Camping and Fishing chapters for more information about Frisco Cove's offerings.

Hatteras Wind N Surf - Avon Boathouse
NC 12, Avon
(252) 995–4525, (888) WND–SURF
www.windnsurf.com

Just across from the Avon Pier, this is the only public boat ramp and marina in Avon. You can launch your craft from the ramp for $5.00 in and $5.00 out. Dock space is also available for $20.00 a day or $100.00 a week. Ask about long-term rates.

Hatteras Harbor Marina
NC 12 and Gulfstream Way, Hatteras Village
(252) 986–2166
www.hatterasharbor.com

This marina can accommodate boats up to 68 feet for a day, month, or year. Rates are $1.00 per foot per day or $10.00 per foot per month. Call for annual charges. Hatteras Harbor also has five apartments available for customers to rent. A full-service deli and ship's store are located at the marina. Diesel fuel is available. Hatteras Harbor is open year-round. Hatteras Harbor Marina has the only public laundry facilities on the island, open 24 hours a day.

Willis Boat Landing
NC 12, Hatteras Village
(252) 986–2208

This marina accepts small craft up to 25 feet for short-term stays. Charges are $15 per night. About 20 boats can be accommodated at a time. Boat and motor repairs can be done on-site. Bait and tackle are available for sale. Willis Boat Landing is open year-round.

Hatteras Landing Marina
NC 12, Hatteras Village
(252) 986–2205, (800) 551–8478

Hatteras Landing offers a complete ship's store with tackle, fresh and frozen baits, lures, sportswear, and a market with beer, ice, and groceries. Gas and diesel fuel are available. Hatteras Landing offers fully metered slips and has laundry facilities, bathrooms, and a fish-cleaning service. It's open year-round.

Oden's Dock
NC 12, Hatteras Village
(252) 986–2555
www.odensdock.com

Oden's Dock has a deep draft that can accommodate vessels up to 65 feet. Of the 27 slips at the marina, 20 are deep draft. Slips cost $1.00 per foot per day, $4.50 per foot per week, and $10.00 per foot per month. Rates include water and electric. Reservations are suggested during the peak season.

You will also find a seafood market and Breakwater restaurant at Oden's Dock. Diesel fuel and gasoline are sold at the on-site ship's store, along with bait, tackle, food, and beverages. Showers are available during business hours, and fish-cleaning facilities are also available for anglers. One headboat and a charter fishing fleet dock here. Oden's is open year-round. Hours vary during the off-season. Please call ahead for details.

Teach's Lair Marina
NC 12, Hatteras Village
(252) 986–2460
www.teachslair.com

This year-round, full-service marina has 95 slips that can accommodate boats up to 65 feet. Depending on the size of your boat, rates range from $15 to $35 a day, $75 to $200 a week, and $200 to $450 a month. Two launching ramps are also located at the marina. Teach's Lair has a bathhouse, dry storage, and a ship's store on-site. Fuel (diesel and gasoline), oil, and tackle are all available at the store. A head-

The Outer Banks's wide, shallow sounds are a boater's paradise. PHOTO: MOLLY HARRISON

boat, charter fishing fleet, and two dive boats dock here. Parasailing adventures leave from the marina.

Ocracoke Island

**The National Park Service Dock
Silver Lake, Ocracoke Village
(252) 928–4531**

From April through November, dockage costs 80 cents per foot plus $3.00 a day for 110-volt electricity hookups, or $5.00 a day for 220-volt connections. During the rest of the year, the cost is 40 cents per foot, while the electric hookups stay the same price. There's a two-week limit on summer stays, and dock space is assigned on a first-come, first-served basis. No water is available in the winter season. If no ranger is on site when you arrive, pay at the visitor center across the street.

**Anchorage Marina/Ocracoke Fishing Center
NC 12, Ocracoke
(252) 928–6661**

Right in the heart of Ocracoke on Silver Lake, Anchorage Marina has 35 slips accommodating boats up to 120 feet long. In-season rates are $1.50 foot, off-season rates are 75 cents per foot, and mid-season rates are $1.00 per foot. Rates include electricity, water, showers, and pool access. Cable TV is available at the slips for an extra $3.00. Diesel fuel and gas are available. The marina is open year-round, and there is no limit on the length of stays. The dockside Smacnally's Raw Bar is next door, and Anchorage offers bike rentals and small-boat rentals. This location is accessible to practically everything in this perfectly walkable village.

Boat Rentals

If you don't own a powerboat but want to explore the vast waters of this region, you can rent one. Lots of places, even marinas or rent-all services, will often rent boats. Following are some reliable sources if you're looking for motorboats.

Duck

Sunset Watersports
NC 12, Duck
(252) 261–7100
www.barrierislandboats.com

Sunset is on the Currituck Sound at the pier behind Sunset Grille and Raw Bar. You can rent motorboats, day sailers, or catamarans hourly, by the half-day, or daily. For fishing, skiing, or just exploring, try out the 18-foot Nautica twin-hull or an 18-foot Carolina Skiff. For pure leisure, rent the pontoon boat. Call for rates. It's open May through October.

North Duck Watersports
NC 12, Duck
(252) 261–4200

North Duck Watersports is on the west side of Duck Road, directly on the Currituck Sound. Sport boats, pontoon boats, kayaks, and bicycles are all available here. North Duck is open spring through fall. Call for rates.

Kitty Hawk

Promenade Watersports
US 158, MP¼, Kitty Hawk
(252) 261–4400

Right across from the Wright Memorial Bridge on the Currituck Sound, Promenade bills itself as the only full-service watersports center in the Southern Shores, Kitty Hawk, and the Kill Devil Hills area. If you want to rent a boat, you are quite likely to find just what you want at this complete fun spot. Sailboats, kayaks, pontoon boats, and 16-foot fishing and crabbing skiffs are all available for rent here. Sunset cruises are offered aboard pontoon boats or a 20-foot trimaran sailboat. Call the number listed for information and rates. Promenade is open spring through fall.

Nags Head

The Waterworks
US 158, MP 16½, Nags Head
(252) 441–8875
www.obxwaterworks.com

Not only can you rent 19-foot powerboats, pontoons, and jet boats at The Waterworks, you can also get any kind of watercraft supplies at this site, plus a complete line of bike, kayak, and beach equipment rentals. This watersports center is the only one in the area that sells and repairs Yamaha watercraft and boats. It also sells Yamaha outboard motors. It is open daily year-round.

Nags Head Water Sports & Kawasaki
Nags Head–Manteo Causeway, Nags Head
(252) 480–2236

Watersports rental equipment at NHWS&K includes Kawasaki three-seat JetSkis, a Donzi jet boat, 16-foot fishing skiffs, and Aquacycles. There's a small picnic area, a boat dock, and a sandy beach for the kids on the premises. Rental operations run from mid-May through October. Call for rental reservations in season.

Bodie Island Adventures
Nags Head–Manteo Causeway, Nags Head
(252) 441–6822
www.bodieislandadventures

Bodie Island Adventures rents 24-foot pontoon boats and 19-foot center-console fishing boats. The pontoon boats rent for $129 for two hours and $279 a day, fuel included. The fishing boats, outfitted with depth finders and rod holders, rent for $89 for two hours and $199 for the whole day.

Hatteras Island

Hatteras Jack Inc.
NC 12, Rodanthe
(252) 987–2428

Right on the Pamlico Sound, Hatteras Jack is a year-round angler's haven. Six fiberglass Carolina Skiffs can be rented from March through December. Equipped with a 20-horsepower motor, the 14-foot skiff, which can hold 5 passengers, rents for $75 a half-day and $110 for 8 hours. The six-passenger, 16-foot skiff with a 25-horsepower motor rents for $80 a half-day and $120 for the full day. Hourly rates are available. A $100 deposit is required on all boats.

The price does not include gas, but it does include a short instruction course and safety gear. Boats are available from dawn to dusk. A bait and tackle shop with a full line of custom-built rods is on-site. You can also charter soundside fishing trips at Hatteras Jack.

Frisco Cove Marina
NC 12, Frisco
(252) 995–4242
www.friscove.com

You can rent motorboats at this full-service marina. Carolina Skiffs (21 or 24 feet) and 14- and 16-foot aluminum boats equipped with outboard motors can be rented by the day or week. Call for rates.

Ocracoke Island
Island Rentals
Silver Lake Rd., Ocracoke Village
(252) 928–5480

Island Rentals rents fiberglass flat-bottom boats and catamarans ranging from 16 to 19 feet. Rates range from $85 for a half-day to $575 for a week. Boats are rented on a half-day, daily, three-day, and weekly basis. Island Rentals is open Easter through Thanksgiving.

Anchorage Marina
NC 12, Ocracoke
(252) 928–6661

Anchorage Marina rents 16- to 24-foot skiffs for half-days, whole days, and weekly. Call for rates. The Marina is right on Silver Lake and is open year-round.

Personal Watercraft

If you feel a need for speed and enjoy the idea of riding a motor-powered vehicle across the water, more than a dozen Outer Banks outposts rent personal watercraft by the hour. Personal watercraft are most well-known and commonly referred to by their brand names—Sea Doo, JetSki, and Wave Runner.

No experience is necessary to ride these powerful boat-like devices, although a training session is a must if you've never before piloted a personal watercraft. Unlike land-locked go-carts and other speedy road rides, there aren't any lanes to stick to on the open sound or ocean. But that doesn't mean you should go out and ride with reckless abandon. With more and more people riding personal watercraft, it is imperative that each person practice responsible and safe riding.

Several styles of personal watercraft have developed over the past decade. Wave Runners allow drivers to maneuver these crafts sitting down and a second passenger to hold on, also sitting, from behind. Most JetSkis don't have seats and can accommodate only one person at a time in a standing or kneeling position. Newer Runabouts, also known as blasters, give riders the choice of standing or sitting. Wave Runners are the easiest style craft to balance and control because you don't have to worry as much about tipping over. JetSkis are, however, more suitable for tricks—and prone to spills—and better able to leap ocean waves. Almost all of these motorized vessels can cruise for up to two hours on five gallons of fuel.

Personal watercraft are akin to motorboats with inboard motors that power a water pump. There aren't any propellers or outside engine parts, so fingers and toes generally stay safe. Like other motorized boats, however, personal watercraft are loud and can be dangerous if you don't know what you're doing. Most rental outposts include brief instructions and sometimes even a video on how to handle Wave Runners, JetSkis, and Runabouts.

Practicing on Personal Watercraft

Basic operations of a personal watercraft (PWC) include an ignition and stall button on the left handle; the throttle on the right. Push the start button on the left to take off. Your right hand can control the speed by turning the throttle forward or back. If you fall off, a wrist lanyard that wraps around your hand automatically snaps away from the handle and shuts off the engine. To get aboard again, climb on from the back. Always steer to the right when approaching another personal watercraft—just as you would on the road. A quick, easy trick on JetSkis and Wave Runners, if you're game, is to throw the throttle open and then turn hard. It's like doing a 360-degree doughnut on the water. As the back of the personal watercraft comes around, the front submerges. Gun the throttle again and you can fly out over your own wake.

While most rental shops are on the sound side of the Outer Banks, where the water's surface is generally slicker and depths are much more shallow, a few personal watercraft outlets will let you take the vessels into the ocean. There, shore break and offshore waves provide great takeoffs and challenges to more experienced JetSki drivers. Remember to watch out for surfers, swimmers, and other Jet-Ski drivers who might not see you coming.

Those who own their own PWCs can launch their craft at any of the public boat ramps. Be aware, however, that PWCs are banned in certain areas of the Outer Banks. The National Park Service does not allow the launching of PWCs anywhere in Cape Hatteras National Seashore. The Town of Southern Shores requires PWCs launchers to get a permit from the police department. To get this permit, you must show proof of insurance and that you have taken a boating-safety course. You must stay at least 400 yards offshore in Southern Shores. In Nags Head, PWCs must stay at least 600 yards offshore and away from piers. Ocracoke Island forbids the use of PWCs.

Renting Personal Watercraft

New PWCs sell for $5,000 to $10,000. Several Outer Banks rental shops also sell used personal watercraft for cheaper prices at the end of the summer season. Remember, you'll probably need a trailer to haul these vessels behind your vehicle.

If you're just here on vacation, or don't think you'd ride one enough for the price to pay off, shops from Corolla to Hatteras Island rent personal watercraft beginning at $30 a half-hour. Price wars will occasionally result in very low prices. More powerful models are generally more expensive. Additional charges also sometimes apply for extra riders. Personal watercraft also can be rented by the hour, day, or even week at some spots.

When you're out riding through the waves, keep in mind these personal watercraft rules:

- Stay in designated buoyed areas at all times.
- Stay at least 50 yards away from other personal watercraft, swimmers, and boaters.
- Give sail craft, such as windsurfers and sailboats, the right of way.
- Do not excessively flip your vehicle.

- Wear a life jacket.
- Keep the lanyard attached to your wrist at all times.
- Be aware that PWCs are low profile and often difficult for others to see. Stay a safe distance away.
- Return to shore immediately if gas has turned to "reserve" or if any mechanical problems are apparent.
- Do not wake jump, splash, race, or interact in any way with other watercraft.
- Check local regulations before using a PWC in a new area. Some municipalities, such as Ocracoke Island, strictly forbid their use.

Corolla

Corolla Watersports
at the Inn at Corolla Light
1066 Ocean Trail, Corolla
(252) 453–8602

A sister store to North Duck Watersports, Wave Runner III can be rented here. Call for rates and more information. Corolla Watersports is open May through October.

Kitty Hawk Watersports
NC 12, Corolla
(252) 453–6900
www.khsports.com

Kitty Hawk Waters-ports, behind Tim-Buck II Shopping Village, and affiliated with Kitty Hawk Sports, runs a complete watersports store. You can rent Wave Runners by the half hour and hour. Call for prices and more information. Waterbikes, paddleboats, kayaks, and parasailing are also offered through this store. Kitty Hawk Watersports is open in Corolla from early spring through fall. The Nags Head location at Milepost 16 on US 158 is open longer.

Duck

North Duck Watersports
NC 12, Duck
(252) 261–4200

Three miles north of the village on the Sanderling border, this watersports center rents Wave Runners to race across the nearby Currituck Sound. Call for information on rates. North Duck Watersports is open April through October.

Sunset Watersports
NC 12, Duck
(252) 261–7100
www.barrierislandboats.com

Sunset Watersports, on the sound behind Sunset Grille and Raw Bar, rents Wave Runners and Sea Doo jet boats. Wave Runners rent for $48 for a half hour to $77 for an hour. Sea Doos rent for $145 an hour. Sunset is open spring through fall.

Kitty Hawk

Promenade Watersports
US 158, Kitty Hawk
(252) 261–4400

Even before you hit the sandy Outer Banks from the Wright Memorial Bridge, you'll see the Promenade on your right. A watersports and kiddie recreational park, Promenade includes enough to keep everybody delighted on land while you're racing around on the Currituck Sound on a personal watercraft. Wave Runners and Runabouts can be rented by the half hour, hour, half-day, or full day. Early-bird specials are offered on Wave Runners. Call for price information. The Promenade says it has the largest riding area of any other personal watercraft rental business because its share of the Currituck Sound is not restricted by municipal regulations. Promenade closes in winter.

Nags Head

The Waterworks
US 158, MP 16½, Nags Head
(252) 441–8875
www.obxwaterworks.com

One of the many watersports activities and services Waterworks offers is rental of personal watercraft. JetSkis, Sea Doos, and Wave Runners are available at half-hour and hourly rates. Call for prices. Waterworks also sells personal watercraft, including Yamaha and Sea Doo. Personal watercraft rentals are offered from March through November.

Nags Head Water Sports & Kawasaki
Nags Head–Manteo Causeway, Nags Head
(252) 480–2236, (252) 480–3444

Nags Head Water Sports & Kawasaki is a Kawasaki PWC dealership with such water-sports rental equipment as Kawasaki three-seat JetSkis, a Donzi jet boat, fishing skiffs, kayaks, and Aquacycles. JetSki 750 rents for $78 an hour, and the 900 rents for $95 an hour. Prices are less in the off-season. In addition to rentals, you'll find a substantial amount of retail goods, including PWC accessories, sandals, and sportswear. There's a small picnic area, a boat dock, and a sandy beach for the kids on the premises. Rental operations run from mid-May through October. Call for PWC sales and service information throughout the year or for rental reservations during the summer.

Kitty Hawk Watersports
US 158, MP 16, Nags Head
(252) 441–2756
www.khsports.com

This complete watersports store offers Wave Runners for rent by the half hour and hour. The store is right on the sound in Nags Head, so launching is easy. Waterbikes, paddleboats, and kayaks are available for purists. Call for prices. There are also Kitty Hawk Watersports locations in Corolla, Duck, and Avon. The Nags Head location is open well into the fall.

Hatteras Island

Rodanthe Watersports and Campground
NC 12, Rodanthe
(252) 987–1431

This soundfront campground and watersports operation rents Wave Runners starting at $58 an hour. They also rent surfboards, bikes, kayaks, and sailboats.

Hatteras Watersports
NC 12, Salvo
(252) 987–2306

Hatteras Watersports rents Wave Runner personal watercraft. The Wave Runner 650, which seats one to two persons, rents for $48 per half-hour and $68 per hour. The Wave Runner 700, which seats three riders, rents for $54 per half-hour and $78 per hour. Hatteras Watersports is on the sound side, across from the Salvo Volunteer Fire Department.

Outer Banks fishing is the stuff of which dreams are made.

Fishing

Welcome to our waters. If fishing is your passion, your options along these barrier islands should be enough to send you reeling. Situated as we are in the Atlantic, not only do we have fabulous close-range ocean and inlet fishing, but we're so close to the Gulf Stream and all its bounty that offshore trips are just as popular. Half-day and full-day charters are available year-round, or if you're a seasoned boater with an ocean-worthy vessel, you can make the trip yourself. If you're looking to spend only a couple of hours' worth of angling, you can surf fish along nearly 100 miles of wide sandy beaches, or you can wet a line at any one of a number of fishing piers. And that's just covering the ocean. Our sound waters are home to a number of different finned species, and even interior freshwater ponds are stocked with fish. Whether you yearn for surf, sound, inshore, offshore, pier, or fly-fishing, this is your place. Outer Banks angling is the stuff of which dreams are made. And these fish stories are for real.

The International Game Fish Association lists 92 world records for fish caught in Outer Banks waters, though some of those are now retired. These record-holders include a 405-pound lemon shark caught off of Buxton, a 67-pound amberjack caught in Oregon Inlet, a 41-pound bluefish, and a 72-pound red drum landed off Hatteras. There was a 348-pound bluefin tuna caught in Hatteras waters as well, along with black sea bass, Spanish mackerel, oyster toadfish, bigeye tuna, kingfish, and sheepshead landed in waters from Kill Devil Hills to Ocracoke. Even if you don't tip the scales with a record-breaking catch, you're bound to fill your coolers with anything from albacore to wahoo. Depending upon the season, where you fish, and your choice of bait, you'll also find speckled trout, gray trout, flounder, striped bass (or rockfish), black drum, largemouth bass, tautog, cobia, a variety of pan fish, and the big-daddy challenge: billfish.

You might think that the variety here draws expert anglers, hence the great catches. Well, there's more to the story. Chances of a good catch are enhanced by physical conditions existing here that you won't find anywhere else. And that's no fish story! Read on. We outline these characteristics in the offshore section that follows.

Another factor that hugely influences the catch is our charter fleets. Many consider the local sportfishing boats, called Carolina boats, the most beautiful in the world, and these vessels house the complete package of brains, talent, and beauty. Our experienced captains are without peer, and their charter mates will awe you with their knowledge, skill, and the manner in which they work. Some mates move as if their actions are choreographed: simultaneously working lines, assisting members of the fishing party, keeping the captain apprised of catches-in-progress, arranging poles, gaffing fish, and encouraging you to keep reeling when it feels as if your arm just won't manage another revolution. A good mate is worth his or her weight in gold.

While anyone who's ever gone fishing knows you can't predict catching fish, the local charter boat captains know what species should be in the area, and they will help you make wise choices on the morning of your trip. Charters leave the docks for inshore and offshore fishing every day that the weather permits. When you call to book a boat (see our Marinas listings in this chapter), you may find it hard to decide what kind of trip to choose unless you've fished before. Booking agents at each marina will guide you.

In the following sections, we describe offshore and inshore angling, backwater, surf, fly, and pier fishing. Offshore trips generally leave the docks at 5:30 A.M. and return no later than 6:00 P.M. Inshore trips are half-day excursions that leave twice daily, generally at 7:00 A.M. and again around noon. Intermediate trips can last all day but generally don't travel as far as the Gulf Stream.

Whether you venture out to sea or remain with your feet in the sand, you're bound to have a memorable experience. If you decide to fish without a guide or charter captain, the North Carolina Division of Marine Fisheries, (800) 682-2632, is a wealth of information. It's your resource for all available licenses, including recreational, commercial gear, and standard commercial licenses. A license to land flounder is only available through this Morehead City office. The division publishes an annual recreational fishing handbook, the *2000 North Carolina Coastal Waters Guide for Sports Fishermen*, a comprehensive guide to licenses, limits, and sizes. The helpful staff will also direct you to the appropriate contacts for obtaining federal permits for tuna and other controlled species.

For information on freshwater fishing permits and regulations, you'll need to contact the North Carolina Wildlife Resources Commission in Raleigh. The number for hunting and fishing licenses is (919) 662-4370. A regulations digest is available at sporting-goods stores and tackle shops. Call either Wildlife Resources or the North Carolina Division of Marine Fisheries for information on motorboat registration. Official weigh stations are listed toward the end of this chapter.

Offshore Fishing

The Outer Banks has been referred to as The Billfish Capital of the World. Though other fishing destinations would debate that point, the Outer Banks waters are home to an incredible number of billfish—white and blue marlin and sailfish. These fighting fish are caught from spring through early fall, with peak catches for blue marlin in June and peak catches for white marlin and sailfish in August and September. In order to protect the species, billfish are almost always caught and released. You still get bragging rights for your released fish, though; the mate flies one flag per released billfish on the outriggers of the boat so everyone at the dock can see how many your party reeled in that day.

Next to billfish, some of the most pursued Gulf Stream fish are the yellowfin tuna and bluefin tuna. Other fish you're likely to catch are bigeye tuna, blackfin tuna, dolphin (mahi mahi), king mackerel, wahoo, and mako shark.

The majority of Outer Banks captains who lead you to offshore fishing grounds have been working these waters for years. Many are second- and third-generation watermen. They generally choose the daily fishing spot depending on recent trends, seasons, and weather. Occasionally, when there's a slow spell, a captain will move away from the rest of the fleet to play out a hunch. If the maverick meets with success, it's common for him/her to share this find with the rest of the fleet. In other words, the area fleets have a brother- or sisterhood that visiting anglers say they've experienced nowhere else. This camaraderie can't help but enhance the fishing experience, plus, fishing together is safer.

Anglers fishing offshore for big game fish generally troll (drag bait behind the moving boat). If you run into a school of fish, such as dolphin (mahi mahi), the

Reeling in a big tuna, wahoo, or billfish will fully test your strength and stamina. PHOTO: COURTESY OF LINDA LAUBY

captain will stop the boat so the party can cast into the water that's been primed with chum, or fish bits. Chumming also is used on bluefin tuna trips. All these techniques are explained the day of the trip. Expect to pay from $800 to $1,200 for six people to charter an offshore fishing excursion. Bluefin tuna trips cost a bit more. Gulf Stream charters leaving from Hatteras marinas tend to be less expensive than those near Oregon Inlet.

One offshore area that's frequented with great regularity is called The Point (not to be confused with Cape Hatteras Point). Approximately 37 miles off the Outer Banks, this primary fishing ground for local boats is rich in game fish such as tuna, dolphin, wahoo, billfish, and shark. Blue marlin, wahoo, and dolphin show up at The Point in April and May. Yellowfin, bigeye, and blackfin tuna are the anglers' mainstay year-round. A significant population of yellowfin inhabits this area in the winter, providing a tremendous seasonal fishery. You have to be patient to fish in the

winter because plenty of bad weather days make traveling offshore a waiting game.

The Point has unique characteristics that give it a reputation for attracting and harboring a variety and quantity of fish from the tiny baitfish to massive billfish. Deep-swimming reef fish, such as grouper, snapper, and tilefish, also inhabit The Point. Because of the strong current, however, you must travel a little bit south of The Point to fish for them effectively.

What also helps set this spot apart is its proximity to the edge of the Continental Shelf. Where there's a drop-off, you'll find a concentration of baitfish because of the nutrient-rich waters and the currents playing off the edge to stir things up. Anglers don't have to travel far to get to The Point since the Continental Shelf is particularly narrow off Cape Hatteras. The Point is the last spot where the Gulf Stream appears near the Shelf before it veers off in an east-northeasterly direction. Weather permitting, there are some days when the Gulf Stream entirely covers

The Point. Other days, prevailing winds can push it farther offshore.

At about 50 miles wide and a half-mile deep, the Gulf Stream has temperatures that rarely drop below 65 to 70 degrees, providing a comfortable habitat for a variety of sea life. The Gulf Steam flows at an average rate of 2.5 mph, at times quickening to 5 mph. This steady flow carries millions of tons of water per second, continually pushing along sea life in its path, including fish, microscopic plants and animals, and gulfweed. Gulfweed lines the edge of the Gulf Stream when the winds are favorable, creating a habitat for baitfish. You can pull up a handful of vegetation and find it teeming with miniature shrimp and fish. Anglers fish these "grass lines" as well as the warm-water eddies that spin off from the Gulf Stream. These warm pockets, which vary in size from 20 to 100 miles long by a half-mile to a mile wide, are sometimes filled with schools of dolphin, tuna, and mako shark. The Gulf Stream is about 30 miles off the Outer Banks. It takes about two hours to get there from Oregon Inlet, and about an hour and a half from Hatteras Inlet, depending on the prevailing winds and the speed of your boat.

Catch-and-release fishing for bluefin tuna has anglers from across the globe traveling to Hatteras Island to partake in a bonanza that has really revived winter offshore charter fishing along the Outer Banks. In 1994, captains began noticing a massive congregation of bluefin tuna inhabiting the wrecks about 20 miles from Hatteras Inlet. We've seen the action firsthand, and the quantity of bluefin available and the frequency with which they bite are phenomenal. Bluefin fishing takes place on the southern Outer Banks, with trips leaving from Hatteras and Ocracoke marinas. Charter boats that ordinarily dock on the northern Outer Banks make their home base on Hatteras during the bluefin months. Many motels on Hatteras Island gladly stay open year-round to accommodate bluefin anglers.

Bluefin tuna weighing from 200 to more than 800 pounds have been caught in these waters. These giants are a federally protected species, so anglers almost always must release them. Restrictions state that during bluefin tuna season anglers may keep one fish from 27 to 73 inches per boat per day. The length of the tuna season is determined annually by National Marine Fisheries and is contingent on overall poundage caught.

But just reeling in a bluefin of any magnitude will make the blood of an avid angler run hot! The bluefin seem to strike with less provocation on the choppy days—plus there are fewer boats present during rougher weather. On days when the fish are spooked by excessive boat traffic or simply aren't biting for whatever reason, mates will chum the water to increase the chance of a strike. These giants often jump 4 feet out of the ocean just to bite a bloody bait.

Local anglers troll, chum, and use live or dead bait. Many anglers even catch bluefin tuna and other game fish on a fly. We've seen great success with 130-pound test line. Some folks like to use lighter tackle for the sport of it, but the heavier the line, the better the condition of the fish when it's released. Circle hooks are also recommended, for they tend to lodge in the mouth cartilage rather than in the fleshy gullet or gills.

Even though most of the fish are caught on heavy tackle, carefully handled, and subsequently released, recreational charter boat captains are contemplating a self-imposed quota for catch and release to try to protect the fish even further. When there are large groups of boats present day after day, it's likely the same fish will have to do battle over and over.

You can enjoy offshore fishing year-round, but for bluefin fishing off Hatteras, you should book a trip from January through March. Some fish may show up earlier, and there are bluefin available in early April, but by then, captains begin concentrating on yellowfin again. Bluefin boats leave the dock between 5:30 and 7:00 A.M.

Offshore fishing charters accommodate six people. If your party is shy of six, tip them at least 10 percent and up to 20 percent of the cost of your trip.

If you really love offshore fishing, consider entering one of the fishing tournaments listed in our Annual Events chapter. If you're not up for Gulf Stream fishing but want to see the fish, show up at these docks at about 4:00 P.M. to watch the boats unload their catches. You'll see dolphin, tuna, wahoo, cobia, and others, but no billfish since those are catch-and-release species.

Inshore and Small-Boat Fishing

A variety of inshore opportunities abound that will strike the fancy of the novice or expert angler. Inshore generally refers to inlet, sound, lake, river, and some close-range ocean fishing on a boat.

Inshore captains generally book half-day trips but also offer intermediate all-day trips to take you farther out. If you're interested in bluefish, Spanish mackerel, cobia, king mackerel, bonito, trout, flounder, croaker, and red drum, you can book trips from virtually any marina. Half-day trips are a little easier on the pocketbook.

Spanish mackerel are a mainstay of the area. Ocracoke Island captains begin looking for them in late April and typically enjoy catches through late October. Farther north on the Outer Banks, Spanish mackerel usually arrive the first or second week in May, depending on the water temperature. Casting to them is the most sporting way of catching them. We suggest that you use 8-pound test on a medium to medium-light spinning rod with a pink and white Sting-silver. Other colors work well also; if the people next to you are catching fish and you aren't, see what kinds of lures they are using.

If it's flounder you're after, you can find these flat fish in both Hatteras and Oregon Inlets, in clear water. Anglers drift bottom rigs on medium-light spinning tackle.

Offshore fishing is a big-time thrill. PHOTO: MARY ELLEN RIDDLE

many times the booking agents or captain can hook you up with another small party. Anglers are expected to bring their own food and drinks on the trips. Coolers for any fish you want to take home can be left in your car at the dock to save room on the boat. Fish-cleaning facilities are available at all docks, and fish-cleaning services (for a fee) are available at most. Don't forget to bring sunscreen and seasickness remedies (see our section on Preventing Seasickness). All bait, tackle, instruction, and advice are included in the price of your charter. Mates work for tips, so be sure to

Croakers are found in the sounds around deep holes, oyster rocks, and sloughs.

You can dine on almost all inshore species. There's one bony fish with little food value that cannot be overlooked: the tarpon. A release-category fish, the tarpon is probably one of the strongest fighting fish available inshore. While the Outer Banks is not a destination spot for tarpon, a handful of locals fish for them around Ocracoke in the Pamlico Sound and south to the mouth of the Neuse River. We recommend fresh-cut bait, such as spot or trout, and very sharp hooks to penetrate the tarpon's hard mouth. Remember, it's one thing to hook up and a whole other to bring a tarpon to the boat. Good luck!

Outer Banks anglers enjoy fishing for rockfish (also called striped bass or stripers) year-round. They are fun to catch and make a great-tasting dinner. Though stripers are a regulated species, they've steadily been making a comeback during the last decade or so. Each year stripers spawn inland, and the young live in estuaries for several years before joining the Atlantic migratory population. A moratorium initially was placed on the fish in summer 1984, when striper stocks in the Chesapeake Bay started to decline rapidly. This was significant since about 90 percent of the Atlantic migratory stock comes from the Chesapeake Bay. Marine fisheries experts blamed overfishing and water quality for the drop. A widespread East Coast moratorium gave the species a chance to thrive again. There was a partial lifting of the moratorium in 1990, and today, while the species still is closely monitored, they afford Outer Banks anglers a hearty catch-and-release recreational fishery.

The ocean season for stripers is open year-round, but limits vary according to season. Though stripers are present in our waters year-round, the sound inhabitants are protected by restrictions. Since the sound fishing season fluctuates, the best thing to do is call your favorite tackle shop for up-to-date regulations. If you just want to catch and release, go at it anytime.

When a cold snap hits the Chesapeake Bay area, stripers migrate down past Corolla into Oregon Inlet. November is one of the best months to fish for them around the Manns Harbor bridge that connects Roanoke Island to the East Lake community. Anglers also fish in the winter for stripers behind Roanoke Island in East and South lakes.

Stripers tend to congregate around bridge pilings. They cluster near these nutrient-covered supports that entice smaller baitfish. You can troll, use spinning tackle with lures, fly-cast, or surf fish for them. Stripers are bottom feeders, so a planer can be used to catch them. Insiders suggest using a butter bean with a white bucktail on the end or Rat-L-Traps. You can catch these fish on slick calm days and in rougher weather, but a little current seems to help.

Summertime finds Outer Bankers fishing the sounds from Manteo to Ocracoke for speckled trout. Insiders suggest you move to the surf or a pier to catch them in fall. The speckled trout fishing is excellent in early fall around Oregon and Hatteras Inlets. They are best enjoyed on light tackle with artificial lures or on a fly rod. Light spinning tackle is another good choice. Artificial lures are the norm. Insiders suggest using a lead head jig with a soft plastic twister tail for sound, bridge, and inlet fishing. For the beach, try MirrOlures. Currently the fish must be a 12-inch total length minimum to be a keeper. Call your local tackle shop for more information.

Offshore and Inshore Charters

To book offshore and inshore charters, contact one of the marinas listed below. You can request a certain boat and captain or let them offer you one. All of these marinas represent reputable, licensed captains. It's best to call at least a month ahead, but call earlier if you know your schedule. Fishing trips are offered year-round. If everything is booked up, ask to be put on a waiting list; somebody might cancel. You should know that it is the captain's call on whether to go out in inclement weather. Always defer to the captain's judgment.

Pirate's Cove Yacht Club
Nags Head–Manteo Causeway , Manteo
(252) 473–3906, (800) 367–4728

Pirate's Cove is a world-class fishing center known for its boats, captains, and large-purse tournaments. It's by far the most modern marina on the Outer Banks, and its prices reflect its high quality. Seventeen sport-fishing boats operate out of this marina, each at a price of $1,200, plus mate's tip, for a full day of Gulf Stream fishing. Booking is centralized through the marina. Pirate's Cove Yacht Club is about a 15- to 20-minute boat ride from Oregon Inlet, the northernmost ocean-sound inlet on the Outer Banks. From there the Gulf Stream is about a two-hour ride. Pirate's Cove is the central booking agent for four inshore boats. Half-day trips cost $400, with a maximum of six people per boat. Trips run year-round. Pirate's Cove sponsors several fishing tournaments each year; see our Annual Events chapter.

Custom Sound Charters
152 Dogwood Trail, Manteo
(252) 473–1209
www.customsoundcharters.com

Captain Rick Caton has long been fishing the Outer Banks waters, both inshore and offshore, and he offers a wide variety of trips. Year-round, you can charter sound-fishing trips with Caton, who specializes in catching striped bass. He'll take you fly-fishing or light-tackle fishing for trout, puppy drum, flounder, striped bass, and bluefish. Everything you need is furnished.

Caton's inshore trips are offered on the 42-foot *Free Agent,* and he charges $400 for a maximum of six people for a half-day, $700 for a full day. Caton also offers shrimping and crabbing trips,

inshore Spanish mackerel trolling trips, plus light-tackle bottom fishing over wrecks for triggerfish and black sea bass. Or, you can choose to anchor up and chum for sharks, cobia, and king mackerel. Call for more information.

Inlet Charters
(252) 441–2174, (252) 202–2174

Capt. Billy Griggs offers inshore full or half-day inlet trips for red drum, large stripers, bluefish, Spanish mackerel, king mackerel, and cobia onboard his 24-foot custom Carolina-style boat. Half-day trips range from $275 to $350, and full-day trips range from $550 to $600.

The Hobo
Thicket Lump Marina, Wanchese
(252) 473–5297
www.hobofishing.com

The 40-foot *Hobo* is the one of the largest boats in the inshore charter fleet. It holds six anglers comfortably, with room to spare. Inshore and intermediate trips are offered for half and full days. Prices range from $350 to $700. You can also charter the *Lil' Hobo* for shrimping and crabbing trips for one to four people.

Tideline Charters
Thicket Lump Marina, Wanchese
(252) 261–1458
www.tidelinecharter.com

Full- and half-day inshore and intermediate trips are offered on this 34-foot custom Carolina boat called the *Tideline.* Half-day inshore trips cost $350, and half-day intermediate trips cost $400. Full-day intermediate trips cost $750.

Thicket Lump Marina
212 Thicket Lump Rd., Wanchese
(252) 473–4500

The no-frills Thicket Lump Marina represents three offshore fishing vessels. The boats leaving from Thicket Lump offer a bit of a bargain, at $875 for a full-day trip. Thicket Lump is about a 10-minute boat ride from Oregon Inlet.

Nags Head Guide Service
(252) 475–1555
www.nagsheadfishing.com

Captain David Dudley offers light-tackle inshore trips for stripers, flounder, trout, bluefish, mackerel, cobia, drum, and largemouth bass. Rates range from $150 to $425, depending on the number of people on board and the length of the trip.

Oregon Inlet Fishing Center
NC 12, Bodie Island
(252) 441–6301

The Oregon Inlet charter fishing fleet is a historic landmark on the Outer Banks. Most of the 31 sport-fishing boats in this marina were locally made, giving a good representation of the famous Carolina flared bow. Some of the Outer Banks's most seasoned captains fish from this marina and have done so since it opened in the 1960s. All offshore trips from this marina cost $1,100 for a party of six. Five boats offer inshore and intermediate trips from Oregon Inlet Fishing Center. Inshore trips cost $360 a half-day and $695 for a full day. Intermediate trips to ocean wrecks cost $412 for a half-day and $720 for a full day. Each boat accommodates up to six people. The Fishing Center is next to Oregon Inlet, which saves precious traveling time when heading to the fishing grounds.

Hatteras Harbor Marina
NC 12, Hatteras Village
(252) 986–2166, (800) 676–4939

This marina represents about 20 vessels that take anglers to the Gulf Stream via Hatteras Inlet. Trips cost from $650 to $1,100, depending on the size of the boat. Winter bluefin tuna trips cost $1,200. The Gulf Stream is about 90-minute boat ride from Hatteras Inlet. Inshore fishing trips can be chartered year-round from this marina on one of two 24-foot boats. Half-day trips cost $180 to $200 for up to three people, with an extra $25 charge for each additional passenger.

Hatteras Landing Marina
NC 12, Hatteras Village
(252) 986–2205, (800) 551–8478

Hatteras Landing Marina represents 12 offshore fishing boats. Prices range from $600 to $1,100, depending on the size of the boat. If you don't have a full party, Hatteras Landing can put one together for you if you're willing to wait on standby for a couple of days. Winter bluefin tuna trips cost about $100 to $200 more. Three boats offer inshore charters from this marina, with prices ranging from $300 to $400. Capacity is limited to six. Morning trips run 7:00 A.M. to noon and afternoon trips run 1:00 to 5:00 P.M.

Oden's Dock Marina
NC 12, Hatteras Village
(252) 986–2555

Around five or six offshore charter boats operate out of Oden's Dock. Prices range from $850 to $1,000, and winter bluefin tuna trips usually cost around $1,000. Oden's books inshore charters on a 22-foot boat and a 24-foot that can each handle four people. These boats fish in the sound only and charge $250 for a half-day. A larger 42-foot boat can operate in the sound or ocean and can accommodate six people for $325 a half-day.

Teach's Lair Marina
NC 12, Hatteras Village
(252) 986–2460

Fourteen boats operate out of Teach's Lair. Full-day offshore trips cost between $700 and $950, and make-up charters are available for $175 per person. Bluefin trips are more expensive. Teach's Lair books inshore charters on morning or afternoon half-day trips. Morning trips run from 7:00 A.M. to noon, and afternoon trips run from 12:30 to 5:30 P.M. Prices range from $300 to $350, depending on the boat.

Albatross Fleet
Foster's Quay, Hatteras Village
(252) 986–2515

The Albatross Fleet of Hatteras, established

The marsh and creeks behind the Bodie Island Lighthouse are good fishing grounds. PHOTO: HORSLEY/GARDNER by Capt. Ernal Foster in 1937, was the first charter fishing operation on the North Carolina coast. The original boat, the *Albatross*, is still taking anglers to the Gulf Stream. The *Albatross* was designed by Foster to perfectly accommodate offshore fishing parties, and it was built across the sound in Harkers Island. The fleet now consists of three boats, all named *Albatross*, and is now operated by Foster's son, Ernal Foster Jr., who began working as a mate on his father's boat in 1958. The *Albatross I, II,* and *III,* all 44 feet, dock at Foster's Quay. Offshore trips begin at $750 for a full day. Inshore half-day trips cost $350.

Ocracoke Fishing Center and Anchorage Marina
NC 12, Ocracoke Village
(252) 928–6661

Three boats offer full-day offshore charters out of this marina. Full-day trips cost $800 to $850. Bluefin tuna fishing packages, including lodging and food, are available for $1,500 for four people and $1,800 for six people. These boats use Ocracoke Inlet when heading to the Gulf Stream.

Offshore and Inshore Headboat Fishing

Headboat fishing can give you a great fishing experience without the expense of chartering a private boat. Several large boats take parties into the intermediate waters (in the ocean, though not as far as the Gulf Stream) all day, while others ply the inshore waters for half-days. Ocean trips typically track bottom species, such as black sea bass, triggerfish, tilefish, amberjack, snapper, tautog, grouper, and occasionally small sharks. The species vary slightly from north to south. Generally on these trips you're dropping a line down over artificial and natural reefs and wrecks, not trolling. Inshore trips ply the sounds and inlets and sometimes go several miles offshore to the wrecks on calm days. The trips usually yield croaker, trout, spot, flounder, sea mullet, blow toads, and pigfish. There is one head-

boat, the *Country Girl* out of Pirate's Cove, that takes trips to the Gulf Stream.

Headboats are built to accommodate a multitude of passengers, each person paying "by the head," hence the name. Open deck space from bow to stern holds anglers comfortably, and sometimes there is an enclosed cabin area. The boats are generally between 60 and 75 feet long and can hold up to 50 anglers. All gear and bait is supplied. All you have to bring is food, drinks, and sunscreen. Some boats provide snacks and drinks, so you should check when making reservations. You don't even need a fishing license. If you're new to fishing, the mates will help you with everything from baiting your hook to identifying your catch. Be sure to dress in layers if you're fishing any time other than summer. Mornings and evenings can be cool, even when days are warm.

Inshore headboat trips are the most suitable choice for families with young children, mainly because they're shorter. Deep-sea trips are full-day trips that can be as long as 8 to 10 hours, and the captain will not turn around except in a real emergency. Seasickness is not an emergency. Inshore trips are typically a half-day. Watch the kids carefully on the boats. The decks are often slippery, so you should enforce a no-running policy. Plus, these boats carry large crowds of people and fishing gear. Getting hooked can ruin a trip. That said, headboats are great places to teach children how to fish for a very small amount of money. Remain positive when fishing with kids. Everywhere in the world, there are days when the fishing is slow. If you're having one of those days, let the trip be a positive lesson in nature, patience, and people. A positive attitude will go far in hooking your kids on fishing for life. Besides, you often see dolphins, birds, turtles, and sometimes whales on these trips, so the day won't be a total loss.

Crystal Dawn
Pirate's Cove Yacht Club
Nags Head–Manteo Causeway, Manteo
(252) 473–5577

This 65-foot, two-story vessel offers inshore (inlet and sound) bottom-fishing trips from May through October. The boat holds up to 55 passengers. All bait and tackle are provided, but you have to bring your own snacks and drinks. Tickets cost $30 per person for everyone older than 10, and $25 per child age 10 and under. In peak season (Memorial Day to Labor Day), trips run from 7:00 A.M. to noon or 12:30 to 5:00 P.M. The rest of the time, the boat heads out from 8:00 A.M. to 1:00 P.M. The *Crystal Dawn* also takes sight-seeing trips in the evenings (see our Recreation chapter).

Country Girl
Pirate's Cove Yacht Club
Nags Head–Manteo Causeway, Manteo
(252) 473-5577

The *Country Girl* heads offshore from 5 to 35 miles, depending on the weather and the fishing. The 57-foot boat holds 27 passengers, each paying $75. This is a full-day trip, lasting from 7:00 A.M. to 5:00 P.M. Older children and teenagers are welcome, but younger children are not. The *Country Girl* offers trips from May through October.

Rosanne
Manns Harbor Marina, US 64
Manns Harbor
(252) 453-5150

Capt. Budgie Sadler offers half-day inshore fishing trips leaving from the Manns Harbor Marina. Trips cost $30 per person, and the boat can hold up to 16 people. There must be at least six people on board to leave the docks. Make reservations in advance.

Miss Oregon Inlet
Oregon Inlet Fishing Center, NC 12, Bodie Island
(252) 441-6301

The *Miss Oregon Inlet* is a 65-foot headboat that offers half-day, inshore fishing trips for $31 per person or $21 for kids age six and under. In early spring and fall, the boat makes one trip per day (except Sunday), leaving at 8:00 A.M. and returning at

12:30 P.M. From Memorial Day through Labor Day there are two trips: 7:00 to 11:30 A.M. and noon to 4:30 P.M. Buy tickets one day in advance, if possible, because the boat often fills up.

Miss Hatteras and Captain Clam
Oden's Dock, NC 12, Hatteras Village
(252) 986-2555

The *Miss Hatteras* headboat ties up at Oden's Dock in Hatteras Village and operates from February through November. She offers half-day fishing trips for $30 per person on Monday, Tuesday, and Thursday mornings from 8:00 A.M. to noon and Tuesday and Thursday afternoons from 1:00 to 5:00 P.M. On Wednesday, Friday, Saturday, and Sunday, she offers full-day bottom-fishing trips from 6:30 A.M. to 4:30 P.M. for $75 per person. The boat accommodates 45 people. In late October and early November, she offers full-day king mackerel fishing trips for $95 per person. All gear is included in the cost of the trip, and a snack bar is on board. In the summer, when the *Miss Hatteras* is booked, Oden's Dock also offers the *Captain Clam*, a 40-person-capacity headboat offering half-day, inshore sound, and inlet fishing trips for $30 a person. These trips run Monday through Saturday from 8:00 A.M. to noon and 1:00 to 5:00 P.M.

As the Stomach Turns: Battling and Preventing Seasickness

Almost everyone who has ever been on the water for any length of time has gotten seasick or at least battled that unmistakable queasy feeling. Seasickness is a one-of-a-kind experience. We've spent plenty of time on the water and know what it's like to want to throw yourself overboard. Here are some suggestions to help you avoid that feeling. Experiment to find what works best for you.

1. Take an over-the-counter remedy for motion sickness the night before

your trip and again an hour before departure. This allows time for the medicine to get into your system. Ask your pharmacist about the specifics on these medications. Some will make you more sleepy than others. If you're bringing children along, you'll need to find out whether the medication you are taking is safe for them too.

2. Topical patches are also available over the counter. The patch fits behind your ear or on your wrist and administers medication through your skin.

3. Eat nongreasy food the night before the trip (and go easy on the alcohol), and always eat a nongreasy breakfast. Pancakes and toast are good choices. Despite what you may think, a full stomach is much better than an empty one.

4. Pack a lunch that is neither spicy nor greasy. It also helps to nibble on saltines or ginger snap cookies all day. Ginger is an Asian remedy for motion sickness. Some people actually take ginger capsules, but we like the cookies.

5. Some swear that you should drink a lot of fluids while offshore. This makes sense when it comes to dehydration, but we've seen plenty of people get even sicker by downing a soda hoping to ward off the oncoming surge. Always pack some bottled water. While some people refrain from drinking anything until the latter part of the trip, others replenish fluids all day. Again, this is a highly personal choice.

6. If you do get sick, the worst may be over if you follow this simple rule: always eat immediately after getting sick (so says Hatteras native Capt. Spurgeon Stowe of the *Miss Hatteras*).

7. If you're feeling queasy, stay out on deck in the fresh air. Don't hole up in the salon, and do not go into the head (bathroom). If you're going to throw up, do it overboard. This is common and acceptable. Concentrate on the horizon if possible. Orient yourself with a stable point, and you should feel better. Above all, don't be embarrassed.

Marinas

The Outer Banks is dotted with many marinas that offer slips, boat ramps, gas and diesel fuel, tackle, and supplies. Almost all of them offer fishing charters as well. We've listed the fishing opportunities available at marinas in our Offshore, Inshore, and Headboat categories in this chapter. For information pertaining to slip rental, see our Getting Here, Getting Around chapter; and for information on the amenities offered to boaters, such as boat ramps, gas, and supplies, see our Watersports chapter.

Backwater Fishing

Fishing the backwaters means fishing the more-protected inland sounds, rivers, and lakes, either brackish or freshwater. The Croatan Sound, between Roanoke Island and the mainland, is a popular fishing spot for striped bass, also known as stripers or rockfish in these parts. Striper fishing is a year-round sport on the Outer Banks, though you can only keep those caught in the sound at certain times of the year. The Manns Harbor Bridge is renowned for its striper activity. Stripers congregate at the bridge, feeding around the pilings. They also feed over oyster bars located near the bridge. Be on the lookout for diving gulls and terns, which is a good identifying marker of the location of stripers. Both sides of the bridge have public parking and access for waders, but the western side has a marina with a boat-launch ramp. The new Croatan Sound bridge, just beyond the Manns Harbor Bridge, has already proven itself as a striper-attracting structure, so you should try both bridges. Many anglers fly-fish for stripers. Others swear by live eel, jigging with a bucktail or grub, or casting a Rat-L-Trap.

Backwater fishing also includes the Alligator River and South and East Lakes. You can troll, spin-cast, bait-cast, or fly-fish year-round in the backwaters. You'll find an interesting mix of freshwater and saltwater species, including crappie, striped bass, largemouth bass, flounder, bream, sheepshead, drum, perch, croaker, spot, catfish, and trout. It all depends on the season.

If you'd like a guide, there are a few that offer backwater services. The fishing is so laid-back that you might find the guide throwing in a line with you. Since these waters are more protected and less prone to harsh offshore winds, you can often fish here when you can't elsewhere. This is a nice alternative to ocean fishing, and it's a good choice for families. Bring your camera. You might spot birds, deer, and bears on land and alligators in the water.

You don't have to hire a guide, though. You can launch your own boat from any number of local ramps (see our Watersports chapter) or contact a tackle shop or marina for information.

Backwater Charters

If the following options are unavailable, you can always launch your own vessel from any of a number of local ramps (see our Watersports chapter) or contact the nearest marina or tackle shop for more information.

Phideaux Too
P.O. Box 343, Manns Harbor
(252) 473-3059

Capt. V.P. Brinson uses a 21½-foot twin-engine bateau that he constructed himself six years ago and says that he has a lot of repeat customers, including those who fished with him during his previous 38 years of offshore fishing. Brinson offers spin-casting, fly rod, bait-casting, and trolling charters in lakes, sounds, and rivers. You'll fish for rockfish, trout, red drum, flounder, bass, bream, crappie, and perch. Trips cost $175 for a half-day for two people, and $25 extra for each person up to four. Whole-day trips cost $300 for two people and $50 each for additional people.

Custom Sound Charters
152 Dogwood Trail, Manteo
(252) 473-1209
www.customsoundcharters.com

Light-tackle backwater trips are taken on the *Iron Will*, an 18-foot center-console. Captain Rick Caton books trips on this boat in the spring and fall. Half-day trips are $200 for one person, $225 for two, and $250 for a maximum of three. Full-day trips are $425 for one person, $450 for two, and $475 for a maximum of three.

Fly-Fishing

The Outer Banks has been a top fishing destination for decades, but fly-fishing has only recently caught on here. The fly-fishing bug on the Banks started in the 1960s and '70s, when a few well-known fly anglers and locals cast flies into the surf for bluefish and were quite successful. In 1979 Chico Fernandez fly-fished the Outer Banks, catching a white marlin. In 1981 he set an International Game Fish Association Fly Rod record with a 42-pound, 5-ounce red drum on 12-pound tippet. Since then, anglers have slowly discovered the Outer Banks's varied fly-fishing opportunities. Fly-fishing magazines and television shows now regularly feature the Outer Banks and its fly-fishing guides.

Fly anglers fish in the same places conventional anglers do. Fly anglers catch dolphin, tuna, and marlin in the Gulf Stream. They catch amberjack, mackerel, albacore, and cobia on inshore wrecks. They reap pompano and bluefish in the surf and stripers in the sounds. The most successful and accessible fly-fishing is in the sounds, where speckled trout, stripers, red drum, bluefish, and Spanish mackerel are waiting.

It can be difficult to learn to fly-fish the Outer Banks, especially the vast Pamlico and Roanoke Sounds. Hiring a guide is the quickest way to learn the area. If you'd rather go it alone, ask for advice at local tackle shops, and you're sure to get some solid information and leads.

Outer Banks Fly Shop
US 158, MP 13, Nags Head
(252) 480–FISH
www.outerbanksflyshop.com

The Banks's only full-service fly-fishing shop opened in 1999 to serve the growing number of fly anglers who fish here. Owner Shawn Rollison and the rest of the staff are very knowledgeable about fly-fishing and can give you advice or help you find a guide. The shop is stocked to the gills with top-of-the-line rods (Sage, Orvis, St. Croix), Outer Banks–tested flies, line, and all the gear you'd ever need. Clothing especially suited to fly anglers is available, along with Costa del Mar sunglasses, hats, T-shirts, and gift items. Outer Banks Fly Shop books trips for both wading and boating anglers. They also offer a fly-fishing school, with casting classes on the water and seminars in the shop.

Flat Out Fly-Fishing & Light-Tackle Charters
(252) 449–0562
www.outerbanksflyfishing.com

Captains Brian Horsley and Sarah Gardner are the true Insiders when it comes to Outer Banks fly-fishing. Both halves of this fly-fishing duo are guides and well-known fishing writers. Horsley has the distinction of being the first saltwater fly-fishing guide in North Carolina. He's held a saltwater fly-rod world record in the tippet class for a 16-pound, 9-inch bluefish he caught off Kitty Hawk Beach on 20-pound test. Gardner is also a world–record-holding angler and holds two fly-rod world records in the tippet

class for 12-pound bluefish and 16-pound bluefish. Note to novices: Before moving to the Outer Banks to become a fly-fishing guide, the ever-patient Gardner taught fly-fishing techniques. If you want fishing instruction, she's your captain.

Horsley's *Flat Out* and Gardner's *Fly Girl* dock at Oregon Inlet Fishing Center. They run near-shore fly-fishing/light-tackle charters from April through November, though they move both boats to Harkers Island on the southernmost Outer Banks during October and November for false albacore fishing. They fish the Pamlico, Roanoke, and Croatan Sounds for speckled trout, bluefish, puppy drum, little tunny, flounder, and cobia. Half-day trips cost $275, and full-day trips cost $450.

Fish Trap Charters
(252) 473–2657
www.outerbnksguideservice.com

Captain Tom Wagner of Fish Trap Charters offers light-tackle and fly-fishing charters in the sounds and near-shore waters. Expect to catch drum, trout, stripers, cobia, albacore, and more. Fish Trap offers full- and half-day trips, plus a special two-hour trip that is great for families with children. All anglers are welcome, so don't be shy if you're not experienced. Wagner has 16 years of experience fishing the Outer Banks, so you're in good hands. All equipment, bait, tackle, and ice are provided. His 24-foot boat accommodates up to four people. He stocks the boat with G. Loomis rods and Fin-Nor reels. You can take four-, six-, or eight-hour trips for prices ranging from $250 to $575. Call to arrange a meeting place.

Riomar Fly-Fishing and Light Tackle
(252) 480-6416
www.fish-riomar.com

Captain David Rohde offers inshore, near-shore, and soundside charters onboard his 18-foot Parker boat, the *Riomar*. He offers fly and light-tackle trips for speckled trout, bluefish, stripers, and drum. Rohde operates the *Riomar* in Harkers Island in the fall for albacore fishing. Half-day trips cost $250, and full-day trips cost $450. Call to arrange a meeting place.

Captain Bryan De Hart's
Coastal Adventures Guide Service
507 Barlowe St., Manteo
(252) 473–1575
www.coastaladv.com

Captain De Hart books light-tackle fly-fishing charters inshore, in brackish and saltwater, and in coastal rivers and sounds. He charges $225 for two people to fish a half-day, and $425 to take two people fishing all day. On the backwaters, De Hart uses an 18-foot War Eagle, and in the open sound, he fishes from a 22-foot Javelin. De Hart has been featured on ESPN's *Fly-Fishing America* program and is a regular on *The Carolina Outdoor Journal*.

Outer Banks Waterfowl
67 E. Dogwood Trail, Kitty Hawk
(252) 441–3732
www.outerbankswaterfowl.com

Captain Vic Berg runs sound and inlet fly- or spinning-tackle fishing trips. Everything you need is included, or if you like, you can bring your favorite tackle. Berg also offers instruction on fly- or surf fishing. Family and group rates are available for lessons. For full-day fishing for two people he charges $250; add $75 for a third member. Half-day trips for the same number of anglers run $175. Berg is U.S. Coast Guard–licensed.

Berg is also an experienced hunting guide who leads hunting trips that can yield many species of waterfowl. A typical bag of 10 ducks can contain seven different species. Berg's blinds are located between Oregon Inlet and Pea Island and have proven their success over 25 years. He also offers swan-hunting trips. A rate of $125 per person covers the blind, guide, decoys, and retriever for one day.

Surf Fishing

Surf fishing is a popular Outer Banks pastime for the competitor or amateur alike.

While there are miles of beach from which to cast a line, experienced local anglers say a surf-caster's success will vary depending on sloughs, temperature, currents, and season. One of the hottest surf-casting spots on the Outer Banks is Cape Point, a sand spit at the tip of Cape Hatteras. Anglers often stand waist-deep in the churning waters, dutifully waiting for red drum to strike.

About nine months out of the year, anglers can fish for red drum on the Outer Banks. The best time to catch big drum is mid-October through mid-November. During this period large schools of drum are feeding on baitfish called menhaden that migrate down the coastline. Cape Point is the hot spot for drum, but it tends to be a very crowded place to fish. A good second choice is the beach between Salvo and Buxton. But in the fall, you can catch them from Rodanthe down to Hatteras Inlet. From mid-April through about the third week in May, red drum show up around Ocracoke Inlet, both in the ocean and shallow shoal waters at the inlet's mouth and also in the Pamlico Sound.

Serious drum anglers fish after dark for the nocturnal feeders. Insiders prefer a southwesterly wind with an incoming tide and water temperatures in the low 60s. Big drum are known to come close to the surf during rough weather. Puppy drum (or juvenile drum) are easier to catch than the adult fish. They show up in the surf after a northeast blow in late summer or early fall. Anglers use finger mullet with success as well as fresh shrimp (and we do mean fresh). Red drum are a regulated fish, both in size and limit. Call your local tackle shop for more information. If you're interested in learning more about red drum tag and release programs, call the Division of Marine Fisheries at (252) 473–5734 or (252) 264–3911.

There's a lengthy list of fish regularly caught at Cape Point. Common species include dogfish, bluefish, pompano, striped bass, and Spanish mackerel as well as bottom feeders such as croaker, flounder, spot, sea mullet, and both gray and speckled trout. More uncommon are tar-

It's a mad dash for the blues during the bluefish blitz. PHOTO: COURTESY OF BOB REARDON

pon, cobia, amberjack, jack crevalles, and shark weighing several hundred pounds.

Shoaling that takes place off Cape Hatteras makes Cape Point a haven for baitfish, and the influence of the nearby Gulf Stream and its warm-water jetties also contribute to excellent fishing. The beach accommodates many four-wheel-drive vehicles, and during peak season (spring and fall) it's packed with anglers. If you want to try fishing Cape Point, take NC 12 to Buxton and look for signs to vehicle access ramp 43. (For more information about driving on the beach, please see our Getting Here, Getting Around chapter.)

A section on surf fishing would not be complete without discussing bluefish. For years, anglers enjoyed the arrival and subsequent blitzes of big bluefish during the Easter season and again around Thanksgiving. During a blitz, big blues chase baitfish up onto the beach in a feeding frenzy. This puts the blues in striking distance of ready surf-casters. It's a phenomenal sight to watch anglers reel in these fat and ferocious fish one after the other. Anglers line up along the shore like soldiers, and many a rod is bent in that telltale C-shape, fighting a bluefish. Some days you can see a skyfull of birds hovering, waiting to feast on the baitfish that the bluefish run toward the shore.

The last few years, the blues have not blitzed like they used to. As with most species, population figures (or at least landings) tend to rise and fall in cycles; perhaps they're tending toward a low point in the pattern. Maybe the big bluefin tuna, which feed on bluefish, are taking over these days, but blitz or not, you can usually catch some bluefish in the surf or in greater numbers offshore.

Joe Malat's Outer Banks Surf Fishing School
415 Bridge Lane, Nags Head
(252) 441–4767
www.outer-banks.nc.us/joemalat

If you're interested in learning some pointers from an angler who has certainly put his time into the sport, pick up a copy of Joe Malat's *Surf Fishing*. This easy-to-read, illustrated book outlines methods of catching species common to our area. Malat shares tips on the lures, rigs, baits, and knots favored by local surf anglers. You can also read about catch-and-release techniques and how to locate and land fish. This comprehensive book also includes useful information about tides, currents, wind, and other factors that affect surf fishing. Written in similar style with the same basic format is Malat's book, *Pier Fishing* (Wellspring, 1999). This soft-cover book includes all you should want to know about pier fishing plus information on 15 species of fish. For even more information, read "Joe Malat's Fishing Notebook," which appears weekly in the *Outer Banks Sentinel*.

Malat's Outer Banks Surf Fishing School is the best way to learn this sport—with an experienced angler. The two-and-a-half-day school includes one day of classroom instruction, one-and-a-half-days of on-the-beach instruction (bait included), classroom materials, and a copy of Malat's book. Malat and instructor Mac Currin offer personal instruction in an enjoyable, relaxed atmosphere, teaching students about such things as "reading the beach," fish identification, tackle, bait and lures, knot tying, casting, and beach driving. Cost is $225 per person, and there is a 25-person maximum per school. Two schools are held in the fall, and one is held in spring. There is also a two-day Surf Fishing School for Ladies Only. Malat and his wife, Nell, are the instructors on this weekend that includes one day of classroom instruction and one day of fishing. This school is held once a year, in June, at a cost of $120 per person.

Pier Fishing

Pier fishing is a true Outer Banks institution and has delighted anglers young and old for decades. The appeal is obvious: low cost and a chance to fish deeper waters without a boat. The variety of fish available also lures anglers. Depending on the time of year, you can catch croakers, spot, sea mullet, red drum, cobia, and occasionally a tarpon, king mackerel, sheepshead, or amberjack.

Bait and tackle are sold at each pier, or you can rent whatever gear you need. Avid anglers usually come prepared, but newcomers to the sport are always welcome on the pier, and staff are more than willing to outfit you and offer some fishing tips. Pier fishing is a good way to introduce kids to the sport. Many Outer Banks locals spent their youth on the pier soaking in know-how and area fishing lore. For instance, Garry Oliver, who owns the Outer Banks Pier in South Nags Head, spent many a summer day at the Nags Head Fishing Pier when he was a lad. Today, Garry is a member of an award-winning surf-casters team.

The Outer Banks has no oceanfront boardwalks, but the piers more than make up for it. The smells of salt air and creosote-treated lumber greet you as you walk the wide planks over the ocean water.

On many Outer Banks beaches you can drive right out to the surf-fishing grounds.

Looking down between the cracks, you can see the waves crashing beneath you, which lends an exciting sense of vertigo to the experience. You don't have to fish to appreciate the piers. For a small fee, you can just walk out on the piers to enjoy the vantage points they offer.

Kitty Hawk Fishing Pier
NC 12, MP 1, Kitty Hawk
(252) 261–2772

After you cross the Wright Memorial Bridge and arrive on the Outer Banks, it's a matter of seconds before you get your first glimpse of the ocean at the Kitty Hawk Fishing Pier. The central feature of this pier is the breezeway with a bait and tackle shop on the south end of the building and a diner-style restaurant on the north. From the breezeway, the fishing pier itself extends 714 feet over the ocean.

You don't have to fish to appreciate the Kitty Hawk Fishing Pier. Once an Insiders' best-kept breakfast secret, the pier's restaurant is now a popular tourist—as well as local—spot for breakfast, lunch, and din-

ner. Early mornings during the summer and any time of the day during the spring and fall, it's a colorful locals' haunt. Nothing beats the ocean view, the daily specials, or the pitch and roll of the dining room when the surf's up. Next, pay the $2.00 to walk out to the end of the pier for an eye-opening experience. Peopled with anglers, this structure has endured many powerful storms, and many citation fish have been caught off its weathered railings.

Kitty Hawk Fishing Pier is open April through Thanksgiving from 5:00 A.M. until generally around midnight if the fish are biting. When fish are scarce or the windchill starts to plummet, the pier closes after nightfall. Parking is ample, and daily admission is $5.00 for adults and $3.00 for children; a weekly pass is $25.00; season passes are $125.00. Disabled persons are admitted free. Tackle rental is $5.00 with a $30.00 cash deposit.

Avalon Fishing Pier
NC 12, MP 6, Kill Devil Hills
(252) 441–7494

Avalon Pier, in the heart of Kill Devil Hills, was built in the mid '50s and is 705 feet long. The pier has lights for night fishing, a snack bar, bait and tackle shop, ice, video games, and rental fishing gear. A busy place in-season, the pier is open 24 hours a day. The pier house is open from 6:00 A.M. until midnight. The pier is closed December through mid-March. Admission prices have recently been set at about $7.00 for adults and $3.50 for children younger than 12. A weekly pass is $35.00. A three-day weekend pass is $15.00; ask about their season passes. People with disabilities are admitted free.

Nags Head Fishing Pier
NC 12, MP 12, Nags Head
(252) 441-5141

This is one of the most popular fishing piers on the Outer Banks. It is 750 feet long and has its own bait and tackle shop. Enjoy night fishing, game tables for the kids, and a restaurant. The Pier House Restaurant features fresh seafood and wonderful views of the ocean. The restaurant serves breakfast, lunch, and dinner. (See our Restaurants chapter for more information.) The pier closes in December and reopens in March or April, depending upon whether the fish are biting. It is open 24 hours during the season. Admission is $7.00 per day for adults, $3.50 per day for kids 11 and younger,

and children under 6 are admitted for free. Passes for three or more days cost $18.00. Season rates are $150.00 for singles and $240.00 for couples. Tackle rental is $5.00. Sightseeing costs $1.50 for adults and 75 cents for children. Inquire about cottage rentals near the pier; one- to four-bedroom cottages are available for rentals of three or more nights.

Jennette's Pier
NC 12, MP 16½, Nags Head
(252) 441-6116

Built in 1932, Jennette's is the oldest pier on the Outer Banks, and friends have been gathering here since the last plank was put in place. At this writing, the future of Jennette's Pier is uncertain. There has been talk that the pier will close to make way for more modern development, but there is also a movement afoot to save this historic Nags Head landmark. What will happen with this pier is anybody's guess. Call or stop by when you come to town to find out for yourself. The current rates are $6.00 per day, $15.00 for a three-day pass, and $32.50 for a weekly pass. Children 11 and younger gain access for free if accompanied by a paying adult. Adults can walk out on the pier for $1.00 each. Rod and reel rental is $6.00.

This pier is usually crawling with anglers. But we're told that the crowds here have not put a damper on the fish being caught. It's in the heart of Whalebone Junction—along a hotbed of big catches and tall stories. The pier opens between mid-March and April 1 and closes in December. Hours do vary, but the schedule is generally 6:00 A.M. 'til 6:00 P.M., April 1 through Memorial Day. The pier is open 24 hours a day, seven days a week from Memorial Day through Labor Day. Snacks are available. Jennette's retail store features items to round out all your fishing and beach needs.

Outer Banks Pier and Fishing Center
NC 12, MP 18½, South Nags Head
(252) 441-5740

This 650-foot ocean pier was originally built

in 1959 and rebuilt in 1962 after the Ash Wednesday storm. Owner Garry Oliver has all you need in the bait and tackle shop for a day of fishing along this stretch of beach. A 300-foot sound fishing and crabbing pier is also available on the Nags Head–Manteo Causeway. The piers are open 24 hours a day from Memorial Day until mid-October and close from Thanksgiving through Easter. Rates are $6.00 per day, $15.00 for three days, $30.00 per week, $135.00 per season for one person, and $175.00 per season for a couple. Tackle rental is $5.00. Senior citizen discounts and group rates are available. Snack at the pier's on-site oceanside deli.

Hatteras Island Resort Fishing Pier
NC 12, Rodanthe
(252) 987–2323

After massive poundings by Hurricanes Dennis and Floyd, this pier collapsed in fall 1999. Even the land on which the pier house stood disappeared due to storm erosion. The land was refilled and in fall 2000 the pier reopened, a little farther back from its original location. The pier house sells drinks, snacks, sandwiches, tackle, and bait. The pier and pier house are open every day in the summer, 7:00 A.M. to 11:00 P.M. from Memorial Day to Labor Day and 7:00 A.M. to 10:00 P.M. the rest of the season. The Rodanthe Pier is closed December 1 through April 1. Prices are $6.00 per day to fish and $1.00 to walk on. Weekly and seasonal passes are available.

Avon Golf & Fishing Pier
NC 12, Avon
(252) 995–5480

Avon Golf & Fishing Pier has a reputation for being a hot spot for red drum. The all-tackle world record red drum, weighing in at 94 pounds, 2 ounces, was caught about 200 yards from the pier in 1984, and the record holds to this day. The pier opens at

the beginning of April and remains open through Thanksgiving. You can purchase or rent all your fishing supplies here, buy sandwiches and drinks, and also pick up nautical gifts including T-shirts and sand mirrors. They also offer an 18-hole natural grass putting green on the premises. Play is unlimited, and you can come and go as you please for $6.00 ($7.00 during summer evenings). After Memorial Day, the pier remains open 24 hours a day until it closes for the season. All-day fishing for adults is $6.00, and kids' and seniors' all-day passes are $5.00. Weekly passes are $35.00, and tackle rental is $8.00 plus a $30.00 deposit. Sightseeing passes are $1.00. After you work up an appetite fishing or playing golf, stop in the on-site Dirty Dick's Crab House for lunch or dinner (see our Restaurants chapter for details).

Cape Hatteras Pier
NC 12, Frisco
(252) 986–2533

The Cape Hatteras Pier, locally called the Frisco Pier, is open the end of March through December 1. The pier is noted for its great king mackerel fishing during the summer and sells or rents everything you'll need for fishing, including live bait for those big kings. Snacks and soft drinks are available. The pier is open every day. The Frisco Pier is on the South Beach, and folks who drop a line here often boast about the large quantity of fish that frequent the vicinity. Fishing currently costs $6.00 daily and $32.00 weekly. Tackle rents for $5.00, and for $1.00 you can go sightseeing on the pier.

Citation Fish

Citation fish are caught in the waters off the Outer Banks every year. The North Carolina Division of Marine Fisheries manages the North Carolina Saltwater Fishing Tournament, which recognizes outstanding angling achievement. The tournament runs yearlong from January 1 through December 31. Other than charter boat captains and crews for hire, everyone is eligible for a citation fish award. Eligible waters include North Carolina sounds, surf, estuaries, and the ocean. This tournament is for the hook-and-line angler; use of electric or hydraulic equipment is not allowed. There is one award per angler per species, and all fish must be weighed in at an official weigh station. Anglers receive a certificate after the close of the tournament. There is no registration fee. Following is a list of the area's weigh stations, where you can pick up a species list and receive rules for the tournament. Citations are also awarded for the catch and release of some species.

Official Weigh Stations

Corolla

TW's Bait & Tackle Shop
NC 12, (252) 453–3339

Duck

Bob's Bait & Tackle
NC 12, (252) 261–8589

Insiders' Tip

When buying waders or boots, always buy them one-and-a-half sizes larger than your shoe size. The larger size will enable you to slip them off in the event that you step in a slough or fall overboard.

Kitty Hawk

Kitty Hawk Bait & Tackle
US 158, MP 4½, Kitty Hawk, (252) 261–2955

TW's Bait & Tackle Shop
US 158, MP 4, (252) 261–7848

Whitney's Bait and Tackle
US 158, MP 4½, Kitty Hawk, (252) 261–5551

Kill Devil Hills

Avalon Fishing Pier
NC 12, MP 6, (252) 441–7494

Nags Head

Jennette's Pier
NC 12, MP 16½, (252) 441–6116

Nags Head Fishing Pier
NC 12, MP 12, (252) 441–5141

Outer Banks Pier and Fishing Center
NC 12, MP 18½, (252) 441–5740

Outer Banks Fishing Unlimited
Nags Head–Manteo Causeway,
(252) 441–5028

T.I.'s Bait & Tackle
US 158, MP 9, (252) 441–3166

TW's Bait & Tackle Shop
US 158, MP 10½, (252) 441–4807

Whalebone Tackle Shop
Nags Head–Manteo Causeway,
(252) 441–7413

Manteo

Pirate's Cove
Nags Head–Manteo Causeway,
(252) 473–3906

Salty Dawg Marina
US 64, (252) 473–3405

Oregon Inlet

Oregon Inlet Fishing Center
NC 12, 8 miles south of Whalebone Junction,
(252) 441–6301

Rodanthe

Hatteras Jack
NC 12, (252) 987–2428

Mac's Tackle & Island Convenience
NC 12, (252) 987–2239

Salvo

The Fishin' Hole
NC 12, (252) 987–2351

Avon

Frank and Fran's Fisherman's Friend
NC 12, (252) 995–4171

Buxton

Cape Point Tackle
NC 12, (252) 995–3147

Dillon's Corner
NC 12, (252) 995–5083

The Red Drum Tackle Shop Inc.
NC 12, (252) 995–5414

Frisco

Frisco Rod & Gun
NC 12, (252) 995–5366

Frisco Tackle
NC 12, (252) 995–4361

Hatteras Village

Hatteras Harbor Marina
NC 12, (252) 986–2166

Visually Impaired Anglers—Truly VIPs

Every October, hundreds of visually impaired persons visit the Outer Banks as part of the annual Lions VIP Fishing Tournament. Entering its 19th year in 2002, the tournament not only provides these VIPs (visually impaired persons) with the chance to fish, but a three-day program filled with motivating activities and information.

Scheduled around the fishing highlights are seminars that include job training and placement and introduction to new technology designed to make life easier for the visually challenged. Socializing with peers plays a valuable role in the success of this program that has expanded from a one- to a three-day event. A banquet and dance provide the opportunity to make friends, share personal stories, and swap coping skills. Fishing trophies are awarded at the banquet, which is always

With the help of technology and a little creativity, many disabled anglers can still take to the sea.
PHOTO: COURTESY OF THE SPORTFISHING REPORT

highlighted by an inspirational speaker. Newly blind folks and those with individual struggles gain hope from such testimonials.

One day is set aside for fishing from a host of local piers and headboats for a variety of species, sometimes giving participants their first-ever fishing experience. A day spent casting lines side-by-side provides a hands-on experience that Insiders swear weaves its own magic for the 400 guests enjoying the world-class fishing of the Outer Banks.

Autumn has produced record-breaking fish catches from the surf, boats, and piers. Whether the catch makes its way into the International Game Fish Association (IGFA) world-record ranks or not, the sport yields plenty of fun along with tasty and often feisty species such as sea mullet, croaker, flounder, and spot. Everything needed to fish is provided, including volunteers to give as much or as little help as anglers desire. It's the perfect sport for the visually impaired because it relies less on sight and more on feel.

Volunteers always play a major role in the program that has grown in attendance over the years; however, the VIP tournament is able to target only a fraction of the 21,000-person visually challenged population in North Carolina. The primary reason for this is the lack of a meeting place to accommodate the large group. In the mean-time, generous souls (including visually impaired entertainer Doc Watson, who per-formed for the group in the past) keep the program afloat. Local businesses and civic organizations underwrite most of the tournament costs that in the past have amounted to over $100,000. Piers, boats, restaurants, and motels donate their services; the Lions Club Foundation has made grant money available; and the Dare County Tourist Bureau funded the publishing of a twin-vision brochure in print and Braille.

Individuals can get involved through the adopt-a-fisherman program, which is available year-round. Each donor contributes $25 to sponsor an angler. In turn, they are invited to fish with the individual, but attendance is not required. Because of the outpouring of help, the only cost to the participants in past tournaments has been $35 for the entry fee and the cost for transportation—a small price to pay for a big experience that yields far more than a fish wriggling at the end of a line.

Applications are sent out through the North Carolina Division of Services for the Blind. State social workers that service the visually impaired and Lions Clubs distribute them. For donation or entry information call VIP Director Gwen White at (252) 449–4411.

Oden's Dock
NC 12, (252) 986–2555

Pelican's Roost
NC 12, (252) 986–2213

Teach's Lair Marina
NC 12, (252) 986–2460

Village Marina
NC 12, (252) 986–2522

Willis Boat Landing
57209 Willis Lane, (252) 986–2208

Ocracoke

Ocracoke Fishing Center
NC 12, (252) 928–6661

O'Neal's Dockside and Tackle Shop
NC 12, (252) 928–1111

Tradewinds Tackle Shop
NC 12, (252) 928–5491

Bait and Tackle Shops

Full-service tackle shops are scattered from Corolla to Ocracoke. They are good sources for not only rods, reels, bait, and other fishing equipment and accessories, but also for tips on what's biting and where. You'll find bait and tackle at all Outer Banks fishing piers and most marinas too. Just about every department store and general store on the barrier islands carries some sort of fishing gear, and many shops also offer tackle rental. You can ask for guide information at any one of the following shops:

Duck

Bob's Bait & Tackle
NC 12, Duck
(252) 261–8589
Stop in Bob's if you're looking for advice on where to catch the really big one. The old building is left over from Duck's early days, when a soundside dock out back was the distribution point for shiploads of fresh ocean fish. The shop carries a good supply of rods, reels, bait, and tackle. Bob's will also book your offshore charters and offers a hunting and fishing guide service.

Kitty Hawk

TW's Bait & Tackle
US 158, MP 4, Kitty Hawk
(252) 261–7848
TW's Bait & Tackle, next to the 7-Eleven in Kitty Hawk, is a great place to find the right stuff for your fishing adventure. The gear is top-notch and so is the info on what's biting. Owner Terry "T.W." Stewart has been in business since 1981 and can sell you what you need, including ice and live bait.

T.W. will also book your inshore and offshore charter fishing trips. There is another location in Corolla, (252) 453-3339, at the Food Lion Shopping Center but it's closed January and February. The Kitty Hawk location stays open year-round. TW's has a Nags Head store at MP 10½, (252) 441-4807. The Nags Head location is open all year.

> ### Insiders' Tip
> The Roanoke and Pamlico Sounds are very shallow in places, and many boaters discover this by running aground. If your boat runs aground, call Sea Tow at (252) 473-3465 or Salty Dawg Marina at (252) 473-3405.

Whitney's Bait & Tackle
US 158, MP 4½, Kitty Hawk
(252) 261-5551
Whitney's specializes in custom rods made by Whitney Jones, plus offshore and inshore bait and tackle. The shop also offers rod and reel repairs. The walls at Whitney's are lined with Jones's impressive freshwater and saltwater citations and trophies. Call for Whitney's fishing report.

Kill Devil Hills

Stop N Shop Convenience & Deli
NC 12, MP 8½, Kill Devil Hills
(252) 441-6105
Located on the Beach Road across from the Kill Devil Hills beach access, Stop N Shop has about anything you might need for a day of fishing or a day at the beach. This is a full-service tackle shop, with fishing and beach items that include bait, tackle, local information, beer, ice, gas, and even rental equipment. Owners Tom and Vickie Byers stock a surprising amount of goods for anglers. Make sure to order some of their excellent sandwiches to take along on your fishing trip. Stop N Shop is open seven days a week year-round.

T.I.'s Bait & Tackle
US 158, MP 9, Kill Devil Hills
(252) 441-3166
T.I.'s is an official weigh station and member of the North Carolina Beach Buggy Association. The shop offers quality tackle and fresh bait and is an authorized Penn parts distributor and repair station. T.I.'s is also a factory-authorized Daiwa service warranty center. The shop is open year-round. Check out their other location across from Cahoon's grocery on NC 12, MP 16½, in Nags Head, (252) 441-5242.

Nags Head

Whalebone Tackle
Nags Head–Manteo Causeway, Nags Head
(252) 441-7413

Whalebone is a full-service tackle shop offering ice, fresh bait, tackle, and rod and Penn reel repairs. As they say at the store, "All roads lead to Whalebone Tackle, the center of the universe." The store is open year-round.

Fishing Unlimited
Nags Head–Manteo Causeway, Nags Head
(252) 441-5028
Fishing Unlimited specializes in fresh bait and is a full-service tackle shop. You can purchase live bait, custom rigs, and lures here as well as crabbing supplies, snacks, and drinks. Services include 16-foot outboard and 20-foot pontoon boat rentals. Fish or crab from their 300-foot sound pier for a fee of $2.00. You can rent rods and reels for $5.00 a day. The shop is open from Easter until early December.

Salvo

The Fishin' Hole
NC 12, Salvo
(252) 987-2351
Operating on the Outer Banks since 1976, The Fishin' Hole is a full-service tackle shop that sells live bait, tackle, beach supplies, groceries, and T-shirts. Rod and reel repairs for Daiwa, Penn, and other brands are available here. It's an official weigh station for the North Carolina Beach Buggy Association. The shop is open from the end of March through mid-December.

Avon

Frank and Fran's Fisherman's Friend
NC 12, Avon
(252) 995-4171
A full-service tackle shop, official weigh station, and headquarters for the local Red Drum Tournament held every October, Frank and Fran's is an emporium of fishing gear. This is another official weigh station for the state and the North Carolina Beach Buggy Association.

To get the low-down on what's biting where, call a local tackle shop. PHOTO: HORSLEY/GARDNER

Buxton

Cape Point Tackle
NC 12, Buxton
(252) 995-3147

This shop offers everything you need to fish and have a fun day at the beach. Look here for tackle, bait, waders, drinks and snacks, beach chairs, T-shirts and sweatshirts, and a variety of gifts. Cape Point Tackle is an official weigh station. It's open year-round except for a couple of weeks around Christmas.

Dillon's Corner
NC 12, Buxton
(252) 995-5083

Stop here for an assortment of tackle, including custom rods and bait. The shop also carries a wide selection of gifts, T-shirts, and lighthouse replicas (see our Shopping chapter). The shop also offers rod repairs and has gas pumps. Dillon's Corner is open all year but has shorter hours in winter.

Red Drum Tackle Shop
NC 12, Buxton
(252) 995-5414

Get the latest in fishing information and select gear at Red Drum Tackle Shop. It offers everything you need in the way of custom rods, bait, and tackle, plus reel repairs. They're a Penn warranty center and official weigh station for the state, North Carolina Beach Buggy Association, and the Cape Hatteras Anglers Club.

Frisco

Frisco Rod and Gun
NC 12, Frisco
(252) 995-5366

Frisco Rod and Gun is a one-stop shop for everything you need for a hunting or fishing trip. The owner calls it his "hobby gone wild." You'll find inshore and offshore fishing equipment, fly-fishing gear, custom rods, guns, ice, bait, tackle, and one of the biggest and best selections of

> ## Insiders' Tip
> Always dress in layers for an Outer Banks fishing trip. Cold mornings have been known to transform into a warm afternoon on many fall and winter days. Of course, the opposite is also true, and gales and thunderstorms notoriously appear out of nowhere.

knives you'll ever see. They also offer rod and reel repairs and can help you find a hunting or fishing guide. Taxidermy services can be arranged. Camping supplies, name-brand outdoor apparel, Sperry footwear, T-shirts, groceries, gas, and convenience items round out the offerings.

Ocracoke

Tradewinds
NC 12, Ocracoke
(252) 928-5491

Tradewinds is a one-stop tackle shop that can supply all your fishing needs, including fresh and frozen bait, tackle, clothing items, and plenty of good advice about fishing. The shop also offers tackle rentals and rod and reel repair. Tradewinds is an official North Carolina weigh station and is open seven days a week from March through December.

O'Neal's Dockside Tackle Shop
NC 12, Ocracoke
(252) 928-1111

O'Neal's offers fresh and frozen bait as well as fishing, marine and hunting supplies and can furnish you with any license you need for both sports. They are a full-service tackle shop and offer tackle rentals. These folks have been in business for nearly 20 years and are official North Carolina Wildlife and Marine Fisheries agents. If you have any questions on official regulations, stop here.

Fishing Reports

For the latest word on what's biting, check with the following sources:

Kitty Hawk Fishing Pier, (252) 261–2772
Nags Head Fishing Pier, (252) 441–5141
Pirate's Cove Yacht Club, (252) 473–3906
Oregon Inlet Fishing Center, (252) 441–6301
Red Drum Tackle Shop, (252) 995–5414
Frisco Pier, (252) 986–2533
O'Neal's Dockside, (252) 928–1111

Also read *The Virginian-Pilot* daily North Carolina section and *The Carolina Coast* for Damon Tatem's report. Check out Joe Malat's informative weekly column in the *Outer Banks Sentinel. The ReelFisher News* is a free quarterly tabloid available at retail outlets throughout the Outer Banks that offers folksy fishing editorial plus acts as a directory to area piers, ramps, marinas, and weigh stations. For more Insiders' information, you can pick up a copy of the *Sportfishing Report,* the Outer Banks's first saltwater fishing magazine, which has expanded to cover the entire East Coast. This bimonthly magazine is available on the newsstands. Subscriptions are currently available for free, with a modest charge for postage. For information, call (252) 473–1553 or visit the Web site at www.sportfishing-report.com.

Golf

Whether you're a scratch golfer or a duffer, you'll find play to suit your game and style on or near the Outer Banks, where the number and variety of golf courses have increased dramatically in the past few years. Part of the pleasure of golf almost everywhere is in the lushness of the environment, but few locations outside of this area offer the astounding ocean-to-sound views you'll find at many courses along these barrier islands. Such distraction might not be good for your game, but it'll do wonders for the soul!

In this section, you'll find golf courses from Corolla to Hatteras Island, plus courses on the Currituck mainland, just north of the Wright Memorial Bridge. We've also included an excellent course in Hertford that's only an hour's drive from the heart of the Outer Banks.

Golfers have it made during the off-season and shoulder seasons. Accommodations are a bargain from the fall through the spring, and many hotels, motels, and cottage rental companies package special golf vacations. Depending upon the season, you can usually plan a visit on the spur of the moment if you want to play at off-peak times. The temperatures on the Outer Banks remain fairly moderate throughout the year. A day in January might bring temperatures of 60 degrees or higher, so keep an eye on the weather and your clubs close at hand. To avoid disappointment, call for tee times at your course of choice before your visit: More and more golfers are discovering the Outer Banks in the off-season.

All the regulation courses in the following section are semiprivate, meaning the public can pay to play, and all welcome beginners and newcomers. Yardage and par figures are based on men's/white tees.

Regulation and Executive Courses

The Carolina Club
US 158, Grandy
(252) 453-3588
www.thecarolinaclub.com

More and more Outer Banks golfers are discovering the courses on the Currituck mainland, and The Carolina Club, designed by Russell Breeden, is one of the nicest of the bunch. Located in Grandy, the course is just 13.5 miles past the Wright Memorial Bridge, about a 20-minute drive from Kitty Hawk. The 7,000-yard, par 72 course has, according to the Southeastern director of the U.S. Golf Association (U.S.G.A.), "among the finest putting surfaces in the eastern U.S." Indeed, The Carolina Club management prides itself on its high level of course conditioning, slick bentgrass greens, and plush Tifway Bermuda fairways. Five sets of tees allow you to match your game to an appropriate level of challenge. On this course, you will encounter wetlands, woodlands, water, and bunkers galore. Hole 7, a par 3, has an island green that will challenge your club-selection skills. The par 5 hole 18 offers the ultimate in risk vs. reward. Water and wind direction factor in on this hole, where the tee shot must be right on the mark. There's a snack bar on the premises, plus a pro shop. Rental clubs and carts are available. Individual and group lessons are offered by PGA head professional Doug Kinser. Greens fees, including cart, are a good value,

From the rolling dunes, golfers can enjoy views of the Atlantic Ocean and Currituck Sound. Within the property lie 15 acres set aside for the historic and private Currituck Shooting Club, whose lineage dates back to 1857. The back nine has several holes that offer some of the most beautiful views you'll ever see. The view from the elevated 13th tee offers a panoramic view of the ocean, sound, and the Currituck Beach Lighthouse.

The course features a full driving range. Lessons are offered year-round, along with weekly clinics by PGA professionals. Lessons start at $45 for 45 minutes. Golf schools are offered from June through August on Tuesday, Wednesday, and Thursday from 9:00 to 11:00 A.M. Junior golf school is offered on Thursdays from 5:00 to 7:00 P.M. Rates include golf cart rental and vary according to the season. A brand-new clubhouse opened in September 2001 and includes a restaurant (Bunkers), a bar and lounge with full ABC permits, a pro shop, locker rooms, bag storage, and a private members' lounge.

ranging from $85 in June to $29 in January, but they change monthly so call for accurate prices. Youth rates are available. Tee times are booked up to three months in advance. The course is open all year.

The Currituck Club
NC 12, Corolla
(252) 453–9400, (888) 453–9400
www.thecurrituckclub.com

When The Currituck Club opened in 1997, *Golf Magazine* named it one of the "Top 10 You Can Play." In 1999, *Golf Digest* ranked it as one of the Top 25 courses in North Carolina, a great compliment for a young course in a renowned golfing state. This 6,888-yard, par 72 course is situated on 600 acres of pristine wetlands along the Currituck Sound, surrounded by luxurious homes in The Currituck Club resort community. The natural beauty of this course makes it one of the most peaceful golfing spots around. Prominent golf architect Rees Jones designed the stunningly scenic links-style course with respect to the wildlife and waterfowl that populate the area. While protecting their habitats, he also offers golfers a course set amid dunes, wetlands, and marsh fringes.

Duck Woods Country Club
50 Dogwood Trail, Kitty Hawk
(252) 261–2609

Duck Woods is the club to play on windy days, since it offers more shelter than the soundside clubs. This 18-hole, 6161-yard, par 72 course was built in 1968. Designed by Ellis Maples, Duck Woods features a traditional layout with tree-lined fairways. Shots must be placed with care, especially on the par 5 14th hole, where water dissects the fairway. Water comes into play on 14 holes. You might want to warm up before your round; the course begins with a 481-yard par 5 and ends with a 506-yard par 5.

While the club accommodates 900 members, it accepts public play year-round. Nonmembers can take advantage of the driving range and putting green on the day of play only. Target greens and a practice bunker are available. Duck Woods offers a pro shop, complemented by the presence of golf pro Tommy Wine, and club rentals. Members enjoy clubhouse and locker room privileges and the bar and restaurant. Beer and wine are sold to nonmembers, but no other alcoholic beverages are available, as the club does not hold a liquor license.

Riding is mandatory for nonmembers. Booking is accepted a week in advance for members and two days in advance for nonmembers. Call for more information. Greens fees vary.

Goose Creek Golf and Country Club
US 158, Grandy
(252) 453–4008, (800) 443–4008

Goose Creek, a 5,943-yard par 72 public course, offers an easygoing track complete with a hospitable atmosphere and some of the most affordable greens fees in the area. The greens and fairways on this flat course are blanketed with bermudagrass. Greens are relatively small. Trees line the course, with tighter fairways on the first nine but more undulating and open terrain on the back.

Designed by Jerry Turner and built by Jernigan Enterprises, Goose Creek is a player-friendly golf course. Goose Creek's Class A PGA golf professional is Chris Busbee. Water comes into play on five holes. Hole 13 is considered the signature. The hole plays differently according to the wind (it's generally to your back during the summer and in your face in fall and winter).

The clubhouse is a former hunting lodge that the owners converted into private locker rooms. Take some time to relax in the pine-paneled lounge for a cool drink. The clubhouse menu includes all sorts of sandwiches, plus everything from buffalo wings to crab cakes.

A driving range and practice green are available. Walking is allowed for members only. This is a great course for the entire family, and children are both welcome and encouraged; however, it's recommended that young golfers check in after noon.

Holly Ridge Golf Course
US 158, Harbinger
(252) 491–2893
www.wrightflightgolf.com

Holly Ridge Golf Course is just 1.5 miles north of the Wright Memorial Bridge in Harbinger. Under the new management of Wright Flight Golf, including PGA professional Danny Miller and managing partner Kim Leatherwood, Holly Ridge is making new steps to satisfy golfers of every ability. The new management plans to make the par 63 course significantly longer with the addition of four brand-new holes, including a dogleg par 4, a monstrous par 5, and a scenic par 3. Each new hole will have plenty of water hazards to negotiate. The front nine winds through a peaceful forest of native trees and picturesque ponds, while the more open back nine are affected by winds. Holly Ridge has a full-length, fully lighted grass practice area and putting green. PGA Pro Danny Miller has over 20 years of experience in teaching golfers of all levels. Private lessons and group clinics are available, as are private lessons with video analysis. The pro shop carries a great selection of apparel, accessories, and equipment, and the staff can help you select the right clubs. Walking is allowed on this course. Pull carts, golf clubs, and, of course, golf carts are available to rent. Greens fees are a good value here, and they vary throughout the year, so call ahead. Juniors may play for half-price but must have a valid drivers license to operate a cart.

Mill Run Golf and Country Club
US 168, Currituck
(252) 435–MILL, (800) MILL–RUN

If you're willing to drive a ways, Mill Run Golf and Country Club offers a great bargain for Outer Banks golfers. The course, opened in 1999, is just south of Moyock on US 168, about 50 miles from the Outer Banks and about 5 miles south of the NC/VA line. Greens fees in the summer of 2001 were $25 during the week and $32 on the weekend. You can't beat that. The course is fun and enjoyable, not overly difficult; so if you're looking for a good time game that will leave you feeling good about yourself, not depressed about your

Many Outer Banks golf courses have taken special care to preserve natural environments, so sightings of wildlife are common. PHOTO: HORSLEY/GARDNER

missed shots, come here. It's a great course for beginners. Course architect James Overton Sr. designed the 6,651-yard course to take advantage of the natural terrain and to provide challenging play for golfers of all levels. Mill Run is relatively flat and plays somewhat like a links-style course, though it's nowhere near the ocean or sound. It does offer some challenges with wind, ponds, and woods. Bunkers are still being added to the course. The signature hole is number 17, a par 3 with the carry over water. Greens are in tip-top shape. A driving range, practice putting green, and chipping green are available, and golf professional Chris Busbee offers lessons. Walking is allowed here. The pro shop is well equipped with all you'll need for your game, and the on-site Hackers Grill serves breakfast and lunch.

Nags Head Golf Links
5615 S. Seachase Dr., Nags Head
(252) 441–8073, (800) 851–9404
www.nagsheadgolflinks.com

This soundside 18-hole Scottish links-style course is in the Village at Nags Head just off US 158 at Milepost 15½. Architect Bob Moore left most of the natural setting intact, and the 6,100-yard, par 71 course is a real beach beauty. Golfers enjoy idyllic views of Roanoke Sound from nearly every hole. With the sound to the west and the ocean to the east, wind plays a constant role here.

It doesn't take but one quick gust of wind to blow your ball off course on the 221-yard 15th, a lengthy par 3. The green is fronted by a pond. Of course, on virtually every barrier island track, you'll have to deal with wetlands. All but four holes are affected by water here.

Danny Agapion, the golf director for both this club and The Currituck Club, and Nags Head Golf Links pro Jeff Lewis invite you to try this mercurial course. The environment is so refreshing that we think it's worth a round regardless of what's controlling the shots. As with The Currituck Club, golf school is offered mornings three days a week during the summer.

Golf Digest called the holes along the sound "among the most beautiful in the eastern U.S.," and went on to say that "Nags Head Golf Links is the longest 6,100 yards you'll ever play."

Cart and greens fees vary, and starting times may be reserved up to one year in advance. Special off-season rates are offered to seniors. A nine-hole scramble is played June through August late Sunday afternoons. Please call to sign up.

If you work up an appetite, you can enjoy good food and excellent views of the Roanoke Sound from the Links Grill, which is open for lunch only. Nags Head Golf Links also has a bar, golf shop, driving range, putting green, and rental clubs. The course is open every day, except Christmas, from sunrise to sunset. Call for more information.

Ocean Edge Golf Course
NC 12, Frisco
(252) 995-4100

Ocean Edge is a public, nine-hole executive course that also permits 18-hole play. Look out for the big pond—the first, second, fifth, and eighth holes play over the water.

Ocean Edge is open all year. This 1,400-yard, par 30 Hatteras Island course covers 23 acres of dunes. Tee times are required. Golf carts and club rentals are available. Rates, including cart, are $30.00 for nine holes and $40.00 for 18. Off-season rates are $20.00 for nine-hole play and $30.00 for 18-hole play. On same-day plays, after your first round of 18 holes, your second round is $5.00 for each additional nine-hole play. Walking is permitted.

The Pointe Golf Club
US 158 E., Powells Point
(252) 491-8388
www.thepointegolfclub.com

Golfer's heaven well describes this 5,911-yard, par 71, 18-hole championship golf course. Both the recreational golfer and the professional will find a challenge on this verdant course created by Russell Breeden. Breeden's unique design features

soundfront views from wooded and links-style holes with gentle mounds and slopes. This was the first course in the country to feature A1 bentgrass greens, a new disease-resistant dense grass. It's no surprise really, because the folks at Pointe are grass experts. Pointe owner Keith Hall is the president of United Turf, and he takes his business seriously (he was responsible for growing the grass that blanketed U.S. soccer fields hosting World Cup play). Expect highly manicured, lush greens and concrete cart paths.

In a rural Carolina setting, The Pointe offers a nice respite from the beach scene. The course sports a traditional design, with water hazards coming into play laterally on 15 holes. The signature hole is number 6, a 457-yard par 4 with a carry over wetlands, a blind shot to the fairway, water, bunkers and slopes to the right.

You can fine-tune your game on the driving range, in the practice bunker, or on the full-size putting green. The Pointe offers a full-service pro shop headed by resident golf pro David A. Donovan III. Other amenities include a clubhouse, carts, lessons, sales, and rentals. The Pointe Restaurant, which serves breakfast and lunch, has views of the 9th green and the 10th tee.

Walking is allowed after noon for greens fee pass-holders, October 1 through May 24. Greens fees vary, so it's a good idea to call for timely information. Annual golf packages are offered through Outer Banks Golf Getaways, (800) 916–6244 and Outer Banks Golf Packages, (800) 946–5383; accommodations packages are available through area rental companies.

The Pointe Golf Course is 3.5 miles north of the Wright Memorial Bridge. Call for tee times up to a month in advance.

Sea Scape Golf Links
300 Eckner St., Kitty Hawk
(252) 261-2158
www.seascapegolf.com

Keep your eye on the ball and not the view on this 18-hole, links-style championship course if you don't want to be distracted. You get a real taste of Outer Banks beauty with water vistas from almost every hole, especially from the elevated ninth tee. Sea Scape is cut into Kitty Hawk's maritime forest, just off US 158 East at Milepost 2½. Designed by Art Wall, the 6,052-yard, par 72 course features bentgrass greens and fairways, which are fairly wide. Sea Scape was host of the 2000 North Carolina Open.

Opened in 1965, the links-style course has been modernized, and now you can expect cart paths on all holes. Wind is a factor here, and you may find yourself puttering around in the sand and brush looking for your ball. Expect a challenge on number 11: Look to play against the wind on this 410-yard, par 4 hole. Sea Scape will test your ability as well as your patience, with five par 3s and five par 5s.

A scheduled golf clinic is offered for all ages from June through August. Sea Scape offers club fitting, rental clubs, a driving range, bar, restaurant, and fully stocked pro shop. Longtime Sea Scape pro Bryan Sullivan is available to discuss your game or the course. Sea Scape's new clubhouse features a fully stocked pro shop and Sully's Restaurant, serving breakfast and lunch.

Walking is not allowed. Greens fees range from $45 to $85, including the cart. Call ahead for tee times, especially if you plan to play during the summer (there's no established rule, but we were informed that eight months in advance isn't too soon). The course is open every day except Christmas from 7:30 A.M. until dark.

The Sound Golf Links
101 Clubhouse Dr., Hertford
(252) 426–5555, (800) 535–0704

Tucked within Albemarle Plantation, The Sound is a 6,504-yard, par 72, 18-hole course. It's also a world-class golfing and boating community at the tip of the Albemarle Sound near Hertford. The beautiful 12,000-square-foot clubhouse overlooks the water. Owner and designer Dan Maples stamped his signature here. As with all Maples-designed courses, you get a break on the par 4s and 5s, but the par 3s are extremely difficult. It's a target golf course with a few similarities to a links course.

Fairways are narrow, and marsh must be carried frequently. It's a fair course overall but a tough one from the back tees. On the 7th and 13th holes, the landing areas are extremely small. Both are par 4s.

This course is surrounded by undisturbed wetlands and tall pines. Enjoy the ride from the 16th green to the 17th tee over the wetlands; in fact, you'll probably enjoy all the cart rides over the bridges. The three finishing holes stretch along water and provide breathtaking views.

The golf pro here is Jim Nodurft. The clubhouse includes a golf shop and restaurant, The Soundside Grille, which serves lunch and dinner. A driving range and putting green are also available. The marina, available to the public, is the largest in the area.

Greens fees, including the cart, range from $30 to $49. Walking is restricted, so call for details. Tee times may be booked up to nine months in advance. The course is approximately an hour's drive from Kitty Hawk.

Practice Ranges

The Promenade
US 158 E., MP¼, Kitty Hawk
(252) 261–4900

Fun for the whole family is a sure bet at The Promenade. On the Currituck Sound at the eastern terminus of the Wright Memorial Bridge, this 30-acre adventure spot features a nine-hole chip-and-putt course on natural grass. Separate putting green and target driving range facilities are available. Mini–golf lovers will appreciate the 18-hole themed Waterfall Greens, and youngsters ages 1 through 12 will have a blast at the Smilin' Island playground.

Golf Equipment and Supplies

Besides course pro shops where you can find quality golf supplies, we suggest the following shops for discount equipment. Everyone we have encountered at these places is especially helpful and patient with golfers who are just starting out.

Teed Off
US 158 E., MP 1, Kitty Hawk
(252) 261–4653, (888) 829–4653
www.teedoffgolf.com

Just east of the Wright Memorial Bridge, at Three Winks Shops, Teed Off offers top-quality equipment and apparel at discount prices. Custom-built golf clubs are available. The store is open Monday through Saturday 9:00 A.M. to 5:00 P.M. Closeout sales and specials are advertised on their Web site.

Smash Hit Tennis & Golf
NC 12, Duck
(252) 261–1138
www.smashhittennisandgolf.com

Smash Hit Tennis & Golf, in Duck's Scarborough Faire shopping center, offers a variety of top sports fashions.

Insiders' Tip

In helping to maintain course quality, please remember to repair your ball marks. A repaired mark will take three to five days to heal, while one ignored will take up to three weeks.

Loyal customers claim that Smash Hit has the finest selection anywhere for ladies' clothing. You'll also find men's and children's clothing, gifts, accessories, and some equipment. The helpful, knowledgeable staff will deck you out just right for a round of golf or game of tennis, or you can visit the new Web site and shop online. A great service is Smash Hit's mail-order goodie boxes. They will send you a selection of clothing from which you can keep what you like and return the rest. Smash Hit Tennis & Golf, now in its 15th year, is open year-round; please call for hours.

Day Trips

Nature Adventures
Historic Attractions
Something Different

In your eagerness to reach the beach, you may have kept your eyes straight ahead and not noticed the numerous attractions in the surrounding areas. The Outer Banks can serve as a "base camp," enabling you to easily explore all that is offered nearby, from historic sites to nature sanctuaries to autumn festivals that offer a glimpse into the lives of a small Southern town. Following are some exciting adventures you may wish to take while visiting the Outer Banks, each within a few hours' drive.

Nature Adventures

North Carolina Estuarium
223 E. Water St., Washington
(252) 948–0000
www.partnershipforthesounds.org

Less than two hours from Roanoke Island, this environmental education center offers more than 200 hands-on displays and interactive exhibits about estuarine ecosystems in creative ways kids won't be able to resist. Estuaries—bodies of water with a mixture of fresh- and salt water—are vital marine life breeding grounds. The region's Albemarle-Pamlico system, the second largest in the country after Chesapeake Bay, incorporates seven sounds that several river basins drain into. It totals more than 300,000 square miles. Only Alaska and Louisiana have more square miles of estuarine waters than North Carolina.

The first of several major facilities completed by the nonprofit Partnership for the Sounds, the estuarium teaches kids and grown-ups about the threat of pollution and why marine species couldn't survive without clean estuaries. In addition to the two 130-gallon terrariums and five 130-gallon to 650-gallon aquarium tanks, you'll also find here a number of educational exhibits including a salinity drip where you can actually sample the saltiness of different types of water bodies; a model of animal skulls that asks you to guess which animals are represented; a

working model of wind and tide, where fans are manipulated to move a miniature waterway; and a movie about estuaries that gives an emotional sense of the importance of the system to the coast.

The estuarium also features a nursery area with minnows, shrimp, and flounder, plus exhibits with snakes, turtles, lizards, and other creatures that live in estuarine areas. A glass-enclosed front room overlooking the Pamlico River is available for special educational workshops. Pontoon boat rides on the Pamlico River are available seasonally.

The North Carolina Estuarium is open year-round Tuesday through Saturday from 10:00 A.M. to 4:00 P.M. Hours may be extended in the summer months. Admission is $3.00 for adults, $2.00 for school-age children and free for preschool children.

Merchants Millpond State Park
Access from US 158, NC 32 and NC 37,
Gatesville
(252) 357–1191
www.ncsparks.net

Less than a two-hour drive from the Outer Banks, Merchants Millpond is an isolated, undisturbed wonderland like no other place in the world. This scenic backwater swamp boasts family and wilderness campsites, miles of well-marked hiking trails and canoe runs, and some of the best largemouth bass fishing in eastern North Carolina.

Between the mid-1800s and early 1920s, the 760-acre millpond was a gathering place for farmers and merchants. A grist and sawmill sat on the edge of the pond. Water controlled by wooden gates in a spillway powered the mill. A general store, a post office, and rough-hewn wooden houses also hugged the muddy shores. Today, only fragments of foundations can be found rotting among more than 3,233 acres of surreal state land in the western Albemarle area.

Picnic tables, ranger programs, fishing, and at least 201 species of birds still inspire people to flock into these boggy lowlands from early spring through late fall. More than 85,000 visitors tour the site each year. Poisonous snakes, mosquitoes, and ticks also inhabit the area—so beware.

Merchants Millpond became a state preserve in 1973 after Moyock nature lover A.B. Coleman donated 919 acres to the state of North Carolina. The Nature Conservancy contributed another 925 acres, and additional land has been acquired over the years. The park tries to sponsor at least one activity per weekend from spring through fall, such as talks, slide programs, and moonlit hikes to stargaze or search for screech owls. Most programs are offered in the warmer months.

Campers are welcome on a first-come, first-served basis at 20 drive-in campsites with drinking water and grills. Three-quarters of a mile from the boat-launching ramp are seven rustic canoe-in sites, and 3.5 miles into the woods are five primitive backpack sites. These sites offer more secluded camping and steel fire rings. The park also has three walk-in and three canoe-in sites 1.25 miles from the launching site for organized groups of up to 50 members. Primitive camping permits are sold at the ranger station for $8.00 per family. The tent and trailer area, which has hot showers, costs $12.00 per night. Campsites are closed December 1 through March 15, but primitive camping is available year-round. North Carolina requires anglers to have freshwater fishing licenses, and these are sold at nearby bait shops.

Even inexperienced boaters can manage to maneuver canoes around these serene, scenic waters. Canoes rent for $3.00 for the first hour and $1.00 for each additional hour. Canoes can also be rented overnight at canoe campsites for $15.00 for 24 hours. Both Merchants Millpond and the adjoining Lassiter Swamp, about a two-hour paddle away, have miles of water trails well-marked by brightly colored buoys. The park is best observed by boat, but it's easy to get lost in this eerie area after dark.

With knobby knees sticking out of the coffee-colored water and long, spiraling Spanish moss beards, the bald cypress in this enchanted forest look like old, wizened wizards wading through the swamp. Some of the ancient trees here are more than 1,000 years old. Their gnarled trunks tower up to 120 feet and grow up to 8 feet in diameter.

Mistletoe has deformed the branches of tupelo gums into zigzags, circles, and fantastic spiderweb patterns. Pink swamp rose, white water lilies, and purple pickerel weed form a floating garden around the edges of this murky millpond. Red and green duckweed weave weird mosaics across the center of the wide, winding waterway.

In canoes, your paddles make thick slurping noises as they drag through this flannel-like blanket of vegetation; the only other sounds are croaking cricket frogs happily munching on mosquitoes.

The deepest fishing spot in the state park is known as the "Polly hole." Here, at the most narrow part of the swamp, a makeshift boardwalk of cypress planks once ran from tree to tree. Legend has it an elderly midwife named Polly drank too much whiskey, stumbled, and fell in as she made her way home through the tangled tree trunks.

Beneath the still, dark waters, bluegill, chain pickerel, black crappie, catfish, and long-nosed gar lurk between the roots and reeds. Fly-fishing is probably the park's most popular pastime. River otter, beaver, and mink also make the millpond their home. Mallards, swans, and herons hover

at 6:00 P.M. November through February and is closed Christmas Day.

Alligator River National Wildlife Refuge
US 64, near East Lake
(252) 473-1131

Stands of 6-foot-wide juniper stumps sparkle with the gray-green tentacles of sphagnum moss. Bobcats, wolves, bears, bald eagles, and alligators thrive amidst these tangled thickets. Remnants of a century-old railroad track wind 100 miles through the thick forest, and rotting ties lead to a 19th-century logging town that has long since been swallowed by the swamp.

On the Dare County mainland off US 64 between East Lake, Manns Harbor, and Stumpy Point, about a half-hour drive west of Manteo, Alligator River National Wildlife Refuge stretches across the Hyde County line into Alligator River. The U.S. Air Force owns a 46,000-acre Dare County Bombing Range in the center of the refuge, but the rest of this sprawling preserve is federally protected.

Endangered species including the peregrine falcon, red-cockaded woodpecker, and the American alligator roam freely through the preserve. Dozens of red wolves, extinct in the wild less than two decades ago, have been reintroduced into this region (see our Natural Wonders chapter). The refuge also is reputed to have one of the biggest black bear populations in the mid-Atlantic region.

The U.S. Fish and Wildlife Service has called the Alligator River Refuge one of the largest and wildest sections of land left on the East Coast.

The entire 151,000-acre refuge is accessible to four-wheel-drive vehicles, and jeep trails traverse much of the flat, sandy marshlands. Two half-mile hiking trails and 15 miles of well-marked canoe and kayak trails also are open.

Activities are free and available year-round throughout daylight hours. Parking is available at the well-marked Milltail Road paved lot or at the end of the dirt Buffalo City Road off US 64. Two houses

overhead, and turtles line up lethargically to sun themselves on logs.

There's plenty of free parking at the canoe launching and picnic areas. The rangers supply paddles, life jackets, and trail maps. You must bring your own food and drinks into the park, although there is a snack and beverage machine on-site if you run out. Don't forget your camera—the strange sights in this secluded swampland speak thousands of unwhispered words.

Merchants Millpond State Park's new entrance includes a picnic area with a shelter, tables, and a bathroom. Large groups can reserve the area for $50. The park is open from 8:00 A.M. to 7:00 P.M. in March and October. Evening hours extend to 8:00 P.M. in April, May, and September and to 9:00 P.M. June through August. It closes

still stand alongside this dusty path leading to Milltail Creek, but only remnants of human existence remain. Once the Albemarle's largest logging town, Buffalo City had two hotels, a school, general store, scores of moonshiners, a tavern, and more than 3,000 people.

Buffalo City thrived along the sandy banks of Milltail Creek from the late 1870s through the early 1940s. It was built by three men from Buffalo, New York, who bought 168,000 acres to begin a modest logging operation. Shortly after the turn of the century, they sold the remaining white cedars, cypress, and juniper to the Dare Lumber Company. Loggers built wooden railroads through the peat bogs and carted their plankings as far as New York and Atlanta. A thriving town grew up around the growing clearing.

When the trees ran out, the lumber company went broke, and townsfolk turned to making moonshine. It was the peak of Prohibition, and the town had an isolated outpost with a built-in rail and water transportation system along the wide Alligator River, so the area became famous for its liquor. By 1936, experts estimate that East Lake had produced one-and-a-half million quart bottles of liquor, which showed up on the shelves of saloons from Philadelphia to Charleston.

Liquor became legal again, and the government took over small stills. After World War II, residents of what is now Alligator River Refuge returned to farming for a while, but the swamp and snakes reclaimed the land too quickly. The government would not let people drain the marshes, so in 1984 then-owner Prudential Life Insurance donated 118,000 acres to the Nature Conservancy, which later turned the substantial parcel over to the U.S. Fish and Wildlife Service.

Today, there are a variety of ways for visitors to see the refuge. About 4 miles west of the US 64/264 split, travelers can stop at a wooden kiosk and pick up brochures about trails, wildlife, and flora. Behind the kiosk there's a paved 15-space parking lot, where the old, dirt Milltail

Road ends. Here, a half-mile paved walkway with a boardwalk overlooking the water begins. This Creef Cut Wildlife Trail and Fishing Area is wheelchair-accessible. It opens at a public fishing dock and culminates in a 50-foot boardwalk atop a freshwater marsh.

Interpretive plaques depicting the area's unusual flora and fauna are nailed along freshly plowed pathways. Beaver cuttings, wood duck boxes, rare sundew flowers, and warbler nesting areas are among the hidden attractions. Look closely: In some places, the forest is so thick you can't see 20 feet ahead.

Refuge workers estimate there are about 100 alligators in this preserve, which marks the northernmost boundary of the American alligators' habitat. On the Milltail Creek Road, there's a platform winding around the creek. The waters surrounding that platform are supposed to be among the gators' favorite haunts. If you wait quietly, you might catch a glimpse of a scaly, dark green snout.

Sandy Ridge Wildlife Trail is a little more rugged. It starts where Buffalo City Road dead-ends off US 64 about 2 miles south of East Lake. Rough wooden pallets help hikers traverse swampy spots, but if rain has fallen during the past week, walkers are bound to get wet. Sweet gum, maple, and pine trees reach 30 feet high around this path.

Canoe and kayak trails through Sawyer Lake and connecting canals include four main routes marked by colored PVC pipe. Trails range from 1.5 to 5.5 miles, all along a wide waterway that is smooth with no rapids. You can bring your own boat in and paddle for free. On the Outer Banks, several rental outlets lease canoes and kayaks by the day (see our Watersports chapter). Guided canoe tours are also offered at the refuge. Call Pea Island Visitor Center at (252) 987-2394 for schedule and prices. Several times a year and regularly in the summer, the refuge staff holds Wolf Howls, leading visitors deep into the refuge at night to hear the red wolves howl (see our Attractions chapter for more details).

If you enjoy nature, isolation, and abundant wildlife, there is no better place to spend a day away from the Outer Banks than at Alligator River National Wildlife Refuge.

Lake Mattamuskeet National Wildlife Refuge
Hyde County mainland
(252) 926–4021
mattamuskeet.fws.gov

About a 90-minute drive southwest of Manteo down lonely US 264 is the 50,000-acre Lake Mattamuskeet National Wildlife Refuge, home to sprawling marshland and the state's largest natural lake, which spans 40,000 acres and averages only three feet and never dips below five feet. In addition to the lake, the refuge includes freshwater marsh, forested wetlands, managed impoundments, croplands, and forested uplands, providing a safe habitat for migratory waterfowl and other birds, including endangered species of bald eagles and peregrine falcons. This is also a refuge for endangered American alligators.

Nearly half of the nation's tundra swans swoop into this rare wilderness refuge to feed, nest, and wait out the winter. From November through March, Lake Mattamuskeet is filled with thousands of the regal white birds. Watching them is amazing. Feeding on the foliage and duckweed that thrives in the shallow, murky waters, the swans dip their black beaks and long necks underwater, upending their tail feathers in a comical fashion. They swim gracefully, making barely a ripple through the still water. They sleep sitting atop the steely gray water, their long necks curled and a head tucked under a wing. Their constant honking, a din of chatter, is unforgettable.

Each fall, an estimated 100,000 tundra swans make a cross-continent trek from the wilds of western Canada and Alaska to the warmer waters of North Carolina and the Chesapeake Bay. Lake Mattamuskeet, a world of isolated flatlands surrounded by 400 acres of wheat farms, is North Carolina's most popular roosting area. Between 20,000 and 40,000 swans winter here every year.

Photographers, bird-watchers, and people with only a casual curiosity can drive through the refuge, across the lake on a two-lane causeway, to get a good glimpse of the birds. Swans usually swarm around the water at sunrise and sunset. They spend their days eating in the nearby fields. Besides these big birds, which can live 20 years or longer, you'll also see a huge variety of ducks, Canada geese, and snow geese.

If you can't get here in the winter, come anyway. The refuge is beautiful year-round, and you will always see a variety of birds, including wading birds, shorebirds, raptors, and bald eagles, depending on the season. You can walk the roads along the lake or on the designated trail or stand atop two observation towers for a sweeping view of the flatlands.

The lake is also famous for its blue crabs. The crustaceans creeping around this waterway in the summer can grow twice as big as the Outer Banks variety. Some say that's because the crabs feed off the unusually rich lake bottom, which was cultivated farm land at one time. If you make the trek to the refuge in the summer, be sure to buy some crabs at an area seafood shop and sample them for yourself. The lake and nearby canals have significant fishery resources, including largemouth bass, bream, white perch, crappie, and herring. The lake is open to public fishing from March through November, and three boat ramps give anglers access to the lake.

The old pumping station near the center of the refuge was built between 1915 and 1918. The pumping station was used to drain the lake so that people could farm the lakebed. The lake was drained and farmed on three occasions, but each company that did this went bankrupt. The pumping station was then sold to the U.S. Government, and the lake was converted into the Lake Mattamuskeet National Wildlife Refuge, a division of U.S. Fish and Wildlife, in 1934. The Civilian Conservation Corps renovated the building, adding rooms, bathrooms, and balconies and turning it into a hunting and fishing lodge. It was closed in 1974. See the Close-up in this chapter for more about the history of the pumping station/lodge.

Public hunting opportunities are available in fall and winter for deer (October) and waterfowl (December and January). The refuge has 16 blinds that are assigned by a drawing for two-day hunts. Call the refuge office for details.

A popular event at Lake Mattamuskeet is Swan Days, held the first weekend in December. The Swan Quarter Service Group, in cooperation with the U.S. Fish and Wildlife Service and the staff of the Lake Mattamuskeet National Wildlife Refuge, puts on the celebration to welcome the thousands of tundra swan and other waterfowl. The event, which began in 1994, offers a variety of activities for the whole family, including guided tours of the refuge, workshops and lectures on a variety of wildlife and history topics, local arts and crafts, kids' activities, and delicious food. Many of the guided tours and workshops require reservations, so make plans early by visiting the Web site or calling the refuge and asking for a brochure.

Edenton National Fish Hatchery
1104 West Queen St. (exit 224 off US 17),
Edenton
(252) 482–4118
www.fws.gov/FWSFH/NFHS

Run by the U.S. Fish and Wildlife Service on the grassy banks of the Chowan River, the Edenton National Fish Hatchery includes an expanse of outdoor ponds and a small aquarium. This fascinating hatchery is only about 90 minutes from the Outer Banks.

Officials opened a waterfront walkway and pier at the facility in spring of 1995, providing access to Pembroke Creek for people with disabilities. The 15-acre area also gives nature lovers a look at some of the native wildlife and waterfowl indigenous to the surrounding wetlands.

The Hatchery expanded in 2001. Inside, groups of aquariums house fish native to local waters. Kids will love seeing three alligators kept in one tank. A question and

> ## Insiders' Tip
> Check the gas tank before you drive off into the wild blue yonder of eastern North Carolina. This is sparsely populated farm country, and there are not—thank heaven—filling stations around every corner.

answer computer touch screen helps people learn about the fish and environment.

The most popular attraction, "Pathway to Fishing," is a 12-station, one-hour tour that teaches youngsters the basics of fishing. Included are brief talks on angler ethics and safety, live baits and lures, ecology, rods and reels, knot-tying, casting, and local fish species.

The fish hatchery is open 7:00 A.M. to 3:30 P.M. Monday through Friday in the off-season, and Monday through Sunday from 8:00 A.M. to 5:00 P.M. April through August. There is no admittance charge.

Cape Lookout National Seashore
Southern barrier islands of NC
(252) 728–2250
www.nps.gov/calo

Low, unpopulated and much less visited than the Outer Banks, the southern stretches of North Carolina's barrier islands extend 55 miles southwest from Ocracoke Inlet and include Portsmouth Island, Core Banks, Cape Lookout, and Shackleford Banks.

These remote sand islands are untouched by development and linked to the mainland and other barrier island beaches only by private ferries or private boats. (Call the listed number for ferry schedules and reservations.) In 1976 they came under the control of the National

Park Service when a separate national seashore was established south of the Cape Hatteras holdings. Each year, more than 300,000 nature lovers visit these sparse strips of beach.

If you have your own boat, you can get to Cape Lookout by launching from ramps at marinas throughout Carteret County or from Silver Lake on Ocracoke. The easiest access to Cape Lookout is from Harkers Island. Concession ferries and private boats for hire also are available from Harkers Island to the Cape Lookout Light area, from Davis to Shingle Point, from Atlantic to an area north of Drum Inlet and from Ocracoke to Portsmouth Village. Boats are also available from Beaufort.

There are no roads on these islands, but four-wheel-drive vehicles can cruise on the Core Banks or Portsmouth Island. There are few facilities along this sparse stretch of sand, however, the islands are perfect for primitive camping year-round, four-wheel driving, fishing, bird-watching, and photography. Stay alert for sudden storms, because there is little shelter. To help foreshadow bad squalls, call the National Weather Service, (252) 223-5327, before you set out on an excursion. Visitors must supply their own water and food, and pets are not allowed.

Deer ticks, chiggers, deer flies, mosquitoes, gnats, and other annoying insects are also abundant around the islands, so bring repellent and wear long sleeves even in the summer months. Water is available from pitcher pumps around Cape Lookout, but campers are encouraged to bring their own supplies. Primitive camping is allowed throughout the park, but there are no designated sites.

The Cape Lookout grounds include a lighthouse that was first illuminated in 1859, a lighthouse keeper's quarters that has been converted to a visitor center, and a Coast Guard station that is no longer active. Cape Lookout is closed Christmas and New Year's Day.

Portsmouth Island, site of the only ghost town on the Eastern Seaboard, is just a 20-minute boat ride south of Ocracoke Island. What was the biggest, most bustling town on the Outer Banks for more than a century is now uninhabited, except for two volunteer rangers. Owned by the National Park Service since 1976, the 23-mile-long, 1.5-mile-wide isolated outpost attracts about 10,000 visitors a year. Most come to camp, watch birds, scan for seashells on miles of wide empty beaches, or just hike through the remnants of the historic village and re-enter a long-forgotten world. Two-dozen cottages, a weather-beaten post office, and an old church still remain of the former shipping community that was populated by more than 700 people in its prime before the Civil War.

Although about 1,400 ships used to dock at the rough-hewn piers annually, Portsmouth Island was eventually done in by a storm-narrowed Ocracoke Inlet and Civil War evacuations. By 1950 only 14 inhabitants remained on the still-primitive island. The last few holdouts finally abandoned their homes for good in 1971. Although most of the houses remain in relatively good condition, considering their exposure to the elements and years of being uninhabited, only one is open for public perusal: the turn-of-the-20th-century Salter/Dixon House that now serves as the National Park Service Visitor Center. Beyond the center lies the post office, a cemetery, and a cluster of buildings that includes the homes of the most recent residents. A short hike from the village, a visitor will see the Methodist Church, the best-preserved structure on the island. Built in 1914, the church has seen quite a few couples take the vow of marriage in recent years. You don't have to get married to see inside, though—like the visitor center, it is open to the public.

Rudy Austin ferries visitors to Portsmouth Island most of the spring, summer, and fall. The boat departs Ocracoke Island at 9:30 A.M. and costs $15 per person. For reservations and further information, call (252) 928-4361 or (252) 928-5431. Whichever way you visit this remote land, make sure you bring plenty of bug spray, snacks, and drinks.

For more information about Portsmouth Island and Cape Lookout National Seashore, call or write the National Park Service, Cape Lookout National Seashore, 131 Charles Street, Harkers Island, North Carolina 28531. Also, pick up a copy of the *Insiders' Guide® to North Carolina's Central Coast* from any area bookstore or by calling the Globe-Pequot customer service number listed at the back of this book.

Historic Attractions

Museum of the Albemarle
1116 US 17 South, Elizabeth City
(252) 335–1453
www.northeast-nc.com

About 50 miles inland from the Outer Banks, on the west side of Elizabeth City, this state-owned museum preserves the Albemarle area's past with exhibits, photographs, and maps.

The Museum of the Albemarle includes permanent interpretive displays depicting Native American tribes and their tools and exhibits on the food, folk tales, crafts, and hunting artifacts of early English-speaking colonists. A 19th-century hearth exhibit allows visitors to contrast Colonial living with modern American amenities. Other offerings trace the development of boating, logging, and the U.S. Coast Guard in surrounding sites.

With two weeks' notice, the museum can provide guided tours, lectures, and audiovisual programs for groups and individuals. A small gift shop sells memorabilia. Admission to the museum is free, and the building is wheelchair-accessible with assistance at the front door.

The museum is open Tuesday through Saturday from 9:00 A.M. until 5:00 P.M. and Sunday from 2:00 until 5:00 P.M. It is closed Mondays and holidays. Please call the number listed for program schedules and reservations.

Historic Hertford
Intersection of US 17 and NC 1336, Hertford
(252) 426–5657
www.perquimans.com

One of the oldest towns in North Carolina, Hertford was incorporated in 1758 to serve as the Perquimans county seat and commercial center of the surrounding Albemarle area.

About 50 buildings dating from the early 1800s stand as stalwart sentries along the tree-lined lanes of the downtown. These magnificent mansions and well-kept gardens serve as reminders of the early inhabitants who spent their lives fishing, farming, and felling trees for lumber. Later, cloth was manufactured in nearby factories.

This tiny town is toured easily by car. We also advise walking around the shady streets to get a closer perspective. Hertford is about an hour's drive from the Outer Banks.

The Newbold-White House
110 Newbold-White Rd., off US 17 South, Hertford
(252) 426–7567
www.albemarle-nc.com/newbold-white

About 60 miles from the Outer Banks in historic Perquimans County, North Carolina's oldest house was built in 1730 and is still open for tours today.

The Newbold-White House is an outstanding example of early American domestic architecture. It's set about a mile off the road across an immense cotton field. The former plantation home is built entirely of handmade brick molded from the clay that can be found 12 inches below the soil on the grounds surrounding the house.

Joseph Scott, the original landowner, was a magistrate, legislator, and Quaker. The original owner of the home was Abraham Sanders, who built this elegant brick abode on a 600-acre tract along the Perquimans River and surrounded it with tobacco fields. Tobacco was frequently used as currency during the 18th century. Later, peanuts and other products also were farmed in these fields.

Numerous other families occupied the house, and Thomas Elbert White bought it in 1903. In 1943, his heirs sold the property to John Henry Newbold, whose heirs in turn sold it to the Perquimans County Restoration Association in 1973. Since

Lake Mattamuskeet—Not Just for the Birds

Heading west on US 264 out of Manteo, you will enter Hyde County and eventually come to a sign for Lake Mattamuskeet National Wildlife Refuge. Take the turn and explore this extensive marshland that draws migrating tundra swans to its shores each winter. (See our daytrip in this chapter for more information.) Within this refuge you'll come upon Mattamuskeet Lodge, built in 1915–16 by the Mattamuskeet Drainage District to house the world's largest pumping station.

In 1909, Hyde County landowners decided to drain 100,000 acres of wetlands, including Lake Mattamuskeet, for what they referred to as "productive purposes." In other words, the landowners wanted to develop the land, encouraging people to move to Hyde County and farm. The Southern Land Reclamation Company took over the project in 1911. The president of the company, Douglas Nelson Graves from Massachusetts, along with three Asheville residents decided to divide the lakebed into farms and residential lots and sell them. Graves envisioned development of a model community unmatched anywhere else.

To build the drainage system, the Drainage District sold 500 $1,000 drainage bonds to the New First National Bank of Columbus, Ohio. A dredging contract was awarded to A. V. Wills & Sons from Illinois to dredge 130 miles of canals. Work was begun in April of 1914, and a network of canals was cut to bring the water from the lake to the pumping plant where it could be pushed into the Pamlico Sound.

The plant was built by Morris Machine Works of Baldwinsville, New York, and installation of the pumps was done by Erie City Iron Works of Erie, Pennsylvania. The Drainage District paid $205,000 for the plant, $30,000 for the building, and $175,000 for the pumps. These huge centrifugal pumps could move 1,200,000 gallons of water per minute. Four coal-fired Lentz steam engines, rated at 850 horsepower each, powered the pumps.

In 1915, Southern Land Reclamation Company changed its name to New Holland Farms, Inc. and launched a strategy around a Dutch theme. They laid out an 850-acre town called New Holland around the pumping plant, built a first-class hotel, and started their own fleet of freight and passenger boats called the New Holland Boat Lines.

Pumping operations began in May of 1916, and initially they failed, causing the soft canal banks to cave in and block the water flow. Faced with higher coal cost than originally anticipated, the pumps were shut down in 1917 until the pumping efficiency could be increased and the canals cleaned out. The lake began to refill. Of course, lakebed property could not be sold, and in 1918, New Holland Farms sold the lake property to private owners in Ohio. Graves returned to Massachusetts.

The new owners, called the North Carolina Farms Company, continued development, and the pumps were redesigned and the canals dredged. Pumping operations resumed and the lake was drained for the second time. The company built houses, stores, and roads, along with a 35-mile private railroad called the New Holland, Higginsport, and Mount Vernon Railroad. Nine miles of the line ran through the drained lake bed. The independently financed company went bankrupt in 1923. Pumping operations were once again shut down, and the lake refilled for the third time.

In 1925 August Heckscher, a wealthy New York philanthropist and real estate developer, purchased the property and assets and formed the New Holland Corporation; he hired Graves to return to the lake to manage the project. Abandoning the original idea for the property, Heckscher decided to create a commercial farm in the lakebed. An overhaul of the pumping plant was called for and pumping resumed in May 1926. By late fall, Lake Mattamuskeet was once again empty. After enormous improvements, in 1929 the New Holland Corporation had 5,000 acres in cultivation, mostly soybeans, corn, and wheat.

Excessive rain and wet soil conditions often interfered with planting and harvesting over the next several years, and in 1932 the New Holland Corporation offices based in New York decided to discontinue the farming operation. Everything was shut down and the lake began refilling, flooding many of the buildings.

In 1934 the property was sold to the U.S. Government for $311,943, which led to the creation of Lake Mattamuskeet Bird Refuge. The Civilian Conservation Corps helped to set up the refuge and convert the pumping plant into a rustic hunting and fishing lodge. They installed a spiral staircase in the old smokestack to create a 112-foot observation tower for viewing the lake and waterfowl.

Mattamuskeet Lodge was first opened to the public in 1937, and the lake became known as the "Canada Goose Hunting Capital of the World." Over the course of many years, the climate altered and there were changes in land use in the Atlantic flyway. Both of these significantly reduced the number of geese that would frequent the Mattamuskeet Refuge. An effort was made by the U.S. Fish and Wildlife Service to protect the declining birds by closing the refuge to hunters in 1972. Because of the loss of the hunting business, the lodge was forced to close in 1974.

In 1981 the lodge building was listed on the National Register of Historic Places, and 10 years later the Greater Hyde County Chamber of Commerce realized the importance of the lodge and formed the Friends of Mattamuskeet Lodge Committee to begin restoration of the building by arresting deterioration and stabilizing the building. A field station for coastal studies is now housed in a portion of the building for use by the East Carolina University. Partnership for the Sounds, a nonprofit organization, is working with other community groups to raise funds to help further renovate the structure. And another nonprofit group, The Mattamuskeet Foundation, is involved in preserving and publishing the history of the lake and helping to recover artifacts from the lake drainage area.

Plans are in the works for more renovations to the lodge in hopes that it will become a center for educational activities, interpretative exhibits, community gatherings, and administrative offices. For additional information on the Mattamuskeet Lodge contact The Mattamuskeet Foundation at (252) 746–4221 or toll free at 888–MAT–LAKE.

then, the house has been beautifully restored to its original condition.

A tour of this three-century-old structure is well worth the trip. Sturdy and sophisticated, the dwelling is of English bond construction on the lower portions and Flemish bond-brick construction higher up. Its first floor consists of the traditional great hall and a more intimate parlor, both with cavernous fireplaces, great wooden mantles, and superb original pine woodwork.

Winding wooden stairs tucked in the corner of the main first-floor room lead to two dormer-lighted, second-floor rooms. During restoration, the leaded window casements with diamond-shaped panes were restored with glass shipped in from Germany. Artisans made these windows by copying a piece of the panes found on the floor of the Newbold-White House before restoration work began.

When you visit the house, be sure to stop at the Perquimans County Restoration Association headquarters on the way. This visitor center of sorts offers an informative audiovisual journey into the house's heyday and inhabitants. Hours at the Newbold-White House are 10:00 A.M. to 4:30 P.M. Tuesday through Saturday and 2:00 to 5:00 P.M. on Sunday. The museum is closed on Mondays. The museum is closed in December, January, and February, but special tours can be arranged in advance during the winter months. Admission is $2.00 for adults, and children and students pay 50 cents each.

Albemarle Plantation
1 Plantation Lane, Hertford
(252) 337–8029, (800) 535–0704
www.albemarleplantation.com

Albemarle Plantation, a golfing and boating community, is just off US 17. Visiting this sprawling complex of recreational and dining facilities along the waters of the Albemarle Sound makes a great daytrip. Albemarle Plantation is part of an upscale residential development that also includes a swimming pool, tennis courts, and fitness center. Sound Golf Links, an 18-hole golf course that's open to the public, is one of the most popular venues in the region for dedicated golfers (see our Golf chapter for more information). Call the number listed for tee times. After a couple of rounds, you may be ready for lunch or dinner at the Soundside Grille, which has great views of the water.

The 200-slip marina, also open to the public, offers all the amenities and hookups a boater could wish for. The 1,600-acre secured community is designed for 1,000 single-family homes with a few townhomes and condominiums as well. If you're interested in staying for several days, call about the Albemarle Plantation's getaway packages. Follow US 17 from Elizabeth City to Hertford. Drive time from Kitty Hawk is just over an hour.

Historic Edenton
US 17, Edenton
(252) 482–2637
www.edenton.com

Edenton is the oldest town in North Carolina and one of the oldest towns in America. It was settled in 1690 along the shores of the Albemarle Sound and Edenton Bay. It was incorporated in 1722 and established as the Colonial capital of North Carolina in 1782.

Edenton is a charming historic town that's perfect for a daytrip or an overnight stay. It's an easy daytrip from the Outer Banks by boat or by automobile, a little over an hour's drive. It's a town with a Colonial past, similar to Williamsburg, Virginia, in its historic significance but much less commercial and "touristy." Historic homes are the star attractions of this waterfront town. Twenty-five homes and public buildings encompass this North Carolina State Historic Site, though there are hundreds of magnificent historic homes in the town. Along with the homes, antiques stores inhabit iron-gate–sheltered alleys, grand bed-and-breakfasts offer extraordinary escapes, and a walk along the waterfront beckons. Everything is this quaint town is readily accessible by walking.

The Historic Edenton Visitor Center,

an East Lake–style Victorian built in 1892, is at 108 West Broad Street, across the street from St. Paul's Episcopal Church. A short audiovisual presentation on the history of Edenton is offered throughout the day at the visitor center, plus there is a gift shop. The visitor center offers self-guided walking tour maps. Or you can choose to take a guided walking or trolley tour, which begin and end at the visitor center. Trolley tours last 45 minutes and are led by an experienced interpreter. Trolley tours are offered year-round, Tuesday through Saturday at 10:00 A.M., 11:00 A.M., 3:00 P.M., and 4:00 P.M. They cost $7.00 for adults and $2.00 for K–12 students. Guided walking tours are offered at 10:30 A.M. Monday through Saturday and 2:00 P.M. every day, year-round. Walking tours also cost $7.00 and $2.00.

This Colonial community had its own tea party in 1774 when 51 women gathered at Elizabeth King's home and signed a petition protesting British taxes. A journey through town reveals the restored homes of James Iredell, an attorney general during the Revolutionary War who served as U.S. Supreme Court justice from 1790 to 1799; Samuel Johnston, a state governor and post Revolutionary War–era U.S. senator; Dr. Hugh Williamston, who signed the U.S. Constitution; Joseph Hewes, who put his own John Hancock on the Declaration of Independence; and Thomas Barker, a North Carolina agent to England and husband of Penelope, the reputed leader of the infamous Edenton Tea Party.

Other 18th-century buildings with unsurpassed Colonial architecture include the Chowan County Courthouse and St. Paul's Episcopal Church. An easy walk along King Street uncovers a remarkable collection of Georgian, Federal, and Greek Revival homes nestled among impeccably kept gardens and centuries-old trees.

From 1771 to 1776, Edenton was a prosperous port town. More than 800 ships linked Carolina and Virginia colonists with supplies from Europe and the West Indies. Blackbeard often sailed into Edenton Bay to unload—and pilfer—pirate goods. Sailors continue to cruise into this historic harbor today.

Edenton is well-known for its romantic bed-and-breakfast inns, so you may want to plan to spend the night. The Lords Proprietors' Inn at 300 North Broad Street comprises three restored homes in the heart of the historic district, and 20 guest rooms are available for nightly accommodations. Each home is graced with grand parlors and stately front porches. Guests are served breakfast daily and both breakfast and dinner Tuesdays through Saturdays, except in the month of January, when dinner is not served. Reservations are available year-round by calling (252) 482-3641.

Just down the street is the Governor Eden Inn, 304 North Broad Street. This neoclassical home is fronted by massive Ionic columns and unusual oval portals of beveled glass. There is a lovely, upper-story front balcony overlooking North Broad Street. A large wraparound porch is another great place for guests to meet. All rooms have private baths and TVs, and rates are very reasonable. Breakfast is served each morning. To make reservations, call (252) 482-2072.

Granville Queen Inn also offers exquisite accommodations in the historic district. This abode at 108 South Granville Street features furnishings from around the world. Guest rooms are named for their individual themes, including the Queen of Queen's bedroom and Egyptian Queen bedroom. A five-course gourmet breakfast featuring filet mignon and chicken tarragon is served on the plantation porch. The inn is closed the month of January. For more information, call (252) 482-5296.

At the Captain's Quarters Inn at 202 West Queen Street, you get more than just a bed and breakfast. Guests are treated to two-night "sail and snooze" specials or golfing trips from March through October that include three-hour sailing excursions on the Albemarle Sound or a golfing expedition. On Saturday nights, dinner is served at this 1907 home in the historic district. Guests also may take a two-hour guided walking tour of the town or help solve a mock murder mystery during Murder Mystery weekends. Reservations can be made by calling (800) 482–8945.

The Trestle House Inn, at 632 Soundside Road, is part of a wildlife refuge that is a magnet for migratory birds. Just outside Edenton, the estate was built in 1972. This bed and breakfast inn features five guest rooms and redwood beams that were milled from old railroad trestle timbers. Guests can fish in a small pond that is part of the Albemarle Canoe and Small Boats Trails System or wander the inn's extensive grounds, which are also part of the North Carolina Biking Highway. Canoes can be rented for $10 a half-day or $20 a full day. The inn is open year-round. For reservations call (252) 482–2282 or (800) 645–8466.

Edenton can be reached from Roanoke Island via US 64 by driving 40 miles west until you come to NC 32, and then turning right and following the signs.

The Historic Edenton Christmas Candlelight Tour is a favorite annual event held the second weekend in December. Holiday visitors are guided through about a dozen beautifully decorated homes, both historic and contemporary. Tickets cost $20 each.

Historic Columbia
US 64, Columbia
(252) 796–0723
www.albemarle-nc.com/columbia

Visitors traveling to the Outer Banks on US 64 through eastern North Carolina used to completely overlook the isolated outpost of Columbia, whizzing through the town in their rush to get to the beach. In years past there wasn't really a reason to stop. But that's all changed today. Many visitors now stop in this burgeoning waterfront town to stretch their legs and soak up a healthy dose of ecotourism. More and more Outer Bankers are making a special trip to Columbia for the day; it's about a 30-minute drive from Manteo on US 64.

The beautiful, $1.1 million Tyrrell County Visitor Center, right on the Scuppernong River and visible from the road, opened in 1995. It's a combination rest area, welcome center, and environmental education center. The center is dedicated to the preservation and understanding of North Carolina's coastal wetlands, which are abundant in this area. A three-quarter-mile raised boardwalk winds along the river behind the visitor center, providing breathtaking views of coastal wetlands and the Scuppernong River as it slides slowly into Bull Bay. For thousands of feet along the river's edge, tiny electric lights twinkle across the dark water, illuminating the walkway that creeps through unspoiled timber wetlands. Interpretive signs tell you what you're looking at. Visitors are greeted with sounds from scurrying wildlife, jumping minnows, and fat, quacking ducks. Bullfrogs clear their throats with resonating croaks. Opossum, raccoon, and nutria scuttle for cover beneath the reeds and marsh grasses. A black bear cub ambling along the boardwalk in broad daylight, apparently too lazy to struggle through the swampy underbrush below, astonished a walker we know one day.

A fountain, gazebo, and wide turnouts to accommodate wheelchair passengers are among the other attractions along this zigzagging boardwalk that twists around towering forest giants and squatty flowering bushes that would have soon disappeared in more chainsaw-oriented communities. If you want to see the wetlands closer than this, rent a kayak at the visitor center.

Columbia has many other attractions. At the visitor center, pick up a brochure of the Columbia on the Scuppernong Walking Tour, which will lead you through town past 20 houses and churches built around the turn of the twentieth century.

One of the most surprising residents of Columbia is the Pocosin Arts Gallery, an art museum, gift shop, gallery, and arts education center on the corner of Main and Water streets. Pocosin is a highly evolved cultural center, and it holds a variety of classes and special events. Call (252) 796-2787 for information, or stop by to see what great things they have going on while you're there.

Another great attraction is the Columbia Theater Cultural Resources Center on Main Street. Housed in the town's renovated movie theater, it's an environmental and cultural history museum that highlights the general way of life in Tyrrell County, including fishing, farming, and forestry. The museum has a gift shop and welcomes group tours. Admission is $2.00 for adults, $1.00 for students, and free for kids five and younger. It's open Tuesday through Saturday from 10:00 A.M. to 4:00 P.M. Call (252) 766-0200.

The Columbia Marina is a charming marina that houses mostly permanent boats. There is one slip for transient sailors. If you're walking around town, be sure to walk by the marina and have a look at the beautiful boats docked there. If you're hungry, there are a couple of restaurants and the Columbia Pharmacy for snacks. If you're having so much fun you want to stay the night, Columbia has a couple of great bed-and-breakfast inns.

If you happen to be here on the second weekend of October, you're in luck. The Scuppernong River Festival is a delight, featuring water tours, boat rides, kids' activities, arts and crafts vendors, and yummy food.

Somerset Place
Off US 64, Creswell
(252) 797-4560
www.ah.dr.state.nc.us/hs/somerset/
somerset.htm

On the swampy stretch of marshland surrounding Phelps Lake, bordered by handdug canals and majestic stands of sycamore, Somerset Place is a historic plantation in Washington County where visitors can learn about antebellum lifestyles of wealthy plantation owners and their slaves.

This state-funded site is 5 miles outside Creswell, near Pettigrew State Park, and about an hour's drive from the Outer Banks. Guides offer free tours and special arrangements for school groups. Grounds include isolated walking trails and wooden boardwalks to the water, where nearby fishing is excellent. About 25,000 people visit the site annually.

When the ongoing restoration is complete, this historic place will be the only plantation in the country that documents how both owner and slave populations lived. Planning has begun to rebuild a two-story, four-bedroom house that the field laborers inhabited. Two families shared each small room and helped to wrest the fertile farmland from the ever-encroaching swamp. At this writing, reconstruction has been completed on one building in the slave community, and the remains of five other buildings can now be seen.

Once one of North Carolina's four biggest plantations, Somerset Place used more than 300 slaves to grow corn and rice and work in the expansive wetlands. An incredible collection of the plantation's slave records is open at the house for genealogical research. In August 1996 more than 2,000 descendants of Somerset's slaves gathered for a 10th anniversary homecoming reunion.

Josiah Collins built the elegant, two-story mansion in 1830 to entertain the cultivated elite of the state's planter aristocracy. Nearby, North Carolina's first Episcopal bishop–elect, Charles Pettigrew, his congressman son, and Confederate brigadier general grandson lie buried beneath sprawling live oak trees. The plantation home itself has 14 rooms and six original outbuildings and is furnished with period furniture.

When students tour Somerset, they grind corn by hand, haul water from distant streams, and make corn bread in a black iron skillet over an open fire. They wash dishes in homemade lye soap, gather broom straw, and bind stalks together to clean wood floors. They dip wax and make candles two at a time, clean cotton by hand, weave baskets, and sew pincushions. The idea, curator Dorothy Redford says, is to simulate experiences of the period slaves and see what it was like to live on an antebellum plantation.

Somerset Place is open April through October from 8:00 A.M. to 5:00 P.M. Monday through Saturday and from 1:00 to 5:00 P.M. on Sunday. From November through March, it's open Tuesday through Saturday 10:00 A.M. to 4:00 P.M., Sunday 1:00 to 4:00 P.M. and closed Monday. To make reservations for large groups, write to 2572 Lake Shore Road, Creswell, North Carolina 27928. There is no admission fee.

Hope Plantation
NC 308, Windsor
(252) 794–3140

In the 1720s, the Lord Proprietors of the Carolina Colony granted abundant Albemarle-area acreage to the Hobson family. David Stone, a delegate to the North Carolina Constitutional Convention of 1789, began building an impressive plantation home on the site around 1800. About a two-hour drive west of the Outer Banks, this Federal period mansion is included on the National Register of Historic Places and is open to the public for guided tours.

Stone was a judge, representative, senator, trustee of the University of North Carolina, and governor of the new state from 1808 until 1810. A contemporary of Thomas Jefferson, he shared many of his Virginia friend's interests, especially in books. When the Hope Mansion was completed in 1803, it included a 1,400-volume library. Copies of these works are being assembled from an inventory of Stone's belongings at the time of his death. They will be stored in a fireproof room inside the Roanoke-Chowan Heritage Center on the site.

A well-preserved Federal residence furnished with period furniture, Hope Plantation reminds some visitors of Jefferson's Monticello estate and reminds others of Scarlett O'Hara's beloved Tara. The Historic Hope Foundation purchased the home and 18 acres around it in 1966. Now restored, the property includes two smaller structures, the King-Bazemore and Samuel Cox houses. Lovely 18th-century style gardens surround the homesites, and the 16,600-square-foot J.J. Harrington Building nearby includes a museum-like center that promotes the area's history and culture.

To get to Hope Plantation, take US 64 out of Roanoke Island west to its intersection with US 13; go north on US 13 and you'll find the house 4 miles west of the US 13 Bypass. From Roanoke Island, it is about a 90-minute drive. Summer hours are Monday through Saturday from 10:00 A.M. to 5:00 P.M. and Sunday from 2:00 to 5:00 P.M. Winter hours are the same, except that it closes at 4:00 P.M. Monday through Saturday. Admission is $6.50 for adults and $2.00 for students.

Something Different

Currituck County's Produce Stands
Along US 158
on the Currituck County mainland

If you're looking for a little lushness near the barren barrier island beaches—or if you're hungering for something sweet to eat on the long, last leg of your drive to the Outer Banks—Currituck County's mainland has the stuff to make your mouth water.

Visitors arriving from Hampton Roads areas travel through fertile farmlands on the last hour of their trip. Like an oasis in a desert of desolation, wooden produce stands pop out of the flatlands. Hand-painted signs hawk the homegrown wares: just-ripe melons, cucumbers, corn, blueberries, tomatoes, butter beans, and peaches so juicy they should be sold with bibs.

More than 10 markets are strewn in sporadic fashion from the Virginia border in Chesapeake to just west of the Wright Memorial Bridge. Each has a personality—and produce—all its own. Many are run by local families who began selling vegetables from the backs of pickup trucks parked along the roadside. Some stands include frozen yogurt, dried flowers, and even seafood stalls, and almost all sell produce grown within a few miles of the open-air markets.

Decor includes the hospitable deep-green awnings of Grandy Greenhouse and

Farm Market, the baby-blue exterior of Tarheel Produce, and the pink-and-purple polka dots of S & N Farm Market. Margaret and Alton Newbern have been running the Hilltop Market for more than 43 years. Morris Farm Market is one of the larger outposts along the Currituck stretch. Rufus Jones Farm Market features colorful fruits stacked in tilted wooden troughs and large-wheeled carts. And Soundside Orchard specializes in peach sales beneath a pointy-roofed wooden gazebo.

Whether you know produce or not, local farmers and their families are always glad to give free advice. They can thump a watermelon, peruse a peanut display, or just feel a pumpkin and know how long ago it was picked. And they'll load you up with bursting berries, just-jarred apricot preserves, and even local lore if you stick around long enough.

The produce of Currituck County is so good, you just might want to come back for more—they're only a half-hour jaunt from the barrier island beaches.

Hampton Roads and Williamsburg, Virginia

If you're in the mood for more citified fun after days at the beach, head to Hampton Roads, Virginia, home to the urban cities of Norfolk, Virginia Beach, Chespeake, Portsmouth, Hampton, and nearby Williamsburg. Outer Bankers are constantly making the 90- to 120-minute drive to this area to stock up at the superstores, fly somewhere, or attend a cultural or entertainment event. Norfolk is home to the Chrysler Museum of Art, the Harrison Opera House, and other performing arts centers that bring in top-name performers. MacArthur Center is Norfolk's premier shopping mall, and it's near the city's waterfront, which also has many attractions, museums, historic buildings, restaurants, and accommodations. Virginia Beach is a busy tourist resort, but it also has a wealth of cultural offerings, an outdoor amphitheater that features national acts, and many shopping opportunities. Williamsburg, Virginia, is about 45 minutes from Virginia Beach. It's famous for its historic attractions and for Busch Gardens, Water Country USA, and its endless shopping opportunities.

Elizabeth City, North Carolina

Our nearby neighbor to the northwest, Elizabeth City, North Carolina, offers more than enough beautiful scenery; historic, architectural, and natural attractions; and cultural and culinary options to make for a great daytrip—and it's all just about an hour from the Outer Banks. The area chamber of commerce is your best source for more information.

Elizabeth City Area Chamber of Commerce
502 Ehringhaus St., Elizabeth City
(252) 335–4365, (888) 258–4832
www.elizcity.com

The chamber offices are jam-packed with information on all there is to see and do in this Pasquotank County jewel of a city, and a friendly staff is on hand to provide assistance. Elizabeth City is steeped in history. The first Grand Assembly of North Carolina met in this county in 1665, the state's first public school opened its doors here 40 years later, and the nation's oldest operational canal—the one snaking through the Dismal Swamp—opened in the early 1800s.

The chamber can get you started on your explorations of these fascinating facts and has also developed a self-guided walking tour through the city's historic districts. Elizabeth City has five designated districts listed with the National Register of Historic Places. Chamber personnel can also point you toward the Museum of the Albemarle (see previous listing in this chapter), with its collections, exhibits, and artifacts that document the history of northeastern North Carolina.

Other great ideas to include on your daytrip or weekend getaway (there are at least a dozen great places to stay in the city; again, ask at the chamber for more information) include the dynamite dirt-track excitement of the Dixieland Motorsports complex; the Elizabeth City State

University Planetarium, art galleries, and professional theater; and dining from fast-food to four-star finery. And remember, the Pasquotank River rolls right through town, so there are a number of water-related activities available as well.

If you prefer to write for more information, send correspondence to Elizabeth City Area Chamber of Commerce, P.O. Box 426, Elizabeth City, North Carolina 27907.

Insiders' Tip

If you're visiting Cape Lookout National Seashore, insect repellent is a must. Cape Lookout and Portsmouth Island are notorious for their blood-thirsty mosquitoes.

Real Estate

There's a certain feeling that many of us get when we cross a bridge to the Outer Banks. It's excitement mixed with awe, blended with the spirit that something wonderful might happen at any moment. It's also a feeling of coming home. Any visitor to these shores who has that feeling should know one thing: It only gets stronger, and it makes leaving increasingly difficult. When you get that feeling, you know that it's time to look at Outer Banks real estate.

It's the desire to belong here, as much as the desire to own here, that puts the ink on all those real estate contracts. Before you take up a pen, however, realize that no matter how much experience you have buying and selling real estate in other areas, you need a deep understanding of the Outer Banks and its unique real estate market in order to make a sound decision. There's a lot to learn about seasonal vs. residential neighborhoods, coastal and wetlands regulations, investing in an income-producing property vs. buying a second home, buying an existing home vs. building—you get the picture. It's not unusual for real estate agents to work with prospective buyers for two or three years before it all comes together. Then again, you may find exactly what you want your first day out looking.

So if you're serious about buying on the Outer Banks, begin by reading this chapter, and when you're done, consider that you've learned just enough to be dangerous. Do two things: (1) start interviewing real estate professionals, and (2) begin collecting and reading everything you can get your hands on that will help you decipher the real estate market. Subscribe to the local newspapers (see our chapter on Media) and get to know the areas, the issues, and the prices. Read the weekly column in *The Virginian-Pilot* by Shirley Mozingo, who has been writing about Outer Banks real estate for a number of years and who imparts substantive information helpful to both buyers and sellers. Surf the Internet and pick up the free real estate magazines. Smart buyers begin performing this due diligence well before they're ready to make a purchase.

Understanding the Local Market

The last several years have seen a strong, healthy real estate market all over these barrier islands. Some recent hot spots have been Currituck's northern beaches, soundside in Duck, South Nags Head, and, of course, anything oceanfront. With the declining availability of raw oceanfront land, we're seeing a trend toward buying older existing homes and either remodeling the outdated structures or moving them off altogether and starting anew. Each year, prices continue to appreciate, and those who put off buying in the past have usually regretted their delay. If you want to buy, buy now, for the same piece of real estate will probably not be available next year and prices are guaranteed to be higher. In a nutshell, a purchase of Outer Banks real estate has never been a bad investment.

As you learn about the Outer Banks, you'll come to understand that the market

Large, multilevel homes are becoming the dominant architectural style along the Outer Banks oceanfront.
PHOTO: MOLLY HARRISON

varies quite a bit by township and by proximity to water. Nowhere is the old adage about location, location, location more important than here on the Outer Banks. The rules of supply and demand apply, period. The closer to the ocean, the greater the demand—and nothing is more precious than an oceanfront lot. Bear in mind that all oceanfront lots aren't created equal. The shoreline along the entire East Coast is in a constant state of flux. With such a dynamic scenario, some areas of the beach will experience erosion, some will experience accretion, and it's all subject to change. There's always an element of risk in owning property in a coastal environment.

The priciest real estate on the Outer Banks is in Corolla—especially in Pine Island—where the few oceanfront lots that haven't been built upon currently list from $740,000 to more than $800,000 and the newer oceanfront homes sell for up to $2.1 million. Still, there are many excellent, established neighborhoods in other areas of the Outer Banks where you

can buy a cottage for the low $100,000s and still walk to the ocean. This chapter touches upon the flavor of the various sections of the beach; for more information on townships, see our Area Overviews chapter.

Working with a Real Estate Agent

Whether you decide to buy an existing home or build your own, a good real estate agent can supply you with the information you need to make a smart decision and can save you a great deal of time and, very often, money. You are wise to enlist the services of a knowledgeable agent when you buy real estate on the Outer Banks given the uniqueness of the market economics and the local environment.

Interview a few agents before you decide with whom you'd like to work. Ask around for referrals. It's important for you to know that any real estate agent or broker can represent your interests, but be careful to select an agent with expertise in the communities in which you're most interested. Generally, you're better off to work with an agent whose office is located near your preferred areas. An agent who understands the market in Corolla probably won't be quite as knowledgeable of markets in Hatteras or Manteo.

Real estate agents and brokers are licensed by the State of North Carolina and are subject to its laws and regulations. A Realtor® is an agent or broker who also belongs to the Board of Realtors, represented in our area by the Outer Banks Association of Realtors. What sets a Realtor apart from any licensee is the Realtor Code of Ethics, a set of stricter rules of conduct to which members subscribe, and access to the Multiple Listing Service, the most comprehensive database of properties for sale. For a listing of local Realtors, contact the Outer Banks Association of Realtors, P.O. Box 1070, Kill Devil Hills, North Carolina 27948, (252) 441-4036; www.outerbanksrealtors.com. This organization represents over 600 Realtors on the Outer Banks.

When you choose an agent or broker, technically you're entering into an agreement not only with that agent but also with the agent's firm. You'll need to decide whether you want exclusive representation from a buyer's agent, whether you're content to work with the seller's agent, or whether under certain circumstances you'll allow your buyer's agent to represent both you and the other party to the transaction, which makes your agent a "dual" agent. There are specific rules governing these relationships, and all agents and brokers are required to explain these rules at the first substantive contact with a prospective client or customer. You will be asked to sign an agency agreement; make sure you understand your options and your obligations to your agent as well as her or his obligations to you. Most agents collect their fees from the proceeds of the sale, but this is not always the case. Make sure you understand the compensation arrange-

ment before you commit to an agent. According to North Carolina Statute, even if an agent does not represent you, the agent must still be fair and honest and disclose to you all material facts that the agent knows or reasonably should know.

A conscientious, hard-working agent or broker will supply you with extensive information on the market—including comps (comparable properties currently listed and recently sold), neighborhood amenities and covenants, and financing options—and will be conversant in the pros and cons of building your own vs. buying an existing home. She or he can also help you estimate the costs of ownership and what you might expect to realize in terms of income if you decide, as many owners do, to rent your home to others.

At the end of this chapter are listings of real estate companies and the areas they specialize in. Along with some community listings, we've supplied contact information for the developer, but do be aware that you don't have to work with the developer or the developer's agent directly; you should feel free to use your own buyer's agent if that's your preference.

Building Your Own

If you decide to build, your agent can help you choose a building contractor, or you can ask for a list of members from the Outer Banks Homebuilders Association, 105 W. Airstrip Road, Kill Devil Hills, North Carolina 27948, (252) 449-8232.

If you decide to build your own home, first be clear about its intended use: do you want a second home, rental property, or year-round residence? Your answer to that question will determine where you build and the style of home. If you're designing for the rental market, you'll have to keep in mind not only your preferences, but those of others as well. Talk with your builder and property managers to learn the features that will make your home a popular rental. You'll be wise to listen to their advice.

Ask your builder to not only show you floor plans but also to take you through other houses he or she has built. (If you do this in the off-season, you'll have a better chance of viewing homes, for they will probably be vacant. Understandably, property managers try not to interrupt their guests' summer vacations.) If your goal is to achieve the maximum income, ask a property manager whose firm represents a lot of homes in your area to show you the most popular rentals in their inventory, but be careful to focus on homes similarly located to the lot you've selected. You can't compare income on an oceanfront to income on a house four rows back from the ocean!

You'll want to familiarize yourself with the building codes and regulations unique to our area, including regulations relating to environmental protection set by the North Carolina Coastal Management Authority (CAMA). Throughout the process, keep in mind that your intended use of the property will dictate its design and construction. A home intended for weekly rental is usually substantially different in design than a home intended for year-round residential use. Wandering through open houses and model homes is a fun and informative way to refine your ideas before you begin to set them down on paper.

Tune in to Reality

Many prospective buyers wander into real estate offices insisting they be shown properties that will "pay for themselves." Trust this Insider: If that many properties paid for themselves, there would be precious few for sale. Even if you're planning to rent out your new home at the beach, know that in 99 percent of cases you'll have to shell out more money than you'll take in for the privilege of owning it. Just how much you'll have to pay is highly variable. It depends upon how much you paid for the property, the financing terms you've arranged, and how much rental income it generates.

When you buy a beach cottage with the intention of realizing rental income, what you're really doing is operating a business, so learn about it. As an owner, you have a great deal of influence over how much income your property generates. Participate in setting your rates. Keep your home in good repair, and be realistic about the funds you'll need to designate for annual maintenance and periodic replacement of housewares and furnishings. Discuss your goals with your agent and speak with property managers at a few carefully selected real estate firms (see our chapter on Weekly and Long-Term Cottage Rentals). You'll also want to consult your tax adviser, since the IRS has specific rules you must follow depending upon how you use your property.

Once you place your property in service, review its performance at least annually with your property manager and pay close attention to any complaints or comments from renters. Keep a guest book in the cottage for renters' comments and think of it as a quality control device.

Nearly all owners realize that by renting out their cottages, they are letting others subsidize their dream of owning a home by the sea. Over time, as property values and rental rates creep up and other costs stabilize, many cottages will operate at break-even or better. Your best bet is to be conservative in your expectations and be pleasantly surprised when they're exceeded.

What follows is a brief overview listing the main residential resort communities, as well as information on timeshare properties and a listing of real estate companies. Please also refer to the Area Overviews chapter for more information.

Residential Resort Communities

We've listed a combination of newer and more established oceanside and soundside residential communities to give you an idea of what's here on the Outer Banks. We start our journey in the four-wheel-drive beaches north of Corolla and then move south through the Outer Banks, ending on Ocracoke Island. These communities include resorts and developments that offer recreational amenities and easy access to the ocean and sound, those that provide a mixture of both seasonal and year-round living, and neighborhoods with more of a year-round lifestyle.

Most developments have strict architectural guidelines, or covenants, to ensure quality development. It should also be noted that there are many one-road (cul-de-sac) subdivisions scattered throughout the Outer Banks. Some of these subdivisions offer private roads and private ocean or sound accesses. These neighborhoods offer great rental opportunities but fewer amenities. Call your local real estate professional for more information about sales or rentals (see the Real Estate Sales section at the end of this chapter).

The Four-Wheel-Drive Beaches

Carova, North Swan Beach, Swan Beach, Seagull, and Penny's Hill Subdivisions Off the paved road north of NC 12

Access to these subdivisions is by four-wheel-drive vehicle only. Depending upon how far north you're heading, you'll be in for a 5- to 20-minute drive once you cross the beach access ramp just north of The Villages at Ocean Hill. (Be sure to read the rules of the road.) Although there's no paved road linking these communities to the asphalt in Corolla, once you drive up the beach, you'll discover a network of dirt roads throughout the four-wheel-drive area. Many of these will have standing water after heavy rains, so watch for puddles and deep holes. Even though these are some of the widest beaches anywhere, we recommend that you drive at low tide. Some parts of the beach are home to the remains of a petrified forest—an indication of how much this bar-

rier island has migrated throughout the centuries. The black stumps are eerily beautiful, but can easily puncture a tire if you drive over them. Use extra caution in these areas, especially at night. At one time, the beaches were open to vehicular travel clear past the northernmost town of Carova up to Virginia. Driving into Virginia is no longer permitted from here, and there's a fence and a gate to prevent crossing the border. Watch for the wild horses!

Virginia's False Cape State Park borders Carova on the north, and North Swan Beach borders Carova on the south. As you continue southward, you'll come to Swan Beach, Seagull, and Penny's Hill subdivisions. Development began in Carova Beach in 1967, followed by development in North Swan Beach and Swan Beach. Carova Beach is the largest subdivision off the paved road.

Carova consists of approximately 2,000 lots. Resales are available in most areas. There are approximately 400 improved lots from Ocean Hill to the Virginia line and 2,500 property owners, of which a small number are year-round residents. The Seagull and Penny's Hill subdivisions are much smaller than Carova, which offers lots fronting the canals, sandy trails, and open water between Currituck Sound and the Atlantic Ocean. Swan Beach and North Swan Beach are ocean-to-sound developments. Ocean Beach and Penny's Hill do not include sound frontage. Basic amenities are offered, including electricity and telephone service and water/sewer by individual well and septic system. Cable television is not available, but we've been told that television reception from the Hampton Roads network affiliates is excellent. There is no garbage pickup; you must take your trash to a nearby dump. Some mail delivery is available to a bank of locked boxes.

Real estate agents working in Corolla tend to be the most knowledgeable about this area; make sure you find one that specializes. The quality of lots varies widely, and some areas are more prone to erosion than others.

Corolla

Ocean Hill and The Villages at Ocean Hill
NC 12, Corolla

Ocean Hill and The Villages at Ocean Hill lie at the northernmost end of the paved road in Corolla. The Villages at Ocean Hill is a unique resort community covering 153 acres, including lakefront, oceanfront, and soundside lots. This development of primarily rental homes is still very much available to the buying public. Amenities include oceanfront and lakefront pools, tennis courts, and a freshwater lake. Wide, white, sandy beaches are also part of the package. There are strict architectural guidelines to ensure quality development. The adjacent Ocean Hill has no amenities to speak of, although lot sizes are larger.

Corolla Light Resort Village
NC 12, Corolla

More than 200 acres comprise this northern Outer Banks resort. Construction began in 1985, and some very large luxury homes were built here as well as elegant three-bedroom condos and four-bedroom villas. Home sizes range from 1,300 square feet to 3,600 square feet. When it all began, Corolla village was a sleepy, well-hidden oceanside community with a lighthouse, post office, and a small general store. This beautiful ocean-to-sound resort boasts an oceanfront pool complex, tennis courts scattered throughout the resort, a soundside pool, and an indoor sports center that houses a competition-size indoor pool, tennis courts, racquetball courts, and exercise rooms.

Whalehead Beach
NC 12, Corolla

Whalehead Beach is the most established beach neighborhood in Corolla. Its wide beaches stretch for more than 3 miles along the ocean and have a dozen public beachfront walkways. Public parking lots are scattered throughout. Though Whalehead doesn't have a central water system (properties have individual wells) and there are few other amenities, its 20,000-square-foot lots are a remarkable draw.

Monteray Shores
NC 12 , Corolla

While Whalehead Beach occupies only the east side of NC 12, Monteray Shores is situated on the soundside (or west side) of this northern Outer Banks area. Its Caribbean-style homes have red tile roofs, arched verandas, spacious decks, and an abundance of windows, contrasting with the wooden structures found in most Outer Banks residential communities. But if you prefer Outer Banks–style homes, they also are available here. The community features single-family residences and offers sound or ocean views from every homesite. While there are no oceanfront lots, the full gymnasium, soundside clubhouse, junior Olympic swimming pool, hot tub, four tennis courts, jogging trails, stocked fishing ponds, boat ramps, and other recreational amenities provide a dash of sophistication.

Buck Island
NC 12, Corolla

In a small section of the northern Outer Banks lies the exclusive community of Buck Island. This development is across from the TimBuck II Shopping Village on Ocean Trail. It is an oceanfront and oceanside development.

Buck Island is reminiscent of the nautical seaside villages of Kiawah and Nantucket and boasts timeless Charlestonian architecture along a promenade of hardwood trees and turn-of-the-20th-century streetlights. Amenities include a guarded entrance, pristine ocean beach, beach cabana, spa, pool, and tennis courts.

Crown Point
NC 12, Corolla

Crown Point is 1 mile north of Ocean Sands and 10 miles north of Duck. This is a single-family subdivision with oceanfront and oceanside properties. It is completely separate from the Ocean Sands subdivision. There are approximately 90 homes here. Amenities include a swimming pool, tennis courts, and private beach access walkways.

Ocean Sands
NC 12, Corolla

Ocean Sands is an oceanside and oceanfront planned unit development, or PUD, considered to be a model of coastal development by land-use planners, government officials, and environmentalists alike. The Ocean Sands concept is centered around clusters of homes that form small colonies buffered by open space. This design eliminates drive-through traffic while increasing privacy and open vistas. Clusters are devoted to single-family dwellings, multifamily dwellings, and appropriate commercial usage. Many of the approximately 600 residences at Ocean Sands are placed in rental programs. Amenities include tennis courts, nature trails, and a fishing lake stocked with bass. The development has guarded private roads. Tucked within Ocean Sands is Ocean Lake, a little neighborhood with a three-acre lake, tennis courts, and a large swimming pool.

Ocean Sands is a family-oriented community buffered on the east by the Atlantic Ocean and on the west by the exclusive Currituck Club community. Lots are 6,000 square feet.

Spindrift
Ocean Trail, near the Currituck Club, Corolla

Spindrift is a small gated community with about 30 40,000-square-foot lots—large in comparison to neighboring developments. The single-family residential development offers few amenities, but the privacy here can't be beat. You can build a dream home and be assured you will not be within an arm's length of your neighbor.

The Currituck Club
NC 12, Corolla
(252) 453-9445
www.thecurrituckclub.com

This 600-acre world-class golfing community is bordered by the Currituck Sound and sports an 18-hole championship golf course (see our Golf chapter). Single-family homes, villas, and patio homes are available. The upscale, gated community features tennis, basketball, and volleyball courts; swimming pools; lighted bike and jogging paths; and a full fitness center. Private ocean access is available with a trolley system, and there's even a beach valet service. Overall density is just more than one family per acre. Located in a maritime forest environment, on the grounds of the historic Currituck Shooting Club, the scenery can't be beat. Don't miss touring the development's Mainstreet Corolla model homes.

Pine Island
NC 12, Corolla

Pine Island resort is on 385 acres, with 300 single-family homesites and 3 miles of oceanfront. This planned oceanfront and oceanside community is bordered on the west by 1,500 acres of perpetually preserved marsh, islands, and uplands that comprise the National Audubon Society Pine Island Sanctuary. Homesites are generous, and there are strict architectural guidelines. Central water and sewer and underground utilities are available.

Residents have access to a tennis court, two community swimming pools, beach club, jogging paths, and more. Property owners also have access to a private landing strip.

Duck

Palmer's Island
NC 12, Duck

Located between Pine Island and Sanderling, the exclusive Palmer's Island is a 15-year-old ocean-to-sound community with fewer than 15 homesites. Beach frontage ranges from 120 feet to 225 feet per lot, and the enormous homes are magnificent. This is the narrowest stretch of land on the Outer Banks, and residents have breathtaking views of both the ocean and the Currituck Sound. Although no property is available in Palmer's Island, home values begin at several million dollars.

Sanderling
Duck Rd. (NC 12), Duck

This ocean-to-sound community several miles north of Duck consists of nearly 300 homes and lots and is one of the most desirable residential communities on the Outer Banks. The heavy vegetation, winding lanes, and abundant wildlife offer the most seclusion of any resort community on the beach. Developers have taken care to leave as much natural growth as possible, and there are strict building covenants to ensure privacy and value. The Sanderling Inn Resort is just north of the residential area.

Homeowners have their own recreational amenities, including miles of nature trails, the Soundside Racquet and Swimming Club, and sailing and canoeing opportunities.

Port Trinitie
Duck Rd. (NC 12), Duck

Port Trinitie, situated on 23 acres of ocean-to-sound property, stretches across Duck Road and offers some gorgeous soundfront views. Located 2 miles north of Duck village, amenities include two swimming pools, two tennis courts, a soundside pier and gazebo, and an ocean-front sitting area. This development began with condominiums, which are co-ownership properties, but Port Trinitie now offers an even mixture of whole ownership single-family dwellings (cottages and townhomes) and co-owned condos.

Sea Ridge and Osprey
Duck Rd. (NC 12), Duck

This area, 1.5 miles north of the village of Duck, claims to have the best views on the Outer Banks and has lots and three- and four-bedroom single-family homes available. Natural beauty is this development's calling card.

NorthPoint
Duck Rd. (NC 12), Duck

Fractional ownership is popular at North-Point, though some lots remain for individual ownership and development. You'll enjoy an enclosed swimming pool, tennis and basketball courts, and a long soundfront pier for fishing, crabbing, and small boat dockage. One of the first fractional ownership developments on the northern Outer Banks, NorthPoint has enjoyed good values on resales.

Ships Watch
1251 Duck Rd. (NC 12), Duck
(252) 261-2231, (800) 261-7924
www.shipswatch.com

Mid-Atlantic Country magazine portrayed this community as "the Palm Beach of the Outer Banks." Ships Watch is a community of luxurious seaside homes on the northernmost end of the village of Duck. Complete service, home maintenance, and attention to details are characteristics of this resort. Carefully placed on high rolling dunes, the homes offer spectacular views of either the ocean, the Currituck Sound, or both. An Olympic-size pool, tennis courts, jogging trail, soundside pier and boat ramp, and weekly socials offer entertainment options for the whole family. Full concierge service includes arranging tee times, dinner reservations, and babysitting. The resort provides rentals, along with fractional and whole ownership. Fractional, one-tenth deeded ownerships are available. Parlayed as a high-end property, developer Buck Thornton and his associates have experienced great success with this resort. Contact Ships Watch for sales and rental information.

SeaPines
Duck Road (NC 12, Duck

SeaPines is a 61-lot development tucked away in the heart of Duck. Lot sizes for this oceanside village range from 15,000 to 20,000 square feet. There still are some lots to choose from, including some with ocean views from upper-level living areas. Amenities include a swimming pool and tennis court.

Schooner Ridge Beach Club
Duck Rd. (NC 12), Duck

Schooner Ridge is in the heart of Duck, but its oceanfront/oceanside homes are well hidden from the hustle and bustle. The high, sandy hills fronting the Atlantic Ocean are perfect for these large single-family homes with ample windows and decks. All lots are sold, but resales are available. The community offers indoor and outdoor recreational amenities. Bike paths wind through the area, and all the shops in the village are within walking distance.

Nantucket Village
Duck Rd. (NC 12), Duck

Nantucket is an upscale private resort consisting of 35 large condominiums with garages and spacious decking. Situated on a high hill overlooking Currituck Sound, these units have panoramic views and magnificent sunsets. The year-round development offers an indoor pool and tennis court as well as sandy soundfront beaches, a pier with gazebo, and boat launch facili-

ties. The sound beach is ideal for wading, children's activities, crabbing, fishing, wind-surfing, and other watercraft sports.

Units in two luxury duplex condominium buildings have approximately 1,750 square feet of living space, two-car garages, three bedrooms, two-and-a-half baths, gas fireplaces, and panoramic water views.

Ocean Crest
Duck Rd. (NC 12), Duck

Near Nantucket Village, Ocean Crest is an ocean-to-sound resort consisting of 54 lots that hit the market in August 1992. Lots are 15,000 square feet or larger and are zoned for single-family dwellings. This is an upscale neighborhood with strict architectural guidelines. Homes must be 2,000 square feet or larger. Amenities include a swimming pool, tennis courts, private ocean access, and good water views.

Kitty Hawk

Martin's Point
US 158, MP 0, Kitty Hawk

Martin's Point is an exclusive waterfront community of custom homes and homesites. There are stringent building requirements, a guarded entry, and some of the most beautiful maritime forests found anywhere. Homes range from 1,200 square feet to 13,000 square feet. This is primarily a year-round neighborhood featuring a marina, dock, and pier on the Currituck Sound. Owners here have easy access to the local elementary school, shopping, and golf.

When you arrive on the Outer Banks at the eastern terminus of the Wright Memorial Bridge, the entrance to Martin's Point is on your immediate left. The community is closed to drive-through inspections, but if you're considering a permanent move to the Outer Banks, it's an upscale area you'll want to look at.

Southern Shores
US 158 and NC 12, Kitty Hawk

Southern Shores is a unique 2,600-acre incorporated town with its own government and police force. Although there is a shopping center on its western boundary, commercial zoning/development is not allowed elsewhere. The town has dense maritime forests along the soundside fringe, wide-open sand hills in the middle, and beachfront property. The substantial year-round population attests to the popularity of Southern Shores. Kitty Hawk Land Company has carefully paced development through the years, and there are still many vacant lots. One of the newest developments within Southern Shores is Ginguite Woods, a neighborhood just south of Martin's Point. Southern Shores is considered one of the most desirable places to live on the Outer Banks.

Kitty Hawk Landing
W. Kitty Hawk Rd., Kitty Hawk

This is a residential community with mostly year-round homeowners. It's on the far western edges of Kitty Hawk. To get there, turn west off US 158 at MP 4 onto West Kitty Hawk Road and just keep driving until you see the signs. The community borders Currituck Sound. It has deep canals, tall pines, and gorgeous sunsets.

Sandpiper Cay Condominiums
Sand Dune Dr., Kitty Hawk
(252) 261-2188

This resort community consists of 280 condominium units and is near Sea Scape Golf Course. About 155 of the units are second homes; some 40 percent of the units are either long-term rentals or primary residences, making this a year-round resort. Some units are available for short-term or weekly leases. All the original inventory has been sold, though some resales are available. Amenities include a large outdoor pool, clubhouse, and tennis court. Homeowner fees apply. Contact Sandpiper Cay for more information.

Kill Devil Hills

First Flight Village
First St., Kill Devil Hills

This is one of the Outer Banks's most pop-

ular year-round neighborhoods in the central area of the beach. The entrance to First Flight Village is on the west side of US 158 at MP 7½. This is a family-oriented neighborhood, so if you're considering a permanent move to the Outer Banks with kids in tow, you should investigate this community. First Flight Village real estate is considered moderately priced.

Colington Island

Colington Harbour
Colington Rd., Colington Island

Development on Colington Island began more than 20 years ago. To get there, turn off US 158 at the stoplight just south of the Wright Brothers Memorial onto Colington Road. Colington Harbour is about 4 miles down the winding road.

The community has some 12 miles of bulkheaded deepwater canals and soundfront lots, all easily accessing Albemarle Sound. Oregon Inlet, the closest ocean inlet, is approximately 25 miles by boat south of Colington Island. There is quite a range of choices here, from extremely affordable "starter" homes to upscale soundfront or canalfront homes with private boat docks. This community combines a year-round population of more than 2,000 with seasonal and weekly renters. The picnic area, playground, sandy beach on Kitty Hawk Bay, boat ramp, boat slips for rent, and fuel dock are available to all residents, including year-round renters. Clubhouse activities, the Olympic-size swimming pool, children's pool, and a tennis court are available to club members. What makes Colington Harbour popular is its private entry and the many canals that offer waterfront living to many residents. Colington Harbour is one of the best places to keep a deep-draft boat.

Colington Heights
Colington Island

This is the last developable subdivision within Colington Harbour. And it's still possible to enter on the ground level here. There are 23 lots on approximately 35 acres. The inventory includes wooded interior lots, waterview lots, and waterfront properties. Essentially, this is a maritime forest development. Large three-acre lot sizes contribute to the privacy of the area. Roads are private, and there is private beach access on Albemarle Sound. Architectural controls are in effect, and the developer has paid all of the water-impact fees, making the real estate even more attractive.

WatersEdge
off Colington Rd., Colington Island
(252) 261–2131, (800) 488–0738
www.khlc.com

WatersEdge is a gated, year-round residential neighborhood on Colington Island. The community has a swimming pool, marina and boat ramp with access to Roanoke Sound and its own owners' association. Sales are handled exclusively by Kitty Hawk Land Company.

Nags Head

South Ridge
Off US 158, MP 13, Nags Head
(252) 441–2800

This 42-acre parcel is a no-frills community with 140 homesites on the hill behind the Nags Head Post Office. The development features quarter-acre ocean- and soundview lots but no soundfront property. Three models are available for viewing. Square footage for new houses runs between 1,600 and 1,900 for three- and four-bedroom homes. Construction features cathedral or vaulted ceilings, lots of open space, and light and bright interiors.

The Village at Nags Head
US 158, MP 15, Nags Head
(252) 441–8533, sales
www.villagerealtyobx.com

The Ammons Corporation began developing this ocean-to-sound community about a decade ago, and it has become one of the best sellers on the Outer Banks. The golf course (with a beautiful clubhouse and popular restaurant) and the oceanfront recreational complex with tennis courts and an outdoor pool make this attractive residential community most desirable. Single-family homes and townhomes provide something for everyone. The oceanfront homes are some of the largest and most luxurious anywhere. There's plenty to do whether you live or vacation here. It's an excellent choice for beach living, vacation rentals, or investment. There is a great variety here, from townhomes to luxurious oceanfronts.

Roanoke Island

Pirate's Cove
Manteo–Nags Head Causeway, Manteo
(252) 473–1451, (800) 762–0245

Pirate's Cove is a distinctive residential marina resort community. Hundreds of acres of protected wildlife marshlands border Pirate's Cove on one side, while the peaceful waters of Roanoke Sound are on the other. Deepwater canals provide each owner with a dock at the door, and the centrally located marina is home to many large yachts and fishing boats.

Pirate's Cove offers homesites, homes, condominiums, and even "dockominiums" fronting deepwater canals. There's always activity here. Fishing tournaments

> **Insiders' Tip**
> Learn to love the outdoor showers that come as a standard feature with most cottages these days. They're essential for washing off after a day at the beach, but lots of Insiders swear by them in place of a mundane indoor shower when the weather turns warm.

seem as important as sleeping to many of the residents, and locals and visitors can get in on the fun. Other recreational amenities include a hot tub, sauna, fitness center, restaurant, and a beautifully appointed clubhouse, plus swimming pools and lighted tennis courts. Scheduled recreational activities for all ages are available. One of the prettiest settings on the Outer Banks enhances the Victorian nautical design of these homes.

Shallowbag Bay Club
US 64/264, Manteo
(252) 261-5500, (800) 395-2525
www.manteocondos.com

The Shallowbag Bay Club is Manteo's newest development. It's a luxury condominium complex and marina with views that will take your breath away. There are 60 luxury three-bedroom condominiums in The Harbor and 17 condominium suites in The Point. The Shallowbag Bay Club's amenities include 91 private boat slips, a full-service marina, a waterfront restaurant, a fitness center, a pool and hot tub, a meeting room, a water taxi to downtown Manteo, and a clubhouse. Association fees are charged to owners. The entrance to Shallowbag Bay Club is on US 64/264, right behind McDonald's.

Roanoak Village
Manteo

Roanoak Village offers options for building a variety of homes ranging in size from 860 to 2,100 square feet. The development is being built in three phases and encompasses nearly eight acres with a potential of 57 homesites. Interiors range from two-bedroom, one-bath styles to four-bedroom, two-and-a-half-bath homes. Some models even feature hardwood floors.

For the new neighborhood, local architect John Wilson IV designed approximately 10 house plans in keeping with the older building styles still evident in downtown Manteo. It gives the project a homey feel with a historic thrust.

The neighborhood is within walking distance of Roanoke Island's bike trails,

the public library, local churches, the town hall, and the Manteo waterfront.

Heritage Point
Pearce Rd , Northern Roanoke Island
(252) 473-1450

This year-round resort community is subdivided into 111 lots off US 64/264 next to Fort Raleigh National Historic Site. Restrictive covenants are in place. Interior, soundview, and soundfront lots overlooking the Croatan and Albemarle Sounds are available. Lot sizes range from a half-acre to more than three-and-a-half acres. Each lot has a boat slip, and there is a fishing pier for homeowners. The community sports two tennis courts, and a parking area, and common beach are provided. Homeowner association fees apply. Contact Ware Realty and Construction Inc. for more information; the company has an exclusive sales listing in this development.

The Peninsula
Russell Twiford Rd., Manteo
(252) 453-3600

This exclusive boating community includes 34 private waterfront homesites with a lighted dock in excess of 2,000 feet, a boat ramp, pump-out station, deepwater canals, and three gazebos over the water. These homes are on the Manteo sewage system and feature looped water lines to prevent sediment buildup. Homes have direct access to the sound. Some covenant restrictions apply. Call BD&A at the above number for more information.

Hatteras Island

Rodanthe
Resort Rodanthe
Resort Rodanthe Dr. off NC 12, Rodanthe

This resort consists of one building featuring 12 two-bed and eight one-bed condominium units. Views of the ocean and sound vary by unit. Lower floor units have sound views. The condos are for sale, but owners also rent them. Amenities include a swimming pool and private ocean access.

Hatteras High Condominiums
Resort Rodanthe Dr., off NC 12, Rodanthe

Hatteras High features four oceanfront condominium buildings with 12 units in each. These two-bed, two-bath condos connect to the beach by boarded walkway. A swimming pool is behind the buildings.

Mirlo Beach
NC 12, Rodanthe

This sound-to-oceanfront resort community is 12 miles south of the Oregon Inlet Bridge, adjacent to Pea Island National Wildlife Refuge. There are approximately 10 large oceanfront cottages in Mirlo Beach, each of which can comfortably sleep an average of 12. Amenities include tennis courts and private beach and sound accesses. This resort has a solid rental history.

Waves
St. Waves
NC 12, Waves

This subdivision, developed during the 1980s, consists of approximately 55 lots and 20 houses. Homes and homesites are available for sale. Properties offer ocean, sound, and lake views. The homes are upscale, and architectural controls are in effect. Amenities include a swimming pool, tennis court, and a centrally located lake. St. Waves maintains an excellent rental history.

Avon
Kinnakeet Shores
NC 12, Avon

Once a desolate stretch of narrow land between the Atlantic Ocean and Pamlico Sound, Kinnakeet Shores is a residential community that is being carefully developed. It consists of 500 acres next to beautiful marshlands and one of the best windsurfing areas in the world. Recreational amenities include swimming pools and tennis courts. This is the largest development on Hatteras Island, and the homes tend to be big, reminding us of the ones on the northern beaches. This is primarily a second-home development, offering one of the most popular rental programs on the island. A small shopping plaza with a Food Lion grocery store is in Avon, as are a handful of restaurants. The village of Buxton is only 5 miles away.

Buxton
Hatteras Pines
NC 12, Buxton

This 150-acre subdivision is nestled in a maritime forest in the heart of Buxton. It consists of 114 wooded lots rolling along the dunes and ridges. The roads for this development are intact, along with protective covenants. A pool and tennis court are part of the package.

Frisco
Sunset Village
Sunset Strip, Frisco
(252) 995-3313
www.landsendinc.com

There are only a few homesites currently available in this new soundside community, but the area is beginning to develop. Lots come with a deeded boat slip.

Hatteras Village
Hatteras Landing
NC 12, Hatteras Village

This development features 41 homesites, a restaurant, clothing stores, gift shop, bookstore, deli, convenience store, coffee shop, and other retail opportunities. Homeowners have access to the on-site Holiday Inn Express pool. Oceanfront and soundfront lots are available. Homeowners build the homes of their choice.

Hatteras By The Sea
NC 12, Hatteras Village

This rather small community of 36 lots on 25 acres is one of the last oceanfront areas available for residential living. There's not much land on the southern end of the Outer Banks, and a good portion is preserved by the National Seashore designation. A large pool and some carefully designed nature paths are included. Sunrise and sunset views are unobstructed here.

Waterfront living will cost you a pretty penny, but it's worth every cent. PHOTO: MOLLY HARRISON

Ocracoke Island

Ocracoke Horizon Condominiums
Silver Lake Rd., Ocracoke Village
(252) 928–5711

These five soundfront condominiums were developed by Midgett Realty in Hatteras but are handled by Sandy Shores Realty on Ocracoke Island. Features include two two-bedroom and three three-bedroom units with either two or two-and-a-half baths and whirlpool tubs. The units overlook Pamlico Sound and Portsmouth Island. Sales and rentals are available.

Timesharing

Timesharing is a deeded transaction under the jurisdiction of the North Carolina Real Estate Commission. A deeded share is 1/52 of the unit property being purchased (one week of a year). This deed grants the right to use the property in perpetuity. Always ask if the property you're inspecting is a deeded timeshare because there is such a thing as undeeded timeshares—these give the right to use a property, but the property reverts to the developer in the end.

What you are buying in a timeshare is the right to use a specific piece of real estate for a week per year. The weeks are either fixed at the time of sale or they rotate yearly. Members trade their weeks to get different time slots at a variety of locations around the world. Qualifying for the purchase of a timeshare unit can be no more difficult than qualifying for a credit card, but be aware of financing charges that are higher than regular mortgages.

Most timeshare resorts on the Outer Banks are multifamily constructions with recreational amenities that vary from minimal to luxurious and sometimes include the services of a recreational director. Timeshare units usually come furnished and carry a monthly maintenance fee. Tax advantages for ownership and financing are not available to the purchaser of a timeshare, so investigate this angle.

Many timeshare ventures offer "free weekends"—you agree to a sales pitch and tour of the facilities in exchange for accommodations. Listen, ask questions, and stay in control of your money and your particular situation. If you get swept away, you'll only have five days to change your mind, according to the North Carolina Time Share Act that governs the sale of timeshares.

It is best to keep the purchase of timeshares in proper perspective; your deeded share only enables you to vacation in that property during a designated time period each year for as long as you own that share. This makes timeshare very different from other potential investments.

All real estate investment decisions require thorough research and planning, and timeshare is no exception. Timeshare salespeople are licensed (to everyone's advantage), and they earn commissions. Some great arrangements are out there, while others are not so good. Check thoroughly before you buy. Several Outer Banks companies specialize in timesharing. The following list includes some of these.

Barrier Island Ocean Pines
NC 12, Duck
(252) 261–3525

Ocean Pines offers timesharing opportunities featuring oceanfront one- and two-bedroom condominiums. Amenities include an indoor pool, tennis courts, whirlpool tubs, and, of course, the beach.

Barrier Island Station
NC 12, Duck
(252) 261–3525

Barrier Island, one of the largest timeshare resorts on the Outer Banks, is on a high dune area of ocean-to-sound property. These are multifamily units of wood construction. There is an attractive, full-service restaurant and bar with a soundside

sailing center, in addition to the beach. A full-time recreation director is on board here for a variety of planned activities and events. Indoor swimming, tennis courts, and other recreational facilities round out a full amenities package. This is a popular resort in a just-as-popular seaside village.

Barrier Island Station at Kitty Hawk
1 Cypress Knee Trail, Kitty Hawk
(252) 261–4610

Barrier Island Station at Kitty Hawk is a multifamily vacation ownership resort set in a maritime forest. The 100 acres of private land sport a million-dollar sports complex featuring an indoor pool, free weights, circuit training, and aerobic and massage facilities. You can also shoot pool or play table tennis in the game room. Condominiums have one, two, or three bedrooms. The community is near two shopping centers.

Bodie Island Realty
NC 12, MP 17, Nags Head
(252) 441–2558
NC 12, MP 7, Kill Devil Hills
(252) 441–9443

This company manages timeshares in the Bodie Island Beach Club in Nags Head. The Beach Club features two pools, an oceanfront sundeck, a game room, miniature golf, and a playground. The units are two-bedroom, two-bath condos with full kitchens, dining rooms, living rooms, wood-burning fireplaces, whirlpool tubs, and private decks. The company also handles resales of timeshare units in complexes up and down the Outer Banks.

Dunes South Beach and Racquet Club
NC 12, MP 18, Nags Head
(252) 441–4090

Townhome timesharing at this resort features two- and three-bedroom units with fireplaces, washers and dryers, and whirlpool tubs. There are 20 units, and most are oceanfront; the remainder of the units are oceanside. A pool, tennis court, putting green, and playground make up the recreational amenities.

Outer Banks Beach Club
NC 12, MP 9, Kill Devil Hills
(252) 441–6321

The round, wooden buildings of the Outer Banks Beach Club were the first timesharing opportunities built and sold on the Outer Banks. The 160 units include oceanfront and oceanside units, plus clubhouse units across the Beach Road, near the clubhouse and its indoor pool. There are two outdoor pools in great oceanfront locations. One-, two-, and three-bedroom units have access to whirlpools, tennis courts, and a playground. There is a full-time recreation director offering a variety of activities and games.

Outer Banks Resort Rentals
Pirates Quay Shopping Center, US 158, MP 11, Nags Head
(252) 441–2134

This company deals exclusively with time-shares, handling rentals and resales at all the timeshare complexes on the Outer Banks. All the units this company represents are furnished and self-contained, and all have swimming pools.

Sea Scape Beach and Golf Villas
US 158, MP 2½, Kitty Hawk
(252) 261–3837

There are plenty of recreational opportunities here: tennis courts, three swimming pools, an indoor recreation facility, exercise room, and game room. The Villas are next to the Sea Scape golf course. The two-bed, two-bath units are of wood construction, and they are on the west side of US 158. Sea Scape offers a unique opportunity for timeshare ownership and an active rental program.

Real Estate Sales Firms

Following are some Outer Banks real estate sales companies, their locations, and contact information. While this list is not all-inclusive, it is representative of reputable real estate sales companies on the Outer Banks. Most, if not all, of these companies are members of the Outer Banks Association of Realtors.

20/20 Realty Ltd.
516 US 64, Manteo
(252) 473–2020

Roanoke Island properties are the focus for 20/20 Realty.

Beach Realty & Construction/Kitty Hawk Rentals
790-B NC 12, Corolla
(252) 453–3131
1450 NC 12, Duck
(252) 261–6600
US 158, MP 2, Kitty Hawk
(252) 261–3815, (800) 849–9888
US 158, Kill Devil Hills
(252) 441–1106
www.beachrealty.com

Beach Realty handles real estate sales, rentals, and construction. Offices are in Corolla, Duck, Kitty Hawk, and Kill Devil Hills. It represents properties from Carova to South Nags Head.

Bodie Island Realty
NC 12, MP 7, Kill Devil Hills
(252) 441–9443, (800) 839–5116
NC 12, MP 17, Nags Head
(252) 441–2558, (800) 862–1785
www.bodieislandrealty.com

Bodie Island Realty offers general real estate, timeshare, and timeshare resales covering Corolla to north Hatteras.

Brindley & Brindley Real Estate, A Resort Quest Company
Brindley Bldg., NC 12, Corolla Light
(252) 453–3000
www.brindleyandbrindley.com

Brindley & Brindley represents property from Carova to Southern Shores.

Cape Escape
NC 12, Salvo
(252) 987–2336, (800) 996–2336
www.capeescaperealty.com

Cape Escape, across from the local post office, handles sales in Rodanthe, Waves, and Salvo.

Coastland Realty
NC 12, Corolla
(252) 453–2105, (888) 207–4209
Coastland offers real estate sales only. It represents the northern Outer Banks—specifically, Ocean Sands and Crown Point.

Colington Realty
2141 Colington Rd., Colington Island
(252) 441–3863
www.kittydunes.com
Colington Realty specializes in Colington Harbour properties.

Cove Realty
Between NC 12 and US 158, MP 14, Nags Head
(252) 441–6391, (800) 635–7007
www.coverealty.com
Cove represents Nags Head and South Nags Head and specializes in Old Nags Head Cove.

Duck's Real Estate
NC 12, Duck
(252) 261–2224, (800) 992–2976
Duck's Real Estate represents property from Corolla to Nags Head.

Harrell and Associates
US 158, MP 7, Kill Devil Hills
(252) 441–7887
www.harrellandassociates.com
This company specializes in property throughout Dare County including commercial and residential listings, plus lots of condominiums.

Karichele Realty
66 Sunset Blvd., Corolla
(252) 453–2377
TimBuck II, NC 12, Corolla
(252) 453–4400
www.karichele.com
Karichele covers properties from the Virginia line to Nags Head.

Hatteras Realty
NC 12, Avon
(252) 995–5466, (800) HATTERAS
www.hatterasrealty.com
Hatteras Realty covers residential and commercial lots and homes on Hatteras Island.

Joe Lamb Jr. & Associates, Realtors
US 158, MP 2, Kitty Hawk
(252) 261–4444, (800) 552–6257
www.joelambjr.com
Joe Lamb represents properties from northern Duck to South Nags Head.

Kitty Dunes Realty
US 158, MP 5, Kitty Hawk
(252) 261–2173
Corolla Light Village Shops , Unit 1110, Corolla
(252) 453–DUNE
www.kittydunes.com
Kitty Dunes represents Corolla to South Nags Head. This company also owns Colington Realty. Residents of Canada should contact the Canadian representative at (514) 252-9566.

Kitty Hawk Land Company
US 158, Kitty Hawk
(252) 261–2131, (800) 488–0738
www.khlc.com
Kitty Hawk Land Company has been in the real estate business for more than 50 years. KHL is credited with developing Southern Shores, Spindrift on the Currituck Outer Banks, WatersEdge on Colington Island, SeaPines and Oceancrest in Duck, and The Currituck Club in Corolla. They offer properties within these developments as well as select listings of outside properties on the Outer Banks.

Frank Mangum Realty
US 158, MP 10½, Nags Head
(252) 441–3600, (800) 279–5552
www.mangumrealty.com
Frank Mangum handles sales covering the entire Outer Banks.

Nags Head Realty
US 158, MP 10½, Nags Head
(252) 441–4311, (800) 222–1531
www.nagsheadrealty.com
Nags Head Realty represents property from Corolla to Oregon Inlet.

Midgett Realty
NC 12, Rodanthe
(252) 987–2350
NC 12, Avon
(252) 995–5333
NC 12, Hatteras Village
(252) 986–2841, (800) 527–2903
vacations@midgettrealty.com

Midgett Realty represents properties on the southern end of the Outer Banks.

Ocean Breeze Realty
100 E. Third St., Kill Devil Hills
(252) 480–0093, (800) 633–4491

Ocean Breeze specializes in sales of improved and unimproved property from Southern Shores to Manteo.

Ocracoke Island Realty
NC 12, Ocracoke
(252) 928–6261, (252) 928–7411
www.ocracokeislandrealty.com

Ocracoke Island Realty represents Ocracoke Island properties.

Outer Banks Ltd.
US 158, MP 10, Nags Head
(252) 441–7156
www.outerbanksltd.com

Outer Banks Ltd. represents property from Kitty Hawk to South Nags Head.

Outer Banks Resort Rentals
Pirates Quay, US 158, MP 11, Nags Head
(252) 441–2134
www.outerbanksresorts.com

Marvin Beard represents the sales and rentals of timeshares only. Beard offers timeshare options from Duck all the way to South Nags Head as well as a few in Hatteras. (See our Weekly and Long-term Rentals chapter for further details.)

Outer Banks Vacation Realty
Seagate North Shopping Center Parking Lot
Kill Devil Hills
(252) 449–9034, (888) 685–9581
www.vacationouterbanks.com

Properties from Kitty Hawk to South Nags Head are offered through Outer Banks Vacation Realty.

Outer Beaches Realty
NC 12, Waves
(252) 987–1102, (800) 627–3750
NC 12, Avon
(252) 995–6041, (800) 627–3150
NC 12, Hatteras
(252) 986–1105, (888) 627–3650
www.outerbeaches.com

Outer Beaches Realty specializes in properties throughout Hatteras Island.

Jim Perry & Company
Executive Center, US 158, MP 5½ , Kill Devil Hills
(252) 441–3051, (800) 222–6135
www.jimperry.com
Jim Perry represents properties in all areas of the Outer Banks.

Pirate's Cove
Manteo–Nags Head Causeway, Manteo
(252) 473–1451, (800) 762–0245
www.pirates-cove.com
The realty arm of Pirate's Cove Yacht Club represents properties in this boating paradise.

Properties at the Beach
The Dunes Shops, US 158, MP 4½, Kitty Hawk
(252) 261–2855, (800) 245–0021
Formerly Century 21, Properties at the Beach represents property from Carova Beach to South Nags Head.

RE/MAX Ocean Realty
US 158, MP 6, Kill Devil Hills
(252) 441–2450
www.obxrealtor.com
RE/MAX represents properties from Corolla to Hatteras Village.

Riggs Realty
Austin Bldg., NC 12, Corolla
(252) 453–3111
Riggs specializes in northern beach land and home properties.

Sandy Shores Realty
NC 12, Ocracoke Village
(252) 928–5711
www.ocracoke-island.com
Formerly Sharon Miller Realty, Sandy Shores represents Ocracoke Island properties.

Sea Oats Realty
P.O. Box 3399, Kill Devil Hills
(252) 480–2325
www.seaoatsrealty.com
Sea Oats handles real estate sales from Duck to South Nags Head.

Southern Shores Realty
NC 12, Southern Shores
(252) 261–2000, (800) 334–1000
www.southernshores.com
Southern Shores Realty represents properties from Corolla to Nags Head.

Stan White Realty & Construction
812 Ocean Trail, Corolla
(252) 453–3161, (800) 753–6200
US 158, MP 10½, Nags Head
(252) 441–1515, (800) 753–9699
www.builderouterbanks.com

Stan White represents properties from Corolla to Hatteras Village.

Surf or Sound Realty
NC 12, Rodanthe
(252) 987–1444, (800) 237–1138
NC 12, Avon
(252) 995–6052
www.surforsound.com

Surf or Sound represents properties from Rodanthe to Hatteras Village.

Mercedes Tabano Realty
NC 12, Rodanthe
(252) 987–2711

Mercedes Tabano represents properties on Hatteras Island.

Twiddy & Company Realtors
NC 12, Duck
(252) 261–8311, (800) 342–1609
NC 12 and Second St., Corolla
(252) 453–3325, (800) 579–6130
www.twiddy.com

Twiddy represents properties from Carova through Kitty Hawk.

An old ramshackle fish camp is not necessarily prime real estate, but you can find sound island property for sale once in a while. PHOTO: MOLLY HARRISON

Village Realty
US 158, MP 14½, Nags Head
(252) 480–2224, (800) 548–9688
www.villagerealtyobx.com

Village Realty represents properties from Corolla through South Nags Head.

Sun Realty
US 158, MP 9, Kill Devil Hills
(252) 441–8011
NC 12, Corolla
(252) 453–8811

NC 12, Duck
(252) 261–4183
US 158, Kitty Hawk
(252) 261–3892
NC 12, Salvo
(252) 967–2755
NC 12, Avon
(252) 995–5821
www.sunrealty.com

This realty represents properties anywhere on the Outer Banks.

Retirement

Senior Centers
Senior Services
Senior Housing

When some people dream of retirement, they might picture themselves strolling along stretches of deserted beaches on a mild winter afternoon. Perhaps later, they would enjoy a round of golf with friends on an award-winning course to be followed by a good meal at one of many area restaurants. Sound too good to be true? It's possible right here on the Outer Banks. But beware, this isn't your normal retirement community! The retirees here eagerly pursue an active lifestyle, participating in the many activities the beach has to offer. Many seniors also enjoy working with the public filling a spot in the workplace through retail sales or other tourist-oriented jobs. As for fun activities, the senior centers offer all kinds of group trips and classes. And with the hospital under construction here (see our Healthcare and Wellness chapter), the Outer Banks now offers all the benefits of places on the mainland.

If you're thinking of retiring to the Outer Banks, you're in good company. Each year, it seems that more retirees are lured to these barrier islands by some sort of siren call. Moderate winters (remarkably quiet due to the small year-round population) provide for a tranquil environment, and 90-plus miles of broad, soft-sand beaches might figure into the equation as well. North Carolina is now the third most attractive state to retirees, after Florida and Arizona.

In 1998 *The Wall Street Journal* published an article called "Your Next Address," in which five atypical retirement communities were highlighted. "This ain't your father's Florida," the introduction reads. No, these are retirement locations that tend to attract early-retiring baby boomers who are seeking out relatively remote areas on the water where outdoor recreation is an integral part of life. Not surprising to anyone who has retired to the Outer Banks, Corolla was one of the five communities showcased in the article. Corolla, with property taxes of $.66 per $100 of assessed value, tends to draw the retirees and second-home owners who are looking for upscale housing, although options for any type of dwelling abound all along the Outer Banks. If you're looking for a seaside mansion in a gated community, you'll find it. And if your tastes lean more toward a bungalow in the woods or to a traditional three-bedroom home with a yard, you'll find those too.

You won't find any county retirement housing communities on the island, but within this chapter is some information about federally subsidized housing that may prove helpful to those on a fixed income. If you're looking for property, check out our chapters on Real Estate and Area Overviews before you start shopping. For information on our community's senior services, read on.

Seniors are encouraged to participate in the Outer Banks Senior Games sponsored by Dare County Older Adult Services. But be warned, these senior athletes are a dedicated and talented bunch, capable of putting much younger athletes to shame. This is a year-round program to promote health and fitness for Dare County residents age 55 and older. Competition events include track and field, bicycle racing, swimming, tennis, bowling, golf, softball and football throwing, basketball shooting, archery, shuffleboard, billiards, horseshoes, and croquet. Medal winners automatically qualify to compete at the North Carolina Senior Games in September. Besides athletics, there is a Silver Competition for the visual and performing arts. See our listing for the Outer Banks Senior Games in the Annual Events chapter under April, or call the Thomas A. Baum Center, (252) 441–1811, for more information.

Senior Centers

Thomas A. Baum Center
300 Mustian St., Kill Devil Hills
(252) 441-1181

Turning 14 years of age in 2002, the Thomas A. Baum Center is as bright and full of life as the many seniors who cross its threshold each and every day. The center is named after a Dare County native who was a pioneer in ferry transportation. His daughter, Diane Baum St. Clair, arranged for the town of Kill Devil Hills to purchase the land, known locally as the Baum Tract, on very generous terms. Dare County bought a section of the land, which today is home to the senior center, a water plant, a library, two public schools, the local chamber of commerce, and the town's administration and water departments.

The senior center was dedicated on December 7, 1987, and cost more than $600,000 to construct. The more-than-10,000-square-foot building houses the senior center and the county's older adult services. A handful of paid staff and countless senior volunteers operate the center, which is the hub for senior activity north of Hatteras Island. Dare County residents or property owners who are 55 or older may use the center for free; if you are younger than 55 but your spouse meets the age requirement, you also may use the center.

The facility includes a multipurpose room with a stage where the center's drama group, Center Front, performs various productions annually. Past plays include *Li'l Abner*, which sold out all four evenings. The Outer Banks Senior Chorus, which performs two concerts per year, also uses this room for practice sessions. The Baum Center is home to the Wright Tappers, a seniors tap-dancing group, and the Dare Devils, the official cheerleaders for the Outer Banks Senior Games. Line- and square-dance groups round out the foot-tapping activities. And going hand in hand with its name, the multipurpose room does double-duty for aerobic classes three days a week.

A full-service kitchen is used for social

Insiders' Tip

You don't have to limit yourself to the senior centers to socialize. Dare Voluntary Action Center is always looking for community volunteers, (252) 480-0500. Our cultural arts nonprofit groups such as the Theatre of Dare, Dare County Arts Council, and the Outer Banks Forum offer plenty of opportunities for you to volunteer your time and offer your expertise. See our Arts & Culture chapter for more information.

functions and fund-raisers such as the popular annual eat-in or take-out spaghetti supper. The center does not cook daily lunches on the premises.

You can head to the lounge to chat, relax, or read a book borrowed from the center's honor-system library that is filled with a variety of paperbacks. Adjacent to the lounge is the game room where you can play bridge weekly, work puzzles, play cribbage or canasta, or sit in on seminars in history, tax aid, or health education, just to name a few. The center also hosts support group meetings for such organizations as the Outer Banks Cancer Support Group and the Amputee Coalition of Coastal Carolina. Twice a month, seniors gather at the center for an afternoon movie and popcorn.

If you're an outdoor lover, move to the deck to eat lunch or watch for resident deer and foxes. Five picnic tables and various chairs encourage relaxation or conversation. The nearby yard is host to a football target to test your throwing accuracy, horseshoe pits, and spin-casting targets. Outer Banks Senior Games contenders practice discus and shot put as well as archery using bales of hay for targets.

The recreation room comes alive as competitors play a leisurely game of billiards, table tennis, or shuffleboard. There's plenty of elbow room in this spacious area complete with three pool tables, two Ping-Pong tables, and several huge, floor-painted shuffleboard games. Coffee is available in the kitchenette just off the recreation room, and cups are in the cabinet. Donations are welcome. Feel free to bring your lunch and store it in the refrigerator or heat it in the microwave.

Off the rec room is a craft room complete with two sinks, projector, storage space, seven tables with four chairs each, and a sewing machine. Check the center's newsletter, *Senior Soundings*, for craft courses and special activities that take place in this room. The newsletter comes out by the 15th of the month and is available at both county senior centers and the three public libraries.

The center has an information and referral room where you can sign up for programs on preparing healthful food, bird-watching, growing perennials, and acrylic painting. Some activities have a small supplies fee; scholarships are available. There's a wall of pamphlets that cover such topics as taxes, health, and fire safety. Countywide information is available via the computerized Senior Connection information and referral system. Questions on Alzheimer's disease, in-home services, marriage licenses, and the like can be answered by using this program staffed by trained volunteers.

A small computer room is set up with a Packard Bell unit. An exercise suite features a treadmill, rowing machine, and four stationary bicycles, and a staff exercise specialist offers regular exercise programs.

Seniors also can take advantage of the center's 20-seat conference room complete with a telephone and white marker board. Community groups also use this space from time to time.

Insiders' Tip

The local chapter of SCORE (Service Corps Of Retired Executives) offers free counseling on business matters such as putting together a marketing plan, starting a business, compiling financial statements, computerizing an office, obtaining small business loans, and expanding business plans. Weekly sessions are held on Tuesdays at the Outer Banks Chamber of Commerce in Kill Devil Hills. For more information, call the Chamber of Commerce, (252) 441-8144.

The senior center plays a vital role in providing transportation for elderly and disabled Dare County residents. A paid staff member is on hand at the center to schedule free rides to doctor appointments and hospitals in Chesapeake and Norfolk, Virginia, as well as Greenville, North Carolina. The transportation volunteer needs 24-hours' notice.

Rides also are available for shopping trips and getting to and from the center to attend activities and to lunch at the nutrition site at Mount Olivet United Methodist Church in Manteo, where lunch is served Monday through Friday. Seniors are asked to make a 75-cent donation, but it's not mandatory. Menu selections may include herb-baked chicken with a mixed vegetable and rice pilaf or spaghetti with a tossed salad. Two-percent milk and dessert top off the meal. The meals are prepared off the premises by Best Steaks of Elizabeth City. Twenty-six seniors may participate per day. A day's notice is all they need to make sure the food count is correct. If you can't make it to the luncheon, home delivery is available.

The Baum Center is open Monday through Friday from 8:30 A.M. until 5:00 P.M. and for special functions.

Fessenden Center
NC 12, Buxton
(252) 995-3888

The Fessenden Center offers services and programs for county residents and property owners of all ages, although you must be 55 or older to participate in the older adult activities for free. However, the center schedules activities, such as aerobic classes, for adults of all ages for various fees.

The building has a gym with a basketball court. The center operates as a senior center and a site for youth athletic activities. Open gym time is held from 3:00 to 5:00 P.M. Monday through Friday. You can enjoy basketball and volleyball at the center as well as fishing, believe it or not. Throw a line in the creek off the back deck—chances are you'll snag a puppy drum (small channel bass).

The full service kitchen/conference room is available for preparing meals. Every second and fourth Thursday of the month, seniors can attend a luncheon there. The second Thursday lunch is prepared at the center by seniors; the fourth Thursday lunch is a covered-dish affair. Funds for the lunches are provided by Fesstivities, a volunteer senior group that raises money by running the center's concession stand at athletic functions. Seniors contribute a $1.00 donation if they are able. The kitchen/conference room does double-duty as a county meeting facility.

The center also sports an activity room, sitting room, and library. Seniors are invited to hone their skills at the outdoor tennis courts or play with grandchildren at the on-site playground. The soccer and baseball fields give them plenty of room to stretch or jog.

Adults can participate in organized step aerobics, toning and stretching, abdominal exercise, tae kwon do, tai chi, walking, basketball, and dance. You can take Spanish or sign language classes; attend seminars, workshops, and classes on fire safety, cardiac rehabilitation, credit fraud, nutrition, home decorating, quilting, and painting; or take cultural arts trips to shows and parks outside the area. Minimum fees are attached for supplies in the $5.00 to $10.00 range.

Transportation is available through the center's coordinator by calling the center's main number. Shopping trips are scheduled for seniors and disabled adults who have transportation problems. Rides are available to medical appointments and out-of-town hospitals and doctors' offices in Norfolk and Chesapeake, Virginia, as well as Elizabeth City, Nags Head, and Greenville, North Carolina.

The Fessenden Center is open Monday through Friday from 8:30 A.M. until 5:00 P.M. and weekends for youth and special activities.

Senior Services

Helping Hand
Manteo Police Department,
410 Ananias Dare St., Manteo
(252) 473-2069

Working from a list of voluntary participants, Manteo officers check on more than 70 elderly or disabled citizens twice a week in person or by phone to make sure they are healthy and that their needs are being met. The town list is divided among the officers, who prefer to go in person but will telephone from time to time. Participants include seniors, disabled individuals, and persons who live alone. This program is particularly useful in a community like the Outer Banks, where storms occasionally threaten the coast and require residents to evacuate. The officers are in

Put Some Harmony in Your Life With the Sea Notes

Music is a big part of life on the Outer Banks, from rock and roll bands to the acousti-cal performers and swinging jazz singers that can be found performing at numerous nightspots any night of the week. But a barbershop quartet on the beach? Absolutely! Who doesn't like four-part harmony?

When four distinct voices of the Sea Notes (an offshoot of the Chorus of the Outer Banks) combine with four different personalities, *usually* in perfect harmony, their expertise in the art of musical sound turns to magic, infecting everyone around them.

The Sea Notes' melodies are led by Mike Buchko and anchored by Ron Snell singing bass. At the other end from Ron is Bob Watson, tenor. Singing the leftover notes is Bill Brobst, baritone. Each Sea Note has been performing for several years, many of those years spent in four-part harmony. For the past six years, they have per-formed at civic functions, contests, and social gatherings. Their bright spirit and musi-cal talent has brought them a local reputation for adding high quality a cappella music to just about any kind of occasion. Last year, this talented foursome won the Senior Performing Arts Championship, and they have been invited to sing the National Anthem at the opening of the North Carolina Senate this April.

The term "barbershop" denotes a chromatic four-part harmony sung by four unaccompanied voices. The melody is sung by the lead, while the tenor part is sung above the lead. The bass sings in a range an octave below the lead, and the baritone

In a land of flip-flops and shorts, the Sea Notes look pretty spiffy in their barbershop garb. PHOTO: COURTESY OF BILL BROBST

provides the in-between notes that complete the chords. The lyrical emphasis of the majority of barbershop music has always been on simple, heartfelt emotion: love, lost love, friendship, mother, moon, June, and the girl next door. Recently, modern songs have been arranged in the barbershop style to provide more appeal to younger listeners.

The Sea Notes' repertoire includes songs from the full range of the past century, from barroom ballads to ragtime, along with some favorite songs that have been sung since the 1800s. One of the group's personal favorites is the National Anthem, which they have performed at sporting events as well as special occasions and celebrations. Music from the Beatles, Rodgers and Hammerstein, Cole Porter, and even Elvis are some of their most requested songs. The Sea Notes also sing a variety of Valentine selections, Mothers' Day greetings, marching songs, novelty songs, and inspirational music. So for a special way to celebrate a birthday, anniversary, wedding, or any other event, just call the Sea Notes, (252) 261–3068. Who wouldn't appreciate a little harmony in their life?

such close contact with the community they are able to alert homebound individuals in the event of a weather emergency. If you're interested in being on the Helping Hands list, call the police department. Anyone there will be glad to assist you with more information. This is a free service.

Hatteras Island Adult Care
(252) 995–5208, (252) 995–4890

This meals-on-wheels program offers lunch to needy seniors and disabled individuals on Hatteras Island. The year-round program serves meals Monday through Friday, including holidays. Meals are prepared by several local restaurants and markets.

Little Grove United Methodist Church
Monthly Luncheon
NC 12, Frisco
(252) 986–2149

Little Grove usually has a luncheon the third Thursday of the month for anyone interested in food and fellowship. The luncheon includes singing and storytelling that begins at 11:30 A.M. You need to call the above number on the Monday before the third Thursday of the month to reserve your space. Donations are appreciated.

Senior Housing

Bay Tree Apartments
10 Bay Tree Dr., Manteo
(252) 473–5332

Bay Tree is a subsidized housing community designed for seniors and disabled citizens aged 62 or older. The fee to live here is figured according to annual income. Primarily Social Security–dependent citizens occupy these apartments.

Each of Bay Tree's 40 units can accommodate one or two individuals, and small pets are welcome. Each living space has one bedroom and one bathroom with a kitchen/dining area and a storage room. The floor space measures 580 square feet and includes wall-to-wall carpeting, range and refrigerator, heat pump, and air conditioning. Each home has two emergency cords set up so seniors can alert neighbors in case of emergency. A bell rings and a light flashes outside the home when a cord is pulled. Four Bay Tree units are fully wheelchair-accessible, with wide doorways, low counters, walk-in showers, and ramps. A separate laundry facility is available with two washers and two dryers.

Bay Tree has a community room with a kitchen that can be used for fellowship

The Rev. John Wreford and his wife, Dorothy, take a four-wheel-drive break from their usual activities.
PHOTO: COURTESY OF LINDA LAUBY

or other activities. The community also has a resident manager. The complex has sidewalks, small front yards that can be cultivated by the residents, and a few benches scattered among the units. The complex is minutes from a grocery store, two pharmacies, restaurants, and a video and camera store. Also nearby are a commercial laundry, dry cleaners, a movie theater, and various gift shops. Residents can arrange transportation to the Mount Olivet nutrition site by calling the Thomas A. Baum Center phone number. This housing community operates under the U.S. Department of Agriculture's HUD program. If seniors don't qualify for Bay Tree housing, they can ask the resident manager about other options at Harbourtowne Apartments next door, where income can be higher and the age restrictions do not apply.

Healthcare and Wellness

Ah, paradise. Beach umbrellas instead of bus shelters, shingled cottages instead of skyscrapers, communing with nature instead of commuting to work. Yes, it is idyllic—until an accident or illness disrupts your life. Don't worry. In the event of an emergency, the Outer Banks has a multitude of trained medical personnel, both staff members and volunteers, who can be on-site in a remarkably short time after they receive a call from the 911 dispatcher. Local EMTs, firefighters, and ocean rescue workers can all provide immediate medical assistance and continued care while patients are transported to a local medical facility.

The biggest news in Outer Banks healthcare is the brand-new Outer Banks Hospital, scheduled to open in early 2002. Believe it or not, this is the first and only hospital on the Outer Banks. It is centrally located in a big new building in Nags Head. This is really exciting for locals and visitors because one of the biggest complaints about this area for years was the lack of medical facilities. Pregnant women had to travel to Elizabeth City or Virginia to have their babies, and many babies were born en route to the hospital. Many retirees hesitated to move here because of the lack of medical facilities. Anyone who ever experienced a major emergency or illness in the past has had to be flown by helicopter or transported by ambulance to a hospital at least 50 to 100 miles away. The hospital may still be a long distance from Corolla or Ocracoke, but it's a heck of a lot closer than Virginia.

In addition to the new hospital, there are a number of medical centers and clinics on the Outer Banks, along with an ever-increasing roster of alternative medical service providers.

Hospital

The Outer Banks Hospital
4800 US 158, MP 14, Nags Head
(252) 449-4500, (877) 359-9179
www.theouterbankshospital.com

This 73,500-square-foot facility is the Outer Banks's first and only hospital, a welcome addition to the community. At this writing it was under construction, but officials were confident of an early 2002 opening date. The hospital is a partnership between Chesapeake Health of Chesapeake, Virginia, and University Health Systems of Eastern Carolina. The two entities have collaborated on Outer Banks emergency and primary healthcare in the past with HealthEast Medical Centers in Nags Head, Avon, and Hatteras Village.

The Outer Banks Hospital is a 24-hour facility with 19 acute-care beds and emergency services. Rooms include emergency observation rooms for monitoring patients, two labor/delivery rooms, and two operating rooms. A helipad is on-site. Patients with serious emergencies or major trauma will be stabilized on-site, then flown to a hospital in North Carolina or Virginia for further medical care. The hospital employs 55 physicians and 125 employees. Services include cardiology, dermatology, urology, endrocrinology, ophthalmology, obstetrics and gynecology, pulmonology, ENT (ear, nose, and throat), and senior services.

The hospital provides services that in the past people had to travel off the Outer Banks for. More sophisticated lab tests are performed here. Two operating rooms accommodate general surgery (in- and outpatient), orthopedic surgery, oral surgery, cesarean sections, and vascular surgery, among others, and there are pre- and postoperative recovery rooms. Diagnostic services include anesthesia, pharmacy, lab and pathology, and physical and respiratory therapy. Oncology services and support groups are available, as well as radiology, including CT scans, ultrasound, and mammography. Wellness and preventative medicine programs are another service provided by this community-minded hospital.

For more information about The Outer Banks Hospital, visit the Web site or call the numbers above.

Medical Centers and Clinics

Tarheel Internal Medicine Associates
1123 Ocean Trail, Corolla
(252) 453–8616

Tarheel Internal Medicine Associates offers year-round family healthcare on the northern beaches. Walk-ins are welcome and summer hours are Monday through Friday from 9:00 A.M. to 6:00 P.M. Call for winter hours.

Chesapeake Health
Medical Offices
The Marketplace, US 158, MP 1,
Southern Shores
(252) 261–5800

Physician specialists form the framework for this affiliate of Virginia's Chesapeake General Hospital. Services include oncology, urology, endocrinology, audiology, nutrition counseling, diabetes education, rheumatology, dermatology, allergy care, and ear, nose, and throat care. Minor office surgery is performed on the premises, and surgeons specializing in colon/rectal and

plastic surgery see patients at this complex. This is not an emergency-care facility. Call for insurance information. The facility serves patients by appointment Monday through Friday from 9:00 A.M. to 5:00 P.M. and is open year-round.

Regional Medical Center
US 158, MP 1½, Kitty Hawk
(252) 261–9000

The communities of the Outer Banks rely on this medical center for convenient, high-quality healthcare. The facility offers a wide range of services and strives to provide quick and easy access to the appropriate diagnostic and healthcare departments for those in need. Preventive and educational programs are also offered here.

Family Medicine and Urgent Care (open 9:00 A.M. to 9:00 P.M.) are located in the Regional Medical Center along with a rotation of more than 50 medical specialists, who include gastroenterologists, allergists, OB/GYNs, a rheumatologist, a neurosurgeon, and cardiologists. A directory of physicians and specialties can be obtained by calling (252) 261–9000. In addition to outpatient surgery, a diagnostic laboratory is on-site, and blood tests are handled quickly for in-house diagnosis. Outer Banks Radiology, (252) 261–4311, provides routine as well as diagnostic services such as mammograms, ultrasounds, fluoroscopy, CT, and MRI. Regional Medical Center is an affiliate of Albemarle Hospital in Elizabeth City.

The Surgery Center
Regional Medical Center, US 158, MP 1½,
Kitty Hawk
(252) 261–9009

This is an outpatient surgery center. Procedures such as breast biopsy, hernia repair, laparoscopy, tonsillectomy, adenoidectomy, oral surgery, cataract surgery, colonoscopy, and tendon repair, among many others, are performed here.

Virginia Dare Women's Center
US 158, MP 10½, Nags Head
(252) 441–2144

Appointments are available for female-related medical needs. Patty Johnson is the center's certified nurse-midwife and family nurse practitioner. Baby and youth care and pap smears are offered along with generalized care. Call for an appointment.

HealthEast Outer Banks Medical Center
US 158, MP 11, Nags Head
(252) 441-7111 Urgent Care
(252) 441-3177 Primary Care
HealthEast Outer Banks Medical Center provides both urgent and primary care in Nags Head. Walk-in emergency care is available 24 hours a day, with attention provided by on-staff board-certified emergency physicians. Also available 24 hours a day are laboratory, X-ray, and CT scan services. Please call the non-emergency number above to make an appointment for primary care. This medical center is an affiliate of University Health Systems of Eastern Carolina.

HealthEast Medical Specialists, (252) 449-4141, in the same building as the medical center, has a variety of specialists, including family practice, mammography, and radiology, among others. Call for an appointment.

Insiders' Tip

When you check into your rental cottage, write down the street address (which will differ from your rental company's house identification number) and phone number and keep them next to the phone. That way you'll have the address handy in case of an emergency.

Outer Banks Center for Women
4917 US 158, MP 14, Nags Head
(252) 449-2100
Outer Banks Center for Women occupies a brand-new building just across the street from The Outer Banks Hospital in Nags Head. The new building features something never before seen on the Outer Banks—a birthing center. With two birthing rooms, hot tubs, lounges, and living quarters, this is truly an exciting prospect for women giving birth on the Outer Banks.

The Outer Banks Center for Women is affiliated with Chesapeake General Hospital of Chesapeake, Virginia. It offers a broad spectrum of women's care, including obstetrics and gynecology, midwifery, women's health maintenance, menopausal care, hormone replacement, pelvic ultrasounds, and infertility issues. Minor surgical procedures are performed here.

The new birthing center is an extraordinary service for Outer Banks families. The center features two birthing suites with family rooms, a full-size kitchen, and a library. With state-of-the-art equipment, it is staffed by professional nurses and midwives who promote natural birthing with hydrotherapy and water birthing. Women who give birth at this center are required to take educational classes while they are pregnant. In case of complications, patients are transferred to The Outer Banks Hospital directly across the street.

Island Medical Center
715 US 64, Manteo
(252) 473-2500
Dr. Johnny Farrow and nurse practitioner Janice Jenkins provide complete family medical care at this office. X-ray services are available, and some lab work is done on the premises. Walk-ins are welcome, or you can call for an appointment. The center's hours are 8:30 A.M. to 5:30 P.M. Monday, Tuesday, Thursday, and Friday and 8:30 A.M. to 12:30 P.M. on Wednesday. Island Medical Center is across the street from the Elizabethan Inn in Manteo.

Engaging in a relaxing hobby, such as gardening, has been shown to reduce stress and promote overall wellness. PHOTO: COURTESY OF ROANOKE ISLAND FESTIVAL PARK

HealthEast Family Care/Avon and Hatteras
NC 12, Avon
(252) 995-3073
NC 12, Hatteras Village
(252) 986-2765

The two Hatteras Island HealthEast Family Care offices offer comprehensive family medical care and urgent care from board-certified physicians. Dr. Seaborn Blair III, Dr. J. Al Hodges, Dr. Bentley Crabtree, and nurse practitioner Carey Le Sieur staff both of these offices. X-ray and lab services are available. Walk-ins are accepted, but appointments are preferred. Hours for both offices are weekdays from 8:30 A.M. to 5:00 P.M. and Saturday from 9:00 A.M. to 3:00 P.M. On Saturdays and Thursdays, only one office is open. HealthEast maintains 24-hour emergency call coverage at one of the two locations.

Dare Medical Associates
US 64, Manteo
(252) 473-3478

Dr. Walter Holton provides family service and acute care from this office. X-ray services are available. Hours are 8:00 A.M. to 5:00 P.M. Monday through Thursday, and Friday from 8:00 A.M. until noon.

Dare County Health Department Clinic
109 Exeter St., Manteo
(252) 475-1089
NC 12, Buxton
(252) 995-4404

The Dare County Health Department Health Care Services Clinic has a maternal health program, a family planning program, and outreach for pregnant women and new mothers. It also has a full-time nurse who deals with communicable diseases and sexually transmitted diseases (STD). Flu-shot clinics are held every fall. For diabetics, an education program, support group, and dietician are available. Fees are paid on a sliding-scale basis according to income.

Ocracoke Health Center
Back Rd., adjacent to the school playground, Ocracoke Island
(252) 928-1511

A physician's assistant and nurse practitioner provide general medical care for all ages at this small island clinic, which is overseen by Dr. Seaborn Blair of HealthEast Family Care on Hatteras Island. Walk-ins are accepted, but appointments are preferred. Hours are Monday, Wednesday, and Friday from 8:30 A.M. to 5:00 P.M. (closed at lunch hour), Tuesday from 4:00 to 9:00 P.M., and Thursday from 1:00 to 5:00 P.M. Hours may change for summer 2002, so call ahead. For emergencies after hours, call the office number and you will be given a pager number to call. This is a Blue Cross Blue Shield of North Carolina provider.

Emergency Helicopter Transport

Dare Medflight
Dial 911

The Dare County Emergency Medical Service runs this service. It offers advanced life support air ambulance service for flying major trauma and emergency cases to

Albemarle Hospital in Elizabeth City; Chesapeake General Hospital in Chesapeake, Virginia; Norfolk General Hospital in Norfolk; and Virginia Beach General Hospital in Virginia Beach. The helicopter flies from Outer Banks clinics or from the trauma scene.

Alternative Healthcare

Chiropractic Care

Wellness Center of the Outer Banks
The Marketplace, US 158, MP 1, Southern Shores
(252) 261–5424

Daniel Goldberg, DC, offers a full range of chiropractic services and nutrition management, including family chiropractic care and sports injury treatment. The Wellness Center of the Outer Banks is the exclusive participant in this area for many health care plans. The office is in The Marketplace shopping center. Hours are Monday, Wednesday, and Friday from 8:30 A.M. to noon and 3:00 to 6:00 P.M., Tuesdays from 3:00 to 6:00 P.M., and Thursdays from 9:30 A.M. to 1:00 P.M. Massage therapy is also offered here. Please call for an appointment.

Family and Sports Chiropractic Center
Overseas Bldg., 2400 US 158, Ste. I, MP 6, Kill Devil Hills
(252) 261–8885
www.obxchiro.com

Dr. Eugene Flynn offers affordable chiropractic care for the entire family. He has extensive specialized training in sports and fitness injuries, work-related injuries, and auto injuries. He stresses regular chiropractic care as a means to overall well-being and health. Office hours are Monday, Wednesday, and Friday from 10:00 A.M. to 1:00 P.M. and 3:00 P.M. to 7:00 P.M., Tuesday and Thursday from 3:00 to 7:00 P.M., and Saturday from 10:00 A.M. to noon. No appointment is necessary.

Outer Banks Chiropractic Clinic
US 158, MP 10, Nags Head
(252) 441–1585

Craig Gibson, DC, offers all chiropractic services. Office hours are Monday, Tuesday, Thursday, and Friday from 8:00 A.M. to noon and 1:30 to 5:30 P.M. and Wednesday from 8:00 A.M. to noon and 2:00 to 6:00 P.M.

Massage Therapy

Massage therapy is available in a variety of forms, including Swedish massage, shiatsu, and reflexology. Since each therapist's techniques differ, it may help to have a conference to clarify your needs and to determine if the individual's area of specialization will suit you. Massage therapy can be invaluable in helping to recover from physical trauma or simply to relax.

Insiders' Tip

At the height of the summer season, area restaurateurs often tell tales of tourists who pass out at the tables merely because they didn't drink enough water during the day. Remember that alcoholic beverages and drinks with caffeine are diuretics and will aggravate dehydration. Make sure to drink plenty of water throughout the day, especially when it's sweltering outside.

Helpful Phone Numbers

AIDS Hotline:
   (800) 342–AIDS
   (800) 344–7432 (Spanish)
   (800) 243–7889 (TTY Hearing Impaired)

Al/Anon:
   (252) 480–3896

Albemarle Hospital Referral Services:
   (252) 384–4610

Alcoholics Anonymous:
   (252) 261–1681, Kitty Hawk
   (252) 261–4818 (if no answer at above number)
   (252) 441–2769 (if no answer at above number)
   (252) 995–4240, Hatteras Island

Albemarle Mental Health Center:
   (252) 473–1135, Manteo
   (252) 441–9400, Nags Head
   (252) 995–4951, Avon
   After hours and holidays:
   (252) 261–1490 (north of Oregon Inlet);
   (252) 995–4010 (south of Oregon Inlet)

Dare County Health Department:
   (252) 473–1101, ext. 220
   (252) 995–4404, Buxton

Dare County Home Health Services:
   (252) 473–1101

Dare County Emergency Medical Facilities:
   (252) 441–1551 (north of Oregon Inlet)
   (252) 473–3444 (south of Oregon Inlet)

Dare Home Health and Hospice:
   (252) 473–5828

Dare County Social Services:
   (252) 473–1471

Dare County Older Adult Services:
   (252) 441–1181

HIV Support Group:
   (252) 473–6151

Hotline Crisis Intervention:
   (252) 473–3366
   (252) 473–9814, Main Office

Narcotics Anonymous:
   (252) 480–4931

N.C. Community Child Abuse Educator:
   (800) 982–4041

Outer Banks Crisis Pregnancy Center:
   (252) 480–4646 (pro-life counseling)

Poison Control Center:
   (800) 848–6946

Senior Connection Information and Referral Service:
   (252) 480–1100

Veterans Services Office:
   (252) 473–1101

Hatha yoga has been proven to aid in health and wellness. Many classes are offered on the Outer Banks each week. PHOTO: MOLLY HARRISON

We've listed a smattering of services available. Check the local phone book for a complete list.

Fitness centers, salons, and resort facilities often have massage therapists on staff. Check with them for that possibility.

David Henderson, CMT
Hammerheads Gym, NC 12, MP 6,
Kill Devil Hills
(252) 480–6459
David Henderson offers Swedish massage, sports massage, neuromuscular therapy, deep muscle therapy, and lymph drainage therapy on location or in a quiet room at Hammerheads Gym. Call for an appointment.

Healing Hands Massage Therapy
Sea Holly Sq., NC 12, Kill Devil Hills
(252) 480–0524
Martha David, AMTA/LMT, offers massage for stress release, pain relief, and injury rehabilitation. She also offers foot reflexology, aromatherapy, and moist steam-pack therapy. Her office is in Sea

Holly Square, but she also makes house calls. Call for an appointment.

Outer Banks Integrated Massage Therapy
2405 US 158, Nags Head
(252) 449–8307
Nancy Salvatore, BA, CMT, offers an alternative approach to wellness through massage therapy. She employs a combination of techniques, including Swedish and deep tissue massage, trigger point therapy, and shiatsu. Call to make an appointment or for information and help in organizing oceanside wellness retreats.

Dianna Carter and Associates, CMT
208 W. Ocean Acres Dr., Nags Head
(252) 441–0698
Dianna Carter specializes in Swedish as well as therapeutic massage, cranio-sacral therapy, and neuromuscular trigger point therapy. Pre-natal and infant massage are also offered. Dianna Carter and Associates also has locations in Kitty Hawk and Corolla, or you can arrange for home or office visits. Call the Nags Head number

for information on services at all sites or to schedule an appointment with any of the certified therapists.

Dhanyo Merillat-Bowers, CMT
NC 12, Buxton
(252) 995-4067

Dhanyo Merillat-Bowers's massage techniques center around neuromuscular work, deep tissue massage, relief from pain and injury, relaxation and stress reduction. Merillat-Bowers is nationally certified in therapeutic massage and body work and is a member of the American Massage Therapy Association. Call for an appointment.

Health-related Services

Dare Home Health and Hospice
106 Sir Walter Raleigh St., Manteo
(252) 473-5828

DHHH offers skilled nursing, speech therapy, physical and occupational therapy, and home health aid. This group is Medicare-certified and accredited by the Accreditation Commission for Home Care. The services are available for Dare County citizens who are homebound. DHHH will bill Medicare, Medicaid, and other insurance companies, or fees can be set on a sliding scale, depending on income.

Insiders' Tip

Since most of the medical offices on the Outer Banks are urgent care facilities, you may wish to call ahead for non-emergency visits to inquire as to how long the wait might be. The receptionist might be able to suggest a less hectic time to come in.

Outer Banks Hotline
US 64, Manteo
(252) 473-3366

Hotline is a 24-hour crisis counseling service that also provides shelter to victims of abuse. To generate funds, Hotline operates thrift shops in Manteo, Kill Devil Hills, Kitty Hawk, and Hatteras Island. Hotline conducts regular public-awareness seminars and training. For crisis counseling, please call.

Education and Child Care

Public Schools
Private Schools
Higher Education
Preschool/Day-care
  Facilities
Child Care Centers and
  Services

Children take top priority in the county of Dare, and the proof is everywhere you look, from numerous educational activities offered outside of school to parents and teachers who truly care about the future of each child.

Education has evolved a lot since the days when some Outer Banks kids paddled their skiffs to the one-room schoolhouse. Today there are more than 4,500 students attending 10 schools on the Outer Banks, 9 in Dare County and 1 on Ocracoke Island. Two new schools will open in the coming years to the deal with the demands of a growing population.

Higher education opportunities on the Outer Banks include a community college campus, College of the Albemarle, in Manteo. COA provides associates degrees, certificates, and diplomas, and many of the hours are transferable to other colleges. Some students make a 45-minute commute to Elizabeth City to attend that city's College of the Albemarle campus or Elizabeth City State University. Other students have been known to commute over an hour and a half to attend Old Dominion University in Norfolk, Virginia, or up to two-and-a-half hours to attend East Carolina University in Greenville, North Carolina.

For children who are not school-age or who need care after school, Outer Banks parents depend on a patchwork of day-care providers ranging from grandparents, teenagers, and the neighborhood retiree who cares for one or several children in the home; to licensed home providers who care for a number of children in their homes; to after-school care service at their child's school; to day-care centers that watch dozens of children in a more controlled and regulated setting. We cannot provide listings for grandparents, teenagers, and neighborhood retirees here, but we have provided information about area preschools, day-care facilities, and baby-sitting services.

Education

Public Schools

Dare County Schools
(252) 473–1151
www.dare.k12.nc.us

More than 4,500 elementary and secondary students from Corolla to Hatteras Island attend one of the nine Dare County schools—four elementary schools, two middle schools, one combination middle and high school, one high school, and one alternative high school.

There are some unusual situations in the Dare County Schools. One is that the only high school is at the far end of Manteo, up to an hour's drive for students who live in Corolla, Duck, and Kitty Hawk. Another has to do with students who live in Corolla. Corolla is in Currituck County and does not have its own school. The Currituck County schools are across the sound, an easy trip by boat but a lengthy trip by land. Corolla had its own small two-room school that opened in the

Area schools combine book learning with educational field trips. PHOTO: COURTESY OF ROANOKE ISLAND FESTIVAL PARK

late 1800s, but it was closed in 1958 when the population of the village dwindled. Dare County transports students to and from the Currituck Outer Banks to its schools via bus—all the way to Manteo for the high school students! Corolla students can spend several hours a day on the bus.

As the population of year-round residents grows, the Dare County Board of Education is constantly besieged with finding new ways to meet the demands of more students. With almost every one of the current schools at, near, or over capacity, the biggest goal is more space. Two new schools are planned to supplement the nine existing Dare County schools in upcoming years. One is a new elementary school on Hatteras Island, a 63,000-square-foot facility with a capacity for 600 students. This school will be ready for students in the 2002–03 school year. The other new school is a $30 million high school that will be located in Kill Devil Hills, much to the pleasure of families who live in the beach communities. The new high school will be a 156,000-square-foot facility with classrooms, a gymnasium, a cafeteria, and athletic fields.

Planned for a September 2004 opening, the school will have a 1,200 student capacity, though the board of education expects 800 students at opening. Work will begin on the new high school in the summer of 2002. Manteo High School will remain open when the beach high school opens.

But for all the concerns over raising enough funds and providing better classrooms, Dare County offers children a quality education, one of the top-scoring districts statewide, some of the best teachers around, and involved parents. Despite the area's remoteness and distance from cultural and educational hubs, schools here have measured up exceedingly well. Dare County schools have consistently ranked in the top five on student achievement among school systems statewide. The district, one of the first to connect to the state's Information Highway in 1994, provides computers in every classroom, Internet access for students, and a commitment to technological advancement. Cape Hatteras and Manteo high schools are linked through a computer network that allows each school to transmit and share information. Each school has an interactive room with audio and visual equipment.

Dare County schools open after Labor Day and close in mid-June. All elementary schools have after-school day care available on-site until 6:00 P.M. (See the Child Care section of this chapter for information.)

For more information about these nine Dare County schools, contact the Dare County Board of Education at (252) 473-1151.

Kitty Hawk Elementary (K–5)
US 158, MP¹⁄₂, Kitty Hawk
(252) 261-2313

First Flight Elementary School (K–5)
Run Hill Road, off Colington Rd.,
Kill Devil Hills
(252) 441-1111

First Flight Middle School (6–8)
Run Hill Road, off Colington Rd., Kill Devil Hills
(252) 441-8888

Manteo Elementary School (K–5)
NC 64/264, Manteo
(252) 473-2742

Manteo Middle School (6–8)
NC 64/264, Manteo
(252) 473-5549

Manteo High School (9–12)
Wingina Avenue, Manteo
(252) 473-5841

Dare County Alternative School (9–12)
NC 64/264, Manteo
(252) 473-3141

Cape Hatteras Elementary School (K–5)
NC 12, Buxton
(252) 995-5730

Cape Hatteras Secondary School (6–12)
NC 12, Buxton
(252) 995-5730

The Ocracoke School
1 Schoolhouse Rd., Ocracoke Island
(252) 928-3251

Part of the Hyde County school system, The Ocracoke School is one of the smallest public schools in the United States, serving an island where the entire year-round population is only 700. It is a K–12 school and in 2001 had 65 students, with only two graduating seniors that year. The Ocracoke School was built in 1931. For the last several years it has been designated a School of Excellence, a state honor awarded to schools where more than 90 percent of students are performing at or above their grade level. The Ocracoke School is also repeatedly honored as an Exemplary School, in which academic growth exceeded expectations by more than 10 percent. Though small, The Ocracoke School is sophisticated. Every classroom is equipped with computers that are linked to the rest of the state via the Information Highway. Student clubs, a student newspaper, and a basketball team provide extracurricular activities for students. The basketball team is not in a league but does play numerous independent games throughout the season.

Private Schools

The Wanchese Christian Academy
39 The Lane, Wanchese
(252) 473-5797
www.wcacademy.org

The oldest private school on the Outer Banks, this K–12 facility was founded in 1978 by members of the Wanchese Assembly of God church who wanted to be able to teach their children moral values and Bible studies. This Christian school, however, is open to members of any religion. About 110 students from Currituck to Avon attend. (Transportation is not provided.) The Wanchese Christian Academy meets North Carolina private-school requirements.

Higher Education

College of the Albemarle,
Dare Campus
132 Russell Twiford Rd., Manteo
(252) 473–2264
www.albermarle.cc.nc.us

The Manteo campus of the College of the Albemarle (COA) was established in 1984 as a second branch of the main campus in Elizabeth City. A third branch is in Edenton. The College of the Albemarle is part of the state's 59-member North Carolina System of Community Colleges. This is the only institution of higher learning on the Outer Banks, and it is a great asset to the citizens of these remote islands. The campus overlooks the marsh on the east end of Roanoke Island near the junction of US 64/264 and NC 345. The campus includes classrooms, laboratories, offices, a library, a student lounge, a new technology building, and a new auditorium and conference facility.

Certificate, diploma, and associate degrees are offered in numerous areas. For example, associate degrees are offered in arts, fine arts, and general education; associate of applied science degrees are offered in business administration, office systems technology, information systems, early childhood education, criminal justice, electronics, and computer engineering; diplomas are offered in heating and air conditioning; certificates are offered in nursing assistance, real estate, and medical transcription. This of course does not cover all areas of study. A new Cisco Systems Academy prepares students to work with Cisco Systems network. The campus is connected to the North Carolina Information Highway so that students may take classes or seminars from remote locations while remaining on campus. The school has an active Student Government Association. Students at the Dare branch can apply credits earned at COA toward degrees at other state colleges and universities. Day, evening, and weekend classes are offered during the school year and during the summer. Federal financial aid and other student assistance is available.

Continuing education programs are wide-ranging at COA. Certifications, trainings, and just-for-fun classes are offered in nursing assistance, notary, effective teacher training, computers, Spanish, science, English as a second language, yoga, cooking, photography, art, and more. The college's Small Business Center, based in Elizabeth City, loans videos, books, audio tapes, and CD-ROMs. A list of publications is available by calling (252) 335–0821 ext. 223.

Child Care

North Carolina law mandates child/staff ratios at licensed day-care centers and home providers that are different for each age group and type of facility. The state also requires that all teachers meet certain criteria for health and continuing education. Anyone who watches more than two children (who are not relations) for more than four hours a day must be licensed. Home-care providers can care for a maximum of eight children with no more than five preschoolers in the group, including the provider's own kids (if the provider has school-age children, they are not counted toward the eight children). Regulators inspect facilities and teacher records on an annual basis. For information on ratios and license requirements, call the state Division of Child Development at (800) 859-0829.

Recently some centers have stretched their hours to accommodate parents who work nights in one of the restaurants across the barrier islands. Others have put out the welcome mat for tourists who need child-free time during their vacations. A running list of registered and licensed providers is available from the Dare County Department of Social Services. Contact the office at (252) 473-5857 to request the current list of day-care providers.

Dare County schools offer the After School Enrichment Program to serve working parents of K–5 students. Children are cared for in the same building where they attend school, but their after-hours time is spent in free play inside or out on the playground. Crafts and games are on hand for kids to play with one another and the staff. Help with homework is also available, and an optional homework period is set aside every day. Call the Dare County Board of Education, (252) 473-1151, for scheduling and information.

The North Carolina Cooperative Extension 4-H provides summer camp programs for elementary and middle school youth, rolling child care and supervised fun activities into one service. And 4-H also offers day care at the schools during spring and winter breaks. Contact the Cooperative Extension office in Manteo at (252) 473-1101, ext. 243. Also see our Kidstuff chapter for a list of summer camps.

Additional day-care options are also available through a Head Start program run by the Economic Improvement Council, (252) 473-5246.

Preschool/Day-care Facilities

First Assembly of God Preschool and Daycare
812 Wingina Ave., Manteo
(252) 473-2664

Founded as a "Christ-centered" facility, children here are given Bible lessons daily. Attendees do not have to be Christian. Children age three through kindergarten are taught preschool three times a week, including phonics and numbers. The kids are also taken on regular field trips to educational attractions, such as the aquarium or the Norfolk Zoo. The school invites members of the community, such as firefighters or police officers, to give on-site presentations.

The school is conducted Tuesday, Wednesday, and Thursday from 8:30 A.M. to noon. Full-time day care, which includes preschool, is available. Sessions include lunch and two snacks daily. A transitional class for children not quite ready for kindergarten is also offered. The day care is state-certified. Hours are 7:30 A.M. to 6:00 P.M. Monday through Friday. Drop-off service is not available.

Heron Pond Montessori School
3910 Poor Ridge Rd., Kitty Hawk
(252) 261-6077
831 Herbert Perry Rd., Kitty Hawk
(252) 261-5358

Based on the philosophies of Italian physician/educator Maria Montessori, Heron Pond offers half-day and full-day licensed day-care programs, kindergarten programs, and junior elementary programs through the third grade. Both locations of the school are in historic Kitty Hawk village, one of them in the Unitarian Universalist Church building. The staff of nine well-trained teachers has extensive child-care and educational experience and is trained in the Montessori method.

The Montessori spirit of education is rooted in the belief that children are naturally eager to learn, and all the teaching tools at Heron Pond are centered on encouragement of the child's ability to teach him- or herself. The school has a summer program.

Munchkin Academy
NC 12, across from Cape Hatteras School, Buxton
(252) 995–6118

This state-certified facility offers preschool, prekindergarten, after-school care, and full-time, and drop-in child-care service. The only A-licensed child-care facility on Hatteras Island, Munchkin Academy also offers 4-H summer camp programs for school-age youth. A homey center with an unusually large playground, the academy provides care for children ages birth through 12 years. All teachers are certified in first aid and CPR and have state child-care credentials. According to director Kyle Williams, the facility far exceeds state standards for teacher/child ratio. A registered nurse is also on-site. Preschool and preK are held Monday through Friday from 7:45 A.M. to 5:15 P.M. Two-, three-, and four-day schedules are also available. Call ahead to reserve a drop-in space. Munchkin Academy is open Monday through Friday year-round from 7:45 A.M. to 5:15 P.M.

Child-care Centers and Services

At Your Service
(252) 261–5286

The oldest baby-sitting service on the Outer Banks, At Your Service offers bonded adult baby-sitters who drive themselves to your home. Sitters are screened thoroughly, and all references are checked. Owner Barbara Hall attracts most of her business from referrals and repeat business from happy clients. At Your Service is the only business of its kind recommended by the Outer Banks Chamber of Commerce. Rates are based on the number of children and number of hours (there is a four-hour minimum). Parents must also pay the travel expenses of the sitter. The service was expanded in 1995 to also provide linen, maid, housekeeping, delivery, chef, and grocery shopping services. At Your Service is available year-round. Call for rates and off-season information.

(See also the listing in the Weekly and Long-Term Cottage Rentals chapter.)

Better Beginnings, Inc.
108 W. Sibbern Dr., off US 158, Kitty Hawk
(252) 261–2833

This child-care center has been in business on the Outer Banks for nearly 20 years. State-licensed, Better Beginnings provides full-time or after-school care in a safe, educational environment for children ages 6 weeks to 12 years. The daily schedule is geared to provide structure but allows for flexibility, establishing a rhythm of active play between quiet periods. In addition to the regular curriculum, the center also has a music program, an after-school program, a preschool class, and a full-time summer program for school-age children. Nutritional snacks and meals are provided. Call for a complete rate schedule. Better Beginnings is open 8:00 A.M. to 6:00 P.M. Monday through Friday year-round.

Ferris Wheel Day Care and Preschool
109 E. First St., off US 158, Kill Devil Hills
(252) 441–3808

Ferris Wheel take pride in providing a warm, stable environment that encourages learning. Licensed by North Carolina, the center offers full-day child care for infants, toddlers, and preschoolers. An early education program is held for toddlers and preschoolers. Field trips are also part of the curriculum here. Healthy snacks and lunches are provided, drop-in rates are available. Ferris Wheel is open from 7:30 A.M. to 6:00 P.M. year-round.

Rocker Room Child Care Center
US 158, MP 10½, Nags Head
(252) 480–0241

Family-oriented and state-licensed, Rocker Room Child Care Center provides full developmental play programs with inside and outside activities for infants through five-year-olds. According to director Sallye Hardy, the facility meets the National Association for the Education of Young Children ratio standards, the highest in the country. Rocker Room's motto is "Care that works for working families," a philosophy that's reflected in the center's flexible approach to child care. For instance, rather than having set hours, the facility tries to work around the needs and schedules of its customers. In the summer the center is open seven days a week from 6:30 A.M. until midnight. Drop-ins are welcome year-round, if there's room. Vacationers are provided with their own beeper, so the staff can find them if they're needed—a real worry reducer and relaxation enhancer.

In the slower season, Rocker Room usually operates between 7:00 A.M. and 6:00 P.M. daily. Reservations for drop-ins must be made by noon the day before.

Sandcastle Child Care Center
117 W. Sea Chase Dr., The Village at Nags Head, Nags Head
(252) 480–3388

Sandcastle, a licensed day-care center, caters to both residents and tourists. A large center with a capacity for 137 children, the center offers full-time, part-time, and drop-in rates for children ages birth through five years. All employees are screened and certified in CPR and first aid. Hot meals and snacks are included for full-time attendees. Drop-in care requires 24-hour advance notice. Sandcastle Child Care Center is open daily from 7:30 A.M. to 5:45 P.M. year-round. In the summer the facility is open until 11:15 P.M. on Monday and Wednesday through Saturday. Winter hours are extended until 10:00 P.M. on those same days.

Ocracoke Child Care, Inc.
45 Beach Rd., Ocracoke
(252) 928–4131
www.ocracokechildcare@ocracoke.net

The only licensed, four-star center on Ocracoke Island, this facility moved to a new location in 1998. What's unique about Ocracoke Child Care is that it is owned by its members. For an annual fee, participants are entitled to attend membership meetings and receive the quarterly newsletter. The center, which has a capacity of 40 children, is overseen by a six-member Board of Directors, which sets rules and policies. Children ages 6 weeks to 12 years are cared for by a fully trained staff who prefer to think of themselves as teachers rather than baby-sitters. The new facility has a special infant-toddler room and an age-3-and-older preschool room. Based on the motto "Peace begins in the playground," Ocracoke Child Care has structured playtime as well as indoor and outdoor play areas and revolves activities around a different theme each week. Visitors to the area are asked to come in a day in advance to fill out forms and will be served if there is room available. Immunization records are not necessary for out-of-towners. Ocracoke Child Care is open from 7:45 A.M. to 5:15 P.M. Monday through Friday year-round.

Media

Newspapers

Magazines and
  Miscellaneous
  Publications

Television

Radio Stations

Online Media and
  Internet Service
  Providers

If you happen upon two contractors leaning out of their truck windows while stopped on NC 12, one facing north and the other facing south, you'll witness how most information is passed on in this part of the world. Insiders generally disseminate information by talking to each other—either on the roads, at the post office, or over the telephone. More options are available, including newspapers, magazines, radio stations, telephone information lines, Internet sites, and, of course, the TV. This chapter highlights those sources.

Solid selections of daily papers can be found at the Stop 'n' Shop convenience market, (252) 441-6105, on NC 12 at MP 8½, Kill Devil Hills, and in Duck at Wee Winks Market, (252) 261-2937, 213 Duck Rd. (NC 12). Costs may be inflated for some papers as the Outer Banks is considered a remote distribution area.

Before we turn you on to what's available, we'd like to share a little bit of radio history. Despite being an Atlantic Ocean outpost of sorts, the Outer Banks boasts of being the site from which the first wireless telegraph signal was sent by Reginald Fessenden in 1902 (see our History chapter). While Guglielmo Marconi has been credited with developing wireless telegraphy, Fessenden was experimenting on the Outer Banks during the same time period with transmitting sound using an entirely different system that's credited as the true basis for radio broadcasting. Read our section in this chapter on radio stations to see how it's progressed on the Outer Banks since Fessenden's day.

Newspapers

We have a variety of newspapers that range from a daily Virginia paper with a North Carolina section where Outer Banks news appears coupled with coastal Virginia news, to weekly, tri-weekly, quarterly, and biannual periodicals with Outer Banks–only coverage. The writing styles vary in these publications, ranging from highly editorialized and a more laid-back approach to a tighter, stricter journalistic structure.

Even though a couple of the smaller papers frequently disregard *The Associated Press Stylebook* rules, these publications offer a wealth of local information. You'll find that the pages are loaded with community news—educational, political, environmental, and civic happenings that you won't find anywhere else.

The Virginian-Pilot
Nags Head Bureau, US 158, MP 10, Nags Head
(252) 441–1620

This Norfolk, Virginia–based daily broadsheet combines "big-city paper" experience with local knowledge to cover national news and regional news from northeastern and coastal North Carolina and, predominantly, Hampton Roads, Virginia. The *Pilot's* total circulation is about 230,000, with close to 16,000 of that number going to the Outer Banks and northeastern North Carolina.

A separate North Carolina section is published daily, with articles and photographs composed by an Outer Banks–based news staff, but this section also includes lots of coastal Virginia news due to our proximity to the state line and the small amount of hard news the Outer Banks generates. (If you're looking for lighthearted community news such as wedding coverage, civic club updates, job promotions, and social stuff, you'll want to pick up one of the weekly or tri-weekly publications listed in this chapter.)

The Virginian-Pilot is available at area newsstands and convenience stores for 50 cents Monday through Saturday and $1.25 for Sunday's edition. Home delivery is available by subscription.

The Coast, a free, weekly entertainment and news publication produced by *The Virginian-Pilot*, is available each weekend at grocery and general stores and other locations throughout the Outer Banks from March through December. It is published monthly in January and February. Winter circulation is 20,000, while height-of-summer circulation soars to around 45,000. *The Coast* also is delivered as part of the Sunday edition of *The Virginian-Pilot* to North Carolina newsstands and subscribers.

The Coastland Times
501 Budleigh St., Manteo
(252) 473–2105
US 158, MP 7½, Kill Devil Hills
(252) 441–2223

Touting itself as the "Journal of the Walter Raleigh Coastland of North Carolina," *The Coastland Times* has been continuously published since 1935. This local paper is published on Sundays, Tuesdays, and Thursdays, and is available at area newsstands and convenience stores for 50 cents; mail delivery is available by calling the above numbers.

Reporters cover Currituck, Dare, Hyde, and Tyrrell Counties. You'll find the most extensive local classifieds here, including yard sale ads (mostly in Thursday's issue). Pick up this paper for wedding, birth, obituary, reunion, community, and civic club information. It's famous for "big fish," public school, and other grip-and-grin photographs that give locals and visitors, young and old, a brief step into the limelight.

The Outer Banks Sentinel
Central Sq., US 158, MP 11, Nags Head
(252) 480–2234
www.obsentinel.com

The Outer Banks Sentinel is a weekly broadsheet newspaper owned by Sentinel Publishing that has been operating since March 1996. With a weekly circulation of 9,000, it covers news occurring from Corolla to Ocracoke and on Roanoke Island and the Dare County mainland. This industrious paper makes an effort to include everything from hard news to poetry.

The Sentinel provides news and features on area personalities, editorials, and columns about the Outer Banks. Insiders laugh themselves silly while reading local humorist Jack Sandberg's satiric column "Uncle Jack." Special calendars and listings include information on weather, fishing, tides, surf conditions, entertainment, and community events.

The Sentinel is published every Thursday and Sunday and is sold for 50 cents at area newsstands and bookstores. Mail delivery is available to subscribers.

Ocracoke Observer
P.O. Box 427, Ocracoke, NC 27960
(252) 928–3291

Ocracoke Observer is a tabloid newspaper published once a month for distribution to Ocracoke and connecting points. This free publication is a handy resource for tide charts, cable TV listings, library hours, ferry schedules, and almanac reports. It also includes interesting editorial regarding Ocracoke Island and is available free at Ocracoke retail and grocery stores.

The Island Breeze
NC 12 and Dunes Dr., Hatteras Village
(252) 986–2421

The Island Breeze, an award-winning Hatteras and Ocracoke tabloid published by *The Virginian-Pilot*, comes out monthly February through December. This publication features a variety of articles on local personalities, businesses, the environment, and community-related news. It is free and available at area shops and restaurants.

ReelFisher News
P.O. Box 1146, Kitty Hawk, NC
(252) 261–8210

The *ReelFisher News* is published four times a year by Gulfstream Graphic Arts & Publishing. It's a free tabloid available at retail outlets throughout the Outer Banks that offers folksy fishing editorial while acting as a directory to area piers, ramps, marinas, and weigh stations.

The *North Beach Sun*
1106 NC 12, Kill Devil Hills
(252) 449–2222

Covering the northern beaches—predominantly, but not limited to, Southern Shores to Corolla—the *North Beach Sun* is a free quarterly publication. It is mailed to local residents from Nags Head north to Corolla and is available in racks in retail outlets in the beach communities. The tabloid-style paper features recaps and announcements of local events, feature stories, arts articles, a wine column, a spiritual column, tennis tips, and more.

Magazines and Miscellaneous Publications

There are quite a few specialty magazines published on the Outer Banks, though only two that qualify as regional publications. They focus on either the specific—fishing, playing golf, dining—or the general—Outer Banks living. We have included several free guides in this section that contain lots of restaurant and shopping coupons to help you stretch your vacation dollars, as well as a fun newsletter from one of our favorite bookstores.

The Edge Outer Banks
Outer Banks Press
P.O. Box 2829, Kitty Hawk, NC
(252) 261–0612, (888) 261–4411
www.outerbankspress.com

The Edge Outer Banks is a slick four-color annual magazine focusing on the entire Outer Banks with brief forays into surrounding geographical areas. This four-year-old regional magazine is distinctive for its quality, both in appearance and in its lively editorial content. Readers of this publication will find informative, entertaining articles on aviation, food and wine, architectural design, golf, high-energy recreation, and area destinations. Everything about *The Edge* is cutting-edge: design, photography, art, and editorial. It's available at area retail outlets and grocery stores for $4.00, or by subscription by calling or e-mailing Outer Banks Press.

Sportfishing Report
P.O. Box 3806, Kill Devil Hills, NC
(252) 473–1553
www.sportfishing-report.com

Sportfishing Report was first published in the winter of 1991 and has gradually expanded from an Outer Banks–only magazine to also include the coastal areas from Virginia Beach to Georgia. Readers of this bimonthly publication will find informative saltwater fishing tips; profiles and history of surf, sound, and sea venues; plus product reviews and information on shows and tournaments. Gorgeous color photography brings the fishing experience into your living room. The magazine is available at most local news and magazine stands, or by subscription. For information, call the above number or visit the Web site.

Hatteras Monitor
18 Baccus Ct., Frisco
(252) 995–5378

The *Hatteras Monitor,* a news magazine, is published nine times a year, April through December, and is filled with historical stories and photographs, real estate planning, fishing reports, poetry, environmental news, a telephone guide, visitors' guide and map, community news, and want ads for Hatteras and Ocracoke islands. Copies are free.

Outer Banks Kid Connection
P.O. Box 1451, Kill Devil Hills, NC
(252) 480–2939

This free publication is distributed from September through May. A Visitors Edition covers the entire summer's worth of kids' activities. The tabloid-style paper includes a calendar of events, family-friendly attractions, parks and recreation programs, information for parents, an advice column, and more. For kids, there's a special pull-out section of fun pages with mazes, word puzzles, and other games. The *Kid Connection* can be found in grocery stores, schools, libraries, doctors' offices, and various businesses on the Outer Banks.

The Beach Book
Central Sq., US 158, MP 11, Nags Head
(252) 480–2787, (800) 844–3128
www.beachbook.com

Don't overlook our first "local" phone book for useful information. Owners Jeff Graham and Tom Chisholm host an art contest each year to determine the next year's cover design and also highlight artwork by local children throughout the book. The phone book includes a vacation guide and restaurant menu section; articles on history, nature, and flight; plus information on first aid, governing officials, and hurricane preparedness; maps; and a calendar of events. Business as well as residential phone numbers are listed including Coinjock, Mamie, Corolla, Duck, Kitty Hawk, Southern Shores, Kill Devil Hills, Nags Head, Manteo, Hatteras Island, and Ocracoke Island. Free copies of *The Beach Book* are available at either the Outer Banks Chamber of Commerce or at *The Beach Book* offices.

Big Game Tournaments Magazine
Pirate's Cove Yacht Club,
Nags Head–Manteo Causeway, Manteo
(252) 473–3906, (800) 537–7245

This free magazine covers offshore Gulf Stream fishing from a tournament angle. It features Pirate's Cove Yacht Club–sponsored and North Carolina Governor's Cup tournament schedules, rules, and guidelines and their histories. The tournaments are nonprofit, charitable functions. You can pick up a copy of *Big Game* at the Pirate's Cove Yacht Club's Ship's Store.

Television

WITN
P.O. Box 775, Manteo NC 27954
(252) 473–4705

WITN is an NBC affiliate based in Washington, North Carolina, and it's the only TV station that has made the commitment to place a full-time news bureau on the Outer Banks. Other TV stations only pay attention to the Outer Banks when something big happens, like a hurricane or a lighthouse moving. WITN's local reporter and Outer Banks general manager, Tom Skinner, is always on the go, tracking stories. Monday through Friday you can see his local reports on the CNN Headline News station every half-hour, at 24 and 54 past each hour. Skinner's reports are also aired on WITN, which is broadcast throughout eastern North Carolina. NBC national news picks up Skinner's reports when something nationally newsworthy occurs on the Outer Banks.

Charter Cable Television
NC 12, MP 10½, Kill Devil Hills
(252) 441–2881

This company supplies cable connection service for most of the Outer Banks, except Ocracoke Island. Most motels, hotels, and cottages have cable connections. Some add special features such as HBO, Showtime, Cinemax, or Disney Channel. Charter also offers pay-per-view movies, sporting events, and concerts with the proper equipment obtained from the company. Charter service includes the Prevue Channel, providing a continuous update on all programming carried on its channels; The Weather Channel, one of the most-watched stations on the Outer Banks; Beach Channel 12, with information on restaurants, real estate, and recreational opportunities; and Government Access Channel 20, with programming by the local townships. Digital cable access is available; call the office for details.

Local media cover a wide variety of topics related to the Outer Banks, but it usually takes a hurricane to attract attention from the national media. PHOTO: HORSLEY/GARDNER

Radio Stations

As we stated earlier, Outer Banks radio began when Reginald Fessenden sent the first transmissions between two 50-foot towers, one near Cape Hatteras and the other on Roanoke Island, in the early 1900s. Sixty-eight years later, the first Outer Banks radio station, WOBR-1530 AM, went on the air, joined three years later by WOBR-95.3 FM. We now have nine local stations featuring country, gospel, album and alternative rock, adult contemporary, and oldies formats. One company owns four of these stations. Since the FCC opened up new frequencies in the mid-'80s, radio stations have multiplied, creating a highly competitive field when it comes to maintaining listeners and achieving advertising dollars. That's a whole lot of radio in one little seasonal area.

Several local stations have informative talk shows once a week that share information on community events such as upcoming symphonies, art shows, entertainment, plays, and more. We have one Christian station on the AM frequency and two stations that unfailingly cover live local high school basketball. Formats often shift annually as stations try to capture listeners and as the music world evolves on a national level, but the primary listening target is the adult population ranging from age 25 to 54.

National Public Radio is broadcast to transmitters in Manteo and Hatteras from Chapel Hill.

WNHW-97.1 FM, WYND-92.3 FM
637 Harbor Road, Wanchese
(252) 475-1888

WNHW 97.1 plays all the familiar classic country hits and bluegrass. CNN and the North Carolina News Network air daily as do local news and fishing reports. WYND 92.3 is an easy-listening oldies station. Together the stations reach numerous counties in eastern North Carolina.

WOBR-95.3 FM and 96.7 FM
2046 NC 345, Wanchese
(252) 473-3434

These stations—95.3 and 96.7 The Rock—are simulcast stations featuring AOR: album-oriented rock. Each day you can listen to morning radio personalities John Boy and Billy, who have their own brand of Southern redneck, irreverent humor. Saturday mornings feature "best of" John Boy and Billy, while on Sundays, this dynamic duo stars in the *John Boy and Billy Rock-n-Roll Racing Show*. The music is speckled with frequent weather reports, public service announcements, and morning surf reports. WOBR is owned by East Carolina Radio, Incorporated. The contest and request line is (252) 473-2444.

WOBX-98.1 FM
2046 NC 345, Wanchese
(252) 473-3434

This is the Outer Banks's newest radio station. OBX 98.1 plays "hot" adult contemporary hit radio. Mornings kick off with Rick Dees from 5:00 to 10:00 A.M. Local and national news are aired throughout the day.

Insiders' Tip
The Currituck Chamber of Commerce, (252) 453-9497, and the Outer Banks Chamber of Commerce, (252) 441-8144, provide area information booklets for the asking. Call to request vacation or relocation materials.

WOBR-1530 AM
2046 NC 345, Wanchese
(252) 473–5402

This was the first station on either band to hit the Outer Banks. Today, WOBR airs daytime Christian music and programming plus USA Network news, weather, and local obituaries.

WRSF-105.7 FM
US 158, MP 10¹/₂, Nags Head
(252) 441–1024, (800) 553–DIXI

Dixie 105.7 plays "today's hottest country" and also airs local and world news and weather broadcasts. The contest and request line numbers are (252) 441–4566 and (800) 422–3494.

WVOD-99.1 FM
Manteo Waterfront,
Queen Elizabeth Ave., Manteo
(252) 473–1993, (252) 473–9863 request line

This station, known as The Sound, broadcasts from a studio on the Manteo waterfront. Announcers play a varied format centering around adult rock and alternative music. Tune in Sunday for a morning of classical music. Then at 1:10 P.M., listen to *Dateline Carolina*, which features guests who discuss upcoming theater productions, art shows, and a wide variety of community happenings.

The Sound features a Coastal Calendar airing area events. You'll also find reports on fishing, surf conditions, weather, and hourly national news. Local news is broadcast several times a day. This community-minded station also offers air time for public service announcements and personnel for charitable causes. The Sound is a great source for information on local school closings, lost pets, and road conditions.

WCXL-104.1 FM
104 Radio Rd., Powells Point
(252) 491–9295

This 100,000-watt boomer of a station, Beach 104, covers the Outer Banks and Hampton Roads with an adult contemporary and beach music mix that makes for great listening during a day by the ocean.

One minute you'll be grooving to such pop divas as Mariah Carey, Whitney Houston, or Celine Dion; the next you'll be flashing back with the Beach Boys. Every morning on this station there's a radio auction called Best Buys on the Beach, in which local goods and services are often sold for a fraction of their regular prices. WCXL also offers regional and national news and fishing and farm reports.

WERX-102.5 FM
US 158, MP 10¹/₂, Nags Head
(252) 441–1025, (888) 75–SHARK

If you like oldies, The Shark supplies plenty of hits from the '50s, '60s, '70s, and '80s to accompany you on your trip down memory lane. Couple this with their *Charlie Byrd Beach Blast* on Sundays from 4:00 until 8:00 P.M., and you'll never want to come back. Killer classics air right after Byrd's segment right on up until midnight. CNN, regional, and local news air daily. Traffic updates and seasonal fishing reports round out their Good Times–Killer Oldies format. The Shark is owned by East Carolina Radio, Incorporated.

WUNC 90.5 and 91.9 FM
(919) 966–5454, (800) 962–9862

WUNC is a National Public Radio station based in Chapel Hill, North Carolina. The station has two transmitters on the Outer Banks, one in Manteo and one in Buxton. Most local announcements are for the Triangle area, but Outer Banks weather and public service announcements do get coverage. The station switched formats in 2001 to become a predominantly news and talk station. Two music shows still air on the weekends: *Back Porch Music* (bluegrass) and *Thistle and Shamrock* (Celtic music). The news and talk lineup includes, among others, *BBC World News, Morning Edition* from 5:00 to 9:00 A.M., *The Connection, Fresh Air, Talk of the Nation, All Things Considered, Marketplace,* and *The State of Things,* a show covering issues in the state of North Carolina. On the weekends look for special shows like *Car Talk, The People's Pharmacy,* and *Prairie Home Companion.*

Online Media and Internet Service Providers

Beach Access
www.beachaccess.com
(252) 441–1521 voice line,
(252) 480–0817 modem line for users only

Beach Access is a 56K and ISDN digital-access Internet provider, which also provides web design services, hosting, and domain name hosting. Call for rates and information.

Aginet
1245 NC 12, Duck
Ocean Plaza, US 158, MP 4½, Kitty Hawk
(252) 261–2675
www.obxonline.com

Aginet provides Internet service ranging from T-1 lines to 56K dial-up service, including ISDN service. Weekly accounts are available. They also operate three Cybercades on the Outer Banks at the locations listed above. The Cybercades are set up so that anyone can come in, set up an account, and use the Internet. Cost is $10.00 an hour or $6.00 for a half-hour. Locals can set up an account for $30.00 a month.

Beachlink
3915 Welch St., Kitty Hawk
(252) 261–0744, (800) EAT–SPAM
www.beachlink.com

Beachlink provides 56K and broadband connections, technical support, and vacation accounts. Soundwaves, a division of the company, provides custom design programs.

> **Insiders' Tip**
> For free National Park Service news and information, pick up a copy of *In The Park*, published once a year and available at the National Park Service visitor centers.

The Outer Banks's beautiful beaches offer peaceful retreat.

Worship

The freedom to worship as we please is a right and privilege many people take for granted. But for those early settlers to the Outer Banks, this freedom was worth risking everything for, worth a dangerous trip across a vast ocean to unexplored lands filled with unknown perils. It wasn't important that there were no churches to worship in when they arrived. After all, God had gotten them safely across the ocean and deposited them in this wild and beautiful land He had created. What better way to thank Him for their blessings than under a canopy of leaves or a star-studded sky?

The first recorded religious event in the area was the baptism of Manteo, an Algonkian Native American for whom the town of Manteo is named. The event happened on August 13, 1587, on Roanoke Island. However, it wasn't until approximately 200 years later that formal buildings were erected where people could gather together to worship in the way they saw fit. These early churches were mostly Baptist, Methodist, and Pentecostal.

The Outer Banks now can boast numerous churches ranging from simple wooden structures to modern buildings that have kitchens, day-care rooms, and meeting rooms. Some of the older churches are undergoing renovations to keep pace with the continued development that brings more people to services. The interdenominational Corolla Chapel experienced such rapid growth that it was forced to expand its tiny 100-seat setting. On summer Sundays, more people would be standing outside than in. Pastor John Strauss led an expansion effort that included building a new facility across the street and moving the old, historic chapel over to it and combining the two. The new church facility, open in spring 2002, will seat 250. It will also allow the addition of a ministry to teens as well as a senior citizens group along with other outreach programs.

The Holy Redeemer Church in Kill Devil Hills, which burned down in 1998, was rebuilt at a new site in Kitty Hawk on Kitty Hawk Road. The new church is much larger and more modern than the old one was. For up-to-date information on service times, call the church information line, (252) 261–1168. Another addition to the Holy Redeemer is Father Michael Butler, who arrived two years ago.

If you're a fan of stained glass, be sure to see the exquisite windows of Mount Olivet United Methodist Church in Manteo. Late-afternoon light provides the best viewing time. If you're into the natural beauty of the Outer Banks, stop by the Duck United Methodist Church, designed by architect Greg Frucci. As the story goes, Frucci had a difficult time convincing the powers that be to forgo conventional stained glass for a natural view. Why not have a perpetually changing scene fashioned by the Maker Himself, Frucci argued. The church eventually agreed, enabling worshipers to admire a wooded soundside landscape through a huge bay window behind the altar. The view obviously inspired the late Reverend Bill Ruth, for one Sunday he invited the entire congregation up to the altar to see a red-tailed hawk perched on a tree limb.

Our varied array of religious congregations includes Baptist, Southern Baptist, Catholic, Charismatic, Christian Scientist, Assembly of God, Methodist, United Methodist, Jehovah's Witnesses, Lutheran, United Church of Christ, Mormon, Episcopal, Full Gospel, Seventh-Day Adventist, Presbyterian, Unitarian Universalist, and Interdenominational. Still, there are some missing (spiritual) links. If you wish to attend services other than those mentioned above (Jewish, Greek Orthodox, etc.), you must drive to Virginia Beach or Norfolk.

The natural beauty of the Outer Banks brings out the spiritual side in many people. PHOTO: HORSLEY/GARDNER

Most of our Outer Banks churches have full-time year-round pastors who are assisted by visiting clergy during the peak season, when attendance increases several-fold. It's not uncommon for a summertime congregation to spill out of a church and into the parking lot. Hatteras Island has a host of United Methodist parishes, and often one minister will travel to two or more communities to conduct Sunday services.

As in the islands' early days of worship, nature provides some special alternatives to indoor church services. It's not unusual to find oceanfront services, and, on occasion, *The Lost Colony's* outdoor amphitheater serves as a venue. If you're here on Easter Sunday, you're in for an early-morning treat: Scores of people flock to the ocean for nondenominational sunrise services in many communities along the Outer Banks. Favorite locales include Kitty Hawk Pier, Jockey's Ridge, and the Corolla Chapel Sunrise Service held at Corolla Light Homeowners Association oceanfront swimming pool. When attending one of these, allow yourself plenty of time to vie for parking and be sure to bring a coat or a blanket, as the early hours can be on the chilly side.

Some religious groups are branching out beyond traditional Sunday services, offering Christian counseling, athletic opportunities, thrift-store shopping, and even entertainment. The Dream Center in Nags Head, (252) 441-1155, has mostly Christian-oriented theater and musical performances during the summer season as well as a coffeehouse, a small Christian gift shop, and a bookstore. The environment is nonsmoking and no alcoholic beverages are served on the premises. (See our Shopping chapter for more Christian gift store information.)

Since worship schedules vary seasonally for the many churches on the island, pick up the most recent Sunday edition of *The Coastland Times* for comprehensive information on worship services and locations.

Index of Advertisers

Index

About the Author

Molly Harrison is a North Carolina girl through and through. Born in the Piedmont, she has gradually been pulled eastward throughout her life, first to the coastal plains of Greenville for an education in English and writing at East Carolina University and finally as far east as she could go, to the Outer Banks, on a spit of land that sticks far out into the Atlantic.

Her first trip to the Outer Banks was to visit her sister in mid-winter of 1989. The Outer Banks seemed harsh and rugged, with a nor'easter blowing and even the fast-food restaurants and convenience stores closed due to the dearth of humans. She returned to the Outer Banks many times and spent a summer here in 1991, working the early morning shift at The Dunes Restaurant and spending afternoons on the beach. When she met her husband-to-be, Patrick, in 1992, they traveled often from Greenville to Nags Head to spend time at his family's cottage on the Roanoke Sound.

In 1994 Molly started working as a reporter with *The Coastland Times*, the area's longest-running newspaper. Covering commissioners' meetings, superior court cases, traffic accidents, political fish fries, boat launchings, fishing tournaments, bear killings, Christmas parades, hurricanes, and whale beachings plunged her headfirst into Outer Banks culture, and soon she was hooked, in love with the people, charm, quirkiness, beauty, and seasons—quiet winters, unpredictable springs, crazy summers, and absolutely magical falls.

A year and a half later, she met Beth Storie and Michael McOwen and ended up working as an editor for their series of travel guides called The Insiders' Guides. She worked in their Manteo offices for three years, editing Insiders' Guides to places all over the country, but never to the Outer Banks. Molly loved working in "downtown" Manteo, where she was on a first-name basis with everyone from the sandwich maker to the UPS man to the mayor to the garbage collector.

Since 1998 Molly has been a freelance writer, working for a variety of local publications such as *The Virginian-Pilot* and *The Coast, Outer Banks Magazine, The Edge Outer Banks,* and numerous tourist publications and businesses. She is the author of *The Manteo Walking Tour and Roanoke Island Guide,* published in 2001. She is also a freelance editor and project manager and works for many national publishers.

Molly lives in Nags Head with her husband, whom she married on Ocracoke Island, and two dogs. She is blessed to have many family members living on the Outer Banks as well. She spends her time writing in her home office, walking the beach and running through Nags Head Woods with her dog, teaching hatha yoga, reading anything she can get her hands on, fishing and cooking with her husband, camping on Little Tim's Island, searching for beach glass, volunteering, and helping to restore an old cottage she and her husband saved from destruction.